Setting the Table

An Introduction to the Jurisprudence of Rabbi Yechiel Mikhel Epstein's *Arukh HaShulhan*

Setting the Table

An Introduction to the Jurisprudence of Rabbi Yechiel Mikhel Epstein's *Arukh HaShulhan*

Michael J. Broyde
and Shlomo C. Pill

Boston
2021

Library of Congress Cataloging-in-Publication Data

Names: Broyde, Michael J., author. | Pill, Shlomo C., author.

Title: Setting the table : an introduction to the jurisprudence Rabbi Yechiel Mikhel Epstein's Arukh HaShulhan / Michael J. Broyde, Shlomo C. Pill.

Description: Boston : Academic Studies Press, 2021. | Includes bibliographical references and index.

Identifiers: LCCN 2019050093 (print) | LCCN 2019050094 (ebook) | ISBN 9781644690703 (hardback) | ISBN 9781644690710 (adobe pdf)

Subjects: LCSH: Epstein, Jehiel Michael ben Aaron Isaac, Halevi, approximately 1829-approximately 1908. ʿArukh ha-shulḥan. | Israel Meir, ha-Kohen, 1838-1933. Mishnah berurah. | Jewish law--Codification. | Jewish law--Interpretation and construction.

Classification: LCC BM521 .B767 2020 (print) | LCC BM521 (ebook) | DDC 296.1/8--dc23

LC record available at https://lccn.loc.gov/2019050093
LC ebook record available at https://lccn.loc.gov/2019050094

Copyright © Academic Studies Press, 2021

ISBN 9781644690703 (hardback)
ISBN 9781644690710 (adobe pdf)
ISBN 9781644693810 (ePub)
ISBN 9781644695173 (paperback)

Book design by Kryon Publishing Services, Ltd.
www.kryonpublishing.com
Cover design by Ivan Grave

Published by Academic Studies Press
1577 Beacon Street
Brookline, MA 02446, USA

press@academicstudiespress.com
www.academicstudiespress.com

In memory of:
הרב חיים דוב בן משה אהרן ודבורה בראיודע
Dr. Barret (Barry) Broyde
Who returned his soul to his Maker on September 30, 2018
יצא נשמתו בהושענא רבא תשע"ט
Most beloved and loving father, husband,
grandfather, and great-grandfather,
a kind heart, a sweeping intellect,
a broad and deep Torah scholar,
an astonishing memory, truly a role model
for his family and all who knew him.
His loss will be felt by his family for decades to come.

In memory of:
ר׳ צבי בן שמואל יהודה
Hersh "Heshy" Aron
Who returned his soul to his Maker on September 29, 2018
יצא נשמתו בשבת חול המועד סוכות תשע״ט
A Holocaust survivor who remained deeply committed
to the faith and traditions of his ancestors after
experiencing incredible loss, and together
with his wife, Ella, built a family of children,
grandchildren, and great-grandchildren committed
to continuing that legacy. In life, Hersh Aron exemplified
a simple, deep dedication to Torah and *halakhah*
of a kind that recalls a Jewish past now lost.
May his memory be a blessing.

Contents

Acknowledgments	viii
Introduction	x
Part I—Setting the Table: The Codification of Jewish Law	1
Chapter One: Codifying Jewish Law	2
Chapter Two: Rabbi Yechiel Mikhel Epstein's *Arukh HaShulchan*	33
Chapter Three Competing Models: The *Arukh HaShulchan* and *Mishnah Berurah*	45
Part II—The Methodological Principles of the Arukh HaShulchan	69
Introduction	70
Chapter Four: The Rule of the Talmud	83
Chapter Five Rabbinic Consensus	98
Chapter Six Resolving Doubtful Cases	110
Chapter Seven Non-Normative Opinions	135
Chapter Eight Supererogatory Religious Conduct	157
Chapter Nine Law and Mysticism	172
Chapter Ten Law and Custom	185
Chapter Eleven Temporal Rationalization of *Halakhic* Rules	208
Chapter Twelve Law and Pragmatism	223
Part III—Illustrative Examples from the *Arukh HaShulchan*	249
The *Arukh HaShulchan's* Methodological Principles for Reaching *Halakhic* Conclusions	250
The Ten Methodological Principles of the *Arukh HaShulchan*	252
Bibliography	395
Index of Biblical and Rabbinic Works Cited	405
Index of Names and Subjects	409
Index of Examples by Methodological Principle	413

Acknowledgments

Many people have contributed in different ways to the writing of this book, and we would like to thank them: Thank you to the Emory University Center for the Study of Law and Religion, the Emory University Law School, Emory University Candler School of Theology, and the Judish London Evans Directors Fund at the Tam Institute of Jewish Studies, which all supported us in writing this work. In particular, we would like to thank Professor John Witte Jr. and Professor David R. Blumenthal, whose vision and hard work created the Center and the Institute, which continue to support excellent research, teaching, and publishing in Jewish law. We would like to thank the editors at *Dinei Israel*, who published portions of this work as an article in volume 33 of the journal. Portions of this book were also presented at the Jewish Law Annual Moscow Conference in 2018 and various other academic and popular lecture forums. We thank participants in those conversations, whose attendance, questions, and insights have enhanced this work. We also note that this work owes an intellectual debt to a prior work that one of us co-authored; some small portions of this work derive from Michael J. Broyde & Ira Bedzow, The Codification of Jewish Law and an Introduction to the Jurisprudence of the Mishna Berura (2014).

We particularly also want to thank Jerry and Chaya Weinberger, who supported our work in dedication to their lovely children, Goldi and Mordechai Reisman, Shmuel, Bailey, and Shevi. The Weinberger family's support is a demonstration of the ideal that parents wish for their children to continue to grow and study works of Torah and *halakhah* and also that their learning enhances their practice and observance.

We would like to thank the many different people who helped with production of the manuscript. In particular, the very capable editorial team at Academic Studies Press helped us in many different ways. Thank you as well to the many fine research assistants who helped edit the collection of examples, including Tzipporah Machlah Klapper, Carl Johnson, Noah Notis, Ben Notis,

Jacob Pesachov, Vera Wexler, Rami Schwartz, Ashley Stern-Mintz, and Moshe Unger, and to Yael Klausner, who provided valuable editorial and research assistance. Many people—too many to name and thank individually—read different portions of this work; their comments and criticisms have helped clarify and sharpen many of our arguments, and we are grateful to each of them. All errors are, of course, our own.

We also thank our wives, Channah Broyde and Tzivie Pill—without whose support and advice this project could not have been completed—and our children Joshua, Aaron, Rachel Irene, and Deborah Malka Broyde, and Arial, Minnie, and Delphine Pill, who make it all worthwhile.

This book is dedicated in memory of Rabbi Eitam Henkin, who was murdered before completing his work on the biography of Rabbi Yechiel Mikhel Epstein, the author of the *Arukh HaShulchan*. This work has recently appeared under the title *Ta'arokh Lefanai Shulchan* (Set a Table Before Me: The Life, Times, and Works of Rabbi Yechiel Mikhel Epstein, Author of the *Arukh HaShulchan*, Maggid Press, 2019). We—along with the whole community—deeply mourn his murder and the murder of his wife Na'ama on October 1, 2015. We thank the extended Henkin family, and particularly Rabbi Yehuda Herzl and Rabbanit Chana Henkin, for sharing the above manuscript with us, and we cite it extensively in the biographical sections of this work. Rabbi Eitam Henkin indicated in this above manuscript an intent to address the many topics we discuss in this work,[1] but he sadly did not live to write those sections. We are certain he would have done a better job at this book than we have done, and it is only with tears in our eyes that we attempt to undertake this task. We relied heavily on Rabbi Henkin's research and used material from his biography in chapter two of this book. His work was groundbreaking, pathbreaking in its insights, and astonishing for one so young. If we have accomplished anything novel in this work, it is because we are midgets on the shoulders of a young giant taken from our community before he could grow to his full height.

Each of us suffered losses in our family while writing this book, and we note with sadness the passing of Rabbi Dr. Barret Broyde, father of one of us, and Hersh Aron, grandfather-in-law of one of us. They both returned their souls to their Maker on *Chol HaMoed* Sukkot 5779, one on Hoshana Rabbah and the other on Shabbat *Chol HaMoed*. Their losses are deeply felt, and we dedicate this volume to their memories.

---

1 See Eitam Henkin, Ta'arokh Lefanai Shulchan: Chayo Zemano U'Mepaalo Shel HaRav Yechiel Mikhel Epstein Baal Arukh HaShulchan 309 (2019).

Introduction

This book is about the magnum opus of Rabbi Yechiel Mikhel Epstein, the *Arukh HaShulchan*, focusing particularly on *Orach Chaim*, the section of his work that is most extensive and complete, and which addresses matters of normative daily Jewish law, such as prayers, Sabbath observance, and festival celebrations.

In this work, we do not focus on specific rulings or on Rabbi Epstein's social or linguistic presentations. Rather, we are interested in understanding how the work functions as a law book—the jurisprudence of the work and the way it reaches its *halakhic* (Jewish law) conclusions. How does the *Arukh HaShulchan* decide matters of Jewish law in light of the panoply of rabbinic sources, such as Talmudic texts, Maimonides's code, the *Shulchan Arukh*, the glosses of the *Rema*, and the many other great authorities who came before the *Arukh HaShulchan*? How does this seminal restatement of *halakhah* navigate and resolve tensions between text, interpretation, precedent, tradition, custom, spirituality, and pragmatism? By the time Rabbi Epstein first raised his pen to write about 150 years ago, Jewish law was far from a *tabula rasa*. Indeed, by the mid-1800s, the classical code of Jewish law, the *Shulchan Arukh*, had spawned dozens of commentaries and related works, many of which had become deeply integrated into the ways that rabbinic scholars approached Jewish law such that the *Shulchan Arukh* could not be approached without also engaging a multivocal chaos of commentary and legal disagreement. Yet the *Arukh HaShulchan* undertook to write a new and completely different restatement of Jewish law, not a commentary, nor a set of responsa proposing new answers to a few very specific questions. Instead, he wrote whole new code because he had a deeply important methodological contributions to make to how Jewish law is determined. This *halakhic* methodology—like that of so many major figures in the annals of rabbinic law—is never explicitly or fully explained by Rabbi Epstein, but it becomes clear upon a close examination of the *Arukh HaShulchan*. In this book, we explain that his basic approach—although it has much nuance and complexity—was that of an innovative traditionalist. Rabbi Epstein was a fiercely independent *halakhic* decisor and did not view himself bound to follow the precedential opinions of past rabbis, preferring instead to address legal issues by direct appeal to his own understandings of the Talmud. This independence, combined with Rabbi Epstein's commitment to viewing *halakhah* contextually as a normative system whose rules must achieve their stated goals given local realities, often resulted in the *Arukh HaShulchan*'s disagreeing with even the most important rabbinic scholars of earlier eras. At the same time, Rabbi Epstein's *halakhic* jurisprudence is also deeply traditional and cautious. The *Arukh HaShulchan* rarely rejects standards of practice supported by broad rabbinic consensus, even when Rabbi Epstein himself thought the consensus view was wrong. The rulings of the *Arukh HaShulchan* evince a deep respect for legal normativity of traditional customs, even when such customs are not required by—or are in tension with—Talmudic norms. Our study of the *Arukh HaShulchan* reveals an approach to *halakhic* judgment that recognizes the *de facto* and *de jure* independence of rabbinic decisors to offer the *halakhic* guidance they think is best under the circumstances, but which cautions prudence, humility, and a measure of conservative respect for tradition in order to keep Jewish law vibrant, relevant, and alive, as well as grounded and authentic.

As we will explain in Part II, much of the *Arukh HaShulchan*'s methodological approach to determining Jewish legal norms revolved around four basic ideas. First, Rabbi Epstein was deeply committed to the notion that the right answers to *halakhic* questions are inherent in the qualified rabbinic scholar's independent analytic understanding of the Talmud itself and cannot be determined by the mechanistic reliance on post-Talmudic codes and precedents. While Rabbi Epstein does often defer to the Talmudic readings reached by a consensus of other scholars, the jurisprudence of the *Arukh HaShulchan* is fundamentally rooted in the idea that the *halakhah* is the law of the Talmud and that one must turn to the Talmud in the first instance, rather than to later codes and commentaries. Second, the jurisprudence of the *Arukh HaShulchan* is rooted in the realization that while legal inquiries must begin with an understanding of "the law of the Talmud," they do not always end there. Oftentimes the Talmud itself does not admit a single correct legal standard; instead, doubt-resolving rules that serve to cut through analytically irresolvable Talmudic uncertainties determine the correct *halakhic* norm. Third, the *Arukh HaShulchan* recognizes that *halakhah* is not merely a matter of determining Talmudic prescriptions but is part of a broader normative religious universe that includes other spiritual values. Thus, when determining what the *halakhah* is in practice—rather than solely focusing on what the right Talmudic rule is in the abstract—the *Arukh HaShulchan* considers the legal import of mysticism and the religious imperative to act at times with heightened piety. Fourth, central to the *Arukh HaShulchan*'s legal methodology is the idea that *halakhah* must be practiced by real people in the real world. Thus, for Rabbi Epstein, *minhag*—the religious customs of ordinary Jews and of rabbinic scholars, which reflect the real-world experience of how *halakhah* is actually practiced—is an important factor in legal decision-making. Likewise, when deciding what Talmudic standards entail in practice, the *Arukh HaShulchan* regularly considers social, economic, and geographical contexts in which Jewish law must be observed and the practical difficulties of upholding various potential *halakhic* standards. Of course, as we will explain in greater detail throughout this book, there is much more at play. In the upcoming chapters, we divide the insights into the methodology of the *Arukh HaShulchan* into ten distinct principles.

This book is made up of twelve chapters and an appendix of more than two hundred examples that apply these methodological principles to the *Arukh HaShulchan*. The first chapter traces the codification of Jewish law from the Talmud to around the year 1850. This chapter explains how Jewish law became overly complex and multivocal such that it became difficult for even experts to discern the correct course of conduct for any hard question. Chapter two explains the dilemmas confronted by Jewish law in the second half of the nineteenth century and how this gave rise to two very different proposed solutions: one response took the form of the *Mishnah Berurah*, a legal work written by Rabbi Israel Meir Kagan; the other solution was Rabbi Yechiel Mikhel Epstein's monumental restatement of *halakhah*, the *Arukh HaShulchan*. To better explain these different approaches and highlight some of the unique features of Rabbi Epstein's work, chapter three compares the approaches of the *Mishnah Berurah* and the *Arukh HaShulchan* on *halakhic* questions of common interest by focusing on four examples.

The remaining chapters of the book provide a broad overview of the ten principles that animate Rabbi Epstein's *halakhic* methodology in the *Orach Chaim* section of the *Arukh HaShulchan*, providing a detailed explanation of how each principle is applied and its relationship with other principles. Each methodological principle is discussed in turn; its significance, rationale, and historical usage in rabbinic jurisprudence is explained; and salient examples of Rabbi Epstein's use of each principle are elucidated.

The third and most ambitious part of this work provides a comprehensive review of the data upon which the foregoing assessments of Rabbi Epstein's *halakhic* methodology are based. This part analyzes and explains more than two hundred instances in which Rabbi Epstein reaches definitive *halakhic* conclusions in the *Orach Chaim* section of his *Arukh HaShulchan*. For each ruling, this work traces earlier rabbinic disputes over the issue, identifies Rabbi Epstein's conclusion, and presents the reasons he gives for reaching that determination. In doing so, this work identifies the methodological principles and secondary rules of decision that drive Rabbi Epstein's legal rulings, which are then summarized at the end of our presentation of each discrete issue. These examples are intended to show that the division of the methodology of the *Arukh HaShulchan* that we propose is not mere speculation or conjecture; rather, it is a data-driven, inductive assessment of the many disputes resolved by the *Arukh HaShulchan* while writing his work on *Orach Chaim*.

Part I
Setting the Table: The Codification of Jewish Law

CHAPTER ONE

Codifying Jewish Law

The Jewish Legal System: Then and Now

*H*alakhah, or Jewish law, is a system of rules, standards, practices, texts, traditions, interpretive and methodological principles, and institutions that constitutes the behavioral normative thrust of Judaism.[1] The rabbinic tradition understands *halakhah* as being rooted in the divine revelation of both the written text of the Torah—the first five books of the Hebrew Bible—and an oral tradition of explanations, qualifications, and expansions on the relatively sparse legal content of the biblical text.[2] In rabbinic thought, God communicated both the Oral Torah and Written Torah to Moses, who in turn conveyed these teachings to the Israelites. Subsequently, the text and these traditions were preserved and further developed by generations of prophets, priests, and (beginning in the later Second Temple period) by rabbis, who studied, taught, interpreted, and applied the Torah's teachings.[3] By the second century CE, the Rabbis—the scholarly heirs of the Pharisees—had become the primary keepers of the Torah's oral tradition of law, ethics, and theology.[4]

---

1   *See generally* Chaim Saiman, Halakhah: The Rabbinic Idea of Law (2018).
2   *See* Aaron Kirschenbaum, Equity in Jewish Law: Halakhic Perspectives on Law 10 (1991) ("The ultimate principle [*Grundnorm*] is the rule that the Torah, the Five Books of Moses, is of binding authority for the Jewish legal system. Parallel to this Written Torah is the Oral Tradition, which Jewish theology traces back to Moses [receipt of the tradition] from God."). *See also* Menachem Elon, Jewish Law: History, Sources, Principles 233 (Bernard Auerbach & Melvin J. Sykes trans., 1994); Mishneh Torah, *Introduction*.
3   *See* Mishnah, Avot 1:1.
4   *See* Rabbi Adin Steinsaltz, The Essential Talmud 22 (Chaya Galai trans., 2006).

CHAPTER ONE • Codifying Jewish Law | 3

In the early centuries of the Common Era, Jews experienced a series of major upheavals, including internal political and religious conflicts, the expansion of Roman control over Judea and the Galilee, the destruction of Jerusalem and the Second Temple during the Great Revolt of 66-73 CE, and the destructive suppression of the Bar Kokhba Revolt of 132-135 CE.[5] Largely in response to these events, the Rabbis determined that the preservation of Torah knowledge required fixing in formal texts the previously fluid and open-ended tradition.[6] Rabbi Judah the Prince edited the Mishnah at the beginning of the third century, which provided a topically organized textual outline of the Jewish legal tradition as it then stood. More a digest than a code, the Mishnah includes numerous rabbinic opinions on many issues and typically determines singular standards of *halakhic* conduct only by implication.[7] In the subsequent centuries, successive generations of *Amoraim*, rabbis who lived and worked in Jewish centers in both Palestine and the Persian Empire, subjected the text of the Mishnah to close analysis.[8] These scholars used the Mishnah as a focal

---

5   *See* Lawrence H. Schiffman, From Text to Tradition: A History of Second Temple and Rabbinic Judaism 157–76 (1991).

6   *See Introduction* to Mishneh Torah:

> Why did our holy teacher [Rabbi Judah the Prince] do this [i.e. compose a textual restatement of Jewish law] rather than leaving the matter as it was [with a more fluid, orally transmitted tradition]? This is because he recognized that the number of students was diminishing while new troubles were constantly arising; the Roman Empire was spreading across the world and becoming ever stronger, and the Jewish people were spread in a wandering diaspora across the world. He therefore composed a single text that would be readily available to everyone—and which could be studied quickly—so that it would not be forgotten.

7   *See* Lawrence H. Schiffman, From Text to Tradition: A History of Second Temple and Rabbinic Judaism 177-200 (1991). The Mishnah was redacted in Galilee at the end of the second century CE by Rabbi Judah the Prince, who served as both the religious and political head of the Jewish community at the time. The Mishnah distills the teachings of the Oral Torah into rule-like formulations, some attributed to particular scholars and others left unattributed. Generally, these rules are organized topically by individual Mishnah (lit. "teaching"), chapter, tractate, and groups of tractates. *See* Menachem Elon, Jewish Law: History, Sources, Principles 1048-56 (Bernard Auerbach & Melvin J. Sykes trans., 1994). In addition to the Mishnah, a variety of other compilations of Oral Torah teachings were compiled around the same time and with substantial overlap with the Mishnah itself. *See* ibid., 1078-79. For a variety of reasons, however, the Mishnah came to be regarded as the most authoritative of these works—a status concretized by the Talmud's being ultimately formulated as a commentary on the Mishnah. *See* ibid., 1057, 1061.

8   *See* Lawrence H. Schiffman, From Text to Tradition: A History of Second Temple & Rabbinic Judaism 214-27 (1991).

point of interpretation, a source of law, and a framework through which the far more expansive and untextualized contents of the *halakhic* tradition could be recalled, analyzed, and further developed. The content of these rabbinic discussions, which are referred to as *gemara* (lit. "studies"), were ultimately collected, organized, edited, and appended to the text of the Mishnah.[9] Together, the Mishnah and *gemara* comprise the Talmud. There are in fact two Talmuds: the Jerusalem Talmud is a relatively shorter text compiled in the latter half of the fourth century, and it reflects the rabbinic learning of *Amoraim* living in the Land of Israel; in contrast, the Babylonian Talmud is a much longer and generally more authoritative text compiled in the sixth century that records the scholarship of the rabbis living in the Persian Empire.[10] Importantly, as a legal text, the Talmud is even less determinative than the Mishnah. The text of the Talmud often reads like a meandering discussion that flexibly incorporates jurisprudence, theology, ethics, and biblical interpretation. Talmudic Rabbis debate issues and offer proofs and counterproofs, although usually these discursive deliberations end without having reached a definitive legal ruling.[11]

In rabbinic jurisprudence, the redaction of the Babylonian Talmud in the sixth century represents an important watershed event that divides Jewish legal history into Talmudic and post-Talmudic periods.[12] This event, known as the "sealing" of the Talmud, established the Talmud as the principal and authoritative text of rabbinic Jewish law. Subsequent to the sealing of the Talmud, rabbinic scholars read earlier texts and traditions only through a Talmudic lens and regarded the Talmud as setting the inviolable boundaries of *halakhic* practice and discourse.[13] Post-Talmudic developments and understandings of Jewish

---

9   See Menachem Elon, Jewish Law: History, Sources, Principles 1084 (Bernard Auerbach & Melvin J. Sykes trans., 1994). *See also* Rabbi Adin Steinsaltz, The Essential Talmud 3 (Chaya Galai trans., 2006) ("The formal definition of the Talmud is the summary of oral law that evolved after centuries of scholarly effort by sages who lived in Palestine and Babylonia until the beginning of the Middle Ages.").

10 See Menachem Elon, Jewish Law: History, Sources, Principles 1095-98 (Bernard Auerbach & Melvin J. Sykes trans., 1994).

11 See Rabbi Adin Steinsaltz, The Essential Talmud 57 (Chaya Galai trans., 2006).

12 See Babylonian Talmud, Bava Metzia 86a.

13 *See Introduction* to Mishneh Torah:

> All those things contained in the Babylonian Talmud—all Jews are obligated to follow them. Every town and country must observe all the customs, obey all the decrees, and uphold all the enactments of the Talmudic sages, for the entire Jewish people have accepted upon themselves all the things contained in the Talmud. The Sages who adopted the enactments and decrees, instituted the practices, rendered the rulings, and derived the laws [contained in the Talmud] included all or most of the scholars of Israel.

law must be grounded in sound readings of the Talmud and cannot be inconsistent with Talmudic standards.[14] Within these wide parameters, however, there was room for the *de facto* existence and *de jure* justification of a great diversity of legal opinion and religious practice. The move from abstract *halakhic* norms to practical standards of religio-legal conduct required substantial analysis and interpretation of Talmudic sources. Yet rabbinic scholars disagreed widely about how best to understand discursive and indeterminate Talmudic sources, and they also disagreed about the right methodological principles to be used in reaching conclusive legal rulings.[15] Additionally, the relatively wide normative boundaries established by Talmudic materials left substantial room for different Jewish communities to develop a range of customary religious expressions and extralegal practices.

As Jewish law developed in the centuries following the sealing of the Talmud, rabbinic scholars came to recognize a loose periodization of post-Talmudic *halakhic* development that helped establish further parameters for acceptable Jewish legal practice. The post-Talmudic era is conventionally divided into three periods. The period of the *Geonim* ("brilliant ones") is generally understood to have lasted from the seventh century until the mid-eleventh century and is characterized by the rabbinic dominance of the *Geonim*, the heads of the great Talmudic academies of the Persian Empire, who filled the roles of authoritative transmitters and interpreters of the Talmud.[16] As Jewish communities in Franco-Germany, Spain, and North Africa became more established while the Persian centers of Jewish learning were experiencing a decline,

---

They were the recipients of the tradition of the fundamentals of the Torah in an unbroken chain of transmission back to Moses.

14 *See, e.g.*, Rabbi Yitzchak Yosef, Ein Yitchak, vol. 1, 55 (2009); Biur HaGra *to* Shulchan Arukh, Choshen Mishpat 25:6; Rabbi Yom Tov Lipmann Heller, Tosafot Yom Tov, Sheviit 4:10 ("Even though the Torah can be interpreted in numerous different ways . . . when it comes to legal rulings, however, a decisor must rely on what the scholars of the Talmud have said."). *Cf.* Avraham Derbaremdiker, Seder HaDin 305-308 (2010) (discussing the parameters for the base-line legitimacy of *halakhic* rulings).

15 *See* Chaim Saiman, Halakhah: The Rabbinic Idea of Law 141-62 (2018). *See also* Moshe Halbertal, People of the Book (1997) (describing and explicating three distinct schools of rabbinic thought on how to view and understand the Talmud).

16 *See generally* Robert Brody, The Geonim of Babylonia and the Shaping of Medieval Jewish Culture (1998) (for an overview of the *Geonim*, their work and context). *See also* An Introduction to the History and Sources of Jewish Law 203-14 (Neil S. Hecht et al., eds., 1996) (discussing the legal literature produced by the *Geonim*); *id.* at 228-34 (describing the lives and works of several major Geonic scholars); *id.* at 239-41 (explaining the perceived authority of Geonic rulings within rabbinic jurisprudence).

the era of the *Geonim* gave way to the period of the *Rishonim* ("first ones").[17] The period of the *Rishonim* lasted until the end of the fifteenth century and was characterized by furious scholarly activity that produced voluminous Talmudic commentaries, codifications of Talmudic law, and responsa literature in which rabbis answered legal inquiries posed to them by private individuals and communities.[18] The third period, that of the *Acharonim* ("last ones"), is usually dated from Rabbi Joseph Karo's publication of his seminal code, the *Shulchan Arukh*, around which nearly all subsequent *halakhic* developments and discussions revolve. Following the precedent established by the *Arbah Turim*, a fourteenth century restatement of Jewish law authored by Rabbi Jacob ben Asher, the *Shulchan Arukh* divided Jewish law into four main branches: *Orach Chaim* addresses the daily ritual routine, including laws governing the observance of the Sabbath and holidays; *Yoreh Deah* deals with those areas of ritual law—such as dietary observances—that do not relate chiefly to one's daily routine; *Even HaEzer* concerns family law matters; and *Choshen Mishpat* addresses torts, contracts, property, and other civil law matters along with judicial procedure.[19] Throughout the period of the *Acharonim*, many significant scholars—themselves as important as Rabbi Karo in status and authority—wrote annotations to the *Shulchan Arukh*, which solidified the place of the work and its surrounding commentaries as the modern touchstone of Jewish law.[20]

* * * * *

According to the rabbinic jurisprudential tradition, long ago, during the biblical and Second Temple periods, Jewish law functioned much like most modern legal systems. Indeed, by many measures, the *halakhah* was very progressive for its time.[21] As described—perhaps aspirationally—in traditional rabbinic

---

17 *See* An Introduction to the History and Sources of Jewish Law 271-358 (Neil S. Hecht et al., eds., 1996).
18 *See* An Introduction to the History and Sources of Jewish Law 359-96 (Neil S. Hecht et al., eds., 1996).
19 *See* Living the Halakhic Process 16-18 (Daniel Mann, ed., 2007) (providing an overview of the topics covered in each of these four sections of Rabbi Karo's *Shulchan Arukh*).
20 Ibid., 18-26.
21 *See, e.g.,* Gerald J. Blidstein, *Capital Punishment—The Classic Jewish Discussion,* 14 Judaism 159 (1965) (on capital punishment); Samuel J. Levine, 1 Jewish Law and American Law: A Comparative Study, 133-39 (2018) (on self-incrimination); Ephraim Glatt, *The Unanimous Verdict According to the Talmud,* 3 Pace International Law Review 316, 321-28 (2013); Shlomo Pill, *Recovering Judicial Integrity: Towards a Duty-Focused Disqualification Jurisprudence Based on*

sources, the Jewish legal system had an executive authority as well as a federalized system of local courts answerable to regional appellate courts. These lower courts operated under the jurisdiction of a high court known as the *Sanhedrin*,[22] which functioned as a joint legislative and judicial assembly that resolved questions of Jewish law by majority vote. The king or other executive authority was ultimately bound to obey the law as determined by the *Sanhedrin*, as were all other subjects.[23] The *Sanhedrin* crafted rules of law that bound all, both by engaging in binding interpretations of the canonical texts of the Torah and by enacting legislative decrees of many different types, be they fences to protect Torah law, new decrees out of whole cloth to reflect differing realities, or even on rare occasions the suspension of the duties of Jewish law in response to exigencies.[24] Importantly, within this system, disputes and uncertainties about what the law was or required, as well as those about the relevant facts to which the law was to be applied, were ultimately subject to adjudication in the rabbinic courts—litigants were both obligated and obliged to obey the courts' rulings. Here, the *Sanhedrin* functioned as the court of last resort; it resolved any persistent doubts about the law by issuing authoritative interpretations of the Torah and tradition, and it unified Jewish legal practice by resolving inconsistent rulings by lower courts.[25] The determinations of the *Sanhedrin* were final, legally infallible, and binding upon all those subject to the Jewish legal system. In short, the Jewish legal system looked very much like any other legal system.

In rabbinic thought,[26] this system began to unravel at the beginning of the Common Era, a time when a number of factors contributed to the decline of Jewish law's ability to continue functioning like any other public law system. Most importantly, Rome expanded its control over Judea and Galilee, and Jewish legal and political authority eroded rapidly in the early decades of the

---

Jewish Law, 39 Fordham Urban Law Journal 511 (2011) (on judicial bias); Shlomo Pill, *Jewish Law Antecedents to American Constitutional Thought*, 85 Mississippi Law Journal 643 (2016) (on checks and balances, equal application of law, government by consent); Shlomo Pill, *The Political Enforcement of Rabbinic Theocracy? Religious Norms in Halakhic Practice*, 2 Studies in Judaism, Humanities, and the Social Sciences 23 (2018) (on religious liberty).

22 The Hebrew and Aramaic word is commonly thought to derive from the Greek *Synedrion*, a translation of the Hebrew term "Men of the Great Assembly."
23 *See* Mishneh Torah, Hilkhot Melakhim, 1:1-2:6. *See also* An Introduction to the History and Sources of Jewish Law 41-43, 127-30, 147-50 (Neil S. Hecht et al., eds., 1996).
24 *See* Mishneh Torah, Hilkhot Mamrim 1:1, 2:1-9. On rabbinic legislation generally, *see* Menachem Elon, Jewish Law: History, Sources, Principles 477-544 (Bernard Auerbach & Melvin J. Sykes trans., 1994).
25 *See* Mishneh Torah, Hilkhot Mamrim 1:4.
26 Aaron M. Schreiber, Jewish Law and Decision-Making 226-77 (1979).

Common Era. According to the Talmud, the *Sanhedrin*'s criminal jurisdiction lapsed around 30 CE.[27] It ceased formally functioning as the supreme judicial and legislative authority of the Jewish legal system altogether following the destruction of Jerusalem in 70 CE.[28] Various rabbinic assemblies and proto-*Sanhedrin* bodies continued to meet in the following centuries in order to debate and determine various pressing issues of Jewish law, but even these august bodies never wielded the kind of top-down juridical authority to determine the law possessed by the legislatures or high courts of other systems.[29] The *Sanhedrin* could no longer impose uniformity of practice among the now widely scattered and largely independent communities of the Jewish diaspora. By the mid-fourth century, any formal juridical authority to determinately decide the substance and requirements of Jewish law ceased to exist altogether.[30] The Mishnah (c. 200 CE) bears witness to this phenomenon and illustrates the devolution of the Court by routinely recounting various conflicts among the Sages without attempting to resolve them.

Due to its exilic development since the beginning of the Common Era, without a *Sanhedrin* or centralized system of judicial authority, Jewish law has evolved for the last two thousand years and developed without any clear method for resolving disputes. Talmudic, medieval, and contemporary debates about Jewish law linger, since direct, categorical rules of resolution (such as, for example, majority votes of the Supreme Court in the United States or Papal pronouncements in Canon law) do not exist. The exact reason for this is beyond the scope of this introduction,[31] yet some methodological explanation will allow the reader to have a better understanding of the relationship of the modern classical work of Jewish law, the *Arukh HaShulchan*, to other jurisprudential approaches to Jewish law and other legal systems. Frequently, the methodology of Jewish law is unintelligible to those well familiar with other legal systems but who lack a crisp understanding of the functioning of Jewish law on a practical and historical level.[32]

---

27 *See* Babylonian Talmud, Avodah Zarah 8b.
28 *See* Babylonian Talmud, Sanhedrin 37b.
29 *See* A History of the Jewish People 317-23 (H. H. Ben-Sasson, ed., 1985).
30 *See* Babylonian Talmud, Bava Kamma 84b.
31 For one account of the intentional multivocality of Jewish law, see Shlomo Pill, *Law as Engagement: A Judeo-Islamic Conception of the Rule of Law for Twenty-First Century America* (2016) (Dissertation). *See also* Avi Sagi, The Open Canon (2007). For historical explanations for rabbinic legal disagreement, see, e.g., *Introduction* to Beit Yosef *to* Arbah Turim.
32 Until the modern era, rabbinic scholars have been relatively unconcerned with producing systematic accounts of the philosophy and methodology of Jewish law. Unlike Islamic law,

From the time of the disbanding of the *Sanhedrin* through the centuries following the redaction of the two Talmuds, disputes as to what the Jewish law should be in any specific case were resolved by an informal, consensus-based voting process in which the ordained rabbis of the generation participated.[33] Not every dispute, however, was resolved, and since there was no consensus on what the normative practice should be, the law was sometimes left open with more than one practice considered reasonable and legitimate.[34] Indeed, one who studies Talmud sees that most of the Talmudic disputes are left unresolved textually, and most are not resolved through inferential logic even when the text is studied as a whole.[35]

From the early eighth century until modern times, the process for resolving Jewish legal disputes further deteriorated to the point that even informal consensus was no longer possible. Absent the ability to reach deliberate, consensus-based conclusions about what Jewish law should be, diverse *halakhic* opinions gradually proliferated, and the range of different legal views and practices on many issues steadily expanded. As a result, indeterminacy and disagreement became both an unavoidable fact of Jewish law that made it increasingly difficult to know the correct rule or standard of practice, as well as a serious impediment to the Jewish legal community's ability to settle on any

---

Canon law, Roman law, and Common law systems, pre-modern rabbinic thinking, with only a few exceptions, never produced systematic accounts of its own jurisprudence and methods of legal decision-making. Some indications of specific *halakhic* scholars' own decision-making methods can be found in the introductions to those rabbis' major *halakhic* works (for instance in Maimonides's introduction to his code, *Mishneh Torah*, and Joseph Karo's introduction to his *Beit Yosef*), as well as scattered throughout various responsa (*see, e.g.,* Responsa Masat Binyamin, no. 62) and commentaries (*see, e.g.,* Rabbi Shabbatai HaKohen, Klalei Horaah B'Issur V'Hetter).

33 Thus, for example, the Talmud sometimes concludes a dispute with the word *"vehilkheta,"* which is generally understood to mean "and this is the proper practice," denoting the consensus that is mentioned above.

34 In some instances, a consensus developed, but uncertainty has since arisen as to what that consensus ruling actually was, or to what extent a consensus had actually formed on certain points of law, which is itself often a matter of Talmudic interpretation itself. *See generally* Arbah Turim, Choshen Mishpat 25; Beit Yosef *to* Arbah Turim, Choshen Mishpat 25 (discussing variant views among early medieval authorities on the extent of Talmudic consensus).

35 *See, e.g.,* Rabbi Moses ben Jacob of Coucy, Introduction to Sefer Mitzvot Gadol (1547) (noting that the length, complexity, and dialectic nature of Talmudic material prevents it from being a source of determinate legal directives). *See generally* Shlomo Pill, *Law as Engagement: A Judeo-Islamic Conception of the Rule of Law for Twenty-First Century America*, Ch. 5 (2016) (Dissertation).

very widely accepted methodology for resolving *halakhic* disputes. The lack of doubt-resolving institutions and methods made increased legal disagreement inevitable; at the same time, the proliferation of legal disagreement made it impossible to garner widespread acceptance of any particular doubt-resolving institutions or methods.

There are several reasons for this substantial deterioration of the rabbinic jurisprudential system's ability to resolve legal doubts and clarify *halakhic* uncertainties. First, as the Jewish diaspora became more dispersed throughout Europe, Africa, Asia, and eventually the Americas, geography made communication across communities difficult. Building consensus through discourse and interaction is difficult even if all the scholars are in one location and interested in consensus; as the Jewish community became spread out over vast areas of land, it became virtually impossible.[36] Second, by the era of the *Rishonim*, increased interest in Talmud study in geographical areas with very diverse living conditions led different Jewish communities and schools of rabbis to very different ways of understanding the legal implications of Talmudic texts based on their respective social, cultural, environmental, political, economic, and religious contexts.[37] This not only resulted in different ways of thinking about and practicing Jewish law, but this also meant that even attempts at reaching rabbinic consensus across geographic bounds were stymied by scholars in different contexts speaking very different jurisprudential languages. Consensus remains possible when disputants merely disagree, but it becomes an increasingly remote possibility when discussants are merely speaking past each other with fundamentally different understandings of the subject matter at hand.[38] Third, diverse social and economic conditions began to make it harder to apply the Talmudic rules to new realities with consensus. Regionalism became a significant complexity in climate, community, economy, and many other factors. Finally, diversity increased the degree to which classical rabbinic texts became corrupted through copying and printing errors, which led different

---

36 *See, e.g., Introduction* to Beit Yosef *to* Arbah Turim.
37 *See, e.g.,* Rabbi Menachem Meiri, *Introduction* to Responsa Meiri Magen Avot (drawing on the Aristotelian idea that people tend to think and act like those around them to explain the proliferation of rabbinic disagreement over *halakhah*); Rabbi Israel Salanter, Ohr Yisrael, no. 30 (arguing that "subjective emotional forces which human beings cannot fully eradicate from their cognitive processes" prevent *halakhic* scholars from understanding anything more than "what their own eyes see").
38 For a discussion of some of the fundamentally different understandings about the nature of Jewish law and the proper methods for reaching *halakhic* decisions, see generally Moshe Halbertal, People of the Book (1997).

communities to sometimes work with different versions of the authoritative sources of Jewish law. Other texts disappeared entirely from certain regions, while some texts were deemed authentic and binding in some communities and not so much in others.[39]

Many other factors and reasons were present as well. The truth is obvious to anyone invested in law: absent a binding mechanism for forcing a consensus, such as voting or a high court of final jurisdiction, legal systems are rarely able to avoid the specters of widespread legal disagreement, indeterminacy, and uncertainty. Ponder for a minute what would happen in the United States with its fifty state supreme courts and thirteen federal circuit courts of appeal if the United States Supreme Court ceased resolving disputes between these various judicial authorities about what federal law is and what it requires. Even with a functioning Supreme Court, there is substantial diversity in how federal law is understood and applied in the courts of various states and circuits. Absent a final arbiter to "say what the law is,"[40] as Chief Justice John Marshall put it, grand diversity would take shape in a very short amount of time.[41] In this sense, the Jewish legal tradition is no different than any other; it once functioned with a relatively high degree of legal determinacy, but in the absence of institutions empowered to force uniform legal resolutions and the conditions necessary to support the development of widespread consensus, Jewish law in the medieval and modern periods can be characterized as a complex, messy universe of texts, traditions, authorities, and opinions that make it notoriously difficult to determinatively conclude what the law is and what it requires on most issues.

* * * * *

Regardless of the precise reasons, Jewish legal disputes became common by the early Middle Ages. In the absence of a widely accepted procedural method or judicial institution for resolving *halakhic* disagreements, legal decision-making became highly analytical. The principal method for determining legal uncertainties and resolving disputes was to demonstrate that one conclusion or line of reasoning substantially represented the more analytically correct

---

39 *See generally* Rabbi Moshe Walter, The Making of a Halachic Decision 163-66 (2013).
40 Marbury v. Madison, 5 U.S. 137, 177 (1803).
41 Indeed, many scholars maintain that among the most important jobs the United States Supreme Court does is enforce uniformity of federal law on important matters. For more on this, see Michael J. Broyde, Note: *The Intercircuit Tribunal and Perceived Conflicts*, New York University Law Review 62, 610-50 (1987).

understanding of the Babylonian Talmud. Support for any one *halakhic* opinion over others rested upon which view was seen by any particular scholar to be more consistent with accepted and authoritative Talmudic sources.⁴²

The opinion shown to be a more accurate and analytically persuasive interpretation of Talmudic intention, given the particular context in which it was being applied, was accepted as normative. The significance of relying on such an analytic approach to resolving *halakhic* questions, in contrast to earlier models of dispute resolution that were utilized while the *Sanhedrin* still functioned or when widespread consensus remained possible, should not be underestimated. In earlier eras, Jewish legal normativity rested less on the analytic correctness of a given ruling or determination and much more on the institutional or procedural provenance of the legal conclusion in question. Judgments of the *Sanhedrin* were per se correct, and rabbinic consensus provided its own self-referential and independent justification for accepted legal conclusions.⁴³ To use Justice Robert Jackson's famous description of the authority of the United States Supreme Court, *halakhic* rulings determined by consensus or by the *Sanhedrin* were not final because they were infallible but rather were regarded as infallible because they were final.⁴⁴ In the absence of such institutions and mechanisms, however, the normativity of any claimed rule of Jewish law had to rest on its substantive correctness in analytic terms.

Nevertheless, in many cases, the analytic tools used to evaluate the plausibility of competing Talmudic understandings and applications were insufficient to answer *halakhic* questions or resolve rabbinic disagreements—oftentimes more than one answer was deemed plausibly true within the confines of the Talmudic discourses. Indeed, there are many cases where post-Talmudic discourse reached an impasse and was unable to provide an intellectually honest determination of which view should be considered more analytically correct. For instance, regarding a Talmudic discussion of whether the daughter of a non-Jewish man and a Jewish woman is permitted to marry a *kohen*, a member of the priestly families of the tribe of Levi, three equally legitimate readings

---

42 *See* Rema *to* Shulchan Arukh, Choshen Mishpat 25:1-2.
43 Consider the rabbinic dictum that the rulings of the *Sanhedrin* (and possibly of other courts staffed by judges possessing biblical ordination) were authoritative, binding, and "correct," even when they may be analytically "wrong," e.g., "even when they tell you that right is left and left is right." Sifri Deuteronomy §17:11.
44 *See* Brown v. Allen, 344 U.S. 443, 540 (1953).

(and rulings) emerge among the post-Talmudic jurists.[45] The variances depend on whether one considers the authority of the Talmudic statements in question to be of equal weight or not. The inability to draw a single, unequivocal ruling is partially the result of the open-textual nature of the Talmud, which, while allowing flexibility for adaptation, may also at times create ambiguity by permitting two or three positions to be seen as reasonable.[46] Determining which of those reasonable positions normatively ought to be followed cannot be done in many cases through the use of first-tier principles of analytical jurisprudence alone; close Talmudic analysis simply fails to determine a single most correct result. Indeed, anyone with a reasonable familiarity with the Talmud could quickly provide dozens of examples of such.

To further complicate matters, determining Jewish law analytically on the basis of a close study of relevant Talmudic sources is only possible where the Talmud speaks to the issue in question. The Talmud remains silent on many issues, thus making any analytic determination of the correct *halakhic* standard impossible. Even when some Talmudic sources like the Jerusalem Talmud, *Midrash Halakhah*, or other Mishnaic and Talmudic materials outside the Babylonian Talmud do speak to an issue, the Babylonian Talmud itself is sometimes silent or cryptic. This too makes analytic resolutions difficult and has rendered disputes largely intractable, especially since there was little agreement among rabbinic scholars about the proper normative weight that should be accorded to these other primary rabbinic texts.[47]

The limitations of analytically determining Jewish law induced rabbinic decision makers, Talmudic commentators, and codifiers to develop various second-order rules of decision that provided guidelines for reaching *halakhic* conclusions in the many cases in which textual analysis and logical reasoning alone could not adequately indicate the correctness of one opinion over others.[48] As

---

45 Babylonian Talmud, Yevamot 44a-45b. It is worth noting that conflicting conclusions may be reached in this case despite the appearance of the term *vehilkheta*, discussed *supra* note 34.
46 *See* H.L.A. Hart, The Concept of Law 121-32 (2nd ed., 1997) (describing the nature of open-textual nature of law); H.L.A. Hart, *Positivism and the Separation of Law and Morals*, 71 Harvard Law Review 593, 607 (1958) (providing examples of what is meant by the "open-textual nature of laws").
47 *See* Michael J. Broyde, *The Yerushalmi as a Source of Halacha*, TorahMusings.com, https://www.torahmusings.com/2011/05/the-yerushalmi-as-a-source-of-halacha/ (last visited Dec. 25, 2018).
48 For compendia of such rules, *see, e.g.*, Rabbi Malachi HaKohen, Yad Malachi; Rabbi Yitzchak Yosef, Ein Yitzchak, 3 vols. (2009).

may be intuited from our previous discussion of first-order analytic approaches to determining Jewish law, these second-order principles once again shifted the focus of legal decision-making from finding the right Talmudic norm to reaching some singular legal determination, regardless of its substantive correctness in light of Talmudic precedents. To paraphrase Justice Louis Brandeis, these second-order rules of decision recognized and responded to the fact that it is sometimes more important that legal questions be clearly and definitively resolved than that they be resolved correctly.[49] Rather than purporting to ascertain which competing *halakhic* viewpoint is right, these second-order guidelines offer a framework for cutting through analytically unresolvable doubts to reach clear and determinative *halakhic* conclusions. These second-order guidelines include many nuanced and complex principles directing *halakhic* judgments in cases of doubt (such as doubts about biblical or rabbinic obligations, ritual or civil duties, which rabbis and authorities should be followed regarding various kinds of issues, and so on).[50]

It may be helpful to think about the foregoing discussion in terms of the following hierarchy of jurisprudential ideas that have been used to determine specific rules of *halakhah*. Some disputes are resolved—and some uncertainties are clarified—by groups of specially appointed scholars and jurists determining the correct legal standard, either individually or collectively, through formal procedures and majority votes. This was generally the way Jewish law disagreements were addressed prior to the destruction of the Second Temple: officially ordained rabbinic decision makers, courts, and ultimately the *Sanhedrin* itself had the judicial authority to determinatively decide what the law was. Even in the absence of such institutional frameworks, however, legal questions may be resolved by formal or informal consensus among recognized scholars whose reputations, constituencies, and affiliations with important centers of rabbinic learning are sufficient to command popular respect for their collective judgments. This was roughly the way Jewish law was determined following the demise of the *Sanhedrin* until after the sealing of the Talmud, with the Talmudic text itself representing the last instance of such rabbinic consensus determining the acceptable parameters of *halakhic* practice and discourse. In the absence of these formal and informal mechanisms for determining *halakhic* norms, some legal disputes are resolved

---

49 Burnet v. Coronado Oil & Gas Co., 285 U.S. 393, 406 (1932) (Brandeis, J., dissenting).
50 *See* Shulchan Arukh, Yoreh Deah 110-11, 242 *and* Shulchan Arukh, Choshen Mishpat 25, each of which codifies many of these rules. For a one-volume review of these rules, see Rabbi Chaim Hezekiah Medini, Sdei Chemed, Klalei HaPoskim.

analytically by determining which possible solution reflects the best analytic understanding of the primary sources—the Torah, Babylonian Talmud, and other Talmudic sources. In some instances, particular analytic legal conclusions may be buttressed and further legitimated as rabbinic consensus over time gradually endorses and builds around some rulings while marginalizing others. Many *halakhic* issues are not fully determinable analytically, however, because oftentimes primary rabbinic sources are multivocal and speak ambiguously, lending themselves to numerous equally reasonable interpretations. Additionally, even when a scholar concludes that a particular viewpoint is analytically compelling, many others are likely to disagree. As the thirteenth century rabbinic scholar Nachmanides famously observed, Jewish law is not like math or the natural sciences; it is quite light on determinative proofs and far more dependent on arguments.[51] In some such cases, questions may be resolved by resorting to doubt-resolving, second-order guidelines that establish decisional preferences based on a variety of different factors: doubts about biblical laws are resolved strictly to avoid any possible violation; doubts regarding rabbinic obligations are resolved leniently; the rulings of locally appointed rabbinic authorities and courts determine local practice; the law follows the more recent scholars; doubts in litigious disputes are resolved in the favor of defendant; and so on. In many cases, however, even these secondary, doubt-resolving principles are insufficient to reach a single conclusive result. Sometimes, competing secondary rules urge different results in the same cases. Other times, the strict rules of law determined through Talmudic analytics or second-order principles come into conflict with other important religious values or social, economic, and pragmatic concerns. In such instances, reaching determinative *halakhic* prescriptions requires mediating such tensions in principled and consistent ways that support the integrity, workability, and objectives of Jewish law.

Two Models of Codification

The lack of central organization and decision-making authority, and the legal indeterminacy and uncertainty it engenders, is a direct and substantial hindrance to the ability of Jews—and even of rabbis—to easily know and

---

51 *Introduction* to Milchamot Hashem *to Rif*.

properly observe Jewish law.[52] With the start of the medieval era, *halakhic* decision-making gradually moved away from the relatively centralized authority of the Babylonian *Geonim* to the widely dispersed rabbinic authorities across the Jewish diaspora. In response to this challenge, various scholars sought to produce codifications, restatements, and other kinds of secondary sources designed to make *halakhic* norms more clear and consistent and to make observance more feasible.[53] Broadly speaking, two general approaches to codifying *halakhah* developed in the early Middle Ages that roughly paralleled the two different models of recording Jewish tradition utilized during the Talmudic era—the Mishnah and the *gemara*.[54]

One school of thought, which arose principally among the Sephardic Jewish scholars of medieval Spain and North Africa, advocated for the production of codes of Jewish law in which indeterminate and ambiguous Talmudic discourses would be distilled into clear-cut, accessible rules of law.[55] In an important sense, this approach followed the precedent of the Mishnah. While the Mishnah does often include several variant opinions on any given issue, and while it routinely avoids clearly prescribing a particular course of conduct, it presents Jewish law in relatively terse rule statements. In a similar vein, the Sephardic codifiers sought to distill the complex dialectics of the Talmud into definitive statements of *halakhic* rules and standards devoid of excessive argumentation, prooftexts, and extralegal discussions. This process of codification began with the work of the Moroccan jurist Rabbi Isaac Alfasi (1013-1103), who was the first to attempt to craft a complete code of Jewish law. Rabbi Alfasi, also known as the *Rif*, started this process by deleting all the sections of the Talmud he thought to be non-normative or non-legal stories, as well as discursive materials that he viewed as merely the Talmud's means of reaching

---

52 *See* Babylonian Talmud, Chagigah 3b:

> "The masters of the assemblies" (Ecclesiastes 12:11): These are the students of the wise scholars who sit in many different assemblies and are engaged with the Torah. Some pronounce [the subject of legal inquiry] unclean, while others pronounce it clean; some prohibit, while others permit; some disqualify it, while others rule it fit. A person might say, "How can I study the Torah under these circumstances [where the law is so uncertain]?"

See generally Menachem Elon, Jewish Law: History, Sources, Principles 1144-49 (Bernard Auerbach & Melvin J. Sykes trans., 1994).

53 *See generally* Menachem Elon, Jewish Law: History, Sources, Principles 1149-79 (Bernard Auerbach & Melvin J. Sykes trans., 1994).

54 *See* Rabbi Moshe Walter, The Making of a Halachic Decision 39-64 (2013).

55 *See* Moshe Halbertal, People of the Book 73 (1997).

halakhic conclusions. He also occasionally shifted Talmudic texts from one place to another, and even more rarely, he incorporated into his work texts that are not found in the Babylonian Talmud. He combined this with his writing of minimal, terse notes that helped to explain the Talmudic rules as he understood them.[56] The resulting work, consisting of what was left of the text of the Babylonian Talmud after Rabbi Alfasi's deletions and together with his new additions, amounted to a substantially abridged version of the Talmud that could be read containing only normative law.[57]

The *Rif*'s work was widely admired and served as the intellectual catalyst for Maimonides's legal magnum opus, the *Mishneh Torah*.[58] Maimonides (1135-1204) was a preeminent philosopher, jurist, and physician, and he is universally acknowledged as one of the foremost arbiters of rabbinic law in all of Jewish history. By building on the conceptual goals of *halakhic* codification developed by Rabbi Alfasi and then actively writing an independent, self-standing, and complete codification of Jewish legal rules that is distinct from the Talmud, Maimonides sought to change the basic structure of *Halakhah* into an ordered, hierarchical system in which every question has one—and only one—correct answer. He organized this code around fourteen volumes, eighty-four subvolumes, and one thousand chapters in total. Had this approach alone taken hold, Jewish law could have conceivably developed into a law code similar, at some level, to many other legal systems.[59]

At the same time as the *Rif* was embarking on his project of simplification and codification of Talmudic law, however, another school of thought on the matter was emerging among the Ashkenazic Jews of Franco-Germany. This approach, led by the prominent French rabbinic scholar Rabbi Solomon

---

56 *See* Menachem Elon, Jewish Law: History, Sources, Principles 1167-73 (Bernard Auerbach & Melvin J. Sykes trans., 1994).

57 We would not claim that the *Rif* was the first to ponder such a code. Handbooks of legal rules and practical directives culled from Talmudic discussions existed in a few areas of Jewish law prior to the *Rif*, such as those written by Rabbi Saadia Gaon and Rabbi Hefetz Gaon. *See* Menachem Elon, Jewish Law: History, Sources, Principles 1150-66 (Bernard Auerbach & Melvin J. Sykes trans., 1994). These works were incomplete, however, and addressed only specific narrow areas. The *Rif* undertook to write a systemic Talmudic code.

58 Literally "Repetition of the Torah," subtitled *Sefer HaYad HaChazakah*, or "The Book of the Strong Hand." Compiled between 1170 and 1180, the *Mishneh Torah* consists of fourteen books, subdivided into sections, chapters, and paragraphs. It is the only Medieval-era work that details *all* of Jewish observance, including those laws that are only applicable when the Temple is in existence.

59 *See generally* Menachem Elon, Jewish Law: History, Sources, Principles 1180-215 (Bernard Auerbach & Melvin J. Sykes trans., 1994).

Yitzchaki (1040-1105), also known as *Rashi*,[60] as well as his disciples and descendants, rejected the priority of taking a systematic approach and creating a clearly delineated code of determinative *halakhic* rulings. Instead, proponents of this school focused on creating coherency and harmony throughout the Talmud but without attempting to then supplant the Talmud's own dialectics with their own conclusory understandings of its normative import. This school's major endeavor was to write commentaries and supercommentaries to explain the Talmud page by page, issue by issue, in attempt to harmonize the diverse strands of thought found within its often meandering, ambiguous debates.[61] When it came to these scholars discussing practical *halakhic* rulings, they tended to emphasize legal discourse—as distinct from determinate legal conclusions—as an important *halakhic* value in and of itself. Thus they tended to prefer preserving a plurality of rabbinic opinions, all kept in conversation with each other, to the prescription of singular rules of law.[62] This approach recalls the rabbinic model of *gemara*—unlike the Mishnah, the focus is on the meandering give and take of *halakhic* disputation and discussion rather than on the determination of clear-cut rules of conduct.[63]

While in theory this approach sought to make sense of the complex and often uncertain dialectics of the Talmud, unsurprisingly it largely gave rise to the opposite conclusion. Instead of clarity, even more confusion arose. In attempting to unify the Talmud, diverse theories and approaches to creating harmony developed. Within this approach, the *Tosafot* (Tosafists), a group of Franco-German scholars who lived and worked in the two centuries following *Rashi*'s death (and who included several of *Rashi*'s own descendants), created a style of legal discourse that flourished under diverse models of analytical thought with only the occasional narrowing of focus. Frequently, these scholars posited modes of Talmudic and *halakhic* analysis that, instead of contracting, vastly expanded many of the substantive disagreements in Jewish law into even greater and even more irresolvable disputes.[64]

---

60 Rabbi Solomon Yitzchaki authored comprehensive commentaries on both the Hebrew Bible and the Talmud. *Rashi*'s prominence and wide acceptance has made his work the point of departure for much of Talmudic scholarship over the last nine hundred plus years.
61 See Menachem Elon, Jewish Law: History, Sources, Principles 1118-22 (Bernard Auerbach & Melvin J. Sykes trans., 1994).
62 *See, e.g.,* Rabbi Solomon Luria, *Introduction* to Yam Shel Shlomo *to* Chullin.
63 *See* Rabbi Moshe Walter, The Making of a Halachic Decision 40 (2013); Rabbi Yom Tov Lipmann Heller, *Introduction* to Ma'adnei Yom Tov.
64 *See generally* Warren Zev Harvey, *Law in Medieval Judaism,* The Cambridge Companion to Judaism and Law 157 (Christine Hayes, ed., 2017).

Despite Maimonides's great influence, many—indeed most—of the great commentators who followed forsook Maimonides's approach to systematically codifying Jewish law. Instead, many rabbinic luminaries, including Rabbi Asher ben Yechiel, or the *Rosh*,[65] Rabbi Yom Tov Assevilli, known as the *Ritva*,[66] Nachmanides,[67] Rabbi Solomon ben Aderet, or the *Rashba*,[68] and Rabbi Menachem Meiri,[69] adopted the model of the *Tosafot* over that of Maimonides by expressing legal views in the medium of Talmudic novella or commentaries rather than in codifications of Talmudic conclusions. These scholars frequently concluded that more than one approach was viable on any given issue and as a result steadfastly refused to write definitive conclusions to Talmudic matters. By the fourteenth century, one who wished to determine what Jewish law was on a given topic would have encountered the problem that there was not one definitive legal book to consult to answer that question. Rather, there was a compendium of opinions which one would have to consider. This compendium was not organized by topic; rather, it was found in various places as commentary to the Talmudic sources.[70] Of course, Maimonides's code could be consulted, but even if it was regarded as a useful starting point for *halakhic* inquiry, its conclusions were rarely viewed as the final word on any given topic, and its rulings were not widely followed in many communities.

---

65 Rabbi Asher ben Yechiel (Ashkenazi) was born in Germany and died in Spain, where he served as a prominent rabbi for the latter half of his life. His abstract of Talmudic law focuses only on the legal (non-*aggadic*) portions of the text and specifies the final, practical *halakhah*, leaving out the intermediate discussions and entirely omitting areas of law that are limited to the Land of Israel.

66 Rabbi Yom Tov ben Avraham Asevilli of Spain is known for his clarity of thought and his commentary on the Talmud, which is extremely concise and remains one of the most frequently referred to Talmudic works today.

67 Rabbi Moses ben Naḥman Girondi, also known as Nachmanides, was born in Gerona, Spain and died in Israel. A leading medieval philosopher, physician, kabbalist, and commentator, his commentary to the Talmud, *Chidushei HaRamban*, often provides a different perspective on a variety of issues addressed by the French *Tosafot*.

68 Rabbi Solomon ben Aderet of Spain was the author of thousands of responsa, various *halakhic* works, and the *Chidushei HaRashba*, his commentary on the Talmud.

69 Rabbi Menachem Meiri of Barcelona authored his commentary, the *Beit HaBechirah*, which is arranged in a manner similar to the Talmud, presenting first the Mishnah and then the discussions and issues that arise from it. He focuses on the final upshot of the discussion and presents the differing views of that upshot and conclusion.

70 For a bibliography of such major medieval rabbinic legal works, see Menachem Elon, Jewish Law: History, Sources, Principles 1236-308 (Bernard Auerbach & Melvin J. Sykes trans., 1994).

Rabbi Asher ben Yechiel's son, Rabbi Jacob ben Asher (1250-1327), recognized this lacuna and sought to fill it by writing another, different type of restatement of Jewish law that sought to blend the very best of Maimonides's innovative systemizations while also maintaining the Tosafist preference for preserving rabbinic discourse and recognizing a plurality of different but reasonable Talmudic understandings on most issues. Unlike the *Mishneh Torah*, which was much broader in that it attempted to restate all of Jewish law—including both those laws which could be practiced absent a Temple and those which needed a Temple and Davidic monarchy to function—Rabbi Jacob covered only those areas of *halakhah* that were in force in his contemporary, pre-messianic times. It was written to be a practical and convenient *halakhic* guide for Jews living in an era with no Temple or Jewish king. His four-volume work, the *Arbah Turim* ("Four Pillars"), divided all of Jewish law into four broad subject areas: daily life, including the laws of Sabbath and festivals, family law, commercial law, and ritual law.[71]

Another major difference between the *Arbah Turim* and the *Mishneh Torah* is that the former work, unlike the latter, was not written as a definitive, univocal legal code. While Maimonides approached legal questions with the assumption that there was only one right answer, Rabbi Jacob ben Asher wrote a compendium in which every legal question admitted several reasonable answers, which he culled from the various Talmudic commentaries and Maimonides's code. As such, while the book is extremely useful, it rarely resolves disputes. The reader of the *Arbah Turim* finds that the work greatly assists in the task of collecting and organizing the many opinions on any topic, but it does not prescribe a single correct rule of law. Rabbi Joseph Karo's classic sixteenth century commentary on the *Arbah Turim*, the *Beit Yosef*, is an expansion of Rabbi Jacob ben Asher's methodology. It embellishes the *Arbah Turim*'s relatively laconic text by recording the views of many early scholars and decisors that Rabbi Jacob ben Asher did not directly reference, and it also connects these various opinions to their Talmudic sources. The *Beit Yosef* does not, however, systematically provide a mandate as to what the normative law should be. The same can be said for other major commentaries on the *Arbah Turim*, including Rabbi Joel Sirkis's *Bayit Chadash*, or the *Bach*, and Rabbi Joshua Falk Kohen's dual commentary, *Drisha U'Prisha*. Although both Sirkis and Falk Kohen broadly seek to defend the classical practices of the Ashkenazic communities of Europe from the

---

71 *See* Menachem Elon, Jewish Law: History, Sources, Principles 1277-302 (Bernard Auerbach & Melvin J. Sykes trans., 1994).

intellectual challenges of Maimonides and his followers, the reader of their works immediately senses that these are not codes but intricate Talmudic discourses on law and theory, which only sometimes reach a conclusion of law. They are unreadable to all but the best trained scholars, and they serve mainly to complicate and further obscure efforts to cut through rabbinic disagreements and assert definitive *halakhic* conclusions on most questions.[72]

Building the Set Table: Rabbi Joseph Karo's *Shulchan Arukh*

To rectify this situation and to return to the code model, Rabbi Joseph Karo undertook the responsibility of writing yet another legal code, the *Shulchan Arukh*, which was meant to follow the organizational structure of the *Arbah Turim* while using the methodology of Maimonides.[73] In other words, Rabbi Karo set out to write a work that provides one—and almost always only one—answer to questions of Jewish law in the areas covered by the *Arbah Turim*.[74] In fact, the *Shulchan Arukh* derives most of its rules from Maimonides's earlier code, though it does frequently deviate from Maimonides's rulings, especially when a unanimous consensus from other authorities rejects those views. Significantly, Rabbi Karo chose to call his work the *Shulchan Arukh*, or "Set Table,"[75] to suggest that everything was prepared for its user. Here, Rabbi Karo was playing off of a famous rabbinic interpretation of the biblical verse that

---

72　*See generally* ibid.
73　*See generally* ibid.
74　There are instances in the *Shulchan Arukh* where Rabbi Karo will give a ruling and will then give another opinion using the phrase, "There are those who say," or something to that effect. When this occurs, Rabbi Karo is not seeking to avoid giving a definitive normative position. Rather, he does this in circumstances where he concluded that, due to the historical difficulties of the time, as discussed above, a truly definitive decision has not been reached. Therefore, Rabbi Karo tries to account for veritable alternatives even while indicating the position he deems normative.
75　Regarding the work's title, and as noted by Broyde and Bedzow, some background on the names of Jewish books is needed, if for no other reason than to explain why the single most significant work of Jewish law written in the last five hundred years, the *Shulchan Arukh*, should have a name which translates into English as "The Set Table" (*see generally* Michael J. Broyde & Ira Bedzow, The Codification of Jewish Law and an Introduction to the Jurisprudence of the Mishna Berura 379-81 (2014)). Unlike the tradition of most Western law, in which the titles to scholarly publications reflect the topics of the works (consider John T. Noonan, Jr. and Edward McGlynn Gaffney, Religious Freedom: History, Cases and Other Materials on the Interaction of Religion and Government (3rd ed., 2011)), the tradition in Jewish legal literature is that a title rarely names the relevant subject or subjects. Instead, the title usually consists either of a pun based on the title of an earlier work on which

introduces one of the Torah's main recitations of the law: "These are the laws that you [Moses] shall place before them [the people]."⁷⁶ The Mishnaic sage Rabbi Akiva understood that the verse's seemingly superfluous instruction to "place" the law in front of the people should be understood as an exhortation to make the law readily understandable to those who are expected to practice and

---

the current writing comments, or a literary phrase, into which the authors' names have been worked (sometimes in reliance on literary license), or some other literary device.

A few examples demonstrate each phenomenon. Rabbi Jacob ben Asher's classical treatise on Jewish law was entitled "The Four Pillars" (*Arbah Turim*) because it classified all of Jewish law into one of four areas. A major commentary on this work that to a great extent, supersedes the work itself is called "The House of Joseph" (*Beit Yosef*), since it was written by Rabbi Joseph Karo. Once Karo's commentary (i.e., the house) was completed, one could hardly see "The Four Pillars" on which it was built. A reply commentary by Rabbi Joel Sirkis, designed to defend "The Four Pillars" from Karo's criticisms, is called "The New House" (*Bayit Chadash*). Sirkis proposed his work (i.e., the new house) as a replacement for Karo's prior house.

When Rabbi Karo wrote his own treatise on Jewish law, he called it "The Set Table" (*Shulchan Arukh*), which was based on (i.e., located in) "The House of Joseph," his previous commentary on Jewish law. Rabbi Moses Isserles's glosses to Rabbi Karo's "Set Table"—which were really intended vastly to expand "The Set Table"—are called "The Tablecloth" (*Mapah*) because no matter how nice the table is, once the tablecloth is on it, one hardly notices the table. Rabbi David HaLevi Segal's commentary on the *Shulchan Arukh* was named the "Golden Pillars" (*Turei Zahav*), denoting an embellishment on the "legs" of the "Set Table." This type of humorous interaction continues to this day in terms of titles of commentaries on the classical Jewish law work, the *Shulchan Arukh*.

Additionally, there are book titles that are mixed literary puns and biblical verses. For example, Rabbi Shabbatai ben Meir HaKohen wrote a very sharp critique on the above-mentioned *Turei Zahav* (Golden Pillars), which he entitled *Nekudat HaKesef*, "Spots of Silver," a veiled misquote of the verse in Song of Songs 1:11, which states "we will add bands of gold to your spots of silver." Thus, HaKohen's work is really "The Silver Spots on the Golden Pillars," with the understanding that it is the silver that appears majestic when placed against an entirely gold background.

Other works follow the model of incorporating the name of the scholar into the work. For example, the above-mentioned Rabbi Shabbatai ben Meir HaKohen's commentary on the *Shulchan Arukh* itself is entitled *Sifsei Kohen*, "The Lips of the Kohen," a literary embellishment of "Shabbatai HaKohen," the author's name, as well as a veiled reference to Malachi 2:7, which reads, "*Ki sifsei kohen yishmeru da'at*," or "the lips of the Kohen [priest] guard knowledge." Rabbi Moses Feinstein's collection of responsa is called *Igrot Moshe*, "Letters from Moses." Hundreds of normative works of Jewish law follow this model.

Of course, a few leading works of Jewish law are entitled in a manner that informs the reader of their content. Thus, the Fourteenth Century Spanish sage Nahmanides wrote a work on issues in causation entitled "Indirect Causation in [Jewish] Tort Law" (*Grama B'Nezikin*), and the modern Jewish law scholar Eliav Schochetman's classical work on civil procedure in Jewish law is called "Arranging the Case," a modern Hebrew synonym for civil procedure.

76 Exodus 21:1.

observe it. It should be taught thoroughly so that it will be "systematically organized in their mouths" and presented "like a set table" from which the people may consume the law without any need for further analysis.[77] Rabbi Karo set out to do the same. Drawing on his more elaborate and analytically involved work in the *Beit Yosef* commentary on the *Arbah Turim*, he sought to produce a comprehensive codification of Jewish legal rules and principles ready-made for easy use. Rabbi Karo describes his reasons for writing the book as follows:

> I saw in my heart that it would be good to put the numerous statements [in the *Beit Yosef*] in a condensed form and in a precise language so that the Torah of God will be continuous and fluent in the mouth of every Jew ... so that any practical ruling about which he may question will be clear to him when this magnificent book which covers everything is fluent in his mouth.... Moreover, young students will study it continuously so that they memorize it. Its clear language regarding the practical *Halakhah* will be set on their young lips so that when they get older, they will not deviate from it. Also, scholars will take care of it as if it was light from the Heavens easing them from their troubles, and their souls will be recreated when studying this book which contains all the sweet *halakhot*, decided without controversy.[78]

According to Rabbi Karo, those who would read the *Shulchan Arukh* would be able to discern the laws of daily living and would not need to consult other opinions. He accomplished his goal—the *Shulchan Arukh* is written in fairly simple Hebrew and is in a simple, rule-based manner understandable to people who have neither studied Talmud nor learned law. It is a code similar in style to Maimonides's *Mishneh Torah*.

The codification, however, succeeded only if the underlying assumption for its commentators was that it was in fact a "set table" and needed only a few minor adornments or adjustments. In the case of the *Shulchan Arukh*, this impression was not to be. Consistent with the historical development of Jewish Law, immediately after the publication of the *Shulchan Arukh*, other Jewish law authorities began to write extensive commentaries on it, both to explain Rabbi

---

77 *See* Mekhilta D'Rabbi Shimon bar Yochai 21:1.
78 *Introduction* to Shulchan Arukh.

Karo's relatively terse text, and more frequently, to correct what these scholars saw as its errors.[79]

The first to comment was Rabbi Moses Isserles (1520-1572), who appended his own views—which reflected the Ashkenazic *halakhic* traditions in contrast to Rabbi Karo's nearly exclusive presentation of accepted rules and practices of Sephardic Jewry—to the *Shulchan Arukh* so as to provide alternative positions.[80] Rabbi Isserles, known as the *Rema*, also authored a commentary on the *Arbah Turim* titled *Darkhei Moshe* that paralleled Rabbi Karo's *Beit Yosef*, supplementing and embellishing the *Arbah Turim*'s restatement of Jewish law without systematically providing the normative *halakhah*. Additionally, Rabbi Isserles wrote a legal work called *Torat HaChatat* which was more similar to a code, albeit only on a few areas of Jewish law.[81] In his thousands of glosses on Rabbi Karo's *Shulchan Arukh*, Rabbi Isserles incorporated Ashkenazic Jewry's practices into the predominantly Sephardic-oriented work.[82] These glosses, however, revert back to the practice of accepting juridical ambiguity. The *Rema* is inclined to cite more than one opinion as normative, both in theory and in practice, and he frequently cites conflicting views without offering any clear direction about how to resolve such contradictions.[83] Unlike Rabbi Karo, who generally follows a secondary rule of decision that prefers any *halakhic* position adopted by the majority of his preferred precedential decisors, such as the *Rosh*, Maimonides, and Rabbi Alfasi,[84] Rabbi Isserles never provides a clear set of rules as to how he decides matters of Jewish law. Indeed, the *Rema* criticizes Rabbi Karo's reliance on this secondary rule for resolving *halakhic* disputes in the introduction to his glosses to the *Shulchan Arukh*, and he explains his

---

79 For a review of these commentaries, see Menachem Elon, Jewish Law: History, Sources, Principles 1423-43 (Bernard Auerbach & Melvin J. Sykes trans., 1994).
80 *See* Rabbi Moses Isserles, *Introduction* to Darkhei Moshe.
81 *See* Menachem Elon, Jewish Law: History, Sources, Principles 1357-59 (Bernard Auerbach & Melvin J. Sykes trans., 1994).
82 *Ibid. See also* Rabbi Moses Isserles, *Introduction* to Rema *to* Shulchan Arukh:

> [Rabbi Joseph Karo's] books are full of rulings that do not follow the interpretations of the [Ashkenazic] scholars from whose waters we drink—the important authorities among the Ashkenazic Jews, who have long been our eyes, and upon whom the earlier generations relied . . . which are built upon the words of the *Tosafot* and the French scholars from whom we are descended."

83 *See, e.g.*, Rema *to* Shulchan Arukh, Orach Chaim 111:1, 232:2, 467:12; Rema *to* Shulchan Arukh, Yoreh Deah 89:1, 391:2; Rema *to* Shulchan Arukh, Even HaEzer 27:1, 165:1.
84 *See* Beit Yosef *to* Arbah Turim, *Introduction* to Orach Chaim.

criticism of Rabbi Karo in this exact way in his *Darkhei Moshe*. After advancing two different reasons for his work, he explains:

> The third and primary reason for writing this work is, as is known, that the author of the *Beit Yosef* was enamored with the giants of Jewish law and ruled normatively like two or three of the great Jewish law scholars testified: these are the beloved *Rif*, Maimonides, and *Rosh*, so that when all three of them adopted one approach, then he paid no attention to other great scholars of Torah at all. In the place of other scholars, he would rule like two of them . . . and based on this he discarded all of the customs of our communities . . .[85]

Indeed, it is quite common for the Rema to cite—with no clear indication of which view he adopts—more than one reasonable view, even when these views are completely contradictory.[86]

Upending the Set Table: The Rise of the Commentators

In the century and a half following the appearance of the *Shulchan Arukh*, many additional commentaries to Rabbi Karo's code appeared.[87] These works provided the Talmudic and early rabbinic bases for Rabbi Karo's clear-cut rulings, suggested rationales for his decisions, applied the *Shulchan Arukh*'s rules to new cases, and voiced disagreement with Rabbi Karo's conclusions. Very often, these various commentaries disagreed with each other as well, and as a result they added to the uncertainty about how to determine normative rules of Jewish law.

The most significant early commentaries that grew up around the *Shulchan Arukh* include Rabbi Mordechai ben Abraham Yaffe of Prague's (1530-1612) *Levush*;[88] Polish Rabbi David HaLevi Segal's (1586-1667) *Turei Zahav*, or *Taz*; Rabbi Samuel Feibush's (1650-1706) *Beit Shmuel*; Rabbi Shabbatai HaKohen's

---

85 See Darkhei Moshe to Arbah Turim, *Introduction*.
86 For an excellent example of this, see the simple rule found in Shulchan Arukh, Even HaEzer 21:5, where the *Rema* cites five views, some stricter and some more lenient than the view of the *Shulchan Arukh*. In truth, many cases such as this abound, and thus the *Rema* is much less of a "code" than *Shulchan Arukh*.
87 *See generally* Menachem Elon, Jewish Law: History, Sources, Principles 1423-43 (Bernard Auerbach & Melvin J. Sykes trans., 1994).
88 The claim could be made that the *Levush* is a rival code and not a true commentary, but this strikes us as incorrect for the purposes of this work, since the *Levush* assumes that the reader

(1621-1662) *Sifsei Kohen*, or *Shakh*; Rabbi Joshua Falk Kohen's (1555-1614) *Sefer Meirat Einayim*, or *Semah*; Rabbi Moses ben Isaac Judah Lima's (1615-1670) *Chelkat Mechokek*; and Rabbi Abraham HaLevi's (1633-1683) *Magen Avraham*. Within a relatively short time, many of these texts were printed on the same page alongside the text of Rabbi Karo's *Shulchan Arukh* and the *Rema*'s glosses.[89] In particular, on the *Orach Chaim* section of the *Shulchan Arukh* (which deals with daily laws and which is the subject of this book), the *Taz* and the *Magen Avraham* wrote detailed commentaries that incorporate a variety of positions found neither in the *Shulchan Arukh* nor in the *Rema*'s glosses. These include citations from the Talmud, the mystical traditions embodied in the text of the *Zohar*,[90] opinions of many additional early rabbinic authorities, and religious customs practiced in Central and Eastern Europe. The *Shulchan Arukh*, along with its commentaries, was transformed over the relatively short period of time of a century—from a set table to a crowded one—in which the right answer was no longer clear.[91]

---

has read the *Shulchan Arukh* and *Rema* and is referring to his work as an additional source of information.

89   *See* Menachem Elon, Jewish Law: History, Sources, Principles 1417-1419 (Bernard Auerbach & Melvin J. Sykes trans., 1994).

90   Meaning literally, "splendor"; the *Zohar* is the foundational work in kabbalistic literature. The *Zohar* first appeared in Spain in the thirteenth century and was published by a Jewish writer named Moses de Leon. De Leon ascribed the work to Rabbi Shimon bar Yochai, a second-century *Tanna*, who hid in a cave for thirteen years studying the Torah to escape Roman persecution and, according to legend, was inspired by the Prophet Elijah to write the *Zohar*.

91   Of course, there were always those Jewish law authorities who highlighted the de-codification and insisted that this was a—or even the—central feature of Jewish law. This school of thought was pressed most vigorously by Rabbi Solomon Luria in his anti-*Shulchan Arukh* polemic in the beginning of his commentary, *Yam Shel Shlomo* to both *Bava Kamma* and *Chullin*. Rabbi Luria makes three important points. First, he states that diversity is a central feature of the Talmudic discourse, and that searches for the "correct" answer is methodologically fruitless, because there is frequently no single correct answer. Second, he argues that even when a single answer could be correct, the process of following the majority of a group of decisions—even as great as the *Rif*, Maimonides, and the *Rosh*—is methodologically invalid. All opinions need to be considered. Third, he claims that Talmudic discourse is central, while codes serve as shortcut for weaker authorities to defer to putatively greater authorities without directly confronting the central Talmudic texts in order to determine which answer is actually most suited for the question in front of them.

A modern example of this sentiment is Rabbi Nathan Lopez Cordozo's recent plea for decodification:

> One of the Talmud's greatest contributions to Judaism is its indetermination, its frequent refusal to lay down the law. Talmudic discussions consist primarily of competing positions, often lacking a clear decision on which view is authoritative. The reason is obvious: *there*

Precisely by adopting the *Shulchan Arukh* as a central organizational model of Jewish law—and not the Mishnah, Talmud, or *Mishneh Torah*—the authors of these voluminous commentaries ensured that the *Shulchan Arukh* would become the central touchstone document of Jewish law. However, by adopting the model of writing commentaries on Rabbi Karo's code, and by declining to venerate the substantive rules adopted by the *Shulchan Arukh*, the commentators ensured the continued relevance—even primacy—of the Tosafist tradition of diverse and confusing Jewish law with no certain rules and no clear processes for determining what to do in practice.[92] The *Shulchan Arukh* thus made a deep and lasting contribution to Jewish law, but it was not at all the contribution that

---

      should not be one. The well-known Talmudic statement *"Elu ve-elu divrei Elokim Chaim"* (These and those are the words of the Living God) supports this position. Halachic disagreement and radically opposing opinions are of the essence. There is a profound reason for this principle. The Torah, which is the word of God, can only be multifaceted. Like God Himself, it can never fit into a finalized system, for it is much too broad in scope. Every human being is different; the Torah must therefore be different to each one of them, showing nearly infinite dimensions and possibilities. *This is one of the most fascinating aspects of Jewish Tradition, making it strikingly distinct from the religions of the world.*

Nathan Lopes Cardozo, *The In-Authenticity of Codifying Jewish Law*, CardozoAcademy.org, https://www.cardozoacademy.org/thoughts-to-ponder/codifying-jewish-law-not-authentic/ (last visited May 16, 2019).

But we think that, whatever the objective merits of this argument, this controversy is long since over – and both sides won. Rabbi Luria lost the battle against codification, although he might have won the war in his observation that the codes are not "binding" (in the same way that the United States Code is binding). Thus, while the *Shulchan Arukh* and the glosses of the *Rema* have become both a canonical text (and the *Yam Shel Shlomo* remains an important but marginal text), neither of these texts—nor any other code, including Maimonides's code, are generally binding: they are just a starting point in the development of Jewish law. As we show in this work, frequently the code is just a format, and the author—in this case, the Arukh HaShulchan—sees neither the formulation of the *Shulchan Arukh* nor the *Rema* as binding at all. Rather, the organizational framework of the *Shulchan Arukh* is a valuable one through which to ponder questions of normative Jewish law.

92 This point is worthy of emphasis. When an American law scholar writes a commentary on the United States Code, the starting point is to explain the U.S.C., which is always "correct" in the sense that it is truly "the law," but which is sometimes in need of explanation or even resolution of conflicts. When a modern Catholic scholar writes a commentary on the 1983 (most recent) Code of Canon Law, it is to explain the code; the author will never and cannot argue that the Code is not "the law." Such is not the case in commentaries on the *Shulchan Arukh*, each of which repeatedly argues for the incorrectness of the code in specific cases. Rabbi Karo's commentary on Maimonides's *Mishneh Torah*, titled *Kessef Mishnah*, is closer to the model of defending a canonized code. In certain ways the modern Sephardic Code, *Yalkut Yosef* by Rabbi Yitzchak Yosef, is an attempt to treat the *Shulchan Arukh* as a canonized text, although a more detailed study would reveal this to be a woefully incomplete explanation of that work.

Rabbi Karo had hoped for. Instead, he and Rabbi Isserles contributed an organizational structure for Jewish law that has stood the test of five hundred years. Ever since the publication of the *Shulchan Arukh* in the mid-1500s, virtually all major and comprehensive treatments of Jewish law have been organized around, in response to, and founded upon both the structure and content of Rabbi Karo's text—even as they often vigorously disagree with his and each other's *halakhic* conclusions.[93] Jewish law is divided into four basic groupings: daily law, family law, commercial law, and ritual law, and each of these basic groupings is divided into many different topic subgroups to allow ease of access and understanding. This division is a basic contribution in itself.

Consider the rules of daily ritual law, which is the focus of this work. The *Orach Chaim* section of the *Shulchan Arukh* is divided into 696 smaller chapters, grouped into twenty-nine topical sections that address common topics in a shared theme—for example, laws of morning prayers, the laws of *tzitzit*, and so on—which allow the reader to readily find the exact topic desired. This reference type access, with an intuitive organization reflective of the sequence in which topics naturally arise in a home governed by Jewish law, has made the *Shulchan Arukh* a simple work to use.[94] A huge proportion of all subsequent works of Jewish law are organized around its practical organizational system, but Rabbi Karo's text is not formally binding on its own.

Even as Jewish law became organizationally simpler, it became legally much more complex with every passing year. After the first wave of commentaries on the *Shulchan Arukh* was completed in the early eighteenth century, a new generation of scholars began to produce supercommentaries on these

---

93 But, see Rabbi Solomon Ganzfried's *Kitzur Shulchan Arukh*, which provides extremely abbreviated and clear-cut rules on those areas of Jewish law that relate to the ordinary lives of lay people, and is a stand-alone *halakhic* work.

94 This is a frequently missed idea. Maimonides's work is hard to use and deeply counter-intuitive in its organizational structure. The Talmud is even more disorganized. Such is not the case for the *Shulchan Arukh*. Its first section, *Orach Chaim*, follows the simple three cycles approach. The first 241 chapters codify all of daily Jewish law, starting from when a person wakes up and concluding with when a person goes to sleep. Topics are covered in the order a person would encounter them during the day. Chapters 242 to 417 cover the Sabbath laws, starting with bringing in the Sabbath and concluding with the rituals that one does to end the Sabbath, followed then by the very technical rules related to building an *eruv*. The third cycle is the festival cycle, which starts with the most common and routine monthly new moon festival, and then discusses Passover, Shavuot, the Fast days, the New Year celebration, Yom Kippur, Sukkot and Lulav, Hanukkah and then Purim, exactly in the order one would encounter them if one started the year with the first Hebrew month, Nissan. Ease of use is a central feature.

earlier commentaries. Rabbi Joseph ben Meir Teomim (1727-1792) authored the *Pri Megadim* commentary on the *Shulchan Arukh* itself, as well as the *Mishbetzot Zahav* and *Eshel Avraham* as supercommentaries on the *Taz* and *Magen Avraham*, respectively. These works created yet another layer of new analysis and elaboration on many areas of Jewish law and life. Indeed, the list of important supercommentators who lived from the late seventeenth century through the early nineteenth century is both long and impressive. It includes Rabbi Judah Ashkenazi (1730-1770), author of the well-known *Be'er Heitev*; Rabbi Hezekiah da Silva (1659-1698), who wrote the *Pri Chadash*; Rabbi Chaim Margoliyot (1780-1823), author of *Shaarei Teshuva*; Rabbi Samuel ben Nathan HaLevi Loew (1720–1806), who wrote *Machatzit HaShekel*; and many others who wrote derivative commentaries[95] on the *Shulchan Arukh*. Rabbinic legal scholarship was flourishing, but these new works left Jewish law more confused—it grew harder and harder to determine what Jewish law really mandated of its adherents as the commentaries grew longer, more nuanced, and less clear. Furthermore, deciding which commentary was "correct" became almost impossible for even well-trained rabbis to do, never mind laypeople who could read Hebrew and were interested in topics of Jewish law and practice.

By 1830, three detailed additions to the *Orach Chaim* section of the *Shulchan Arukh* had appeared. These were the *Biur HaGra* by Rabbi Elijah ben Solomon Zalman Kramer (1720-1797), also known as the Vilna Gaon; the *Shulchan Arukh HaRav*, written by Rabbi Shneur Zalman of Liadi (1745-1813), the first Rebbe of the Chabad-Lubavitch Hasidic dynasty; and Rabbi Akiva Eiger's (1761-1837) *Hagahot*. The methodological gaps between these three works are wide, but all three substantially contributed to the further complication and multivocality of Jewish law and jurisprudence that made discerning the "right" *halakhic* rule on any given issue even more difficult and uncertain. The Vilna Gaon's *Biur HaGra* consists of a combination of reference notes and brief comments appended directly to the text of Rabbi Karo's *Shulchan Arukh*. It focuses on citing Talmudic texts, including the Jerusalem Talmud, that constitute the jurisprudential foundations of the topics discussed by Rabbi Karo in his own work in a style that is at once concise, cryptic, and not deferential to the precedent of post-Talmudic authorities that came before it. The *Shulchan Arukh HaRav*, written by the first Lubavitcher Rebbe, is a classic synthesis of prior codes, albeit with a slight Hasidic, mystical slant. Importantly, while Rabbi

---

95 By this term, we mean that the writer of the commentary assumes that the reader has seen other earlier commentaries and is looking for further explanation.

Shneur Zalman of Liadi's work is organized around the general structure used by Rabbi Karo, it is fundamentally a stand-alone text that, in some circles, rivals even the *Shulchan Arukh* itself as a basic text of Jewish law. *Hagahot Rabbi Akiva Eiger*, written as a supercommentary on the prior works of the *Magen Avraham* and the *Taz*, brings sharp insights and the methodology of the *Tosafot* back into the legal discussion. On complex and nuanced questions, these three important authorities on the *Shulchan Arukh* rarely agree. The reasons are obvious: one of them is reaching back into the whole of the Talmudic rabbinic corpus; one is reaching back only to the traditions of *Rashi* and his disciples while adding a mystical outlook; and one is continuing the work of the *Magen Avraham* and *Taz*, commenting on and complicating the work of the last generation of commentators. There is no reason to assume that complex matters would be resolved identically by each of these three works.

By the mid-1800s, two additional, short, but important self-standing legal codes had become popular—the *Chayei Adam* by Rabbi Abraham ben Yechiel Mikhel of Danzig (1748-1820) and Rabbi Solomon Ganzfried's (1804-1886) *Kitzur Shulchan Arukh*—which attempted to resolve all disputes and provide a singularly correct *halakhic* directive that could be easily comprehended and observed by laypeople. While both of these works of Jewish law were written by eminent Jewish scholars, each has a totally different style and approach to codification. The *Kitzur Shulchan Arukh* is both simple to use and practically strict, whereas the *Chayei Adam*, whose author was a disciple of the Vilna Gaon, is deeply analytical in its approach to Jewish law. Both, however, were revolutionary for their time in that they abandoned the organizational structure of the *Shulchan Arukh* and crafted their own structure while aiming for simplicity in codifying Jewish law. These were an attempt to "set a new table" so that their readers would not be confused by the crowded table that Rabbi Karo's *Shulchan Arukh* had become. That these two new codes were well received despite—or perhaps because of—the fact that neither of them even followed the basic organizational structure of the "Set Table" of the *Shulchan Arukh* was reflective of the problems that the commentators' crowding of Rabbi Karo's table had engendered.

This approximately three-hundred-year period of "crowding the table" also saw the rejuvenation and development of responsa literature, which was a separate genre from the commentaries. The responsa literature, comprised of questions and answers on matters of *halakhah* collected into volumes, formed an alternative to the model of discerning normative law through codes and Talmudic commentaries. While the genre had been dormant—though not extinct—for many years in acquiescence to the focus on writing commentaries, by the 1700s the responsa literature was the primary vehicle used by some rabbinic authorities for determining and communicating *halakhic* norms.[96] For instance, Rabbi Ezekiel Landau (1713-1793) and Rabbi Moses Sofer (1762-1839), as well as many other highly regarded European scholars and decision makers, chose to write responsa—rather than commentaries or stand-alone codes—as their primary vehicle for sharing their views of Jewish law, adding a whole other set of literature to the melting pot of Jewish law. This literature also rarely followed the set-table organizational model and contributed further to the complication and indeterminacy of *halakhic* jurisprudence.[97]

Conclusion: The Table in Disarray

By the year 1880, a little more than three hundred years after the initial 1577 publication of Rabbi Karo's *Shulchan Arukh* with the *Rema*'s glosses,[98] Jewish law in Eastern Europe was anything but clear. There were more than a dozen significant codes, commentaries, and other texts illuminating a myriad of topics, from minor customs and practices to major matters of Torah law.[99] It was difficult for a legal scholar, let alone a layperson, to discern what was normative *halakhic* practice on even simple matters. Needless to say, it was much harder to find where to turn when deciding complicated issues.

Generally speaking, one can say that until the late 1800s, works of Jewish law generally fell into one of five categories.[100] First, there were the major restatements like the *Arbah Turim* and *Beit Yosef*, which provided broad, comprehensive surveys of rabbinic opinions spanning across particular geographic and temporal spaces, often ruling based on minimal rules of authority and

---

96 Rabbinic authorities had always written responsa to answer *halakhic* questions. The difference is that at this time writing responsa went from being a practical method of discerning *halakhah* for individuals to being the primary genre used by rabbis to demonstrate what the normative *halakhah* should be in general.

97 Two indices to the responsa literature—*Pitchei Teshuva* and *Shaarei Teshuva*—are an attempt to organize the responsa literature around the organizational structure of the set table. Of course, both further crowd the table.

98 *See* Joseph M. Davis, The Shulchan Arukh and Sixteenth Century Jewish Law (2012).

99 For a comprehensive listing and brief descriptions of the main codes and commentaries on Jewish law, see Shlomo M. Pereira, *Codes of Jewish Law and their Commentaries: Historical Notes* (5763), *available at* http://www.lookstein.org/resource/jewish_law_codes.pdf.

100 *See generally* Michael J. Broyde & Ira Bedzow, The Codification of Jewish Law and an Introduction to the Jurisprudence of the Mishna Berura 13-14 (2014) for a similar discussion of the history of the rabbinic codification of *halakhah*.

provenance.[101] The second category, exemplified by the *Shulchan Arukh* and Maimonides's *Mishneh Torah*, consists of works which clearly delineate the laws without commentary or explanation. Rabbi Ganzfried's *Kitzur Shulchan Arukh*—though much smaller and less influential—falls into the category as well. The works intend to provide an easy guidebook for proper action. Some, like the *Mishneh Torah*, were meant to stand independent of any other work; others, such as the *Kitzur Shulchan Arukh*, are meant for younger students and for quick review and presuppose that their audience will look elsewhere for greater in-depth analysis.[102] The third category includes works like the *Rema's* glosses on the *Shulchan Arukh* and Rabbi Abraham ben David of Posquieres's (1125-1198) (known as the *Raabad*) glosses on the *Mishneh Torah*, as well as the many other commentaries that grew up around the *Shulchan Arukh*. These texts are primarily editorial or commentative works that add to, update, or correct information contained in foundational works written by others.[103] The fourth category contains works, such as the Rabbi Solomon Luria's (1510-1574) *Yam Shel Shlomo*, which attempt to collect all relevant information on a topic, from the Talmud to contemporary times, in order to evaluate the subject properly and determine the correct decision independent of the structure and substance of the major codes and commentaries. Finally, a fifth category includes the voluminous responsa literature which, rather than seeking to systematize Jewish law and determine *halakhic* norms from within some conceptual framework, focused instead on providing concrete answers and directions on how to legally address specific real-world questions on discrete topics in rabbinic jurisprudence. Of course, these categories are not always so distinct such that a work need only fit into one of them. For example, works like those of the *Magen Avraham*, *Taz*, and *Shakh* use a hybrid method of commentary, such that they can fit into more than one category, while some writers wrote responsa, which they turned into commentary on the codes.

---

101 For Rabbi Jacob ben Asher, the final decision (if he adopts one) is that of his father Rabbi Asher ben Yechiel; for Rabbi Karo, the decision is determined by the majority opinion cited.

102 Whether such is the actual case or not is irrelevant to the author's intention (referring to the *Mishneh Torah* standing independent of any other work).

103 In the *Rema's* case, additions are meant to include the local practices of Ashkenaz, which are omitted in the *Shulchan Arukh*. In the *Raabad's* case, additions are meant to correct what are seen as errors.

CHAPTER TWO

Rabbi Yechiel Mikhel Epstein's *Arukh HaShulchan*

Introduction

The Jewish legal landscape in the second half of the nineteenth century was thus a veritable quagmire of conflicting texts, commentaries, authorities, and competing opinions that made determining the correct course of conduct on any particular question difficult for laypeople and scholars alike. The *halakhic* uncertainty engendered by the state of rabbinic jurisprudence was further exacerbated by the fact that by the late 1800s, the Jewish world was undergoing sustained and cataclysmic changes. The Enlightenment had posed substantial challenges to many aspects of traditional rabbinic thought,[1] and Emancipation and the gradual transformation of Jews into members of European civil society during the nineteenth century raised new questions about the interaction of Jewish legal norms with the prevailing cultural mores and practices of the general societies into which Jews sought to integrate.[2] New modes of thinking and

---

1 *See generally* Eliyahu Stern, *Enlightenment Conceptions of Judaism and Law*, 215, in The Cambridge Companion to Judaism and Law (Christine Hayes, ed. 2017); Jacob Katz, Out of the Ghetto: The Social Background of Jewish Emancipation, 1770-1870, pp. 142-160 (1998); Michael A. Meyer, *Modernity as a Crisis for the Jews*, 9:2 Modern Judaism 151 (1989).

2 On Jewish Emancipation in Europe generally, see Pierre Birnbaum & Ira Katznelson, eds., Paths of Emancipation: Jews, States, and Citizenship (1995). On the impacts of emancipation on European Jewish life, see generally Michael Goldfarb, Emancipation: How Liberating Europe's Jews from the Ghetto Led to Revolution and Renaissance (2009); David Ellenson, After Emancipation: Jewish Religious Responses to Modernity (2004); J.M. Hess,

ideologies—secularism, historical criticism, nationalism, socialism, and liberalism, among others—made substantial inroads into various aspects of Jewish life and into various segments of the Jewish community.[3] All this served to challenge many traditional rabbinic responses to legal and theological questions and indeed raised many new and unprecedented questions that for traditional Jews often demanded *halakhic* answers.[4]

The stage was thus set for a fresh reconsideration of the great body of diverse *halakhic* thought and opinion that had grown up around Rabbi Karo's *Shulchan Arukh* during the preceding centuries. In much the same vein as Maimonides's *Mishneh Torah* attempted to cut through the accumulated mass of rabbinic thinking that had accumulated from the close of the Talmudic era up to his own time,[5] and similarly to how both the *Arbah Turim* and *Shulchan Arukh* served to take stock of and systematize the messy expanse of conflicting *halakhic* literature that had developed in the preceding centuries,[6] by the end of the 1800s the state of Jewish law demanded a fresh attempt to reorder the by then very crowded and disordered table.

In fact, in response to this exigency, two different new codifications of Jewish law were produced around the turn of the twentieth century. Importantly, and perhaps not surprisingly, these two works reflect and continue the two different—but longstanding and well-established—traditions of *halakhic* codification discussed in the previous chapter. One work, Rabbi Israel Meir Kagan's (1839-1933) *Mishnah Berurah*, follows the Mishnaic model of offering relatively simple and clear-cut legal prescriptions that attempt to cut through and are unencumbered by the multivocality and complexity of rabbinic discourse

---

Germans, Jews, and the Claims of Modernity (2002); Carol Iancu, *The Emancipation and Assimilation of the Jews in the Political Discourse Regarding the Granting of French Citizenship to the French Jews During the French Revolution*, 18 Studia Judaica 89 (2010).

3   *See generally* Leora Batnitzky, How Judaism Became a Religion: An Introduction to Modern Jewish Thought (2011); Noah H. Rosenbloom, Tradition in an Age of Reform: The Religious Philosophy of Samson Raphael Hirsch (1976); Michael A. Meyer, Response to Modernity: A History of the Reform Movement in Judaism, 3-224 (1988); David Ellenson, *Antinomianisn and Its Responses in the Nineteenth Century*, 260 *in* The Cambridge Companion to Judaism and Law (Christine Hayes, ed. 2017).

4   *See* Menachem Lorberbaum, *Rethinking Halakhah in Modern Eastern Europe: Mysticism, Antinomiansim, Positivism*, 232, *in* The Cambridge Companion to Judaism and Law (Christine Hayes, ed. 2017).

5   *See generally* Menachem Elon, Jewish Law: History, Sources, Principles 1180-215 (Bernard Auerbach & Melvin J. Sykes trans., 1994).

6   Ibid.

and disputation.[7] Published between 1884 and 1906, the *Mishnah Berurah* is a *halakhic* work of relatively limited scope and was written as a supercommentary on the *Orach Chaim* section of Rabbi Karo's *Shulchan Arukh*. In it, Rabbi Kagan collects and summarizes the *halakhic* conclusions of the many important commentaries and other legal works that had sprung up around the *Shulchan Arukh* in the preceding centuries, and he provides clear, practical instruction to his readers about what norms they should observe in practice.[8] The other major restatement of Jewish law to appear at this time was Rabbi Yechiel Mikhel Epstein's (1829-1908) *Arukh HaShulchan*, the principal subject of this book. Written between 1873 and 1903, Rabbi Epstein's work covers the full expanse of Jewish law topics dealt with in Rabbi Karo's *Shulchan Arukh*. It also follows the *gemara* model of Jewish law codification, which traces the development of *halakhic* rules and doctrines through biblical, Talmudic, and later rabbinic sources without shying away from the complexities and uncertainties engendered by legal disagreement.[9] Significantly, both texts sought to signal their attempts to clarify Jewish law in an uncertain age. Rabbi Kagan named his work *Mishnah Berurah*, or "Clear Teachings"; and Rabbi Epstein made his intent to recover the clarity of Rabbi Karo's *Shulchan Arukh* amidst the messiness of accumulated commentaries by calling his restatement *Arukh HaShulchan*—"Setting the Table."[10]

This chapter focuses on Rabbi Epstein's life and career, as well as on a preliminary introduction to the *Arukh HaShulchan* itself. Chapter three, however, also draws attention to the similarities and differences between Rabbi Epstein's *halakhic* magnum opus and the *Mishnah Berurah*. As both are seminal attempts to clarify the complexity and diversity of *halakhah* written at roughly the same time and in response to very similar concerns, the significance and importance of Rabbi Epstein's *Arukh HaShulchan*, and its place within the ongoing development and periodic codification of Jewish law, can be better understood in comparison with its principal alternative work. In particular, as this work

---

7   *See* Michael J. Broyde & Ira Bedzow, The Codification of Jewish Law and an Introduction to the Jurisprudence of the Mishna Berura 21 (2014).

8   For analyses and discussions of the *Mishnah Berurah*, see ibid.; Simcha Fishbane, The Method and Meaning of the Mishnah Berurah (1991); Simcha Fishbane, An Analysis of the Literary and Substantive Traits of Rabbi Israel Mayer Hacohen Kagan's Mishnah Berurah (1998) (Dissertation).

9   For discussions and analyses of the *Arukh HaShulchan*, see Simcha Fishbane, The Boldness of an Halakhist (2008); Eitam Henkin, Ta'arokh Lefanai Shulchan (2019).

10 *See* Arukh HaShulchan, *Introduction* to Choshen Mishpat; Eitam Henkin, Ta'arokh Lefanai Shulchan 232-234 (2019) (discussing the provenance and meaning of the work's title).

focuses on the jurisprudential methodology of the *Arukh HaShulchan* and the principles and guidelines Rabbi Epstein used to reach *halakhic* conclusions in the face of a vast diversity of rabbinic opinion and indeterminacy of legal sources, a very general analysis of the chief differences between the methodological approaches of the *Mishnah Berurah* and the *Arukh HaShulchan* can help highlight the significance of Rabbi Epstein's jurisprudential approach to deciding Jewish law.

The Life and Times of Rabbi Yechiel Mikhel Epstein

Rabbi Yechiel Mikhel Epstein was born into a relatively wealthy family on January 24, 1829 in Bobriusk, Russia. Rabbi Epstein's father was a successful businessman and competent Torah scholar who made sure that his son—who by many accounts demonstrated intelligence and aptitude for Talmudic studies at a young age—received a thorough rabbinic education.[11] Rabbi Epstein spent his formative years studying Torah under the direction of Rabbi Elijah Goldberg, the Chief Rabbi of Bobriusk, as well as a brief stint in the famous Volozhin Yeshivah from 1842 through 1843.[12] While Rabbi Epstein briefly pursued a business career,[13] he was appointed a rabbinical judge and assisted his teacher, Rabbi Goldberg, in his hometown of Bobriusk and ultimately decided to become a communal rabbi.[14] He received his first appointment in 1865 when he was selected to become the rabbi of Novozybkov, a Russian town in which a few thousand Jews lived. These included Orthodox, Secular, and Hasidic Jews, as well as Jews who resisted the Hasidic movement (*Mitnagdim*).

At some point prior to his first rabbinical appointment at the age of thirty-five, Rabbi Epstein married Roshka Berlin, the daughter of Rabbi Jacob Berlin and sister of the famous Rabbi Naftali Tzvi Yehudah Berlin, who would later become head of the Volozhin Yeshivah.[15] The couple ultimately had five children: Rabbi Baruch Epstein (1860-1941), a bookkeeper by trade and an accomplished Torah scholar and author in his own right;[16] Rabbi Dov Ber

---

11 See Eitam Henkin, Ta'arokh Lefanai Shulchan 37-43 (2019); Simcha Fishbane, The Boldness of an Halakhist 2-4 (2008).
12 See Simcha Fishbane, The Boldness of an Halakhist 5 (2008). On Rabbi Epstein's time in the Volozhin Yeshivah, see Eitam Henkin, Ta'arokh Lefanai Shulchan 57-58, 321-322, 349-351 (2019).
13 See Eitam Henkin, Ta'arokh Lefanai Shulchan 43-44 (2019).
14 Ibid., 349-361 (2019).
15 See Simcha Fishbane, The Boldness of an Halakhist 6 (2008).
16 See Eitam Henkin, Ta'arokh Lefanai Shulchan 198-204 (2019).

CHAPTER TWO • Rabbi Yechiel Mikhel Epstein's *Arukh HaShulchan* | 37

Epstein, who became an important communal figure in Jerusalem after moving to Palestine in 1902;[17] Braynah Velbrinski, who was twice widowed before settling into her parents' home and managing the publication and distribution of the *Arukh HaShulchan*;[18] Batyah Miriam Berlin, who divorced her first husband after only a few months of marriage and subsequently married her uncle, Rabbi Naftali Tzvi Yehudah Berlin;[19] and Eidel Kahanov, who married into a wealthy family of Jewish merchants from Odessa.[20]

Rabbi Epstein spent ten years as rabbi of Novozybkov, during which he spent some time in Lyubavichi visiting with Rabbi Menachem Mendel Schneersohn of Lubavitch, the third Rebbe of the Chabad Hasidic court.[21] According to Rabbi Epstein's son, Baruch, the trip was made on Rabbi Epstein's own initiative; he wished to meet and study with Rabbi Schneerson, who was an important scholar and *halakhic* decisor in his own right, and who led the Chabad Hasidic group to which many of Rabbi Epstein's Novozybkov constituents belonged.[22] While it is unclear how long Rabbi Epstein spent in Lyubavichi, it is known that he studied with Rabbi Schneerson and received an additional rabbinic ordination from him.[23] Later, when writing his *Arukh HaShulchan*, Rabbi Epstein would often quote the *Shulchan Arukh HaRav*, a code written by Rabbi Schneerson's grandfather, Rabbi Shneur Zalman of Liadi, and he took seriously the kabbalistic traditions so central to much of Hasidic thought.[24] Also during this time, Rabbi Epstein published his first book, *Or LaYesharim*, a commentary on the medieval text *Sefer HaYashar*, which was written by the Tosafist Rabbeinu Tam. While the *Sefer HaYashar* itself is a relatively obscure and not well-studied work, Rabbi Epstein's commentary gained the attention of many important Eastern European rabbis, many of whom gave the book fine reviews.[25]

The publication of *Or LaYesharim* improved Rabbi Epstein's rabbinic reputation, and in 1874 he accepted a position as Rabbi of Lubcha, a small town on the outskirts of Novogrudok in southern Lithuania. Shortly after arriving in Lubcha, the communal leaders of Novogrudok offered the recently vacant

---

17 Ibid., 204-207 (2019).
18 Ibid., 207-213 (2019).
19 Ibid., 213-218 (2019).
20 Ibid., 218 (2019).
21 Ibid., 55-58 (2019).
22 *See* Rabbi Baruch HaLevi Epstein, Mekor Baruch 1234 (1954).
23 *See* Simcha Fishbane, The Boldness of an Halakhist 7 (2008).
24 *See. e.g.*, Arukh HaShulchan, Orach Chaim 442:23.
25 *See* Eitam Henkin, Ta'arokh Lefanai Shulchan 259-262 (2019).

position of city rabbi of their own community to Rabbi Epstein. At this time, and indeed until the city's Jewish population was almost completely annihilated during the Second World War, Novogrudok was an important center of Lithuanian Jewish life.[26] Novogrudok was home to several thousand Jews, numerous synagogues and study halls, the important Novogrudok Yeshiva headed by Rabbi Joseph Yozel Horwitz (a student of Rabbi Israel Salanter and a major figure of the Mussar Movement), and a city whose previous rabbis included the famed Rabbi Isaac Elchanan Spektor.[27] Rabbi Epstein continued to serve as Rabbi of Novogrudok until his death in 1908. During this time, he led the community, delivered sermons, and answered *halakhic* questions posed by local residents. Over time his leadership extended to Jews throughout Europe, Palestine, and the United States—he ran the local rabbinical court and interacted with Russian authorities on behalf of the Jewish community.[28] Most importantly, it was during his time in Novogrudok that Rabbi Epstein wrote his magnum opus: the multivolume restatement of Jewish law, the *Arukh HaShulchan*.

Setting the Table: The *Arukh HaShulchan*

Rabbi Epstein's crowning literary achievement is his monumental compendium of Jewish law titled *Arukh HaShulchan*, or "Setting the Table." As explained earlier, by the second half of the nineteenth century (nearly three hundred years after the widespread publication of Rabbi Karo's *Shulchan Arukh*), Jewish law had once again become a very complex field. Rabbis Karo and Isserles's relatively straightforward prescriptions were still central, but primarily as the hub around which an ever-expanding universe of multivocal, discursive, and often contradictory commentaries, responsa, and other *halakhic* texts revolved. Rabbi Karo's once pristine table needed to be reset, and Rabbi Epstein was determined to fill this need.[29]

---

26 On the significance of Jewish life in Novogrudok, see generally Yehudah Leib *Nekritz*, "*Yeshivot Beit Yosef Navaredok*," in Mosdot Torah B'Yiropah [Hebrew] (S. K. Mirsky ed, 1956); Eitam Henkin, Ta'arokh Lefanai Shulchan 51-63 (2019); Eliezer Yerushalmi, Pinkas Navaredok Memorial Book (Alexander Harkavy, ed., 1963).

27 *See* Eitam Henkin, Ta'arokh Lefanai Shulchan 65-93 (2019); *see also id.* at 162-166 (on Rabbi Joseph Yozel Horwitz).

28 *See* Simcha Fishbane, The Boldness of an Halakhist 8-13 (2008). For an overview of Rabbi Epstein's rabbinic activities in Novogrudok based on allusions to his work in the *Arukh HaShulchan* itself, see generally Eitam Henkin, Ta'arokh Lefanai Shulchan 83-93 (2019).

29 *See* Arukh HaShulchan, *Introduction* to Choshen Mishpat.

In his *Introduction* to the first published volume of the *Arukh HaShulchan*, Rabbi Epstein noted that the complexity and diversity of thought in rabbinic jurisprudence had led earlier scholars—specifically Rabbis Joseph Karo and Moses Isserles—to collect and analyze the diverse views of their predecessors so as to determine clear standards of *halakhic* conduct.[30] Rabbi Karo recorded his own rulings drawn from the Sephardic tradition of rabbinic jurisprudence and heavily relied on the pillars of Sephardic *halakhic* thought and practice, and Rabbi Isserles contributed his own conclusions, which drew on the texts, traditions, and customs viewed as fundamentally important among Ashkenazic Jewry.[31] "Together," Rabbi Epstein writes, "the two built the entire house of Israel with [their clarifications] of the laws that apply in contemporary times."[32] However, Rabbi Epstein argues, the *Shulchan Arukh* was never meant to be the last word on Jewish law; it was instead meant to serve as a helpful framework for studying the law in depth using primary sources in the Talmud and earlier codes and commentaries.[33] Consequently and unsurprisingly then, the publication of the *Shulchan Arukh* engendered the production of voluminous commentaries and *halakhic* texts that utilized the framework and guidance of Rabbi Karo and the *Rema*'s works to further explain, analyze, and apply Jewish legal norms and principles.[34] As a result, Rabbi Epstein writes, "In the current generation . . . the uncertainty and confusion [about the law] have returned."[35] Observing this state of affairs, Rabbi Epstein took it upon himself to try to rectify and clarify what he saw as the proper rules and standards of *halakhic* practice by, as he says, "writing this book entitled *Setting the Table*, which I have set with all manner of delicacies."[36] Thus, the purpose of the *Arukh HaShulchan* is simple: it aims to clarify the confused state of Jewish law at the end of the nineteenth century by resetting the crowded and messy table built by earlier scholars.

The *Arukh HaShulchan* was not written to replace the *Shulchan Arukh*; indeed, Rabbi Epstein recognizes the central and esteemed place occupied by the organizing structure of Rabbi Karo's *Shulchan Arukh* in modern *halakhah*.[37]

---

30 Ibid.
31 *See supra* Chapter One, *Building the Set Table*.
32 Arukh HaShulchan, *Introduction* to Choshen Mishpat.
33 Ibid... For other rabbinic scholars who adopted this view of Rabbi Karo's *Shulchan Arukh*, and of *halakhic* codes generally, see Menachem Elon, Jewish Law: History, Sources, Principles 1407-1417 (Barnard Auerbach & Melvin J. Sykes trans., 1994).
34 *See supra* Chapter One, *Upending the Set Table*.
35 Arukh HaShulchan, *Introduction* to Choshen Mishpat.
36 Ibid.
37 *See* ibid.

Instead, the *Arukh HaShulchan* seeks to reset Rabbis Karo and Isserles's table by presenting both prior and subsequent developments in rabbinic literature in a clear, comprehensible manner that lends itself to use as a tool for knowing and practicing Jewish law. To accomplish this end, Rabbi Epstein did not set out to write a true *code* of Jewish law in the same vein as the largely determinate rule prescriptions of the *Shulchan Arukh*.[38] The *Arukh HaShulchan* follows the same four-part division of *halakhah*, created by the *Arbah Turim* and confirmed by the *Shulchan Arukh*, into daily observances (*Orach Chaim*), ritual practices (*Yoreh Deah*), family law (*Even HaEzer*), and civil law (*Choshen Mishpat*). Likewise, within each section, the *Arukh HaShulchan* utilizes the subject headings of the *Shulchan Arukh* and generally follows the same chapter numbering system utilized by Rabbi Karo such that the content of each chapter of the *Arukh HaShulchan* broadly corresponds to the substantive issues addressed in each corresponding chapter of the *Shulchan Arukh*. However, while the *Shulchan Arukh* and Rabbi Moses Isserles's glosses present Jewish legal norms in terse, determinate, rule-like formulations, utilizing the Mishnaic model of *halakhic* codification discussed earlier, Rabbi Epstein's work takes the alternative Talmudic approach.[39]

In addressing each legal issue, Rabbi Epstein begins by presenting the foundational sources for the rule or doctrine under discussion in the Torah and Talmud, and he traces early understandings of the topic and rabbinic interpretations of those primary Talmudic sources through Maimonides, other scholars of the period of the *Rishonim*, the *Arbah Turim*, the *Shulchan Arukh*, and later commentaries as well. In doing so, Rabbi Epstein analyzes these views, presents his own questions and counterarguments, and provides his own alternative interpretations of the Talmud and other primary rabbinic sources. He also records points of rabbinic disagreement and often resolves such disputes, takes note of customary practices, and ultimately reaches and defends his own *halakhic* determinations.[40] Thus, rather than a code like Rabbi Karo's *Shulchan Arukh*, the *Arukh HaShulchan* reads as a compressive review and analysis of rabbinic legal literature on every topic covered. But importantly, it reads as one ultimately interested in reaching practical legal conclusions rather than just offering a digest of rabbinic opinions or learned study of Talmudic dialectics.

---

38 *See* ibid.
39 *See* Rabbi Moshe Walter, The Making of a Halachic Decision 39-64 (2013).
40 Arukh HaShulchan, *Introduction* to Choshen Mishpat.

CHAPTER TWO • Rabbi Yechiel Mikhel Epstein's *Arukh HaShulchan* | 41

Rabbi Epstein began writing the *Arukh HaShulchan* in late 1869 or early 1870, shortly after establishing himself in the rabbinate of Novogrudok. He continued working on writing and publishing the work for the next thirty-seven years with the final published volume of the *Arukh HaShulchan* finally appearing shortly after Rabbi Epstein's death in February 1908.[41] According to Rabbi Epstein's grandson, Rabbi Meir Bar-Ilan, the former worked on this major project systematically and incessantly:

> My grandfather sat each day in the room designated as the local rabbinic courtroom together with his two rabbinic judge colleagues from morning until night, save for two hours in the afternoons . . . He sat at his table with a chair next to him upon which he kept four books related to the topic he was currently dealing with: a volume of Maimonides's *Mishneh Torah*, a volume of the *Arbah Turim*, the *Shulchan Arukh*, and a small edition of the Talmud. And thus, looking here and there, he wrote his book, *Arukh HaShulchan*, page after page. Occasionally, he would get up and take out another book to look at . . . This book, the *Arukh HaShulchan*, which is foremost in its genre, was printed directly from the first draft manuscripts, exactly as they were initially produced by the author . . . without edits, erasures, or rewrites.[42]

Despite the pace and quality of Rabbi Epstein's work described above, it took decades to finally complete the publication of the ten original volumes of the *Arukh HaShulchan*.[43] There are two primary reasons for this very long publication schedule. First, the high cost of publishing and Rabbi Epstein's own commitment to fund the publication of his books on his own meant that funds were often lacking and publication delayed.[44] As Rabbi Epstein himself wrote in an 1886 letter, "To my great distress, I am unable to publish [the next installment of the *Arukh HaShulchan*] due to the lack of funding . . . publishing is

---

41 For a publication history, see Eitam Henkin, Ta'arokh Lefanai Shulchan 229-230 (2019).
42 Rabbi Meir Bar-Ilan, MiVolozhin Ad Yerushalayim: Zikhronot [From Volozhin to Jerusalem] 269-71 (1939).
43 Two additional volumes were published in the four years following Rabbi Epstein's death, and a thirteenth volume—the third of four volumes covering the *Yoreh Deah* section of the *Shulchan Arukh*—was not published at all during this period, and was only rediscovered in manuscript form and published along with Rabbi Epstein's written sermons by Simcha Fishbane in 1992.
44 For a detailed discussion of the publication difficulties and schedule of the *Arukh HaShulchan* see Eitam Henkin, Ta'arokh Lefanai Shulchan 229-257 (2019).

exceedingly expensive."[45] The high cost of publishing with limited funding actually led to Rabbi Epstein initially publishing the *Arukh HaShulchan* in numerous short pamphlets with each covering just a few of the *Shulchan Arukh*'s topic headings rather than in larger volumes. Eventually, as funds became available, these pamphlets were combined into larger volumes organized around the "four pillars" framework of *halakhah* used by other rabbinic jurists since Rabbi Karo.[46]

The second reason for the long and often delayed publication schedule of the *Arukh HaShulchan* was the intense process of scrutiny and censorship by the Russian government that manuscripts were required to undergo before they could be published and distributed within the Russian Empire.[47] Rabbi Epstein began his work on the *Arukh HaShulchan* with *Choshen Mishpat*, the last of the four main sections of the *Shulchan Arukh*, dealing with civil and criminal law and rabbinic court procedure. In his introduction to the *Arukh HaShulchan*, Rabbi Epstein explains that he began his restatement of Jewish law with *Choshen Mishpat* specifically because its treatment of Jewish civil and criminal law is particularly complex, as well as because it had received less sustained rabbinic attention than other sections of the *Shulchan Arukh* that address ritual laws, giving him a greater opportunity to say something significant and new and to make a mark on rabbinic jurisprudence.[48] However, one of the reasons why *Choshen Mishpat* seemed less thoroughly treated in rabbinic legal literature was because in much of Eastern Europe, it was a good deal more difficult to obtain publication permits from the government for writings on Jewish civil and criminal law than for works dealing with *halakhic* ritual. Since *Choshen Mishpat* addresses areas of law also covered by the laws of secular government, the Russian imperial authorities in particular were suspicious of legal works purporting to expound and explain a competing system of public law and regulation.[49] Many rabbinic works on *Choshen Mishpat* were banned, heavily edited by government censors, and in any case were subject to exhaustive and

---

45 Kitvei Arukh HaShulchan, no. 104.
46 *See* Eitam Henkin, Ta'arokh Lefanai Shulchan 234-235 (2019).
47 *See* ibid.
48 *See* Arukh HaShulchan, *Introduction* to Choshen Mishpat.
49 On the practices of Czarist censorship of Jewish religious publications in the nineteenth century, *see generally* Richard Gottheil, *Censorship of Hebrew Books* 650-52, *in* The Jewish Encyclopedia, vol. 3 (1906); Ben-Tzion Katz, *L'Toldot HaTzenzurah Shel HaSifrut HaYisraelit: Reshamim V'Zikhronot*, 9 HaToren 41-48 (1923), 10 HaToren 43-51 (1923), 12 HaToren 48-60 (1923); John D. Klier, *1855–1894: Censorship of the Press in Russian and the Jewish Question*, 48 Jewish Social Studies 257-268 (1986).

lengthy reviews by Russian bureaucrats.[50] Rabbi Epstein's works were no different, and thus nearly thirteen years elapsed from the time that Rabbi Epstein began writing his first volume of the *Arukh HaShulchan* on *Choshen Mishpat* until the text was finally published in 1883.[51] Another decade elapsed before the second volume of *Choshen Mishpat* appeared, and Rabbi Epstein himself noted in a letter to Rabbi Chaim Berlin that the delay was due to the manuscript's being held up in the government censor's office in St. Petersburg.[52] Ultimately, however, Rabbi Epstein's manuscripts gradually received government approval—though sometimes only after some necessary editing—and as funds were procured to finance the printing and distribution of the books, ten volumes of the *Arukh HaShulchan* were published before the author's death in 1908 with another two volumes appearing in 1908 and 1911. An additional volume was published using Rabbi Epstein's manuscripts in 1992.

The *Arukh HaShulchan* seems to have been generally well received during and in the years following Rabbi Epstein's life.[53] At the very least, the *Arukh HaShulchan*'s comprehensive overviews of the *halakhic* topics it addresses, as well as Rabbi Epstein's own juristic independence and willingness to disagree with his predecessors and draw his own legal conclusions, quickly made the *Arukh HaShulchan* a relevant and important text—and Rabbi Epstein himself an important authority—in rabbinic discourses. There are to date no firm figures for the numbers of copies of each volume of the *Arukh HaShulchan* that were printed or distributed in the late nineteenth and early twentieth centuries. However, the fact that four of the ten volumes of the *Arukh HaShulchan* were reprinted in two or three editions during Rabbi Epstein's lifetime is indicative of the demand for these books.[54] Rabbi Epstein noted in a letter to Rabbi Chaim Berlin that "the work [*Arukh HaShulchan*] is found in many places so that anyone who wishes can examine them,"[55] and he made similar observations in other correspondence.[56] Rabbi Epstein's daughter, Braynah, who after

---

50   *See, e.g.,* Arukh HaShulchan, Choshen Mishpat 388:7 (discussing the impact of censorship on formulations of rules governing the turning over of Jewish criminals to non-Jewish authorities in the *Shulchan Arukh*). *See also* Eitam Henkin, Ta'arokh Lefanai Shulchan 236 (2019).
51   *See* Eitam Henkin, Ta'arokh Lefanai Shulchan 231-234 (2019).
52   *See* Kitvei Arukh HaShulchan, no. 56.
53   *See generally* Eitam Henkin, Ta'arokh Lefanai Shulchan 248-249 (2019).
54   *See* Eitam Henkin, Ta'arokh Lefanai Shulchan 287-309 (2019) (listing the printing dates of various editions of the *Arukh HaShulchan*).
55   Kitvei Arukh HaShulchan, no. 20.
56   *See* ibid. no. 96.

being twice widowed returned to her father's house around 1900 and thereafter managed the continued publication of the *Arukh HaShulchan*, wrote in 1911 that "the *Arukh HaShulchan* has spread throughout the diaspora; it has been sold in the tens of thousands throughout Europe, Asia, and America."[57] Even if this last description may be hyperbolic or not based on hard data of the *Arukh HaShulchan*'s actual distribution, it is clear that Rabbi Epstein's work became a common feature of rabbinic libraries and writings.

Since it was not a simple code of clear-cut rules of *halakhic* behavior, but rather a complex restatement and analysis of the state of Jewish legal discourse at the end of the nineteenth century, the *Arukh HaShulchan* was not a widely popular text among the laity. It was geared towards those who were at least competent students of Talmud and *halakhah*. Evidence of its reception and impact is thus most evident in the scholarly discourses of Rabbi Epstein's contemporaries as well as those of latter generations of rabbinic decisors. The *Arukh HaShulchan* is referenced numerous times in various late nineteenth and early twentieth century *halakhic* writings produced both in Rabbi Epstein's own Russia as well as in other parts of Eastern and Western Europe, England, the United States, and Palestine.[58] Of course, not all references to the *Arukh HaShulchan* were positive; many scholars took issue with Rabbi Epstein's tendency to ignore precedent and independently suggest alternative rulings based on his understandings of the Talmud and other primary sources. In such cases, some rabbinic decisors leveled harsh criticism against both Rabbi Epstein and his approach to *halakhic* decision-making.[59] Being the subject of strong rabbinic pushback, however, only indicates that other rabbis—even those who fundamentally disagreed with Rabbi Epstein's methodology and conclusions—viewed the *Arukh HaShulchan* as a work with which they had to contend and account for in their legal deliberations. It was sufficiently well regarded that it could not simply be ignored or dismissed as to those issues of ongoing *halakhic* discussion to which it spoke. In the decades after Rabbi Epstein's death, the impact and reputation of the *Arukh HaShulchan* within the rabbinic community continued to grow, especially in relation to its main competitor, another late nineteenth century evaluation of Jewish law, the *Mishnah Berurah*.

---

57 Bentzion Katz, HaZman 2:68, 6 (19 Nissan 5672).
58 For an exhaustive list of references to the *Arukh HaShulchan* in Jewish legal literature of this period, *see* Eitam Henkin, Ta'arokh Lefanai Shulchan 248-254 (2019).
59 *See* ibid. 254.

CHAPTER THREE

Competing Models: The *Arukh HaShulchan* and *Mishnah Berurah*

This chapter highlights the differences in *halakhic* methodology between Rabbi Epstein's *Arukh HaShulchan* and Rabbi Kagan's *Mishnah Berurah*. This contrast is particularly valuable as a preface to the more detailed consideration of Rabbi Epstein's *halakhic* jurisprudence in the *Orach Chaim* section of the *Arukh HaShulchan* because these two important and influential Jewish law authorities—Rabbi Epstein and Rabbi Kagan—shared much in common yet produced two starkly different kinds of codifications of Jewish law. Consider that both Rabbis Epstein and Kagan lived and worked in Eastern Europe during the nineteenth century and wrote their major *halakhic* restatements during the same overlapping decades.[1] While the two seem to have never met

---

1   The *Mishnah Berurah* was published in six distinctly different times, from 1884 to 1906. According to Rabbi Eitam Henkin, in his yet unpublished work on the *Arukh HaShulchan*, the first volume of the *Arukh HaShulchan* on *Orach Chaim* (chapters 1-241) was published in 1903, the second (Chapters 242-428) was published in 1907, and the third was published right after the death of Rabbi Epstein in 1909.
    Although there is an aspect of speculation in this next sentence, we suspect that *Arukh HaShulchan* wrote his work much before its publication and was delayed in publication for economic reasons, as Rabbi Eitam Henkin notes. Volume one of the *Mishnah Berurah* was published in 1884 and the *Arukh HaShulchan* cites it and uses it. The third volume of the *Mishnah Berurah*, which was published six years later, is cited as well by the *Arukh HaShulchan* on occasion (*see, e.g.*, Arukh HaShulchan, Orach Chaim 245:18), but he cites none of the other four volumes, which indicates that he did not have them. That, together with the fact that the *Mishnah Berurah* published his works out of order, with volumes one and three published first, indicates that the *Arukh HaShulchan* wrote his work before

in person, they lived only about sixty-five miles apart for most of their lives under the same secular government, in the same Jewish and general culture, speaking the same languages. The two had access to nearly identical libraries of rabbinic texts, though they made very different choices about how to weigh and prioritize the importance of these texts in *halakhic* decision-making. They also understood the general hierarchy of these works from within the same general religious frame of reference—unlike, say, a Sephardic jurist who may have given special preference to the writings of Maimonides, or a Hasidic rabbi who would have placed more significant weight on the rulings of the Rabbi Shneur Zalman of Liadi's *Shulchan Arukh HaRav*. They confronted very similar issues and problems of Jewish law and served similar constituencies, yet despite the impressive and extensive commonalities, Rabbis Epstein and Kagan approached matters of Jewish law completely differently in their respective codes.

Rabbi Yechiel Mikhel Epstein's *Arukh HaShulchan* is very widely acknowledged to be a remarkable and singularly important work.[2] As discussed earlier, the *Arukh HaShulchan* is a comprehensive restatement of rabbinic law that is firmly grounded in the Talmud, authoritative codes, and commentary literature, which seeks not merely to present a dispassionate survey of the state of *halakhic* literature—in the style of the *Beit Yosef*—but rather to provide concrete determinations of the correct rules and standards of Jewish practice as Rabbi Epstein understood them to be. While the *Arukh HaShulchan* follows the familiar organizational structure of Rabbi Karo's *Shulchan Arukh*, it is a stand-alone work rather than a commentary on Rabbi Karo's code; and in truth Rabbi Epstein does much more: his discussion of each topic begins with a summary of the biblical, Talmudic, and post-Talmudic code sources on the issue and further surveys the views of the important major commentators on these primary sources. Like the Vilna Gaon, Rabbi Epstein seeks to ground any *halakhic* discussion or determination in the relevant Talmudic literature; and like Maimonides, he sought to comprehensively organize and address the full breadth of *halakhic* topics. Indeed, in testament to his awesome breadth, he and Maimonides are the only two writers in the last two thousand years

---

1885, when volume two of the *Mishnah Berurah* (the third to be printed), which the *Arukh HaShulchan* does not have, was published.

2 See Eitam Henkin, Ta'arokh Lefanai Shulchan 248-254 (2019). *See also* Responsa Bnei Banim 2:8 (citing Rabbi Yosef Eliyahu Henkin, a preeminent twentieth century American *halakhic* authority, as maintaining that the *Arukh HaShulchan* is the most definitive and authoritative contemporary restatement of Jewish law).

who undertook to provide a comprehensive code of Jewish law, one which would encompass both contemporary *halakhic* issues as well as those not presently practiced, which also would become relevant in a future Messianic Age.[3] Perhaps most importantly, the *Arukh HaShulchan* proceeds with its treatment of Jewish law with the implicit assumption that despite the tumultuous sea of rabbinic discourse and disagreement on virtually all topics, the vast majority of *halakhic* questions can be correctly resolved analytically—that is, by correctly discerning which views accord more with the best understanding of the relevant Talmudic sources.

Rabbi Israel Meir Kagan's *Mishnah Berurah* is a very different kind of work. At the foundational level, the *Mishnah Berurah* assumes that virtually all disputes of Jewish law and Talmudic understanding are analytically irresolvable.[4] Whereas Rabbi Epstein considers most *halakhic* questions susceptible to analytically correct resolutions, Rabbi Kagan rarely does so. For the latter, determining correct legal practice is a matter of mediating between the myriad discordant views that have been expressed by post-Talmudic—and especially post-*Shulchan Arukh*—scholars and commentators using second-order rules of decision rather than those of determining which existing (or new) opinion is analytically correct through a Talmudic lens. According to Rabbi Kagan, even the *Shulchan Arukh*, the supposed "set table of easily understood rulings for daily practice," is not really as clear-cut as Rabbi Karo asserted, even without the multitude of commentaries and other works associated with it. Thus, when explaining the primary reason for choosing to write the *Mishnah Berurah*, Rabbi Kagan writes:

> The *Shulchan Arukh*, even when one also learns the *Arbah Turim* along with it, is an obscure book, since when [Rabbi Karo] ordered the *Shulchan Arukh*, his intention was that one would first learn the essential laws and their sources from the *Arbah Turim* and the *Beit Yosef* in order to understand the rulings, each one according to its reasoning. Since the *Arbah Turim* and *Beit Yosef* bring numerous differing opinions for each law, he thus decided to write the *Shulchan Arukh* to make known the ruling in

---

3   While the *Arukh HaShulchan* itself covers only those contemporarily relevant topics dealt with in the *Shulchan Arukh*, Rabbi Epstein also wrote a companion work, *Arukh HaShulchan HaAtid* ("Setting the Future Table") in which he addresses the broad range of agricultural, purity, and Temple laws only applicable in the Messianic Era.

4   *See* Michael J. Broyde & Ira Bedzow, The Codification of Jewish Law and an Introduction to the Jurisprudence of the Mishna Berura 27 (2014).

practice for each issue. It was not his intention, however, that we would learn it alone, since the law is not able to sit well with a person unless he understands the reasoning behind it.[5]

The *Mishnah Berurah* is thus Rabbi Kagan's attempt to elucidate for the Hebrew-reading educated layperson (and not only for the legal scholar) both what should be the normative *halakhic* practice and why it should be so—for complicated *halakhic* matters and for simple daily life alike.

In undertaking this task, the *Mishnah Berurah*'s approach to addressing and resolving a *halakhic* dispute was to first ask four central questions: First, what is the spectrum of answers provided by prior *halakhic* decisors to the question at hand? Second, what is the common *halakhic* practice of the community on this issue? Does the general religious practice accord with any one of the existing rabbinic views on the questions? Does more than one custom exist? Third, what are the minimum *halakhic* requirements one should try to fulfill when seeking to observe the law in question? Fourth, how can one maximize observance in order to enhance his relationship with God?[6]

Note that there is one seemingly critical and obvious question that does not actually feature in Rabbi Kagan's framework: what is the right legal standard? Because Rabbi Kagan was methodologically committed to not resolving rabbinic disputes analytically, the *Mishnah Berurah* did not seek to answer this question and did not seriously attempt to reach a single, unequivocally correct ruling on most issues. In truth, while such an approach to legal decision-making may appear strange and counterintuitive, it is well grounded in the rabbinic tradition of respect for the stature, capabilities, and judgment of the great scholars of the past. If veritable legends of *halakhic* decision-making and Talmudic learning could not settle on an analytically clear conclusion, who am I to presume to assert the truth of the matter? Or, to use a famous rabbinic aphorism, "Shall I stick my head between the mountains?" Declining to assert analytically correct resolutions to questions that vexed and divided generations of scholars would be to hubristically disrespect them, and thus Rabbi Kagan preferred to seek ways of cutting through the confusing quagmire of rabbinic disputations

---

5   *Introduction* to Mishnah Berurah. For a similar discussion of Rabbi Kagan's approach, *see also* Michael J. Broyde & Ira Bedzow, The Codification of Jewish Law and an Introduction to the Jurisprudence of the Mishna Berura 15-17 (2014).

6   *See* Michael J. Broyde & Ira Bedzow, The Codification of Jewish Law and an Introduction to the Jurisprudence of the Mishna Berura 27-28 (2014).

to reach practical directives for *halakhic* observance without taking a strong position on which view is correct in an analytic sense.

To do so, Rabbi Kagan developed a complex set of second-order guidelines of decision-making, which would allow him to determine what to do in a given situation without having to answer the fundamental question: which rabbinic opinion on the issue is right? The following are the *Mishnah Berurah*'s second-order methodological rules for determining normative *halakhic* practice in the face of entrenched rabbinic disagreement:[7]

1. When a settled ruling no longer seems to fit the current reality, the *Mishnah Berurah* provides alternative explanations for the ruling, changes its language, or adapts practices so that they fit with the ruling's spirit.[8]
2. When the codes record both lenient and strict positions, the *Mishnah Berurah* advises when one should be strict and when one may be lenient.[9]
3. When the codes record more than one normative view without excluding the validity of either, the *Mishnah Berurah* accepts the validity of different practices in different locations and suggests manners of fulfillment that incorporate the different views.[10]
4. When the codes record two mutually exclusive opinions, the *Mishnah Berurah* suggests ways to avoid transgression according to either view.[11]
5. When the early codes are lenient, and the later commentators are strict, the *Mishnah Berurah* inclines towards the strict position.[12]
6. When the major codes adopt a lenient position, yet other codes are stricter, the *Mishnah Berurah* suggests qualifying one's intention to act so as to avoid transgression according to the strict position.[13]
7. When people have adopted an unsupported custom, the *Mishnah Berurah* disapproves of it yet attempts to justify it for those who will nevertheless continue to follow it.[14]

---

7 *See* ibid. 28-29.
8 *See* ibid. 30-31.
9 *See* ibid., 31-35.
10 *See* ibid., 35-37.
11 *See* ibid. 38-40.
12 *See* ibid. 40-46.
13 *See* ibid. 46-50.
14 *See* ibid. 50-51.

8. When the codes are easily misunderstood, the *Mishnah Berurah* clarifies misunderstood rulings and defends widespread practices.[15]
9. When the codes and the mystical traditions and teachings of the *Kabbalah* conflict, the *Mishnah Berurah* minimizes the tension between the two positions.[16]
10. When the codes are in tension and the Vilna Gaon has expressed strong support for a particular view, the *Mishnah Berurah* allows one to rely on the position of the Vilna Gaon.[17]

In many cases, the *Mishnah Berurah* used more than one of these guidelines or principles at a time and balanced them, along with the four central questions discussed above, in order to provide the proper ruling given his jurisprudential objectives.[18] Frequently, the *Mishnah Berurah*'s rulings are actually a series of options presented to the reader as minimally acceptable, acceptable, better, and best, rather than simply "this is the correct answer."

As the reader of this book will see, the methodology of the *Arukh HaShulchan* is distinctly different. The goal of Rabbi Epstein's code was to distill the practice of individuals into one "correct" approach to Jewish law whenever possible. This is not a mere stylistic difference of the sequence of ideas quoted or what is summarized; instead, it is a much deeper and more robust difference in terms of what a code of Jewish law is supposed to do and what modern authorities of Jewish law are capable of doing. The *Arukh HaShulchan*'s methodology—to start with the central Talmudic texts and summarize the literature on each topic—is not for the reader to merely use as a cheat sheet to avoid reading all the prior literature. Rather, the *Arukh HaShulchan* is insistent that only by deeply digesting the prior literature—what is said by which scholars, and what is right or wrong with each argument—can anyone determine the correct way to conduct oneself.[19]

---

15 *See* ibid. 51-56.
16 *See* ibid. 56-57.
17 *See generally* ibid. 57-60.
18 *See* ibid. 29.
19 Concomitantly, the *Mishnah Berurah* does not summarize the Talmudic literature precisely because neither what the Talmud truly states nor which *Rishonim* correctly understood it is important to his approach. If a group of *Rishonim* adopt a view, Rabbi Kagan avers, we can neither prove it correct nor incorrect, consistent or inconsistent with the Talmudic texts. We simply note what was said and who said it, and we formulate Jewish law in light of our inability to resolve disputes analytically.

Indeed, absent this regurgitative exercise of closely chewing through every single dispute that the *Arukh HaShulchan* ponders through close and tight readings of the various Talmudic texts and the exact parsing of the early and later rabbinic authorities, codifiers, and commentators, it is difficult to imagine how the *Arukh HaShulchan* could have become the classical work that it is. The *Arukh HaShulchan* on *Orach Chaim* summarizes what Rabbi Epstein viewed as the most central Jewish legal literature literally from the time of God's revelation of the Torah at Mount Sinai through the late 1800s on hundreds and hundreds of complex matters. In doing so, Rabbi Epstein notes the various opinions that are taken on these issues and presents what he determines to be the single correct way to understand Jewish law. The remaining chapters of this book deconstruct the methodology of the *Arukh HaShulchan* based on carefully tracking and closely reading Rabbi Epstein's readings and treatments of the Talmud, codes, and commentaries, as well as the ways that his understandings of these materials contribute to the manner in which he resolves *halakhic* disputes. Based upon a database, we share a collection of two hundred diverse rulings from across the *Orach Chaim* section of the *Arukh HaShulchan* to illustrate for the reader the unstated rules of decision that drive *Arukh HaShulchan*'s substantive *halakhic* choices and conclusions.

Reasoning inductively from the data points provided by Rabbi Epstein's *halakhic* determinations, his rulings can be understood in light of ten distinctly different principles, which do not overlap with the basic approach of the *Mishnah Berurah*. In the next chapters, we provide detailed examples and robust explanations of each of them. For now, we list them and briefly explain:

1. Rabbi Epstein follows his own independent understanding of the correct meaning of the relevant Talmudic sources, even against the precedential rulings of important authorities of previous generations. Often, Rabbi Epstein's independent judgment involves innovating creative explanations of Talmudic sources, novel reasons for particular laws, and entirely new rules of *halakhic* conduct. This independent judgment incorporates an impressive command of the Jerusalem Talmud, which Rabbi Epstein often deploys as an important source of *halakhah*.[20]
2. Rabbi Epstein declines to follow his independent judgment of the correct understanding of the relevant Talmudic sources when his

---

20 *See infra* Chapter Four.

own view is incompatible with the established rule of a broad consensus of past authorities, or when the views of all the major pillars of *halakhic* jurisprudence, such as Maimonides, the *Shulchan Arukh*, or the *Arbah Turim*, adopt a rule more stringent than his own or the contemporary practice.[21]

3. When considering the views of past authorities in the absence of a clear independent understanding of the Talmudic sources or a strong *halakhic* consensus, Rabbi Epstein tends to give primary weight to the views of Maimonides and then to the rulings of the *Shulchan Arukh*.[22]

4. Rabbi Epstein closely follows the standard *halakhic* rule that in cases of doubt regarding biblical laws, one should act strictly, whereas in cases of doubt regarding rabbinic rules, one should act leniently—but only in cases where Rabbi Epstein is himself unsure of the correct Talmudic rule, and past rabbinic consensus and major authorities do not provide clear guidance on the issue.[23]

5. Rabbi Epstein generally does not rule that one should act strictly in order to satisfy particular *halakhic* opinions that have been rejected in accordance with the ordinary rules of *halakhic* decision-making, but he does make use of such rejected opinions to resolve complex *halakhic* questions or disputes among past authorities, to justify common practices that are at odds with standard *halakhic* norms, and to permit non-normative behavior in extenuating circumstances.[24]

6. Rabbi Epstein generally encourages—but does not mandate—supererogatory behavior that goes beyond the minimal requirements of the *halakhah*, but only when there is a genuine benefit to such conduct in terms of Torah values and observance. When he believes such extralegal practices will have negative religious or material repercussions, Rabbi Epstein discourages supererogatory conduct.[25]

7. Rabbi Epstein tries whenever possible to reconcile the mystical prescriptions of the *Zohar* with standard *halakhic* norms, though he

---

21 See *infra* Chapter Five.
22 See *infra* Chapter Six.
23 See *infra* Chapter Six.
24 See *infra* Chapter Seven.
25 See *infra* Chapter Eight.

CHAPTER THREE • The *Arukh HaShulchan* and *Mishnah Berurah* | 53

affirmatively rejects the *halakhic* relevance of mystical practices that are incompatible with Talmudic sources. Moreover, Rabbi Epstein generally permits or even recommends the adoption of mystical practices innovated by the *Zohar* as long as they do not contradict *halakhic* requirements.[26]

8. Rabbi Epstein upholds the *halakhic* normativity of what he sees as *minhag*—the customary practices of his own time and place—even when such customary practices are inconsistent with precedential *halakhic* rulings or Rabbi Epstein's own preferred understanding of the Talmudic sources, provided that the *minhag* is not unavoidably incompatible with basic *halakhic* norms or based on mistaken factual premises.[27]

9. Rabbi Epstein insists that *halakhic* issues need to be decided in the present time and place. Thus, he holds that when the underlying reasons for established *halakhic* stringencies or leniencies no longer apply, the practical rules once produced by those reasons change in response to present circumstances. So too, he notes changes in sociology, technology, and the like and their relevance for religious observance.[28]

10. Rabbi Epstein recognizes that *halakhah* must be practiced by real people in the real world and is therefore willing to adapt seemingly impracticable *halakhic* norms to better account for the real-world practical challenges attendant to trying to uphold such standards. So too, he is unwilling to mandate *halakhic* practices that are too complex for normal people.[29]

Four Illustrative Examples

Although a longer study is needed of every case in which the *Arukh HaShulchan* and the *Mishnah Berurah* provide different rules of decision in identical cases, it is worthwhile to share four examples of important decisions of Jewish law that both the *Mishnah Berurah* and the *Arukh HaShulchan* make and discuss and to contrast them with each other in order to understand the most basic methodological distinctions between these two great decisors of Jewish law of the last

---

26 See *infra* Chapter Nine.
27 See *infra* Chapter Ten.
28 See *infra* Chapter Eleven.
29 See *infra* Chapter Twelve.

century. In each of these examples, Rabbi Epstein and Rabbi Kagan examine a complex and indeterminate *halakhic* problem and come to distinctly different conclusions in ways that highlight their deep methodological differences.

1. *Tefillin* on *Chol HaMoed*

Our first example focuses on whether one may or should don *tefillin* (phylacteries), the black leather boxes worn during prayers,[30] on *Chol HaMoed*, the intermediate days of the major Jewish holidays that have both holiday and weekday qualities.[31] This case is a prime example of the *Mishnah Berurah* and *Arukh HaShulchan*'s competing understandings of how Jewish law ought to work.

The *halakhic* data available to both Rabbis Epstein and Kagan is simple and similar: the *Shulchan Arukh* rules that it is prohibited to wear *tefillin* on *Chol HaMoed* because, like the Sabbath and full holiday days, *Chol HaMoed* itself is considered a "sign" of the relationship between Man and God. Since the *tefillin* too serve as such a sign of the covenant with God, and because displaying two signs at once would derogatorily imply that one of the signs was somehow deficient, one should not wear *tefillin* on *Chol HaMoed*.[32] The *Rema*, on the other hand, rules that a person *is* required to don his *tefillin* on *Chol HaMoed*, since he is of the opinion that *Chol HaMoed* is not considered a sign. Since there is nothing that would prohibit donning *tefillin* during those days, one is required to do so.[33] By the time that Rabbis Epstein and Kagan are writing, their communities include both traditional Ashkenazi Jews who, following the *Rema*, did wear *tefillin* on *Chol HaMoed*, as well as Hasidim who followed the Kabbalah-influenced practice of not donning *tefillin* on *Chol HaMoed*. The issue was thus open both in theory and in practice with no clear or obvious normative or right *halakhic* rule.

---

30 *See* Exodus 13:9, 16; Deuteronomy 6:8, 11:18; Shulchan Arukh, Orach Chaim, ch. 25-45. For an overview of the laws of *tefillin* in English, see Moshe Chanina Neiman, Tefillin: An Illustrated Guide to Their Makeup and Use (1995).
31 *See generally* Mishneh Torah, Hilkhot Yom Tov 6:22-24, 7:1-25, 8:1-21; Shulchan Arukh, Orach Chaim, ch. 530-548.
32 *See* Shulchan Arukh, Orach Chaim 31:2. The reason one must not have two signs together is that it shows contempt for each one. It is also considered a transgression of *"baal tosif,"* the prohibition of adding to the commandments given in the Torah in such a way that it is perceived as though one is denying the perfection of the prescribed performance, i.e., like saying, "This alone is not good enough."
33 *See* Rema *to* Shulchan Arukh, Orach Chaim 31:2.

It is worth noting here that at first glance it is impossible to simply dispose of the matter by ruling strictly. Those who say one must wear *tefillin* maintain that not donning is a sin, and those who rule that one must not wear *tefillin* maintain that donning is a sin, just like donning *tefillin* on the Sabbath is a sin.

The *Mishnah Berurah* seeks to compromise since this dispute cannot be resolved. Rabbi Kagan adopts the following argument: With respect to the *Shulchan Arukh*'s reasons for prohibiting the donning of *tefillin* during *Chol HaMoed*, the *Mishnah Berurah* writes that the prohibition of displaying two covenantal signs simultaneously and of "*baal tosif*" (adding unprescribed observances to Torah obligations)[34] applies only to times when a person would don *tefillin* for the sake of observing the Torah commandment to do so. If he dons them without such intention, however, wearing the *tefillin* would neither show contempt for any other covenantal sign, nor would it be a transgression of "*baal tosif*." Therefore, Rabbi Kagan recommends that during *Chol HaMoed*, a person should don his *tefillin* without saying a blessing and have in mind the following intention: "If I am obligated to wear *tefillin*, then I am donning them for the sake of fulfilling the commandment, and if I am not obligated to wear *tefillin* today, then I am donning them without any intent to observe a religious duty."[35] In this manner, the *Mishnah Berurah* claims, one can satisfy both schools of thought in Jewish law and need not resolve this issue or decide which view—that of the *Shulchan Arukh* or the *Rema*—is actually correct. The matter is thus practically resolved without being legally resolved.

---

34 See 3 Encyclopedia Talmudit (s.v. *baal tosif*), especially text accompanying footnotes 18-19.
35 Mishnah Berurah 31:8. The *Mishnah Berurah*'s explanation of the *Shulchan Arukh*'s reasoning gives him the tools to deal with a blatant contradiction and create a compromise in the following way. He first mentions that the *Acharonim* agree with the *Turei Zahav* that a blessing on donning *tefillin* during *Chol HaMoed* should not be said. The reason not to say the blessing is that its requirement in the first place is in doubt, since there is a doubt as to whether or not one must don phylacteries at all on these days; and also, even if there is a requirement to don them, missing blessings do not actually have an impact on the fulfillment of a commandment. Thus, one need not make the blessing. Having removed this otherwise necessary verbal indication that donning *tefillin* is certainly required, i.e., the saying of a blessing, which implies that this, the putting on of *tefillin*, is a required act, *today*, the *Mishnah Berurah* advises that a person have a particular intention while donning his phylacteries, which would allow him to fulfill the potential obligation without running into a possible transgression if donning them *were* really prohibited. He writes that before a person dons his phylacteries, he should think to himself that if he is obligated to do so, then his donning is for the sake of fulfilling a commandment, and if not, it is not. This stipulation removes the possible transgression of "*baal tosif*" since one acts without definitiveness, yet it provides enough intention to be considered efficacious if necessary, even, as we said, without a blessing.

In his discussion of wearing *tefillin* on *Chol HaMoed*, after reviewing the different opinions on the matter and summarizing the data no differently than did the *Mishnah Berurah*, the *Arukh HaShulchan* writes:

> The *Beit Yosef* rules that one should not don *tefillin*, but the *Rema* writes that there are those who do don them but make the blessing in a whisper. No Sephardic Jew dons, and all Ashkenazic Jews don; but today they don without a blessing, and so it seems proper to act accordingly. And many great later authorities have already written at length regarding this, one saying one thing, and another saying another. Thus, each should continue according to his custom. And now, many—even among the Ashkenazic Jews—do not don, and we will not continue at length on this.[36]

The *Arukh HaShulchan* encourages all to do as their custom directs with no other instruction provided.

This case serves as an excellent example of how these two works resolve disputes differently even as they understand both the social and *halakhic* data identically. The *Mishnah Berurah* recognizes that there are two competing claims made by two different schools of thought in Jewish law and that these competing views are—at first glance—incompatible with each other: either the law is "yes, every man must put on *tefillin* on *Chol HaMoed*" or "no, it is a sin to don *tefillin* on *Chol HaMoed*." In the face of this seeming unresolvable dispute, the *Mishnah Berurah* works very hard to craft a resolution that he thinks actually works according to both schools of thought, which entails a very complex thought process of "doing X while thinking Y" and intending to conditionally fulfill the *mitzvah* of donning *tefillin*. It is jurisprudentially unwise, the *Mishnah Berurah* must posit, that no matter which option of Jewish law a pious Jew chooses, sin will result according to an important school of thought. So, he crafts a resolution that solves this problem.

This is not the approach of the *Arukh HaShulchan*. Since the Talmud itself is completely silent on this issue, Rabbi Epstein recognizes that no direct Talmudic resolution of this dispute is possible, and there are thus two competing customs in practice. So, he simply notes that each person and community should continue their custom and practice. Rabbi Epstein upholds the *halakhic* normativity of what he sees as *minhag*—the customary practices of his own time and place—and he is completely comfortable with the idea that one

---

36 Arukh HaShulchan, Orach Chaim 31:4.

person's custom is another person's sin. Furthermore, he runs away from overly complex resolutions like the one offered by the *Mishnah Berurah*, since Rabbi Epstein recognizes that *halakhah* must be practiced by real people in the real world and is therefore unwilling to adopt the seemingly impracticable practice of "doing X while thinking Y" in order to bridge the gap between two competing *halakhic* norms.

2. *Prayer in Front of Fully Uncovered Hair of a Married Woman*

The second example concerns the problem of married women who come to synagogue with their hair uncovered, a practice that became common around the time that Rabbis Epstein and Kagen were writing their works.[37] The *Shulchan Arukh* rules that a man may not recite the *Shema* prayer while standing in view of a woman's hair which she is accustomed to covering,[38] and elsewhere he notes that women ought to cover their hair.[39] In this context, Rabbi Epstein laments that for many years married woman have been ignoring the *halakhic* requirement to cover their hair. Indeed, he decries the fact that in his own day, this shameful state of affairs had become endemic.[40] As a result of this social change for the worse, however, Rabbi Epstein rules that men may now pray and recite the *Shema* in front of a married woman's uncovered hair, since seeing such hair is no longer potentially erotic.[41] To support this contention, Rabbi Epstein cites the thirteenth-century authority Rabbi Mordechai ben Hillel HaKohen (1250-1298), known as the *Mordechai*, who himself quotes the earlier authority Rabbi Eliezer ben Joel HaLevi (1140-1225), known as the *Raavyah*. The *Mordechai* rules that an unmarried woman's hair is not considered a form of *ervah*, or "nakedness," in the presence of which prayers cannot be said because the common custom is for unmarried women to uncover their hair, and men are therefore so accustomed to seeing women's hair that it does not lead to improper thoughts.[42] The *Arukh HaShulchan*

---

37 On the history of Jewish women and hair covering, see generally Amy K. Milligan, Hair, Headwear, and Orthodox Jewish Women (2014); Lynne Schreiber, ed., Hide and Seek: Jewish Women and Hair Covering (2003). For an exhaustive discussion of rabbinic opinions on female hair covering, see Michael J. Broyde, *Hair Covering and Jewish Law: Biblical and Objective (Dat Moshe) or Rabbinic and Subjective (Dat Yehudit)?*, 42:3 Tradition 97-179 (2009).
38 *See* Shulchan Arukh, Orach Chaim 75:2.
39 *See* Shulchan Arukh, Even HaEzer 21:5.
40 *See* Arukh HaShulchan, Orach Chaim 65:7.
41 *See* ibid.
42 *See* Mordechai *to* Berakhot, end of the third chapter.

extends this logic to a married woman's hair as well. Because men are long accustomed to seeing uncovered hair of even married women, he argues, there is no fear of improper thoughts upon seeing such during prayer. Thus, a married woman's hair is not considered "nakedness," and prayers may be said while in sight of it.

The *Mishnah Berurah* takes the exact opposite approach to this issue. Indeed, quoting his words might help highlight his approach. He states:

> And you should further know that, even if this woman and her friends in that place have a practice of going out with their hair [literally "head"] uncovered in public in the way of those who are immodest, it is still forbidden [to pray in their presence] no differently than the case of uncovered thigh, which is forbidden under all circumstances. As we have explained in note two above, since this woman is required to cover her hair by operation of Jewish law (and this involves a Torah prohibition, because the verse says, "And he shall uncover the woman's head," which implies that her hair was covered initially), and also, since all Jewish women who observe Torah law have been careful about this from the time of our ancestors a long time ago until the present day, uncovered hair is considered a nakedness, and it is forbidden to pray in its presence.... And, do not say that such is permitted since once one is used to it exposed [or that] it does not generate erotic thoughts, as I explain later on.[43]

The contrast between the two approaches is obvious: the *Arukh HaShulchan* delves into the Talmudic and classical Jewish law sources and comes to a novel conclusion of Jewish law which, while grounded in the sources, is unfound in this exact case in any prior source that he was aware of.[44] While unprecedented, Rabbi Epstein's conclusion does derive from those Talmudic and classical sources, although only when studied and broken down to basic principles that the original authors of those sources never explicitly considered. Furthermore, the *Arukh HaShulchan* neither bothers to share with the reader that this is a novel idea of his own nor note that others might not agree.[45] Nor does he encourage one to be strict on this matter, since the leniency he is providing appears to him to be analytically correct. Rabbi Epstein views his determination

---

43 Mishnah Berurah 75:10.
44 We now know that this approach was first noted by the Ben Ish Chai, Year 1, Parshat Bo, no. 12.
45 Indeed, *Arukh HaShulchan* has *Mishnah Berurah* Volume One, so he knows that Rabbi Kagan disagrees.

here as correct as a matter of law and not merely as practical instruction for how to navigate a complicated *halakhic* issue. The *Mishnah Berurah*, however, is simply unaware of any Jewish law authority who has adopted the—unknown to him—view which will be propounded by the *Arukh HaShulchan*.[46] Rabbi Kagan does not see the mandate of this work as being to provide novel explanations of Jewish law, and he is not prepared to extend the leniency of the *Shulchan Arukh* beyond its text since others have not done so before him. Rather, his mission is to reinforce the universal status quo that such conduct is both prohibited and may not be allowed in the synagogue under any circumstances. The "custom" discussed here is neither legitimate nor sanctioned by Jewish law authorities, nor permitted in the synagogue. The absence of precedent makes the matter easy to the *Mishnah Berurah*.

3. The Minimal Size for Tzitzit

The *Shulchan Arukh* explains simply and concisely that "the size of the garment that is obligated in *tzitzit* [the ritual fringes worn on four-cornered garments] is one large enough to cover in length and width the head and most of the body of a child who can go alone in the market and does not need an adult to watch him."[47] The problem with this formulation is at first glance clear: the standard needs elaboration, since the measure is imprecise and hard for the reader to apply.

This is exactly the problem the *Mishnah Berurah* confronts, and he discusses the spectrum of opinions. *Mishnah Berurah* summarizes the views of those who came before him simply, and he explains both the best way to conduct oneself and the most lenient way to conduct oneself, as well as other standards in between, and concludes with a recommendation for what people should do in practice.[48] First, he cites the view of the *Pri Haaretz* that the minimal size of a *tzitzit* garment is three quarters of a cubit in length and a half a cubit wide; the *Mishnah Berurah* notes that the *Machatzit HaShekel* and others find that this view is inconsistent with the Talmud and should not be relied on, particularly with respect to *tzitzit* garments needing to be only a half a cubit wide. Rabbi Kagan then notes the practice of what he called "*anshai ma'aseh*," or "people who engage in [execeptional religious] action," who held that one's

---

46 Which was published a few years after the *Mishnah Berurah*.
47 Shulchan Arukh, Orach Chaim 16:1. On the practice of wearing *tzitzit*, see Numbers 15:38-40; Deuteronomy 22:12; Mishneh Torah, Hilkhot Tzitzit.
48 *See* Mishnah Berurah 16:4.

garment should be at least one cubit in width and length and that this satisfies the views of the *Pri Haaretz* and others. The *Mishnah Berurah* goes on to add that certainly one should not wear a garment smaller than three quarters of a cubit in length and width—such a garment may well not be obligated to have *tzitzit*, and reciting the blessing for wearing *tzitzit* when donning such a garment might be a blessing in vain.

The *Arukh HaShulchan* approaches this topic totally differently. He notes that a huge cultural change has taken place between the Talmudic era and his own time. *Tzitzit*-wearing Jews, he observes, actually wear two such garments: one during prayer on top of one's clothes and one under their shirt that they wear all the time.[49] Furthermore, the *Arukh HaShulchan* posits that the Talmudic discussion and the rules formulated in the major codes speak to the minimal size for the larger garment worn during prayer, which needs to cover one's head and body. But, he argues, the smaller *tzitzit* garment worn by Jews of his own time under their clothes can be of any size. He thus writes:

> In my humble opinion, this whole discussion of the size of *tallit* is unneeded, and all fulfill their obligation to wear *tzitzit* with small garments, for we have already explained in the opening section of chapter eight that . . . as a matter of Torah law, every garment one wears with four corners needs *tzitzit*, and this is the opinion of the *Beit Yosef*. The requirement to fully wrap oneself with a *tallit* is only with a prayer *tallit*, which was like a handkerchief [with no neck hole] in the center . . . But, our small *tallit* which is worn under the shirt needs no minimal size at all; rather it only has to have four corners to be obligated in *tzitzit*.[50]

Here, the *Arukh HaShulchan* and the *Mishnah Berurah* again disagree, and their disagreement is about a few things. First, in light of the changed reality of how the commandment of wearing *tzitzit* is observed in practice, the *Arukh HaShulchan* concludes that when the *Shulchan Arukh* speaks about the minimum size for a *tzitzit* garment, he has in mind a very different kind of garment than the one with which Rabbi Epstein is concerned; one is speaking about the large prayer shawl worn during prayers while the other is addressing the issue of the small *tzitzit* clothes worn under one's shirt. The *Mishnah Berurah* follows the simple text of the codes before him and refuses to modify these

---

49 *See* Arukh HaShulchan, Orach Chaim 16:5.
50 Arukh HaShulchan, Orach Chaim 16:5.

codified standards in light of the changed reality of how Jews observe the *tzitzit* commandment. Second, the *Mishnah Berurah* organizes and cites—and places in order from best to worst—the many precedential views on the issue with little commentary on which view he thinks is "correct"; even with respect to the view that he says one should not rely on, Rabbi Kagan declines to recommend adopting that opinion only because others have rejected it and not because of any Talmudic proof that it is actually incorrect. The *Arukh HaShulchan*, however, cites the views that he thinks are correct, leaving out the various different "wrong" views of those who came before him, and then he updates the *halakhah* to reflect the society he is living in. Third, the *Mishnah Berurah* cites no authorities from the period of the *Rishonim* in his discussion of this topic, whereas the *Arukh HaShulchan* is essentially only discussing the views of Jewish law authorities in the era of the *Rishonim* and that of the *Shulchan Arukh*.

4. Validating the Custom of Building Citywide Communal Eruvin

An *eruv* (pl. *eruvin*) is a ritual enclosure around a community which allows Jews to carry objects on the Sabbath when they would otherwise be forbidden to do so.[51] The *eruv* is meant to symbolize a wall around the community in order to turn it into one unified domain for the purpose of carrying on the Sabbath when carrying objects in public spaces is prohibited.[52] The *Shulchan Arukh* rules that an *eruv* built to enclose a genuine public domain is ineffective; an *eruv* can only be built to permit carrying in areas that are neither genuinely private property nor truly public spaces.[53] To define what constitutes a public domain, Rabbi Karo writes in the *Shulchan Arukh* that a public domain is defined as streets and markets that are sixteen cubits wide and which are not roofed or walled. The *Shulchan Arukh* adds that there are those who say that any place that does not contain six hundred thousand people in it every day is not considered a public

---

51 For general overviews of the laws of *eruv*, see Rabbi Shlomo Francis & Rabbi Yonason Glenner, The Laws of Eruv: A Comprehensive Review of the Laws of Eruvin and Their Practical Applications (2013); Adam Mintz, It's a Thin Line: Eruv from Talmudic to Modern Culture (2014); Rabbi Yosef Gavriel Bechhoffer, The Contemporary Eruv: Eruvin in Modern Metropolitan Areas (2002).

52 *See* A.B. Buchman, *King Solomon's Takanah: Rambam's Eruv*, 3 Hakirah: The Flatbush Journal of Jewish Law and Thought, 181-212 (2006); J.R. Searle, The Construction of Social Reality (1995).

53 *See* Shulchan Arukh, Orach Chaim 364:2. (He admits, however, that some say if an area is not closed at night, an *eruv* around it may still be valid on the condition that it is at least *able* to be closed at night.).

domain, no matter the size of the area. It is clear from Rabbi Karo's writing style and methodology that he does not accept this view, and it is likewise rejected by both Maimonides and the *Rif*.[54] Importantly, the Talmud makes no mention of the six-hundred-thousand-person requirement for public domains in its own discussion of the issue.

However, despite the lack of textual justification, by the 1800s, the prevalent custom among European Jews had in fact become to build *eruvin* that enclosed very wide streets that stretched from one end of the city to the other based on the opinion that only areas traversed by at least six hundred thousand people daily are considered genuine public domains that cannot be enclosed by an *eruv*. Based on that disputed requirement, even the very wide streets of nineteenth century European cities would not be public domains, and the construction of symbolic *eruvin* would be effective at permitting Jews to carry items in these areas on the Sabbath. Indeed, by the time of the *Arukh HaShulchan* and the *Mishnah Berurah*, the common custom among Europe's Ashkenazic Jews was to actually build such public *eruvin* in many different larger communities, where the streets were certainly larger than sixteen cubits but where the population was less than six hundred thousand. The question presented was whether this was a valid approach or not. Without this leniency, both the *Mishnah Berurah* and the *Arukh HaShulchan* understood that no larger communal *eruvin* could be built, as city streets are all wider than sixteen cubits.

As an initial matter, with respect to how to define a public domain, the *Mishnah Berurah* writes that he has searched through all the opinions of those scholars who defined a public domain in terms of six hundred thousand people, but he could not find the stipulation that the people must be present every day. Rather, Rabbi Kagan argues, these authorities meant that a public domain is an area in which there is a possibility that six hundred thousand people may be found in general.[55] In the *Biur Halakhah*—Rabbi Kagan's own gloss on the *Mishnah Berurah*—he notes that if the actual presence of six hundred thousand people were a necessary condition, the Talmud would not have omitted mentioning it.[56] The *Mishnah Berurah* writes that even though many early authorities disagree with this opinion, one cannot protest against those who act leniently and use *eruvin* that enclose areas larger than sixteen cubits but without six hundred thousand people. Nevertheless, Rabbi Kagan writes, a *baal*

---

54 *See* ibid. 345:7.
55 *See* Mishnah Berurah 345:24.
56 *See* Biur Halakhah 252 (s.v. *she'ein shishim ribo*).

nefesh—a religiously conscientious person—should be stringent upon himself and not use an *eruv* that enlaces spaces wider than sixteen cubits.[57]

By stating that one cannot protest against those who follow the lenient custom, the *Mishnah Berurah* demonstrates that he does not believe that the lenient position is the essential normative opinion that should be followed. However, because some rabbinic authorities have found the more lenient view to have legal worth, and in order to spread the net of *halakhic* legitimacy as widely as possible and not label those many Jews who follow the common custom of carrying in such an *eruv* as sinners, the *Mishnah Berurah* somewhat condones it and maintains a steady ambiguity as to what the right rule of law really is. A *baal nefesh*, on the other hand, should follow what he thinks is the true *halakhic* position, which is not to carry in such an *eruv*.[58] Thus, the *Mishnah Berurah* writes that a *baal nefesh* should, and will, act stringently. *Mishnah Berurah* encourages people not to carry in all modern communal *eruvin*, but he will not label as sinful the decision to carry.

Like the *Mishnah Berurah*, the *Arukh HaShulchan* understands the difficulty of the established custom to use an *eruv* enclosing a street wider than sixteen cubits. On the contrary, he believes that most Jewish law authorities prior to him understand the *halakhah* to be according to the opinion that does not consider population when defining a public domain, which would mean that he thinks using an *eruv* to enclose areas wider than sixteen cubits would be ineffective. Rabbi Epstein makes this point simply by recounting the various authorities who fall into either camp on this issue[59]

> All of the permissible *eruvin* in our communities rely on this view [that public domains must have six hundred thousand residents], and since our cities do not have six hundred thousand people passing through them, thus they are not public places, and a *tzurat hapetach* [symbolic wall] is effective. According to the first view [that public domains do not require six hundred thousand inhabitants], since our streets are sixteen cubits wide [or more], no such leniency is allowed, and they need doors that close at night with doors [that is, actual walls, instead of a merely

---

57 See Mishnah Berurah 345:23; 364:8.
58 Thus we see that Rabbi Kagan believes that 600,000 is not the normative view, yet he foresees that the practice cannot be changed as it has been deeply ingrained and is a predicate for how the community actually functions in this area.
59 See Arukh HaShulchan, Orach Chaim 345:17.

symbolic *tzurat hapetach* post and lintel].⁶⁰ Those who are lenient on this matter include the *Sefer HaTerumah*, the *Semag* [*Sefer Mitzvot Gadol*], *Semak* [*Sefer Mitzvot Katan*], *Maharam MeRutenberg*, *Rosh*, and *Arbah Turim*—all of whom accept the view of *Rashi* [that public domains require six hundred thousand inhabitants]. Those who prohibit include the *Rif*, Maimonides, Rabbeinu Tam, *Rashbam*, Raavan, Nachmanides, *Rashba*, *Ritva*, *Ran*, *Magid Mishnah*, *Rivash*, many of the *Tosafot*, including the first *Rashbam*, the *Riva*, the *Ri HaLevi*, the *Ran*, and the *Riaz*. So too, the *Maharshal* in the *Yam Shel Shlomo* in tractate *Beitza* also resolves this matter not consistent with this [the lenient] view.⁶¹

Despite the long list of important authorities who rejected the minimum population requirement for public domains, however, Rabbi Epstein is acutely aware that all of the communities in his time and place actually adopt the more lenient position; like the *Mishnah Berurah*, he wants to accept the more lenient opinion out of a desire to incorporate those who follow it into the realm of observance. After explaining how the requirement that public domains have six hundred thousand people actually present at one time is not accepted by any of the early authorities, the *Arukh HaShulchan* writes:

> But in any case, what good will result from continuing at length now that the *eruvin* that have spread throughout the majority of cities of the Jewish people for many hundreds of years are based only on this leniency, and it is as if a *bat kol* (Heavenly Voice) came forth and said that the *halakhah* is according to this opinion; and if we come and restrain it, not only will they not listen, but it will seem as if they have gone crazy.⁶²

Of course, the *Arukh HaShulchan* does not rely solely on the assumption that a Heavenly Voice went forth and said that the *halakhah* is according to this opinion; rather, after making this statement, he also goes back and attempts to support the leniency via his detailed textual analysis of the Talmud and the early rabbinic decisors of the period of the *Rishonim*. His textual analysis, however, seems to serve primarily a justificatory purpose; it is predicated on the legitimacy of the established custom, reflecting his basic methodology of

---

60 Which was factually impossible to implement.
61 Arukh HaShulchan, Orach Chaim 345:17.
62 Ibid. 345:18.

CHAPTER THREE • The *Arukh HaShulchan* and *Mishnah Berurah* | 65

reading the Talmudic texts consistent with the common practice. But, a look at what he does and how he does this serves a very important insight into his methodology.

The *Arukh HaShulchan* opens his discussion by stating that it is "a *mitzvah* and a duty to find virtue in the conduct of the Jewish people. Thus, I focused my heart to find some justification."[63] He then proceeds to list three excellent justifications for accepting the six-hundred-thousand-person requirement grounded in the Talmud itself.

First, Rabbi Epstein argues that a close read of the Talmudic sources indicates that a city can have only one public thoroughfare—a single central street that runs straight across the entire city, or at most two such streets, one going east-west and one going north-south. However, "our cities" are not designed that way, the *Arukh HaShulchan* notes, but instead have many smaller streets, none of which—even when wider than sixteen cubits—are the single main street. Thus, a city without a main street can never be a public domain no matter how matter how wide the streets are.[64]

Second, Rabbi Epstein argues that the Talmudic paradigm of public domains assumes that a city has one central marketplace, which constitutes its public domain. Rabbi Epstein points out that cities in his own time have many, many marketplaces and stores with no centralized single market; instead, stores are scattered here and there, each of which is then not defined as a public place at all. This is true, the *Arukh HaShulchan* claims, even according to those scholars that reject the six-hundred-thousand-person requirement. Indeed, the *Arukh HaShulchan* notes that the Jerusalem Talmud and the *Bahag*—an important Geonic-era collection of *halakhic* rules—provide some support for this insight.[65]

Third, the *Arukh HaShulchan* reflects on the implications of the modern use of railroad systems, which certainly carry more than six hundred thousand travelers daily, and he concludes that railroads are indeed genuine public domains. Moreover, Rabbi Epstein indicates that perhaps railroads are the only modern example of a genuine public domain, since in modern times, this is the method of public transportation akin to the major city thoroughfare of Talmudic times. Interestingly, it is a reasonable read of the *Arukh HaShulchan* that in his view, in the cities of his time, only the railroad tracks are places through which Jews

---

63 Ibid. 345:18.
64 *See* ibid. 345:19-21.
65 *See* ibid. 345:21-24.

may not carry objects on the Sabbath. The *Arukh HaShulchan* thus has given a modern application of the Talmudic concept of a public space.[66]

Having concluded with three plausible justifications, the *Arukh HaShulchan* spends another fifteen hundred words and ten paragraphs dealing with this same topic from other angles, adding Talmudic proof after proof to the idea that even those authorities who rejected the six-hundred-thousand-person test would nonetheless refuse to consider modern cities "public spaces" where *eruvin* cannot be built.[67] The sheer tenacity he brings to bear on this problem—from the variety of Talmudic and medieval sources, as well as the radical and novel readings of some of them—causes one to see that the *Arukh HaShulchan* is not content to recite to the reader that a Heavenly Voice ruled this way or to cite other authorities who rule that six hundred thousand is needed, but rather he is seeking a plausibly honest reading of the binding texts which validates the custom of the community. Furthermore, the *Arukh HaShulchan* does not conclude that it is better to be strict. He is content to simply validate the custom.

The contrast between the *Mishnah Berurah* and the *Arukh HaShulchan* is distinct and noticeable here and manifests in six distinct values. First, the *Mishnah Berurah* is more comfortable than the *Arukh HaShulchan* in actually discouraging people from carrying in modern *eruvin*. The fact that everyone builds them and that the custom is to rely on this is less important to the *Mishnah Berurah* than it is to the *Arukh HaShulchan*. Second, the *Arukh HaShulchan* is prepared to reexamine well-worn Talmudic texts to find intellectually reasonable but novel ways to validate the common custom. The breadth and depth of the material he digests in order to validate a custom in new and novel ways, from the Jerusalem Talmud onward, is not something the *Mishnah Berurah* is prepared to do. Third, the *Mishnah Berurah* is much more deeply connected to the traditions and decisions of the scholarly community that resides around him and defers to their judgments in many ways, large and small. Fourth, the *Arukh HaShulchan* is more prepared to apply the *halakhic* rules to the modern world in ways that allow greater function—the discussions of modern city structure and his discussion of railroads reflect that. Fifth, the *Mishnah Berurah* is more nuanced and complex, prepared to both share that one should not rebuke people who carry but that pious people should be strict, leaving some uncertainty as to whether this conduct is permissible as a

---

66 *See* ibid. 345:26.
67 *See* ibid. 345:27-36.

matter of Jewish law. The *Arukh HaShulchan* here (and in other places as well) has more of a tendency to be binary than the *Mishnah Berurah* with regard to whether something is permissible or prohibited. Finally, and relatedly, is the tendency of the *Arukh HaShulchan* to record one view and rarely more than one view which he thinks is correct, whereas the *Mishnah Berurah*'s methodology tends to record all of the different reasonable views and then rank them from best to acceptable.

Conclusion

We noted at the beginning of this section that the *Mishnah Berurah* and the *Arukh HaShulchan* confronted the same problem: the "set table" had become very crowded and messy, and Rabbi Karo's *Shulchan Arukh* was no longer the practical guide to Jewish practice it was meant to be because it had evolved into the hub of a very diverse collection of other scholars' opinions, thoughts, and insights. The "set table" stopped being an effective code of Jewish Law as it had become confusing to use, and it was thus hard to determine what was normative amidst the clutter of rabbinic opinions and learned discourses. Both the *Mishnah Berurah* and the *Arukh HaShulchan* sought to reset the table—both were deeply committed to the organizational structure of the *Shulchan Arukh* and that work's important place in the rabbinic corpus, but both recognized the need for *halakhic* jurisprudence to go through yet another round of systemization and synthesis in order to make it more practical to know and follow the law.[68]

While both Rabbis Epstein and Kagan sought to address the same basic challenge, each set out to solve the crowded-table problem in a different way. The *Mishnah Berurah* set about to tidy the very crowded table by ordering the prior works that developed around the *Shulchan Arukh*, imposing important ordering values on each opinion and sharing with the reader a structure for determining the proper place of each view in practice so that all could be used and all could be useful. Everything is processed and placed properly, and little is discarded—almost nothing is labeled wrong. This was not the methodology of the *Arukh HaShulchan*. Rabbi Epstein set out to clear the crowded table and reset it in his own vision. He removed from the table those commentaries and opinions that he thought did not belong, reinforced the correctness of that

---

68 The *Mishnah Berurah* more so than the *Arukh HaShulchan*, because his is a commentary which follows not only chapters but subchapters of the *Shulchan Arukh*.

which remained, and provided concrete direction for how to use the remaining utensils on the table so that the table would have fewer settings—but everything on it would be correct.[69]

With this understanding of the purpose and function of Rabbi Epstein's work in hand, we turn to explore in greater detail the methodology of the *Arukh HaShulchan*.

---

69   Although beyond the scope of this book, it is worth noting that the basic intellectual insight of the *Mishnah Berurah* (that current authorities cannot resolve intellectually the disputes among giants of previous generations), and the basic intellectual insight of the *Arukh HaShulchan* (that the job of Jewish law authorities is to provide a single correct opinion for conduct), while contrasted here, can be combined into a work that resolves questions of Jewish law, like either of these works. The current Sephardi Code by Rabbi Yitzchak Yosef titled *Yalkut Yosef* is such a hybrid work. It tends to function like an *Arukh HaShulchan* type code with one correct opinion, but does so by following the *Mishnah Berurah*'s view that disputes cannot be intellectually resolved, and should be determined by the rule of majority instead, with approaches crafted that satisfy a majority of decisors being the dominate test: no need to present to the reader with "better" approaches, and no *halakhic* value in minority approaches.

Part II
The Methodological Principles of the *Arukh HaShulchan*

Introduction

The nine chapters in this part of this book explain and provide examples of the ten methodological principles that guide Rabbi Epstein's *halakhic* determinations in the *Orach Chaim* section of his *Arukh HaShulchan*. Taken together, the ten principles that comprise Rabbi Epstein's *halakhic* methodology respond to the critical questions that lie at the heart of Jewish law and rabbinic jurisprudence: what is the correct *halakhic* rule or standard for any given issue, and how should a rabbinic decisor go about making such determinations?

This question has animated virtually every attempt to codify Jewish law, and Rabbi Epstein's comprehensive restatement of *halakhah* in the *Arukh HaShulchan* is no exception. If there is a perennial theme running through virtually all the introductions of major post-Talmudic compendiums of Jewish law, it is that the author concluded that some codification of correct *halakhic* rules and standards is necessary because it has become exceedingly difficult—indeed, nearly impossible—for ordinary Jews and even rabbis and scholars to reliably know the correct legal norms and standards prescribed by Jewish law.[1] As discussed earlier, there are at least three different reasons for this difficulty. First, the primary sources of Jewish law—the Torah and Talmud—are, on their faces, notoriously ambiguous; cognizing what these texts mean entails a great deal of interpretation, and often that interpretive effort is global as seemingly unrelated passages from different corners of the rabbinic corpus relate to and impact each other in important ways.[2] Thus, in earlier times, correct

---

1   See, e.g., Introduction to Mishneh Torah; Introduction to Beit Yosef to Arbah Turim; Introduction to Rema to Shulchan Arukh; Introduction to Arukh HaShulchan.
2   See generally Menachem Elon, Jewish Law: History, Sources, Principles 1144-49 (Bernard Auerbach & Melvin J. Sykes trans., 1994).

understandings of the Torah and Talmud were communicated through close teacher-student relationships, which allowed the primary sources of Jewish law to serve more as outlines or lecture notes used to format and recall the substantive content of countless instructional encounters.[3] This, then, leads to the second main cause for the ongoing need for textual restatements to clarify the contexts of the *halakhah*, namely the travails and insecurities of diaspora life—the social upheavals and pressures caused by war, drought, and economic and political instability made it increasingly difficult for Jews to form and maintain the kinds of close, long-standing teacher-student relationships needed to effectively transmit extratextual knowledge of the *halakhah*.[4] Left to rely on interpretive understandings of the primary sources, and without any formal hierarchy of religious or legal authority to establish correct understandings of the Talmud, disagreements over what Jewish law is, how it applies, and what it entails in practice arose and persisted in perpetually new and developing factual contexts.[5] The Talmudic text spawned dozens of commentaries and *halakhic* analyses offering different accounts of the law.[6] Thus, the third problem: the existence of numerous competing conceptions of correct *halakhic* rules left Jewish law practitioners and decision makers uncertain as to which views were correct and which ought to be observed in practice.[7] Making such determinations would require even accomplished scholars to have a prodigious command of these interpretive commentaries as well as of the Talmudic sources themselves so as to make informed judgments about which opinions best expressed the right legal standards. The proliferation of such rabbinic material, however, made it difficult for even accomplished scholars to have an adequate knowledge of the relevant literature.[8] This in turn led to the compilation of restatements

---

3 *See* Menachem Elon, Jewish Law: History, Sources, Principles 1084 (Bernard Auerbach & Melvin J. Sykes trans., 1994). *See also* Rabbi Adin Steinsaltz, The Essential Talmud 3 (Chaya Galai trans., 2006).

4 *See* Lawrence H. Schiffman, From Text to Tradition: A History of Second Temple and Rabbinic Judaism 157-76 (1991).

5 *See* Chaim Saiman, Halakhah: The Rabbinic Idea of Law 141-162 (2018). *See also* Moshe Halbertal, People of the Book (1997) (describing and explicating differing schools of rabbinic thought regarding how to view and understand the Talmud).

6 For a review of many major early Talmudic commentaries and a discussion of their various approaches, see Menachem Elon, Jewish Law: History, Sources, Principles 1357-59 (Bernard Auerbach & Melvin J. Sykes trans., 1994).

7 *See* Babylonian Talmud, Chagigah 3b (discussing the apparent challenges of studying Torah given the uncertainty generated by the proliferation of differences of opinion, all of which claim to correctly represent the tradition).

8 *See Introduction* to Beit Yosef *to* Arbah Turim.

of *halakhah* that collected, synthesized, and accounted for these myriad scholarly opinions and set forth clear conclusions about what the law is and what it requires. Codes and restatements, however, merely invited renewed commentary and discussion—within a short time, any *halakhic* compendium found itself swallowed up by a sea of new rabbinic discussion and disputation, which in turn invited yet another round of codification, and so on.[9] With each attempt to organize existing *halakhic* literature and authoritatively and concisely formulate the correct rules and standards of Jewish law, rabbinic authors thus had to begin their projects by answering some very fundamental questions: What is it that they are looking to restate? What are the right *halakhic* rules? Where do they inhere? How does one identify them and know when they have gotten it right?

Answering these questions requires a framework for legal *methodology*; or invoking H.L.A. Hart's famous jurisprudential theory, it requires a set of *secondary rules* of Jewish law.[10] Hart famously observed that the chief distinguishing characteristic of legal systems—what sets them apart from other kinds of normative regimes, such as custom, etiquette, morality, and social convention—is that legal systems are composed of both what Hart terms *primary* and *secondary* rules.[11] Primary rules (and standards, principles, values, and other such norms) directly regulate behavior; they are the proscriptions and duties that comprise the basic substantive structure of any normative system.[12] Systems composed exclusively of primary rules suffer from several critical deficiencies, however. As Hart notes, primary rule systems lack any mechanism for determining whether a given norm is prescribed by the system or is a standard external to the system itself.[13] Primary rule systems likewise lack any means of changing their own rules by enacting, repealing, or adjusting primary rules of conduct within the system.[14] Additionally, systems composed exclusively of primary rules of conduct do not include any means of determining whether such primary rules of conduct have been complied with

---

9   See Rabbi Solomon Luria, *Introduction* to Yam Shel Shlomo, Bava Kamma (arguing that every time one attempts to author an account of the *halakhah*, "there is an even greater need for clarifications, and clarifications upon clarifications. For it is impossible that the initial clarification of the law would be free of all doubts and nuances such that there would be no need for further elaboration").
10 See H.L.A. Hart, The Concept of Law 81, 96-98 (2nd ed., 1997).
11 *See generally* ibid. 81-99.
12 *See* ibid. 81.
13 *See* ibid. 91-92.
14 *See* ibid. 92-93.

or violated in any given situation, or how and when to sanction infractions or reward observances of primary rules.[15] Secondary rules help rectify these deficiencies. Rules of Recognition define what it takes for a norm to count as a rule within the system; Rules of Change prescribe the means of adding, removing, and changing primary rules; and Rules of Adjudication provide means for interpreting and applying abstract rules to specific cases in order to determine whether primary rules have been violated and how such violations should be addressed.[16]

Jewish law, or *halakhah*, follows the same jurisprudential patterns identified by Hart. The *halakhic* universe includes very many primary rules that speak to required, recommended, discouraged, or proscribed modes of conduct in virtually every sphere of Jewish public and private life. As Hart observed, however, no legal system can function based on such primary rules alone. Primary rule systems lack an effective mechanism for identifying what norms and standards the law actually prescribes; they include no way of adapting existing rules to new conditions by enacting, repealing, and changing the law, and they offer no means for determining whether and how abstract norms and standards apply to particular factual situations. Jewish law is no exception to Hart's theory of law, and in addition to primary rules, *halakhah* also encompasses a broad range of secondary rules that address these concerns.[17] The Jewish legal system includes various doctrines and principles for recognizing which primary rules are part of the *halakhah* and which are not, as well as what kinds of *halakhic* rules these are, whether biblical, rabbinic, customary, supererogatory, to name a few such categories.[18] *Halakhah* also includes enabling rules that create opportunities for legislating new laws to deal with developing problems, as well as interpretive and analytic devices for effectively changing existing rules—in practical application,

---

15 *See* ibid. 92-94.
16 *See* ibid. 94-98.
17 For two important and comprehensive compendia of such secondary rules designed to guide the determination of practical *halakhic* rulings from the complex array of Talmudic and post-Talmudic sources that comprise rabbinic legal materials, see Rabbi Malachi HaKohen, Yad Malachi; Rabbi Yitzchak Yosef, Ein Yitzchak, 3 vols. (2009).
18 *See, e.g.*, Deuteronomy 17:8-10 ("If there is a matter of law that is too profound for you . . . you shall come to . . . the judge that will be in those days . . . and you shall act in accordance with what he instructs you."); Babylonian Talmud, Bava Kamma 113b ("The law of the state is the law."); Mishneh Torah, *Introduction* ("All matters decided by the Babylonian Talmud are incumbent on the entire Jewish people to follow."); Shulchan Arukh, Yoreh Deah 214:1 ("Things that are permitted, but which people—knowing they are permitted—customarily treat as prohibited, are as if they were undertaken as a vow, and cannot be permitted to them.").

if not always in theory—to better address new contingencies and contexts.[19] Finally, Jewish law prescribes a comprehensive system of judicial and political authorities tasked with interpreting and applying its abstract and general primary rules to specific cases in order to determine what *halakhah* is and requires in practice.[20]

Thus, secondary rules function as a mechanism for bridging the gap between legal theory and practice. They allow legal actors and decision makers to cognize what the law really is, how it applies, and what it entails in specific cases. These are critical concerns for any legal system and not any less so for *halakhah*. Furthermore, a system of secondary rules plays the important role of controlling—though not eliminating—the role of subjective human discretion in the interpretation, application, and determination of legal rules and principles.[21] Providing a framework of metarules that regulate which norms are actually legally binding, as well as how to determine what those norms are and how they apply secondary rules of decision, creates an external standard against which legal judgments and opinions can be assessed and even predicted despite the indeterminacy of primary sources. Secondary rules thus constitute a sort of metalaw; they are *laws about law*, and they help legal actors and decision makers determine and apply the correct rules of legal conduct.

* * * * *

The importance of such methodological rules of decision within Jewish law and jurisprudence is well evidenced by the many attempts made over the centuries by various rabbinic scholars and jurists to comprehensively list, organize, and explain the secondary rules that help guide *halakhic* decision-making.[22] The

---

19 *See, e.g.*, Mishneh Torah, Hilkhot Mamrim 2:2 ("If a court issued a decree . . . and another court seeks to nullify it . . . it cannot do so unless it is greater in wisdom and numbers of adherents."); Rema *to* Shulchan Arukh, Choshen Mishpat 25:2 ("If the town follows a lenient view because one scholar had ruled thusly for them, we follow his opinion; and if later another scholar arrived and prohibits what they permit, one must act in accordance with the prohibition.").
20 *See generally* Arbah Turim, Choshen Mishpat, ch. 1-25.
21 *See* H.L.A. Hart, The Concept of Law 81, 94-95 (1961).
22 *See, e.g.*, Rabbi Shmuel HaNagid, Introduction to the Talmud, *as printed and translated in* Aryeh Carmel, Aids to Talmud Study 65-73 (4th ed., 1980); Rabbi Malachi HaKohen, Yad Malachi; Rema *to* Shulchan Arukh; Choshen Mishpat 25:1-2; Rabbi Shabbatai HaKohen, Sifsei Kohen *to* Shulchan Arukh, Yoreh Deah, Klalei Horaah B'Issur V'Heter; Rabbi Zvi Hirsch Chajes, Darkhei Horaah, vol. 2, *in* Kol Kitvei Maharitz Chajes, vol. 1, (1958); Rabbi Yitzchak Yosef, Ein Yitzchak, 3 vols. (2009).

existence of secondary rules of decision in Jewish law goes as far back as the Torah itself, which provides what are ostensibly very straightforward directives for determining correct *halakhic* standards. The Torah, for instance, outlines secondary rules of adjudication by instructing that when people are unsure about the correct legal rule or *halakhic* resolution to a particular question, they should go and inquire from "the priest, the Levite, and the judge that will be in those days."[23] These authorities will answer the question, and that answer, the Torah says, is final and determinative of the law: "And you shall act in accordance with the law that they teach you and the judgment that they tell you; do not turn aside from that which they tell you, whether to the right or to the left."[24] In rabbinic interpretation, this provided both a rule of recognition and a rule of adjudication that established certain formally qualified judicial authorities as the ultimate legal authorities, so much so that their judgments are per se the *halakhah* – "even if they say that left is right and right is left."[25]

In practice, during much of the Second Temple period, when rabbinic Judaism and *halakhah* began to form as a comprehensive system of religious law, the role of the "judge that will be in those days" was taken up by the *Sanhedrin*, a deliberative body that met on the Temple Mount in Jerusalem and exercised legislative and supreme judicial authority within the Jewish law system.[26] While it functioned, the word of the *Sanhedrin* was law, at least in theory. Its legislative measures were considered religiously binding on all Jews; its judicial rulings represented the final legal determinations of the highest court within the *halakhic* system; and its legalistic interpretations of biblical texts and traditions were absolutely definitive. As Maimonides put it: "The *Sanhedrin* in Jerusalem is the source and root of the law. It is the pillar of instruction from which statutes and judgments issue forth for the entire Jewish people. And in it the Torah puts its trust and security, as it says, 'You shall do according to the laws which they shall instruct you.'"[27]

Following the destruction of the Second Temple in 70 CE and the suppression of Jewish religious life in Judea and Galilee following the Bar Kokhba Revolt in the early second century, the *Sanhedrin* ceased functioning—the hierarchical system of formal judicial authority previously

---

23 Deuteronomy 17:9.
24 Deuteronomy 17:10-11.
25 Sifri Deuteronomy 17:11.
26 *See* An Introduction to the History and Sources of Jewish Law 41-43, 127-30, 147-50 (Neil S. Hecht et al., eds., 1996).
27 Mishneh Torah, Hilkhot Mamrim 1:1.

used to determine correct *halakhic* norms disappeared.[28] Concerned that these pressures were compounded by the ever widening dispersion of Jews around the world, Rabbi Judah the Prince compiled the *Mishnah*, a shorthand compendium of the rabbinic legal tradition, around 250 CE.[29] The *Mishnah* is a relatively terse text that often records several rabbinic opinions on any given issue. Almost immediately, rabbinic scholars began closely parsing the text, debating its meaning, and considering how its rules and standards should apply in a wide range of theoretical and practical factual contexts.[30] These discussions, which took place in the rabbinic academies of the Persian Empire, were collected and organized into another text, the *gemara*, which was compiled around 550 CE.[31] Together, the *Mishnah* and the *gemara* produced in the Persian academies comprise the Babylonian Talmud, which, after its completion, came to be regarded as the final authority on *halakhah*. Importantly, the completion and widespread acceptance of the Talmud gave rise to yet another important secondary rule of Jewish law—one that offered a viable alternative to the Bible's rules of recognition and adjudication in the absence of a formal religious hierarchy and *Sanhedrin*. As Maimonides notes, after its completion, the Talmud became *the* locus for *halakhic* norms and standards; rules prescribed by the Talmud were regarded as inviolable, and any later legal opinions that contradicted the Talmud would be treated as outside the scope of Jewish law.[32] In addition to this critical rule of recognition, post-Talmudic scholars also developed a complex array of additional secondary rules designed to guide Jewish law practitioners in their attempts to determine what rules the Talmud actually prescribes. The Talmud is written in a rambling discursive style, not organized by subject matter, and it only rarely reaches explicit legal conclusions. Determining the right Talmudic rule is thus often quite difficult. Rabbinic scholars therefore composed lists of Talmudic principles that could be used to properly decode the Talmudic text and distill the right

---

28 *See* Menachem Elon, Jewish Law: History, Sources, Principles 19 (Bernard Auerbach & Melvin J. Sykes trans., 1994).
29 *See* ibid.
30 *See* Lawrence H. Schiffman, From Text to Tradition: A History of Second Temple and Rabbinic Judaism 177-200 (1991); Menachem Elon, Jewish Law: History, Sources, Principles 1048-56 (Bernard Auerbach & Melvin J. Sykes trans., 1994).
31 *See* Lawrence H. Schiffman, From Text to Tradition: A History of Second Temple and Rabbinic Judaism 214-27 (1991).
32 *See Introduction* to Mishneh Torah.

halakhic conclusions from its web of different opinions, arguments, proofs, rebuttals, and rejoinders.[33]

Gradually, and as discussed earlier, direct rabbinic engagement with Talmudic sources gave rise to various attempts to codify Talmudic rules. As major codes and restatements of Jewish law like Maimonides's *Mishneh Torah* and Rabbi Joseph Karo's *Shulchan Arukh* gained traction, commentators began to formulate similar sets of rules and principles to better decode and understand these texts.[34] These attempts at codification also gave rise to voluminous commentaries that both attempted to explain and often disagreed with the rulings they examined.[35] At the same time, rabbinic decision makers across the Jewish world produced volumes of responsa, written responses to legal questions posed to them for resolution.[36] Gradually, additional works of secondary rules of decision were formulated that contained principles designed to help *halakhic* practitioners assess the relative weight of various rabbinic authorities, decide whether to follow the legal rulings found in relevant responsa or alternative formulations of correct *halakhic* rules found in codes, determine when and how Talmudic rules can change, and reach determinate conclusions in cases where the right rule is genuinely uncertain.

* * * * *

In the *Orach Chaim* section of his own comprehensive restatement of Jewish law, the *Arukh HaShulchan*, Rabbi Epstein relies on ten methodological principles to navigate the complex waters of rabbinic jurisprudence and reach determinate *halakhic* conclusions. These ten methodological principles can be organized into four different groups, each of which speaks to a different important question of Rabbinic jurisprudence: How does one determine what the right *halakhic* standard is in principle? How does one determine the right standard of *halakhic* practice where the correct legal norm is unclear? What is the relationship between observing the right *halakhic* standard and

---

33 *See, e.g.*, Rabbi Shmuel HaNagid, Introduction to the Talmud, *as printed and translated in* Aryeh Carmel, Aids to Talmud Study 65-73 (4th ed., 1980).
34 *See, e.g.*, Rabbi Yitzchak Yosef, Ein Yitzchak, vol. 3 (2009); Michael J. Broyde & Ira J. Bedzow, The Codification of Jewish Law and an Introduction to the Jurisprudence of the Mishna Berura 3-5 (2014).
35 *See* Michael J. Broyde & Ira Bedzow, The Codification of Jewish Law and an Introduction to the Jurisprudence of the Mishna Berura 2-3 (2014).
36 *See* ibid. 12.

other religious values? What is the relationship between following the correct *halakhic* rule and other rationalistic, social, material, and pragmatic concerns?

The *Arukh HaShulchan*'s ten methodological principles for reaching *halakhic* conclusions, sorted by the four jurisprudential questions they address, are as follows:

Principles for Determining the Ideally Correct *Halakhic* Standard

1. *Dina D'Talmuda: The Normativity of Talmudic Norms*

Rabbi Epstein maintains that in the abstract, the correct *halakhic* standard is the one that emerges from each qualified rabbinic scholar's independent and confident understanding of the relevant Talmudic sources—even against the precedential rulings of other important *halakhic* authorities of previous generations. Thus, when Rabbi Epstein is confident in the correctness of his own Talmudic interpretations, he rules in accordance with his own understanding of these materials, which for him include not only the Babylonian Talmud, but also the Jerusalem Talmud, which Rabbi Epstein often deploys as an important *halakhic* source. This approach often leads Rabbi Epstein to express disagreement with the rulings of other important rabbinic scholars. He often offers new and creative Talmudic readings to explain his conclusions, proposes novel reasons for established *halakhic* norms, and prescribes entirely new standards of *halakhic* conduct.[37]

2. *Intellectual Humility in the Face of Teachers and Colleagues*

Rabbi Epstein's commitment to following his own independent understandings of the Talmudic sources is tempered by epistemic humility. Even where Rabbi Epstein is personally confident in his legal opinion, he declines to follow his independent understanding of the relevant Talmudic sources when his own view is incompatible with the established rule of a broad consensus of past authorities or when the views of major pillars of *halakhic* jurisprudence adopt a rule more stringent than his own. In such cases, Rabbi Epstein becomes less certain about the correctness of his own Talmudic understandings and tends to either defer to the collective weight of rabbinic consensus or to cautiously

---

37 *See infra* Chapter Four.

prescribe the adoption of the more ritually restrictive standard adopted by particularly significant *halakhic* authorities.[38]

Principles for Resolving Doubts about the Ideally Correct *Halakhic* Standard

3. *Reliance on Precedent in Cases of Doubt*

In cases where Rabbi Epstein is himself unsure about the right Talmudic norm, and in the absence of a strong *halakhic* consensus regarding the correct meaning of the Talmudic sources, Rabbi Epstein tends to give primary weight to the rulings of Maimonides and then to the determinations of Rabbi Joseph Karo as recorded in his works, the *Beit Yosef* and the *Shulchan Arukh*.[39]

4. *Reliance on Secondary Rules for Resolving Doubts*

In cases where Rabbi Epstein is himself unsure of the correct Talmudic rule, and past rabbinic consensus and major precedential authorities do not provide clear guidance on the issue, Rabbi Epstein resorts to the application of standard, doubt-resolving secondary rules of *halakhic* decision-making. Most prominently, Rabbi Epstein follows the standard *halakhic* rule that in cases of doubt regarding biblical laws, one should act strictly, while in cases of doubt regarding rabbinic rules, one should act leniently.[40]

Principles for Mediating Between the Talmudic Standard and Other Religious Values

5. *The Relevance of Non-Normative Halakhic Opinions*

Rabbi Epstein generally does not rule that one should act strictly in order to satisfy *halakhic* opinions which he regards as mistaken, whether because he rejects the Talmudic interpretations upon which they rely, because they have been marginalized by rabbinic consensus, or because they have been otherwise rejected in accordance with the ordinary rules of *halakhic* decision-making. However, Rabbi Epstein does make use of such rejected opinions to

---

38 See *infra* Chapter Five.
39 See *infra* Chapter Six.
40 See *infra* Chapter Six.

resolve complex *halakhic* questions or disputes among past authorities, to justify common practices that are at odds with standard *halakhic* norms, or to permit non-normative behavior in extenuating circumstances.[41]

6. Supererogatory Religious Conduct

Rabbi Epstein generally encourages—but does not mandate—supererogatory behavior that goes beyond the minimal requirements of what he thinks is the correct normative *halakhic* standard, but only in cases where he believes there is a genuine religious or social benefit to doing so. In cases where Rabbi Epstein thinks that supererogatory behavior offers no appreciable religious or social benefits, or where he believes that such conduct is likely to have negative religious or material consequences, Rabbi Epstein discourages extra-*halakhic* observances.[42]

7. Halakhah and Mysticism

Rabbi Epstein tries whenever possible to reconcile the mystical prescriptions of the *Zohar* and other kabbalistic sources with standard *halakhic* norms, though he affirmatively rejects the *halakhic* relevance of mystical practices that are incompatible with Talmudic sources. Moreover, Rabbi Epstein generally permits—and often recommends—the adoption of mystical practices innovated by the *Zohar*, as long as they do not contradict *halakhic* requirements.[43]

Principles for Mediating Between Talmudic Standards and Pragmatic Concerns

8. Minhag: The Role of Custom in Determining Halakhah

Rabbi Epstein upholds the *halakhic* normativity of what he sees as *minhag*—the customary practices of the Jewish people living in his own time and place—even when such customary practices are inconsistent with precedential *halakhic* rulings or Rabbi Epstein's own preferred understanding of the Talmudic sources. However, Rabbi Epstein rejects the legal validity of customary practices that

---

41   See *infra* Chapter Seven.
42   See *infra* Chapter Eight.
43   See *infra* Chapter Nine.

are irreconcilably incompatible with basic *halakhic* standards, as well as those which are based on mistaken factual or legal assumptions.[44]

9. Contemporary Rationalization of Halakhic Norms

Rabbi Epstein insists that *halakhic* issues need to be decided in the present time and place. Thus, he holds that when the reasons for established *halakhic* rules no longer apply due to changed circumstances, those rules likewise change so as to respond effectively to achieve the same objectives in the circumstances posed by current realities.[45]

10. Real-World Pragmatism: The Torah Was Not Given to the Ministering Angels

Rabbi Epstein recognizes that *halakhah* must be practiced by real people in the real world; therefore, he adapts seemingly impracticable *halakhic* norms to better account for the real-world practical challenges that come with trying to actually uphold such standards.[46]

* * * * *

These ten principles address four distinct but interrelated jurisprudential questions—and some of them relate to more than one of these questions. First, as discussed in chapters four and five, some principles speak to the way in which one ought to determine the genuinely correct *halakhic* rule for any given issue. For Rabbi Epstein, as for many other *halakhists* throughout history, this is principally about determining the correct understanding of relevant Talmudic materials in order to arrive at an independent assessment of the *dina d'Talmuda*, the legal rule determined by the Talmud. Secondly, some principles speak to the fact that knowledge of the right legal rule may be obscured at times, usually because Talmudic sources can often be genuinely ambiguous or irreconcilably contradictory, and because competing post-Talmudic interpretations of the primary sources may all be equally reasonable with no single understanding of the Talmudic rule being especially more credible than the others. Thus, chapter

---

44 See *infra* Chapter Ten.
45 See *infra* Chapter Eleven.
46 See *infra* Chapter Twelve.

six addresses how Rabbi Epstein determines in practice the appropriate course of *halakhic* conduct in cases where there are genuine and unresolvable doubts and uncertainties about the right Talmudic rule. Finally, no system of law exists in a vacuum; law must be practiced and implemented in the real world where pragmatic concerns—as well as competing normative commitments—often create tensions with abstractly posited legal standards. Jewish law is no different, and chapters seven through nine thus address the methodological principles that Rabbi Epstein uses to address the third question—regarding how to determine the correct course of *halakhic* conduct in cases where the right Talmudic rule is known, but where that rule stands in tension with other religious concerns and values. Chapters ten through twelve, in turn, explore the secondary rules that Rabbi Epstein uses to address the final question of how to resolve tensions between the theoretically correct Talmudic rule and social, economic, and practical pressures.

CHAPTER FOUR

The Rule of the Talmud

This chapter explains and illustrates several of the secondary rules that Rabbi Epstein uses to determine the correct *halakhic* standard in the *Orach Chaim* section of his *Arukh HaShulchan*. The basic jurisprudential premise of Rabbi Epstein's methodological approach is the view that, in principle, the correct *halakhic* rule for any given issue is the norm or standard prescribed by the Talmud.[1] We say that according to Rabbi Epstein the Talmudic rule is the right one "in principle" to highlight and caution that often Rabbi Epstein does not rule in accordance with what he believes is the legal standard embraced by the Talmud. In Rabbi Epstein's jurisprudence, the Talmudic standard is the right *halakhic* norm in theory; it is a kind of platonic ideal form of the right legal rule. The theoretically correct Talmudic rule is often genuinely unclear, however, and chapter six considers the ways in which Rabbi Epstein reaches practical *halakhic* determinations when such Talmudic indeterminacy precludes his arriving at an analytically correct ruling. Moreover, even when the Talmudic rule is clear and known, this standard often gives way to alternative standards in practice as theoretically correct and abstractly formulated Talmudic standards come into conflict with various religious, social, and pragmatic concerns in real-world *halakhic* practice. As discussed later in chapters seven through twelve, such tensions often call for a reconsideration of what the *halakhah*, broadly defined, requires in practice. Such analyses often result in some substantial modification of the Talmudic rule itself or at least some alternative expression of what that standard entails when applied to complex, real-world conditions.

---

1   See Arukh HaShulchan, *Introduction* to Choshen Mishpat.

Before considering how he addresses the very complex issue of how to interpret and apply *halakhic* standards in actual practice, this chapter addresses the methodological principles that Rabbi Epstein uses to determine the ideally correct *halakhic* norms that form the theoretical foundation for practical, applied *halakhic* rulings. At this initial stage of the *halakhic* decision-making process, every rabbinic decisor must contend with the pivotal issue of how much he trusts his own *halakhic* judgment in the face of contrary rulings by other authorities. If a contemporary scholar's judgment leads him to one legal conclusion, but the judgment and analysis of other, perhaps highly regarded—even legendary—decisors of past eras reached alternative *halakhic* conclusions, should the contemporary scholar follow his own judgment, or should he defer to the rulings of those who preceded him? Rabbi Epstein addresses these concerns through two secondary rules of recognition and adjudication. First, as discussed in this chapter, Rabbi Epstein maintains that the ideally correct *halakhic* rule is the one that emerges from his own independent understanding of the relevant Talmudic sources, even where his own conclusions differ from those of important *halakhic* authorities of previous generations.[2] Importantly, in reaching his own understanding of the correct Talmudic rule, Rabbi Epstein considers the Jerusalem Talmud as an important source of legal material and often utilizes it alongside the more well-known and widely used Babylonian Talmud.[3] This direct engagement with the Talmudic corpus often leads Rabbi Epstein to prescribe entirely new *halakhic* rules and to offer novel rationales and explanations for well-settled *halakhic* norms not previously articulated by other major rabbinic scholars. Second, as discussed in chapter five, Rabbi Epstein tempers his willingness to independently derive *halakhic* norms directly from the Talmud with a healthy dose of epistemic humility. Thus, when his own understanding of the Talmudic sources conflicts with the *halakhic* conclusions expressed by a broad consensus of other authorities, or when certain major authorities express more ritually stringent legal opinions, Rabbi Epstein sets aside his own potentially mistaken judgment and defers to his peers.

* * * * *

Principle One: Rabbi Epstein maintains that the correct halakhic rule is the one that follows from the qualified scholar's independent understanding of the relevant

---

2 *See* ibid.
3 *See, e.g.,* Arukh HaShulchan, Orach Chaim 345:21-24.

CHAPTER FOUR • The Rule of the Talmud | 85

Talmudic sources, even against the precedential rulings of important authorities of previous generations.

Before considering how Rabbi Epstein approaches the very complex question of how to interpret and apply the right rules of law in practice, we consider his thinking on what the right rule of law is, where it comes from, and how he knows it. As to these fundamental issues, Rabbi Epstein's approach is clear: at bottom, he approaches each *halakhic* issue with the conviction that the correct legal standard is the one articulated by the Talmud—his goal, then, is always to determine the rule or standard evinced by the relevant Talmudic sources.[4]

In explaining the roots, workings, and historical usage of this approach to rabbinic jurisprudence, it is helpful to contrast this methodological model with another general jurisprudential outlook, which helps highlight the significance

---

4   In truth, this approach is, at least in theory, undisputed in rabbinic jurisprudence. Following the redaction of the Talmud in the sixth century, virtually all *halakhic* decision makers have maintained that at least in principle all *halakhic* determinations must be made by direct reference to the Talmud itself. Maimonides stridently promoted this view when he emphasized that the only truly binding and authoritative statements of Jewish law are those found in the Talmud itself. *See* Mishneh Torah, *Introduction* ("All matters decided by the Babylonian Talmud are incumbent on the entire Jewish people to follow."). Indeed, Maimonides explicitly rules that in all matters of Jewish law, it is the Talmud itself that is binding rather than the opinions of post-Talmudic authorities, no matter how erudite or well regarded they might be. Thus, he writes that, even if one has available the Talmudic interpretations of the *Geonim*, who Maimonides himself viewed as the most reliable heirs of the Talmud, one should not follow those precedential rulings if one concludes that they misunderstand the correct Talmudic law. "So too, if one of the *Geonim* understood that the law was such and such, and it became clear to another court afterwards that this was not the correct rule of law determined by Talmud, the earlier [Geonic] court is not to be obeyed, but rather what seems the more correct [understanding of the Talmud], whether earlier or later." Mishneh Torah, *Introduction*. Maimonides, as well as other codifiers thus explained that their attempts to reformulate Talmudic norms were merely a concession to the pressures of the age, which prevented students of the Talmud from gaining adequate facility with this difficult text in order to reliably determine practical legal rules. *See, e.g.*, Beit Yosef to Arbah Turim, *Introduction* ("However, if we were to demand that in every matter one must investigate the roots of the law in the Talmud and commentators, the task would be overly difficult."). The important twentieth century scholar, Rabbi Moses Feinstein, likewise asserts that proper *halakhic* decision-making involves a qualified decisor's reaching a legal conclusion on the basis of his own understanding of the Talmudic sources, rather than by deferring to existing precedent: "Legal truth is that which appears correct to the scholar after he has toiled and studied to clarify the law in the Talmud and in the words of the authorities according to his abilities ... and that is how he should—and must—rule in practice." Rabbi Moses Feinstein Igrot Moshe, Orach Chaim, vol. 1, *Introduction*. Rabbi Epstein follows this tradition in his *Arukh HaShulchan*, ruling in accordance with what he independently views as the correct understanding of the Talmud, rather than deferring to the precedential rulings of prior scholars.

of Rabbi Epstein's approach. As post-Talmudic rabbinic literature—including codifications and restatements of *halakhic* rules, as well as voluminous responsa providing specific legal replies to actual questions—proliferated during the Middle Ages,[5] *halakhic* scholars began to debate the implications of these new materials for *halakhic* decision-making. Two schools of thought developed. One group of scholars, which we call here the precedentialist school, maintained that while in principle the *halakhah* follows the prescriptions of the Talmud, in practice, *halakhic* decision makers should rely on and apply the legal rules and standards found in authoritative secondary works like Maimonides's major twelfth century code, the *Mishneh Torah*, or Rabbi Joseph Karo's sixteenth century *halakhic* code, the *Shulchan Arukh*.[6] These scholars maintained that independent reasoning and direct engagement with the Talmud is not a virtue; on the contrary, it is likely to lead to mistaken understandings and erroneous legal conclusions, and therefore rabbinic decision makers should rely on the well-formulated *halakhic* rulings found in accepted secondary sources.[7] This view is grounded in a number of different textual, conceptual, and practical jurisprudential considerations put forth by rabbinic scholars.

Accepted secondary rules of rabbinic jurisprudence include doctrines governing the incidence of judicial error, which help determine whether a *halakhic* ruling is erroneous as well as the decision maker's liability for any losses caused by that mistaken judgment.[8] One such doctrine called *ta'ut b'davar mishnah*, or "mistake in Mishnaic matters," maintains that *halakhic* rulings that contravene clearly established rabbinic norms are null and void.[9] While most scholars have confined the reach of this rule to only those norms clearly prescribed by Talmudic sources, some have extended the doctrine to apply to widely accepted and authoritative post-Talmudic expressions of Jewish legal standards, which establish binding precedents of Jewish law and thereby limit later scholars' legal authority to draw *halakhic* rulings directly from the Talmud.[10]

---

5   On the development of post-Talmudic *halakhic* materials, see Chaim Saiman, Halakhah: The Rabbinic Idea of Law 140-194 (2018).
6   *See, e.g.*, Rabbi Refael Yosef Chazzan, Responsa Chikrei Lev, Choshen Mishpat 3:49; Rabbi Jacob ben Joseph Reischer, Responsa Shevut Yaakov 2:64.
7   *See e.g.*, Rabbi Joseph ibn Migash, Responsa Ri Migash no. 114.
8   *See generally* Shulchan Arukh, Yoreh Deah 142; Shulchan Arukh, Choshen Mishpat 25.
9   *See* Shulchan Arukh, Choshen Mishpat 25:1 ("A judge who rules in a monetary matter and errs: if the error is in matters that are revealed and well known, such as explicit rulings of the Mishnah or *gemara*, or in the rulings of the [post-Talmudic] decisors, the judgment is reversed and the case retried.").
10 *See generally* Beit Yosef *to* Arbah Turim, Choshen Mishpat 25:1.

For instance, Rabbi Abraham ben David of Posquieres (1125-1198) ruled that scholars of his own time were obligated to read the Talmud through the interpretive lens of the *Geonim*, a school of rabbinic authorities that flourished in what is today Iraq between the eighth and eleventh centuries.[11] Similarly, in Rabbi Joseph Karo's major sixteenth century *halakhic* code, the *Shulchan Arukh*, he ruled that contemporary rabbinic judgments that conflict with "matters that are well known, such as . . . the words of the [major post-Talmudic] *halakhic* decisors," are void.[12] And some more recent scholars have argued that the *Shulchan Arukh*'s codification of Jewish law itself constitutes such binding precedent.[13] Even according to scholars who reject the applicability of the doctrine of *ta'ut b'davar mishnah* to post-Talmudic legal opinions, another judicial mistake principle known as *ta'ut b'shikul hada'at*, or "error in judgment," may help create highly persuasive *halakhic* precedents that preclude later scholars' direct engagement with the Talmud as a primary source of Jewish law.[14] "Errors in judgment" occur when contemporary *halakhic* decision makers reach legal conclusions that are not inconsistent with Talmudic norms, but which fail to account for the development of post-Talmudic consensuses in support of more specific and contrary standards.[15] This concept functions to create a kind of historical periodization of *halakhic* authority, which, while somewhat ill-defined at the edges, has become fairly widely accepted. There are three such generally accepted periods of post-Talmudic *halakhic* development: the Geonic period lasted roughly from 700-950 CE and was characterized by the *halakhic* hegemony of the *Geonim*, the heads of the rabbinic academies of Babylon, where the Talmud itself had been compiled; the Rishonic period lasted from the eleventh century through the mid-sixteenth century, and it involved the development of major restatements, codifications, and collections of responsa by the *Rishonim* ("first ones"), the rabbis who lived and worked in Europe and North Africa during this time; the Acharonic period began in the latter half of the

---

11 Raabad, *quoted in* Rosh *to* Babylonian Talmud, Sanhedrin 4:6. *See also* Mishneh Torah, Hilkhot Sanhedrin 6:1.
12 Shulchan Arukh, Choshen Mishpat 25:1.
13 *See* Chavot Yair, *as quoted in* Rabbi Tzvi Hirsch Eisenstadt, Pitchei Teshuva *to* Shulchan Arukh, Choshen Mishpat 25:2.
14 *See generally* Shulchan Arukh, Choshen Mishpat 25:2.
15 *See* Shulchan Arukh, Choshen Mishpat 25:2 ("Errors in judgment: Such as an issue which is a matter of dispute among the *Tannaim* or *Amoraim* where the law has not been clearly decided like either of them [by the Talmud], and he [the decisor] followed one of them without realizing that a rabbinic consensus has already developed in support of the other one . . .").

1500s and continued until roughly the turn of the twentieth century, during which rabbis known as *Acharonim* ("last ones") commented on and applied the texts produced during the Rishonic era.[16] According to some, the doctrine of *ta'ut b'shikul hada'at* instructs that at the close of each of these historical eras, the *halakhic* rulings from that period constitute a kind of strongly persuasive—if not truly formally binding—precedent, which restricts the *halakhic* freedom of later decision makers to render independent rulings based directly on the Talmud.[17]

The force of post-Talmudic precedent is reinforced, according to the precedentialist school, by an important Talmudic dictum and secondary rule of *halakhic* decision-making that prescribes "*halakhah k'batrai*," or that "the law follows the latter [view]."[18] According to many rabbinic commentators, this important principle teaches that present practitioners and adjudicators of Jewish law should look to the more recent expressions of *halakhic* norms and standards for the most authoritative statements of Jewish law, rather than the more ancient expressions.[19] Indeed, the Talmud itself seems to suggest that it should not be used directly as a source of practical *halakhic* norms: "We do not derive the law from specific incidents or from Talmudic teachings, but only from rulings issued as practical law."[20]

Buttressing the foregoing normative claims regarding the possibility of a post-Talmudic binding precedent is a strong sense, at least among some rabbinic scholars, that the history of Jewish legal and religious learning is one of

---

16 See generally Robert Brody, The *Geonim* of Babylonia and the Shaping of Medieval Jewish Culture (1998), for an overview of the *Geonim*, their work and context. See also An Introduction to the History and Sources of Jewish Law 203-14 (Neil S. Hecht et al., eds., 1996) (discussing the legal literature produced by the *Geonim*); id. at 228-34 (describing the lives and works of several major Geonic scholars). For background on the Rishonic era, see generally An Introduction to the History and Sources of Jewish Law 271-358 (Neil S. Hecht et al., eds., 1996); id. at 359-96. For an overview on major Acharonic works, see generally Living the Halakhic Process 18-26 (Daniel Mann, ed., 2007).

17 See, e.g., Shulchan Arukh, Choshen Mishpat 25:1 (arguing that contemporary rabbinic judgments which conflict with the rulings of major post-Talmudic *halakhic* decisors are void); Chavot Yair, *as quoted in* Rabbi Tzvi Hirsch Eisenstadt, Pitchei Teshuva *to* Shulchan Arukh, Choshen Mishpat 25:2 (arguing that the *Shulchan Arukh*'s codification of Jewish law itself constitutes a similarly binding precedent).

18 See, e.g., Rema *to* Shulchan Arukh, Choshen Mishpat 25:2; Tosafot *to* Babylonian Talmud, Berakhot 39b (s.v. *mevarech al haptitin vepoter et hashlemin*); Rosh *to* Babylonian Talmud, Bava Metzia 4:21.

19 For an academic overview, *see* Israel Ta-Shma, Hilchata K'batrai: Historical Observations on a Legal Rule, 6–7 Jewish Law Annual (1979–1980), 405–23 [Hebrew].

20 Babylonian Talmud, Bava Batra 130b.

gradual decline.²¹ This concept is known as *yeridat hadorot*, or "the decline of the generations," and it generally teaches that the rabbinic scholars and *halakhic* decision makers of later generations are less competent than those of earlier generations. This is due to a decline of scholarly ability, political upheavals and economic instability, and temporal distance from the original point of revelation at Sinai.²² Belief in this proposition, at least in the realm of *halakhic* insight and knowledge, helps explain why, according to the precedentialists, post-Talmudic legal rulings should be the primary source of binding *halakhic* norms rather than the Talmud itself. Based on this view, rabbinic decision makers must always view themselves as less qualified and less capable than their predecessors and should therefore defer to precedential rulings of earlier *halakhic* authorities. In doing so, however, contemporary scholars should not refer all the way back to the Talmud itself—while Talmudic sources are the earliest and most authoritative, the historical periodization of *halakhic* development established by the doctrines of judicial error, as well as the principle of *halakhah k'batrai*, urge against such direct engagement with the Talmud as a source of law. They instead suggest that precedential rulings of more recent major rabbinic scholars should be the primary reference point for practical Jewish law decision-making.

As discussed earlier, many rabbinic scholars severely criticized and rejected the general approach that post-Talmudic precedent, whether in codes, restatements, or responsa, could establish binding norms of Jewish law.²³ According to some opponents of ruling based on post-Talmudic codes and precedents, such materials are inadequate because they are merely expressions of their authors' legal opinions rather than the law itself.²⁴ Thus, Rabbi Judah Loew (1526-1609) argued that relying on post-Talmudic precedents is mistaken because such texts "were merely authored for practical instruction, and not to learn the law from,"²⁵ meaning that post-Talmudic accounts of the *halakhah* are useful handbooks of practical instruction for the times and places in which they were written, but they cannot be regarded as the law itself. "It is more appropriate,"

---

21 *See, e.g.*, Menachem Marc Kellner, Maimonides on the "Decline of the Generations" and the Nature of Rabbinic Authority (1996).
22 *See, e.g.*, Babylonian Talmud, Shabbat 112b ("If the earlier [scholars] were sons of angels, we are sons of men; and if the earlier [scholars] were sons of men, we are sons of asses. . . .").
23 For a comprehensive explanation of why *halakhic* rulings should not merely follow existing precedents—whether in the codes or other rabbinic materials—see Rabbi Zvi Hirsch Chajes, Darkhei Horaah, vol. 2, 249-250, *in* Kol Sifrei Maharitz Chajes, Vol. 1 (1958).
24 *See, e.g.*, Rabbi Chaim ben Betzalel, Vikuach Mayim Chaim, sec. 1, 94.
25 Rabbi Judah Loew, Netivot Olam, Netiv HaTorah, ch. 15.

Rabbi Loew continues, "to rule based directly on the Talmud, for while there is room to fear that in doing so one may . . . rule incorrectly . . . nevertheless, a wise man has only what his own mind understands from the Talmud," and he may thus rely on his own judgment.[26] Others maintained that, in reality, the seemingly determinate rulings found in various post-Talmudic works were no more clear-cut than the meandering discourses of the Talmud itself; therefore, they offered little real advantage to rabbinic scholars seeking knowledge of correct *halakhic* norms.[27] According to this view, *halakhic* decision makers may as well engage directly with the Talmud—the true repository of the law—and rule in accordance with their respective understandings of the primary sources. Because relying on secondary works also requires substantial interpretation and analysis as abstract rules are applied to specific cases, it is better that such legal reasoning engage the law itself through independent Talmudic analysis rather than rely on secondary sources several steps removed from the ultimate source of *halakhic* authority.[28] Moreover, some scholars opposed ruling from post-Talmudic precedent because they thought that such reliance on such secondary sources was bound to lead rabbinic decisors to reach incorrect results in practice. For instance, Rabbi Joel Sirkis (1561-1640) argued that "those who [mechanistically] issue rulings based on the [precedential authority] of the *Shulchan Arukh* are ruling not in accordance with the *halakhah*, for they do not know the roots of the *halakhah* from which these specific rules emerge."[29]

More recently, two important twentieth century *halakhic* authorities firmly rejected the possibility that rabbinic scholars can be bound by any precedent; they instead affirmed that each must rule in accordance with his own independent judgment of the issue.[30] Rabbi Moses Feinstein (1895-1986), the preeminent *halakhic* authority in the United States during the latter half of the twentieth century, wrote that the scholars of later generations are permitted, and indeed required, to resolve *halakhic* questions in accordance with their own considered understanding of the relevant sources, even if their rulings

---

26 Ibid. *See also* Rabbi Judah Loew, Derekh Chaim 6:7.
27 *See* Rabbi Solomon Luria, Yam Shel Shlomo, *Introduction* to Bava Kamma (arguing that every time one attempts to author an account of the *halakhah*, "there is an even greater need for clarifications, and clarifications upon clarifications. For it is impossible that the initial clarification of the law would be free of all doubts and nuances such that there would be no need for further elaboration").
28 *See, e.g.,* Rabbi Solomon Luria, Yam Shel Shlomo, *Introduction* to Bava Kamma.
29 Responsa Bach (yashanot), no. 80.
30 *See generally* Jeffrey Woolf, The Parameters of Precedent in Pesak Halakhah, 27 Tradition 4, 41 (1993).

conflict with the opinions of earlier authorities, and even if they themselves might be objectively less qualified and learned than scholars of earlier generations.[31] Rabbi Chaim David HaLevi (1924-1998), Chief Rabbi of Tel-Aviv, put this view even more stridently. Speaking about contemporary *halakhic* decisors, he wrote, "No precedent binds him, even a ruling of a court composed of scholars greater than he, and even of his own teachers."[32]

It is this school of thought to which Rabbi Epstein belongs. Rabbi Epstein rejects the view of some scholars that one must not issue *halakhic* judgments without investigating what is written in post-Talmudic texts. This approach, he says, "is irrational."[33] In his view, while various post-Talmudic works are impressive and important, the fundamental and primary source of *halakhah* is the Talmud. Legal rulings not grounded in direct knowledge of the Talmudic sources themselves are therefore necessarily deficient, and those who issue *halakhic* rulings directly from codes like the *Shulchan Arukh* do so without adequate knowledge of the underlying reasons and rationales of the rules they are applying. This, Rabbi Epstein maintains, leads to errors unless one's legal knowledge is solidly grounded in a direct understanding of the Talmudic sources themselves.[34] Indeed, Rabbi Epstein explains that a primary motivation in undertaking the task of writing his *Arukh HaShulchan* was to counter the trend of his own time, which saw competent *halakhic* scholars treating Rabbi Joseph Karo's code, the *Shulchan Arukh*, as the primary source of Jewish law, and as the starting point—if not always the final word—for *halakhic* decision-making. His own work was intended to counter this trend by presenting not only his own *halakhic* conclusions grounded in his own understandings of the relevant Talmudic materials, but also to do so in such a way that would present to his readers the underlying Talmudic discussions, thereby better equipping others to understand and determine the *halakhah* based on the Talmud itself.[35]

One example of Rabbi Epstein's primary reliance on what he thinks is the right Talmudic norm, even against the contrary views of other authorities, concerns the question of whether or not one should recite the usually prescribed blessing upon ritually washing one's hands in the morning in a situation where

---

31 See *Introduction* to Rabbi Moses Feinstein, Igrot Moshe, Orach Chaim, vol. 1. *See also* ibid., Yoreh Deah 2:88.
32 Aseh Lecha Rav 2:61 (1989).
33 Arukh HaShulchan, Yoreh Deah 242:35.
34 *See* ibid. 242:36.
35 *See Introduction* to Arukh HaShulchan.

one stayed awake the entire previous night. Ritual morning handwashing was originally prescribed as a means of cleansing the body of ritual impurity and uncleanliness that one contracts while sleeping, and which must be removed before one can recite the morning prayers.[36] Thus, the case of someone who did not sleep during the night poses a question: should the handwashing be performed with the ordinary blessing recited; or is washing in such a situation unnecessary, and would the recital of a blessing thus be a violation of the prohibition against taking God's name in vain? The *Shulchan Arukh* and the *Rema* both rule that one should not recite a blessing in such a case because Jewish law generally instructs that when one is in doubt about whether to recite a blessing, a blessing should not be recited.[37] Here it is doubtful whether a blessing should be recited—on one hand, the Talmudic Sages decreed that one wash one's hands in the morning with a blessing, and they did not distinguish between one who was awake the night before and one who slept the night before; on the other hand, both of the reasons given for washing one's hands in the morning potentially do not apply to one who was awake the night before.[38] Despite the assertion by these two preeminent *halakhic* authorities that a blessing should not be recited, Rabbi Epstein rules, to the contrary, that there is no doubt at all; therefore, a blessing should be recited.[39] Rabbi Epstein bases this conclusion on his own understanding of the relevant Talmudic sources. He argues that the correct Talmudic rule is that everyone must wash their hands with a blessing each morning, even someone who did not sleep at all the previous night. This is because the Talmudic Rabbis did not specifically exempt a person who remained awake all night from the general obligation to wash one's hands every morning with a blessing; if the Rabbis had intended such an exception, they could have provided as much in the Talmudic discussion of handwashing.[40] Rabbi Epstein was indeed so confident in his own read of the Talmudic norm that he went so far as to prescribe the recital of what the *Shulchan Arukh* and the *Rema* feared may be a blessing made in vain, which is a severe prohibition.[41]

---

36 *See* Rosh *to* Babylonian Talmud, Berakhot 9:23; Rabbi Solomon ben Aderet, Responsa Rashba 1:191.
37 Shulchan Arukh, Orach Chaim 4:13.
38 *See* Beit Yosef *to* Arbah Turim, Orach Chaim 4:13.
39 *See* Arukh HaShulchan, Orach Chaim 4:12.
40 *See* ibid. 4:12.
41 In fact, according to the Talmud, one who recites a blessing in vain thereby violates one of the Ten Commandments. *See* Babylonian Talmud, Berakhot 33a; Exodus 20:6.

Another example of Rabbi Epstein's rejection of precedent in favor of his own Talmudic understanding pertains to the question of whether one may leave the synagogue during the public Torah reading service. The Talmud rules that the congregation may not leave the prayer service taking place in a synagogue until after the Torah scroll used for public congregational Torah reading has been rolled up, covered, and returned to the ark.[42] While this rule is codified by the *Shulchan Arukh*, the *Rema* qualifies this prohibition as applying only to instances where the entire congregation leaves the synagogue at once; individuals, however, may leave one-by-one, even before the Torah scroll is returned to the ark.[43] The *Arukh HaShulchan* rejects the *Rema*'s permissive view.[44] Rabbi Epstein asserts that a correct understanding of the relevant Talmudic passage shows that the prohibition on leaving the synagogue prior to the Torah's being returned to the ark applies to each and every individual member of the congregation and not merely to the congregation as a whole. This, Rabbi Epstein says, is implicit from the context of the Talmudic ruling, which involves several discussions about individuals' obligations as good members of a prayer congregation, and it is likewise consistent with *Rashi*'s explanation of that Talmudic passage.[45]

Notably, Rabbi Epstein's methodology is unique and independent even within the originalist school—Rabbi Epstein does not only rely on the text of the Babylonian Talmud when forming his judgments about correct, Talmudically prescribed *halakhic* rules. Rather, he makes substantial use of the Jerusalem Talmud as well, of which he has an impressive command. Traditionally understood to have been compiled and composed by Ravina and Rav Ashi, the heads of the main rabbinic academies in Persia around the first half of the sixth century CE, the Babylonian Talmud includes the text of the Mishnah and a record of the discussions, interpretations, and applications of Mishnaic and other tannaitic materials by Babylonian rabbinic scholars over the course of the several preceding centuries. It also includes a wealth of homiletic and ethical content, as well as social, historical, economic, medical, and other insights and commentaries on Jewish living.[46] The Jerusalem Talmud—so called because it was compiled by scholars in the Land of Israel—is a much shorter work that was completed around 150 years before the Babylonian Talmud. It too is based around the text of the Mishnah, but

---

42 *See* Babylonian Talmud, Sotah 39b.
43 *See* Rema *to* Shulchan Arukh, Orach Chaim 149:1.
44 *See* Arukh HaShulchan, Orach Chaim 146:1.
45 *See* ibid.
46 *See generally* Menachem Elon, 3 Jewish Law: History, Sources, Principles 1087-1092 (Bernard Auerbach & Melvin J. Sykes trans., 1994).

it comprises the rabbinic discussions, textual analyses, and insights of the rabbis who lived in the Land of Israel during the third and fourth centuries.[47]

Traditionally, the Babylonian Talmud has been the primary touchstone of *halakhic* discourse and decision-making.[48] For instance, Rav Hai Gaon maintained, "With respect to *halakhic* matters decided by our [Babylonian] Talmud, we do not rely on any contradictory statements of the Jerusalem Talmud."[49] This view was widely accepted and repeated by many other prominent authorities, such as Rabbi Isaac Alfasi who rules, "We rely on our [i.e. the Babylonian] Talmud."[50] Maimonides refers only to the Babylonian Talmud when discussing the absolutely binding nature of Talmud norms, implicitly downplaying the *halakhic* significance of the Jerusalem Talmud.[51] Likewise, *Tosafot* explicitly rule that the Babylonian Talmud takes precedence over the Jerusalem Talmud in cases of conflict.[52] Scholars have given a number of reasons for this *halakhic* preference for the Babylonian Talmud. Rabbi Isaac Alfasi argued that the Babylonian Talmud is superior to the Jerusalem Talmud because it was completed at a later date, and thus the editors of the Babylonian Talmud already had access to and accounted for materials and rulings contained in the Jerusalem Talmud.[53] Others point to the fact that the Babylonian Talmud is a much larger, comprehensive work; it covers more Mishnaic material, includes more rabbinic interpretation and discourse, and is several times the size of the text of the Jerusalem Talmud. This simply makes the Babylonian Talmud a better work for use as a primary source of *halakhic* norms.[54] In a similar vein, some have argued that the Jerusalem Talmud is a less complete and less edited work than the Babylonian Talmud, since it was composed hastily and under conditions of religious persecution and economic and political instability at the end of the fourth century in Judea and Galilee.[55]

---

47 *See generally* ibid. 3.
48 *See* ibid. 3.
49 Gaonica: Gaonic Responsa and Fragments of Halachic Literature from the Geniza and Other Sources 125 (Simchah Assaf, ed., 1933) [Hebrew].
50 Rabbi Isaac Alfasi, Rif, Eruvin 35b.
51 *Introduction* to Mishneh Torah. *See also* Rosh *to* Sanhedrin 4:5.
52 *See* Tosafot *to* Babylonian Talmud, Berakhot 39a (s.v. *batzar lei shi'ura*); Tosafot *to* Babylonian Talmud, Sukkah 26b (s.v. *v'lo birech acharav*). *See also* Tosafot *to* Babylonian Talmud, Berakhot 11b (s.v. *she'kevar niftar*).
53 *See* Rabbi Isaac Alfasi, Rif, Eruvin 35b. *See also* Responsa Maharik nos. 84, 91.
54 *See* Rabbi Naftali Tzvi Yehudah Berlin, HaEmek Davar, Shemot 34:1.
55 *See* Rabbi Isaac HaLevi Rabinowitz, Dorot Rishonim ch. 20.

While the general *halakhic* consensus has thus long favored the Babylonian Talmud, many rabbis of the Rishonic period were clear masters of the Jerusalem Talmud and deployed it often—if not dispositively—in their *halakhic* writings.[56] Moreover, many of those authorities that have expressed their preference for the Babylonian Talmud have even noted that the teachings of the Jerusalem Talmud do carry normative import, even while they do not take precedence over the rulings of the Babylonian Talmud in cases of conflict between the two. For instance, Rav Hai Gaon maintained that while the rulings of the Babylonian Talmud are most authoritative, "Whatever we find in the Jerusalem Talmud that does not contradict our own [Babylonian] Talmud, or which provides a nice explanation for its matters of discourse, we can hold on to it and rely upon it."[57] Similarly, Rabbi Joseph Karo wrote that "any way that we can interpret the Babylonian Talmud in a manner that will prevent it from conflicting with the Jerusalem Talmud is better, even if that interpretation is somewhat forced."[58] Maimonides, too, often relies on legal rulings contained in the Jerusalem Talmud on matters where the Babylonian Talmud is silent or where the *halakhic* standard prescribed by the Babylonian Talmud is unclear.[59]

Rabbi Epstein also views the Jerusalem Talmud as an important source of *halakhic* standards. Throughout his writings in the *Arukh HaShulchan*, Rabbi Epstein demonstrates an impressive command of the Jerusalem Talmud. He quotes it frequently, quoting passages not previously referenced by other authorities, identifying misquotes and mistaken references to the Jerusalem Talmud made by other *halakhic* writers, and often using passages in the Jerusalem Talmud to elucidate ambiguous discussions in the Babylonian Talmud. For instance, the *Arbah Turim* rules that if one blows a full three-sound series of blasts from a *shofar* in a single breath without taking a new breath in between each of the three sounds, the sounds are not ritually valid and do not count towards the fulfillment of the obligation to blow the proper number of sounds with a *shofar* on Rosh Hashanah.[60] This is also the view of the *Rosh*, and this is supported by a Tannaitic *Tosefta*, which explicitly invalidates a series of *shofar* sounds if the individual sounds were not separated from each other by separate breaths. Rabbi Epstein

---

56 *See* Michael J. Broyde, May the Jewish Daughter of a Gentile Man Marry a Kohen? 52 Journal of Halacha and Contemporary Society, 97, 100, n. 6 (2009).
57 Rav Hai Gaon, *as quoted in* Rabbi Abraham Isaac of Narbonne, Sefer HaEshkol, vol. 2, 49 (s.v. *Hilkhot Sefer Torah*) (Benjamin Hirsch Auerbach, ed., 1868).
58 Kessef Mishnah *to* Mishneh Torah, Hilkhot Gerushin 13:18.
59 *See* Rabbi Shabbatai HaKohen, Shakh *to* Shulchan Arukh, Yoreh Deah 145:1.
60 *See* Arbah Turim, Orach Chaim 590.

notes, however, that the Jerusalem Talmud offers a contrary ruling, holding that if all the sounds were produced with a single breath, one still fulfills the obligation to hear the *shofar* through those blasts. Rabbi Epstein rules in accordance with the Jerusalem Talmud and against the *Arbah Turim* and the *Tosefta*, since the Babylonian Talmud does not directly contradict the Jerusalem Talmud's ruling.[61]

Rabbi Epstein's impressive command of the Jerusalem Talmud—itself a function of the importance with which he regards this work as a source of *halakhic* norms—is well demonstrated by an additional example, namely his disagreement with Rabbi Joseph Karo regarding the correct explanation for the fact that an unusual number of Torah verses are read as part of the public Torah reading service on the holiday of Purim.[62] It is well settled that on Purim the congregation reads only nine verses from the Torah during the public Torah reading service.[63] This practice requires an explanation because normally, by Talmudic rule, a minimum of ten verses are read during communal Torah readings. Rabbi Karo seeks to explain this practice as derived from a passage in the Jerusalem Talmud, which teaches that we "cut off" the reading to symbolize Haman's attempt to "cut off" the lives of Jewish people in the Purim story, as told in the book of Esther.[64] However, the *Arukh HaShulchan* points out that this explanation is not found in the Jerusalem Talmud at all.[65] In fact, Rabbi Epstein notes, the Jerusalem Talmud provides a completely different explanation for the practice, namely that the subject matter of the Torah reading ends after nine verses, and there is thus no need to read more than that.[66] Here, Rabbi Epstein shows an impressive command of the Jerusalem Talmud by pointing out that the explanation attributed to the Jerusalem Talmud by Rabbi Karo is not found in the text at all, as well as by providing an alternative explanation of the practice at hand that actually is presented by the Jerusalem Talmud.[67]

Importantly, Rabbi Epstein's reliance on his own independent understanding of both the Babylonian Talmud and the Jerusalem Talmud leads him to occasionally prescribe entirely new *halakhic* rules and to sometimes offer novel rationales and explanations for well-settled legal norms. Thus, to offer an additional example, Rabbi Epstein utilizes the Jerusalem Talmud to

---

61 *See* Arukh HaShulchan 590:14.
62 *See* Arukh HaShulchan, Orach Chaim 137:1.
63 *See* Rabbi Isaac Alfasi, Rif, Megillah 12a.
64 *See* Shulchan Arukh, Orach Chaim 137:1.
65 *See* Arukh HaShulchan, Orach Chaim 137:1.
66 *See* Arukh HaShulchan, Orach Chaim 137:1.
67 *See* Shulchan Arukh, Orach Chaim 137:1.

suggest a new explanation for the well-established obligation to pray three times each day and to prescribe a new prayer rule not previously prescribed by other authorities. In contrast to the more commonly known view expressed by the Babylonian Talmud—that the three daily prayers were established by the three patriarchs, Abraham, Isaac, and Jacob[68]—Rabbi Epstein cites the Jerusalem Talmud, which maintains that the three daily prayers correspond to the three times each day that our environment changes around us. Rabbi Epstein goes further, however, and notes that this passage of the Jerusalem Talmud also prescribes a short prayer to be said as part of each of the three daily prayers to mark each of these three daily transitions. Rabbi Epstein appears to endorse this practice and the reason for the daily prayers offered by the Jerusalem Talmud, even though he notes that no other *halakhic* decisors reference this idea or endorse this practice.[69]

* * * * *

Thus, the *Arukh HaShulchan* is a thoroughly independent work of Jewish law in which Rabbi Epstein reaches *halakhic* conclusions by directly engaging the breadth of Talmudic sources without feeling bound to follow the rulings of even very prominent rabbinic decisors of earlier eras.

---

68 *See* Babylonian Talmud, Berakhot 26b.
69 *See* Arukh HaShulchan, Orach Chaim 1:29.

CHAPTER FIVE

Rabbinic Consensus

The previous chapter explored the first and most fundamental of the methodological principles that guide Rabbi Epstein's *halakhic* determinations in his *Arukh HaShulchan*. First and foremost, Rabbi Epstein thinks the *halakhah* should follow the analytically correct norms and standards that arise from each competent decisor's understanding of the relevant Talmudic sources. This chapter explains how Rabbi Epstein tempers his willingness to independently derive *halakhic* norms directly from the Talmud with a healthy dose of epistemic humility. Thus, when his own understanding of the Talmudic sources conflicts with the *halakhic* conclusions expressed by a broad consensus of other authorities, or when certain major authorities express more ritually stringent legal opinions, Rabbi Epstein sets aside his own possibly mistaken judgment and defers to his peers.

* * * * *

Principle Two: Rabbi Epstein declines to follow his own understanding of the relevant Talmudic sources in cases where that understanding is incompatible with a halakhic rule agreed upon by a broad consensus of past authorities, or when major halakhic scholars adopt a rule more stringent than his own.

Rabbi Epstein's confident and independent approach to reaching *halakhic* conclusions on the basis of his own understanding of the relevant Talmudic sources does not mean that he is convinced that his assessments of the Talmudic materials are necessarily always correct. On the contrary, while he does not recognize the legal formulations of prior *halakhic* authorities as formally binding, Rabbi Epstein does regard the precedential opinions of major rabbinic figures as sources of persuasive precedent and as carrying jurisprudential weight (this follows the nearly universal approach of rabbinic scholars). In practice, Rabbi Epstein's regard for such *halakhic* precedents leads him to second-guess his own Talmudic understandings in cases where a broad consensus of past rabbinic scholars has reached a contrary conclusion, or where major individual authorities, such as Maimonides or Rabbi Joseph Karo, prescribe more ritually stringent *halakhic* norms.

Rabbi Epstein's epistemic humility and self-doubt in this regard are deeply rooted in the rabbinic tradition of *halakhic* jurisprudence. A famous Mishnaic dictum instructs that good rabbinic practice requires one to be "deliberative in judgment."[1] Commentators explain this to mean the following:

> Those who teach legal rules, issue legal decisions, and judge litigious disputes . . . should not rule based on their first impression, but only after great deliberation and incisive investigation . . . For error is found in all people . . . and about this matter, King Solomon said: "If you see a man who thinks himself wise, there is more hope for a dullard than for him" (Proverbs 26:12). Therefore, it is incumbent upon someone who makes legal decisions to go back and forth on the matter and that their thoughts sit and ripen . . . for through ripening and deliberation, we add reasoning to our reasoning and sharpness to our sharpness, until we thereby judge true and honest judgments.[2]

The same Mishnaic passage continues and urges rabbinic scholars to "raise many students."[3] Once again, commentators on this passage have understood this imprecation as a means of inducing scholarly caution and humility.[4] Students, the commentators note, serve as a check on scholarly hubris and misplaced self-confidence. Knowledge and self-assurance in one's own scholarly accomplishments and abilities can lead to error as one too quickly assumes that one's views are correct and fails to fully engage in scholarly debate and questioning the underlying premises and logic of one's views owing to one's presumed academic excellence. By directing even accomplished scholars to teach and raise students less knowledgeable and competent than themselves, the Mishnah intends to force scholars into a position where they will be required to clarify and second-guess their own conclusions in the face of naïve

---

1 Mishnah, Avot 1:1.
2 Rabbi Jonah Gerondi, Commentary on Mishnah Avot 1:1.
3 Mishnah, Avot 1:1.
4 *See, e.g.* Rabbi Judah Loew, Derekh Chaim *to* Avot 6:6.

and basic questions from their pupils. Moreover, having to teach, interact with, and persuade students helps situate the rabbinic scholar within a community of learners with different perspectives and Ideas. This compels the accomplished scholar to genuinely listen and respond to questions and alternative points of view with understanding and humility.[5]

The importance of humility in *halakhic* decision-making is underscored by the importance rabbinic sources have placed on *yirat horaah*, or the "fear of deciding" legal matters. This concept is well sourced in the Talmud and in later rabbinic literature—it refers to a degree of fear, apprehension, and awe that good *halakhic* decision makers are expected to have when making legal judgments or presuming to say what the law is or means.[6] This, in turn, is rooted in a profound awareness that rendering *halakhic* decisions is qualitatively different from reaching other kinds of normative or even legal judgments. Unlike human law where judges are responsible to litigants and legislators, *halakhah* at its core is fundamentally religious; thus, rabbinic decisors see themselves also as duty-bound to God, and they see their rulings as having cosmic implications beyond the specific matter at hand.[7] Thus, "Judges should know whom they judge, and before Whom they judge, and Who it is who judges with them [God], and Who [if they reach a false verdict] will exact punishment from them [God]. And it says in Scripture, 'God stands in the congregation of the Divine, and in the midst of judges He judges.'"[8] Rabbinic discussions of judicial ethics likewise caution decision makers to imagine themselves—when judging *halakhic* matters—as though they are standing before a gaping pit leading to hell with a sharp sword resting on their necks.[9] They are likewise urged against articulating their legal opinions until "the matter is clear like the shining sun."[10] This "fear of deciding" thus stems from a religious concern—*yirat shamayim*, or "fear of Heaven"—which constitutes another important touchstone of *halakhic* decision-making.[11] In rabbinic thought, getting *halakhah* right matters not only because a wrong decision fails to correctly uphold parties' genuine rights and obligations, but because the law—while a product of rabbinic

---

5   *See* Rabbi Judah Loew, Derekh Chaim *to* Avot 6:6.
6   *See* Babylonian Talmud, Sanhedrin 7b.
7   *See* Yuval Sinai, *The Religious Perspective of the Judge's Role in Talmudic Law*, 25 Journal of Law and Religion 357, 357 (2009).
8   Tosefta, Sanhedrin 1:9; Psalms 82:1.
9   *See* Babylonian Talmud, Yevamot 109a.
10 Mishneh Torah, Hilkhot Sanhedrin 20:7; Shulchan Arukh, Choshen Mishpat 10:1-2.
11 *See* A. Yehudah Warburg, Rabbinic Authority: The Vision and the Reality 57-63 (2013).

interpretation and application—is ultimately God's law, and pious decision makers should proceed with extreme caution lest they presume to misrepresent the divine will through their erroneous *halakhic* rulings.

The importance of humility and caution when rendering *halakhic* rulings should not be debilitating and paralyzing, however. The Talmud itself clarifies that while rabbinic scholars faced with the gravity and significance of reaching legal decisions may balk at the responsibility, they must do so nevertheless—"A decisor might say to himself, 'For what do I need all this [personal responsibility for correctly discerning the right *halakhic* standards]?' Scripture thus responds, 'I [God] am with you in judgment,' meaning that a judge should follow his own understanding [and rule accordingly]."[12] In other words, while the responsibility for reaching correct *halakhic* conclusions is serious indeed, rabbinic decisors should take confidence in the fact that God has ultimately entrusted them to give expression to the law. As Rabbi Aryeh Leib Heller (1745-1812) puts it, "Human decisors fear lest they err with respect to the Torah . . . But the Torah was not given to the angels, but to human beings with human reason . . . and God said, 'Truth shall spring from the earth.' (Psalms 85:11)"[13] Since God has entrusted the law to mankind, human beings may—and truly must—proceed to determine the *halakhah* despite the possibility of error. They are responsible to do so carefully, responsibly, and with due humility, of course, since intellectual hubris may make them more prone to error. But even so, "The judge only has what his own eyes see,"[14] and one may rule on the basis of one's own well-considered judgment. Rabbi Chaim Volozhin (1749-1821) put it as follows:

> A person must be cautious [when offering his own *halakhic* conclusions] lest he speak arrogantly and stridently simply because he has found a reasonable basis for disagreement, or lest he come to think he is as great as his teachers or as the author of the book that he wishes to dispute. Rather, a person must know in his heart that sometimes he has not fully understood the author's words and intent. Therefore, he should take an attitude of great humility; and [when offering his own view] he should say, "Although I am not worthy [to disagree], nonetheless it is Torah [and I cannot but offer my own considered understanding]."[15]

---

12 Babylonian Talmud, Sanhedrin 6b.
13 Rabbi Aryeh Leib Heller, Introduction *to* Ketzot HaChoshen.
14 Mishneh Torah, Hilkhot Sanhedrin 23:9.
15 Rabbi Chaim Volozhin, Ruach Chaim on Avot 1:4.

Following this traditional approach, Rabbi Epstein's jurisprudence exhibits appropriate confidence in his own knowledge and ability to reach his own independent *halakhic* conclusions while also recognizing that his understandings of often ambiguous Talmudic sources may be mistaken—and that other scholars' conclusions may be more correct than his own. Specifically, Rabbi Epstein begins to question his own conclusions when they conflict with the *halakhic* position endorsed by a consensus of other authorities.

Rabbinic consensus has long been considered a weighty authority in *halakhic* jurisprudence and an important indicator of which legal viewpoints are correct. Thus, it makes good sense that despite Rabbi Epstein's confidence in his own ability to interpret and derive *halakhic* norms directly from Talmudic sources, he becomes less confident and more deferential to other scholars in the face of a consensus of opinion upholding a contrary understanding of the Talmud reaching an alternative legal standard. The Hebrew Bible itself affirms the normative weight of a majority opinion over and against minority views. "Follow the majority"[16] is understood as an important secondary rule of adjudication in Jewish law, and it instructs that in cases of dispute over the law, the majority view should be regarded as correct.[17] Technically, rabbinic jurisprudence generally understands this secondary rule as applying only to the judicial deliberations of sitting courts.[18] Rabbinic courts traditionally comprise three, twenty-three, or seventy-one judges, and this principle prescribes that a court's ruling follows the opinion of a majority of its judges.[19] The importance of majority opinions in rabbinic jurisprudence has gone far beyond its earlier technical meaning, however. Especially with the decline of formal judicial institutions like the *Sanhedrin* as the principal repositories of *halakhic* authority following the destruction of the Second Temple in 70 CE,[20] the principle of majority rule took on the character of an informal decisional principle for resolving rabbinic disputes about *halakhah*.[21] Thus, when the Mishnaic text records disputes between individual scholars and "the Rabbis," such disputes are generally resolved in favor of "the Rabbis," though the disputants did

---

16 Exodus 23:2.
17 *See* Mishneh Torah, Hilkhot Sanhedrin 8:1.
18 *See* Exodus 23:2; Babylonian Talmud, Chullin 11a; Torah Temimah, Shemot 23:2, n. 23.
19 *See* Babylonian Talmud, Sanhedrin 3b.
20 *See* Menachem Elon, Jewish Law: History, Sources, Principles 19 (Bernard Auerbach & Melvin J. Sykes trans., 1994).
21 *See* Babylonian Talmud, Chullin 11a; Maimonides, *Introduction* to Commentary on the Mishnah.

not typically sit together on the same courts; thus, the "follow the majority" principle did not technically apply. Rabbi Nissim Gerondi (1320-1380) thus explained that the scriptural command "'follow the majority' . . . constitutes a general command to follow the view of the majority of scholars in the legal rulings and judgments of the Torah."[22] Likewise, Rabbi Moses Isserles ruled, "If there is an individual view and a majority view, we follow the majority view."[23]

The normative weightiness of consensus or majority opinion also contributes to the jurisprudential concept of *ta'ut b'shikul hada'at*, or "error in judgment." As discussed earlier, post-Talmudic rabbinic legal thought has recognized the legal significance of consensus by positing that even *halakhic* issues not clearly decided in a particular way by the Talmud can be more or less authoritatively resolved by a post-Talmudic scholarly consensus supporting a given legal rule. Rabbi Joseph Karo defines such an "error in judgment" as occurring:

> Where there is a matter that is subject to dispute among Mishnaic or Talmudic authorities, and those sources did not explicitly determine the correct rule in accordance with any of them, and he [the erring rabbinic decision maker] ruled in accordance with one of them, not knowing that the general practice throughout the world is in accordance with the other view. . .[24]

Legal consensus, in other words, determines correct legal norms. Scholars have offered a variety of rationales for the *halakhic* normativity of consensus beyond the formalistic rule of "follow the majority." One important and presently pertinent explanation suggests that rabbinic decisors should generally follow the weight of consensus because the formation of scholarly consensus, along with the absence of significant scholarly debate, gives some strong indication that the consensus view is in fact the right one.[25] The presence of a scholarly consensus on an issue thus gives Rabbi Epstein pause. This broader application of "follow the majority" has typically been treated more as a broad decisional principle than a hard and fast secondary rule of decision; it lends weightiness and authority to *halakhic* positions endorsed by a majority of scholars but

---

22 Drashot HaRan, no. 12. *See also* Babylonian Talmud, Avodah Zarah 7a.
23 Rema *to* Shulchan Arukh, Choshen Mishpat 25:2.
24 Shulchan Arukh, Choshen Mishpat 25:2.
25 *See* Rabbi Baruch Efrati, *Tokfam Shel HaMinhagim B'Yisrael* (2005), daat.ac.il, http://www.daat.ac.il/daat/toshba/maamarim/tokpam-2.htm (last visited Dec. 31, 2018).

does not completely foreclose the possibility that competent rabbinic decisors may still disagree.[26] Nevertheless, even Rabbi Epstein's usual intellectual confidence and independence typically gives way in the face of a rabbinic consensus opposing his own *halakhic* view.

One example of this tendency concerns the recital of multiple blessings upon sequentially donning several pairs of *tzitzit*, the ritual fringes worn on the corners of four-cornered garments in fulfillment of the biblical commandment to "make fringes on the corners of your garments."[27] The *Rema* rules that if a person has many four-cornered garments with *tzitzit* and removes one such garment that he had previously donned after saying the appropriate blessing, and afterwards he seeks to put on another four-cornered garment, he must recite a second blessing on fulfilling the commandment of *tzitzit* before putting on the second garment.[28] The *Arukh HaShulchan* expresses his support for the *Rema*'s ruling here, reasoning that when it comes to repeating the same blessing on numerous successive performances of the same *mitzvah*, the operative concern is whether or not the person in question has broken his intent to continue to fulfill that same *mitzvah*.[29] If one has continuous intent to fulfill the *mitzvah*, the original blessing suffices for all subsequent performances of that *mitzvah*; but once one concludes the performance of a *mitzvah*, then a subsequent performance of that *mitzvah*—even if temporally linked to the earlier performance—requires a new blessing. Thus, Rabbi Epstein writes that when one removes a four-cornered garment, one has demonstrated that he has concluded the performance of that *mitzvah* and must therefore make a new blessing when putting *tzitzit* back on thereafter.[30] Despite his agreement with the *Rema*'s ruling in principle, however, in practice Rabbi Epstein prescribes that one should not recite a new blessing when putting on a pair of *tzitzit* after having previously removed another pair of *tzitzit*. This is because Rabbi Epstein notes that the consensus of *halakhic* authorities disagrees with the *Rema*'s view, and "the law follows the majority."[31] Rabbi Epstein's respect for the consensus view stands even as he presents his own arguments for the weaknesses in the

---

26 *See* Rema *to* Shulchan Arukh, Choshen Mishpat 25:2; Biur HaGra *to* Shulchan Arukh, Choshen Mishpat 25:15 (s.v. *elah im hu*); Rabbi Moses Feinstein, Igrot Moshe, Yoreh Deah 1:136.
27 Deuteronomy 22:12. *See also* Numbers 15:38-40.
28 *See* Rema *to* Shulchan Arukh, Orach Chaim 8:12.
29 *See* Arukh HaShulchan, Orach Chaim 8:18.
30 *See* ibid. 8:19.
31 Ibid. 8:19.

reasoning of those authorities that disagree with the *Rema*. Thus, while the *Arukh HaShulchan* is generally willing to rule in accordance with his own understanding and against individual yet important authorities like the *Shulchan Arukh*, he is far more deferential to the *halakhic* consensus, even when it runs counter to his own preferred understanding of the substantive issue.

Another instance of Rabbi Epstein's deference to consensus concerns the ritual validity of a cracked *shofar* for use on Rosh Hashanah.[32] Rabbi Joseph Karo rules that if a *shofar* is cracked around most of its width, it may not be used for ritual purposes on Rosh Hashanah; if the crack runs across less than half the width of the *shofar*, then the *shofar* may be used. However, even a *shofar* that is cracked around most of its width may be used if the crack is situated far enough away from the horn's mouthpiece that the *shofar*, measured from the mouthpiece to the crack, is large enough to be ritually valid even if the cracked section were removed.[33] This view is supported by the *Rosh, Ran, Baal Ha'Ittur, Semak, Semag*, and possibly Maimonides.[34] Rabbi Karo also records another position, however, which maintains that a *shofar* that is cracked along most of its width is usable—even if there is not enough length from the mouthpiece to the crack to constitute a valid *shofar*—so long as the crack does not produce a distortion in the sound the *shofar* makes when blown.[35] Rabbi Epstein endorses the first view because, as he says, it is supported by a consensus of authorities as well as the Talmudic text.[36]

Rabbi Epstein also relies on rabbinic consensus to support a permissive ruling regarding one's liability for eating on Yom Kippur. While the Torah prohibits eating and drinking on Yom Kippur,[37] one who violates this stricture is punished for their sin only if they ate or drank more than a certain minimal amount (as with all Torah-based dietary prohibitions). In the case of Yom Kippur, one is liable only for eating more than the size of a large date and for drinking more than a cheek-full.[38] There is an early dispute, however, over the amount of time within which one must have consumed the requisite minimum amount of food or drink to be liable. According to *Rashi*, one is liable for eating or drinking on Yom Kippur only if one consumes the requisite amount within

---

32   *See generally* Babylonian Talmud, Rosh Hashanah 27a.
33   *See* Shulchan Arukh, Orach Chaim 586:9.
34   *See* Be'er HaGolah *to* Shulchan Arukh, Orach Chaim 586:21:2 (quoting those *Rishonim*).
35   *See* Shulchan Arukh, Orach Chaim 586:9.
36   *See* Arukh HaShulchan, Orach Chaim 586:21.
37   *See* Leviticus 16:29-31; Babylonian Talmud, Yoma 74b.
38   *See* Babylonian Talmud, Yoma 80b; Arukh HaShulchan, Orach Chaim 612:1, 8.

the amount of time it takes to eat a piece of bread—approximately a few minutes.[39] According to Maimonides, however, one is liable for eating or drinking on Yom Kippur only if the minimum amount is consumed during the amount of time it takes to drink a *revi'it*, about four fluid ounces, which represents a stricter view.[40] Rabbi Epstein notes that many authorities question Maimonides's position here—although this issue is a question of biblical law, he ultimately rules against Maimonides and in accordance with *Rashi*'s more permissive opinion, since the latter is supported by a strong consensus of other authorities.[41]

Rabbi Epstein also mistrusts his own understandings of Talmudic materials—instead he defers to the alternative readings and rulings of other rabbinic scholars, especially in cases where particularly prominent *halakhic* authorities have reached more ritually stringent conclusions. In such instances, Rabbi Epstein errs on the side of caution and rules that one should follow the more demanding *halakhic* standard prescribed by others, just in case their understanding of the Talmudic sources is correct and his own is mistaken. For instance, Rabbi Epstein declines to follow his own independent judgment and instead endorses a more stringent view proposed by other authorities regarding the correct blessing to recite upon cleaning one's hands with a medium other than water. Ordinarily, one is obligated to wash one's hands in the morning with water and to recite the blessing of *"al netilat yadayim"* ("on the washing of the hands").[42] If water is not available, however, the Talmud instructs that one should wipe one's hands on a stone, the earth, a beam, or any other abrasive surface that would clean one's hands.[43] Rabbi Epstein's own independent judgment leads him to the conclusion that upon wiping one's hands in this manner, one may recite the blessing of *"al nekiyut yadayim"* ("on the *cleanliness* of the hands") instead of the usual *"al netilat yadayim."* However, Rabbi Epstein notes that the *Arbah Turim* and the *Rosh* both reject such an alternative blessing. Instead, they require one to recite the blessing of *"al netilat yadayim,"* whether one washes one's hands with water or cleans them with another medium. Since these authorities adopt a more restrictive view as to which blessings are acceptable upon cleaning one's hands without water, the *Arukh HaShulchan* advises that one accordingly recite only *"al netilat yadayim"* and not *"al nekiyat yadayim."*[44]

---

39   *See* Rashi *to* Babylonian Talmud, Keritot 13a (s.v. *iy amart bishlema rabbi meir lechumra*).
40   *See* Mishneh Torah, Hilkhot Yom Kippur 2:4.
41   *See* Arukh HaShulchan, Orach Chaim 612:9.
42   *See* Shulchan Arukh, Orach Chaim 4:1.
43   *See* ibid. 4:19.
44   *See* Arukh HaShulchan, Orach Chaim 4:19.

Another example of Rabbi Epstein's deference to more stringent opinions in cases where he considers his Talmudic understanding less than fully dispositive involves the validity of a *sukkah* built under a retractable roof. Rabbi Epstein observes that in his own time, many people build their *sukkah* beneath a removable roof by installing ritually valid *skhakh*—a temporary covering for the *sukkah* made from cut foliage—beneath a regular permanent roof and then later removing the permanent roof in order to sit and eat in the *sukkah* under the *skhakh* as prescribed by Jewish law.[45] Rabbi Epstein notes that this practice could be viewed as problematic because the *halakhah* requires that a *sukkah* be ritually valid at the time of its construction; if the *sukkah* was built in a ritually invalid manner, it remains invalid even after the impediment to its ritual validity is later removed.[46] Here, the *sukkah* is built beneath a roof, which renders it invalid; therefore, the later removal of the roof should not succeed in validating the originally invalid *sukkah*. Based on his analysis of the Talmudic principle that a *sukkah* must be valid at the time of construction, however, Rabbi Epstein, argues that this requirement applies only to invalidating features of the *sukkah* itself rather than to external factors present at the time of construction that are later removed.[47] Thus, for instance, a *sukkah* that is covered with foliage that is still attached to the ground is invalid at the time of construction, and cutting the foliage from the ground later will not make the *sukkah* ritually valid. By contrast, the presence of a permanent roof hanging over an otherwise valid *sukkah* does indeed render the *sukkah* presently invalid. This invalidating factor is distinct from the *sukkah* itself, and so the later removal of the roof, which leaves the otherwise valid *sukkah* sitting properly beneath the open sky, will render the *sukkah* ritually fit for use.[48] Ultimately, however, Rabbi Epstein declines to apply this speculative understanding of the Talmudic principle that a *sukkah* must be valid at the time of construction, which ultimately enjoys no explicit support in the Talmudic text itself. Instead, he defers to the more stringent interpretation of this principle offered by Rabbi Moses Isserles, who rules that the post-construction validation of a *sukkah* is ineffective, even with respect to the removal of invalidating features external to the *sukkah* itself.[49]

The practice of deferring to the more ritually stringent rulings of prominent authorities—even in the face of one's own self-confident and fully

---

45 *See* ibid. 626:25.
46 *See* Babylonian Talmud, Sukkah 11b.
47 *See* Arukh HaShulchan, Orach Chaim 626:25.
48 *See* ibid.
49 *See* ibid.

qualified understanding of the primary sources of Jewish law—is deeply rooted in rabbinic tradition. While the Talmud often adopts a "better safe than sorry" approach to addressing *halakhic* doubts (as discussed further in chapter six), in several other instances the Talmudic Rabbis also commend the adoption of legal strictures even in cases where one believes that a different, more lenient *halakhic* standard is correct.[50] For instance, in the course of a Talmudic discussion regarding various religious strictures designed to prevent illicit sexual relationships, the Talmud records a dispute between two rabbis, Rav Assi and Shmuel. According to Rav Assi, while a man may not be alone with a woman in order to forestall any improper sexual contact between the two, a man may be alone with his sister, mother, or daughter, since there is relatively little risk of such improper behavior between close relations. Shmuel disagrees, however, and says that one may not be alone with any person with whom sexual relations are religiously prohibited, and he even goes so far as to proscribe seclusion between a human being and an animal since bestiality is likewise biblically prohibited.[51] After presenting these two opinions, the Talmud records that several scholars acted in accordance with Shmuel's stricter rule and avoided being alone with close relatives or animals. These rabbis acted strictly in this regard, even though—as post-Talmudic commentators make clear—there was little doubt that Rav Assi's *halakhic* rule permitting such conduct is the correct legal norm.[52] Some commentators explain that, in fact, these Talmudic Rabbis did not disagree with Rav Assi's opinion; they too understood the law as permitting seclusion with close relatives or animals. Nevertheless, in practice they set aside their own judgment of the correct rule and instead adopted Shmuel's more stringent position because they viewed doing so as religiously pious and proper.[53] One read of this issue is that while the referenced Talmudic Rabbis concluded that Rav Assi's view is indeed normative, Shmuel's disagreement provided some basis for uncertainty about the correct *halakhic* standard. In such a situation, these scholars deemed it prudent to follow Shmuel's stricter standard just in case their own understanding of the issue turned out to be mistaken.

The Talmud attributes this deferential approach to none other than the prophet Ezekiel who declared, "My soul has not been polluted, for from my youth until today I have not eaten [the meat of an animal] that died on its

---

50 *See generally* Daniel Goldstein, *The Role of Humrot*, 1 Hakirah 11 (2004).
51 *See* Babylonian Talmud, Kiddushin 81b.
52 *See* Shulchan Arukh, Even HaEzer 21:1.
53 *See* Rosh *to* Babylonian Talmud, Kiddushin 4:24.

own or was torn."⁵⁴ Anticipating the question of why Ezekiel would consider himself particularly praiseworthy for merely adhering to basic biblical dietary rules that prohibit the meat of animals that have not been properly slaughtered, the Talmud explains that Ezekiel is referring to his decision to avoid any meat whose *halakhic* permissibility was subject to some question, even if ultimately it was ruled permitted as a matter of law.⁵⁵ As one commentator explained, "There are, of course, many things that are subject to dispute among *halakhic* authorities; one scholar permits while another prohibits. Ezekiel [is saying that he] would not have eaten food whose legal status was subject to such disputes . . . even though some scholars ruled it permitted."⁵⁶ Legal disputes, in other words, raise questions and doubts about correct *halakhic* standards even in cases where a competent decisor has a good personal sense of what he thinks is the right rule of law. In such cases, there is ample reason—grounded in prudence, piety, and a more localized instance of Pascal's wager—to err on the side of caution by setting aside one's own *halakhic* viewpoint and instead adopt the more stringent understanding of the issue endorsed by other important authorities.⁵⁷

* * * * *

Thus, while Rabbi Epstein's approach to reaching *halakhic* conclusions in the *Arukh HaShulchan* entails direct and independent engagement with Talmudic sources, Rabbi Epstein also recognizes the importance of situating himself and his *halakhic* opinions within the broader context of rabbinic discourse and decision-making. The kind of independent legal judgment exhibited in the *Arukh HaShulchan* is therefore tempered by Rabbi Epstein's prudential regard for the collective weight of rabbinic consensus. Even where Rabbi Epstein thinks that he has arrived at the most correct understanding of the relevant Talmudic sources, he typically defers to alternative *halakhic* opinions endorsed by a broad consensus of other competent authorities.

---

54 Ezekiel 4:14.
55 *See* Babylonian Talmud, Chullin 44b.
56 Rabbi Elijah de Vidas, Reishit Chochmah, Shaar HaKedushah, ch. 15.
57 *See, e.g.*, Rabbi Moses Chaim Luzzatto, Mesilat Yesharim, ch. 11.

CHAPTER SIX

Resolving Doubtful Cases

This chapter explores the way in which Rabbi Epstein resolves doubts about the correct *halakhic* standard in order to reach determinate legal rulings in his *Arukh HaShulchan*. The previous chapters looked at several secondary rules that Rabbi Epstein follows when determining what he thinks is the ideally correct *halakhic* rule on any given issue, especially in light of the collective weight of past rabbinic scholarship. As discussed there, Rabbi Epstein maintains that, in principle, the right legal rule is the standard that emerges from a correct understanding of the relevant Talmudic sources and discussions rather than any *halakhic* norm expressed by post-Talmudic authorities, no matter how prominent or widely accepted. While in practice Rabbi Epstein tempers his willingness to follow his own understandings of Talmudic sources in cases where the Talmudic interpretations and *halakhic* conclusions of groups of rabbinic scholars differ from his own, in principle, Rabbi Epstein maintains that the *halakhah* follows the standards prescribed by the Talmud.

The Talmud, however, often does not yield up *halakhic* knowledge easily. Oftentimes, the correct Talmudic rule is uncertain. In some cases, uncertainty about the correct Talmudic standard arises because, while one may have a good sense of what they think the Talmud's *halakhic* rule is, one may still not be completely confident in this conclusion—or at least not confident enough to adopt that view against the competing Talmudic understandings of other important authorities. When Rabbi Epstein remains personally unsure about the correct legal meaning of the relevant Talmudic sources—and there is an absence of some rabbinic consensus on the issue—he tends to follow the precedential rulings of Maimonides; however, when he finds Maimonides's view problematic, he tends to follow those of Rabbi Joseph Karo's *Shulchan Arukh*.

Uncertainty about the right Talmudic norm arises in another way as well. Sometimes, the correct *halakhic* standard is genuinely in doubt.[1] This typically occurs in the following cases: where the Talmudic sources themselves are fundamentally indeterminate, thereby lending themselves to a number of equally reasonable and justifiable legal understandings;[2] where there is no post-Talmudic consensus on the correct meaning of the Talmudic sources;[3] where there is no strong tradition of customary practice endorsing any particular resolution; and where major *halakhic* authorities have offered a range of different rulings on the issue. In such cases, the typical sources and methods of *halakhic* jurisprudence run dry without providing any way of analytically determining a legal conclusion from the available array of reasonably justifiable *halakhic* alternatives.

Rabbinic jurisprudence, however, has long appreciated that the primary sources of *halakhic* norms sometimes fail to yield any determinate answers no matter how deeply they are plumbed and no matter how exhaustively they are analyzed.[4] The Talmudic Rabbis themselves anticipated this problem and prescribed a variety of secondary rules of decision used to determine the correct rule of law in cases where—to the mind of the decision maker—the primary sources do not lend themselves to any particularly persuasive understanding and thus fail to determine a *halakhic* conclusion.[5] Providing one such second-

---

1 For discussions of the legal indeterminacy of the Talmud, see Daniel Reifman, *Teaching Talmudic Hermeneutics Using a Semiotic Model of Law* 81, *in* Turn It and Turn It Again: Studies in the Teaching and Learning of Classical Jewish Texts (Jon A. Levisohn & Susan P. Fendrick, eds., 2013); Richard Hidary, Dispute for the Sake of Heaven: Legal Pluralism in the Talmud, ch. 1 (2010); Rabbi Adin Steinsaltz, The Talmud: A Reference Guide, 2-3 (1989); Shlomo Pill, *Leveraging Legal Indeterminacy, The Rule of Law in Jewish Jurisprudence*, The Journal Jurisprudence 221 (2017).
2 *See, e.g.,* Babylonian Talmud, Berakhot 27a; Babylonian Talmud, Shabbat 61a; Babylonian Talmud, Shevuot 48b. In each of these instances the Talmud directly endorses two competing legal opinions as equally valid and legitimate bases for *halakhic* practice.
3 For a fine example of this, see Michael J. Broyde & Avika R. Berger, Jewish Ethics in Torah Reading: Balancing Hatred, the Ways of Peace, Holiness, Communal Dignity, and the Obligation to Read Torah on Shabbat when Five Israelite Men are not Present, 23 Hakirah 181 (2017).
4 *See, e.g.,* Nachmanides, Milchamot Hashem, *Introduction* (discussing the indeterminacy of Talmudic sources and modes of analysis). *See generally,* Shlomo Pill, Leveraging Legal Indeterminacy, The Rule of Law in Jewish Jurisprudence, The Journal Jurisprudence 221 (2017).
5 For collections of such rules, known as *Klalei HaTalmud*, or "principles of the Talmud," see Rabbi Elijah David Rabinowitz Teomim & Rabbi Tzvi Judah Rabinowitz Teomim, Shevet Achim 7-58 (1994); Rabbi Yitzchak Yosef, Ein Yitzchak, vol. 1, 7-342 (2009).

ary rule, the Talmud thus prescribes that in cases where the correct legal norm is genuinely uncertain and the principle of majority rules is inapplicable, "One should follow the strict view in matters of biblical law and the lenient view in matters of rabbinic law."[6]

* * * * *

Principle Three: When he is unsure about the correct meaning of Talmudic sources, and in the absence of a strong halakhic consensus, Rabbi Epstein tends to follow the precedential rulings of Maimonides, or, where he finds Maimonides's view problematic, of Rabbi Joseph Karo's Shulchan Arukh.

Rabbi Epstein's humble originalist approach to *halakhic* decision-making, which generally relies on and follows his own independent understanding of the legal implications of primary Talmudic sources, is viable only in cases where Rabbi Epstein is indeed confident in the correctness of his Talmudic interpretations. But what about those cases in which Rabbi Epstein is not so certain about his own *halakhic* understanding of the Talmud? As discussed later, there are many instances in which the *halakhic* import of particular Talmudic discussions is genuinely indeterminate such that no particular legal understanding is more or less persuasive than any other. Even when this is not the case, however, there is a wide epistemic space between absolute certainty in the correctness of one's *halakhic* understandings of the Talmud and genuine, irresolvable doubt about the right Talmudic rule of law. Oftentimes, a *halakhic* decisor may have a strong sense that a particular standard or Talmudic understanding is correct without being absolutely certain of this conclusion. In such cases, several legal norms are simultaneously reasonably plausible: each *halakhic* possibility has reasons and justifications both commending and undermining it, and while one result may appear more compelling, alternative rulings remain plausible. Reaching independent *halakhic* conclusions requires a very high degree of confidence in the correctness of a given legal rule. As Rabbi Joseph Karo instructs, "A decisor must be deliberative in judgment such that he does not issue a ruling until he discusses the issue and lets his reasoning ferment so that the matter is clear to him like the sun."[7] The absence of such certainty and confidence thus poses an important question for *halakhic* scholars like Rabbi Epstein who are committed to reaching legal conclusions on the basis of their own independent

---

6 Babylonian Talmud, Avodah Zarah 7a.
7 Shulchan Arukh, Choshen Mishpat 10:1.

understandings of the primary sources: how should one rule when the right *halakhic* standard is not "as clear as the sun?"

Rabbi Epstein addresses this dilemma by falling back on established precedents and the prominent rulings of major *halakhic* authorities of past generations. This approach is a well-settled method of determining *halakhic* norms in the face of Talmudic uncertainties, even according to authorities that generally reject relying on legal precedent in *halakhic* decision-making and instead prefer direct engagement with the Talmud as the primary source of *halakhic* standards.[8] The Mishnaic sage Rabbi Gamliel advised, "Make for yourself a teacher and thereby remove yourself from doubts."[9] Maimonides and others explained this statement as an exhortation to rely on the legal rulings of competent teachers and mentors in order to resolve *halakhic* uncertainties.[10] Rabbi Jacob ben Asher (1250-1327), author of the *Arbah Turim*, thus maintained that if a scholar believes he knows the right *halakhic* standard, he should of course follow his own qualified independent judgment, regardless of any precedential opinions to the contrary. But, "If he does not, he should choose one of the codes of Jewish law written by the great authorities that he admires, and he should act in accordance with the rulings set forth therein."[11] This is so, even though Rabbi Jacob ben Asher himself opposed mechanically relying on *halakhic* precedent.[12] Competent scholars, he thought, are duty-bound to rule only in accordance with their considered independent understanding of the primary Talmudic sources of Jewish law. Nevertheless, he recognized that even exceptional rabbinic decisors cannot be expected to know the law with sufficient certainty in every case. Sometimes, they will be less than fully confident that their own understanding of the Talmudic law is the right one. In such cases, Rabbi Jacob ben Asher offers, the scholar may fall back on the precedential rulings found in widely accepted codes and restatements of Jewish law. The rationale for this approach is relatively simple: the prominent authors of such works must have been sufficiently confident in their *halakhic* opinions to have recorded them for posterity. When the right *halakhic* rule is unclear or

---

8   *See* Menahem Elon 3, Jewish Law: History, Sources, Principles 1157-58 (Bernard Auerbach & Melvin J. Sykes trans., 1994).
9   Mishnah, Avot 1:16.
10 *See* Maimonides, Commentary on the Mishnah, Avot 1:16 (s.v. *Rabban Gamliel*). *See also* Bartenurah *to* Mishnah, Avot 1:16 (s.v. *aseh lecha Rav*).
11 Quoted in Rabbi Joseph ibn Nachmias, Commentary on Pirkei Avot 1:16.
12 *See* Rosh *to* Babylonian Talmud, Sanhedrin 4:6 (ruling that judges should determine the law as they see fit, and not consider themselves bound to follow the views of even very important scholars or earlier authorities).

uncertain to one decisor but is clear and certain to another decisor, one should follow the legal opinion of the scholar who is confident in the correctness of his ruling.[13]

In an important sense, this approach is reminiscent of one of the chief jurisprudential justifications for the authority of post-Talmudic codifications of *halakhah*. Rabbi Joseph ibn Migash (1077-1141) defended the *halakhic* authority of codes in response to a question posed to him about whether a scholar who was not sufficiently conversant in the Talmud itself and could not reliably derive legal conclusions from Talmudic discussions could be allowed to render *halakhic* judgments on the basis of post-Talmudic rulings found in codes, restatements, and other secondary literature.[14] According to ibn Migash, such a scholar may—indeed, should—issue legal rulings on the basis of the *halakhic* norms and standards formulated in post-Talmudic codes precisely because he is unable to do so through direct engagement with the Talmud. True, ibn Migash admits, the Talmud is the primary repository of correct *halakhic* rules, and in principle, rulings should be based on Talmudic analysis. But what can a person do if he—like virtually all scholars of his own time, ibn Migash asserts—is unable to arrive at correct understandings of the legal import of complex Talmudic dialectics on the basis of his own analysis? Such a scholar cannot determine the law based directly on the Talmud; he is not sufficiently learned and is likely to err. Instead, ibn Migash writes, he should apply the *halakhic* rules formulated by prominent scholars of past generations and set forth in widely accepted and highly regarded secondary works of Jewish law. As he puts it, "Someone who does not rely on his own reasoning, but instead bases his *halakhic* decisions on the rulings of the [post-Talmudic] Geonic scholars, which are authoritative and well settled, and which are set forth clearly and succinctly, such a person is more praiseworthy than one who [today] presumes to base his rulings directly on the Talmud."[15] In other words, major post-Talmudic compendiums and codes of Jewish law exist precisely so that scholars can refer to and rely on them when those scholars themselves are uncertain about the correct Talmudic rule.

From this perspective, it seems that support for or opposition to direct legal engagement with the Talmud is less a matter of fundamental disagreement over whether the law inheres in the Talmud itself or in post-Talmudic

---

13 *See* Rabbi Jonah Gerondi, Commentary on Mishnah Avot 1:16 (s.v. *Rabban Gamliel*).
14 *See* Rabbi Joseph ibn Migash, Responsa Ri Migash, no. 114.
15 Ibid. no. 114.

rulings (all scholars in the rabbinic tradition recognize that the *halakhah* is derived from the Talmud) and is more a matter of dispute over when contemporary scholars must accept that their own ability to correctly cognize the law from its Talmudic sources has reached its limits. For proponents of the precedential approach (like Rabbi Joseph ibn Migash, for example), who prescribe reliance on post-Talmudic codes and eschew rendering legal judgments on the basis of direct engagement with Talmudic materials, the ability of contemporary scholars to correctly derive the law from Talmudic dialectics runs out before any attempt to do so can even be made: "No one in our time has achieved sufficient facility with the Talmud so as to be able to make correct and authoritative *halakhic* determinations [on the basis of the Talmud itself]."[16] Proponents of the propriety of reaching *halakhic* decisions on the basis of the Talmud do not fundamentally disagree with this concern. Some scholars are simply not skilled enough or qualified to correctly interpret complex Talmudic discussions, and even those who are generally qualified to do so sometimes find themselves unsure about what rule they think the Talmud is prescribing. Even those who generally reject the authority of post-Talmudic codes, such as Rabbi Asher ben Yechiel, nevertheless agree that in the absence of a sufficiently certain legal understanding of the Talmud on a given issue, one can and should revert to relying on well-regarded *halakhic* codes and restatements.[17] Thus, rather than disputing the essential *halakhic* value of post-Talmudic rulings, the two camps may simply differ in their assessment of the ability of later scholars to successfully derive legal rules from Talmudic texts. For both proponents and opponents of the *halakhic* authority of post-Talmudic precedent, however, decisors can and should rely on the well-settled norms found in accepted *halakhic* texts when they find themselves unable to reach a Talmud-based ruling.

Rabbi Epstein follows this sensible approach. When not fully convinced that his own understanding of the correct Talmudic law is correct—even absent any legal counterpressure from a contrary *halakhic* consensus—he reverts to relying on existing precedents, most prominently on the rulings of Maimonides's *Mishneh Torah* and Rabbi Joseph Karo's *Shulchan Arukh*. While Rabbi Epstein himself rejects the precedential authority of post-Talmudic materials as binding, including that of such influential works as the *Mishneh Torah* and the *Shulchan Arukh*, he nevertheless relies on these works when his

---

16 Ibid. no. 114.
17 *See* Mark Washofsky, Taking Precedent Seriously: On Halakhah as a Rhetorical Practice 1, 19-20, *in* Re-Examining Reform Halakhah (Walter Jacob & Moshe Zemer, eds., 2002).

own Talmudic judgment leaves uncertainty as to the correct legal standard. Additionally, in cases where he is himself unsure about the correct Talmudic standard, Rabbi Epstein regards Maimonides's rulings as especially weighty and tends to give precedent to Maimonides's *halakhic* opinions over those of the *Shulchan Arukh* or other important authorities.

For example, the *Shulchan Arukh* rules that water that is disqualified for use for washing before a meal—such as water that looks like another liquid, is dirty, smells bad, or was used for some kind of labor[18]—may nonetheless be used to fulfill the rabbinic obligation to wash one's hands before praying.[19] Rabbi Karo reasons that, while washing before a meal is a ritual requirement and therefore requires ritually clean water, washing before morning prayers is merely a functional practice to ensure cleanliness while praying, a purpose for which any liquid that results in clean hands will suffice. The *Arukh HaShulchan*, exercising independent judgment, rejects the *Shulchan Arukh*'s ruling and rules that water used for washing one's hands before prayer must meet the same qualifications as water used for washing before meals. Rabbi Epstein argues that the *Shulchan Arukh* is mistaken in distinguishing between pre-prayer and pre-meal handwashing in light of the fact that Maimonides appears to have held that the same rules apply to both kinds of handwashing.[20] Maimonides is fairly explicit on this point and writes that the Rabbis legislated that one should wash one's hands and recite the blessing of *al netilat yadayim* "whether for eating, for reciting the *Shema*, or for prayer,"[21] thus indicating that washing before prayer and washing before a meal are manifestations of the same rabbinic enactment and subject to the same conditions.[22]

Another example of Rabbi Epstein's preference for the rulings of Maimonides in cases of doubt regarding the correct Talmudic rule involves the various types of animal horns that may be used as a *shofar* on Rosh Hashanah.[23] There is a basic dispute between Maimonides and Rabbi Joseph Karo regarding the proper characteristics of the kind of *shofar* that is suitable for ritual use on Rosh Hashanah. According to Maimonides, only the curved horn of a

---

18 *See* Shulchan Arukh, Orach Chaim 160:1-4.
19 *See* Ibid. 4:1.
20 *See* Arukh HaShulchan, Orach Chaim 4:9.
21 Mishneh Torah, Hilkhot Berakhot 6:2.
22 *See* Arukh HaShulchan, Orach Chaim 4:9.
23 *See* Babylonian Talmud, Rosh Hashanah 16a; Mishnah, Rosh Hashanah 3:2; Mishnah Rosh Hashanah 3:4; Babylonian Talmud, Rosh Hashanah 26b.

male ram may be used.²⁴ According to Rabbi Karo, however, any horn is ritually fit except for that of a cow—although it is preferable to use a curved ram's horn if possible.²⁵ This dispute is rooted in a disagreement about the correct understanding of several Talmudic passages that provide a number of different formulations of the ritual requirements for the Rosh Hashanah *shofar*. In one passage, the Talmudic sage Rabbi Avahu indicates that the Rosh Hashanah *shofar* should be a ram's horn: "Why do we blow with a ram's horn [on Rosh Hashanah]? [It is as if] God said, 'Blow a ram's horn before Me so that I will recall the sacrifice of Isaac, the son of Abraham [who was exchanged for a ram at the last minute], and I will consider it as though you have offered yourselves as sacrifices before Me.'"²⁶ However, the Mishnah rules, "All horns are fit for use as a *shofar*, except the horn of a cow."²⁷ Another Mishnah teaches, "The *shofar* of Rosh Hashanah is a straight horn from an Ibex . . . and Rabbi Judah said, 'On Rosh Hashanah we blow a male ram's horn.'"²⁸

According to Maimonides, the law follows the view of Rabbi Avahu and Rabbi Judah, who both held that the *shofar* must be a curved horn from a ram since the Talmud expressly endorses that view in its discussion of the relevant Mishnah.²⁹ The contrary view—that all kinds of horns may be used as a shofar, except for cow horns—is grounded in another secondary principle of *halakhic* methodology and Talmudic interpretation, which holds that the law follows the view expressed by an anonymous Mishnah.³⁰ Since the Mishnah anonymously states that "All horns are fit for use as a *shofar*, except the horn of a cow,"³¹ Rabbi Karo maintains that this is the correct *halakhic* rule.³² The correct Talmudic rule is thus uncertain. While the principle of Talmudic interpretation that instructs that the law follow anonymous Mishnaic opinions indicates that any horn not from a cow may be used as a *shofar*, the Talmudic text itself strongly indicates—though does not absolutely and determinately prescribe—that the law follows Rabbi Judah's view that a *shofar* must be a curved ram's horn. Rabbi Epstein notes that there is no rabbinic consensus supporting either view: *Rashi, Tosafot*, the *Semag*, and *Hagahot Maimoni* all agree with Maimonides's view

---

24 *See* Mishneh Torah, Hilkhot Shofar, Sukkah, V'Lulav 1:1.
25 *See* Shulchan Arukh, Orach Chaim 586:1.
26 Babylonian Talmud, Rosh Hashanah 16a.
27 Mishnah, Rosh Hashanah 3:2.
28 Mishnah, Rosh Hashanah 3:4.
29 *See* Babylonian Talmud, Rosh Hashanah 26b. *See also* Arukh HaShulchan 586:3.
30 *See* Babylonian Talmud, Beitza 37b; Babylonian Talmud, Bava Metzia 33a.
31 Mishnah, Rosh Hashanah 3:2.
32 *See* Shulchan Arukh, Orach Chaim 586:1.

that only curved rams' horns are avoided for use as a *shofar* on Rosh Hashanah; the *Rosh*, *Raabad*, *Ran*, and *Arbah Turim*, however, line up in support of Rabbi Joseph Karo's view that any non-bovine horn may be used as a *shofar*, though there is a preference for using a curved ram's horn *ex ante*.[33] Rabbi Epstein ultimately adopts Maimonides's opinion over that of the *Shulchan Arukh* and rules that one must use a *shofar* made from a curved ram's horn.[34]

A third example of this principle concerns the conditions under which a *sukkah*—a ritual hut used to fulfill the biblical commandment to "dwell in huts" during the seven-day holiday of Sukkot, the Festival of Booths—is ritually valid when built beneath a tree.[35] The Talmud states that a *sukkah* built beneath a tree is invalid because one of the central requirements of a ritually valid *sukkah* is that it be covered exclusively with *skhakh*, natural foliage that has been detached from the ground.[36] Rabbi Joseph Karo cites two different understandings of the parameters of this Talmudic rule.[37] First is the view of *Rashi* and *Tosafot*, who qualify the Talmudic rule by maintaining that the Talmud actually intends to distinguish between two different kinds of *sukkah* coverings: one which is mostly closed, creating more shade than sunlight within the *sukkah*, and one which is mostly open, letting in more sunlight than shade. According to this view, the Talmudic rule requiring *skhakh* alone applies categorically only if the canopy of the overhanging tree creates a covering that is mostly closed; in that case, the tree itself constitutes a "roof" over the *sukkah*, and the *sukkah* is therefore invalid. If, however, the tree's canopy is mostly open, the *sukkah* standing under the tree will be valid, provided that the *skhakh* covering the *sukkah* is itself mostly closed. In that case, the dense *skhakh* provides a ritually valid covering for the *sukkah* when the sparse foliage of the overhanging tree does not constitute a genuine "roof" over the *sukkah*, thereby leaving the *sukkah* ritually valid. Moreover, if both the tree canopy and the *skhakh* are sparse (i.e. mostly open), the *sukkah* will still be valid if one lowers the branches of the overhanging tree so that they intermingle with the foliage of the proper *skhakh*. In that case, the tree foliage is too sparse to qualify as an invalidating "roof," and as long as most of the *sukkah* covering is made of proper *skhakh*, the *sukkah* can be considered covered in accordance with the *halakhah*. In addition to the foregoing understanding of the Talmudic invalidation of a *sukkah*

---

33 Ibid. 586:3.
34 *See* Arukh HaShulchan, Orach Chaim 586:3.
35 *See* Leviticus 23:42-43.
36 *See* Babylonian Talmud, Sukkah 9b.
37 *See* ibid. 626:1, 4.

built under a tree, Rabbi Karo also references the more stringent opinion of the *Rosh*.[38] According to the *Rosh*, the *sukkah* is invalid if the *skhakh* foliage lines up under the tree canopy, even when the canopy of the overhanging tree is sparse and the *skhakh* is mostly closed. In that case, the fact that the valid *skhakh* covering lines up directly under the tree foliage means that, in effect, the *sukkah* is ultimately covered by the tree rather than the *skhakh* and is therefore invalid.

Commenting on Rabbi Karo's treatment of this issue, Rabbi Epstein cites two additional opinions—those of Maimonides and the *Baal HaMaor*—which offer alternative understandings of the Talmud's proscription against building a *sukkah* under a tree.[39] Based on the Talmud's permission to use a *sukkah* built under a tree only when one has "cut off" the tree's branches, Maimonides argues that a *sukkah* built under a tree is only valid if one cut off the branches of the tree and placed them on top of the *sukkah* together with the original *skhakh*. The *Baal HaMaor*, by contrast, reads the same words in the Talmud as permitting the use of a *sukkah* built beneath a tree only if one "shook" the branches. He takes this to mean that a *sukkah* built under a tree can be rendered ritually fit only by shaking the leaves off the tree's branches, which demonstrates that one does not desire to use the overhanging tree to provide shelter or shade for the *sukkah*.[40]

The Talmudic passage discussing this issue is thus genuinely ambiguous and easily lends itself to at least four different understandings, as demonstrated by the competing explanations of *Rashi* and *Tosafot*, the *Rosh*, Maimonides, and the *Baal HaMaor*. While Rabbi Karo does not include Maimonides's opinion in his *Shulchan Arukh*, Rabbi Epstein himself regards Maimonides's view as significant and not so easily dismissed.[41] Ultimately, Rabbi Epstein rules that one should build one's *sukkah* in a manner that conforms to all four of these views so as to absolutely ensure that the biblical obligation to sit in a valid *sukkah* is properly fulfilled.[42]

Rabbi Epstein's special regard for Maimonides's rulings does not negate his willingness to deferentially adopt the views of Rabbi Joseph Karo's *Shulchan Arukh* in cases where Rabbi Epstein is unsure about the right Talmudic rule and where Maimonides does not definitively resolve the issue. One example of Rabbi Epstein's deference to the *Shulchan Arukh* relates to the question

---

38 *See* Shulchan Arukh, Orach Chaim 626:4.
39 *See* ibid. 262:9.
40 *See* Arukh HaShulchan, Orach Chaim 262:9.
41 *See* Arukh HaShulchan, Orach Chaim 262:9.
42 *See* ibid. 262:9.

of whether one may respond "amen" upon hearing someone else complete a blessing where the respondent himself had simultaneously completed the same blessing.[43] The *Shulchan Arukh* rules that one should not respond "amen" if one completes the blessing of *Baruch She'Amar*, part of the morning prayer service, at the same time that the *chazzan*, the prayer leader, recites that blessing aloud. Rabbi Karo explains that because the respondent finished saying the blessing at the same time as the *chazzan*, responding "amen" in this scenario would be like responding "amen" to one's own blessing, which is forbidden.[44] The *Arukh HaShulchan* does not believe that Rabbi Karo is correct here because, in truth, one is responding "amen" to the blessing of the *chazzan* and not to one's own blessing, even if one happened to conclude the blessing simultaneously with the *chazzan*.[45] Nevertheless, Rabbi Epstein is not absolutely certain that his own logical argument accurately reflects the correct Talmudic norm; therefore, he defers to the authority of the *Shulchan Arukh*, ruling that in practice one should not recite "amen" when completing the blessing together with the *chazzan*.

Another case concerns the proper approach to reciting the first blessing of the daily *Amidah* prayer.[46] The first blessing of the *Amidah* is so important that the Talmud rules that if one recited it without the proper intention, one has not fulfilled one's obligation.[47] Rabbi Moses Isserles, the *Rema*, points out that despite this Talmudic statement, if one did recite the first blessing of the *Amidah* without the proper intentions (and thus did not fulfill the obligation to recite the *Amidah*), one should not repeat the *Amidah*. This is because any such repetition is likely to prove unhelpful, as one is likely to simply repeat the error.[48] Rabbi Epstein reasons that, although Rabbi Isserles rules that one need not repeat the *Amidah* after having improperly recited the first blessing, one should still not recite the first blessing if he knows in advance before beginning the prayer that he will not recite it with the proper intent.[49] Rabbi Epstein, however, declines to follow this line of reasoning in practice. He notes that the *Shulchan Arukh* does not explicitly prescribe such a prohibition against reciting

---

43 *See* Ibid. 51:4.
44 *See* Shulchan Arukh, Orach Chaim 51:2.
45 *See* Arukh HaShulchan, Orach Chaim 51:4.
46 On the *Amidah* prayer generally, see Cyrus Adler & Emil G. Hirsch, *Shemoneh Esrei*, 270, in 11 The Jewish Encyclopedia (1906).
47 *See* Babylonian Talmud, Berakhot 34b. *See also* Arbah Turim, Orach Chaim 101:1; Shulchan Arukh, Orach Chaim 101:1-2.
48 *See* Rema *to* Shulchan Arukh, Orach Chaim 101:1.
49 *See* Arukh HaShulchan, Orach Chaim 101:2.

the *Amidah* where one does not anticipate being able to recite the prayer with the proper intent and concentration. Rabbi Epstein speculates that Rabbi Karo omits this reasonable standard because most people are no longer capable of reliably reciting the first blessing of the *Amidah* with the proper intentions in any case—therefore, prohibiting the recital of the *Amidah* by those who anticipate being unable to say it properly would result in the widespread, routine omission of this central prayer entirely. While the *Shulchan Arukh*'s implied permission to recite the *Amidah*—even when one anticipates being unable to say it with the proper concentration—thus conflicts with Rabbi Epstein's own preferred standard, Rabbi Epstein defers to the authority of the *Shulchan Arukh* and permits even one who expects to pray without the proper degree of intent and concentration to begin reciting the *Amidah*.[50]

* * * * *

Principle Four: in cases where Rabbi Epstein is himself unsure of the correct halakhic norm and thinks that the right Talmudic rule is genuinely in doubt, and where past rabbinic consensus and major authorities do not provide clear guidance on the issue, Rabbi Epstein follows the standard halakhic secondary rule that in cases of doubt regarding biblical laws, one should act strictly; whereas in cases of doubt regarding rabbinic rules, one should act leniently.

Great legal scholars often have the luxury of spending inordinate amounts of time and energy trying to determine the "right" answers to legal questions.[51] Of course, the "right" answer matters. In a secular legal system, the law is one of the binding agents that makes civil society work. It helps provide people with predictability, security, and confidence as they go about their affairs, and it regulates relations among individuals and between individuals and government. Often, it enshrines and enacts many of a society's deeply held moral and political commitments. From this vantage, resolving legal disputes and answering legal questions correctly—that is, in the manner that the law does indeed

---

50 *See* ibid. 101:2.
51 Of course, whether legal questions have right answers at all is a subject of substantial debate. *See, e.g.*, Ronald Dworkin, *No Right Answer?* 58, *in* Law, Morality, and Society: Essays in Honor of HLA Hart (P.M.S. Hachler & Joseph Raz, eds., 1977); Richard Posner, The Problems of Jurisprudence 197-219 (1993); Douglas Litowitz, *Dworkin and Critical Legal Studies on Right Answers and Conceptual Holism*, 18 Legal Studies Forum 135 (1994); James Q. Whitman, *No Right Answer?* 371, *in* Crime, Procedure and Evidence in a Comparative and International Context: Essays in Honour of Professor Mirjan Damaska (John Jackson, et. al., eds., 2008).

prescribe—is important. Often, this is difficult. Figuring out what the law is and what it requires in novel and difficult circumstances, especially in so-called "hard" cases (which the usual legal sources—constitutions, statutes, regulations, legal handbooks, and past judicial decisions—do not clearly and directly address), requires broad and deep legal knowledge, excellent analytic skills, interpretive knowhow, and the prudent exercise of good judgment.[52] In many such cases, reasonable people—fine legal minds and all—will disagree about the correct legally prescribed course of conduct. In the face of such uncertainty, relying on and conforming to the law becomes difficult indeed. If—as Chief Justice Oliver Wendell Holmes suggested—the law on any given question is really a prediction of how a judge will rule if that case were to come before him for adjudication,[53] then uncertainty about the right answer to legal questions is deeply problematic. The problem goes even deeper, however. While uncertainty is often a serious difficulty for those seeking to conform their behavior and plan their affairs in conformity to the law, in some cases the issue is not so much that the correct legal standard is uncertain or unknown; rather, the issue is that the law itself does not provide any right answer at all.[54] Put simply, not every legal question can be answered analytically, but every legal question does indeed need to be answered.

All legal systems must contend with these sorts of problems; they are inherent and endemic to any normative system that relies on general standards articulated in advance to broadly regulate future conduct.[55] Precisely because such problems are unavoidable, and precisely because no legal system can function without some mechanism for determining standards even in the face of such uncertainty about the "right" legal answer, some have observed that legal regimes

---

52 On judicial process, especially in hard cases, see Benjamin N. Cardozo, The Nature of the Judicial Process (1921); H.L.A. Hart, The Concept of Law 124-136 (2nd ed., 1997); Ronald Dworkin, *Hard Cases*, 88 Harvard Law Review 1057 (1975); Dorota Galeza, *Hard Cases*, 2 Manchester Student Law Review 240 (2013); Chris Guthrie, Jeffrey J. Rachlinski, and Andrew J. Wistrich, *Blinking on the Bench: How Judges Decide Cases*, 93 Cornell Law Review 1 (2007); Henry J. Friendly, *The Courts and Social Policy: Substance and Procedure*, 33 University of Miami Law Review 21 (1978).
53 *See* Oliver Wendell Holmes, Jr., *The Path of the Law*, 10 Harvard Law Review 457 (1897).
54 For a discussion of the theoretical, legal, and political legitimacy problems associated with this uncertainty, see Shlomo Pill, *Law as Engagement: A Judeo-Islamic Conception of the Rule of Law for Twenty-First Century America* 91-126 (2016) (Dissertation).
55 For a brief comparative overview of this issue in different legal systems, see James Q. Whitman, *No Right Answer?* 371, *in* Crime, Procedure and Evidence in a Comparative and International Context: Essays in Honour of Professor Mirjan Damaska (John Jackson, et. al., eds., 2008).

must include mechanisms for reaching legal decisions in cases of doubt. Where the right legal result is uncertain, the system must provide some way for reaching practical legal decisions that, on some level, cut past concerns about finding the "right" result. Some such mechanisms involve rules of decision-making, such as the rule that in litigious contexts, "Doubts must be resolved in favor of the defendant," or the maxim that "Ignorance of the law is no excuse." These examples make clear that when one is in doubt as to whether a particular course of conduct is legal, one should refrain from that conduct. Other mechanisms are institutional, such as the use of courts to reach final judgments that are ultimately binding, largely regardless of whether or not they are legally "correct." Justice Louis Brandeis, for instance, famously observed that in the American legal system, "[I]t is sometimes more important that the applicable rule of law be settled [by the court] than that it be settled right."[56] Likewise, Justice Robert Jackson's view on the function of the Supreme Court—that "we are not final because we are infallible, but we are infallible because we are final,"[57] as noted above—suggests that the Court serves the practical purpose of being the final arbiter of disputed legal questions, but that this is quite different from saying that the Court actually clarifies some platonic legal truth. In other words, the American legal system recognizes that oftentimes the correct answer to a legal question is far from obvious, and that oftentimes legal practitioners, scholars, judges, and citizens will disagree widely and vigorously about the right answer to important normative issues. Given these facts, the United States maintains a system of courts that issue authoritative declarations about what the law is and what it requires in particular cases and prescribes that those judgments must be followed, largely independently from the question of whether or not they are "correct."

What is true of the American legal system (and others) is true of Jewish law as well. As discussed earlier in chapter one, not every normative *halakhic* question can be easily answered by determining the analytically right answer that derives from a correct understanding of Talmudic sources. Sometimes the right Talmudic understanding is uncertain or elusive because Talmudic dialectics are intricate—and Talmudic interpretive and analytic methodologies are complex as well. Other times, doubts about the right *halakhic* answer are the result of there being no apparent Talmudic rule to rely on. After all, the Talmudic corpus—produced in the Middle East around 1,500 years ago—simply does not address all the normative

---
56 Burnet v. Coronado Oil & Gas Co., 285 U.S. 393, 406 (1932) (Brandeis, J., dissenting).
57 Brown v. Allen, 344 U.S. 443, 540 (1953) (Jackson, J., concurring).

issues that are quite relevant today, and analogical reasoning from Talmudic precedents to contemporary cases often admits numerous equally reasonable results.[58]

As early as the Torah itself, Jewish law contemplates this problem. In many ways, it provides a very similar answer to the ones offered by the American and other legal systems. A famous biblical passage in Deuteronomy speaks directly to the issue of how to proceed in cases where the correct legal standard is in doubt:

> If there arises a matter in judgment too baffling for you to decide—be it a controversy between blood and blood, law and law, assault and assault—matters of dispute in your gates, and you shall arise and ascend to the place that the Lord your God will have chosen, and you shall come before the Levitical priests, and to the judge presiding in those days, and you shall inquire, and they shall tell you the matter of judgment. And you shall do in accordance with that which they tell you, from that place which the Lord chose, careful to observe in accordance with all they have instructed you; in accordance with the teaching they have instructed you and the judgment they have told you. You must not deviate from the matter they tell you, neither to the right nor to the left.[59]

Here, the Torah offers an institutional mechanism for reaching legal decisions in cases where the right answer is unknown. When in doubt, go to the Temple priests or the law courts; they will provide a ruling, and that ruling is to be followed. Indeed, as the generally accepted understanding of this passage confirms (like Justice Louis Brandeis's comments about the role of courts in the American legal system), the role of the priest or the judge in the Torah is less about finding the "right" answer and is more about providing an authoritative legal directive that can then be observed in practice. The judge's ruling must be followed not necessarily because it is correct; it must be followed because the *halakhic* system recognizes the judicial determinations of properly constituted courts as authoritative. Explaining the passage's emphatic caution not to deviate from the court's ruling "to the right or to the left," the Talmud teaches that this applies "even if they [the judges] tell you that right is left and left is right."[60] Thus, resorting to the courts in cases where the correct legal standard

---

58 *See generally* Shlomo Pill, *Law as Engagement: A Judeo-Islamic Conception of the Rule of Law for Twenty-First Century America* 131-198 (2016) (Dissertation).
59 Deuteronomy 17:8-11.
60 Sifri Deuteronomy §154.

is unknown is less about getting the right answer and more about resolving the legal doubts with a final and authoritative answer.

Declaring that the priests and judges have the authority to resolve legal questions where the right *halakhic* standard is in doubt is only part of the story, however. This kind of second-order rule of decision helpfully tells us *who* should resolve normative concerns when the right rule of law is uncertain, but it provides little guidance about *how* the priests and judges should reach such determinations. In "easy cases," one would expect these authorized legal decision makers to inform less-learned litigants and questioners about what they understand to be the correct *halakhic* norm or mode of practice. But what about in "hard cases" where the analytically correct legal rule is in doubt, even for the learned rabbinic scholar? How should the judge or priest resolve those legal questions where the right legal result is unclear and perhaps does not even exist at all? Moreover, rabbinic understandings of this second-order rule of decision maintain that the above passage contains only a very specific kind of authorization: it gives ultimate legal decision-making authority—the power to say what the law is—only to duly authorized and properly ordained judges.[61] As discussed earlier in chapter one, however, no such biblically ordained judges have existed within the Jewish law system for at least 1,500 years. Formal rabbinic ordination of the kind that gave rabbinic judges the Torah-based authority to resolve legal queries—independent of the analytic correctness of their rulings—lapsed centuries before the completion of the Babylonian Talmud.[62] In the absence of such "infallible because we are final" judicial authority, the need to ascertain analytically correct answers to Jewish law questions became once again quite important.

The need to resolve legal doubts thus looms large, and it is important to understand that responding to this need involved, by definition, prescribing ways of making singular legal determinations that are not necessarily "correct" in an analytic sense but nevertheless serve the important function of providing a determination when the "right" answer is unknown or may not even exist. As discussed in the previous chapter, one second-order guideline for choosing a *halakhic* standard—in the absence of knowledge of the analytically correct legal rule—is relying on the precedential rulings of certain past rabbinic authorities. This sort of guideline, which identifies a source for authoritative

---

61 *See, e.g.,* Babylonian Talmud, Sotah 7b; Jerusalem Talmud, Horayot 1:1; Sefer HaChinukh, no. 495.
62 *See* Babylonian Talmud, Sanhedrin 37b.

legal determinations that are not tied to the correctness of those determinations in any substantive analytic sense, is akin to the older Torah-prescribed rule that commands that in cases of doubt, one should follow the rulings of "the judge that will be in charge at that time,"[63] whether they are right or wrong. Rabbi Epstein utilizes this guideline, and he has a preferred hierarchy of precedential authorities whose rulings he relies on in cases where he thinks that the analytically correct *halakhic* rule is uncertain—he turns first to Maimonides, then to the Rabbi Karo's *Shulchan Arukh*, followed closely by the *Rema*.

The second part of this chapter addresses another kind of second-order guideline for resolving *halakhic* questions in cases where the right Talmudic norm is doubtful. In addition to rules that determine *who* should decide such questions, Jewish law also includes second-order principles for *how* such questions should be answered. Specifically, when it comes to the determination of standards of ritual conduct in non-litigious contexts—the kinds of issues addressed in the *Orach Chaim* section of Rabbi Epstein's *Arukh HaShulchan*—rabbinic law prescribes that when the "right" answer is unknown or in doubt, questions of biblical law are to be resolved stringently so as to avoid any potential sinful conduct; meanwhile, matters of rabbinic law are to be resolved leniently, such that conduct is permitted unless one knows that it is prohibited.[64] Importantly, like relying on the precedential opinions of certain rabbinic scholars, following this rule is not designed to necessarily produce "correct" *halakhic* rulings. From an analytic perspective, there is no particular reason to think that a lenient resolution to questions pertaining to rabbinic law are necessarily correct any more than there is to think that stringent answers to questions of biblical law are right. Rules like this are designed to produce an answer, which may be relied upon for practical application but not necessarily for *the right* answer.

Rabbi Epstein often utilizes these important secondary rules to resolve *halakhic* doubts and to guide the use of various other methodological principles to reach legal conclusions in cases where either the analytically correct Talmudic rule is unclear, or where the confluence of an abstractly correct Talmudic norm along with other religious or pragmatic concerns makes the correct standard of practice uncertain. One example of the *Arukh HaShulchan*'s reliance on this second-order rule of decision concerns Rabbi Epstein's response to the issue of whether one may use stolen wool to produce strings and then use those strings to fulfill the biblical obligation to tie *tzitzit* fringes on one's

---

63 Deuteronomy 17:9.
64 *See* Babylonian Talmud, Beitza 3b.

four-cornered garment.⁶⁵ Maimonides rules that one cannot make *tzitzit* strings from stolen wool.⁶⁶ Several commentators note that this ruling seems to cut against an established *halakhic* principle stating that changes to a stolen item affect the acquisition of that item by the thief.⁶⁷ In the case of producing *tzitzit* strings from stolen wool, the process of spinning stolen raw wool into strings should affect the thief's acquisition of the strings, rendering the *tzitzit* strings no longer stolen property and thus permitted for use. Commentators therefore offer a variety of explanations for Maimonides's ruling. Rabbi Joseph Karo suggests that Maimonides restricts the use of strings which were made from the stolen wool only prior to the original owner's having given up hope of recovering his lost property, which would prevent the thief from acquiring the wool by virtue of transforming it into *tzitzit* strings. Others suggest that spinning wool into strings is a change that can be undone (by unraveling the strings), which prevents the change from affecting the thief's acquisition of the wool even if the owner has given up hope of recovering his property.⁶⁸ Still others suggest that the *halakhah* imposes more stringent requirements for a thief to acquire stolen property when that property will be used to perform a *mitzvah* than would typically be required, so spinning the wool into strings—coupled with the original owners losing hope of recovering the wool—would still be insufficient to affect the thief's acquisition of wool used for *tzitzit* strings.⁶⁹

The *Arukh HaShulchan* rejects these attempted explanations of Maimonides's view and demonstrates how the premises of each are incorrect.⁷⁰ Rabbi Epstein, however, is hesitant to abandon Maimonides's prohibition on the use of *tzitzit* strings woven from stolen wool and instead offers his own novel explanation of Maimonides's ruling. Rabbi Epstein argues that the reason why one may not use strings woven from stolen wool—despite the change affected in the wool by weaving it into strings, and even after the original owner gave up hope of recovering the wool—is that the thief would not have acquired the wool until after it had been transformed into *tzitzit* strings. Since the spinning of the wool into strings must be done *lishmah* (with the specific intent of using the strings to fulfill the obligation of *tzitzit*), and since at the time of spinning the wool into strings the thief would not yet

---

65 *See* Arukh HaShulchan, Orach Chaim 11:24.
66 *See* Mishneh Torah, Hilkhot Tzitzit 1:11.
67 *See* Babylonian Talmud, Bava Kamma 95a.
68 *See* Arukh HaShulchan, Orach Chaim 11:24.
69 *See* ibid. citing the view of the *Turei Zahav*.
70 *See* ibid.

have acquired it and the wool would still be considered stolen, it would be impossible for the spinning to have been done in a ritually proper manner.[71] Ultimately, Rabbi Epstein seems unconvinced by his own creative justification for Maimonides's ruling. Nevertheless, he is willing to rely on what he views as a possible, reasonable explanation of Maimonides's position rather than discard Maimonides's opinion out of hand—especially because a rejection of Maimonides's rule on this ruling would amount to a serious leniency in a matter of biblical law, effectively permitting one to fulfill the biblical commandment of wearing *tzitzit* with the use of *tzitzit* strings made from stolen wool, which may be invalid.[72]

In another instance, Rabbi Epstein rules strictly on a matter of biblical Sabbath law where he thinks the Talmudic standard is analytically indeterminate. The Babylonian Talmud states that it is forbidden to shake out a black cloak on the Sabbath, as this type of action would constitute a forbidden Sabbath labor.[73] However, the Talmud does not identify the specific kind of forbidden Sabbath labor involved in shaking out a black cloak. The Talmud adds that this prohibition applies only when an individual prefers his clothing to be shaken out. One who does not care whether or not his clothes are shaken out, however, is not prohibited from shaking them.[74] *Rashi* explains that the Sabbath prohibition at issue in the Talmudic discussion is the labor of "whitening," which in this case is violated by shaking dust off the cloak, thereby making it cleaner.[75] According to *Tosafot*, however, the Talmud is prohibiting shaking off dew—not dust—from a cloak as a violation of the prohibition against "whitening," which encompasses forms of laundering; in this view, shaking dust off of a cloak is not sufficiently significant so as to constitute a violation of the prohibition against laundering clothes on the Sabbath.[76]

Rabbi Epstein points out that many medieval authorities—including the *Rosh, Ran, Rashba,* and *Raabad*—followed the interpretation of the *Tosafot*. According to the *Tosafot*, it is forbidden for one to purposely clean one's black clothing by shaking it of dew; however, shaking off dust is permitted.[77] The *Arbah Turim* and the *Shulchan Arukh* both adopted this ruling as

---

71 *See* ibid.
72 *See* ibid.
73 *See* Babylonian Talmud, Shabbat 147a.
74 *See* ibid.
75 *See* Rashi *to* Babylonian Talmud, Shabbat 147a (s.v. *hamena'er talito*).
76 *See* Tosafot *to* Babylonian Talmud, Shabbat 147a (s.v. *hamena'er talito*).
77 *See* Arukh HaShulchan, Orach Chaim 302:1.

well.⁷⁸ Maimonides, however, offers an entirely different understanding of this Talmudic prohibition. According to Maimonides, the Talmud prohibits shaking out a cloak because doing so would violate the prohibition against *makeh bipatish*—doing the final act of production that makes an object usable. Maimonides focuses on the Talmud's concern for the black color of the cloak; shaking tufts of white wool from a black cloak is the final finishing step in producing a usable black cloak, and thus doing so is prohibited on the Sabbath.⁷⁹

Rabbi Epstein rules that the law follows the view of *Tosafot*, since a consensus of scholars support that position,⁸⁰ and because he argues that the views of both *Rashi* and Maimonides are unable to adequately account for the Talmud's prohibition of shaking out specifically a black cloak and its limiting of this prohibition to one who cares to have his cloak shaken out in this manner.⁸¹ Nevertheless, since the issue involves a possible violation of biblical Sabbath laws, and because the Talmudic discussion on the matter is genuinely indeterminate and does not admit an analytically clear standard, Rabbi Epstein rules that in practice one must avoid engaging in any of the acts that the various rabbinic understandings of this Talmudic norm contemplate.⁸²

While questions of what constitutes forbidden labor on the Sabbath address issues of biblical law such that uncertainties must be resolved strictly, performing labor during *Chol HaMoed*—the intermediate days of certain major holidays—is only rabbinically proscribed; thus doubts about such laws are resolved leniently.⁸³ One example of this concerns Rabbi Epstein's treatment of whether and when one may use formalistic tricks in order to circumvent the rabbinic prohibition against performing labor during *Chol HaMoed*.⁸⁴ Following the Talmudic prohibition against doing *melakhah* on *Chol HaMoed* for non-holiday related purposes, the *Shulchan Arukh* rules that while a

---

78 *See* Arbah Turim, Orach Chaim 302; Shulchan Arukh, Orach Chaim 302:1.
79 *See* Mishneh Torah, Hilkhot Shabbat 10:18.
80 *See supra* Chapter Five.
81 *See* Arukh HaShulchan, Orach Chaim 302:2.
82 *See* ibid.
83 On the prohibition of labor on *Chol HaMoed*, see Tosafot *to* Babylonian Talmud, Chagigah 18a (s.v. *ohalo*); Rosh *to* Babylonian Talmud, Moed Katan 1:1; Mishneh Torah, Hilkhot Yom Tov 7:1.
84 Jewish law includes complex doctrines that govern when legal fictions that take advantage of legal technicalities may be used to circumvent normative *halakhic* obligations or prohibitions. Such artifices are known as *har'amot* (singular, *har'amah*), and may or may not be utilized depending on the nature of the law being circumvented and the quality and genuineness of the artifice being deployed. *See generally* 9 Encyclopedia Talmudit 698-713 (2009).

person does not have to specifically limit how much grain he grinds or how much beer he brews on *Chol HaMoed* (in order to ensure he only does just enough *melakhah* as is necessary for the holiday), one may not intentionally use an artifice in order to grind extra grain or brew extra beer on *Chol HaMoed* to use after the holiday.[85] Rabbi Karo further states that one may not use an artifice to produce more flour or beer when one already has some in storage.[86] However, one may bake fresh bread—even if one already has baked bread in storage—because hot bread is preferable to cold bread; once the fresh bread has been made, the older bread may be saved for after the holiday.[87] While it is thus prohibited to use legal artifices to circumvent the Talmudic prohibition against doing *melakhah* for after the holiday on *Chol HaMoed*, if one violated this stricture, one is nonetheless allowed after the fact to partake of the foods or beverages that he produced. Maimonides, however, disagrees with Rabbi Karo's limitations; he instead rules that even one who has already-made foodstuffs may nevertheless circumvent the Talmud's prohibition by producing additional large amounts of those substances "for holiday use" and then saving the inevitable leftovers for after the holiday.[88] Maimonides reasons that this manner of circumventing the Talmudic prohibition against preparing for after the holiday would not be apparent to onlookers as an artifice (since observers do not know whether one has already-prepared foodstuffs available or not), and thus it remains permitted.[89] The *Raabad* disagrees with Maimonides, however, and argues that all forms of artifice used under any conditions to circumvent the rabbinic proscription against performing *melakhah* (biblically prohibited forms of labor) on *Chol HaMoed* for post-holiday use are prohibited.[90] The *Raabad* supports this view by pointing out that the issue is the subject of dispute in the Talmud, where the majority view is that using artifices in this manner is prohibited.[91]

The *Arukh HaShulchan* defends Maimonides's position. Rabbi Epstein points out that the Talmud frames the rabbinic dispute about whether or not one may use artifices to circumvent the prohibition against working on *Chol HaMoed* for post-holiday needs as a conflict between two Tannaitic texts. It

---

85 *See* Shulchan Arukh, Orach Chaim 533:1.
86 *See* ibid.
87 *See* ibid.
88 *See* Mishneh Torah, Hilkhot Yom Tov 7:8.
89 *See* ibid.
90 *See* Raabad *to* Mishneh Torah, Hilkhot Yom Tov 7:8.
91 *See* Babylonian Talmud, Moed Katan 12b.

is true, Rabbi Epstein acknowledges, that one of these texts reflects the view of several Mishnaic rabbis, while the other reflects the view of only a single scholar. However, he argues, since the Talmud presents the dispute merely by quoting the two conflicting texts, the passage is best understood as placing the two Tannaitic texts on equal footing. Since the Talmudic discussion of this issue thus leaves the issue in doubt due to the unresolved conflict between these two Tannaitic sources, the issue should be resolved leniently in accordance with Maimonides's view, as the question of whether an artifice is permitted to circumvent prohibitions is a rabbinic concern and not a biblical concern.[92]

One of the most common uses of these secondary principles relates to the reciting of blessings (or otherwise pronouncing God's name) in cases where the obligation to do so is uncertain. Taking God's name in vain—which includes speaking God's name anytime one is not ritually obligated to do so—involves a likely biblical sin.[93] Almost always, however, any potential obligation to recite a blessing or prayer that includes God's name is only rabbinic.[94] Consequently, in cases of doubt as to the obligation to recite a blessing, Rabbi Epstein routinely rules that one should not recite the blessing. While he treats the rabbinic question of failing to recite a possibly obligatory blessing leniently, he thereby resolves the biblical concern of taking God's name in vain strictly. One such issue concerns the proper blessing to be recited before eating seeds.[95] Rabbi Joseph Karo rules that before eating sweet, edible fruit seeds, one must recite the blessing of *boreh pri ha'etz*, which recognizes God as the "Creator of the fruit of the tree." When eating bitter fruit seeds, however, Rabbi Karo rules that one should not recite any blessing. Moreover, when one eats fruit seeds that are naturally bitter but have become sweet through some kind of cooking process, one should not recite the blessing of *boreh pri ha'etz*, which is only said on fruit itself, and should instead recite the blessing of *shehakol nih'yeh bidvaro*, a residual blessing that is recited upon all foods that do not grow from the ground and which recognizes that "All comes into being through His [God's] word."[96] Rabbi Karo's ruling is based on an earlier rabbinic interpretation of a Talmudic

---

92 *See* Arukh HaShulchan, Orach Chaim 533:4.
93 *See* Exodus 20:7; Babylonian Talmud, Berakhot 33a.
94 *See* Sefer HaChinukh, no. 430; Tosafot *to* Babylonian Talmud, Berakhot 35a (s.v. *lefanav*); Mishneh Torah, Hilkhot Berakhot 1:5.
95 The Talmud makes clear that there is an obligation to recite a blessing before consuming food or drink, and delineates several different blessings tailored to particular kinds of foods. *See* Babylonian Talmud, Berakhot 35a; Mishnah, Berakhot 6:1-8.
96 *See* Shulchan Arukh, Orach Chaim 202:3.

passage that teaches that the shells of nuts and the seeds of fruit are subject to the biblical law of *orlah*, which prohibits the consumption of fruit during the first three years of a tree's productive fruit-bearing.[97] According to *Tosafot* and the *Rosh*, this Talmudic ruling, which is not directly related to the laws of blessings, demonstrates that the *halakhah* views fruit seeds as fruit; therefore, seeds should be subject to the blessing of *boreh pri ha'etz*. Following this understanding of the Talmudic precedent, Rabbi Karo rules that one recites the blessing of *boreh pri ha'etz* on edible seeds just as one would on the fruit itself. The *Rashba*, however, offers an alternative understanding of this Talmudic passage. He maintains that seeds are generally not regarded as fruit, and the Talmud treats them as such for purposes of *orlah* laws only due to special scriptural indication. Consequently, when eating fruit seeds, one should recite the blessing of *boreh pri ha'adamah* ("Who created the fruit of the Earth"), rather than *boreh pri ha'etz*.[98]

Rabbi Epstein rejects Rabbi Karo's ruling and instead adopts the *Rashba's* view that one should recite the blessing of *boreh pri ha'adamah* on fruit seeds.[99] Rabbi Epstein argues that this result is justified because a consensus of important authorities supports the *Rashba's* position, in part because this view is more consistent with the principle that doubts regarding the obligation to recite blessings (which are rabbinic, not biblical, obligations) should be resolved in a manner that avoids reciting possibly unwarranted blessings. As a rule, one may in principle recite the blessing of *boreh pri ha'adamah* on fruit, since they do in fact grow from the Earth; however, one may not recite the blessing of *boreh pri ha'etz* on a food that is not actually considered "fruit." Since the precise status of edible fruit seeds remains doubtful in light of the Talmud's failure to determinately resolve the question, a consensus of rabbinic scholars—as well as Rabbi Epstein himself—concluded that one should err on the side of caution and recite *boreh pri ha'adamah* rather than *boreh pri ha'etz* when eating fruit seeds.[100]

Other examples of this principle relate to the recitation of the *Kaddish* prayer. Rabbi Epstein explains that the Men of the Great Assembly (a rabbinic synod in the early Second Temple period) legislated the recitation of the *Kaddish*, a prayer designed to punctuate the standard prayer liturgy and

---

97   *See* Arukh HaShulchan, Orach Chaim 202:19.
98   *See* ibid.
99   *See* ibid.
100 *See* ibid.

other important occasions with acknowledgments of God's greatness.[101] Rabbi Epstein notes that many people are accustomed to punctuating the morning prayer service by reciting *Kaddish* many times—indeed, more times than the Talmudic Rabbis themselves prescribed. Taking the Talmudic prescription of the correct number of times that *Kaddish* should be said during the morning prayer service as normative, Rabbi Epstein rejects this common custom. While generally Rabbi Epstein treats customs with deference, he notes that according to one major authority, reciting *Kaddish* (which contains God's name) is akin to reciting blessings; therefore, "Just as it is good to be frugal with reciting blessings, it is likewise good to be frugal with the recitation of the *Kaddish* prayer."[102] Thus, following the general principle that one does not recite unnecessary blessings (which involve the possible violation of the biblical injunction against taking God's name in vain), Rabbi Epstein prohibits the unnecessary recital of *Kaddish* and prescribes that *Kaddish* should be said only at those points in the prayer service at which it is legally required.[103] In a similar vein, Maimonides states that after ten or more Jews engage in Torah study—even of non-legal or homiletical matters—one of the group must recite *Kaddish DeRabbanan*, a special *Kaddish* prayer used to mark the end of a public Torah study session.[104] Rabbi Epstein asserts that implicit in Maimonides's statement is a ruling—if fewer than ten Jews learn Torah, they are not permitted to recite *Kaddish*. Indeed—though Rabbi Epstein does not say this explicitly—when Maimonides requires the recitation of *Kaddish*, if "ten or more" study Torah, the qualification "or more" emphasizes that ten is the minimum and excludes the possibility of reciting Kaddish for less than ten. On the basis of his interpretation of Maimonides's rule, Rabbi Epstein rebukes those who customarily recite *Kaddish* alone after learning Torah to commemorate the anniversary of a loved one's death. Moreover, in limiting the recitations of *Kaddish*, Rabbi Epstein rules strictly to prevent future Jews from reciting the name of God in vain.[105]

* * * * *

---

101 *See* Babylonian Talmud, Berakhot 3a; Babylonian Talmud, Berakhot 109b; Tosafot *to* Babylonian Talmud, Berakhot 109b.
102 Arukh HaShulchan, Orach Chaim 55:3.
103 *See* ibid. 55:3.
104 *See* ibid. 55:5.
105 *See* ibid. 55:5.

Normative questions about what Jewish law teaches and requires in practice must be answered. While often—especially for an independent decisor like Rabbi Epstein, who confidently rules in accordance with his own Talmudic understandings—such answers may be derived from the principal primary sources of *halakhah*, in some cases the right *halakhic* standard remains uncertain. Sometimes a rabbinic scholar may not be fully confident in their understandings of the relevant Talmudic sources; other times, the Talmudic materials themselves may prove analytically indeterminate. In order to reach determinate *halakhic* conclusions in his *Arukh HaShulchan*, Rabbi Epstein resorts to several doubt-resolving principles that permit him to arrive at an answer even when the *right* answer remains uncertain. As explained above, when Rabbi Epstein is not fully confident in the correctness of his Talmudic interpretations, he tends to defer to the opinions of major authorities like Maimonides and Rabbi Joseph Karo, especially when these earlier scholars reached more religiously stringent conclusions than Rabbi Epstein's own speculative Talmudic understandings would suggest. Furthermore, when the Talmudic sources are wholly indeterminate, Rabbi Epstein reaches *halakhic* determinations on the basis of well-settled secondary rules of decision, such as the standard doubt-resolving principle that one should act stringently on questions of biblical law and leniently in matters of rabbinic obligations.

CHAPTER SEVEN

Non-Normative Opinions

Chapters four and five considered Rabbi Epstein's preference for ruling in accordance with what he (or a substantial consensus of other authorities) views as the analytically correct understanding of the normative *halakhic* standards prescribed by the Talmud. Most fundamentally, as he does to any given issue, Rabbi Epstein maintains that the right Jewish law standard is the one that emerges from a competent rabbinic scholar's independent understanding of the relevant Talmudic sources. Thus, when determining *halakhic* norms, Rabbi Epstein first and foremost follows his own interpretive understanding of the Talmud. His own sense of the right Talmudic rule gives way, however, when a consensus of prominent rabbinic figures endorses an alternative legal rule—or where major scholars prescribe more stringent standards of conduct—in which case Rabbi Epstein tends to humbly defer to the Talmudic understandings of those other authorities. Chapter six then discussed Rabbi Epstein's use of second order rules of decision, such as the authority of precedent and doubt-resolving principles, to determine *halakhic* standards in cases where there is no analytically correct Talmudic norm to prescribe. When Rabbi Epstein is not fully confident in the correctness of his own Talmudic understandings, he defers to the Talmud-based rulings of preeminent *halakhic* authorities, such as Maimonides, whose Talmudic interpretations Rabbi Epstein trusts as likely correct. Finally, where Rabbi Epstein finds the Talmudic sources genuinely indeterminate, he determines the right *halakhic* standard by applying the well-known principle for resolving doubts in Jewish ritual law, which maintains that one should act strictly with respect to matters of biblical law and leniently in matters of rabbinic law.

Determining the correct legal norm—whether by reference to the Talmud itself, to secondary codes, or by relying on doubt-resolving rules of decision—does not conclude the *halakhic* inquiry, however. The foregoing discussion explains only how Rabbi Epstein reaches determinations of what the law *should be* in an abstract, theoretically ideal sense. The correct Talmudic norm represents a kind of platonic, ideal form of the right *halakhic* standard. But *halakhic* practice in the real world often entails something more than mechanistically following Talmudic rules. *Halakhic* Jewish practice must account not only for the legal niceties of Talmudic rules, but also for an additional variety of religious, social, and other concerns that often push back against the normative import of the idealized legal prescriptions of the *dina d'Talmuda*, the legal rule determined by the Talmud. The remaining discussion of the methodology of the *Arukh HaShulchan* considers the various methodological principles and secondary rules of decision that Rabbi Epstein uses to determine the right standard of *halakhic* practice when theoretically correct Talmudic rules interact with such religious, social, and practical concerns. This chapter begins the discussion by considering how Rabbi Epstein treats what he views as incorrect or non-normative rabbinic opinions in the context of reaching practical *halakhic* judgments.

* * * * *

Principle Five: Rabbi Epstein generally does not rule that one should seek to satisfy halakhic opinions which he regards as mistaken. However, he does make use of such rejected opinions to resolve complex halakhic questions or disputes among past authorities. He does this in order to justify common practices that are at odds with standard halakhic norms and to permit non-normative behavior in extenuating circumstances.

    Legal discourse, argumentation, and debate are central features of *halakhic* jurisprudence.[1] Some rabbinic scholars have understood *halakhic* discourse as a means to an end—they have argued that robust and free debate over how to read primary Jewish texts and about which understandings and applications of those texts are most correct is merely instrumental to achieving the best possible conclusions that most closely approximate *halakhic* truth. Rabbi Samuel Uceda, for instance, argues that in the context of rabbinic jurisprudence, "Disputes between opposing views shed light on the issue, reveal the

---

1   On the role of legal disagreement in rabbinic tradition, see Avi Sagi, The Open Canon (2007); Richard Hidary, Dispute for the Sake of Heaven: Legal Pluralism in the Talmud (2010); Rabbi Zvi Lampel, The Dynamics of Dispute: The Makings of Machlokess in Talmudic Times (1991); Shlomo Pill, *Law as Engagement: A Judeo-Islamic Conception of the Rule of Law for Twenty-First Century America* 199-234 (2016) (Dissertation).

truth, and dispel uncertainties."[2] In a similar but slightly different vein, Rabbi Naftali Tzvi Yehudah Berlin argues that rabbinic arguments about Jewish law are valuable because while only one opinion can actually be legally correct, the mistaken viewpoints can nevertheless teach useful legal concepts. "This is true," he says, "with respect to every opinion recorded in the Talmud, [even those that do not correctly reflect the right legal rule,] which shed light on some issue, and we are therefore obligated to study them."[3] Others have argued that *halakhic* argumentation is good in its own right—even when the correct legal rule is known, the rabbinic debates that underlie that conclusion should be studied for their own sake. Rabbi Meir ibn Gabbai, for example, recognizes that human beings cannot comply with two contradictory views at the same time and that therefore in practice, the law follows one of the various opinions on every given issue. But, he argues, "All the rulings of the rabbis of all times came to them from [God's] voice that emitted from Sinai." Here he speaks of different scholars, living in different contexts, possessing different intellectual abilities, and receiving God's voice in different ways, thereby leading to different legal opinions.[4] Rabbi Solomon Luria advances a similar argument and maintains that revelation, like texts, is inherently ambiguous and open-ended: "Even if all the Heavens were paper and all the seas were ink, they would be insufficient to fully record all the knowledge connected to even one part of the Torah, with all the questions it invites, all the knowledge we draw from it, and all that the scholars derive from it through reasoned interpretation."[5] Thus, even when God communicated Jewish law to the Israelites at Sinai, Rabbi Luria argues, "Each person apprehended and understood the message through his own unique path in accordance with his own understanding… [thus] all these different viewpoints are correct."[6] Looming large in both traditions of rabbinic jurisprudence is the Talmudic dictum of *"elu v'elu divrei Elokim Chaim,"* that "these and those"—that is, the views on both sides of debated *halakhic* questions—"are the words of the living God."[7]

---

2   See Midrash Shmuel *to* Mishnah Avot 5:19.
3   HaEmek Sheilah *to* Sheiltot D'Rav Achai Gaon 19 (Mosad HaRav Kook, ed., 1975). For a more complete overview of this jurisprudential understanding of legal disputes see Avi Sagi, The Open Canon 17-30 (2007).
4   *See* Avi Sagi, The Open Canon 73-75 (2007).
5   Rabbi Solomon Luria, Yam Shel Shlomo, Introduction *to* Bava Kamma.
6   Ibid., Introduction *to* Chullin.
7   *See, e.g.,* Babylonian Talmud, Eruvin 13b; Gitten 6b. *See generally* Avi Sagi, The Open Canon (2007).

Eventually, in *halakhah* (as in the practical application of all legal systems), debate must come to an end—final determinations of the correct rule of law must be made. Some *halakhic* opinions are adopted as normative standards of religious conduct, and other opinions are rejected as practical rules of law. Rabbinic legal opinions may be rejected as normative *halakhic* rules for at least two reasons. Some rejected opinions are excluded from normative practice because they are based on interpretations and applications of Talmudic sources that are considered incorrect. Other rabbinic positions reflect reasonable and justifiable Talmudic understandings but are excluded from standard modes of *halakhic* practice by various secondary rules of decision used to resolve *halakhic* doubts and uncertainties, as well as to reach determinate rulings in the face of otherwise unresolvable *halakhic* disagreement. When Rabbi Epstein concludes that a particular *halakhic* opinion or possible course of action is incorrect—either due to his own independent assessment of the merits of the reasoning and textual interpretations on which that view is based, or because he is genuinely unsure about the correct *halakhic* rule and has excluded this particular view through his application of standard, doubt-resolving, secondary rules—he does not generally think that there is any need to incorporate the rejected view into *halakhic* practice.

Many *halakhic* decisors have rejected the approach adopted by Rabbi Epstein and have instead opted for an alternative model that views rejected opinions as still relevant to *halakhic* practice. Instead of settling on a single rabbinic opinion as the normative *halakhic* standard, this approach seeks to construct modes of religious practice that satisfy as many competing legal opinions as possible. Perhaps one of the most well-known exemplars of this model of *halakhic* decision-making is Rabbi Israel Meir Kagan, author of the *Mishnah Berurah*.[8] As noted in chapter three, Rabbi Kagan often resolves rabbinic disputes and legal uncertainties by recommending the adoption of modes of practice that simultaneously fulfill the *halakhic* opinions of numerous decisors.[9] For instance, there is a dispute between Rabbi Joseph Karo and Rabbi Moses

---

8   Arguably, a form of this approach was also adopted by Rabbi Joseph Karo, at least in the very broad sense that his stated methodology for determining the correct rule of law in his *Shulchan Arukh* involved adopting the rules endorsed by two out of his three preferred authorities—Maimonides, Rabbi Isaac Alfasi, and Rabbi Asher ben Yechiel. This approach ensures that the practical *halakhah* fulfills the opinions of as many of what Rabbi Karo regarded as the most relevant rabbinic authorities as possible. *See* Beit Yosef *to* Arbah Turim, Introduction.

9   *See generally* Michael J. Broyde & Ira Bedzow, The Codification of Jewish Law: An Introduction to the Jurisprudence of the Mishna Berura 35-39 (2014).

Isserles about which kinds of garments must have ritual *tzitzit*, or "fringes," placed on their corners in fulfillment of the biblical commandment to "make twisted cords on the corners of your garments."[10] According to Rabbi Isserles, garments made of any kind of material require fringes, while Rabbi Karo rules that only wool and linen garments are biblically obligated to have *tzitzit*.[11] Rather than reaching a conclusion about which view is correct, Rabbi Kagan recommends wearing a wool garment, which can be used to fulfill the biblical obligation according to both opinions.[12]

Another example of this tendency relates to the particular *halakhic* problem that arises when Passover Eve coincides with the Sabbath. Jewish law requires the consumption of three meals on the Sabbath, one on Friday night and two during the following day,[13] and it also generally defines a *seudah* (a meal) as consisting of bread.[14] The problem is, however, that Jewish law also prohibits the consumption of both leavened and unleavened bread on the afternoon preceding the start of Passover (at the time during which the third Sabbath meal is typically eaten). Regular bread as *chametz* is prohibited because the Passover prohibition on the consumption of leavened bread begins late in the morning on Passover Eve; meanwhile, the consumption of unleavened bread (*matzah*) is prohibited beginning at midday so as to create excitement and anticipation for the ritual consumption of *matzah* at the Passover *Seder* later that night.[15] Some authorities rule that one should eat a third Sabbath meal consisting of unleavened bread made with fruit juices instead of water, since such bread is both not leavened and also not truly *matzah* suitable for consumption at the Passover *Seder* (*matzah* must be made of only flour and water).[16] Others disagree, arguing that unleavened bread made with fruit juices may not be consumed at this time—instead, they rule that the third Sabbath meal should consist of meats, fruits, and other foods, but not bread.[17] Rabbi Kagan does not choose between these two approaches; instead, he prescribes a third model that satisfies both views.[18] He rules that one should eat two meals consisting of proper bread on the morning of the Sabbath, thereby avoiding

---

10 Deuteronomy 22:12. *See also* Numbers 15:38-40.
11 *See* Shulchan Arukh, Orach Chaim 9:1.
12 *See* Mishnah Berurah, Orach Chaim 9:5.
13 *See* Babylonian Talmud, Shabbat 117b.
14 *See* Shulchan Arukh, Orach Chaim 274:1-4, 289:1, 291:1.
15 *See* ibid. 443:1; Jerusalem Talmud, Pesachim 10:1.
16 *See* Arukh HaShulchan, Orach Chaim 444:4.
17 *See* Rema *to* Shulchan Arukh 444:1.
18 *See* Mishnah Berurah, Orach Chaim 444:1.

both the prohibitions on leavened and unleavened bread while also providing for a proper, bread-based *seudah* for the third Sabbath meal.[19]

Rabbi Epstein eschews this general approach. Rather than prescribing modes of *halakhic* practice that succeed in satisfying as many competing rabbinic opinions on the issue as possible, Rabbi Epstein reaches a determinate conclusion about which legal standard is correct and prescribes that mode of religious practice without any serious concern for fulfilling alternative viewpoints. For example, Rabbi Epstein declines to adopt Rabbi Kagan's stringent approach to the question of what kind of garment one should wear in order to fulfill the biblical obligation of wearing *tzitzit*.[20] Rather than recommending that one wear a wool garment in order to avoid resolving the dispute over whether non-wool and non-linen garments are biblically obligated to have *tzitzit* strings attached, Rabbi Epstein comes down solidly in support of the opinion expressed by Rabbi Moses Isserles and others: all garments are biblically obligated in the commandment of *tzitzit*.[21] Rabbi Epstein supports his conclusion with what he is moderately convinced is the correct understanding of the relevant Talmudic discussions,[22] as well as with the fact that this view enjoys substantial support among rabbinic authorities.[23] Importantly, once he concludes that Rabbi Isserles's more permissive view is normatively correct, Rabbi Epstein sees no need to incorporate Maimonides's more demanding opinion into his practical *halakhic* conclusions, even though this means that those relying on Rabbi Epstein's ruling will not have fulfilled the obligation to wear *tzitzit* according to Maimonides.

Similarly, in the case of Passover Eve that coincides with the Sabbath, Rabbi Epstein declines to adopt Rabbi Kagan's approach of prescribing that people eat the second and third Sabbath meals on the morning of the Sabbath so as to satisfy both the *halakhic* opinions of those who think that the third meal on such a Sabbath should consist of *matzah* made with fruit juices, as well as those who reject that possibility and instead recommend eating a meal of fruits and meats without bread. Rather than seeking to satisfy these opinions, Rabbi Epstein prescribes a third approach that rejects

---

19 See Michael J. Broyde & Ira Bedzow, The Codification of Jewish Law: An Introduction to the Jurisprudence of the Mishna Berura 292-93 (2014).
20 See Arukh HaShulchan, Orach Chaim 9:1; Mishnah Berurah, Orach Chaim 9:5.
21 See Arukh HaShulchan, Orach Chaim 9:1.
22 See Arukh HaShulchan, Orach Chaim 9:1. *See also supra* Chapter Four.
23 See Arukh HaShulchan, Orach Chaim 9:1. *See also supra* Chapter Five.

both views.[24] Based on a passage of the *Zohar*, Rabbi Epstein concludes that there is actually no obligation to eat a third Sabbath meal on a Sabbath that coincides with Passover Eve.[25] Since the *halakhah* prohibits the consumption of both *chametz* and *matzah* on the afternoon of Passover Eve, the ordinary obligation to eat a third meal on Sabbath afternoon is suspended, much like it is suspended when the Sabbath coincides with the fast day of Yom Kippur. Since the obligation to eat a third meal is thus suspended, Rabbi Epstein explains that there is no need to figure out ways to eat such a meal given the restrictions on consuming bread or *matzah* at that time.[26]

Rabbi Epstein similarly declines to incorporate a normatively rejected *halakhic* opinion regarding the obligation to verbalize the recitation of blessings. Rabbi Karo codifies the well-settled rule that blessings said prior to eating food must actually be verbalized; the words must "go out from the lips," and ideally should also be recited loudly enough for the one reciting the blessing to hear his own words.[27] If one merely thinks the words of the blessing instead of properly verbalizing them, however, one has not fulfilled the obligation to recite the blessing and must recite the blessing properly. Rabbi Epstein notes that Maimonides disagrees with this view and rules that while blessings should be verbalized, if one merely thought the blessing, one has still fulfilled one's obligation.[28] Moreover, according to this view, since the obligation to recite a blessing is minimally satisfied by thinking the blessing in one's mind, if one did so (though it is not ideal), one should not recite the blessing again verbally, as this would amount to reciting an unnecessary blessing and taking God's name in vain.[29] While Rabbi Epstein is usually deferential to Maimonides's rulings,[30] in this case, he rules that one must recite aloud a blessing that was initially only thought but not verbalized. Rabbi Epstein states that a near-universal consensus of *halakhic* authorities rejects Maimonides's view here based on the well-settled Talmudic principle that thinking something is not the same as verbalizing it, and therefore a blessing that was thought but not verbalized is considered not to have been recited at all.[31] The weight of consensus to establish the correct

---

24 *See* Arukh HaShulchan, Orach Chaim 444:6.
25 *See* ibid.
26 *See* ibid.
27 Shulchan Arukh, Orach Chaim 206:3.
28 *See* Arukh HaShulchan, Orach Chaim 206:5.
29 *See* ibid.
30 *See supra* Chapter Six.
31 *See* Arukh HaShulchan, Orach Chaim 206:5.

Talmudic norm is so strong here that it even overrides Rabbi Epstein's usual concern about making unnecessary blessings.[32] According to Maimonides, the internally thought blessing is sufficient to fulfill one's ritual obligation, and repeating the blessing verbally would thus amount to taking God's name in vain. The rabbinic consensus rejecting Maimonides's view establishes the law, however, and it thus preempts the doubt-resolving rule that instructs one not to make blessings in doubtful cases. Moreover, since Maimonides's opinion is rejected by the countervailing weight of *halakhic* consensus, Rabbi Epstein sees no reason to be concerned about rejecting Maimonides's view and rules that one must repeat a blessing that was previously only thought and not verbalized.[33]

Rabbi Epstein's disinclination to regularly incorporate rejected opinions into his normative *halakhic* determinations does not mean, however, that such rejected rabbinic viewpoints are irrelevant or entirely outside the realm of *halakhic* decision-making. In rabbinic jurisprudence, even generally rejected legal opinions remain legally viable to some degree—they can be relied upon and utilized to reach appropriate conclusions in a variety of cases. This idea is well expressed by the Mishnah, which teaches that even rejected legal opinions are recorded and preserved in classical rabbinic texts because such opinions, while not normative, nevertheless may prove useful in special circumstances. As the Mishnah itself states, "Why . . . preserve the opinion of an individual against that of a rabbinic majority if the law follows the view of the majority? This is so that if another court finds the opinion of the individual compelling, it can rely on it, for a court cannot abrogate the ruling of another court unless it is greater than it in both wisdom and number."[34] In explaining this text, many commentators argue that the Mishnah is confirming that even those *halakhic* opinions that end up rejected due to the ordinary rules of *halakhic* jurisprudence—rules like "follow the majority" against a minority view—remain viable modes of practice in non-normative situations.[35] A parallel Tannaitic text helps explicate this point: "The minority opinions are recorded together with majority opinions so that they can be utilized if ever cases arise where it is necessary to rely on them."[36] Illustrating this principle, the Talmud itself supports reliance on a

---

32 See *supra* Chapters Five and Six.
33 See Arukh HaShulchan, Orach Chaim 206:5.
34 Mishnah, Eduyot 1:5.
35 See Nathaniel Helfgot, *Minority Opinions and Their Role in Hora'ah* 4 Milin Havivin 36, 42-43 (2010).
36 Tosefta, Eduyot 1:5.

non-normative minority view that is otherwise generally not accepted as legally correct in exigent circumstances. For example, Jewish law prescribes the recital of the *Shema* prayer twice each day: once in the morning and once at night.[37] Mishnaic rabbis debated when exactly night turns into day, thereby concluding the permissible time frame for reciting the *Shema* at night. According to a majority of the rabbis, "day" begins at dawn; thus, one may only fulfill one's obligation to recite the *Shema* prayer at night up until the following dawn. Rabbi Shimon bar Yochai disagrees, however. According to Rabbi Shimon, daytime does not begin until actual sunrise sometime after dawn; therefore, the nighttime *Shema* may be recited even after dawn so long as the sun has not yet risen. While Rabbi Shimon's minority opinion is rejected as a matter of normative *halakhah*, which rules that "day" begins at dawn for legal purposes,[38] the Talmud maintains that one may rely on Rabbi Shimon's view in extenuating circumstances, stating plainly that "Rabbi Shimon is worthy of being relied upon in pressing times."[39] For instance, if external conditions prevented one from reciting the *Shema* prior to dawn, one may rely on the opinion of Rabbi Shimon *ex post facto* and fulfill the obligation to recite the *Shema* at night up until sunrise.

The use of otherwise rejected opinions in special cases is a prominent and oft-relied-upon principle of *halakhic* decision-making that is utilized and endorsed by rabbinic decisors. Rabbi Moses Isserles, for instance, rules that *halakhic* opinions which have been rejected by operation of the standard secondary rules of *halakhic* decision-making can nevertheless be utilized to reach acceptable legal conclusions in cases involving pressing needs, as well as cases in which following the normative view would produce substantial financial losses.[40] Several hundred years before Rabbi Isserles codified this standard, Rabbi Isaac ben Moses of Vienna, known as the *Or Zarua* (1200-1270), applied this principle in practice to the case of a rotten citron and dried-out palm branch. Jewish law prescribes that Jews bundle together an *etrog*, or citron, and a *lulav*, consisting of a palm branch, myrtle twigs, and willows, which are then used for ritual purposes during the biblical holiday of Sukkot (the Feast of Tabernacles). Mishnaic rabbis debated whether dried-out specimens were suitable for ritual use; according to an anonymous view recorded in the Mishnah, such dry palm branches and citrons may not be used, while Rabbi Yehudah rules that they

---

37 *See* Mishnah, Berakhot 1:1.
38 Rosh *to* Babylonian Talmud, Berakhot 1:9.
39 Babylonian Talmud, Berakhot 9a.
40 *See* Rema *to* Shulchan Arukh, Choshen Mishpat 25:2.

are ritually valid.[41] Various secondary rules of adjudication and principles of Talmudic interpretation support the less permissive anonymous opinion as normative and reject Rabbi Yehudah's position. Recognizing that Rabbi Yehudah's more permissive opinion, permitting the ritual use of a dry palm branch, is rejected by normative *halakhah*, Rabbi Isaac nevertheless writes:

> In a case of pressing need, where one cannot find a proper palm branch or citron, one may recite the ritual blessing upon a dry palm branch or rotten citron because Rabbi Yehudah is a sufficiently important authority whose opinion can be relied upon in pressing circumstances. While the law is that, in cases of a dispute between a majority and minority, the *halakhah* follows the majority view, here, the Talmud did not explicitly exclude Rabbi Yehudah's opinion [as it is rejected only by operation of accepted secondary rules of decision and Talmudic interpretation], and we may rely on his view in cases of great need.[42]

Rabbi Epstein follows this classic rabbinic model as well and uses normatively rejected opinions to help the *halakhic* system address a variety of unusual or pressing circumstances. Specifically, as we shall see, Rabbi Epstein utilizes rejected opinions to resolve rabbinic disputes, decide complex questions, justify unlawful but widespread common practices, justify prohibited conduct in extenuating circumstances, and justify unnecessarily stringent modes of religious practice.

Halakhah is a deeply interconnected system of law and normative reasoning. Some doctrines and rules are confined to particular subject areas—yet at the same time, ideas, interpretations, and lines of reasoning in one sphere of Jewish law have relevance to and can be utilized to illuminate entirely different areas. For this reason, rabbinic scholars have often expressed the idea that ideally, true competence in *halakhic* decision-making and jurisprudence requires both great depth of legal understanding as well as extreme breadth of Jewish legal knowledge so that rabbinic decisors will fully appreciate and account for this web of interconnected legal subject matter and doctrine.[43] One consequence of this interconnectedness is that rabbinic opinions about

---

41 *See* Babylonian Talmud, Sukkah 31b.
42 Or Zarua 2:306.
43 *See, e.g.*, Rabbi Tzvi Hirsch Eisenstadt, Pitchei Teshuva *to* Shulchan Arukh, Yoreh Deah 242:8, and sources cited therein. For other discussions about the breadth and depth of knowledge expected of competent rabbinic decisors, *see* Responsa Rosh 31:9; Beit Yosef *to*

one area of *halakhah* may have relevance to other questions in different areas of the law.[44] This interconnectedness gives rise to one of the ways in which Rabbi Epstein makes use of normatively rejected rabbinic opinions in his *halakhic* decision-making. Specifically, Rabbi Epstein draws upon *halakhic* viewpoints that were rejected in favor of alternative rulings in some areas of Jewish law, and he uses these rejected positions to help resolve rabbinic disputes and determine legal questions about other issues.

One rather complex example of this kind of use of rejected rabbinic opinions relates to the question of when and under what conditions a person who is interrupted in the midst of the performance of a particular ritual obligation must, when resuming the performance, begin anew from the beginning of that ritual observance. It is generally accepted that if the length of such an interruption is less than the amount of time it would normally take to fully perform the obligation, then one may simply resume performing the interrupted observance, starting from the point at which the interruption occurred.[45] *Halakhic* authorities disagree, however, about how to proceed in cases where the length of the interruption is equal to or greater than the amount of time it would normally take to perform the entire ritual observance that one was engaged in at the time of the interruption.[46] According to Maimonides, the *Rif*, and Rabbi Joseph Karo, the proper approach depends on the kind of ritual observance one was performing before being interrupted. If one was interrupted while in the middle of praying the *Amidah* (the central liturgy of each of the three daily prayer services), and the interruption lasted long enough for one to have said the entire prayer, one must begin reciting the *Amidah* from the beginning of the prayer after the conclusion of the interruption. When it comes to all other observances, however, one need not repeat the entire practice following a lengthy interruption.[47] An alternative view is offered by *Tosafot*, the *Arbah*

Arbah Turim, *Introduction* (describing the broad array of *halakhic* sources with which one must in principle be familiar in order to competently determine the *halakhah*).

44 See, e.g., Babylonian Talmud, Bava Batra 28a (adverse possession rules derived from parameters of negligence liability in property tort law); Rabbi Howard Jachter & Rabbi Michael Broyde, *Electrically Produced Fire and Light and Positive Commandments*, 25 Journal of Halacha and Contemporary Society 89 (Spring 1993) (describing how understandings of the *halakhic* nature of electricity in some areas of Jewish law impact many other ritual practices).

45 See Babylonian Talmud, Rosh Hashanah 34b; Babylonian Talmud, Megillah 11b; Shulchan Arukh, Orach Chaim 65:1.

46 *See generally* Arukh HaShulchan, Orach Chaim 65:1-2.

47 *See* ibid. 65:1.

Turim, and many other authorities: they rule that the *halakhic* standard depends on the nature of the interruption rather than the nature of the ritual observance that was interrupted. If the interruption was voluntary, then one need not restart the observance no matter the length of the interruption, because it is as if the person intended to return and finish the observance the entire time. If, however, the lengthy interruption was involuntary, one must begin the ritual observance anew after the interruption ends.[48] While the Talmudic sources on this issue offer no determinative standard, Rabbi Epstein adopts the second approach of *Tosafot* and the *Arbah Turim* because it is endorsed by a strong consensus of other *halakhic* authorities.[49]

Rabbi Epstein's ruling that one need only restart a ritual observance following a lengthy interruption if the interruption was involuntary does not fully resolve the issue, however. This is because those authorities who endorse the second approach described above disagree amongst themselves about what kinds of interruptions qualify as "involuntary."[50] According to the *Raabad* and the *Baal HaMaor*, only interruptions that are imposed by the *halakhah* are truly involuntary; other interruptions, however, are not.[51] Thus, for instance, since Jewish law prohibits praying in an unclean place, if one interrupts one's prayers in order to use a restroom, the interruption is regarded as involuntary. If the interruption was long enough, one must begin reciting the interrupted prayer from the beginning. By contrast, if one's prayers were interrupted by other, non-legal causes, such as a fire, animal attack, or other phenomena, the interruption would be considered voluntary, and one would not need to restart the prayer afterward, no matter how long the interruption lasted. Many other authorities disagree with the *Raabad* and *Baal HaMaor*.[52] This second view maintains that "involuntary" interruptions include all interruptions that one does not willingly create—including natural events such as attacks by bandits or animals—for which the *halakhah* itself does not prescribe an interruption.[53] On this question, Rabbi Epstein rules in accordance with the first position of

---

48 *See* ibid. 65:2.
49 *See* ibid. 65:4.
50 On the role of *oness*, or involuntarily being prevented from observing a legal obligation, see generally 1 Encyclopedia Talmudit 347-359 (1990).
51 *See* Arukh HaShulchan, Orach Chaim 65:4.
52 *See* ibid. 65:4.
53 *See* ibid. 65:2.

the *Raabad* and the *Baal HaMaor*, which states that only legally imposed interruptions are considered truly "involuntary."[54]

Rabbi Epstein thus rejects the view of Maimonides on the issue of which kinds of interruptions require one to restart an observance, as well as the views of those authorities that rule that all unwilled interruptions are considered "involuntary." Nevertheless, Rabbi Epstein utilizes both of these rejected opinions in the specific case of one who takes a long pause in the recital of the *Amidah* prayer due to an interruption not imposed by the *halakhah*. In such a case, Rabbi Epstein rules that one must begin the *Amidah* prayer anew.[55] This is because the case of an interrupted *Amidah* prayer involves the intersection of both the view that any interruption of the *Amidah* requires one to restart the prayer from the beginning as well as the view that "involuntary" interruptions include even non-legally imposed pauses in a ritual performance. While each of these opinions is normatively rejected in isolation, the confluence of both opinions in the same case (in Rabbi Epstein's view) works to justify the ritually stringent conclusion that one must repeat the entire *Amidah* prayer after an extended, involuntary interruption.[56]

Rabbi Epstein also uses rejected authorities to help decide particularly complex *halakhic* questions, the resolutions of which compound a number of different legal issues. In such cases, Rabbi Epstein is willing to rely on the weight of several rejected opinions on the ancillary legal issues to overrule what he views as the more abstractly correct *halakhic* opinion on the broader issue. This use of rejected authority is illustrated by the following example from Rabbi Epstein's discussion of the laws of *tzitzit*, the ritual fringes worn on the corners of some garments in observance of the Torah commandment to "make twisted cords on the corners of your garments."[57] The *Sifri*, a primary *halakhic* work of the Talmudic period, notes that the Torah's use of the word "cord" (*petil*) in reference to *tzitzit* fringes indicates that these fringes should be made of wool that has been spun into threads, which are then woven together into a cord.[58] Most authorities understand the *Sifri*'s position—that the requirements for both the spinning and weaving of *tzitzit* threads are mandated by the same biblical word—as indicating that the same rules apply to both aspects of the *tzitzit* fringe manufacturing process. Based on this view, just as the wool

---

54 *See* ibid. 65:4.
55 *See* ibid. 65:4.
56 *See* ibid. 65:4.
57 Deuteronomy 22:12. *See also* Numbers 15:38-40.
58 *See* Sifri Numbers §115.

must be spun into thread with the specific intent to use the thread for *tzitzit*,[59] so too, the threads must be woven into cords with the specific intent to use those cords for *tzitzit* fringes.[60] Maimonides disagrees with this understanding of the *Sifri*, however, and he rejects the idea that *tzitzit* fringes must be woven out of several threads.[61] According to Maimonides, the *Sifri*'s reading does not serve to require that *tzitzit* fringes be woven of several threads; instead, it merely permits such strings. Since the Torah prescribes that *tzitzit* should consist of eight fringes on each corner of a garment, one might think that using eight woven cords would be prohibited because each cord is made up of several threads, and this would effectively mean that there were more than eight fringes on each corner of the garment, potentially in violation of the *halakhah*'s eight-string prescription. The *Sifri*, Maimonides says, comes to counter this line of reasoning, confirming that once threads are woven into a cord, that cord is treated as only a single *tzitzit* string.[62] Rabbi Epstein notes that he thinks that the Talmud actually supports Maimonides's view, but virtually all other authorities disagree with Maimonides and rule that *tzitzit* strings must be woven from several threads (though some validate such unwoven strings *ex post*).[63] Rabbi Epstein rules accordingly, following the consensus view against Maimonides's position.

Separate from the question of whether *tzitzit* strings must be woven, rabbinic decisors debated whether such weaving must be done with the specific intent to use the resulting cords for *tzitzit*.[64] The Talmud rules that *tzitzit* must be produced with the intent that the resulting fringed garment is to be used for ritual fulfillment of the Torah's command to wear *tzitzit*.[65] Some authorities, Rabbi Epstein notes, indicate that in contrast to spinning the wool into threads (which must be done with intent to use the threads for *tzitzit*), weaving threads into cords need not be done with such specific intent.[66] This position seems to cut against the plain meaning of the *Sifri*, which equated the spinning and the weaving of *tzitzit* strings. However, Rabbi Epstein suggests that this approach may be justified by viewing the cord-weaving process, even if done

---

59 *See* Babylonian Talmud, Menachot 42b.
60 *See, e.g.,* Magen Avraham *to* Shulchan Arukh, Orach Chaim 11:3.
61 *See* Mishneh Torah, Hilkhot Tzitzit 1:10.
62 Arukh HaShulchan, Orach Chaim 11:2.
63 *See* ibid. 11:3.
64 *See generally* ibid. 11:3.
65 *See* Babylonian Talmud, Menachot 42b.
66 *See* Arbah Turim, Orach Chaim 11; Arukh HaShulchan, Orach Chaim 11:3.

without proper intent, as merely a continuation of the initial wool-spinning process (which would have been done with the necessary intent to produce *tzitzit* strings).[67]

In any case, Rabbi Epstein rules that in cases where a set of *tzitzit* strings is indeed made of woven cords—but those cords have not been woven with proper intent—one may utilize such fringes to fulfill the ritual obligation of *tzitzit*, so long as the wool was initially spun with the proper intent.[68] This conclusion relies both on Maimonides's rejected minority position that weaving is not necessary at all, as well as on the questionable opinion that the weaving of threads into cords need not be done with the specific intent to use the cords for *tzitzit*. While each of these views is rejected in its own right, Rabbi Epstein rules against Maimonides's view that *tzitzit* strings must be woven. He also rules against those who think that the weaving does not require proper intent *ex ante*—instead, he utilizes these rejected opinions in order to resolve the more complex question of the post hoc *halakhic* suitability of *tzitzit* strings woven into cords without proper intent.[69]

Rabbi Epstein also utilizes rejected *halakhic* opinions to provide support for popular customs that cut against normative *halakhic* standards. As discussed later in chapter ten, Rabbi Epstein gives great legal weight to popular modes of religious practice. While in principle Rabbi Epstein does prohibit popular customs that are incompatible with *halakhic* requirements, the high regard in which he views religious custom leads him to attempt to justify customs that are in tension with normative standards of religious conduct. One of the ways in which Rabbi Epstein legitimates such customs is by justifying them in light of the existence of alternative and otherwise normatively rejected *halakhic* opinions.

One example of this use of rejected opinions concerns the recitation of the *Shehechiyanu* blessing on the second day of Rosh Hashanah.[70] While Rosh Hashanah is a two-day holiday, it is different from every other major holiday in that it is celebrated for two days even in the Land of Israel. Other major holidays are celebrated for one day in the Land of Israel and for two days in the diaspora in order to ensure that diaspora communities actually celebrate the holiday on

---

67 See Arukh HaShulchan, Orach Chaim 11:3.
68 See ibid. 11:3.
69 For some other examples of this kind of use of rejected opinions in Rabbi Epstein's jurisprudence, see ibid. 11:8, 65:4.
70 See ibid. 600:1-2.

the correct calendar date.[71] During Talmudic times, the calendar was set by the *Sanhedrin*'s formal declaration of the start of each new month based on a local sighting of the new moon. Since it took time to communicate this information to far-flung communities across the diaspora, the Rabbis declared that Jews outside the Land of Israel should celebrate each one-day holiday for two days, as this would ensure that one of the two celebrated days would be the correct biblically prescribed calendrical date of the holiday. Rosh Hashanah, however, is celebrated for two days, even in the Land of Israel. This is because Rosh Hashanah occurs on the first day of the month of Tishrei, and it was often the case that the *Sanhedrin* would receive testimony about a new moon sighting on the previous night late in the day. This resulted in that entire day having been the first day of Tishrei and thus the holiday of Rosh Hashanah—but without the proper ritual observances having been practiced— since it was not known that the day was Rosh Hashanah until the appearance of witnesses late that afternoon. To avoid this, Tannaitic authorities legislated that all, including those in the land of Israel, should observe Rosh Hashanah for two days following the twenty-eighth day of the previous month of Elul. This practice continued, both in the diaspora and in Israel, even once the calendar was fixed and no longer depended on witness sightings of the new moon.[72]

The extension of Rosh Hashanah into a two-day holiday and the two-day observance of other holidays in the diaspora are thus qualitatively different. While other holidays were observed for two days due to genuine doubts as to the correct calendar day,[73] Rosh Hashanah was observed for two days in order to avoid the religious and ritual concerns that would otherwise result from sometimes beginning a day thinking it was the final day of the previous month, only to discover later that afternoon—following the appearance of witnesses to the previous night's new moon—that the entire day had actually been the first of Tishrei, Rosh Hashanah. Consequently, while each of the two days of other holidays were considered distinct days for ritual purposes—with the second day essentially constituting a complete ritual repetition of the first day due to calendrical doubt—the two days of Rosh Hashanah took on a different character and were in some sense thought of as "one long day."[74]

---

71 *See generally* Jerusalem Talmud, Eruvin 3:9; Mishneh Torah, Hilkhot Kiddush HaChodesh 5:7-8.
72 *See* Mishneh Torah, Hilkhot Kiddush HaChodesh 5:7-8; Arukh HaShulchan, Orach Chaim 600:1-2.
73 *See* Jerusalem Talmud, Rosh Hashanah 2:1.
74 *See* Arukh HaShulchan, Orach Chaim 600:1-2.

CHAPTER SEVEN • Non-Normative Opinions | 151

The hybrid character of the two-day celebration of Rosh Hashanah led to an early rabbinic dispute regarding whether or not one should recite the *Shehechiyanu* blessing, which recognizes the uniqueness of the day, on the second day of the holiday.[75] On other holidays, all agree that the *Shehechiyanu* blessing is recited on both days, since the second day is celebrated out of doubt and thus may be the true and correct date for the holiday celebration. This is not so, however, with respect to the second day of Rosh Hashanah. According to *Rashi*, one should recite the *Shehechiyanu* blessing upon the second day of Rosh Hashanah because the Torah establishes Rosh Hashanah as a one-day holiday, and therefore the blessing should be recited for each of the current two one-day holidays rather than only one time for an extended two-day holiday. Some earlier authorities disagree with *Rashi*, however, and they rule that one should recite the *Shehechiyanu* blessing only on the first day of Rosh Hashanah.[76]

Rabbi Epstein accepts *Rashi*'s view because it is supported by a consensus of *halakhic* authorities, virtually all of whom have endorsed the view that each day of Rosh Hashanah gets a separate *Shehechiyanu* blessing.[77] While adopting *Rashi*'s view, Rabbi Epstein commends the practice of wearing a new item of clothing or including a new fruit as part of the evening meal on the second day of Rosh Hashanah. Since such occasions justify, in their own right, the recitation of the *Shehechiyanu* blessing,[78] one can recite the blessing with the intent that it covers both the incidence of the second day of Rosh Hashanah as well as the new fruit or garment. In this way, one can recite the blessing as required by *Rashi* without having recited an unnecessary blessing, even according to those who hold that no blessing should be recited on the second day of Rosh Hashanah.[79] While Rabbi Epstein does not typically feel the need to construct *halakhic* practices that help satisfy rejected opinions, here he does endorse a practice designed to fulfill the views of both those who support and those who

---

75   On the obligation to recite this blessing, see Babylonian Talmud, Berakhot 54a; Babylonian Talmud, Eruvin 40b; Arukh HaShulchan, Orach Chaim 225:1.
76   *See* Arukh HaShulchan, Orach Chaim 600:4, citing the view of *Rashi*, and noting the disagreement on the matter among authorities.
77   *See* Arukh HaShulchan, Orach Chaim 600:4.
78   *See* Shulchan Arukh, Orach Chaim 223:3 (permitting recitation of the blessing upon purchasing new clothes), 225:3 (permitting the recitation of the blessing upon eating a new fruit).
79   *See* ibid. 600:2.

oppose the recitation of the *Shehechiyanu* on the second day of Rosh Hashanah because, as he notes, "It is the established custom in all our lands" to do so.[80]

As mentioned above, one of the most prominent and common uses of rejected *halakhic* opinions is to reach more acceptable legal outcomes in hard cases with extenuating circumstances or cases where the application of normative *halakhic* standards would produce substantial hardship. Rabbi Epstein, too, uses normatively rejected *halakhic* opinions in this way. For instance, a substantial consensus of *halakhic* authorities rules that if one failed to etch guiding lines into the parchment used to write *tefillin* scrolls (and as a result, the lines of written text on the scroll are uneven or crooked), the *tefillin* are thereby invalid.[81] Maimonides disagrees, however, and he rules that *tefillin* scrolls do not require that guiding lines be etched into the parchment.[82] Rabbi Epstein rejects Maimonides's position as a matter of normative *halakhah* and instead endorses the consensus view that *tefillin* written without guidelines on the parchment are invalid.[83] Nevertheless, he does see fit to draw on Maimonides's normatively rejected opinion to address the extenuating circumstance where the only available *tefillin* contain scrolls written on unlined parchment; in that case, Rabbi Epstein rules that one may rely on Maimonides's rejected view and don such *tefillin* rather than forego observance of this ritual duty entirely.[84]

In another case, the Talmud records that the Rabbis legislated that one may not use wooden planks as *skhakh* to form the roof of a *sukkah* if the planks are wider than four handbreadths.[85] Rabbi Epstein explains that the reason for this rule is that one who uses such wide planks as *skhakh* may come to think that the roof of a *sukkah* is no different than the roof of a house (since regular roofs were also made of wide wooden boards) and may then mistakenly spend the Sukkot holiday in his regular house, which is certainly invalid for ritual use as a *sukkah*.[86] By its own Talmudic terms, however, this rule is limited to wooden

---

80 Arukh HaShulchan, Orach Chaim 600:4, citing the view of *Rashi*, and noting the disagreement on the matter among authorities.
81 Torah scrolls, as well as other copies of biblical texts made for ritual use, such as *mezuzot* and *tefillin*, are handwritten on parchment scrolls. Jewish law demands that such texts be written neatly and respectfully, and requires the parchments on which these texts are written to be scored with guiding lines, or *sirtut*, etched into the parchment. See Babylonian Talmud, Menachot 32b. *See also* Arukh HaShulchan, Orach Chaim 32:17.
82 *See* Mishneh Torah, Hilkhot Tefillin 1:12.
83 *See* Arukh HaShulchan, Orach Chaim 32:18.
84 *See* ibid.
85 *See* Babylonian Talmud, Sukkah 14a.
86 *See* Arukh HaShulchan, Orach Chaim 629:30.

planks that are more than four handbreadths wide; only such wide planks may be confused for regular roofing, and narrower boards may therefore be used as *skhakh* for a *sukkah*.[87] While the Talmudic enactment only invalidates a *sukkah* covered with wide planks, Rabbi Joseph Karo notes that the customary practice is to avoid using even such narrower boards for *skhakh*.[88] In his own ruling on the matter, however, Rabbi Epstein goes even further: keeping with his conviction that Talmudic norms must be applied contextually,[89] Rabbi Epstein rules that in his own time, even a *sukkah* covered with wooden boards narrower than four handbreadths is ritually invalid because narrow planks are regularly used to build regular roofs; therefore, a *sukkah* covered by narrow boards may be easily confused for regular roofing as well.[90] Rabbi Epstein's understanding of the correct application of the Talmudic rule in his own context thus results in the normative rejection of Rabbi Karo's nominal permission to use narrow planks to cover a *sukkah*. Still, Rabbi Epstein rules that in a case where one is unable to find any other *skhakh*, one may rely on Rabbi Karo's understanding of the limits of the original Talmudic decree and build a *sukkah* using narrow planks.[91] While he rejects Rabbi Karo's position that it is merely customary—and not strictly prohibited—to not use narrow planks as *skhakh*, Rabbi Epstein is willing to utilize this otherwise rejected opinion in the extenuating circumstance where one cannot find any other more suitable *skhakh* material.[92]

When deployed to resolve hard cases, rejected legal opinions tend to produce more lenient *halakhic* standards. Rejected opinions can also be used to justify more stringent religious practice, however. As discussed below, Rabbi Epstein generally does not prescribe the observance of supererogatory practices—religious standards that go beyond the demands of normative *halakhah*—and indeed often opposes them when they do not serve some other positive religious purpose.[93] Rabbi Epstein does, however, find acceptable the observance of unnecessarily strict, personal ritual practices when those practices are undertaken in order to satisfy legally significant but normatively rejected *halakhic* opinions.

---

87 *See* Shulchan Arukh, Orach Chaim 629:18.
88 *See* ibid.
89 *See infra* Chapter Eleven.
90 *See* Arukh HaShulchan, Orach Chaim 629:32.
91 *See* ibid.
92 *See* ibid.
93 *See infra* Chapter Eight.

One example of this involves the correct definition of a ritually fit *lulav*, or palm frond, which is one of the four species the Torah commands Jews to "take" during the Sukkot holiday.[94] The Talmud rules that a palm branch with a split *tiyomet* cannot be used to fulfill the biblical obligation.[95] Early rabbinic authorities disagreed over the precise definition of the *tiyomet*. Rabbi Isaac Alfasi and Maimonides note that every leaf on a palm frond is actually made up of two leaves that are joined along one long edge. These scholars maintain that when the Talmud invalidates a *lulav* with a split *tiyomet*, it refers to the long, connected edge where every two *lulav* leaves are joined—a *lulav* is ritually unfit if a majority of its leaves are split along this conjoined side.[96] *Rashi*, however, rules that the *tiyomet* refers not to the conjoined edge of every two leaves on a palm branch; rather, it refers specifically to the spine of the *lulav*, which splits into two separate leaves.[97] Based on this view, a split *tiyomet* refers to a split in the spine of the *lulav* itself between the two leaves that extend from the spine higher up on the branch. Some later authorities note that the palm fronds that they are familiar with do not comport with *Rashi*'s description. Rather than having two leaves protruding from a central spine, every *lulav* has a single double-leaf joined along one side that extends upward from the top of the *lulav*'s spine. In light of this observed reality, and based on a slightly different definition of the *tiyomet* that *Rashi* provides in a different Talmudic discussion, some authorities—including the *Terumat HaDeshen*—define the Talmud's "split *tiyomet*" as a split in the *lulav*'s single, doubled-over middle leaf, which extends upward from the spine.[98] Rabbi Joseph Karo rules in accordance with the position of Maimonides and the *Rif*—which was also adopted by many other authorities—that a *lulav* is only invalidated by a split *tiyomet* if most of its leaves are split along their conjoined edges; he does not even reference the alternative definition of the *tiyomet* offered by *Rashi*.[99] However, the *Rema*—following the accepted custom of his time—rules that a *lulav* is invalid when its middle leaf is split from the top down to the spine and that people should try to find palm fronds on which the middle leaf extending upward from the spine is not split at all.[100]

---

94 *See* Leviticus 23:40.
95 *See* Babylonian Talmud, Sukkah 32a.
96 *See* Arukh HaShulchan, Orach Chaim 645:5.
97 *See* ibid. 645:6.
98 *See* ibid. 645:6.
99 *See* Shulchan Arukh, Orach Chaim 645:3.
100 *See* Rema *to* Shulchan Arukh, Orach Chaim 645:3.

CHAPTER SEVEN • Non-Normative Opinions | 155

Rabbi Epstein expresses great surprise at Rabbi Isserles's decision to adopt *Rashi*'s minority view against the position of Maimonides, which was subsequently endorsed by the vast majority of rabbinic authorities. This is especially astounding, Rabbi Epstein says, because there is not even clarity about what *Rashi*'s definition of the *tiyomet* is, given his two inconsistent comments on the topic and the apparent incongruity between *Rashi*'s description of palm fronds and the actual appearance of *lulav* branches. Thus, Rabbi Epstein rules that as a matter of law, the majority view of Maimonides—that a *lulav* is invalid only if most of its leaves have been split in half—is correct.[101]

Despite this conclusion, however, Rabbi Epstein rules that in practice people should follow Rabbi Isserles's stricter view and find a *lulav* with an intact middle leaf, though he declines to rule that a *lulav* with a split middle leaf is actually invalid.[102] He justifies this conclusion by noting that the mere fact that this position was prescribed by the *Rema*, the preeminent codifier of Ashkenazic practice, justifies encouraging people to adhere to this higher standard for the suitability of *lulav* fronds. Likewise, the *Rema* adopts this view at least in part because it reflects the established practice of Ashkenazic communities, and this lends further support for the standard. Moreover, the obligation requiring ritually fit palm fronds on Sukkot is biblical and thus warrants concern for adhering to the stricter, albeit non-normative standard expressed by Rabbi Isserles.

* * * * *

The *Arukh HaShulchan* thus takes a two-pronged approach to the *halakhic* relevance of legal opinions that Rabbi Epstein regards as non-normative. In cases where Rabbi Epstein concludes that a particular rabbinic viewpoint is not reflective of the correct *halakhic* standard—whether based on his understandings of the Talmud, the existence of rabbinic consensus, or the consequences of his own application of doubt-resolving, secondary rules of decision—he sees no compelling need to account for and comply with that opinion in his own determinations in the *Arukh HaShulchan*. In contrast to some other rabbinic decisors, Rabbi Epstein does not typically prescribe modes of *halakhic* practice that are more rigorous than he thinks are truly and legally required merely to comply with rabbinic rulings he thinks are incorrect. At the same time, Rabbi Epstein does not regard such rejected viewpoints as entirely irrelevant or

---

101 *See* Arukh HaShulchan, Orach Chaim 645:10.
102 *See* ibid. 645:11.

outside the realm of *halakhic* discourse. Specifically, Rabbi Epstein often references opinions he believes are not normatively correct in order to help resolve otherwise intractable *halakhic* disputes, justify popular customs, or find pragmatic legal responses to difficult circumstances.

CHAPTER EIGHT

Supererogatory Religious Conduct

In this chapter, we continue our examination of Rabbi Epstein's methodological guidelines for resolving tensions between what he views as analytically correct Talmudic norms and other religious values. Here we will explain whether and under what circumstances the *Arukh HaShulchan* endorses or discourages supererogatory religious conduct that goes beyond what Rabbi Epstein believes are the strict requirements of the *halakhah*.

* * * * *

Principle Six: Rabbi Epstein generally encourages—but does not mandate—supererogatory behavior that goes beyond the minimal requirements of the halakhah, but only when there is a genuine benefit to such conduct in terms of religious values and observance.

Rabbinic jurisprudence has a long and complex tradition of relating to extralegal, supererogatory practices (modes of religious conduct that impose duties and strictures that go beyond the strict requirements of normative *halakhah*).[1] On the one hand, classical texts of Jewish law and thought contain

---

1 On Jewish pietistic movements that emphasized stringency in *halakhic* practice, see Elisha Russ-Fishbane, Judaism, Sufism, and the Pietists of Medieval Egypt (2015); Peter Schafer, The Ideal of Piety of the Ashkenazi Hasidim and Its Roots in Jewish Tradition, 4 Jewish History 9 (Fall 1990). See also Michael Silber, *The Historical Experience of German Jewry and Its Impact on the Haskalah and Reform in Hungary*, 107, *in* Jacob Katz, ed., Towards Modernity: The European Model (1987); Michael Silber, *The Emergence of Ultra-Orthodoxy: The Invention of a Tradition*, 43, *in* Jack Wertheimer, ed., The Use of Tradition: Jewish Continuity in The Modern Era (1992). *See also* Haym Soloveitchik, *Rupture and*

numerous passages attesting to the value and importance of ritual stringency and extralegal piety—the history of Jewish practice is similarly replete with examples of collective religious movements and individuals who adopted various supererogatory practices as positive expressions of religious devotion.[2] At the same time, some rabbinic sources also speak critically and harshly about the adoption of supererogatory religious practices, which they view as presumptuous, sinful, and likely to result in the disregard of actual *halakhic* requirements.[3]

Rabbinic sources provide endorsements of the positive religious value of—and even the need for—a variety of different kinds of supererogatory religious conduct. One prominent form of supererogatory behavior, which was previously discussed in chapter four, is used to avoid potential violations of Jewish law in cases where the correct *halakhic* norm or standard of practice is in doubt. As explained there, one of the principal doubt-resolving secondary rules of decision that is broadly embraced in rabbinic jurisprudence is the following Talmudic principle: "Doubts regarding biblical law are resolved strictly, and doubts about rabbinic laws are resolved leniently."

Supererogatory behaviors are also viewed as a means of preventing inadvertent violations of genuine legal strictures. Even when the right *halakhic* norms are clear and well known, some rules or concepts are prone to being accidentally violated due to confusion and the very real—though sometimes dismissed—slippery-slope. Recognizing this reality, rabbinic jurisprudence has long recommended the importance of "creating a fence around the Torah,"[4] which many commentators understand as a prescription for recognizing new *halakhic* strictures in order to help people avoid accidental violations of genuine Torah rules. Rabbi Jonah Gernodi (1200-1263) explained that this is a fulfillment of the biblical command "And you shall keep watch over My guarded

---

Reconstruction: The Transformation of Contemporary Orthodoxy, 28 Tradition 64, 64-65, 71-72 (Summer 1994).

2   See Leviticus 18:30; Babylonian Talmud, Moed Katan 5a; Mishnah, Avot 1:1 (directing the creation of "fences" around actual *halakhic* norms in order to ensure adherence to the law through the prescription of stringencies); Bartenurah *to* Mishnah, Avot 1:1 (s.v. *v'asu siyag laTorah*); Mishnah, Berakhot 1:1 (noting that the Talmudic Rabbis ruled that all obligations that may be performed all night must be completed before midnight as a stringency designed to better ensure compliance); Terumat HaDeshen, no. 232; Responsa Minchat Elazar 4:7.

3   *See, e.g.*, Babylonian Talmud, Berakhot 17b. Responsa Mahari Brunah, no. 97. *See generally* Daniel Goldstein, *The Role of Humrot*, 1 Hakirah 11 (2004).

4   Mishnah, Avot 1:1.

thing,"[5] which is understood as an instruction to rabbinic scholars to create sufficient safeguards to ensure that the actual laws of the Torah—God's "guarded thing"—are not transgressed.[6] Such preventative measures, known in rabbinic parlance as "*gezeirot*"[7] (literally meaning "decrees"), were used liberally by rabbinic authorities through the close of the Talmudic era to "make fences for the commandments so that one who fears God will not stumble" by accidentally violating genuine Torah commandments.[8]

In rabbinic tradition, the creation of such extralegal strictures dates back to biblical times. Following the rape of Tamar by her half-brother Amnon, a *gezeirah* designed to better protect single women from such illegal assaults was enacted by King David (their father) and his court.[9] Since Amnon was able to rape Tamar only after the two were secluded in his bedchamber while Tamar nursed Amnon's feigned illness, David's court declared that unmarried men and women may no longer seclude themselves, thereby creating a supererogatory prohibition that went beyond Torah law (which permits such seclusion so long as a secluded, unmarried couple does not engage in sexual conduct). A somewhat different example relates to Jewish dietary laws. While the Torah prohibits the consumption of mixtures of milk and animal meat, it does not prohibit the consumption of milk and fowl. Recognizing the obvious similarities between animal and bird meat, the Talmudic Rabbis enacted a *gezeirah* proscribing the consumption of mixtures of milk and fowl out of concern that those who regularly ate milk and chicken might inadvertently come to eat milk and animal meat, which is biblically prohibited.[10] In another vein, in order to better preserve the character of the Jewish Sabbath as a tranquil day of rest, the Talmudic Rabbis enacted many Sabbath-day ritual obligations and behavioral prohibitions that go far beyond the strict requirements imposed by the Torah itself.[11] For instance, the Torah only prohibits the performance of labors on the Sabbath when such labors are done intentionally, in an ordinary manner, and for constructive purposes. In order to better prevent Jews from inadvertently performing biblically prohibited labor on the Sabbath, the Rabbis extended

---

5   Leviticus 18:30.
6   *See* Rabbi Jonah Gerondi, Commentary on Mishnah Avot 1:1 (s.v. *v'asu seyag laTorah*). *See also* Babylonian Talmud, Moed Katan 5a.
7   Literally, "clean-cut determinations."
8   Rabbi Jonah Gerondi, Commentary on Mishnah Avot 1:1 (s.v. *v'asu seyag laTorah*).
9   *See generally* 2 Samuel 13.
10 *See* Mishnah, Chullin 8:1.
11 *See* Yitzchak Twersky, *Make a Fence Around the Torah* 8 Torah U-Madda Journal 25, 28-29 (1998).

the prohibition even to labors done in an abnormal way for destructive ends.[12] Likewise, in order to help Sabbath-observers maintain a proper focus on the tranquil character of the day, the Rabbis prohibited the handling of items not needed for enjoyment of the Sabbath day itself. They also prescribed the recital of a ritual blessing over a cup of wine recognizing the significance of the day as a commemoration of the creation of the world and the Jewish people's covenant with God.[13] Like the rabbinic prohibitions on seclusion between the sexes and the consumption of milk and chicken, these rules go beyond the legal demands imposed by the Torah itself in order to enhance religious experience and prevent sin.

Gezeirot, or fences built around the Torah, represent a special kind of supererogatory behavior.[14] In rabbinic jurisprudence, the original creation of a *gezeirah* represents the adoption of a new, extralegal religious demand. Once a *gezeirah* is enacted by properly constituted rabbinic authorities, it becomes obligatory and part of the fabric of *halakhah* itself, rendering its subsequent observance no longer truly supererogatory.[15] However, even after taking the totality of *halakhah*—both biblical and rabbinic law—as normative and obligatory, rabbinic thought is replete with calls for the voluntary adoption of religious practices and prohibitions that go "beyond the letter of the law." The principle that one should not merely seek to observe the law itself but should at times act "*lifnim meshurat hadin*" (beyond the letter of the law) is a central feature of rabbinic ethics. When it comes to interpersonal relationships, those who give others only their legal dues—while also demanding from others the full fulfillment of their own rights—are branded as exhibiting the characteristics of the Sodomites. According to rabbinic tradition, the Sodomites were destroyed because of their lack of generosity towards others and their inflexible adherence to law without regard for the values of mercy and equity.[16]

Likewise, the Talmud teaches that the Jews themselves were punished severely for merely seeking to fulfill the technical demands of the law without the willingness to move beyond *halakhic* requirements to adopt

---

12 *See* Mishneh Torah, Hilkhot Shabbat 1:7; Shitah Mekubetzet, Ketubot 5a (s.v. *b'hahi*).
13 *See* Tosafot *to* Babylonian Talmud, Shabbat 126b (s.v. *umedivreihen*); Shulchan Arukh, Orach Chaim 306:1, 307:1.
14 On *gezeirot* as rabbinic legislation, see Samuel J. Levine, 1 Jewish Law and American Law: A Comparative Study 63-82 (2018); Maimonides, *Introduction to the Mishna*, 41-42, *in* Introductions to Commentary on the Mishna (Mordechai Rabinowitz, ed., 1961).
15 *See* Mishneh Torah, Hilkhot Mamrim 2:3.
16 *See, e.g.*, Mishnah, Avot 5:10.

supererogatory behaviors: "Rabbi Yochanan said: Jerusalem [and the Second Temple] was only destroyed because they adjudicated strictly in accordance with the law ... and did not go beyond the letter of what the law required."[17] Furthermore, according to one passage, supererogatory conduct is actually biblically mandated, though the specific kind of extralegal conduct individuals ought to adopt is left open to personal discretion. The Torah states, "And you shall teach them the statutes and the laws and show them the path they shall walk within and the action that they must perform,"[18] which Mishnaic scholar Rabbi Joseph explains as follows: "And you shall teach them" refers to their means of earning a living; "the path" refers to acts of kindness; "they shall walk" refers to visiting the sick; "within" refers to burial; "and the action" refers to acting in accordance with the letter of the law; and "that they must perform" refers to acting beyond the letter of the law.[19]

In an important sense, the adoption of supererogatory religious practices indicates that one does not view Torah and *halakhah* as a burden. Rather than seeking to satisfy one's religious obligations by fulfilling the bare minimum of what the law requires, one who voluntarily engages in supererogatory behavior demonstrates genuine love for God and the divine will. Rabbinic sources thus regularly refer to one who acts more strictly than required by the law as a *baal nefesh*, a spiritual, soulful person. With respect to many supererogatory practices, they state, "One who is strict will be blessed."[20]

This sense of the positive value of supererogatory behavior is well expressed by two biblical commentaries offered by Nachmanides. In response to the Torah's command, "You shall be holy because I, God, am holy,"[21] Nachmanides writes:

> The idea of this commandment is that the Torah warned against forbidden sexual relationships and forbidden foods, but it permitted sexual relations between spouses and the consumption of [kosher] meat and wine. Thus, a person with strong desires could find room within the bounds of the law to become debased in sexual relations with his wife or wives,

---

17 Babylonian Talmud, Bava Metzia 30b.
18 Exodus 18:20.
19 Babylonian Talmud, Bava Metzia 30b.
20 *See, e.g.*, Babylonian Talmud, Pesachim 40a; Babylonian Talmud, Chullin 6a; Sefer HaChinukh, no. 293; Shulchan Arukh, Yoreh Deah 116:7, 148:12, 151:1; Mishnah Berurah, Orach Chaim 285:6, 345:23, 580:1.
21 Leviticus 19:2.

and to become a glutton and guzzler of meat and wine, and to speak however he wishes about all kinds of debased things, since there is no explicit prohibition against such speech in the Torah. And thus, he will become a debased and disgusting person all within the bounds of what is permitted by the Torah![22]

To forestall this eventuality, Nachmanides says, the Torah commands those subject to the law not to merely do as they wish without technically violating the law, but to "be holy." This holiness, as he understands it, entails going beyond the letter of the law and adopting supererogatory behaviors not required by the *halakhah* itself, thereby "sanctifying yourself through [avoiding] that which is permitted to you."[23] In a similar vein, Nachmanides explains that the Torah's instruction to do "that which is good and right in the eyes of God"[24] is a call for people to act with principle and care, even where the Torah's positive directives run out. It would be impossible, Nachmanides points out, for a fixed text like the Torah to clearly prescribe the correct course of conduct in every possible situation. Therefore, to supplement its determinate rules, the Torah also includes broad principles like "Do that which is right and good," which invites Torah law adherents to fill in the gaps left by the Torah's specific directives by reasoning inductively from explicit commandments to intuit correct actions in cases that are not provided for. Nachmanides writes that this includes compromising on one's own legal rights and going beyond the letter of the law when doing so serves to uphold "the right and the good."[25]

Examples of the positively received adoption of supererogatory religious practices abound in rabbinic literature and Jewish history. When discussing the laws governing the obligation to return lost property, for instance, the Talmud records numerous examples of rabbinic scholars returning items that they were legally permitted to keep in order to go beyond the letter of the law.[26] In another Talmudic case, Rabbi Chiya—a money changer by trade—was shown a coin in order to assess its authenticity. Rabbi Chiya confirmed the coin's authenticity and value, but the next day the customer reappeared, complaining that other money changers had disagreed with this assessment

---

22 Nachmanides, Commentary on the Torah: Leviticus 19:2 (s.v. *kedoshim tihyu*).
23 Nachmanides, Commentary on the Torah: Leviticus 19:2 (s.v. *kedoshim tihyu*).
24 Deuteronomy 6:18.
25 Nachmanides, Commentary on the Torah: Deuteronomy 6:18 (s.v. *v'asisah hatov v'hayashar*). See also Rashi ad loc. (s.v. *hayashar vehatov*).
26 See Babylonian Talmud, Bava Metzia 24b, 30b; Shulchan Arukh, Choshen Mishpat 264:1.

CHAPTER EIGHT • Supererogatory Religious Conduct | 163

and refused to honor the coin as valid. Rabbi Chiya proceeded to give the customer a valid coin on his own account in order to cover the loss, despite the fact that the law exempts professional money changers of liability for such ordinary mistakes. The Talmud approvingly notes that Rabbi Chiya did this as a supererogatory measure of personal piety.[27] In another instance, a number of students presented a donkey they had purchased from a Gentile seller to their teacher, the Mishnaic scholar Rabbi Shimon ben Shetach. Upon taking possession of the donkey, Rabbi Shimon discovered a valuable jewel hidden under the animal's saddle, which had certainly been placed there by the previous owners and forgotten prior to the sale. The students told Rabbi Shimon that the purchase agreement specified that the sale included "the donkey and everything that is on it," and indeed Rabbi Shimon acknowledged that by law he was entitled to keep the jewel. Still, Rabbi Shimon determined that he would go beyond the letter of the law and return the jewel, since in truth the owner could not have consciously intended to include the jewel in the sale.[28]

While the rabbinic tradition thus has many positive things to say about the value of supererogatory behavior, as with almost all topics in Jewish thought, the tradition does not speak with one voice. Alongside their substantial praise for supererogatory behavior, the rabbis also offered words of skepticism, caution, and even condemnation of the adoption of extralegal strictures not required by normative *halakhah*. Such attitudes characterize Midrashic treatments of one of the earliest and most foundational narratives of the Hebrew Bible: the story of Adam and Eve's expulsion from the Garden of Eden after eating the fruit of the Tree of Life. The early commentators noted a discrepancy on the biblical account of these events: While God commanded Adam, "Do not *eat* from the Tree of Life," in Eve's discussion with the serpent she relates, "God said that we may not eat *or touch* the fruit of the tree that stands in the middle of the Garden."[29] The Midrash explains the discrepancy in a way that highlights one of the dangers of supererogatory religious strictures:

> Rabbi Chiya taught: [The passage teaches us that] one should not make the fence greater than the primary [rule] in order that one not fall and come to uproot that which has been planted. God said, "On the day that you *eat* from it [you will surely die]," but she [Eve] did not say that. She

---

27 *See* Babylonian Talmud, Bava Kammah 99b.
28 *See* Jerusalem Talmud, Bava Metzia 2:5.
29 Genesis 2:17, 3:3.

said, "God said do not eat from it *and do not touch it.*" When he [the serpent] saw her passing by the tree, he took a fruit and pushed it against her. He said to her, "See, you [touched the fruit and] did not die; just as you did not die from touching it, you will not die from eating it."[30]

This reading of the biblical passage emphasized the fact that Eve expanded God's original prohibition; she went beyond the letter of the law to also restrict touching the fruit of the Tree of Life. Rather than leading to greater spiritual heights, however, Eve's adoption of this supererogatory stricture leads her to ultimately eat the fruit and violate God's actual command.[31]

This Midrashic account of the original sin highlights an oft-reported rabbinic concern about supererogatory behaviors, namely that the adoption of additional obligations and limitations beyond what is actually required by *halakhah* can lead to violations of the *halakhah* itself. In some cases, as with Eve, the adoption of supererogatory duties leads to the confusion of mandatory and elective religious practices, and this results in individuals violating actual legal norms along with supererogatory practices. In another sense, supererogatory behavior can also lead to unnecessary and avoidable rebellion against the law. Some rabbinic scholars have noted that there is a natural human tendency to chafe against restrictions.[32] The genuine duties and proscriptions of Jewish law produce such restrictions, and while some internal desire to rebel against these limitations is to be expected, Jews are charged to control that rebellious impulse and uphold their *halakhic* obligations. Indeed, rabbinic thought maintains that individuals are certainly capable of doing so, since "God does not give people challenges they are not able to overcome." The adoption of supererogatory practices, however, imposes additional, man-made ritual obligations. Such added duties impose greater restrictions, produce a stronger desire to rebel against external limitations, and offer no guaranteed ability to repress that rebellious desire (unlike divinely posited norms). The Talmud thus cautions, "One who prohibits that which is permitted will ultimately come to permit that which is [genuinely] prohibited."[33]

---

30 Midrash Rabbah, Genesis 19:3.
31 See also Avot D'Rabbi Natan 1:5 for a slightly different version in which Adam, not Eve, alters God's command to include the supererogatory stricture against touching the fruit.
32 *Cf.* Avot D'Rabbi Natan 1:7 ("Better a wall that is only ten *tefachim* high that will stand, than a wall one-hundred *amot* high that will collapse").
33 *See, e.g.*, Babylonian Talmud, Yevamot 31a; Niddah 24b.

Some rabbinic sources go even further. Not only can the adoption of supererogatory strictures lead to sin; it *is* sinful in its own right. This idea derives from the presumptuousness of a human being who purports to know what kinds of behavior are right and wrong better than God, as well as a person's decision to abstain from things and actions that God has permitted. The concept is well illustrated by rabbinic explanations of the biblical concept of the Nazarite, an individual who voluntarily undertakes an ascetic lifestyle in which he abstains from wine and other material enjoyments. The Torah prescribes that at the conclusion of one's period of abstention, the Nazarite must bring an offering into the Temple; this offering is the same kind of offering typically brought by one who has committed a sin. While one Talmudic view suggests that this sin offering is brought as a precaution in case the Nazarite mistakenly violated his ascetic vows, another opinion argues that the Nazarite is a sinner in need of atonement merely by virtue of his unnecessary abstention from some earthly pleasures: "Rabbi Elazar HaKapar the Great says: What does the Torah mean when it states, 'And he [the Nazirite] will atone for himself for that which he sinned by the soul'? With what soul did the Nazirite sin? Rather, the verse means that he sinned by the distress he caused himself when he abstained from wine."[34] Based on this, the Talmudic sage Shmuel taught that one who fasts when not legally obligated to do so is called a sinner.[35]

The rabbinic tradition furthermore views the adoption of supererogatory religious behaviors as presumptuous and uncouth. In one sense, an individual who adopts religious strictures that go beyond necessary *halakhic* practices is regarded as haughty, which is not only a widely discussed, negative character trait in rabbinic literature but is also explicitly referred to as "foolish" conduct.[36] The Mishnah thus rules, "In a place where it is customary to work on Tisha B'Av, one should work, and in a place where it is customary to not work, one should not work."[37] But, as the Talmud further discusses, one should not piously abstain from work on Tisha B'Av, a day dedicated to mourning the destruction of the Temple and Jerusalem, if the local custom permits working; doing so would be presumptuous and therefore improper.[38] In another passage, the Talmud relates that one Eliezer Ze'ira was wearing black shoes in the public market as a sign of mourning over the destruction of Jerusalem in

---

34 Babylonian Talmud, Taanit 11a.
35 *See* Babylonian Talmud, Taanit 11a.
36 *See, e.g.,* Terumat HaDeshen no. 1.
37 Mishnah, Pesachim 4:5.
38 *See* Babylonian Talmud, Pesachim 55a.

contrast with the local custom of not wearing black shoes and not mandating such ritual mourning practices. The local authorities regarded this supererogatory religious conduct as presumptuous, and they jailed Eliezer Ze'ira as punishment for his public display of excessive piety.[39] Adopting new supererogatory religious practices is also arrogant in another sense: it casts aspersions on the piety of previous generations of fine Jews who did not maintain such extralegal modes of ritual conduct.

In his *Arukh HaShulchan*, Rabbi Epstein moderates these competing rabbinic perspectives of the value of supererogatory conduct by taking a balanced approach to the role of religious stringency in *halakhic* practice. Rabbi Epstein does not prescribe supererogatory conduct that goes beyond the basic requirements of what he views as the normative standards demanded by the *halakhah* as legally mandatory. This tendency is exemplified by Rabbi Epstein's ruling on whether one may wear *tefillin* in a cemetery.[40] The Talmud rules that one may not wear *tefillin* within four cubits of a dead body because openly displaying one's performance of a *halakhic* obligation mocks (so to speak) the deceased, who are no longer able to do so.[41] In his codification of this rule, Rabbi Joseph Karo writes, "It is forbidden to enter a cemetery or to be within four cubits of a corpse with *tefillin* on one's head because this amounts to mocking the dead."[42] As some authorities note, this formulation suggests that Rabbi Karo went beyond the Talmudic prohibition against wearing *tefillin* within four cubits of a corpse and ruled that if one is merely inside the precincts of a cemetery, then one may not wear *tefillin*, even if one is more than four cubits away in distance from any of the graves.[43] Rabbi Epstein rejects this rule, however. He notes that the Talmudic standard is clear: one may not wear *tefillin* within four cubits of a dead body. For Rabbi Epstein, any added legal strictures above and beyond the Talmudic norm are not binding.[44]

While Rabbi Epstein thus does not require supererogatory practices, he does recommend the adoption of such extralegal practices when he believes that they offer genuine religious or material benefits. The Talmud, for instance, rules that one who is riding an animal while traveling on a journey does not

---

39 *See* Babylonian Talmud, Bava Kamma 59b.
40 *See* Arukh HaShulchan, Orach Chaim 45:1.
41 *See* Babylonian Talmud, Berakhot 18a.
42 Shulchan Arukh, Orach Chaim 45:1.
43 *See* Be'er Heitev *to* Shulchan Arukh, Orach Chaim 45:1.
44 *See* Arukh HaShulchan, Orach Chaim 45:1.

need to dismount and stop their trip in order to recite the *Amidah* prayer.[45] While the *Amidah* prayer must normally be said while standing reverently in place and facing towards Jerusalem, the Talmud explains that these requirements are suspended when one is traveling on the road because a traveler forced to dismount and face a particular direction while praying will not be able to properly concentrate on his prayers. It is thus preferable for the traveler to recite the *Amidah* prayer while still mounted and moving in the direction of their destination while also directing their thoughts towards God and Jerusalem.[46] Following the well-settled *halakhic* rule, Rabbi Epstein says that this dispensation similarly applies to a person traveling on foot: such a person does not need to halt their journey to pray the *Amidah*, since their preoccupation with the journey would impinge on their concentration in any case, and they can instead recite the prayer while continuing to walk.[47] While this is indeed the normatively acceptable view, Rabbi Epstein suggests—but does not require—that those who are able to muster the proper mindfulness and concentration even while traveling should indeed halt their journey and recite the *Amidah* properly—that is, standing in place and facing Jerusalem—since doing so offers the benefit of enhancing one's prayers.[48]

In another case, Rabbi Epstein suggests that people go beyond the letter of the law and treat certain temporary prayer spaces with the dignity legally required only for permanent synagogues. The reason for this is that doing so shows respect to prayer services conducted in that place, and it also helps people develop positive character traits of cleanliness, orderliness, and regard for others.[49] The *Arbah Turim* and the *Shulchan Arukh* rule that houses and courtyards occasionally used as prayer spaces do not have the status or sanctity of a regular synagogue, and thus, people in those spaces do not need to observe the ordinary strictures that come with synagogue sanctity—such as prohibitions on eating and drinking, discussing business matters, or using the space as a shelter from the weather.[50] This ruling is based on a Talmudic standard that, although it was customary for people to gather and pray in the town squares on fast days, such places do not have the kind of sanctified status that normally

---

45 *See* Babylonian Talmud, Berakhot 30a.
46 *See* ibid.
47 *See* Arukh HaShulchan, Orach Chaim 94:4.
48 *See* ibid. 74:17.
49 *See* ibid. 154:1.
50 *See* Arbah Turim, Orach Chaim 154:1; Shulchan Arukh, Orach Chaim 154:1.

attaches to synagogues.⁵¹ According to the Talmud, the reason for this rule is that synagogue sanctity attaches only to regular and permanent prayer spaces. Since prayers were not regularly held in the public square, and the space was only occasionally used to host special prayer gatherings, the public square did not have the status and sanctity of a synagogue.⁵² Like the Talmud's public squares, private homes and courtyards are used as prayer spaces only occasionally and are thereby not endowed with synagogue sanctity.

Rabbi Karo further rules that the same standing—declining to extend synagogue sanctity to temporary prayer spaces—applies to rented homes or courtyards. Even when regularly used as prayer spaces, they are not accorded the *halakhic* status of synagogues.⁵³ Rabbi Epstein notes, however, that while a rented space does not have the full status of a synagogue, it is qualitatively different from the mundane status the Talmud assigns to public squares occasionally used for prayer gatherings.⁵⁴ In the case of public squares, the absence of synagogue sanctity is a consequence of those spaces not being synagogues at all; instead, these spaces serve as convenient locations for ad hoc gatherings for large groups of people. Synagogues located in rented properties, by contrast, are considered impermanent—not because they are infrequently used for prayer, but because they remain subject to the willingness of the property owner to continue to renew the renter's lease.⁵⁵ Rabbi Epstein argues that this difference is important because it means that, while a rented space does not have the full *halakhic* status of a synagogue, such spaces must still be treated with respect while they are used to house a regular and permanent (at least for the duration of the current rental term) prayer gathering. Rabbi Epstein further extends this notion that spaces regularly used for prayer should be treated with respect—even when they do not have the technical *halakhic* status of a synagogue—by ruling that it is properly pious conduct to ensure that residential apartments built above technically impermanent prayer spaces should be kept clean in a manner that respects the holiness of a space regularly used for prayer.⁵⁶

Rabbi Epstein thus encourages supererogatory conduct when such conduct provides positive religious benefits. When supererogatory religious

---

51 *See* Babylonian Talmud, Megillah 26a.
52 *See* ibid.
53 *See* Shulchan Arukh, Orach Chaim 154:2.
54 *See* Arukh HaShulchan, Orach Chaim 154:1.
55 *See* ibid.
56 *See* ibid.

practices do not offer the promise of such benefits, however, Rabbi Epstein maintains that such modes of conduct should be avoided for many of the reasons given in classical rabbinic condemnations of misplaced religious stringency. For instance, based on a passage in the Jerusalem Talmud, the *Arbah Turim* instructs that one should be especially careful to "eat in purity" during the seven days between Rosh Hashanah and Yom Kippur as an expression of piety and special scrupulousness in *halakhic* observance in preparation for Yom Kippur.[57] On one example of such piety, the *Arbah Turim* writes that it is appropriate for those who do not avoid bread baked by non-Jews during the rest of the year to be careful during the Ten Days of Repentance to only eat bread baked by fellow Jews. Whether this additional stricture (which many communities do not regularly follow) is a *halakhic* requirement applicable year-round or not is a matter subject to *halakhic* debate.[58] While Rabbi Epstein recognizes the religious value of the practice of taking on an extra stringency during this auspicious time of year, he makes clear that one should only undertake such added religious strictures with respect to matters that are not actually prohibited by *halakhah*. One should not, however, undertake supererogatory behaviors as expressions of piety during the Ten Days of Repentance by acting strictly in matters that are subject to legitimate *halakhic* dispute, as doing so could have negative consequences.[59] Rabbi Epstein notes, for instance, that there are some practices which some authorities prohibit but which we have customarily treated as permitted in rejection of the more stringent views. One should not conduct oneself strictly in such matters during the Ten Days of Repentance because such supererogatory conduct would amount to undertaking the task of following the more stringent view on that issue, thereby precluding a return to practicing the normatively accepted permissible view after Yom Kippur. In short, while supererogatory behavior during the Ten Days of Repentance can be religiously valuable, Rabbi Epstein discourages such conduct when it could lead to negative results.[60]

Another illustration of Rabbi Epstein's wariness of supererogatory practices that do not offer clear religious benefits involves the custom of standing or staying awake throughout Yom Kippur. Rabbi Epstein notes that some people have the custom to stand on their feet for the full length of all the prayer services on Yom Kippur. Likewise, even many of those who do not stand for

---

57   *See* Arbah Turim, Orach Chaim 603.
58   *See* Beit Yosef *to* Arbah Turim, Orach Chaim 603:1.
59   *See* Arukh HaShulchan, Orach Chaim 603:1.
60   *See* ibid. 603:2.

the entire service make sure to stand while the holy ark is open and when the Torah scrolls are displayed to the congregation. Rabbi Epstein, however, notes that people who find standing for these extended lengths of time to be difficult or impractical, especially while fasting, need not do so. Moreover, he recommends against adopting the supererogatory practice of staying awake the entire night of Yom Kippur in prayer, which he says tends to make it difficult, or even impossible, to properly pray the required prayers during the following day.[61]

Rabbi Epstein's general approach to supererogatory behavior is nicely summed up in the way he addresses the propriety of fasting as a pious religious practice. There is a Talmudic dispute over the religious propriety of fasting when one is not obligated to do so by biblical or rabbinic law.[62] According to one view, someone who undertakes supererogatory fasts is considered "holy," while another view, noted above, holds that such a person is regarded as a "sinner" for depriving themselves of the permitted material enjoyment of God's world.[63] The Talmud does not clearly endorse either of these two views, and Rabbi Epstein therefore concludes that both are correct—that "these and those are the words of the living God." He argues that these two Talmudic opinions do not actually conflict with each other; whether someone who engages in supererogatory fasts is holy or sinful depends on the circumstances.[64] Here, Rabbi Epstein lays out his basic approach to supererogatory religious conduct in general. It is never mandatory to undertake supererogatory fasts, he explains, but where such fasting may prove religiously beneficial for a particular individual, it is commendable to do so. Thus, an individual who is sinful in general should undertake supererogatory fasts in order to cry, pray, and seek forgiveness from God—goals for which fasting is typically conducive. Likewise, any individual who can undertake fasting without adversely impacting their health or ability to conscientiously fulfill their basic religious duties is considered holy for fasting and thereby cleansing their sins. But, when fasting is likely to have negative religious or health effects, one should not undertake supererogatory fasts, and indeed one who does so is called a sinner. Thus, if supererogatory fasting will weaken a person and prevent them from fulfilling genuine *halakhic* obligations, they should not fast. Likewise, Rabbi Epstein recommends that Torah scholars not undertake fasting and instead devote their energies to increased Torah study. Teachers, communal functionaries, and hourly workers

---

61 *See* ibid. 618:9.
62 *See* Babylonian Talmud, Taanit 11a-b.
63 *See* ibid.
64 *See* Arukh HaShulchan, Orach Chaim 571:1.

should also avoid fasting, he explains, since fasting is likely to negatively impact their ability to do their jobs.[65]

* * * * *

Extralegal stringencies can serve important, religiously valuable functions. Rabbi Epstein recognizes this fact, and thus he often recommends the adoption of supererogatory practices that in his judgment enhance Jewish religious, communal, and material life. Religious stringencies can, however, also produce negative consequences; they may impose unreasonable burdens on people's material resources, cause individuals to become obligated in religious practices that they will not uphold, produce religious resentment, or disregard certain *halakhic* and spiritual concerns. Rabbi Epstein appreciates these potential pitfalls and therefore discourages the adoption of supererogatory practices that he thinks will produce negative religious outcomes. In all cases, however, Rabbi Epstein maintains the distinction between genuine legal obligations on the one hand and voluntary extralegal stringencies on the other. He prescribes the former, but he only ever recommends the adoption of the latter by those for whom they provide a positive religious outlet.

---

65   *See* ibid. 571:1.

CHAPTER NINE

Law and Mysticism

In this final chapter addressing Rabbi Epstein's methodological principles for mediating between correct Talmudic rules and other religious values, we consider the *Arukh HaShulchan*'s approach to the legal significance and normativity of mystical teachings and kabbalistic practices.

* * * * *

Principle Seven: Rabbi Epstein tries whenever possible to reconcile the mystical prescriptions of the Zohar with standard halakhic norms, though he affirmatively rejects the halakhic relevance of mystical practices that are incompatible with Talmudic sources. Moreover, Rabbi Epstein generally permits or even recommends the adoption of mystical practices innovated by the Zohar as long as they do not contradict halakhic requirements.

Rabbinic scholars have long recognized tensions between traditional *halakhic* sources on the one hand and kabbalistic texts and mystical tendencies on the other.[1] Of course, such tensions are not surprising. While Jewish mysticism tends to emphasize other-worldly metaphysical realities and aims at deepening the individual's relationship with God by personalizing and customizing ritual practice to achieve spiritual ends, Jewish law focuses on the physical observance of otherwise mundane behavioral norms in the real world in a way that generalizes and standardizes Jewish observance to create unity and

---

1 See generally Jacob Katz, Halakhah and Kabbalah: Studies in the History of Jewish Religion, its Various Faces and Social Relevance (1984); Moshe Hallamish, HaKabbalah B'Tefillah, B'Halakhah, U'b'Minhag [The Kabbalah in Prayer, Jewish Law, and Custom] (2002); Matt Goldish, Halakhah, *Kabbalah, and Heresy: A Controversy in Early Eighteenth Century Amsterdam*, 84 The Jewish Quarterly Review 153 (1993-1994).

community. Tensions between the two are thus virtually unavoidable.[2] The need to address the proper place and significance of kabbalistic ideas and traditions in *halakhic* decision-making became increasingly acute, however, following the appearance of the *Zohar* in the mid-thirteenth century. The *Zohar* is a major work of Jewish mysticism that first appeared after being published by the Spanish rabbi and mystic, Moses de Leon (1240-1305), and which was attributed to the Mishnaic Sage, Rabbi Shimon bar Yochai.[3] The *Zohar* very quickly gained prominence as a core text of the kabbalistic tradition in Judaism and, despite persistent questions about its authenticity and true authorship, remains a primary and mainstream source of Jewish mysticism.[4] Perhaps one of the most significant and lasting impacts of the *Zohar* is the manner in which it brought mystical perspectives and practices into the open. While kabbalistic teachings predate the publication of the *Zohar* itself, of course, these were largely orally transmitted traditions passed from teacher to student in relatively private circles of mystical learning not generally open or known to the general Jewish public or even to most rabbinic scholars, who were generally more concerned with Talmudic dialectics and *halakhic* decision-making than with kabbalistic mysticism.[5] The appearance of the *Zohar*—a concrete, broadly circulated text—opened the world of Jewish mysticism to a wider audience. While this development resulted in substantial rabbinic debate about the wisdom, propriety, and even dangers of general access to and mass study of Kabbalah, from the fourteenth century on, mystical learning and practice became an increasingly visible and widespread feature of Jewish religious life.

The appearance of the *Zohar* and the subsequent mainstreaming of kabbalistic teachings led to the development of a variety of mystical schools and popular movements that broadened and deepened the influence and normativity of kabbalistic ideas and practices in Jewish communities. Some of these movements were led by rabbinic scholars who were also accomplished and highly regarded *halakhic* authorities. The Safed school of Kabbalah,[6] led

---

2 *See, e.g.,* Rabbi Zvi Hirsch ben Yaakov Ashkenazi, Responsa Chacham Tzvi no. 36 (noting that a mystical orientation and focus on Kabbalah tends to lead to "each person following after his own understanding," while the goal of *halakhah* is to create relatively uniform ways of practicing Judaism).
3 *See* Joseph Jacobs & Isaac Broyde, *Zohar,* 689, 690-691 *in* 12 The Jewish Encyclopedia (1906).
4 *See* ibid. 689, 692-693.
5 *See, e.g.,* Mishnah, Chagigah 2:1.
6 *See* Ariel Bension, The Zohar in Moslem & Christian Spain 224-240 (1974); Lawrence Fine, *New Approaches to the Study of kabbalistic Life in 16th-Century Safed, in* Jewish Mysticism

by Rabbi Isaac Luria (1534-1572), whose innovative mystical teachings and ritual practices would make an indelible impression on subsequent kabbalistic approaches to Judaism, also included Rabbi Joseph Karo, author of the seminal and hugely influential *halakhic* code, the *Shulchan Arukh*, who himself kept a kabbalistic diary of his mystical encounters with angels.[7] Rabbi Judah Loew of Prague (1520-1609), one of the most important rabbinic figures of his time in central Europe, was also an accomplished kabbalist whose philosophical writings and biblical commentaries are replete with mystical ideas couched in philosophical terminology.[8] The teachings of Rabbis Luria and Loew became important bases for the later development of Hasidism, an Eastern European spiritual movement started by Rabbi Israel Baal Shem Tov (1698-1760).[9] Hasidism emphasized the spiritual elevation of mundane acts as a means of providing a more religiously enriching experience for the masses of common Jews unable to access the scholasticism-focused religiosity of Talmudism.[10]

However, even the rationalist opponents of the Hasidic movement were deeply ensconced in kabbalistic traditions. Rabbi Elijah of Vilna (1720-1797), an important *halakhic* scholar who is often regarded as the herald of the anti-Hasidic Lithuanian school of rationalist and scholastic Jewish thought and practice, was also a serious kabbalist whose mystical teachings were publicized through the writings of many of his students, including Rabbi Chaim Volozhin (1749-1821), another mainstream Talmudist.[11] Rabbi Epstein, whose brother-in-law, Rabbi Naftali Tzvi Yehudah Berlin (1816-1893), inherited the mantle of Lithuanian leadership from his teacher, Rabbi Chaim Volohzin, was likewise well versed in the kabbalistic traditions of the *Zohar* and of Rabbi Isaac Luria. This widespread acceptance and familiarity with the *Zohar* and other mystical teachings helped create a substantial and well-established corpus of kabbalistic

---

and Kabbalah: New Insights and Scholarship (Frederick E. Greenspahn, ed., 2011); Aryeh Kaplan, Meditation and Kabbalah 167-186 (1986); J. Zvi Werblowsky, *The Safed Revival and Its Aftermath*, in Jewish Spirituality: From the Sixteenth-Century Revival to the Present (Arthur Green, ed., 1989).

7 *See* Rabbi Joseph Karo, Maggid Meisharim; J. Zvi Werblowsky, Joseph Karo – Lawyer and Mystic (2nd ed., 1980).

8 *See* Ben Zion Bokser, The Maharal: The Mystical Philosophy of Rabbi Judah Loew of Prague (1977).

9 *See* Moshe Rosman, Founder of Hasidism: A Quest for the Historical Baal Shem Tov (1996); David Biale, et. al., Hasidism: A New History, 43-75 (2018).

10 *See* David Biale, et. al., Hasidism: A New History, 155-255 (2018).

11 *See* Eliyahu Stern, The Genius, Elijah of Vilna and the Making of Modern Judaism 19-29 (2014); Imanuel Etkes, The Gaon of Vilna: The Man and His Image 12-26, 173-178 (2002).

texts, teachings, and traditions of religious practice with which the rules and standards of normative *halakhah*, derived from non-kabbalistic sources like the Talmud, codes, and responsa literature, had to contend. By Rabbi Epstein's time, the practices and attitudes deriving from Jewish mystical traditions constituted both a lived reality—in terms of the huge numbers of conscientious religious Jews adhering to such approaches to their practice—and also a normative system, given credibility and credence by many important rabbinic authorities and *halakhic* scholars.

Concern for the relative normative weight of *halakhic* and mystical imperatives is not exclusively a product of the post-Zoharic era, however. Long before the publication of the *Zohar* and the development of subsequent mystical traditions, Talmudic and post-Talmudic Rabbis addressed the proper place of *aggadah*—the body of homiletical rabbinic teachings and traditions concerning ethics, biblical narratives, morality, history, and other non-imperative subjects—in *halakhic* discourse and decision-making. Here, too, there is an unavoidable tension. As Rabbi Abraham Joshua Heschel put it quite poetically:

> *Halakhah* deals with the law; *aggadah* with the meaning of the law. *Halakhah* deals with subjects that can be expressed literally; *aggadah* [sic] introduces us to a realm that lies beyond the range of expression. *Halakhah* teaches us how to perform common acts; *aggadah* tells us how to participate in the eternal drama. *Halakhah* gives us knowledge; *aggadah* gives us aspiration. . . *Halakhah*, by necessity, treats the laws in the abstract, regardless of the totality of the person. It is *aggadah* that keeps on reminding that the purpose of performance is to transform the performer, that the purpose of observance is to train us in achieving spiritual ends.[12]

Many have noted that *halakhah* and *aggadah* are, in truth, two aspects of a single rabbinic tradition; they are "two sides of the same coin—a single ideational world and a single literary corpus, all authored by the very same sages—and it is absolutely impossible to distinguish between them."[13] Nevertheless, if, as Heschel writes, "*Halakhah* without *aggadah* is dead, [and] *aggadah* without

---

12 Abraham Joshua Heschel, Heavenly Torah: As Refracted Through the Generations 2 (2005).
13 Yaacov Sussmann, *The Scholarly Oeuvre of Professor Ephraim Elimelech Urbach* [Hebrew], Ephraim Elimelech Urbach: A Bio-Bibliography 7-116, 64-65 (David Assaf, ed., 1993).

halakhah is wild,"[14] these two sources of Jewish rules, principles, and values will inevitably grate against each other in the attempt to determine the norms of religious conduct. According to some rabbis, *aggadic* sources should play no role in the determination of *halakhic* norms. Thus, Rabbi Saadia Gaon held that in legal matters, "We do not rely on *aggadah*,"[15] a position which Rabbi Hai Gaon later explained was based on the idea that *halakhic* materials reflect a transmitted tradition rooted in revelation, while *aggadah* is merely every individual's reflective opinion about the values and lessons that can be derived from Jewish texts and traditions:

> It should be known that the words of *aggadah* do not have the status of oral tradition, and each person conjectures as he pleases . . . For that reason, we cannot rely upon them [in *halakhic* matters] . . . And these *midrashot* [expositions] are not tradition and not *halakhah* but were only stated by way of conjecture.[16]

Many others disagreed with this approach and maintained that *aggadic* sources can and should influence *halakhic* decision-making to various degrees. Thus, Rabbeinu Tam (1100-1171) held that *aggadic* material should be considered normative, at least when it does not directly contradict Talmudic rules,[17] and Rabbi Zvi Hirsch Chajes (1805-1855) maintained that *aggadic* material found in the Talmud itself should be considered alongside more legalistic Talmudic discussions in the determination of *halakhic* norms and standards.[18] Later debates over the role of the *Zohar* and other mystical traditions and practices in the determination of *halakhic* norms are in many ways a continuation of these earlier concerns.[19]

The positions at either extreme of the spectrum of debate over the role of mysticism in *halakhic* decision-making are easily stated. According to some scholars, mystical concepts and kabbalistic practices have absolutely no valid

---

14 Abraham Joshua Heschel, Heavenly Torah: As Refracted Through the Generations 2 (2005).
15 Otzar HaGeonim, Berakhot, Commentaries, §271, 91 (B. M. Lewin, ed.; 1928-1943).
16 Otzar HaGeonim, Chagigah, §67, 59-60, *quoted in* Yair Lorberbaum, Reflections on the Halakhic Status of Aggadah 33.
17 *See* Rabbeinu Tam, Sefer HaYashar no. 619.
18 *See* Rabbi Zvi Hirsch Chajes, Darkhei Horaah, *in* Kol Kitvei Maharitz Chajes.
19 *See* Jacob Katz, *Post-Zoharic Relations Between Halakhah and Kabbalah*, in Divine Law in Human Hands: Case Studies in Halakhic Flexibility, 31, 31-32, 40 (1998).

place in *halakhic* decision-making. Rabbi David ben Solomon ibn Zimra (1479-1573) explained this approach as follows:

> I have a general principle that [for] anything written in the Talmud or in one of the texts of legal rulings—even when this contradicts that which is written in the kabbalistic books—I rule in accordance with them [the *halakhic* texts], and I pay no mind to what is written in those [kabbalistic] books.[20]

While ibn Zimra goes on to note that as a matter of personal religious practice, he chooses to observe kabbalistic stringencies that go above and beyond the ritual demands made by traditional *halakhic* texts, he does not recommend that approach to others, whom he thinks should instead follow only the rulings and prescriptions of strictly legal works. This view is well exemplified by a characteristically hyperbolic—but nonetheless entirely serious—statement by Rabbi Moses Sofer (1762-1839) in a responsum concerning the *halakhic* propriety of reciting a particular ritually prescribed blessing of thanksgiving at night. Regarding this matter, he states, "Anyone who mixes kabbalistic matters with *halakhic* rulings is guilty of [violating the biblical prohibition against] planting mixtures [of different kinds of crops]."[21] Similarly, Rabbi Solomon Luria (1510-1574) declared, "If Rabbi Shimon bar Yochai [the supposed author of the *Zohar*] was standing before us and commanding that we change a *halakhic* practice established by our forebears, we would not listen to him."[22]

On the other extreme end of the spectrum, some authorities have held that practical prescriptions and spiritual concepts contained in the *Zohar* are normative and even outweigh contrary viewpoints put forward by a consensus of post-Talmudic authorities. Rabbi Benjamin Slonick (1550-1619), for instance, argued that the *Zohar* "is weightier than all other post-Talmudic authors, such that if all these writers where placed on one side of a scale and the *Zohar* on the other side, the *Zohar* would outweigh them all."[23] In some sense, Rabbi Slonick's position is not so radical if one accepts the claims of Mishnaic-era authorship of the *Zohar*; the Talmud itself is built on Mishnaic precedent, and the Mishnaic-era text of the *Zohar* might then reasonably outweigh any post-Talmudic authority. Other scholars went further, however, and

---

20 Rabbi David ben Solomon ibn Zimra, Responsa Radbaz 4:80.
21 Rabbi Moses Schreiber, Responsa Chatam Sofer 1:51.
22 Rabbi Solomon Luria, Responsa Maharshal no. 98.
23 Rabbi Benjamin Slonick, Responsa Masat Binyamin no. 62.

maintained that kabbalistic practices that originated in the Lurianic school of Jewish mysticism and other late medieval sources should be given precedence over traditional *halakhic* sources.[24]

Between these poles, there is a range of more nuanced treatments of the *halakhic* significance and weight of ritual practices prescribed by the *Zohar* and other kabbalistic traditions. According to some scholars, kabbalistic ideas and prescriptions are to be ignored when they conflict with traditional *halakhic* sources and norms, and they cannot create new *halakhic* obligations or prohibitions in cases where normative Jewish law leaves behaviors unregulated. Mystical texts can play an important role, however, in resolving disputes between *halakhic* authorities. According to this approach, in cases where the correct legal rule is uncertain due to *halakhic* disagreement, decisors should resolve the matter in accordance with the *halakhic* position that coincides with kabbalistic teachings. This view was adopted by Rabbi Tzvi Hirsch Ashkenazi (1656-1718), who wrote:

> Even if the words of the *Zohar* are contrary to those of the *halakhic* decisors, we may not put aside the words of the decisors in favor of things said in the realm of the secrets of the Torah [i.e., the Kabbalah], for when it comes to law and legal decision-making, there is no cause for involving ourselves in secret matters except for where there is a dispute among the *halakhic* decisors—then it is proper to rely on the determination of the *Zohar*.[25]

Another common approach held that kabbalistic norms can be assimilated into *halakhah* in cases where those mystical practices do not contradict legal sources and when the Talmud itself is also silent on the issue, leaving the matter to personal discretion. This was the approach adopted by Rabbi Abraham Zacuto, a Spanish scholar who served as Royal Astronomer and Historian to King Juan II of Portugal. He stated, "It is agreed among the Jewish people that in matters where the *Zohar* does not disagree with the Talmud, or where the issue is not explicitly addressed by the Talmud but is explicitly prescribed by the *Zohar*, we accept it [i.e. the *Zohar*'s ruling]."[26] A similar view was adopted by Rabbi

---

24　*See, e.g.*, Rabbi Chaim Yosef David Azulai, Birkei Yosef, Orach Chaim 46:11; Ben Ish Chai, Exodus Year 1, Parshat Shemot, no. 6.

25　Rabbi Zvi Hirsch ben Yaakov Ashkenazi, Responsa Chacham Tzvi no. 36.

26　Rabbi Abraham Zacuto, Sefer HaYuchsin HaShalem 45 (1925).

Menachem MiPano (1548-1620), himself an accomplished kabbalist. Rabbi Menachem ruled the following:

> We pay no attention to the words of Rabbi Shimon bar Yochai in matters of law. This is something that all the *halakhic* scholars agree to—that when it comes to legal decision-making, we have only what arises from the Talmudic discussions, and we do not put upon our hearts the words of the *Zohar* with respect to any rule or commandment, whether for purposes of leniency or stringency, if they are contrary to the words of the Talmud. Only where the Talmud does not resolve the matter does the *Zohar* determine the issue.[27]

Another approach held that the *Zohar* should be used not only to resolve rabbinic controversies in matters of *halakhah*, but also to embellish and enrich Jewish practice by adding new observances and strictures, so long as they do not contravene established legal norms. Based on this view, while *halakhic* leniencies based on kabbalistic sources should be rejected in favor of the more rigorous requirements prescribed by traditional legal texts, mystically based *halakhic* stringencies that impose obligations or prohibitions that go beyond what is required by normative Jewish law should be accepted.[28] A variant on this position maintains that kabbalistic prescriptions which result in *halakhic* stringencies need not be followed as a matter of law, but can be adopted by individuals as an expression of personal piety.[29] Thus, Rabbi Shneur Zalman of Liadi, a Hasidic leader and mystic, wrote that "if the kabbalistic masters are [prescribing a] stricter [practice than what is required by traditional *halakhic* standards], there is good reason to act strictly, but we do not compel the community to do so."[30]

Rabbi Epstein's approach to this issue falls neatly within this moderate and balanced position. Although he was educated at the illustrious, anti-Hasidic Volozhin Yeshivah and fully ensconced in the world of Lithuanian Jewish scholasticism, Rabbi Epstein himself had a substantial familiarity with Hasidic teachings and a deep reverence for kabbalistic disciplines and practices. Rabbi Epstein's first rabbinic posting was in Novozybkov, Russia, a city inhabited by large numbers of Chabad Hasidim. This led to several meetings between

---

27 Rabbi Menahem Azariah da Fano, Responsa Rama MiPano no 108.
28 *See* Rabbi Jacob Sofer, Kaf HaChaim 25:75.
29 *See, e.g.*, Rabbi Moses Schreiber, Responsa Chatam Sofer, Even HaEzer no. 85.
30 Rabbi Shneur Zalman of Liadi, Shulchan Arukh HaRav, Orach Chaim 25:28.

Rabbi Epstein and Rabbi Menachem Mendel Schneersohn of Lubavitch (1789-1866), the leader of the Chabad Hasidic sect, for whom Rabbi Epstein apparently had much respect and from whom he sought and received additional rabbinic ordination. Indeed, Rabbi Epstein's regard for the kabbalistic tradition went so far that he followed the lead of many of his rabbinic forebears in maintaining that in principle there are no genuine contradictions between authentic Jewish mysticism and *halakhic* norms. As he viewed it, apparent tensions between the two must be the result of misunderstandings of one or both traditions. Thus, with respect to the *Zohar* Rabbi Epstein writes:

> I received a tradition that the *Zohar* never disagrees with the Talmud . . . Where the Talmud determines the law, the *Zohar*, too, accepts this ruling. If there is a place where the *Zohar* and the Talmud disagree, it is because they failed to understand the *Zohar* correctly, and one must therefore properly expound the view [of the *Zohar*] so that it accords with the Talmud.[31]

Rabbi Epstein thus demonstrated great respect for the kabbalistic traditions recorded in the *Zohar*. Unlike many other *halakhic* scholars, he does not simply dismiss the *Zohar's* mystical prescriptions in cases where they conflict with accepted legal norms. Instead, Rabbi Epstein places the Kabbalah itself on a high pedestal, equal, in fact, with the Talmud and traditional *halakhic* sources. Apparent contradictions between Talmudic rules and kabbalistic teachings are not due to the Talmud being right and the *Zohar* being wrong; rather, they are the result of human misinterpretations of the *Zohar*, which Rabbi Epstein suggests must be reexamined so as to harmonize the Kabbalah with the *halakhah*.

Based on this conviction, Rabbi Epstein follows a well-trodden approach to addressing apparent tensions between Talmudic and kabbalistic norms. As he lays out in his *Arukh HaShulchan*:

> The *halakhic* decisors established a principle with respect to this issue: If the Talmud and the rulings of the *halakhic* authorities contradict the *Zohar*, we follow the rulings of the Talmud and *halakhic* scholars. However, if the contrary prescription of the *Zohar* is stricter [than the normative *halakhic* standard], those who wish to do so may act stringently in accordance with the *Zohar's* ruling, and it is certainly proper to do so if

---

31 Arukh HaShulchan, Orach Chaim 25:29.

the issue is not addressed by the Talmud at all—though we do not force people to do so.³²

Rabbi Epstein puts into practice this approach to the *halakhic* significance of Jewish mysticism and the *Zohar* in numerous cases and contexts. Most often, Rabbi Epstein uses the *Zohar* as a basis for his own independent *halakhic* conclusions, especially when his opinions depart from the rulings of other important scholars. For example, Rabbi Epstein disagrees with Rabbi Joseph Karo's rulings regarding the proper approach to ritual handwashing. The *Shulchan Arukh* rules that when washing one's hands before prayer, one does not need to fulfill all the conditions associated with ritual washing before a meal—such as the need to wash using a cup or other vessel, the requirement that the water wash over the hands as a result of human effort, and the requirement that one use as least a *revi'it* of water to complete the washing.³³ The *Arukh HaShulchan* disagrees, ruling instead that washing before prayer must satisfy all the requirements needed for valid washing before a meal.³⁴ Rabbi Epstein relies primarily on Maimonides's equating washing for meals with washing for prayer, and he relies also on the similar views of the *Rosh* and the *Rashba*, both of whom rule that various requirements associated with washing for food must also be observed when washing for prayer. Finally, Rabbi Epstein notes that the *Zohar*, too, affirms this position.³⁵ Similarly, Rabbi Epstein also draws on the kabbalistic tradition when he strongly recommends that synagogues be built with twelve windows—the *Zohar* teaches that one should not pray at all in a synagogue that does not have windows, and there should ideally be twelve windows in every synagogue so as to correspond with "the heavenly synagogue," which also has twelve windows.³⁶

In another case, Rabbi Epstein rules against the *Shulchan Arukh*'s opinion that while normally the *Amidah* prayer must be recited quietly in an undertone, on Rosh Hashanah and Yom Kippur the *Amidah* should be recited in a slightly louder voice so as to improve one's focus and concentration on the relatively unfamiliar High Holiday prayers.³⁷ Rabbi Epstein rejects this position on the basis of the *Zohar*, which teaches that it is always improper to pray the *Amidah*

---

32 Ibid.
33 *See* Shulchan Arukh, Orach Chaim 4:6-7.
34 *See* Arukh HaShulchan, Orach Chaim 4:9.
35 *See* ibid. 4:10.
36 *See* ibid. 90:7.
37 *See* Shulchan Arukh, Orach Chaim 101:7.

loudly.[38] Rabbi Epstein also utilizes the *Zohar* to support the rejection of part of Maimonides's prescribed order of the morning prayer liturgy. Rabbi Epstein questions the standard custom to recite the Torah passage of *Shirat HaYam* at the conclusion of the introductory *Pesukei D'Zimra* section of the morning prayer liturgy. This is problematic, he says, because *Pesukei D'Zimra* consists of readings from Psalms, and it is inappropriate to place readings from the Torah itself after readings from Psalms during the same sequence of prayers.[39] It is for this reason, Rabbi Epstein suggests, that Maimonides instructs that the *Shirat HaYam* passage be recited not at the conclusion of *Pesukei D'Zimra*, but as the introduction to the recitation of the *Shema*, the liturgy sequence that follows the introductory prayers of *Pesukei D'Zimra*.[40] Nevertheless, Rabbi Epstein notes that accepted contemporary practice does not follow Maimonides's liturgy, and the placement of the *Shirat HaYam* is thus problematic. Despite this concern, Rabbi Epstein accepts the settled custom to recite the *Shirat HaYam* at the close of *Pesukei D'Zimra* and seeks to justify the practice by references to the *Zohar*. The *Zohar* raises the question posed by Rabbi Epstein about the proper placement of the *Shirat HaYam* in the liturgy, responding in a somewhat mystical vein that it is precisely because of the elevated holiness of the *Shirat HaYam* that this passage was placed at the very end of the *Pesukei D'Zimra* as a kind of crescendo in the liturgical lead-up to the recitation of the *Shema*.[41]

Rabbi Epstein also uses the *Zohar* as a determinative factor in the resolution of *halakhic* disputes between rabbinic authorities. For instance, Rabbis Joseph Karo and Moses Isserles disagree about whether one should respond "amen" to the prayer leader's recitation of the blessing of *Gaal Yisrael*, a blessing which concludes the recitation of the *Shema* and introduces the silent recitation of the central *Amidah* prayer during the morning prayer service.[42] Rabbi Karo rules that one may not interrupt one's prayers between the recitation of the blessing of *Gaal Yisrael* and the start of the *Amidah* because the Talmud itself places great importance on the juxtaposition of these two parts of the prayer service.[43] Rabbi Isserles disagrees, however, and rules that one may say "amen" following this blessing because saying "amen" does not constitute a true

---

38 *See* Arukh HaShulchan, Orach Chaim 52:1.
39 *See* ibid.
40 *See* Mishneh Torah, Hilkhot Tefillah 7:13.
41 *See* Arukh HaShulchan, Orach Chaim 52:1.
42 *See* Shulchan Arukh, Orach Chaim 111:1.
43 *See* ibid.

interruption in the prayers, as it is part of the normal responsive liturgy.[44] The Talmud does not definitively resolve this issue, and Rabbi Epstein ultimately endorses Rabbi Karo's more stringent view because it is also supported by the *Zohar*.[45] In a slightly different vein, Rabbi Epstein utilizes the *Zohar* to lend support for the simultaneous legitimacy of both *Rashi* and *Rabbeinu Tam*'s competing rulings about the correct ordering of the various biblical passages written on the parchment scrolls placed within *tefillin*.[46] *Rashi* and *Rabbeinu Tam* each maintain that their own prescription of the correct ordering of the *tefillin* scroll passages is exclusively correct, which leads Rabbi Epstein and others to question how it can be that such a fundamental daily Jewish observance can be subject to such a fundamental dispute. While Rabbi Epstein rules that people should make certain to don *tefillin* that comply with *Rashi*'s view, he notes that the *Zohar* can be reasonably read as supporting either position. Thus, Rabbi Epstein concludes that since both views find support in the kabbalistic tradition, "both are true according to the intentions of the Torah."[47]

Rabbi Epstein does not always follow the prescriptions of the *Zohar*, however. Ultimately, in cases of conflict between kabbalistic teachings and what he believes to be normatively correct *halakhic* practice, Rabbi Epstein maintains that conclusions which follow from the legal sources and methods of the rabbinic legal tradition, rather than from the mystical tradition, have the final say. One such example concerns the appointment of communal prayer leaders for the High Holidays. The *Zohar* instructs that the community should be very careful when choosing an individual to lead the congregation in High Holiday prayers and to blow the *shofar* on Rosh Hashanah. Specifically, as Rabbi Epstein notes, the *Zohar* writes that the designated prayer leader should seclude himself for three days prior to the holiday so as to avoid contracting any ritual impurity and in order to spend time in self-introspection and repentance.[48] While Rabbi Epstein considers the *Zohar*'s suggestion seriously enough to quote it, he nevertheless finds this instruction impractical in his own time, concluding, "Due to our sins, we are unable to demand such." He therefore rejects this instruction as a matter of normative law.[49]

---

44 See Rema *to* Shulchan Arukh, Orach Chaim 111:1.
45 *See* Arukh HaShulchan, Orach Chaim 111:2.
46 *See generally* ibid. 34:1-8.
47 ibid. 34:9.
48 *See* ibid. 581:6.
49 ibid. 581:7.

While Rabbi Epstein is thus willing to dismiss the mystical practices prescribed by the *Zohar* in cases where he is convinced that they are incompatible with the correct *halakhic* standard, he generally prefers to find ways to synthesize kabbalistic and Talmudic instructions in a manner that upholds both norms. One salient example of Rabbi Epstein's interest in reconciling mystical and Talmudic sources relates to the proper modes of decorum around someone who is reciting the *Amidah* prayer. The *Zohar* rules that one may not walk within four cubits in any direction of someone who is in the middle of reciting the *Amidah*. In his discussion of this issue, Rabbi Epstein notes that the *Zohar*'s ruling seems to conflict with the Talmudic proscription that only prohibits someone from walking within four cubits to the front of a person praying the *Amidah*. In order to avoid a direct conflict between the standards prescribed by the *Zohar* and the Talmud, Rabbi Epstein offers a novel reading of the relevant passage of the *Zohar*, which concludes that the *Zohar* actually prescribes the same rule as the Talmud and only restricts movements within four cubits in front of a person praying the *Amidah*.[50]

* * * * *

Rabbi Epstein thus has great respect for the kabbalistic tradition in general and particularly the teachings of the *Zohar*. In the final analysis, however, he is ultimately a scholar of *halakhah*, not a mystic. He considers genuine kabbalistic practices to reflect religious truth, but at the same time, he regards the *halakhic* tradition embodied in the Talmud, the rulings of post-Talmudic legal scholars, and—as will be discussed in chapter ten—the well-settled customary practices of the Jewish community to be more epistemologically reliable carriers of that truth. He determines that conflicts between accepted *halakhic* norms and kabbalistic prescription must therefore be resolved in favor of the *halakhah*. But in doing so, Rabbi Epstein views himself not as subordinating the *Zohar* to the Talmud, but rather as using the *halakhic* tradition to clarify and recover correct understandings of previously misinterpreted kabbalistic teachings.

---

50 *See* ibid. 102:12.

CHAPTER TEN

Law and Custom

Chapters seven, eight, and nine addressed the methodological principles that Rabbi Epstein uses to navigate tensions between standard Talmudic rules and other religious values and concerns. The following three chapters explore a similar issue from a somewhat different angle, asking what secondary rules guide Rabbi Epstein's *halakhic* judgments in dealing with tensions between ideal Talmudic norms and various social and practical pressures and concerns. Specifically, this chapter examines the methodological principles that Rabbi Epstein uses to navigate tensions and determine practical standards of Jewish law in cases where *halakhic* practice follows customary practices rather than the law on the books. Chapter eleven considers how Talmudic norms may become inapplicable when changes in economic, social, political, cultural, or other conditions indicate that the underlying reasons for a given Talmudic rule may no longer apply. Finally, chapter twelve discusses how Rabbi Epstein deals with cases where standard Talmudic prescriptions, if applied, would be substantially impracticable or would lead to significant hardships for Jews seeking to uphold *halakhic* practice.

The chapter begins by explaining Rabbi Epstein's methodological approach to the role of *minhag*, or "custom," in determining Jewish legal norms.[1] This is appropriate because, as is explained more fully below, rabbinic thinking on the legal import of customary practices straddles the line between religious and social counterpressures on straightforward applications of standard Talmudic rules. On the one hand, important streams of rabbinic thought ascribe genuine religious and *halakhic* significance to popular

---

[1] On custom as a source of Jewish law, see generally Menachem Elon, 2 Jewish Law: History, Sources, Principles 895-944 (Bernard Auerbach & Melvin J. Sykes trans., 1994); Rabbi Daniel Sperber, Minhagei Yisrael, 8 vols. (1998-2007).

practices and customary modes of Jewish living, and from this perspective, custom constitutes a religious value that may compete with and shape the *halakhic* standards prescribed by the Talmud. On the other hand, popular customs and modes of practicing Judaism and *halakhah* also constitute social "facts on the ground" that tend to put pressure on the formal rules of Jewish law to adapt and adjust in order to account for the lived experiences and actually practiced ways of observing the obligations and limitations of Jewish law. This chapter thus transitions from the focus on secondary rules, used to deal with tensions between normative *halakhic* rules and other competing religious values, to a consideration of how Talmudic law interacts with social and pragmatic concerns, by exploring Rabbi Epstein's approach to the legal significance of *minhag* as a determinative feature of rabbinic jurisprudence.

* * * * *

Principle Eight: Rabbi Epstein upholds the halakhic normativity of what he sees as minhag—the customary practices of his own time and place—even when such customary practices are inconsistent with precedential halakhic rulings or Rabbi Epstein's own preferred understanding of the Talmudic sources, provided that the minhag is not harmful, incompatible with basic halakhic norms, or based on mistaken premises.

Rabbinic jurisprudence has long recognized *minhag*, or customary practice and usage, as an important source and determinant of correct *halakhic* standards. As it is used in Talmudic and rabbinic sources, *minhag* serves three primary functions.[2] Most narrowly, *minhag* serves a law-determining role in that the customary way of resolving *halakhic* questions or practicing Jewish rituals may determine which one of several competing rabbinic viewpoints should be generally followed on issues subject to legal dispute.[3] In such cases, the existence of a *minhag pesak*, a custom to rule in accordance with a particular authority or in a particular way, is used to cut through rabbinic dispute and determine the correct *halakhic* standard of religious practice. Somewhat more expansively, *minhag* is also widely recognized as helping to fill gaps left by other

---

2 See Michael J. Broyde, *Custom as a Source of Jewish Law: Some Religious Reflections on David J. Bederman's* Custom as a Source of Law, 61 Emory L.J. 1037, 1039 (2012).

3 See Menachem Elon, 2 Jewish Law: History, Sources, Principles 898-900 (Bernard Auerbach & Melvin J. Sykes trans., 1994); Babylonian Talmud, Berakhot 45a; Babylonian Talmud, Taanit 26b; Rabbi Meir Ben Baruch, Responsa Maharam MeRutenberg, no. 386 (Berlin ed.).

primary sources and methodologies of rabbinic jurisprudence.[4] Oftentimes, Jewish legal sources prescribe only broad normative limitations on behavior, requiring or proscribing some specific practices while permissively leaving most things to individual discretion. This second form of custom as a source of *halakhah* functions to create legal duties and prohibitions within the sphere of discretion left open by the technical rules of Jewish law, thereby creating new norms and standards that flesh out the open texture of normative *halakhah*.[5] Third, in some cases, *minhag* creates entirely new norms and standards of Jewish religious practice that cut against the otherwise regular rules of *halakhic* practice.[6]

Customary practices that function in these varied ways fall generally into three categories, each of which is more fully explained below. Some customs are forms of personal religious practice that most typically take the form of personal ritual stringencies, practiced in an effort to either avoid genuine violations of *halakhic* requirements or express and achieve higher levels of personal religious piety.[7] Other customs are not personal undertakings but family traditions. Passed on from parents to children over generations, such customs may, like personal customs, provide more rigorous religious frameworks for everyday life and could also be reflective of a family's unique expressions, preferences, or modes of ritual life.[8] In many cases, what appear to be family customs are actually instances of a third kind of custom known as *minhag hamakom*, or

---

4   *See* Menachem Elon, 2 Jewish Law: History, Sources, Principles 901-903 (Bernard Auerbach & Melvin J. Sykes trans., 1994).
5   *See* H.L.A. Hart, The Concept of Law 121-32 (2nd ed., 1997) (describing the nature of open-textual nature of law); H.L.A. Hart, *Positivism and the Separation of Law and Morals*, 71 Harvard Law Review 593, 607 (1958) (providing examples of what is meant by the "open-textual nature of laws").
6   *See* Menachem Elon, 2 Jewish Law: History, Sources, Principles 903-927 (Bernard Auerbach & Melvin J. Sykes trans., 1994).
7   *See* Babylonian Talmud, Nedarim 15a; Shulchan Arukh, Yoreh Deah 214:1.
8   *See generally,* Daniel Sperber, 1 Minhagei Yisrael, 235-236 1990. *See also* Babylonian Talmud, Beitza 4b ("Their ancestral custom is in their hands."); Rabbi Moses Schreiber, Responsa Chatam Sofer, Orach Chaim, no. 122 ("From all this it seems that the essential law is that while they can nullify it, nevertheless, their children cannot nullify it."); Rabbi Yosef Shalom Elyashiv, He-arot Al Mesekhet Pesachim, p. 293 ("And an individual who accepted upon himself a good custom, this obligates his children as it says, 'Do not abandon the teachings of your mother.' However, an individual does not have to choose all the customs of his father and act like it – only those things that his father accepted also on his children after him."). *But see* Rabbi Tzvi Hirsch Eisenstadt, Pitchei Teshuva *to* Shulchan Arukh, Yoreh Deah 214:5 ("A son is not obligated to follow the customs of his father, besides for those that the son was accustomed to after he became an adult.").

local custom, which may be carried from place to place by families who retain and continue to observe the ancestral practices rooted in their countries of origin.[9] Such local customs include communal preferences for particular rabbinic texts or rulings of particular authorities, cultural practices, and localized ritual preferences. While some *halakhic* authorities have limited the scope of communal customs to those practices formally adopted by local lay and rabbinic authorities,[10] most scholars—including Rabbi Epstein—take a more expansive approach that gives normative *halakhic* weight to popular religious practices and settled standards of *halakhic* conduct, even if they have not been affirmatively enacted by any formal authorities.[11]

Rabbinic authorities have generally accepted that an individual's personal religious practices can, under certain circumstances, create *halakhic* obligations to observe such customs. The Talmudic Rabbis grounded the obligatory nature of such personal religious strictures voluntarily undertaken in the biblical doctrine of personal vows and oaths, which makes certain kinds of formally accepted personal undertakings now obligatory. The Rabbis extended the original biblical rule requiring individuals to fulfill their voluntary oaths to include self-imposed religious practices and stringencies: "You may not permit things to people that are in fact permitted, but which those people customarily treat as prohibited, as Scripture teaches, 'He shall not break his pledge' (Numbers 30:3)."[12] Based on this Talmudic rule, numerous authorities maintain that when an individual adopts specific, non-mandatory religious practices—such as fasting on certain days of the week, beginning the Sabbath early on Friday afternoon or ending the Sabbath late on Saturday night, reciting morning prayers each day at first light, abstaining from meat and wine during the three-week mourning period commemorating the destruction of Jerusalem, and myriad other practices—these modes of conduct become obligatory by operation of an implicit vow in the form of personal custom.[13] Thus, Rabbi Joseph Karo rules, "Things which are permitted, but which people—knowing that they are

---

9   *See, e.g.,* Rabbi Hezekiah da Silva, Pri Chadash *to* Shulchan Arukh, Orach Chaim 496.
10 *See* Mishneh Torah, Hilkhot Mamrim 2:2 (describing customs as being enacted into law by a vote of the *Sanhedrin*); Rabbi Isaac Alfasi, Responsa Rif, no. 13; Nachmanides, Commentary on the Talmud, Bava Batra 144b (s.v. *ha d'amrinan*).
11 *See* Menachem Elon, 2 Jewish Law: History, Sources, Principles 927-929 (Bernard Auerbach & Melvin J. Sykes trans., 1994).
12 Babylonian Talmud, Nedarim 15a. *See also* Shulchan Arukh, Yoreh Deah 214:1.
13 *See, e.g.* Arbah Turim, Yoreh Deah 214:1.

permitted—customarily treat as prohibited, are as if they were undertaken as a vow and cannot be permitted to them."[14]

Personal religious strictures of this kind are by definition elective and personal; they bind only those who voluntarily undertake them, and they do not bind anyone who does not specifically adopt such ritual practices. Consequently, we do not find Rabbi Epstein prescribing the observance of various personal religious stringencies and practices in his *Arukh HaShulchan*—which is obviously a work of generally applicable *halakhic* norms—in which such prescriptions would be out of place. Indeed, as discussed earlier in chapter eight, Rabbi Epstein affirmatively rejects the idea that particular personal stringencies and pious private practices can or should be generally recommended or prescribed as a matter of *halakhah*. Still, while he does not prescribe or recommend the performance of specific personal customs, Rabbi Epstein does endorse the normativity and obligatory nature of personal customs from a *halakhic* perspective if such practices are properly undertaken.[15] Thus, in his discussion of the laws of oaths, Rabbi Epstein, following Rabbi Karo, rules that an individual who wishes to engage in certain ascetic or pious practices like fasting can make such religious strictures legally binding on himself by having the intent to undertake the practice as a permanent feature of his religious life and by then actually engaging in the practice at least once. Alternatively, even absent any affirmative intent to permanently undertake the relevant personal religious stricture, an elective personal practice can become a binding religious obligation (according to Rabbi Epstein) if it is repeated several times and thereby becomes a settled feature of one's ritual life.[16] While Rabbi Epstein does not recommend such undertakings and even goes so far as to minutely explain how a person can engage in occasional elective piety while also avoiding any continuing *halakhic* obligation to continue the practice in the future,[17] he nevertheless accepts that personal custom can become normative and serve as a source of obligatory *halakhic* norms.

Religious strictures that begin as personal customs that bind only the person who affirmatively decides to undertake them often achieve generational longevity as personal modes of religious practice become family traditions, passed down from parents to children. When an individual—especially a head of household—adopts a particular religious practice, that practice may thereby

---

14 Shulchan Arukh, Yoreh Deah 214:1.
15 *See* Arukh HaShulchan, Yoreh Deah 214:1-15.
16 *See* ibid. 214:3-4.
17 *See* Arukh HaShulchan, Yoreh Deah 214:2.

become the standard mode of religious behavior within that person's home. Children growing up in households with such practices and learning to practice Judaism in large part by observing and habituating themselves to their parents' ritual routines thus become accustomed to parents' personal customs as normative modes of Jewish observance.[18] What were originally personal pious undertakings by a distant ancestor may thereby become routine religious practices within particular families, as individual ritual observances are mimicked and adopted by subsequent generations of descendants. Such practices thus become *minhag avot*, or "ancestral customs," modes of religious observance passed down through family lines from generation to generation. According to some authorities, once children become accustomed to regularly observing certain legally permissive religious practices, as a result of a household religious routine determined by their parents' personal ritual customs, the children can become obligated to continue such practices by the same oath-based mechanism that originally bound their parents.[19] The fact that one's parents observed a certain religious stricture does not impose a duty to maintain these traditions in and of itself; however, the fact that children raised in a home with well-settled family customs regularly observe such modes of religious conduct themselves and basically intend to continue doing so in the future may amount to their own affirmative adoption of these traditions as their own personal customs. Rabbi Joseph Steinhardt (1700-1776) explains the mechanism as follows: "A son is not automatically obligated to follow the customary practices of his father except for those practices that the son accustoms himself to observe once he reaches the age of legal majority ... but this is not so where a son never began practicing his father's good customs."[20]

Those who support the normativity of family customs rely on a Talmudic passage that appears to indicate that children are indeed bound by the personal religious strictures of their parents:

> The people of the town of Beishan had the custom to not travel from Tyre to Sidon on Fridays [in order to avoid being caught in the midst of their trip at the start of the Sabbath]. The children [of those who began this

---

18 See generally Haim Soloveitchik, *Rupture and Reconstruction: The Transformation of Contemporary Orthodoxy*, 28 Tradition 64 (Summer 1994).
19 *See, e.g.*, Rabbi Chaim ben Attar, Pri Toar, Yoreh Deah 39; Rabbi Moses Feinstein, Igrot Moshe, Orach Chaim 3:64.
20 Responsa Zichron Yosef, Yoreh Deah, no. 14, *quoted in* Rabbi Tzvi Hirsch Eisenstadt, Pitchei Teshuva *to* Shulchan Arukh, Yoreh Deah 214:5.

practice] came to Rabbi Yochanan and said, "For our fathers this [stringent avoidance of travel on Fridays] was possible, but for us it is not possible [so we would like to discard this custom]." He replied to them, "Your forebears have already accepted this, [and you must maintain the customary practice] as it says, 'Listen my son to the instructions of your father, and do not forsake the teachings of your mother'" (Proverbs 1:8).[21]

Some commentators read this exchange as reflective of the *halakhic* force of family customs.[22] In this passage, Rabbi Yochanan rules that the descendants of those who originally adopted the custom of not traveling on Fridays must continue the practice because they were bound by their forebears' prior adoption of this religious custom. Indeed, this Talmudic narrative suggests not only that family customs set obligatory religious standards, but that they do so in a manner that is even stronger and less flexible than the initial adoption of personal ritual customs. While personal customs legally grounded in the concept of vows can be abrogated when circumstances change in unforeseen ways that make maintaining the custom particularly difficult,[23] here Rabbi Yochanan denies such a request to annul the obligation put forward by the descendants of those who initiated the custom. It is impossible for children to abrogate their obligation to uphold their parents' oath-based customs on the grounds that they regret the original vow in light of changed circumstances because, as Rabbi Epstein himself explains, "Were they the ones who undertook the oath such that they could claim to regret undertaking the obligation?"[24]

Similar indications of the obligatory nature of ancestral customs are found elsewhere in the Talmud. For example, the Rabbis of the Second Temple period legislated that Jews living outside the Holy Land should celebrate each one-day holiday established by the Torah for two days.[25] This was because, in the Jewish lunar calendar, months may consist of either twenty-nine or thirty days, and no one would know which one until the new moon—signaling the start of a new month—was observed by the *Sanhedrin*, the high court in Jerusalem. Once the moon was sighted and a new month formally declared, the *Sanhedrin* sent

---

21 Babylonian Talmud, Pesachim 50b.
22 *See, e.g.*, Rabbi Chaim ben Attar, Pri Toar, Yoreh Deah 39.
23 *See* Shulchan Arukh, Yoreh Deah 228:1-4.
24 Arukh HaShulchan, Yoreh Deah 214:29. *See also* Jerusalem Talmud, Pesachim 4:1.
25 *See* Mishnah, Rosh Hashanah 2:1; Babylonian Talmud, Beitza 4b. *See also* Rabbi Yom Tov Assevilli, Ritva, Commentary on the Babylonian Talmud, Rosh Hashanah 18a; Rabbenu Nissim Gerondi Commentary on the Babylonian Talmud, Sukkah 22a (s.v. *itmar*).

messengers to Jewish communities informing them of the calendrical change so that they would be able to celebrate various holidays on the correct dates.[26] Since it took time for these messengers to bring this information to far-flung Jewish communities in the diaspora, and residents of such communities would therefore sometimes not know on which day a new month had begun in time to celebrate holidays on the correct date, the Rabbis declared that Jews living in the diaspora should celebrate holidays for two days in order to ensure that the current month's holidays would be commemorated on the correct days of the month regardless of whether the previous month had run twenty-nine or thirty days. Recognizing that the obligation to observe two-day holidays was tied to the fact that the calendar was once based on actual moon sightings, the Talmud wonders why the practice should be maintained now that the ritual calendar is based on lunar calculations and does not depend upon messengers sent forth from the *Sanhedrin*.[27] The Talmud's answer is simple: "Be careful to observe the customs of your fathers that have come to your hands."[28] This ruling, which prescribes the continued observance of "the customs of your fathers," even regarding those customs whose underlying rationales are no longer operative, provides substantial support for those who accept the normativity of family customs.[29]

Rabbi Epstein often invokes the doctrine of ancestral *minhag avot* to reinforce what he views as correct *halakhic* standards. One example of this concerns the normativity of customary deprivations observed as signs of mourning during the period commemorating the destruction of the Temple. While the Talmud prohibits laundering clothes during the week preceding Tisha B'Av, it limits this prohibition to only a specific kind of fine laundering, which the Talmud calls *gihutz*.[30] In principle, Rabbi Epstein rules that the Talmud's prohibition on laundering during the week of Tisha B'Av does not apply in his own time and place, since routine modern laundering is not as intensive as the *gihutz* laundering prohibited by the Talmud.[31] While ordinary clothes-laundering is thus technically permitted, Rabbi Epstein notes that the prevailing custom is to prohibit all manner of laundering during the period leading up to Tisha B'Av.

---

26 *See* Mishnah, Rosh Hashanah 2:1-7.
27 *See* Babylonian Talmud, Beitza 4b.
28 Ibid.
29 *See* Babylonian Talmud, Taanit 28b, which employs the same principle of ancestral custom to uphold a local practice of Babylonian Jews seemingly at odds with the normative *halakhah*.
30 *See* Babylonian Talmud, Taanit 29b.
31 *See infra* Chapter Eleven.

He writes, "And since our forefathers accepted this prohibition [on laundering], by default this becomes legally prohibited to us."[32] Rabbi Epstein also emphasizes the binding nature of ancestral customs related to the synagogue. Maimonides rules that the *bimah*, the large lectern from which the Torah scroll is publicly read and lectures given, should be placed in the middle of the synagogue, and Rabbi Moses Isserles rules accordingly.[33] However, Rabbi Epstein notes that in his own time, some agitators were seeking to alter this customary placement of the synagogue lectern and instead position the *bimah* to one side of the sanctuary.[34] Rabbi Epstein takes strong issue with this because, as he writes, "What is right in God's eyes is to not alter our ancestral customs in this matter [of the organization and set-up of the synagogue]."[35] In another instance, Rabbi Epstein defends the common practice of using "wine" made by steeping dry raisins in water for an extended period of time for *kiddush* and other ritual purposes—despite the fact that almost all rabbinic authorities have held that such wine is not fit for ritual use—by simply noting that "it is the custom of our forefathers" to treat such drinks as wine.[36]

While some authorities, including Rabbi Epstein, recognize the normativity of *minhag avot*, the vast majority of *halakhic* scholars contend that ancestral practices and family customs do not carry any independent legal weight. According to these authorities, what may at times look like obligatory family practices passed down from generation to generation are actually examples of the third category of legally recognized customs, *minhag hamakom*, or local communal customs.[37] For instance, those who reject the binding authority of family customs understand the Talmudic narrative regarding the residents of Beishan and their custom to not travel on Fridays[38] as illustrating the normativity of local, not ancestral, customs.[39] Based on this view, those who approached Rabbi Yochanan to request permission to abrogate the travel restriction were not literally the children of those who originated the practice; instead, they were simply residents of the town of Beishan whose prior inhabitants had maintained a local custom of not traveling from Tyre to Sidon on Fridays out of

---

32 Arukh HaShulchan, Orach Chaim 551:14.
33 *See* Mishneh Torah, Hilkhot Tefillah 11:3; Rema *to* Shulchan Arukh 150:5.
34 *See* Arukh HaShulchan, Orach Chaim 150:9.
35 Ibid. 150:9.
36 *See* ibid. 202:15.
37 *See, e.g.*, Responsa Chavot Yair, no. 126.
38 *See* Babylonian Talmud, Pesachim 50b.
39 *See, e.g.*, Responsa Chavot Yair, no. 126.

respect for the approaching Sabbath. These later inhabitants of Beishan found the custom unduly burdensome; therefore, they inquired of Rabbi Yochanan whether they were bound to uphold the practice in light of the present difficulties attendant to doing so and given the fact that they had not themselves ever willingly adopted the custom at issue. Rabbi Yochanan's response affirmed that regional communal customs are binding on the community as a corporate body; once properly established, local religious customs become obligatory on all local inhabitants by virtue of their membership in the community.

Many other Talmudic sources reaffirm that communal customs are legally binding, at least on local residents, and that such customs can resolve *halakhic* disputes, add to and enhance ritual practices in areas otherwise left to individual discretion by positive legal norms, and establish proper standards of religious conduct, even when they touch on matters otherwise regulated by normative *halakhic* standards. The Torah, for instance, proscribes the mixing of meat and milk but by its own terms extends this prohibition only to the meat of livestock, while the Torah itself does not forbid the mixing of milk and fowl.[40] Rabbis of the Mishnaic period disagreed about whether the biblical stricture should be rabbinically extended to include the mixing of milk and fowl, since chicken is quite similar to meat—the two are likely to be easily confused. While nearly all the rabbis of the time ultimately agreed to prohibit the consumption of milk and fowl, at least one, Rabbi Yossi HaGlili, maintained that mixing fowl and milk remains permitted. The near-universal *halakhic* standard thus prohibited mixing fowl and milk. Nevertheless, the Talmud concedes that "in the town of Rabbi Yossi HaGlili, fowl is eaten with milk,"[41] thereby giving normative legal credence to the local *halakhic* custom of following the local *halakhic* authority, even against the near-universal acceptance of the opposing legal view. Several similar passages endorse the localized adoption of the otherwise rejected rulings of local rabbinic authorities on a range of issues, including—among others—the performance of prohibited labor on the Sabbath in order to perform a ritual circumcision on that day and the consumption of certain kinds of animal fats whose *halakhic* permissibility was subject to debate.[42] Moreover, in several places, the Talmud utilizes local customary practices to resolve questions and doubts about the correct *halakhic* norm by instructing, "For all those laws which are unclear ... and with respect to which you do not

---

40   See Exodus 23:19, 34:26; Deuteronomy 14:21. *But see* Mikhilta D'Rabbi Yishmael, ch. 20.
41   Babylonian Talmud, Yevamot 14a.
42   *See* ibid.; Babylonian Talmud, Pesachim 51a.

know what is correct, go out and see what the community practices and practice accordingly."[43]

The Talmudic Rabbis even loosely connected the normativity of custom as a means of resolving *halakhic* uncertainties to a form of revelation. Thus, when the Mishnaic scholars where uncertain as to whether the Passover sacrifice should be offered when Passover Eve fell on the Sabbath, they looked to common custom to resolve the issue.[44] Apparently, the calendrical coincidence of Passover Eve and the Sabbath was a rare enough occurrence that it had not recently occurred. Left unpracticed, the Rabbis simply forgot the correct legal rule: does the slaughtering of the Passover sacrifice, which is generally a type of labor prohibited on the Sabbath, override ordinary Sabbath restrictions, or should the sacrifice not be offered when Passover Eve coincides with the Sabbath? To resolve this question, Hillel of Babylon, an eminent scholar who could not recall the right *halakhic* rule on this issue, declared, "Leave it to the Jewish people [to decide]; for if they themselves are not prophets, they are the children of prophets!"[45] Ultimately, the matter was indeed resolved by waiting to see what in fact the people would do that Passover Eve, affirming that the widespread Jewish customs and practices of the people were understood to be indicative of correct legal norms.

In addition to clarifying the right legal standard in cases of doubt about matters known to be governed by some *halakhic* standard, local customs can also establish new religious norms in areas of life left unregulated by positive *halakhah*. In addition to the previously discussed prohibition against traveling on Fridays adopted by the people of Beishan, the Talmud upholds the *halakhic* normativity of ritual purity practices related to menstruation that were originally adopted as customs by Jewish women for purposes of religious convenience, but which, once adopted, became legally mandatory.[46] In another example, when discussing a variety of different liturgical usages that can be (and in various places are) employed during the congregational recital of *Hallel*, a set of thanksgiving prayers recited on certain special occasions and holidays, the Talmud concludes by noting that the correct way to recite *Hallel* "depends on the local custom."[47] Likewise, while neither the Torah nor rabbinic legislation

---

43 Jerusalem Talmud, Peah 7:5. *See also* Babylonian Talmud, Berakhot 45a; Babylonian Talmud, Menachot 35b.
44 *See* Babylonian Talmud, Pesachim 66a.
45 Ibid.
46 *See* Babylonian Talmud, Niddah 66a.
47 Babylonian Talmud, Pesachim 119a.

formally regulate working on Passover Eve, the Talmud rules, "Where it is customary to work on Passover Eve until midday, one may do so; and where it is customary to not work then, one may not do so."[48]

Post-Talmudic scholars have disagreed about the scope of and underlying rationale for the *halakhic* normativity of communal customs. One school of thought holds that, in fact, communal practices *as such* never really create or establish *halakhic* norms. This view, which was prominent among early medieval scholars of the Sephardic tradition, holds that while local laws can be created, and while such local laws are indeed binding from a *halakhic* perspective, only formal enactment can create such legally valid customs. Based on this view, the normativity of local customs is a function of the more general biblical command to obey the judicial rulings and legislative directives of rabbinic authorities.[49] While this biblical rule is traditionally understood to apply to the legal judgments of the *Sanhedrin*, rabbinic jurisprudence has long held that "every rabbinic court in its own city is like the *Sanhedrin* with respect to all of Israel," which lends substantial religious authority to local practices grounded in formal communal enactments.[50] Nachmanides (1194-1279) thus ruled that "a custom is only binding when the local residents or the communal leaders specifically and formally adopt it."[51] According to this approach, if popular practices carry any *halakhic* weight, it is only because widespread modes of religious conduct are taken as evidence of some communal rule that was once formally enacted but is now long forgotten. The ultimate source of the normativity of such popular religious practices, however, remains the fact that it was formally legislated by local authorities. As Rabbi Isaac Alfasi explains,

> The source of any customary practice that we follow is that a majority of the community consulted with the elders of the community, and they legislated an enactment with respect to some matter . . . and even if after many years one no longer knows the root of a popular custom except that it is well established, it should be maintained on this presumption.[52]

In other words, the fundamental normativity of any popular practice—even if only assumed by virtue of the custom's being well established—is that the local

---

48 Babylonian Talmud, Pesachim 50a.
49 *See* Deuteronomy 17:11.
50 Mishneh Torah, Hilkhot Mamrim 17:11.
51 Nachmanides, Commentary to Bava Batra 144b (s.v. *ha d'amrinan*).
52 Rabbi Isaac Alfasi, Responsa Rif, no. 13.

custom reflects the community's observance of some formally enacted communal norm. A similar view is expressed by Rabbi Solomon ben Aderet (1235-1310), who argued that local customs are legally valid and binding because the fact that they are well established indicates that they were not strenuously opposed by local rabbinic authorities, which in turn supports the conclusion that they are proper applications and expressions of normative *halakhic* standards and practices.[53] Maimonides indicates a similar view and conflates the normativity of customary practices with formal rabbinic legislation, maintaining that both forms of supplementary Jewish law ultimately stem from the findings and determinations of the rabbinic courts of each generation.[54] Based on this view, the scope of obligatory *minhag* and its weightiness in the calculus of *halakhic* decision-making is substantially limited in theory, if not necessarily in practice. The community's religious practices are legally significant and valid determinants of correct *halakhic* norms only to the extent to which they accurately reflect the prior formal adoption of such practices by properly constituted and authorized law and rabbinic communal authorities. *Minhag* as popular practice per se, however, does not carry formal *halakhic* weight.

Another group of scholars rejects this formalistic approach to the authority of *minhag hamakom*. This second school of thought maintains that the popular practices of particular communities are not merely evidence of some ancient formal enactment by communal authorities; rather, they actually create normative obligations in their own right. There are several possible explanations for how and why unlegislated popular practices become mandatory within a given locale. According to some authorities, the normativity of local religious customs is a consequence of the Torah's prohibition against sectarianism, which the Talmudic Rabbis understood to require substantial uniformity of religious practice within a single community.[55] By this view, popularly observed modes of religious practice in a given community become binding by default because normative *halakhah* prohibits individuals from causing divisiveness within the community by maintaining different practices. The simultaneous public observance of different religious practices makes "the Torah appear to be two

---

53 See Rabbi Solomon ben Aderet, Responsa Rashba, no. 3:293. See also Responsa Rosh, no. 55; Responsa Maharik, no. 54.
54 See Introduction *to* Mishneh Torah.
55 See Babylonian Talmud, Yevamot 13b-14a.

Torahs"⁵⁶ and creates discord;⁵⁷ therefore, it is proscribed.⁵⁸ The existence of communal customs is simply a consequence of this prohibition; since dissent from settled communal norms of ritual practice is proscribed as a form of sectarianism, established communal customs are determinative of *halakhic* norms by default.

An alternative—and perhaps more dramatic—account of the normativity of popular practices suggests that the people's widespread and well-settled ways of practicing Judaism are a form of revelation or at least the result of a divinely guided historical process whereby some modes of *halakhic* practice and ruling become dominant in a particular place while others disappear. We have already mentioned the Talmudic endorsement of popular practice as a means of determining correct *halakhic* rules, declaring, "If they are not prophets, they are the sons of prophets," which conveys a sense in which the *de facto* practices of the Jewish people signal a kind of divine assent to the normative correctness of those ritual traditions.⁵⁹ This was a common trope among many Ashkenazic *halakhists* who, when faced with conflict between the law on the books and the way their own communities of otherwise pious Jews acted, sought to affirm the normativity of communal customs, often relying on the assumptions that the Jewish people are fundamentally righteous and that therefore their well-settled religious practices must be correct.⁶⁰ Another variation on this idea suggests that God guides and speaks through history and also helps preserve the Jewish people from inadvertently going astray.⁶¹ Thus, a popular mode of religious practice that has become normative and well settled over time amounts to a kind of expression of the divine will; God has guided historical events and pressures in such a way that the Jewish community adopted this customary practice rather than some alternative observance, and that in and of itself provides the *minhag* with some substantial religious legitimacy.

Rabbi Epstein is a strong proponent of this second understanding of the basis and scope of communal popular customs, and he often upholds the normativity of *minhag*, relying on the assumption that the religious practices of the

---

56 Rashi, Yevamot 13b (s.v. *lo ta'asu agudot agudot*).
57 *See* Mishneh Torah, Hilkhot Avodah Zarah V'Chokot HaGoyim, ch. 13.
58 *See, e.g.,* Rema *to* Shulchan Arukh, Orach Chaim 494:3.
59 *See* Babylonian Talmud, Pesachim 66a.
60 *See* Haym Soloveitchik, *Religious Law and Change: The Medieval Ashkenazic Example*, 12 AJS Review 205 (Autumn 1987).
61 *See, e.g.,* Arukh HaShulchan, Orach Chaim 345:18 (describing how a custom having become widespread throughout the majority of Jewish communities is akin, in his view, to a kind of divine revelation of the correct *halakhic* practice).

Jewish community must not be in error and that established customs reflect God's guiding hand, helping reveal the law through communal practice over time. There is, for instance, a fundamental rabbinic dispute about the legal definition of a "public domain" for purposes of Sabbath restrictions.[62] Jewish law forbids Jews from carrying things from public to private domains or within a public domain on the Sabbath.[63] While some of the characteristics of a *halakhic* public domain are defined by the Talmud, post-Talmudic authorities disagreed about whether there is a minimum population requirement for a space to be considered "public." According to most scholars, there is no minimum population threshold for an otherwise open area accessible to the public at large to be considered a "public domain"; this is in fact the more textually sound position, as the Talmud spends a good deal of space defining the parameters of public domains, but in doing so it makes no mention of any population threshold.[64] Some scholars disagree, including many prominent rabbis of the Ashkenazic tradition. Based on the fact that Sabbath prohibitions are exegetically related to biblical descriptions of the Jews' desert encampment during their forty-year sojourn in the wilderness on the way to Canaan, and based on the fact that the bible describes the Jewish desert population as consisting of six hundred thousand military-age men, these authorities maintain that a space must be used regularly by at least six hundred thousand people in order to be considered a "public domain" in the eyes of *halakhah*.[65] The implications of the dispute are obvious. The less textually justifiable minority view—demanding a population of six hundred thousand before a space will be considered "public"—makes it possible for Jews to carry things into and through the streets on the Sabbath, since almost no public streets are traversed by that many people on a regular basis and are therefore not considered "public domains" where carrying is prohibited. According to the majority position, however, most streets are considered "public domains" where carrying is prohibited on the Sabbath.

By Rabbi Epstein's own time, the dominant practice in Europe's Ashkenazic communities had long accepted the minority position that imposed minimum

---

62 *See generally* Rabbi Yosef Gavriel Bechhoffer, The Contemporary Eruv: Eruvin in Modern Metropolitan Areas 41-50 (2002).
63 *See* Mishneh Torah, Hilkhot Eruvin 1:1-6.
64 *See* Arukh HaShulchan, Orach Chaim 345:14-15.
65 *See* ibid. 345:17 (noting *halakhic* authorities who rule leniently on this matter, including the *Sefer HaTerumah*, the *Semag*, the *Semak*, the *Maharam MeRutenberg*, the *Rosh*, and the *Arbah Turim*).

population requirements on the *halakhic* definition of a "public domain."[66] In his treatment of the issue, Rabbi Epstein expresses serious jurisprudential doubts about the *halakhic* credibility of the more lenient position, first because it is poorly grounded in the Talmud in comparison to the stricter view, second because *halakhic* jurisprudence generally prescribes that minority opinions be defeated by majority rulings, and third because the minority view seems to contradict a biblical passage in which the prophet Nehemiah chastises the people for carrying on the Sabbath at a time when the local population was no larger than forty thousand.[67] Despite these very real *halakhic* difficulties with minority view, Rabbi Epstein accepts it as normative and valid. He writes:

> However, in any case, all this analysis does not matter now that there is widespread acceptance [that carrying in the streets is permitted] in most of the cities of the Jewish people these past several hundred years in reliance on this [minority] viewpoint. And it is as if a voice has gone forth from the Heavens saying that "the *halakhah* is in accordance with this view."[68]

Rabbi Epstein exhibits similar respect for the presumptive validity of popular modes of religious practice in many other places as well, even when such practices stand in real tension with *halakhic* norms grounded in primary rabbinic texts and methods.

The confluence of these various instantiations and applications of the normativity of *minhag* in rabbinic jurisprudence contribute to a broad understanding among many scholars that the customary *halakhic* practices and interpretations of particular Jewish groups constituted along ethnic, cultural, ideological, and geographical lines are important—even primary—sources of *halakhic* norms. The most widely recognized of such traditions are the Ashkenazic customs of the Jewish communities of Christian Europe, the Sephardic traditions of Spain and North African Jews, and the Edot HaMizrach customs of Middle Eastern Jewish communities, as well as a smattering of other traditions of Jewish customs of communities in Yemen, Central Asia, Italy, Germany, and Greece, among other locations. While all of these varied

---

66 *See generally* Adam Mintz, *Halakhah in America: The History of City Eruvin, 1894-1962*, pp. 132-175 (2011) (Dissertation) (discussing the use and justification for the construction of *eruvin* in early modern and modern Europe).
67 *See* Nehemiah 8:7; *see generally* Arukh HaShulchan, Orach Chaim 345:16-18.
68 Arukh HaShulchan, Orach Chaim 345:18.

traditions share broad commonalities in religious practice, they differ in important ways in the details of their respective prayer liturgies and practices, holiday observances, dietary laws, family life, and the relative importance they attribute to various rabbinic texts and *halakhic* authorities. For most of Jewish history, and even in Talmudic times, the practices of each of these communities were regarded as normative for members of that community.[69] For most *halakhic* scholars, the normativity of these distinct customary traditions of Jewish law and practice continues in the modern era, even as the heirs of these once geographically distinct communities now live and practice side by side in places like Israel and the United States.[70]

For Rabbi Epstein, who was raised and educated in the Lithuanian Ashkenazic tradition and lived and worked in Russia,[71] the customary practices and recognized *halakhic* authorities of the European Ashkenazic tradition generally (and of the Eastern European Lithuanian tradition more specifically) carry substantial normative weight. *Minhag* in this sense is both a source of normative *halakhic* standards as well as an honored reservoir of religious living to be defended in cases of tension with other sources of proper Jewish practice.

For Rabbi Epstein, customary practice determines the correct manner of fulfilling ritual handwashing obligations, for instance. There is a disagreement among medieval *halakhic* authorities regarding which parts of the hand must be washed in order to fulfill the obligations of ritual handwashing.[72] According to the *Raabad* and the *Rosh*, one must wash one's fingers up to the "third joint," which commentators understand to mean the knuckles.[73] Maimonides rules similarly, prescribing that for ritual handwashing, one must wash the entirety of the fingers (but no more).[74] Rabbi Isaac Alfasi disagrees, however, and rules that one must wash one's whole hand up to the wrist.[75] Rabbi Epstein rules that the law follows the more lenient view of the *Raabad* and the *Rosh*, which is supported by the *Zohar*, which teaches that when performing ritual handwashing, one must be careful to wash "fourteen joints" on each hand: the two

---

69 *Cf.* Babylonian Talmud, Pesachim 51a.
70 *See, e.g.*, Rabbi Abraham Isaac Kook, Orach Mishpat, Orach Chaim 17; Rabbi Abraham Isaac Kook, Igrot HaRayah no. 576.
71 *See supra* Chapter Two.
72 On the obligation and rationale for ritual handwashing, see generally Babylonian Talmud, Chullin 105b-106a; Babylonian Talmud, Shabbat 13b; Babylonian Talmud, Berakhot 53b.
73 *See* Arukh HaShulchan, Orach Chaim 161:7.
74 *See* Mishneh Torah, Hilkhot Berakhot 6:4.
75 *See* Arukh HaShulchan, Orach Chaim 161:8.

joints on the thumb and the three joints on each of the other four fingers.[76] This supports the view that ritual handwashing must cover the entire finger but need not also cover the hand up to the wrist, as prescribed by Rabbi Alfasi. Rabbi Epstein notes that although the *halakhah* does not require one to wash the entire hand, because the widespread custom is to wash the whole hand in accordance with Rabbi Alfasi's view, he therefore advises people to follow this more stringent practice.

Minhag also establishes the *halakhic* norms of commemorative mourning practices during the period recalling the destruction of Jerusalem and the First and Second Temples. While the Talmud prohibits laundering clothes during the week preceding Tisha B'Av, it limits this prohibition to only a specific kind of fine laundering, which the Talmud calls *gihutz*.[77] Rabbi Epstein rules that in principle, the Talmud's prohibition on laundering during the week of Tisha B'Av does not apply in his own time and place, since routine modern laundering is not as intensive as the *gihutz* laundering prohibited by the Talmud. While ordinary clothes-laundering is thus technically permitted, Rabbi Epstein notes that the prevailing custom is to prohibit all manner of laundering during the period leading up to Tisha B'Av. He writes, "And since our forefathers accepted this prohibition [on laundering], by default this becomes legally prohibited to us."[78] Relatedly, the Talmud rules, "All the commandments that apply to a mourner are practiced on Tisha B'Av."[79] Since the Tisha B'Av restrictions prescribed by the Talmud are tied to mourning practices, the *Rosh* writes that in truth one should be obligated to wear *tefillin* on Tisha B'Av, since mourners are obligated to wear *tefillin* after the first day following the death of a relative, and mourning practices of Tisha B'Av are no more restrictive than those of mourning following the day of death.[80] Nevertheless, despite the lack of any clear Talmudic prohibition against doing so, the general practice is to not wear *tefillin* on the morning of Tisha B'Av. Rabbi Esptein accepts this custom and rules that as a matter of law, *tefillin* should not be worn on Tisha B'Av morning.[81] While the Talmud does not instruct that the regular obligation to wear *tefillin* is suspended on Tisha B'Av, Rabbi Epstein thinks that the widespread popular custom to not wear *tefillin* on Tisha B'Av morning is determinative.

---

76 *See* ibid.
77 *See* Babylonian Talmud, Taanit 29b.
78 Arukh HaShulchan, Orach Chaim 551:14.
79 Babylonian Talmud, Taanit 30a.
80 *See* Rosh *to* Babylonian Talmud, Taanit 4:37.
81 *See* Arukh HaShulchan, Orach Chaim 555:2.

The importance of customary practices as determinate of correct *halakhic* norms leads Rabbi Epstein to find ways to justify established customs, especially when those customs cut against the legal import of other sources of *halakhah*. Rabbi Epstein notes that in his own time, for instance, many communities had the custom to use various synagogue accoutrements for mundane purposes. These practices included using the ark curtains to form marriage canopies and placing the Torah scrolls on the *bimah* and a candle in the ark on the holiday of Hoshana Rabbah.[82] These customs are in tension with standard *halakhic* rules that *tashmishei kedushah*—items used for sanctified purposes—cannot be used for other non-sanctified purposes, and they must be placed in *genizah* storage once their usefulness for their originally designated holy purpose has passed.[83] While many authorities therefore severely criticized the kinds of practices Rabbi Epstein described, Rabbi Epstein himself attempts to justify the custom. He notes that the Talmud itself permits the use of sanctified objects for mundane purposes if the items were originally only designated for sanctity on condition that they could also be used for other functions.[84] Based on this idea, and in an attempt to reconcile the *halakhah* with customary practice, Rabbi Moses Isserles and the *Terumat HaDeshen*, a medieval rabbinic authority, suggest that one may use various sanctified synagogue accoutrements for mundane purposes even without having made any explicit conditions to that effect at the time that the items were initially designated for holy uses.[85] Rabbi Isserles explains that since it is practically very difficult to ensure that such items are not used for any mundane purposes, it is as though "the court initially stipulated conditions on their sanctified use."[86] While Rabbi Epstein notes that it is difficult to justify the *Terumat HaDeshen*'s view that the designation of all synagogue items includes an implicit condition permitting their use for mundane purposes, and while he points out that even the *Terumat HaDeshen* finds the idea suspect, Rabbi Epstein ultimately accepts this line of reasoning in order to provide justification for the common customary practice to use synagogue accoutrements for mundane purposes.[87]

In the face of normative *halakhic* challenges, Rabbi Epstein likewise defends the validity of popular custom in the case of using raisin wine for ritual

---

82 *See* ibid. 154:11.
83 *See* Babylonian Talmud, Megillah 26b.
84 *See* Beit Yosef, Orach Chaim 154:12.
85 *See* Terumat HaDeshen, no. 263; Rema *to* Shulchan Arukh, Orach Chaim 154:8.
86 Rema *to* Shulchan Arukh, Orach Chaim 154:8.
87 *See* Arukh HaShulchan, Orach Chaim 154:11.

purposes. The *Arbah Turim* rules that one may recite the Sabbath *kiddush* over raisin wine.[88] This is based on a Talmudic passage that teaches that raisin wine was even *ex post facto* ritually fit for use as part of the offering services in the Temple.[89] If raisin wine is fit for Temple service, it is surely fit for use to fulfill the rabbinic obligation to recite the Sabbath *kiddush* over a cup of wine.[90] Virtually all authorities include an important caveat to this *halakhic* permission to use raisin wine for *kiddush*: the *Arbah Turim*, Maimonides, Rabbi Isaac Alfasi, and Rabbi Moses Isserles all rule that raisin wine is only ritually fit for use for reciting *kiddush* if it was produced from raisins that themselves still contained some small amount of grape juice within them. If, however, the wine was produced merely by steeping completely dry raisins in water for an extended period of time, the "wine"—which is in fact just raisin-flavored water—may not be used for the Sabbath *kiddush*.[91] In light of the strong consensus of authorities invalidating the use of raisin wine made by steeping dry raisins in water for ritual purposes, Rabbi Epstein raises concerns about how people routinely used raisin wine for *kiddush* in his own time and place. This is problematic, he says, because "everyone knows that the small raisins we use to make raisin wine are extremely dry and have no moisture in them at all," which renders the "wine" made from these raisins unsuitable for ritual purposes.[92] Despite these very serious grounds for objection, Rabbi Epstein seeks to justify the local custom and therefore offers several different justifications for the widespread practice of using this kind of raisin wine for *kiddush*.

First, he suggests that the view that wine made from dry raisins is not legally treated as wine is grounded in another *halakhic* position held by Maimonides and Rabbi Alfasi, though it is rejected by most Ashkenazic *halakhic* authorities. There is a basic dispute among early authorities regarding whether the Torah recognizes the flavor of a food as the substance of the food or if this principle is merely rabbinic in nature. According to Maimonides and others, this is merely a rabbinic rule, and Rabbi Epstein suggests this may be why Maimonides declines to treat drinks made from completely dry raisins—which do not contain any actual juice secreted from the raisins themselves—as wine. Ashkenazic authorities, however, maintain that flavor is regarded as

---

88 *See* Arbah Turim, Orach Chaim 727:1.
89 *See* Babylonian Talmud, Bava Batra 97a.
90 *See* Arukh HaShulchan, Orach Chaim 202:15.
91 *See* ibid. 272:6.
92 Ibid. 202:15.

substance even at a biblical level, and based on that line of reasoning, one might be able to treat even water flavored by dry raisins as wine.

Rabbi Epstein also offers a second justification for the common practice of using raisin wine for *kiddush* by arguing that the legal definition of "wine" actually depends on what people customarily regard as wine. Since people consider wine made from dry raisins to be "wine," it may be used for *kiddush*. Third, Rabbi Epstein argues that it would be impracticable to *not* treat this commonly used raisin wine as ritually suitable wine, since in his time and place, proper wine was simply not readily available to most people, and raisin wine had to serve as an acceptable substitute.[93]

In addition to the normative *halakhic* value of custom as a means of establishing proper *halakhic* standards, customary practices also create social realities and "facts on the ground" that can put pressure on rabbinic decisors tasked with making legal rulings to understand and interpret legal rules in ways that do not too dramatically conflict with the lived realities of their communities. While this will be discussed in greater detail below in connection with Rabbi Epstein's ninth methodological principle, it is important to note here that the *de facto* existence of certain modes of religious practice—or, indeed, of normatively incorrect practice—among Jewish populations establishes an important data point in Rabbi Epstein's *halakhic* calculations.

The *halakhic* import of custom is not limitless, however. Aside from the more skeptical rabbinic perspectives on the normativity of *minhag* discussed above, even Rabbi Epstein's expansive respect for the power of customary practices and usages to establish and determine *halakhic* standards is limited. In Rabbi Epstein's jurisprudence, custom only operates as a legitimate source of religious norms in two ways: first, *minhag* can establish standards of *halakhic* conduct within the neutral permissive space left to personal discretion by ordinary *halakhic* sources and methods; and second, *minhag* may function to resolve disputes over correct standards in areas of life regulated by normative *halakhah*.[94] Customary practices cannot, however, change the law in cases where the correct *halakhic* standard is clear and uncontested. In such instances, in Rabbi Epstein's words, "It is prohibited to follow the *minhag*, and we must eradicate it."[95] True to his methodological leanings, Rabbi Epstein grounds even this secondary rule regarding the scope of legally legitimate customs in a

---

93 *See* ibid. 272:7.
94 *See* Arukh HaShulchan, Yoreh Deah 214:33.
95 Ibid. 214:33.

Talmudic norm: "Where there is a [legal] prohibition, of what matter is it that the people customarily act [in a different way]?"[96]

In several places, following this approach, Rabbi Epstein strongly condemns popular practices which he understands as entirely incompatible with accepted *halakhic* norms. For instance, Rabbi Epstein strongly condemns the popular practice of reciting the *Kaddish* prayer multiple times during the morning prayer service. The early Second Temple period rabbinic synod known as the Men of the Great Assembly legislated the recitation of the *Kaddish*, a prayer designed to punctuate the standard prayer liturgy and other important occasions with acknowledgments of God's greatness. Rabbi Epstein notes that many communities customarily punctuate the morning prayer service by reciting *Kaddish* many times—indeed, more times than the Talmudic Rabbis themselves prescribed. Taking as normative the Talmudic prescription of the correct number of times which *Kaddish* should be said during the morning prayer service, Rabbi Epstein rejects this common custom. While Rabbi Epstein generally treats customs with deference, he views the custom of reciting *Kaddish* more than is legally necessary as a supererogatory practice carrying negative repercussions. Rabbi Epstein notes that according to one major authority, reciting *Kaddish* (which contains God's name) is akin to reciting blessings: "Just as it is good to be frugal with reciting blessings, it is likewise good to be frugal with the recitation of the *Kaddish* prayer."[97] Thus, following the general principle that one does not recite unnecessary blessings, as they involve the possible violation of the biblical injunction against taking God's name in vain, Rabbi Epstein prohibits the unnecessary recital of *Kaddish* and prescribes that *Kaddish* should be said only at those points in the prayer service at which it is legally required.

* * * * *

As this chapter shows, *minhag* is an important factor in the determination of *halakhic* standards in the *Arukh HaShulchan*. Rabbi Epstein embraces the normativity of personal, ancestral, and local and communal customs, and he generally seeks to reinforce the *halakhic* legitimacy of such customs in his rulings. The *Arukh HaShulchan*'s regard for custom leads Rabbi Epstein to use *minhag* as a determining factor in the resolution of otherwise intractable rabbinic disputes and to prescribe as legally normative new practices and modes of religious

---

96 Babylonian Talmud, Rosh Hashanah 15b.
97 Arukh HaShulchan, Orach Chaim 55:3.

conduct not contemplated by primary rabbinic sources. Perhaps most significantly, the weighty role of *minhag* in establishing standards of *halakhic* practice in the methodology of the *Arukh HaShulchan* results in Rabbi Epstein sometimes going to some lengths to justify popular customs, even when they stand in tension with normative practice as prescribed by textual sources of Jewish law. In this sense, Rabbi Epstein's jurisprudence recognizes *minhag* as playing an important balancing role in the determination of Jewish legal norms. The *halakhah* cannot be prescribed merely on the basis of analytic assessments of Talmudic discourses, but it must account for and be responsive to the weight of the religiously observant Jewish community's *halakhic* practice and experience.

CHAPTER ELEVEN

Temporal Rationalization of *Halakhic* Rules

This chapter discusses Rabbi Epstein's approach to one of the most vexing and challenging issues in *halakhic* decision-making: how to determine what settled *halakhic* rules and principles require in practice in contexts and under conditions that are substantially different from the ones in which these standards were originally formulated and prescribed.

* * * * *

Principle Nine: Rabbi Epstein insists that halakhic issues need to be decided in the present time and place. Thus, he holds that when the reasons for established halakhic rules no longer apply due to changed circumstances, those rules likewise change so as to respond effectively to current realities.

Law—all law deserving the name—is ultimately purposive and casuistic.[1] Legal rules and standards that govern society through a variety of functions—

---

1   Casuistry is often associated with the study of biblical law and is contrasted with apodictic legal pronouncements. *See* Alt Albrecht, *The Origins of Israelite Law*, 81, *in* Essays on Old Testament History and Religion (R. A. Wilson, trans. 1966). While apodictic normative prescriptions speak in the abstract, casuistic legal formulations offer legal rulings in response to particular sets of facts— "if A injures B, then A shall be liable to compensate B for his injuries." While casuistry often carries a negative connotation and is viewed as a deceptive means of reasoning to reach improper normative conclusions in specific situations, at bottom, it represents the idea that legal conclusions are ultimately responsive to the specific facts to which general legal standards are to be applied. *See* Brian Z. Tamanaha, *Good Casuistry and Bad Casuistry: Resolving the Dilemmas Faced by Catholic Judges*, 4 University of St. Thomas Law Journal 269 (2006). The law requires different things in different cases

such as regulating behavior, imposing duties, prescribing particular forms by which transactions can be executed and relationships can be created and dissolved, and legitimating decision-making and enforcement processes—are not ends in and of themselves. Instead, legal norms regulate conduct in order to accomplish desired policy goals.[2] In the American context, courts have made clear that arbitrary laws—laws that serve no actual policy end—are constitutionally invalid. Even the most benign legislative or regulatory prescriptions that do not touch on or restrict important individual rights are adjudged invalid if they fail what the Supreme Court has termed basic "rational basis" review. Under this standard, a law is not valid (and is not "law" at all) if at a bare minimum its regulation of behavior is not at least "rationally related" to furthering some "legitimate government interest."[3] Consider, for example, something as simple as a law prescribing that all cars shall drive on the right side of the road or laws imposing a speed limit. Requiring drivers to drive on the right side of the street and prohibiting them from driving on the left side, as well as laws prohibiting driving above a certain speed, are not ends in and of themselves; they are means of achieving a substantive policy preference of creating a safe and orderly environment for operating automobiles. The same is true for

---

because changed circumstances warrant different normative means of reaching the same policy aims.

2   The notion that laws must serve a purpose—that they cannot be arbitrary—is a fundamental assumption of Anglo-American law and is deeply rooted in international conceptions of what it means to have a legitimate rule of law. Put simply, laws that serve no legitimate public policy purpose, laws that regulate merely for the sake of regulating, are not viewed as legitimate. *See, e.g.*, William Blackstone, 1 Commentaries on the Laws of England 126, 129-132 (observing that laws that regulate without serving any public good are destructive of liberty and illegitimate); Jeffrey D. Jackson, *Blackstone's Ninth Amendment: A Historical Common Law Baseline for the Interpretation of Unenumerated Rights*, 62 Oklahoma Law Review 167 (2010); Jeffrey D. Jackson, *Putting Rationality Back Into the Rational Basis Test: Saving Substantive Due Process and Redeeming the Promise of the Ninth Amendment*, 45 University of Richmond Law Review 491, 499-526 (2011). *Halakhic* scholars have made similar observations about Jewish law, arguing that the specific rules and standards that prescribe or forbid certain behaviors must necessarily serve a further purpose, even if at times that purpose remains unknown. *See, e.g.* Maimonides, Guide to the Perplexed 3:31:

> There are persons who find it difficult to give a reason for any of the commandments, and consider it right to assume that the commandments and prohibitions have no rational basis whatever... But the truth is undoubtedly as we have said, that every one of the 613 precepts serves to inculcate some truth, to remove some erroneous opinion, to establish proper relations in society, to diminish evil, to train in good manners or to warn against bad habits.

3   *See United States v. Carolene Products Co.*, 304 U.S. 144, 152-53 n.4 (1938).

virtually all laws; laws aim to regulate conduct in order to achieve goals and create conditions that are deemed desirable from a public policy perspective.

What is true of American law is largely true of Jewish law as well. *Halakhic* obligations are not ends in and of themselves; rather, they seek to regulate behavior (and sometimes thought) in order to achieve certain positive outcomes. This view is well expressed by Maimonides, who asserted that "every one of the 613 precepts serves to inculcate some truth, to remove some erroneous opinion, to establish proper relations in society, to diminish evil, to train in good manners, or to warn against bad habits."[4] Indeed, Maimonides went so far as to criticize those who find it difficult to give a reason for any of the commandments—as well as those who assume that the commandments and prohibitions have no rational basis whatever—as having "a disease of the soul."[5] Rabbinic scholars throughout history have classified Torah laws in a variety of ways and have acknowledged that the policy aims and rationales may be more evident for some laws than for others. The broadly mainstream consensus view, however, has long been that the particular rules and standards of *halakhah* are purposive and are means of achieving certain divinely desired goals rather than ends in themselves.[6]

This is especially true when it comes to new laws and practices legislated by the Talmudic Rabbis and also to rabbinic specifications and interpretations of Torah law norms. When the rabbis legislated and interpreted the law within the "open-texture" spaces of Torah text and tradition,[7] they did so with an eye towards achieving certain religiously, materially, and socially desirable results.[8] The Rabbis prescribed an obligation to light candles outside the door to one's home during the evenings of the eight days of Hanukkah—not because lighting candles in that manner is essentially right, but in order to commemorate and publicize the miracles experienced by the Jewish people in their religious,

---

4   Maimonides, Guide to the Perplexed 3:31.
5   Ibid.
6   *See* Deuteronomy 6:24; Babylonian Talmud, Makkot 24a; Midrash Rabbah, Genesis 44:1; Rav Saadia Gaon, Emunot V'Deot 3:1; Rabbi Judah Loew, Tiferet Yisrael, ch. 7; Samson Raphael Hirsch, Horeb (Isidore Grunfeld, trans., 2002). *But see* Rashi *to* Leviticus 19:19 (s.v. *chukim*).
7   *See* H.L.A. Hart, The Concept of Law 121-32 (2nd ed., 1997) (describing the nature of open-textual nature of law); H.L.A. Hart, *Positivism and the Separation of Law and Morals*, 71 Harvard Law Review 593, 607 (1958) (providing examples of what is meant by the "open-textual nature of laws").
8   *See* Ephraim E. Urbach, The Halakhah: Its Sources and Development 7 (1986).

political, and military struggle against the Seleucid empire.[9] Likewise, the Talmudic Rabbis interpreted ambiguous biblical passages pertaining to judicial procedure, evidence, and the imposition of corporal punishment restrictively in order to avoid being obligated to impose harsh and at times inequitable or ineffective Torah-prescribed penalties for various sins, as well as to create greater latitude and discretion to address social and religious ills in a more tailored and flexible manner.[10] In a similar vein, the Rabbis prohibited clapping and dancing on the Sabbath, the consumption of dairy and poultry together, and drinking water left uncovered overnight. They did so not merely because they viewed these practices as essentially wrong; rather, they did so in order to achieve policy objectives: one may not clap or dance on the Sabbath because doing so may lead one to tune or repair a musical instrument—a biblical sin; milk must be kept separate from poultry because this helps reinforce the biblical mandate to not mix meat and dairy; water left uncovered overnight must be discarded out of concern that a snake may have drunk from the water during the night, leaving behind dangerous poison.[11] Jewish law is thus fundamentally purposive; specific rules are means of achieving certain desirable outcomes, not ends in and of themselves.

In light of this, one of the most central and contentious issues in post-Talmudic Jewish law is the question of whether change in circumstance gives rise to a change in legal rule, or just a change in application. What should a rabbinic decision maker do when, under current conditions, the application of a Talmudic rule or accepted post-Talmudic legal understanding fails to achieve the policy objectives and desired outcomes that underlie that *halakhic* norm? Many important areas of Jewish law are codified in a way that is closely tied to the subjective and nuanced contexts in which they were formulated. Consider, for example, the simple question of a man wearing a woman's garment or the reverse. Following the biblical verse, the rule of Jewish law is relatively clear: people of either sex may not wear garments reserved for those of the other sex.[12] What is unclear is which garments fit into which category. To no one's surprise, a timeless legal system can only articulate a rule like this in a very general way and must leave the application of this rule to the decisions

---

9   See Babylonian Talmud, Shabbat 21b.
10 See Shlomo Pill, *The Political Enforcement of Rabbinic Theocracy? Religious Norms in Halakhic Practice* 2 Studies in Judaism, Humanities, and the Social Sciences 23 (2018).
11 See Babylonian Talmud, Beitza 36b; Babylonian Talmud, Chullin 116a; Babylonian Talmud, Chullin 10a.
12 *See* Deuteronomy 22:5.

of every generation. Grounded in this general rule, the Talmud prohibits men from shaving their body hair, and women from wearing military dress or carrying weaponry.[13] But what about those times and places in which grooming body hair is a routine male practice, or where women routinely serve in militaries and carry personal weapons: do the specific Talmudic rules still apply, or does the application of the underlying rationale for the Talmudic standard (the maintenance of distinct male and female dress and mannerisms) to new conditions warrant different conclusions about what the same laws require in practice? In fact, rabbinic scholars and Jewish law codifiers have repeatedly answered this question by periodically updating and reformulating the specific proscribed practices encompassed by this law in light of their contexts. Thus, in twelfth century Egypt, Maimonides codified this rule as including a prohibition on women wearing turbans,[14] while Rabbi Joseph Karo forbade men from gazing at their reflection in a mirror, and Rabbi Moses Isserles disagreed, arguing that it is only prohibited for a man to groom himself in a mirror if that is an exclusively female practice in his own time and place.[15] This updating of Jewish law is the routine gristmill of what the *Arukh HaShulchan* does in his code regularly, namely taking the timeless principles of Jewish law and applying them to the timely reality of the *Arukh HaShulchan*.[16] Without this regular updating, of course, Jewish law would collapse and be unworkable; it would become an ossified legal system that is not connected the reality of its times. Updating timeless principles with modern applications is what legal systems regularly do and in the Jewish tradition is, in principle, done routinely and without controversy.

There is a second matter, however, which is a source of quite a bit of broad dispute in Jewish law, namely how to determine when reality has changed enough to justify concluding not only that a *halakhic* rule requires a different mode of conduct in practice, but that the rule itself is no longer in force. Perhaps changed circumstances that effectively undermine a rule's usefulness for achieving its desired goals serve to nullify the rule itself. Yet, on the other hand, changing or repealing a rabbinic rule in that way may require a formal judicial quorum and another rabbinic decree, something which frequently cannot be done since the destruction of the Second Temple and the

---

13 *See* Babylonian Talmud, Nazir 59a.
14 *See* Mishneh Torah, Hilkhot Avodah Zarah V'Chokot HaGoyim 12:10.
15 *See* Shulchan Arukh, Yoreh Deah 156:2; Rema *ad loc.*
16 These areas are codified in Shulchan Arukh, Yoreh Deah 182.

abandonment of centralized authority from the end of the Talmudic era.[17] The answers are far from clear.

The general rule of Jewish law, as found in the Talmud, is that a rabbinic decree, once enacted, only expires when it is repealed by a formal enactment of a quorum of authorized rabbis.[18] For example, there was an ancient rabbinic decree that certain fruits could only be eaten in Jerusalem.[19] The logic of this decree was simple: requiring certain kinds of fruit to be eaten in Jerusalem would help ensure those fruits would be regularly available around the Temple and for the Jews of Jerusalem, reducing costs and enhancing the Temple and holiday festivities. When Jerusalem was sacked and the Second Temple destroyed by the Romans in 70 CE, logic would have indicated that the decree would no longer be applicable and would therefore naturally expire; after all, what would be the logic connected with providing plentiful and economically discounted fruits to one's evil occupiers who had destroyed the Temple? Yet, the Talmud discusses this issue in detail and concludes that Jewish law authorities seem to generally mandate that a formal act of repeal is needed to end all rabbinic decrees.[20] The Talmud gives other examples of this legal insight as well, and few doubt that this more formal approach seems to be the Talmudic model.[21]

However, this subject is fraught with nuance and complexity, mostly due to the fact that, for at least the last fifteen hundred years, the rabbinic quorum needed to repeal rabbinic decrees has frequently—really almost always—been unavailable.[22] This reality, coupled with the simple fact that Jewish law is indeed purposive and needs to be periodically updated in order to account for the changing factual conditions and contexts in which it must be applied and practiced, has driven rabbinic scholars to recognize a number of exceptions to the clear Talmudic directive that mandates repeal of rabbinic laws only through a formal judicial-legislative act of a properly constituted *Sanhedrin*. *Halakhic* scholars have advanced at least six different ideas to explain how and when rabbinic decrees and settled legal norms can be updated and changed.

---

17 See Mishneh Torah, Hilkhot Mamrim 2:2.
18 See generally 6 Encyclopedia Talmudit 698-705 (s.v. *davar shebminyan tzarikh minyan acher lehatiro*); Babylonian Talmud, Beitza 5a-b.
19 See Babylonian Talmud, Beitza 5a.
20 Rabbi Menachem Meiri, Beit HaBechirah, to Babylonian Talmud, Beitza 5a.
21 See 6 Encyclopedia Talmudit 698-705 (s.v. *davar shebminyan tzarikh minyan acher lehatiro*).
22 See Babylonian Talmud, Bava Kamma 84b; A History of the Jewish People 317-23 (H. H. Ben-Sasson, ed., 1985).

First and most broadly, some rabbinic scholars have rejected the idea that laws cannot be repealed or changed in response to changing conditions that render such rules ineffective at furthering their own purposes. These authorities argue that many rabbinic decrees were legislated to be time-bound, such that when the reason for the decree expires and the time has passed, the decree naturally expires as well.[23] The claim of this group is that, as a general idea, rabbinic decrees are bound by time and place, absent some expression of deep and permanent intention. As enormous social, political, economic, and cultural change takes place, decrees lose their force and are less valid. This very broad exception to the bar on reconsidering the applicability of rabbinic laws—that rabbinic laws expire as their rationales become irrelevant, unless the Rabbis specifically indicated otherwise—is adopted in several cases by *Tosafot*, who often offer this explanation to justify why their own communities often did not observe certain rabbinic rules, even as they were otherwise fully observant of Jewish law.[24]

A second approach—which includes a number of different variations—distinguishes between *halakhic* rules that change based on the continued relevance of their underlying purposes, and those that do not change, depending on the relationship between any given rabbinic law and its rationale, and whether the rationale is part of the rule itself. According to some rabbinic authorities, the Talmudic mandate that formal approval by a court or *Sanhedrin* is required to change or repeal laws is limited to situations where the initial rabbinic decree did not itself incorporate a rationale as part of the legislated norm, where explanations of the new norm were only offered either contemporaneous with or subsequent to the rule's enactment.[25] In such cases, the rationale itself is not part of the rule; the legislated rule stands on its own, and any stated rationales and objectives the rule means to serve are thereby merely speculative. In such cases, the fact that a rule no longer serves its original purpose due to changes to the factual conditions to which it is applied is insufficient to justify suspension of the rule itself. However, in cases where the initial rabbinic decree directly incorporated a reason into the rule, it is as if the Rabbis who enacted the decree crafted an automatic repeal mechanism, such that when the reason is

---

23 *See, e.g.*, Tosafot *to* Babylonian Talmud, Beitza 5a (s.v. *kol davar shebeminyan tzarikh minyan acher lehatiro*); Rabbi Solomon Luria, Yam Shel Shlomo, Beitza 1:9.
24 *See* Tosafot *to* Babylonian Talmud, Beitza 30a (s.v. *tenan ain*).
25 *See, e.g.*, Rabbi David ben Solomon ibn Zimra (Radbaz), Divrei David *to* Mishneh Torah, Hilkhot Mamrim 2:2.

completely inapplicable the decree does not apply.[26] Other scholars have rejected this distinction between rabbinic laws that include a rationale and those for which reasons are offered separately from the legislated standard itself. These authorities maintain instead that whenever a rabbinic law is rationally tied to a reasonable rationale, the presence of the reason allows lesser rabbinical courts—which may be found in many communities and are not unduly complex to constitute—to repeal the enactment when they adjudge the reason to be no longer applicable.[27] Still other scholars distinguish between cases in which the reason is attached to the decree and widely known to be as such, and cases in which the reason is attached to the decree but is not widely known to be so. This third group only permits the repeal of laws when the reasons for the rule are widely and popularly known.[28] In such cases, there is no serious concern that treating the rule as no longer applicable will lead to general and popular disillusionment with the principled nature of rabbinic jurisprudence—indeed, on the contrary, the continued application of the rule whose well-known rationale no longer applies would likely place *halakhah* in disrepute. When the reason for a rabbinic law is not widely understood, however, disregarding the rule would make Jewish law appear to be merely a function of rabbinic will; such laws may therefore only be changed or repealed by a proper vote of the *Sanhedrin*.[29]

A third approach maintains that laws that apply to facts or situations that are naturally and predictably fluid are presumed to have been legislated with the understanding that the substance of the rule would necessarily need to evolve in order to continue to achieve desired policy ends in changing contexts.[30] Thus, when circumstances predictably change over time, the law's regulatory terms automatically change as well. Based on this view, decrees are repealed in response to changed circumstances only when the rabbis who enacted the rules in question could never have imagined changes of that type. For example, proponents of this approach maintain that the original rabbinic law requiring certain fruits to be eaten in Jerusalem remains in effect even after the destruction of the Second Temple, because the rabbis who legislated that rule could

---

26 *See* 6 Encyclopedia Talmudit 698-699 (s.v. *davar shebminyan tzarikh minyan acher lehatiro*).
27 *See* Ran *to* Babylonian Talmud, Gittin 36b.
28 *See* Responsa Rosh 32:8; Rabbi Israel Lipschitz, Tiferet Yisrael *to* Mishnah, Shabbat 6:1.
29 *See* 6 Encyclopedia Talmudit 698-705 (s.v. *davar shebminyan tzarikh minyan acher lehatiro*).
30 *See, e.g.*, Rabbi Menachem Meiri, Beit HaBechirah *to* Babylonian Talmud, Beitza 5a.

not have reasonably anticipated, imagined, or accounted for the possibility that the city would be sacked and the Temple destroyed.[31]

Fourth, some authorities rule that rabbinic decrees which are geographically grounded and limited to particular locations become presumptively inapplicable in other places.[32] A classic example of this is the rabbinic rule mentioned earlier prohibiting drinking water that has been left out uncovered overnight.[33] This law seeks to protect people from being poisoned and is concerned that snakes or scorpions may have drunk from the water during the night, leaving behind harmful poison. Some scholars have argued that this decree must have been limited to places where snakes abound and was originally inapplicable in places where such concerns did not exist. Just as the decree did not apply to places that never had snakes around, these authorities contend, it likewise does not apply in modern times where snakes do not abound in places where people live.[34]

Related to the previous idea is a fifth basis for change in rabbinic decrees, which holds that when a rabbinic rule is about specific people, then when those people—or those types of people—are no longer present, the decree no longer applies.[35] For example, the Talmud prohibits benefiting from wine touched by a Gentile who performs ritual libations to a pagan deity, even if no such idolatrous rituals were actually known to have been performed with that wine itself. The Talmud did not, however, prohibit deriving benefit from wine touched by a non-pagan, non-idolatrous Gentile. By the Middle Ages, some rabbinic authorities posited that, since in their own times no non-Jews performed idolatrous pagan wine libations, this rabbinic prohibition no longer applies.[36] The core of the view is the same as that of the previous one: whenever the Rabbis

---

31 *See* ibid.
32 *See, e.g.*, Tosafot *to* Babylonian Talmud, Avodah Zarah 35a (s.v. *chada*); Magen Avraham *to* Shulchan Arukh, Orach Chaim 690:22.
33 *See* Babylonian Talmud, Chullin 10a.
34 *See* Tosafot *to* Babylonian Talmud, Avodah Zarah 35a (s.v. *chadah*).
35 *See, e.g.*, Tosafot *to* Babylonian Talmud, Avodah Zarah 57b (s.v. *l'afukei*); Rabbi Nathaniel Weil, Korban Netanel *to* Babylonian Talmud, Beitza 1:3:1.
36 *See* Rema *to* Shulchan Arukh, Yoreh Deah 123:1, 124:24; Rabbi Shabbatai HaKohen, Shakh *to* Shulchan Arukh, Yoreh Deah 123:2; Turei Zahav *to* Shulchan Arukh, Yoreh Deah 123:1 ("Based on this rationale [for the prohibition on Gentile wine], it is now permitted . . . for since true libation wine is not found among us today, the rationale has been rendered null, and the prohibition has become permitted.").

naturally limited their decree to a specific type of situation, a change of situation causes the decree to disappear.[37]

Finally, there is an important group of rabbinic authorities who argue that when the social or cultural or technological reality has changed so drastically that the rabbinic degree no longer reflects a present reality, the decree is no longer applicable. One example of this approach involves using medication on the Sabbath. The Talmudic Sages decreed that one should not take medicines for non-life-threatening conditions on the Sabbath because one might come to grind one's medicine when one runs out, as people ground their own pharmaceuticals in Talmudic times.[38] Because grinding is a biblically prohibited Sabbath labor, the Rabbis prohibited taking such medicines at all, in order to better ensure that people do not inadvertently violate the biblical rule against grinding.[39] In modern times, a group of rabbinic authorities argue that, since no one ever grinds their own medicine at home anymore, one can assume that the rabbinic decree naturally does not apply in the present time and place, and that one may therefore take medications on the Sabbath.[40]

In his *Arukh HaShulchan*, Rabbi Epstein often draws on some of these reasons to argue that various rabbinic decrees are no longer applicable. Frequently he notes differences—whether geographical, social, technical, or practical—between the realities in which rabbinic decrees were made and the realities of his own time. He often concludes that rules which no longer further their original purposes or which are no longer necessary, owing to such changed conditions, are to be regarded as no longer in force. Consider, for instance, Rabbi Epstein's disagreement with the *Shulchan Arukh* and the *Rema*'s rulings that one may not place linen strings on silk garments in order to fulfill the biblical obligation of *tzitzit*.[41] Rabbi Joseph Karo rules that one may not put linen *tzitzit* strings on a silk garment because some kinds of wool look like silk, and one may end up inadvertently tying linen strings to a wool garment, thinking that the garment is made of silk, and thereby violate the biblical prohibition of *shatnez*—wearing garments made of mixed wool and linen threads.[42] The

---

37 Tosafot *to* Babylonian Talmud, Avodah Zarah 57a (s.v. *l'afukei*).
38 *See* Babylonian Talmud, Shabbat 53b.
39 *See* Rashi *to* Babylonian Talmud, Shabbat 53b (s.v., *gezeirah*).
40 *See* Rabbi Abraham Chaim Naeh, Ketzot HaShulchan 134, n. 7.2, drawing on the Magen Avraham *to* Shulchan Arukh, Orach Chaim 173:1, who applied this approach to the rabbinic prohibition of eating fish with meat. This is the subject of an excellent work by Rabbi Neria Gutel, titled Sefer Hishtanut HaTevaim.
41 *See* Arukh HaShulchan, Orach Chaim 9:25.
42 *See* Shulchan Arukh, Orach Chaim 9:6.

Rema takes this concern further, and rules that one should not use linen for *tzitzit* strings at all, and instead the strings should be made out of wool, which may then be used on any garments, except ones made of linen (which in the absence of proper blue-colored *tekhelet* strings, would constitute *shatnez*).[43] The *Arukh HaShulchan* rejects this limitation on the use of linen strings, reasoning that, in his own time and place, there is no known variety of wool with an appearance that could be confused with silk, and therefore the risk noted by both Rabbis Karo and Isserles is no longer a matter of concern. In light of this changed reality, and given his conclusion that the reason for the decree no longer applies, the *Arukh HaShulchan* rules that the rabbinic rule prohibiting the use of linen *tzitzit* strings on silk garments no longer applies as well.[44]

In other cases, Rabbi Epstein recognizes that some rules were formulated with specific assumptions about the factual conditions to which they would apply, and argues that changes to those facts over time warrant a reconsideration of the rule itself. This is true, for example, with respect to the obligation to periodically examine *tefillin* parchments to ensure their continued fitness for ritual use.[45] The *Arbah Turim* and the *Shulchan Arukh* rule that *tefillin* which are already presumed to be properly written and ritually valid need not be opened up in order to examine the scrolls to confirm that the text is properly written and that the ink is still legible.[46] Rabbi Epstein notes, however, that while this is true from a strictly *halakhic* standpoint, in his own time a more stringent practice should be followed. He writes that it is well known that the kinds of ink used to write *tefillin* scrolls in his own time and place tend to become dry and chip off the surface of the parchment over the course of several years. In light of this present reality, he rules that it is not sufficient to rely on the earlier rulings of Rabbi Karo and the *Arbah Turim*, and that instead *tefillin* must be checked from time to time to ensure that the scrolls are still valid, thereby acknowledging that such changes in reality may merit discarding decrees which assume a different reality.[47]

Rabbi Epstein also reconsiders the applicability of Talmudic rules which he views as being originally promulgated to apply to certain kinds of people or particular places, utilizing differences in geographical or social reality as a basis for updating or changing prior rabbinic decrees. Thus, for instance, Rabbi

---

43 *See* Rema *to* Shulchan Arukh, Orach Chaim 9:6.
44 *See* Arukh HaShulchan, Orach Chaim 9:25.
45 *See* ibid. 40:6.
46 *See* Arbah Turim, Orach Chaim 39; Shulchan Arukh, Orach Chaim 39:10.
47 *See* Arukh HaShulchan, Orach Chaim 40:6.

Epstein rules that the Talmud's exemption of grooms from having to recite the *Shema* on their wedding night no longer applies, because the Talmudic rule was predicated on the fact that, in general, people are able to maintain proper mental focus on the *Shema* prayer.[48] In such circumstances, the Talmud gave a special dispensation to grooms, who were expected to be especially distracted on their wedding nights, detracting from their ability to maintain proper concertation on the prayer. In contemporary times, however, *halakhic* authorities had characterized the general population of observant Jews as being unable to maintain proper mental focus on their prayers even under ideal conditions.[49] This does not exempt them from ever having to pray but, Rabbi Epstein argues, it does mean that the special exemption for grooms from reciting the *Shema* no longer applies.[50] The groom on his wedding night is no worse off than anybody else on an ordinary evening, as both are unable to properly concentrate on the *Shema* prayer; and if the general population is expected to recite the prayer anyway, their inability to properly focus notwithstanding, then, Rabbi Epstein concludes, the same should apply to a groom.[51] Essentially, in his view, the types of people which he understood the rabbis to have been envisioning when formulating this rule no longer exist in his own time; therefore, the rule no longer applies.

Sometimes, according to Rabbi Epstein's understanding, rabbinic laws become inapplicable, not because they originally applied only to specific kinds of people, but because they applied to specific kinds of things; and when those things no longer exist, that itself amounts to change in reality, justifying, for Rabbi Epstein, a change in the law. The Jerusalem Talmud, for instance, rules that if a Jew's roof was adjacent to a Gentile's roof, and the Gentile's *chametz* rolled onto the Jew's roof during Passover, one should push away the *chametz* using a stick.[52] One should avoid handling such *chametz* directly, since doing so risks the possibility that one may absentmindedly forget the Passover prohibition on *chametz* and accidentally eat the *chametz* being moved. Rabbi Epstein rules, however, that because the function of roofs has changed from Talmudic times to modern times, the requirement to remove or cover *chametz* on one's roof is now nonexistent.[53] In Talmudic times, roofs were flat and utilized

---

48 *See* Babylonian Talmud, Berakhot 16a.
49 *See* Shulchan Arukh, Orach Chaim 70:3.
50 *See* Arukh HaShulchan, Orach Chaim 70:5.
51 *See* ibid. 70:5.
52 *See* Mishnah, Pesachim 2:2.
53 *See* Arukh HaShulchan, Orach Chaim 446:11.

frequently by the members of the dwelling. In Rabbi Epstein's surroundings, roofs were slanted and inaccessible for such use. Therefore, even if a Gentile's *chametz* found its way onto one's roof, one is not obligated to remove it, since it will not pose a serious temptation to anyone if it remains there.[54] Since the roofs envisioned by the Talmudic Rabbis no longer existed in Rabbi Epstein's time, he concluded that a rule based on the existence of such roofs should no longer apply.

Likewise, Rabbi Epstein turned also to geographic changes as a basis to justify departures from Talmudic laws. For example, the Talmud rules that, because environmental factors can cause dough to leaven more or less quickly than is typical, one should not prepare dough for *matzah* under the sunshine, since the heat from the sun may quicken leavening of the dough, causing it to become *chametz* before the usual eighteen-minute deadline.[55] Kneading the dough outdoors but in the shade, out of the sunlight, should therefore permitted. The Talmud rules, however, that even on cloudy days the sun's rays may be expected to peak through the clouds, and therefore one should not knead *matzah* dough outside at all, even if the sky is currently cloudy.[56] Based on this Talmudic rule, the *Bayit Chadash* rules that *matzah* dough prepared in the sun may not be used on Passover.[57] Rabbi Epstein notes, however, that in northern countries cloudy days are in fact good protection from sun, especially in the early spring, when Passover occurs, when the air is still cool. Consequently, he rules that, in this environment, there is no need to prohibit the use of *matzah* dough that was prepared outdoors on a cloudy day.[58] Rabbi Epstein thus viewed the differences between his own geographical reality and that of the rabbis enacting this decree as sufficiently different in ways relevant and significant enough to render the decree no longer applicable.

Rabbi Epstein's geographic contextualization of rabbinic laws is also evident in his treatment of the issue of laundering clothing during the nine-day mourning period over the destruction of the Temple. As discussed above, while the Talmud prohibits laundering clothes during the week preceding Tisha B'Av, it limits this prohibition to only a specific kind of fine laundering, which the Talmud calls *gihutz*.[59] Rabbi Epstein rules that, in principle, the Talmud's

---

54 *See* ibid. 446:11.
55 *See* Babylonian Talmud 42a.
56 *See* Babylonian Talmud, Yoma 28b; Mishneh Torah, Hilkhot Chametz U'Matzah 5:12.
57 *See* Rabbi Joel Sirkis, Bayit Chadash *to* Arbah Turim, Orach Chaim 459:1.
58 *See* Arukh HaShulchan, Orach Chaim 459:1.
59 *See* Babylonian Talmud, Taanit 29b.

prohibition on laundering during the week of Tisha B'Av does not apply in his own time and place, since routine modern laundering is not as intensive as the *gihutz* laundering prohibited by the Talmud.[60] While ordinary clothes laundering is thus technically permitted, Rabbi Epstein notes that the prevailing custom is to prohibit all manner of laundering during the period leading up to Tisha B'Av. He writes, "And since our forefathers accepted this prohibition [on laundering], by default this becomes legally prohibited to us."[61] This is especially so, Rabbi Epstein says, because the Talmud's reasons for permitting ordinary laundering processes no longer applied in Eastern Europe. According to Rabbi Epstein, the Talmud may have permitted some kind of laundering only because the water in Babylonia, where the Talmud was produced, was generally stagnant and could not clean clothes particularly well. But, Rabbi Epstein writes, this is not true in his own time and place, where the water is fresh and can clean clothing quite well, even using only ordinary laundering processes that are less intensive than the *gihutz* prohibited by the Talmud.[62] Thus the change in geographic reality again justified, for him, a change regarding the rabbinic decree.

Beyond geographical changes, social and cultural changes also served as a basis, in Rabbi Epstein's view, for updating the applicability of certain rabbinic decrees. Another excellent illustration of Rabbi Epstein arguing for changed social realities to entail changes to applicable rabbinic laws relates to the Talmudic proscription against wearing jewelry in public domains on the Sabbath. The Talmud forbids women from walking in a public domain on the Sabbath while wearing certain items of jewelry.[63] While one who wears jewelry is not "carrying" the jewelry and is thus not violating the biblical prohibition against carrying objects in a public domain on the Sabbath,[64] the Rabbis nevertheless prohibited the wearing of some kinds of jewelry because they were concerned that the wearer might remove the piece to show others, while walking in a public area, thus inadvertently violating the biblical proscription against carrying.[65] Rabbi Epstein notes, however, that the common practice of women in his own time was to wear all kinds of jewelry in public on the Sabbath, without

---

60 *See* Arukh HaShulchan, Orach Chaim 551:14.
61 Ibid.
62 *See* ibid.
63 *See* Babylonian Talmud, Shabbat 59b.
64 *See* Shulchan Arukh, Orach Chaim 303:2.
65 *See* Babylonian Talmud, Shabbat 62a; Arukh HaShulchan, Orach Chaim 303:1.

any apparent regard for such Talmudic regulations.[66] The *Arukh HaShulchan* justifies this practice by offering several reasons for which the original Talmudic prohibition may no longer remain in force, due to changes in social practices and norms in contemporary times. First, Rabbi Epstein suggests that since in modern times—unlike in the Talmudic era when jewelry was far rarer and more valuable—women regularly wear jewelry in public, there is therefore no real concern that they might remove their accessories to show them to others.[67] Additionally, Rabbi Epstein suggests that the Talmudic Rabbis were concerned that women might remove and show off their jewelry in public because women did not often leave their homes, and when they did so, there was a reasonable basis for a concern that they might use that opportunity to show their jewelry to each other. In modern times, however, women do leave their homes regularly during the week and on the Sabbath, and thus there is no concern that meeting each other in the street poses any kind of special occasion that may result in their removing and displaying their jewelry.[68]

* * * * *

Rabbi Epstein thus embraces the principle that the practical behavioral standards indicated by settled *halakhic* norms—and in some cases, the established rules of Jewish law themselves—can change in response to evolving social, political, economic, geographic, and other conditions. In many cases, where changed conditions to which the *halakhah* must be applied render the underlying reasons for particular legal rules null, Rabbi Epstein rules that *halakhic* practice must change as well. Such evaluations are, of course, fraught, and Rabbi Epstein himself approaches them with caution. However, when to his mind the mechanistic application of anachronistic standards to changed conditions would undermine the broader religious and material purposes of the law itself, Rabbi Epstein generally rules that what the *halakhah* requires must adapt accordingly.

---

66 *See* Arukh HaShulchan, Orach Chaim 303:22.
67 *See* ibid.
68 *See* ibid.

CHAPTER TWELVE

Law and Pragmatism

This chapter explains the tenth and final principle that drives Rabbi Epstein's *halakhic* determinations in the *Orach Chaim* section of his *Arukh HaShulchan*. This principle—that *halakhah* must be decided in a way that makes it reasonably possible for people to observe the law—is an important one in Rabbi Epstein's jurisprudence. As many have noted, rather than an ivory-tower scholar, Rabbi Epstein spent his career—including the entire period spent writing the *Arukh HaShulchan*—as a communal rabbi whose work routinely required him to provide religious guidance to ordinary Jews as they sought to navigate the complicated situations and many pressures of everyday life. As is evident from many of the other methodological commitments of the *Arukh HaShulchan*, Rabbi Epstein was acutely sensitive to the importance of *halakhah* as a lived tradition of religious practice—thus, his regard for consensus, custom, his sensitivity to the rationales for *halakhic* rules, and his careful evaluation of the costs and benefits of supererogatory religious practices. In a similar vein, in formulating his *halakhic* rulings in the *Arukh HaShulchan*, Rabbi Epstein took care to account for the need for Jewish law to be pragmatic and something that can be reasonably observed by Jews in the real world. This was not only a theoretical goal but a practical model of how Jewish law ought to function. Making demands on people and communities that they cannot bear, in fact, was beyond Rabbi Epstein's sense of mandate. Practically, concepts such as financial loss (*hefsed*) and duress (*oness*) certainly play a role in his understanding of Jewish law.

* * * * *

Principle Ten: Rabbi Epstein recognizes that halakhah must be practiced by real people in the real world and is therefore willing to adapt seemingly impracticable halakhic norms to better account for the real-world practical challenges attendant to trying to actually uphold such standards.

One of the important theological threads running through rabbinic thinking on the nature of Torah and *halakhah* is the idea that Jewish law is fundamentally a worldly and human endeavor. It is true that the Talmudic sages repeatedly affirm that in some sense the Torah is otherworldly, eternal, and superlative. Indeed, according to some sources, the Torah predates the creation of the world; it serves as a primary impetus for creation, and provides the blueprint for God's created universe.[1] At the same time, however, rabbinic scholars—especially more practical *halakhic* scholars—have firmly maintained that the Torah is ultimately concerned with the affairs of human beings rather than the workings of the Heavens, and that the norms and standards of the *halakhah* are relevant principally to real people living in the real world. This idea is alluded to, of course, in the famous biblical passage that affirms the Torah's relevance and jurisdiction over earthly matters, and its accessibility to its human subjects:

> This Torah that I command you today is not too baffling for you, nor is it beyond your reach. It is not in the Heavens, that you might say, "Who among us can go up to the Heavens and get it for us and impart it to us, that we may observe it?" Nor is it beyond the sea, that you might say, "Who among us can cross to the other side of the sea and get it for us and impart it to us, that we may observe it?" Rather it is very close to you, in your mouth and in your heart, to observe it.[2]

Many commentators understand this passage as establishing the permanence and unchangeability of the Torah to which it refers. The Torah is not in the Heavens, and thus, no post-Mosaic prophet may change it, and its meaning resides in the hands of human interpreters rather than continued divine revelations. The Talmudic sage, Shmuel, however, explained this passage as indicating that understanding of the Torah is not found among "astrologers" who concern themselves with heavenly matters and are disconnected from the

---

1   *See, e.g.,* Zohar, Toldot 133b:8; Zohar, Terumah 161a:6.
2   Deuteronomy 30:11-14.

mundane concerns of actual human beings in the real world.³ Instead, Shmuel implies the Torah resides in those whose concerns center on practical worldly matters.

The theological claim that the Torah and *halakhah* are concerned principally with worldly matters is expressed in the Talmudic dictum that "the Torah was not given to the ministering angels."⁴ Angels are perfect creatures lacking in free will, capable only of obeying God's commands, and unencumbered by physical human limitations, needs, and desires. The Torah generally, and the behavioral norms, duties, and proscriptions of the *halakhah* in particular, are suited only for imperfect, sensuous, creatures of flesh and blood who are born, eat, sleep, procreate, and die. This idea is developed at length in a Talmudic passage that embellishes the biblical account of the Sinaitic revelation with a story of Moses's ascending to the Heavens to receive the Torah:

> At the time Moses ascended to the Heavens [to receive the Torah], the angels said before God, "Master of the Universe, what is this one, born of woman, doing among us?" God responded, "He came to receive the Torah." They said before Him, "It is a hidden treasure that you kept concealed for 947 generations before the creation of the world, yet you will give it to a person of flesh and blood? . . . Rather, 'Your majesty [i.e. the Torah] is placed above the Heavens'" (Psalms 8:5). God then said to him [Moses], "Respond to them." . . . He said before Him, "Master of the Universe, the Torah that You are giving me, what is written in it?" [God answered,] "I am the Lord your God Who brought you out of Egypt from the house of bondage" (Exodus 20:2). He [Moses] said to them [the angels], "Did you descend to Egypt? Were you enslaved to Pharaoh? Why should the Torah be yours?" Again, [Moses asked,] "What is written in it?" "You shall have no other gods" (Exodus 20:3). [Moses said to the angels,] "Do you dwell among the nations who worship idols [that you require this special warning]?" Again, [Moses asked,] "What else is written in it?" "Remember the Sabbath day to sanctify it" (Exodus 20:8). [Moses asked the angels,] "Do you perform labor that you require rest from it?" Again, [Moses asked,] "What is written in it?" "Do not take the name of the Lord your God in vain [including through false oaths]" (Exodus 20:7). [Moses asked the angels,] "Do you conduct business with

---

3   *See* Midrash Rabbah, Deuteronomy 8:6.
4   Babylonian Talmud, Berakhot 25b; Babylonian Talmud, Kiddushin 54a.

one another [that may lead you to swear falsely]?" Again, [Moses asked,] "What is written in it?" "Honor your father and your mother" (Exodus 20:12). [Moses asked the angels,] "Do you have a father or a mother?" Again, [Moses asked,] "What is written in it?" God said to him, "You shall not murder, you shall not commit adultery, you shall not steal" (Exodus 20:13-15). [Moses asked the angels,] "Is there jealousy among you? Is there an evil inclination within you?" Immediately they agreed with God [that He made the right decision to give the Torah to the people] . . .[5]

In this passage, the angels object to God's "lowering" the exalted and other-worldly Torah by giving it to mere mortals, beings of flesh and blood. The disdain with which the angels hold humankind is perhaps best explained by rabbinic accounts of the angels' much earlier opposition to God's creating humans during the Genesis narrative. There, the Torah relates that "God said, 'Let us make man in our image, after our likeness.'"[6] According to the Talmud, as early as the writing of the Septuagint, the Rabbis felt compelled to explain God's apparently having to consult or seek permission from some other beings before creating humans, which stands in obvious tension with Judaism's strict monotheism. One Midrashic response to this concern posits that the angels sought to dissuade God from creating man: the angel representing truth argued that human beings are full of falsehood, and the angel representing peace argued that human beings were quarrelsome and warlike.[7] Ultimately, God rejects these arguments, but the biblical narrative's suggestion that God's creating mankind was preceded by some sort of deliberation alludes to the underlying heavenly debate.

In any case, the angels in this narrative find human beings unworthy of the Torah; humans are sinful, self-centered, and physically limited beings whose essential nature is incompatible with the kind of strictly just ordering of reward and punishment demanded by Torah law. God's and Moses's response to the angels' complaints, as presented in the above-quoted passage, is that the Torah and its laws are essentially worldly phenomena. As a normative universe that sets behavioral norms and moral and ethical imperatives, the Torah is suited to human beings who exist in a mundane world of action and physicality, and not to the heavenly abode of the angels. Indeed, almost as if in response to

---

5 Babylonian Talmud, Shabbat 88b-89a.
6 Genesis 1:26.
7 *See* Midrash Rabbah, Genesis 8:5.

the angels' earlier arguments against the creation of mankind, God points out that it is precisely humanity's moral failings that make it well suited—indeed, exclusively suited—to receive the Torah and its laws. As Moses retorts to the angels, "Is there jealousy among you, or is there an evil inclination within you that would render these commandments [proscribing murder and illicit sexual relationships] relevant?"[8] The Torah belongs on Earth, in the imperfect, messy, complex world of human interaction where, thanks to the limitations of human physicality, desires, and free-will, its norms and values are relevant and can be fulfilled.

In the Talmud, the idea that the Torah is properly suited to the limitations of earthly human existence rather than the heavenly perfection of the angels is expressed by the adage, "the Torah was not given to the ministering angels," which is used in four different instances to justify limits on what the *halakhah* demands of people in light of the practical difficulties of observance caused by the physical limitations of earthly human existence. One Talmudic discussion concerns the propriety of reciting the *Shema* prayer while one is naked but immersed in water.[9] It is typically prohibited to recite the *Shema* in the presence of uncovered genitals, and so the Talmud wonders whether and how one might recite the prayer if one finds oneself naked in a bath or pool of water when the proper time for reciting the prayer arrives.[10] The Talmud suggests that in this situation one should immerse one's body in the water up to one's neck, so that the surface of the water forms a "barrier" between his uncovered genitals and his eyes and mouth, in which case the prayer may be recited. The Talmud questions why this arrangement is effective given that one's "heels still see their genitals."[11] The Talmud responds by noting that while one may not recite the *Shema* if one's heels are touching their genitals, the mere fact that one's heels can "see" their genitals does not preclude their praying because "the Torah was not given to the ministering angels."[12] As the preeminent rabbinic commentator on the Talmud, *Rashi*, explains, the Torah was not given to angels "who do not have genitals." Rather, the Torah was given to human beings who, "against our will, have genitals, and [therefore] cannot possibly avoid [parts of their bodies "seeing" their genitals while praying]."[13]

---

8   Babylonian Talmud, Shabbat 89a.
9   *See* Babylonian Talmud, Berakhot 25b.
10 *See* ibid.
11 Ibid.
12 Ibid.
13 Rashi *to* Babylonian Talmud, Berakhot 25b (s.v. *lo nitnah Torah l'malachei ha'sharet*).

Another Talmudic use of this principle relates to the rule prohibiting the recitation of prayers in the presence of excrement. The Talmud records a ruling by Rav Papa, who taught that it is prohibited to recite the *Shema* when there is excrement "in its place" (i.e., in the anus).[14] The Talmud questions the necessity of such a rule: "If it [the excrement] is visible, then it is obvious [that one cannot pray, since this is no different from an ordinary case of praying in the presence of excrement]; and if it is not visible [why is one precluded from praying]? But the Torah was not given to the ministering angels."[15] Here, the Talmud questions how the *halakhah* could possibly prohibit praying when feces—unseen and unknown—is present in the anus, since the law must be kept by human beings and not angels. While angels do not produce waste or defecate, human beings do; it is impossible for human beings to ensure that their bodies are entirely clean of unseen (internal) waste matter, and thus the *halakhah* cannot reasonably impose such a condition on the ability to recite the *Shema*. The Talmud does in fact accept this line of reasoning, and explains Rav Papa's ruling as speaking to a situation where the excrement could be seen—and thus removed—while sitting, but remains unseen while standing; in such a case, one cannot recite the *Shema* even while standing because the excrement present on the body could reasonably be noticed and cleaned off.[16]

Two additional instances in which the Talmud limits the reach of seemingly impracticable legal standards pertain to the use and misuse of items consecrated for use in the Jerusalem Temple. The Torah explicitly prohibits *meilah*, the use of consecrated items for mundane purposes or for personal benefit,[17] and this stricture raises questions about how the Temple itself could be constructed and how the Temple priests should conduct themselves while wearing their ritual vestments. In one case, the Talmud explains that the priests were permitted to wear their consecrated vestments on days that they were serving in the Temple even when not actually performing any Temple rituals. While doing so would, in principle, amount to using consecrated items for personal use—in this case as clothing—the priest may continue wearing the vestments even after completing the services because "the Torah was not given to the ministering angels."[18] As some commentators explain, human priests could not reasonably be expected to change out of their vestments and into ordinary

---

14 Babylonian Talmud, Yoma 30a.
15 Ibid.
16 *See* ibid.
17 *See* Leviticus 5:15.
18 Babylonian Talmud, Kiddushin 54a.

clothes instantaneously upon completing their Temple service, and therefore do not need to do so in an effort to avoid committing *meilah*.[19] In another discussion, the Talmud explains that Temple construction and maintenance projects are performed using unconsecrated funds and building materials, which are only later consecrated for Temple use upon the completion of the project.[20] The reason for this practice is that workers often have to take breaks from their work to sit or rest, and they would be unable to do so if the building stones, scaffolding, and other materials upon which they might sit and rest were consecrated for Temple use or purchased with consecrated money. But, the Talmud says, "the Torah was not given to the ministering angels;" it was given to human beings who do indeed sometimes need to rest while engaged in strenuous labor. To accommodate this reality, the Rabbis prescribed that Temple building materials should not be consecrated until the completion of the project.[21]

The upshot of these four Talmudic applications of the principle that "the Torah was not given to the ministering angels" is that, rather, the law was given to be observed by human beings, with all their usual human frailties, limitations, and needs. When an application of what is assumed to be the right rule of law produces a *halakhic* norm that is impracticable to observe, the law bends to accommodate the human condition. Notably, in none of the Talmudic cases to which this principle is applied is *halakhic* compliance truly impossible. People can be careful not to swim naked in water around the proper time of day for reciting the *Shema*; people can scrupulously clean themselves in order to be certain that no waste is present on the body, even in places not typically seen; Temple construction workers can assiduously avoid resting on building materials set aside for the project; and priests can remove their vestments promptly after completing the service rather than delay doing so in reliance on this principle. "The Torah was not given to the ministering angels" thus functions as a *halakhic* release in situations where normative compliance is possible but impracticable—and perhaps even just difficult—due to the nature of mankind's physical nature. This principle is stated even in matters where it is possible for people to comply with the law, but where doing so is difficult; since it is difficult to observe such laws, "The Torah does not hoist upon people this yolk—[the expectation] that they should be angelic."[22]

---

19 See, e.g., Tosafot *to* Babylonian Talmud, Kiddushin 54a (s.v. *b'ketonet kehunah*).
20 *See* Babylonian Talmud, Meilah 14b.
21 Babylonian Talmud, Meilah 14b.
22 *See* 34 Encyclopedia Talmudit 112.

While this principle is not, of course, a general dispensation from any and all difficulties and burdens posed by compliance with *halakhah*, post-Talmudic authorities have applied the idea to a broad range of cases in which compliance with the law is seriously complicated by essential features of what might be best described as the human condition. Rabbi Epstein, for instance, invokes this principle in the context of the *halakhic* requirement that one may only pray with a "clean body," that is, when one does not need to relieve oneself.[23] Rabbi Epstein writes that one should try to defecate in the morning and evening in order to maintain bodily cleanliness, but that prior to praying it is sufficient to merely check to ensure that one does not have waste collected in one's body.[24] If one does check, and confirms that one does not presently need to relieve oneself, one can – and must – proceed to recite one's prayers, even if he or she has not completely expelled all the urine or feces in one's body. After all, Rabbi Epstein says, "The Torah was not given to the ministering angels."[25] Human beings produce and expel bodily waste, and requiring them to completely expel every bit of waste before praying would be an impracticable standard for the *halakhah* to impose, and would lead to a general disregard for fulfilling the obligation to pray. A similar application of this principle was advanced by some early authorities who argued that, although the *halakhah* prohibits passing gas while wearing *tefillin*, one who is especially prone and cannot avoid flatulence may nevertheless don the *tefillin* while doing his best to avoid passing gas. This is permitted according to these authorities because "the Torah was not given to the ministering angels."[26] Human beings pass gas, and cannot always avoid doing so; in light of this reality, it would be absurd for the *halakhah* to impose a standard of bodily cleanliness that cannot reasonably be met, and one which would merely lead to many people being simply unable to ever fulfill the biblical obligation to wear *tefillin*. For this reason, some decisors have ruled that one prone to flatulence may don *tefillin* anyway.

While most authorities have rejected the idea that a flatulence-prone individual may don *tefillin*, despite expecting to unavoidably pass gas while wearing them, rabbinic decisors have applied the principle of "the Torah was not given to the ministering angels" to soften a number of other strictures tied to respecting the sanctity of *tefillin*. The *halakhah* requires that when wearing *tefillin*, one must focus on one's prayers and the sanctity of the *tefillin*, and not let

---

23 *See* Babylonian Talmud, Berakhot 14b.
24 *See* Arukh HaShulchan, Orach Chaim 2:11.
25 Ibid.
26 *See* 34 Encylopedia Talmudit 127, n. 143-44.

one's mind wander to frivolous matters.[27] According to some authorities, not only is it prohibited to think frivolous thoughts while wearing *tefillin*, but one may not think any unrelated thoughts while wearing *tefillin*.[28] Many of these authorities rule, however, that the prohibition only applies to letting one's mind wander for an extended period of time—the amount of time it would take to walk one hundred cubits. These decisors reason that while it is impracticable to demand that people wearing *tefillin* not permit their minds to wander for even a second—after all, "the Torah was not given to the ministering angels"—it is reasonable to expect those wearing *tefillin* to refocus their attention to holy matters from time to time so that they are not thinking about mundane concerns for extended periods.[29] Additionally, while it is prohibited to pass gas in the presence of *tefillin*, one may remove one's *tefillin*, cover them with a cloth, and place them next to one's head while sleeping.[30] While there is a concern that one may uncontrollably pass gas in the presence of the *tefillin* while sleeping, the *halakhah* recognizes that "the Torah was not given to the ministering angels" but to human beings who need to sleep, and who cannot always do so while maintaining a substantial distance from their precious and valuable *tefillin*.[31]

Other examples of the application of this principle include thinking about weekday matters on the Sabbath, destroying leavened products (*chametz*) found in one's possession during Passover, and writing Torah scrolls. The Talmudic Rabbis legislated a prohibition against speaking about mundane weekday matters on the Sabbath in order to better preserve the restful and holy character of the day.[32] While the Talmud equates thoughts with speech with respect to some matters, this equivalency does not extend to a prohibition against thinking about mundane weekday matters on the Sabbath. According to some commentators, the Rabbis limited their proscription to speech, and did not extend to mundane thoughts, since a prohibition against thinking about weekday-related affairs on the Sabbath would be an unreasonable burden to impose on ordinary people, and "the Torah was not given to the ministering

---

27 See Shulchan Arukh, Orach Chaim 37:2.
28 See, e.g., Magen Avraham *to* Shulchan Arukh, Orach Chaim 28:1 (cautioning against merely "forgetting" that one is wearing *tefillin*).
29 See 34 Encyclopedia Talmudit 128, n. 153-54.
30 See Rabbi Menachem Meiri, Beit HaBechirah *to* Babylonian Talmud, Sukkah 26b.
31 See Rashi *to* Babylonian Talmud, Sukkah 26a (s.v. *d'paris*); *see also* Rashi *to* Babylonian Talmud, Yoma 69a (s.v. *Shema*).
32 See Babylonian Talmud, Shabbat 113a-b.

angels."[33] Additionally, the Torah prohibits seeing or owning leaven products during Passover, and *halakhah* therefore prescribes that any *chametz* found in one's possession during the holiday must be destroyed.[34] Rabbinic scholars have ruled, however, that if one finds *chametz* in their possession during the holiday, one does not violate these prohibitions while one is actively engaged in destroying the *chametz*. While destroying the *chametz* inevitably entails both "seeing" and "possessing" it, it is simply impossible to fulfill the Torah's command to destroy the *chametz* in any other way. Since "the Torah was not given to the ministering angels," these authorities posit that the Torah cannot both impose a duty and also hold one liable for violating a prohibition that must be transgressed in the process of fulfilling the original command.[35]

Moreover, Jewish law requires that *tefillin* and *mezuzah* scrolls must be written "in order;" that is, if the scribe writes or corrects earlier parts of the text after having already written later parts of the text, the scroll is ritually invalid.[36] Because Torah scrolls enjoy a greater degree of sanctity than either *tefillin* or *mezuzot*, it would therefore follow that Torah scrolls too should have to be written in order. The *halakhah*, however, does not impose this requirement on the production of Torah scrolls.[37] Some authorities explain that the reason for this dispensation from having to write Torah scrolls in their proper order is that imposing such an obligation would make it very difficult to produce ritually fit Torah scrolls. While the text of *tefillin* and *mezuzah* scrolls is relatively brief, the length of a Torah scroll makes it virtually impossible for a scribe to complete the entire text without having to go back and occasionally fix earlier scribal errors. Likewise, Torah scrolls, which, unlike *tefillin* and *mezuzah* scrolls, are rolled and unrolled and used regularly often develop textual problems, as ink gets rubbed off the parchment over time. Requiring that Torah scrolls be written entirely in order would preclude being able to fix such errors when they arise, and would also invalidate any scroll in which the scribe erred and then continued writing before later finding and fixing a previous mistake.[38]

Scribes are, of course, human and prone to error, and the realities of the physical world entail that valid Torah scrolls will develop textual problems over

---

33   *See* Rabbi Menachem Meiri, Beit HaBechirah, *to* Babylonian Talmud, Shabbat 113b.
34   *See* Tosafot *to* Babylonian Talmud, Pesachim 4b (s.v. *m'de'oraysah*); Shulchan Arukh, Orach Chaim 446:1.
35   *See* 34 Encylopedia Talmudit 130.
36   *See* Shulchan Arukh, Orach Chaim 32:1.
37   *See* Shulchan Arukh, Yoreh Deah 276:1.
38   *See* Rabbi Abraham Chaim HaLevi, Responsa Ginat Vradim, Orach Chaim 2:4.

time. Since "the Torah was not given to the ministering angels," in the case of Torah scrolls, these realities necessitate a rejection of the standard requirement that scriptures must be written in order.

Rabbi Epstein explicitly utilizes this principle in a number of different contexts. In addition to the requirement that one only pray with a "clean body" discussed above, Rabbi Epstein applies this principle to the *halakhic* obligation to pray with proper mindfulness and attention to one's prayers. Thus, he rules that, if one begins praying with appropriate concentration but in the midst of his prayers finds that his mind had wandered and had become confused, one should not thereafter repeat those parts of the prayer which one has already recited without the proper attention because, as he notes, "the Torah was not given to the ministering angels." The minds of ordinary people wander; attempts to maintain concentration are disrupted, and so, says Rabbi Epstein, "what [more] can be done," given that such is the nature of the human condition.[39]

Rabbi Epstein also applies this principle to explain a ruling of Maimonides regarding the laws of *tzitzit*. Maimonides teaches that one should not tie woolen *tzitzit* strings to a linen garment.[40] While the Torah explicitly prohibits the wearing of garments made of both wool and linen, in principle, this prohibition does not apply to *tzitzit* garments because the positive obligation to wear *tzitzit* overrides the negative prohibition against wearing clothing made of both wool and linen (*shatnez*). Still, Maimonides rules that one should not wear *tzitzit* made of wool and linen because "one might come to wear the garment at night, which is not a time when one is obligated to wear *tzitzit*."[41] Since there is no obligation to wear *tzitzit* at night,[42] there is no basis for permitting the wearing of a wool and linen garment at that time. To avoid the possibility that a wool and linen *tzitzit* garment worn during the day might continue to be worn at night, thereby violating the prohibition, Maimonides rules that *tzitzit* made of a combination of both wool and linen materials should not even be worn during the daytime, as a precautionary measure. Rabbi Epstein, however, questions this ruling on the basis of the previously discussed Talmudic rule permitting the wearing of priestly vestments when not performing Temple services.[43] If the principle that "the Torah was not given to the ministering angels"

---
39 *See* Arukh HaShulchan, Orach Chaim 99:4.
40 *See* Mishneh Torah, Hilkhot Tzitzit 3:7.
41 Ibid.
42 *See* Babylonian Talmud, Menachot 43a.
43 *See* Arukh HaShulchan, Orach Chaim 18:5.

permits priests to continue wearing their vestments after completing their service because it would be impracticable to expect them to remove them immediately,[44] the same rule should obviate Maimonides's concerns about people continuing to wear their wool and linen *tzitzit* after sunset. Due to the thrust of this principle, Rabbi Epstein notes that in fact Maimonides's concerns regarding wool and linen *tzitzit* do not revolve around the possibility that one who was wearing such a garment during the daytime might continue wearing it at night, as that would indeed be permissible due to the impracticability of removing the garment precisely at nightfall. Instead, Rabbi Epstein says, Maimonides prohibits the wearing of wool and linen *tzitzit* during the day out of concern that one might come to put such a garment on at night in the first instance, which would certainly be prohibited.[45]

Another example of Rabbi Epstein's utilization of the concept that "the Torah was not given to the ministering angels" pertains to a person's *halakhic* liability for failing to successfully eradicate all leaven products from one's possession prior to the start of Passover. The *Arbah Turim* rules that immediately after one finishes searching for *chametz* on the evening of the 14th of Nissan, one should verbally nullify one's *chametz* so that one will not violate the prohibition against owning or seeing *chametz*, just in case any *chametz* was not found and left over in one's possession following the required search.[46] Rabbi Epstein, however, questions the validity of this rule on the basis of the *Arbah Turim*'s rationale. How can individuals violate the prohibition on owning *chametz*, Rabbi Epstein wonders, merely because, unbeknownst to them, *chametz* happens to be present in their possession? On the contrary, suggests Rabbi Epstein, since "the Torah and its laws were not given to the angels," a person who has searched his property and possessions for *chametz* in the manner prescribed by *halakhah* should be considered blameless for any *chametz* remaining in his possession afterward.[47] While Rabbi Epstein recognizes that it is of course possible for a person to sin inadvertently (*b'shogeg*), he argues that the characterization of sins as "inadvertent" applies only to reckless or negligent sins, such as where a person who is unaware of any *chametz* in his possession does not bother searching his property to confirm this fact, and ends up discovering some *chametz* in his possession on Passover.[48] In that case, the person

---

44 *See* Tosafot *to* Babylonian Talmud, Kiddushin 54a (s.v. *b'ketonet kehunah*).
45 *See* Arukh HaShulchan, Orach Chaim 18:6.
46 *See* Arbah Turim, Orach Chaim 434:2.
47 *See* Arukh HaShulchan, Orach Chaim 434:7.
48 *See* ibid. 434:7.

is liable for committing an inadvertent sin because he did not even bother to fulfill the Torah's requirement that one search for *chametz* in order to ensure that none is found in his possession during Passover. However, Rabbi Epstein rules, if a person does search in the manner prescribed by the Torah, but nevertheless finds *chametz* in his possession on Passover, that person is considered in *oness*, under duress, and is therefore blameless. Rabbi Epstein thus argues that the rationale offered by the *Arbah Turim* for the obligation to verbally nullify one's *chametz* after properly searching for and removing *chametz* in one's possession—that the nullification serves to forestall possible violations of the prohibition against owning *chametz*—is inadequate.[49]

Instead, Rabbi Epstein suggests that the reason *chametz* should be verbally nullified, even after the search is properly completed, is to prevent a later violation of the law against owning *chametz* in case one finds a piece of *chametz* in one's property on Passover and delays destroying it, or forgets to do so. Although such a person would not be liable for initially having owned that *chametz* (since he had previously searched his property), any delays in removing *chametz* that is found on Passover would amount to an active violation of the prohibition against keeping *chametz* in one's possession on Passover. By nullifying all such *chametz* before Passover, one ensures that any *chametz* found in one's possession on Passover is not actually his, such that delays in removing that *chametz* would therefore not result in any violation of the laws against owning *chametz* on Passover.[50]

In addition to these examples of his direct reliance on the idea that "the Torah was not given to the ministering angels," Rabbi Epstein also redirects the normative thrust of many other *halakhic* rules in a variety of instances in which compliance appears impracticable due to the limits of normal human abilities under real-world conditions. For example, blessings recited when doing *mitzvot* are generally said immediately prior to engaging in the act that constitutes the performance of the obligation.[51] Consequently, the *Shulchan Arukh* rules that one should not say the blessing for *tefillin* until after the *tefillin* box is positioned properly on one's arm; then, one should recite the blessing and immediately affix the *tefillin* to one's arm by tightening the strap, which constitutes the fulfillment of the *mitzvah* of "putting on *tefillin*."[52] The *Rema* adds that Ashkenazic Jews, who recite a second blessing when putting the *tefillin shel*

---

49 *See* ibid. 434:7.
50 *See* ibid. 434:8.
51 *See* Babylonian Talmud, Pesachim 119b.
52 *See* Shulchan Arukh, Orach Chaim 25:8.

rosh on their heads, should likewise recite that second blessing immediately before affixing the *tefillin* to their heads.[53] The *Magen Avraham* explains that, in order to follow the *Rema*'s rule, one should first place the *tefillin* on one's head, then recite the blessing, and then fix the *tefillin* in place so that the blessing is recited immediately before fulfilling the *mitzvah*, without the need for the delay of placing the *tefillin* on one's head after the blessing.[54] The *Arukh HaShulchan* notes that the process prescribed by the *Rema* and the *Magen Avraham* poses practical difficulties. In order to recite the blessing, one must ensure that one's head remains covered, but Rabbi Epstein notes, everyone who has ever tried putting the *tefillin shel rosh* on one's head knows that this is very difficult to do while keeping one's head covered with a hat or *kippah*.[55] While this difficulty might be addressed by placing one's *tallit* over one's head and *tefillin*, providing an additional covering, this solution does not help unmarried men who follow the practice of not wearing a *tallit*. In light of this pragmatic difficulty, Rabbi Epstein rules that one may follow the custom of holding the *tefillin shel rosh* in one's hands, very close to one's head, reciting the blessing while one's head remains covered, and then quickly removing one's head covering and fixing the *tefillin* in place. In light of the practicalities of the situation, Rabbi Epstein rules, this procedure can be regarded as satisfying the requirement to recite a *mitzvah*'s blessings immediately prior to performing the *mitzvah* act.[56]

Another illustration of Rabbi Epstein's *halakhic* response to the impracticability of fully observing normative legal standards relates to the selection of public prayer leaders for High Holiday services. The *Zohar* instructs that a community should be very careful when choosing an individual to lead the congregation in High Holiday prayers and to blow the *shofar* on Rosh Hashanah. Specifically, the *Zohar* writes that the designated prayer leader should seclude himself for three days prior to the holiday so as to avoid contracting any ritual impurity and in order to spend time in self-introspection and repentance.[57] While Rabbi Epstein considers the *Zohar*'s suggestion seriously enough to quote it, he nevertheless finds this instruction impractical in his own time, concluding that, "due to our sins, we are unable to demand such."[58] In another case, Rabbi Epstein notes that some people have the custom to stand on their

---

53 *See* Rema *to* Shulchan Arukh, Orach Chaim 25:8.
54 *See* Magen Avraham *to* Shulchan Arukh, Orach Chaim 25:13.
55 *See* Arukh HaShulchan, Orach Chaim 25:15.
56 *See* ibid. 25:15.
57 *See* ibid. 581:5.
58 Ibid. 581:7.

feet for the full length of all the prayer services on Yom Kippur. Likewise, even many of those who do not stand for the entire service make sure to stand while the holy ark is open and the Torah scrolls are displayed to the congregation. Rabbi Epstein, however, notes that people who find standing for these extended lengths of time to be difficult or impractical need not do so.[59]

A final example addresses the proper location for placing one's *menorah* in observance of the holiday of Hanukkah. The Talmud teaches that, since the purpose of Hanukkah candles is to publicize the miracle of Hanukkah, the Hanukkah candles should not be placed indoors, and should instead be placed outside the home, close to the doorway, so that passersby will see the lit candles.[60] Rabbi Epstein notes, however, that the prevalent practice in his own time and place was to not place the candles outside one's house, even in cases where the Talmud's own dispensation—for situations in which placing the candles outside poses some kind of danger—does not apply. Rabbi Epstein explains that this normative custom, which departs from the Talmudic rule, is justified because conditions in Eastern Europe are very different from those in the Land of Israel. In contrast with the generally dry and mild climate of the Middle East, in Eastern Europe Hanukkah falls in the winter, when heavy snow, rain, and strong winds would surely extinguish any candles one tried to light outside. This makes lighting the candles outdoors entirely impracticable, and justifies the common custom of lighting indoors. While this problem could be remedied by enclosing one's Hanukkah candles in a glass case, Rabbi Epstein notes that such extraordinary measures are unnecessary, especially since enclosing the candles in glass detracts from the ability of passersby to clearly see the number of candles that have been lit, which is an essential feature of the publicizing of the miracle accomplished by lighting outside.[61]

It is interesting to note that Rabbi Epstein's appreciation for the *halakhic* relevance of this sort of impracticability may correlate with some of his other methodological commitments. Christine Hayes has noted the connection between the Talmudic principle that "the Torah was not given to the ministering angels" and the rabbinic rejection of certain kinds of religious aspirationalism. According to Hayes, the theological and jurisprudential assertion that Torah law is meant to exist in the human realm entails a recognition that human beings are not angels, and thus are not expected to seek or aspire to

---
59 *See* ibid. 618:9.
60 *See* Babylonian Talmud, Shabbat 21a.
61 *See* Arukh HaShulchan, Orach Chaim 671:24.

some kinds of angelic perfectionism in their service of God.[62] Indeed, the Talmud deploys this principle exclusively in cases related to prayer and Temple service, two areas of ritual observance that, perhaps more than any others, one might expect God to demand angelic behavior from mankind. It is precisely in these areas, therefore, that the Talmud affirms that the Torah was not given to the angels, but to human beings, and that the *halakhah* therefore does not demand absolute perfection in the face of impracticable difficulties arising from the nature of mankind's earthly existence. In Hayes's assessment, this rabbinic perspective maintains that "[h]umans need not aspire to an angelic perfection because, after all, they are not angels and the Torah does not make extraordinary demands upon its recipients."[63] Put slightly differently, there is a direct relationship between the willingness of rabbinic decisors to reach *halakhic* judgments that account for the occasional impracticability of full observance, and the hesitancy of *halakhic* authorities to require people to observe various demanding religious stringencies and to adopt supererogatory ritual behaviors.

It is perhaps no surprise, therefore, that Rabbi Epstein's acute sensitivity for and responses to the practical difficulties sometimes attendant to the proper observance of normative *halakhic* standards goes hand in hand with his tendency to both eschew demanding supererogatory religious behavior and avoid prescribing stringent modes of ritual conduct designed to simultaneously satisfy numerous divergent rabbinic opinions. The latter tendency is particularly important and is directly linked to the idea that "the Torah was not given to the ministering angels" by Rabbi Aryeh Leib Heller. Explaining why human practitioners of Torah law are not required or expected to perfectly conform their conduct to metaphysically objective but often epistemologically uncertain Torah norms, Rabbi Heller writes that, "the Torah was not given to the ministering angels, but to human beings endowed with human reason . . . to implement in accordance with what human reason understands and determines it to entail, even if those judgments are not consistent with the objective truth."[64] In addition to reassuring rabbinic scholars that their task is to diligently search for—and not necessarily to successfully discover—the objective truth of the Torah, this passage provides a solid basis for not demanding adherence to supererogatory religious stringencies. Such stringencies often seek to

---

62 *See generally* Christine Hayes, *"The Torah was not Given to the Ministering Angels": Rabbinic Aspirationalism*, in Talmudic Transgressions: Engaging the Work of Daniel Boyarin 123 (Charlotte Elisheva Fonrobert, et. al., eds., 2017).
63 *See generally* ibid. 123, 124.
64 Rabbi Aryeh Leib Heller, *Introduction* to Ketzot HaChoshen.

craft modes of religious behavior that successfully respect numerous alternative rabbinic opinions on matters subject to dispute as a means of ensuring that one complies with whatever the truly correct standard happens to really be.[65] But working from the assumption that "the Torah was not given to the ministering angels," such measures may be unnecessary. Human beings are not expected to know or comply with what the law actually demands from God's objective, heavenly vantage; that is the vocation of the angels. Mankind, on the other hand, is tasked with reaching *halakhic* determinations in accordance with their own well-considered judgments and acting accordingly. In this model, supererogatory behaviors are unnecessary, and ritual stringencies used to hedge one's *halakhic* bets and ensure compliance are misplaced.

The idea that "the Torah was not given to the ministering angels" is a particular form of what might be broadly termed "*halakhic* safety valves," jurisprudential mechanisms in rabbinic law that provide releases from the pressure created when normative *halakhic* standards conflict with practical human needs and concerns. Other safety-valve concepts include: situational duress; illness which, depending on its severity, justifies dispensations from a variety of different kinds of laws; financial loss that would result from normative *halakhic* compliance; substantial mental or physical pain; and communal or substantial individual needs that will not be satisfied if regular *halakhic* standards are to be observed. The specific rules and principles governing the use and application of each of these doctrines are beyond the scope of this chapter. The thrust of each of these doctrines, however, is to offer exemptions from legal obligations or restrictions, to provide a basis for relying on normatively rejected *halakhic* opinions, and to resolve unsettled legal questions in pragmatic ways that best account for the worldly needs of Jewish law's human subjects and practitioners.

Rabbi Epstein's regard for the relevance of these concerns in *halakhic* practice is illustrated by his approach to dealing with individuals who miss reciting various daily prayers at their proper times.[66] Jewish law prescribes three daily prayers that one is obligated to recite at particular times of the day.[67] The correct way to address having failed to recite the appropriate prayer during the allotted time of day, however, depends on the reason for which the prayer was

---

65 This approach, as discussed in Chapter Three, tends to be the one favored by Rabbi Israel Meir Kagan in his *Mishnah Berurah*. Rabbi Epstein, on the other hand, as discussed in greater depth above, in Chapter Eight, tends in his *Arukh HaShulchan* to avoid this sort of supererogatory approach.
66 *See* Arukh HaShulchan, Orach Chaim 108:5-6.
67 *See* Babylonian Talmud, Berakhot 26a; Shulchan Arukh, Orach Chaim 233:1.

missed. As Maimonides explains, if "one intentionally failed to pray, he has no way to correct his error and does not recite a make-up prayer. However, if [he missed the prayer] by accident, or was subject to some situational duress, or was otherwise busy, he makes up the missed prayer at the time he prays the next obligatory prayer of the day."[68] In other words, those with some excuse for why they missed a prayer are afforded the opportunity to rectify this by making up the prayer at a later time; those who intentionally skip a prayer, however, are considered more culpable and are therefore not given the benefit of correcting their failure by reciting a make-up prayer. When defining the kinds of excuses that render one less than fully culpable for missing a prayer, thus entitling one to correct the error by making up the prayer later, Rabbi Epstein provides an expansive understanding that takes careful account of the pressures and human issues that may understandably lead people to fail to pray at the proper time.[69] For instance, Rabbi Epstein writes that one's missing a prayer is understandably excusable and not treated as intentional if one missed the prayer time because he mistakenly thought he would finish a task in time to pray, but that task ended up taking much longer than anticipated, causing him to miss the prayer time. Likewise, he treats as excusable one who was busy with work or a business venture and did not halt his activities in order to pray out of concern that doing so would result in a financial loss. Remarkably, Rabbi Epstein even goes so far as to rule that missing prayers is considered excusable if it resulted from one simply forgetting to pray on time, because people do in fact forget things, and such forgetfulness is therefore considered a form of situational duress.[70]

While failing to recite an obligatory prayer at the prescribed time for some excusable reason justifies making up the prayer later, Rabbi Moses Isserles points out that this applies only *after* a prayer has already been missed, and the relevant prayer time has passed. "However," Rabbi Isserles rules, "in the first place, while the prayer can still be recited at the proper time, one may not allow the time to pass [and thus miss reciting the prayer] on account of some financial loss" one expects to suffer if one stops what one is doing to pray.[71] Rabbi Epstein, however, argues that such a categorical rule, failing to account for situations in which praying on time would cause a person to suffer serious financial losses, cannot be correct. He notes that Jewish law clearly maintains that one need not spend inordinate amounts of one's money in order to fulfill

---

68 Mishneh Torah, Hilkhot Tefillah 3:8.
69 *See* Arukh HaShulchan, Orach Chaim 108:5.
70 *See* ibid.
71 Rema *to* Shulchan Arukh, Orach Chaim 108:8.

CHAPTER TWELVE • Law and Pragmatism | 241

even biblical obligations, and the same should certainly be true for rabbinically imposed duties, like praying the daily prayers at their prescribed times.[72] Rabbi Epstein rules, therefore, that while one is not excused from praying at the correct time on account of speculative concerns that one may possibly suffer a financial loss as a result, people are excused from having to pray on time if doing so is reasonably likely to cause a financial loss.[73]

Rabbi Epstein thus recognizes financial pressures (*hefsed*) as a justification for departures from normative *halakhic* standards in a number of contexts. In another example of this approach, Maimonides records the standard rule that on the Sabbath it is prohibited to handle items whose primary use involves activities that constitute disallowed Sabbath labors, unless one is handling the item in order to use it for a permitted activity or because one needs to move the item in order to make use of the space the item was occupying.[74] One may not, however, handle such items "for their own sake."[75] For example, a pepper grinder is an item designed for a use that is prohibited on the Sabbath (grinding is a biblically prohibited Sabbath labor), and may therefore not be handled on the Sabbath. While one may move a pepper grinder off a table in order to eat a meal at the table, or handle the pepper grinder in order to use it to break open the shells of nuts that one wishes to eat, one may not take a pepper grinder that has been left outside in the rain and move it indoors in order to prevent it from rusting. This latter handling of the pepper grinder would amount to moving it "for its own sake," which is normatively prohibited.[76]

Despite this general prohibition against handling "for their own sake" items made to be used to perform activities forbidden on the Sabbath, Rabbi Epstein utilizes a passage in the Jerusalem Talmud to prescribe a method that would permit moving such items to avoid their becoming lost or damaged. The Jerusalem Talmud addresses a situation in which one left nets sitting outside in the sun on the Sabbath and is concerned that the sun will damage the nets.[77] Nets are used for trapping—a prohibited Sabbath labor—and thus cannot be moved "for their own sake," but rather may only be handled if the nets themselves are to be put to some Sabbath-permitted use. The Talmud rules that one might successfully remove the nets from the sun to the shade in the following,

---

72 *See* Arukh HaShulchan, Orach Chaim 108:6.
73 *See* ibid. 108:7.
74 *See* Mishneh Torah, Hilkhot Shabbat 25:1-5.
75 *See* Mishneh Torah, Hilkhot Shabbat 25:3.
76 *See* ibid 25:1-5.
77 *See* Jerusalem Talmud, Shabbat 4:2.

somewhat duplicitous manner: one should think to oneself that one wants to use the nets as a pillow (a Sabbath-permitted use that would allow the handling of the nets), and then, once the nets are being moved for this "reason," they can permissibly be moved to a shaded area.[78] Based on this discussion, Rabbi Epstein rules that one may indeed move items that it is otherwise prohibited to handle on the Sabbath in order to protect them from becoming lost or damaged, provided that one can come up with some permitted pretext for moving the item in the first place. While Rabbi Epstein acknowledges that such a fictitious pretext amounts to a *har'amah*, a kind of formalistic legal trickery, he rules this is justified in order to avoid financial loss.[79]

Indeed, it is neither difficult nor uncommon to find in Rabbi Epstein's writing a distinct realization that economic loss is grounds for adopting an acceptable but less than ideal rule as normative practice[80] and the reverse as well: a person should be strict in practice, since there is no economic cost to being strict.[81]

The same calculus is true for Rabbi Epstein in the area of duress (*oness*): he recognizes that in the world that he is living in, sometimes a violation of Jewish law is forced on people, and such conduct is not sinful at all: when one is coerced, no violation takes place.[82] He understands sickness to be such a case of duress,[83] and he seeks to do his best to allow people to observe Jewish Law in situations in which human frailty is unavoidably present.

Human pain and suffering—even when it falls short of the kind of physical or mental illness that often excuse the disregard of normative biblical and rabbinic rules—can also sometimes justify exemptions for standard *halakhic* rules. Jewish law, for instance, prohibits fasting on the Sabbath.[84] In his *Shulchan Arukh*, Rabbi Joseph Karo notes two important exemptions from this rule. First, one for whom eating is harmful need not eat, and may instead avoid food—effectively fasting—on the Sabbath. Second, regarding "a person who fasts every day such that eating on the Sabbath will cause him pain or distress due to this change of routine," Rabbi Karo writes that "there are those who say

---

78 Ibid.
79 *See* Arukh HaShulchan, Orach Chaim 308:14.
80 *See* ibid. 247:13, 254:17, 277:10 309:9, 467:26 and countless other places. In Yoreh Deah this concept is even more pronounced.
81 *See, e.g.* Arukh HaShulchan, Orach Chaim 156:7, 162:7 and 363:34 as well as countless other places. For a fascinating example of this, see 244:22.
82 *See* ibid. 53:3, and 9, 65:5, 153:47, 185:10, 405:6 and countless other places.
83 *See* ibid. 62:6-7.
84 *See* Shulchan Arukh, Orach Chaim 288:1.

that they saw many pious people who fasted on the Sabbath for this reason."[85] Rabbi Epstein expressly endorses both these rulings, and explains that a person for whom eating is harmful or dangerous is of course exempt from the obligation to eat on the Sabbath. However, he writes that even a person who will not be harmed by eating—and will indeed actually enjoy and be energized by the food, but will be somewhat distressed or suffer some indigestion after eating good food because he is used to fasting—is exempted from the usual prohibition against fasting on the Sabbath.[86]

* * * * *

Consistent with a long rabbinic tradition of approaching *halakhic* decision-making in a pragmatic way that helps ensure that Jewish law can be reasonably practiced by Jews, the jurisprudence of the *Arukh HaShulchan* takes careful account of the real-world difficulties sometimes posed by *halakhic* norms. Rabbi Epstein recognizes that Jewish law must be practiced in the real world, and so, when reaching his own *halakhic* determinations, weighs the practicability of alternative standards of practice. Often, the *Arukh HaShulchan* prescribes Jewish legal standards that are reasonably attainable by ordinary people given physical, economic, and other limitations. This approach is significant in its acceptance of the factual conditions in which *halakhah* must be practiced; rather than positing more ideal contexts in which more "ideal" or stringent modes of *halakhic* practice could be upheld, Rabbi Epstein takes the lived political, economic, physical, and mental realities of those committed to Jewish law as a given, and pragmatically determines workable standards of religious practice accordingly.

---

85 Ibid. 288:3.
86 *See* Arukh HaShulchan, Orach Chaim 288:4.

Conclusion

The purpose of this book is to serve as a methodological and jurisprudential introduction to the *Orach Chaim* portion of Rabbi Yechiel Mikhel Epstein's *Arukh HaShulchan*. Our goal is to identify how Rabbi Epstein goes about reaching his *halakhic* conclusions. What goes into his decision to adopt this rule rather than that rule, and why does he choose to prescribe one course of conduct when any number of other approaches are both textually reasonable and also supported by the precedential decisions of other rabbinic scholars? Moreover, we aim to provide insight into how Rabbi Epstein thought about *halakhah*; where does Jewish law come from, what does it aim to do; is it something piously other-worldly, or concerned with the mundane questions of human experience?

The foregoing discussion has identified and explained each of ten distinct secondary rules of decision that together comprise the jurisprudential methodology through which Rabbi Epstein views Jewish law and reaches his *halakhic* conclusions in the *Arukh HaShulchan*. Briefly summarized, these principles are:

1. The theoretically correct *halakhic* rule on any given issue is reflected in each rabbinic decision maker's considered understanding of the relevant Talmudic sources, even when such contradicts the opinions of other important scholars of previous eras.
2. One's independent Talmudic understandings should be subordinated to alternative opinions embraced by a broad consensus of other rabbinic scholars.
3. When one is uncertain about the correct legal understanding of the Talmud, one should defer to the precedential rulings of the great *halakhic* codifiers, including Maimonides and the *Shulchan Arukh*, particularly when those rulings are more legally stringent than one's own.
4. When a rabbinic scholar is genuinely unsure about the correct Talmudic rule, and where rabbinic consensus and other major codes fail to determine the issue, one should follow standard doubt-resolving rules, such as "doubt regarding biblical laws is resolved strictly, while doubt regarding rabbinic rules is resolved leniently."
5. One should practice in accordance with one's considered understanding of the Talmud, and one need not act strictly in order to satisfy alternative *halakhic* opinions that have been rejected in accordance with the ordinary rules of *halakhic* decision-making.

6. One should—but is not required to—adopt supererogatory practices that go beyond the minimal requirements of the *halakhah*, but only when there is a genuine religious or material benefit in doing so.
7. Authentic mystical traditions are part-and-parcel of the *halakhah*, and one must therefore observe kabbalistic practices that are not irreconcilably incompatible with Talmudic sources while rejecting mystical observances that cannot be squared with *halakhic* sources.
8. *Minhag*—the customary practice of one's own time and place—is a normative source of *halakhah*, and customary practices must therefore be observed and reconciled with standard black-letter Jewish law whenever possible.
9. *Halakhic* rules and standards need to be determined contextually, in the present time and place. Thus, even established *halakhic* norms need to change when the underlying reasons for those standards no longer apply such that in the present context the rules no longer succeed in furthering their purposes.
10. *Halakhah* must be practiced by real people in the real world, and impracticable *halakhic* norms must therefore be adapted to better account for the real-world practical challenges attendant to trying to actually uphold such standards.

These ten principles of *halakhic* jurisprudence speak to four different questions that go to the heart of understanding about what Jewish law and Jewish legal decision-making are all about. Principle one affirms that in Rabbi Epstein's view *halakhah* resides in the considered Talmudic judgment of each qualified rabbinic scholar. Correct rules of law are not determined by post-Talmudic precedents, no matter the stature of the opining scholar; and, importantly, the *halakhah* may be multivocal, with numerous individual scholars reaching different *halakhic* understandings of the Talmudic sources, all of which may be regarded as simultaneously correct and legitimate. At the same time, the second principle affirms that Jewish law is not unboundedly individualistic; *halakhah* is a communal project, and correct legal judgments must be situated within the continuing stream of rabbinic discourse, the outer limits of which are set by rabbinic consensus over time. Likewise, principle three cautions humility in the face of decisional uncertainty. The *halakhah* accords with each scholar's own judgment only when "the law is clear to him as the sun"; when one is uncertain about the right legal rule, deference to the highly regarded and influential scholars of the *halakhic* tradition is appropriate.

Consistent with the jurisprudential thrust of these first three principles, principle four affirms that in an important sense *halakhic* decision-making is not a search for objective legal truth, but an activity aimed at framing Jewish living through a creative but humble encounter with rabbinic texts and traditions. Consequently, normative questions must ultimately be resolved and legal guidance given, even in the face of unresolvable analytic doubts, and sometimes even by resort to seemingly arbitrary rules that succeed in determining the issue without necessarily speaking to the actual correctness of the result. Consistent with the foregoing, principle five indicates that in Rabbi Epstein's jurisprudence *halakhic* practice is about making and acting upon considered judgments about how Jewish texts and traditions apply to given situations. One need not act overly strictly in order to be assured of having gotten it right from an objective or Godly vantage; instead one is merely tasked with following qualified *halakhic* determinations.

Principle six affirms, however, that Rabbi Epstein understands *halakhah* as a normative system designed to accomplish positive religious and material outcomes. Thus, while he thinks that people can only be obligated to fulfill the letter of the law, he also maintains that Jews should strive to do more by engaging in supererogatory practices whenever such extralegal observances contribute to religiously or materially positive outcomes. Moreover, as a religious system, *halakhah* is not concerned solely with this worldly practice. Principle seven affirms that Jewish law also embraces the spiritual insights of Judaism's mystical traditions. When *halakhah* and Kabbalah are not inconsistent, therefore, Rabbi Epstein views the latter as normative.

Finally, while *halakhah* is of course a religious system, Rabbi Epstein embraces the idea that ultimately it is a legal regime grounded in the earthly, rather than spiritual realm. Principle eight incorporates into *halakhah* the lived experiences of the Jewish community, making customs—the local Jewish community's way of actualizing *halakhic* norms in practice—a basic source of law. Principle nine encapsulates Rabbi Epstein's conviction that *halakhah* is not a changeless, other-worldly reality, but a normative system grounded in the real world. The law is often designed to achieve certain religious or material ends, and when evolving social, economic, cultural, political, and other contexts render particular legal rules moot, the rules must be reformulated in order to achieve legally desirable objectives under current circumstances.

In principle ten, Rabbi Epstein affirms that Jewish law is ultimately about living Jewishly in the real world; it is not a pact for financial, mental, or physical ruin, and it does not demand that Jews be anything more than refined, law-abiding human beings. Thus, Rabbi Epstein rejects the normativity of impracticable *halakhic* obligations and of standards of conduct too complex or burdensome to be reasonably upheld by dedicated Jews.

Finally, in closing our discussion of Rabbi Epstein's *halakhic* jurisprudence, we note that the legal methodology of the *Arukh HaShulchan* is complex and defies overly simplistic explanations. In rendering legal determinations in the *Orach Chaim* sections of the *Arukh HaShulchan*, Rabbi Epstein is almost always balancing at least four different ideas that run throughout all of these ten methodological principles. Rabbi Epstein is first and foremost deeply intellectually independent, seeking to determine the mandates of Jewish law as he sees it to the best of his ability. Second, Rabbi Epstein is deeply traditional and committed to keeping both his rulings and their methodology deeply rooted in the history of rabbinic thought and Jewish practice. Third, the *Arukh HaShulchan* is deeply pragmatic: Jewish law has to actually work in the real world that he lives in—unworkable rules are to be avoided, even when reasonable in theory. Fourth, Jewish law, Rabbi Epstein repeatedly avers, needs to be decided in the context of the place, time, and matter, and not in the abstract, as if Jewish law lived independent of its time and place. This paints the picture of a nuanced, complex, and importantly, not-mechanistic approach to *halakhic* decision-making. For Rabbi Epstein, *halakhah* is a very human endeavor, one that strives for religious piety and spiritual heights, but which is ultimately determined by variable, fallible—and ennobling—human judgment.

Part III

Illustrative Examples from the *Arukh HaShulchan*

The *Arukh HaShulchan's* Methodological Principles for Reaching *Halakhic* Conclusions

Part I of this work has explored the development of diversity and complexity in Jewish law and some of the variant approaches that *halakhic* scholars have taken to systematizing and codifying rabbinic legal discourses. We briefly explored the divergent models of *halakhic* codification utilized by Rabbis Kagan and Epstein in their important Jewish law codes, the *Mishnah Berurah* and the *Arukh HaShulchan*, both of which sought to organize several hundred years of *halakhic* development since the appearance of Rabbi Karo's *Shulchan Arukh* and to arrive at singular normative determinations at a time when Jewish life and Jewish law were undergoing substantial changes. In Part II, we took a deep dive into the jurisprudence and legal methodology of the *Orach Chaim* section of Rabbi Yechiel Mikhel Epstein's *Arukh HaShulchan*. We elaborated on ten decision-making principles that Rabbi Epstein uses to reach *halakhic* conclusions in the face of the expansive and at times tumultuous sea of prior rabbinic legal discussion. More specifically, we noted that these ten methodological principles constitute Rabbi Epstein's responses to four fundamental questions of *halakhic* jurisprudence: first, how does a rabbinic decisor go about determining the ideally correct legal standard; second, what should a *halakhic* scholar do when the ideally correct rule remains genuinely in doubt; third, when instructing constituents about how to act in practice, how should a rabbinic decision maker balance observing the ideally correct *halakhic* norms with other religious values; and fourth and finally, how should practical Jewish law decision-making account for pragmatic concerns related to social, economic, political, and other contexts in which the *halakhah* must be observed. Our discussion of these issues in Part II revealed that Rabbi Epstein's *Arukh HaShulchan* employs a complex, multifaceted jurisprudence that is at once independent and creative, as well as traditionalist and firmly situated in the historical and conceptual stream of rabbinic legal discourse. Likewise, the methodology of the *Arukh HaShulchan* is attentive to the need for Jewish law to be practicable and intelligible given current geographic, economic, and social contexts, while also remaining sensitive to the *halakhah*'s goal of cultivating a pious, religiously aware Jewish community.

Part III of this book approaches the issue from a different angle. Unlike the historical perspective offered in Part I, and the conceptual-jurisprudence discussed in Part II, Part III seeks to more fully substantiate our claims about the *Arukh HaShulchan*'s legal methodology with verifiable data. Thus, in Part III, we have collected and elucidated two-hundred examples of Rabbi Epstein's *halakhic* decision-making so that each reader may reach their own conclusions as to whether and to what extent the ten methodological principles we have identified are indeed mainstays of the *Arukh HaShulchan*'s jurisprudence, and whether other secondary rules of decision might be at play as well. The reader need not take our claims about the ten principles animating Rabbi Epstein's *halakhic* judgment at face value; nor do the limited number of examples provided illustrating Rabbi Epstein's use of these principles need suffice to support our understandings. Moreover, by providing numerous examples of how Rabbi Epstein reaches *halakhic* determinations—most of which involve the use of more than one of the previously discussed methodological principles—this part offers the reader a window into the mind of the *Arukh HaShulchan*. Studying these examples not only demonstrates Rabbi Epstein's use of each of the ten principles, but more importantly it offers insights into how the various principles utilized by the *Arukh HaShulchan* interact with each other in practice, especially when they seem to pull in different normative directions.

Part III can thus be treated as an appendix to the earlier sections of this book. It comprises our restatements of Rabbi Epstein's treatment of two-hundred discreet Jewish legal issues taken from across the *Orach Chaim* section of his *Arukh HaShulchan*. Rather than direct translations of Rabbi Epstein's writings—which would prove cumbersome, at times opaque, and overly lengthy—we have elected to present the background of each issue; the relevant sources, opinions, and concerns considered by Rabbi Epstein in his *halakhic* analysis; the *Arukh HaShulchan*'s ruling on the topic; and an explanation of Rabbi Epstein's reasoning that identifies the various methodological principles he uses in reaching his legal conclusion. Each example of Rabbi Epstein's legal methodology in action is identified by the section and paragraph numbers under which his ruling appears in the *Arukh HaShulchan*. This more easily permits the reader to study the relevant passages themselves; and for this reason, we have largely eschewed including extensive references and citations to the sources and rabbinic opinions with which Rabbi Epstein engages in his treatment of each issue. Readers interested in exploring these topics and the relevant Talmudic and rabbinic sources are invited to study Rabbi Epstein's discussions directly, and to work backward from there to earlier *halakhic* materials.

This part begins with a brief restatement of the ten methodological principles that define the jurisprudence of the *Arukh HaShulchan* when considering matters that fall within the scope of the *Orach Chaim* section of the work. Next, this part presents two hundred examples of Rabbi Epstein's decision-making, listed in the order in which they appear in the *Arukh HaShulchan*.

The Ten Methodological Principles of the *Arukh HaShulchan*

Principles for Determining the Ideally Correct *Halakhic* Standard

1. *Dina D'Talmuda: The Normativity of Talmudic Norms*

Rabbi Epstein maintains that in the abstract, the correct *halakhic* standard is the one that emerges from each qualified rabbinic scholar's independent, confident understanding the relevant Talmudic sources—even against the precedential rulings of other important *halakhic* authorities of previous generations. Thus, when Rabbi Epstein is confident in the correctness of his own Talmudic interpretations, he rules in accordance with his own understanding of these materials, which for him include not only the Babylonian Talmud, but also the Jerusalem Talmud, which Rabbi Epstein often deploys as an important *halakhic* source. This approach often leads Rabbi Epstein to express disagreement with the rulings of other important rabbinic scholars; to offer new and creative Talmudic readings to explain his conclusions; to propose novel reasons for established *halakhic* norms; and to prescribe entirely new standards of *halakhic* conduct.

2. Intellectual Humility in the Face of Teachers and Colleagues

Rabbi Epstein's commitment to following his own independent understandings of the Talmudic sources is tempered by epistemic humility. Even where Rabbi Epstein is personally confident in his legal opinion, he declines to follow his independent understanding of the relevant Talmudic sources when his own view is incompatible with the established rule of a broad consensus of past authorities, as well as when the views of major pillars of *halakhic* jurisprudence adopt a rule more stringent than his own. In such cases, Rabbi Epstein becomes less certain about the correctness of his own Talmudic understandings and tends to defer to the collective weight of rabbinic consensus, or to cautiously prescribe the adoption of the more ritually restrictive standard adopted by particularly significant *halakhic* authorities.

Principles for Resolving Doubts about the Ideally Correct *Halakhic* Standard

3. *Reliance on Precedent in Cases of Doubt*

In cases where Rabbi Epstein is himself unsure about the right Talmudic norm, and in the absence of a strong *halakhic* consensus regarding the correct meaning of the Talmudic sources, Rabbi Epstein tends to give primary weight to the rulings of Maimonides and then to the determinations of Rabbi Joseph Karo as recorded in his works, the *Beit Yosef* and the *Shulchan Arukh*.

4. *Reliance on Secondary Rules for Resolving Doubts*

In cases where Rabbi Epstein is himself unsure of the correct Talmudic rule and where past rabbinic consensus and major precedential authorities do not provide clear guidance on the issue, Rabbi Epstein resorts to the application of standard doubt-resolving secondary rules of *halakhic* decision-making. Most prominently, Rabbi Epstein follows the standard *halakhic* rule that, in cases of doubt regarding biblical laws, one should act strictly, while in cases of doubt regarding rabbinic rules, one should act leniently.

Principles for Mediating Between the Talmudic Standard and Other Religious Values

5. *The Relevance of Non-Normative Halakhic Opinions*

Rabbi Epstein generally does not rule that one should act strictly in order to satisfy *halakhic* opinions, which he regards as mistaken because either he rejects the Talmudic interpretations upon which they rely; they have been marginalized by rabbinic consensus; or they have been otherwise rejected in accordance with the ordinary rules of *halakhic* decision-making. However, Rabbi Epstein does make use of such rejected opinions to resolve complex *halakhic* questions or disputes among past authorities; to justify common practices that are at odds with standard *halakhic* norms; and to permit non-normative behavior in extenuating circumstances.

6. *Supererogatory Religious Conduct*

Rabbi Epstein generally encourages—but does not mandate—supererogatory behavior that goes beyond the minimal requirements of what he thinks is the correct normative *halakhic* standard, but only in cases where he believes there is a genuine religious or social benefit to doing so. In cases where Rabbi Epstein thinks that supererogatory behavior offers no appreciable religious or social benefits, or where he believes that such conduct is likely to have negative religious or material consequences, Rabbi Epstein discourages extra-*halakhic* observances.

7. *Halakhah and Mysticism*

Rabbi Epstein tries whenever possible to reconcile the mystical prescriptions of the *Zohar* and other kabbalistic sources with standard *halakhic* norms, though he affirmatively rejects the *halakhic* relevance of mystical practices that are incompatible with Talmudic sources. Moreover, Rabbi Epstein generally permits—and often recommends—the adoption of mystical practices innovated by the *Zohar*, as long that they do not contradict *halakhic* requirements.

Principles for Mediating Between the Talmudic Standard and Pragmatic Concerns

8. *Minhag: The Role of Custom in Determining Halakhah*

Rabbi Epstein upholds the *halakhic* normativity of what he sees as *minhag*—the customary practices of the Jewish people living in his own time and place—even when such customary practices are inconsistent with precedential *halakhic* rulings or Rabbi Epstein's own preferred understanding of the Talmudic sources. However, Rabbi Epstein rejects the legal validity of customary practices that are irreconcilably incompatible with basic *halakhic* standards, or which are based on mistaken factual or legal assumptions.

9. *Contemporary Rationalization of Halakhic Norms*

Rabbi Epstein insists that *halakhic* issues need to be decided in the present time and place. Thus, he holds that, when the reasons for established *halakhic* rules no longer apply due to changed circumstances, those rules likewise change so as to respond effectively to achieve the same objectives in the circumstances posed by current realities.

10. *Real-World Pragmatism: The Torah Was Not Given to the Ministering Angels*

Rabbi Epstein recognizes that *halakhah* must be practiced by real people in the real world, and therefore adapts seemingly impracticable *halakhic* norms to better account for the real-world practical challenges attendant to trying to actually uphold such standards.

Example #1 - *Arukh HaShulchan* §1:24

Rabbi Joseph Karo rules in his *Shulchan Arukh* that it is good to recite the Torah passages known as *Parshat HaAkeidah, Parshat HaMan*, the *Aseret HaDibrot*, and the *Olah, Minchah, Shelamim, Chatat*, and *Asham* passages as part of one's morning prayers.[1] In the *Arukh HaShulchan*, Rabbi Epstein disagrees with this prescription, however, and notes that "our custom" is to say what is typically printed in the prayer books and to not recite *Parshat HaMan*, the *Aseret HaDibrot*, or the *Olah, Minchah, Shelamim, Chatat*, or *Asham* passages (Principles 1 and 8).

Rabbi Epstein provides several explanations for his departure from the *Shulchan Arukh*'s prescribed practice. First, he argues that his view does not really conflict with the *Shulchan Arukh* at all, since in his *Beit Yosef* Rabbi Karo indicates that the recitals listed in the *Shulchan Arukh* only reflect the custom of some Jews, suggesting that other alternative customs omitting these passages exist and are valid modes of practice (Principle 8). Second, Rabbi Epstein offers a creative argument for why one should not say these passages contrary to the preferred practice espoused by the *Shulchan Arukh* (Principle 1). He argues that the only prayers that should be recited as part of the public congregational service are those that correspond to communal practices. Accordingly, why should the congregation recite the passages referring to the *Olah, Minchah, Shelamim, Chatat*, and *Asham* offerings, since these offerings were not communal sacrifices, and were only ever personally obligatory for certain individuals in response to certain conditions? Furthermore, Rabbi Epstein writes, one should not recite the *Aseret HaDibrot*, the Ten Commandments, as part of the daily morning prayers because the Talmud itself establishes that the Rabbis prohibited the congregational recital of the *Aseret HaDibrot* as part of the prayer service as a means of countering heresies that may claim that the Ten Commandments are the only important part of the Torah (Principle 1).

Rabbi Epstein notes that the foregoing reasons nevertheless do not explain the custom to not recite *Parshat HaMan*, which recalls the collective experience of the Jews' receiving food from the Heavens while wandering in the wilderness, and the recital of which is not subject to any Talmudic strictures. He suggests that perhaps the reason it is omitted is because, while the Talmud does not proscribe its recital, it also does not mandate it; and while some claim that *Parshat HaMan* is recorded in the Jerusalem Talmud, Rabbi Epstein says no such reference exists (Principle 1). Additionally, Rabbi Epstein suggests that perhaps *Parshat HaMan* is omitted, contrary to the view of the *Shulchan Arukh*, because the historical receipt of the Manna food by the Israelites in the wilderness was preceded by their complaints to God and Moses and God's displeasure with the people, which should not be raised in the context of prayer (Principle 1). Importantly, overarching Rabbi Epstein's discussion of this issue is his observation that in fact "our custom" is to omit many of the passages that the *Shulchan Arukh* ruled one should say. His subsequent arguments thus reflect his efforts to support the observed practice of his time and place (Principle 8).

Methodological Principles: 1, 8.

Example #2 - *Arukh HaShulchan* §1:26

There is a dispute among some later authorities about whether one should recite the *Korbanot* passages detailing the Temple sacrificial service while standing or if one can do so

---

[1] *See* Shulchan Arukh, Orach Chaim 1:5.

while sitting. According to the *Magen Avraham*, a major commentator on Rabbi Karo's *Shulchan Arukh*, and an important authority in his own right, one must recite *Korbanot* while standing because the actual process of offering the sacrifices in the Temple in Jerusalem could not be done sitting down. Many others disagree, however, and rule that one can recite the *Korbanot* as part of the morning prayer service while sitting.

The *Arukh HaShulchan* rules in accordance with the latter approach. Rabbi Epstein argues that there is no reason to think that the recital of *Korbanot* as part of the daily prayers need necessarily correspond to the way in which the offerings were brought in the Temple; after all, he writes, ordinary, non-*Kohen* Jews—who were not members of the priestly tribe—could not perform the Temple service for these offerings at all, yet such Jews nevertheless recite the relevant passages as part of their daily prayers. Thus, Rabbi Epstein concludes, the contemporary recital of the *Korbanot* passages as part of the prayer service need not mimic the Temple service, and the passages can be said while sitting (Principle 1). At the same time, Rabbi Epstein innovates a new rule, based on this line of reasoning. He writes that a *Kohen*, a priest, who could have performed that actual sacrificial service during the times that the Temple stood and would have had to perform that service while standing, is obligated to stand when reciting the *Korbanot* passages during his daily prayers even today (Principle 1).

Methodological Principles: 1.

Example #3 – *Arukh HaShulchan* §1:29

The *Arukh HaShulchan* draws on a passage in the Jerusalem Talmud to offer a novel explanation for why we pray three times each day. In contrast to the more commonly known view expressed by the Babylonian Talmud, which states that the three prayers were established by the three patriarchs, Abraham, Isaac, and Jacob, the Jerusalem Talmud suggests that the three daily prayers correspond to the three times each day that our environment changes around us (Principle 1). Rabbi Epstein goes further, however, and notes that this passage of the Jerusalem Talmud also prescribes a short prayer to be said as part of each of the three daily prayers to mark each of these three daily transitions. Rabbi Epstein appears to endorse this practice and the reason for the daily prayers offered by the Jerusalem Talmud, despite also noting that no other *halakhic* decisors reference this idea or endorse this practice (Principle 1).

Methodological Principles: 1.

Example #4 – *Arukh HaShulchan* §2:8

The *Shulchan Arukh*, following a ruling by the *Arbah Turim*, instructs that when getting dressed a person should first put on their right shoe, then their left shoe, after which they should first tie their left shoe and then their right shoe.[2] Some rabbinic scholars, including the *Malbim* in his *Artzot HaChaim*, disagree with the *Shulchan Arukh*'s instructions, and all the major early *halakhic* codifiers, including Rabbi Isaac Alfasi, Maimonides, Rabbi Asher ben Yechiel, the *Mordechai*, and *Semag*, make no mention of any obligation to put on one's shoes in any specific order.

Rabbi Epstein, however, endorses the *Shulchan Arukh*'s directive. He first notes that it is in fact the custom to don one's shoes in this manner (Principle 8). Next, Rabbi Epstein reiterates

---

2   See ibid. 2:4.

the common explanation for this rule—that the Torah regularly accords primacy to the right side of the body over the left, and so the right foot should be covered and protected before the left. He also references the Talmud's explanation—that we learn from how to tie *tefillin*, which are tied on the left arm—that when tying things, including shoes, one gives primacy to the left side over the right.[3] Importantly, Rabbi Epstein notes that the more likely correct understanding of the Talmudic discussion of this issue seems to support the view that the order of putting on one's shoes is not *halakhically* important. While the Talmud records that Rav Nachman bar Yitzchak related that the son of Ravana was scrupulous about putting on his shoes in this order, it goes on to note that Rav Ashi testified that Rav Kahana disregarded this practice; and since Rav Ashi lived after the son of Ravana, his rejection of the practice should be determinative under the Talmudic rule that "the law follows the latter authority." Nevertheless, Rabbi Epstein concludes, it is still appropriate to follow the affirmatively prescribed practice of the *Shulchan Arukh* and the *Arbah Turim* who represent important pillars of *halakhic* decision-making (Principle 2). In effect, then, the *Arukh HaShulchan* relies on the importance of the *Shulchan Arukh* and the *Arbah Turim* as precedential authorities to support the existing custom even against what he admits is most likely the correct—but not the only reasonable—understanding of the relevant Talmudic sources. Methodological Principles: 2, 8.

Example #5 – *Arukh HaShulchan* §3:13

Maimonides rules categorically that one may not sleep "between east and west, but rather between north and south."[4] This rule, which is sourced in the Babylonian Talmud, is an expression of reverence and awe for the Jerusalem Temple, the *Beit HaMikdash*, which was built along an east-west axis. In his *Shulchan Arukh* Rabbi Karo instructs that one should ideally be careful to observe this practice. The *Arukh HaShulchan*, however, rejects this prohibition, noting, against the view of the *Shulchan Arukh*, that "we are not careful about this" (Principle 1).

In explanation of his ruling, Rabbi Epstein notes that the meaning of the Talmudic passage that serves as the source for this rule is genuinely unclear. The Talmud records that Rav said that he made substantial efforts to ensure that his bed was not placed between east and west because Rav Yitzchak taught that one who places his bed between north and south will have male children.[5] Rabbi Epstein notes that most fundamentally the language of the Talmudic text is unclear as to whether one's bed should be placed with the head and feet on the north and south points of the compass (so that one sleeps with the length of one's body facing the east or west), or whether one's bed should run from east to west (so that one sleeps with one's body facing north or south). Additionally, Rabbi Epstein observes that early authorities disagreed over the normative implications of the relevant Talmudic passage. While Maimonides appears to have understood the Talmud's recording of Abba Shaul's statement as establishing a firm prohibition, others, including the *Arbah Turim*, hold that the passage merely indicates pious behavior, but it does not impose a strict duty to place one's bed in a certain direction. Moreover, *Tosafot*, scholars of an important medieval French rabbinic school, understand Abba Shaul's statement contextually as limited only to situations in which a husband and wife are sleeping in the same bed. Given the multifaceted uncertainty about this rule, Rabbi Epstein notes that in practice "this rule has fallen into the bonfire." Considering the prevailing practice rejecting this prohibition (Principle 8), and

---

3 *See* Babylonian Talmud, Shabbat 61a.
4 Mishneh Torah, Hilkhot Beit HaBechirah 7:9.
5 *See* Babylonian Talmud, Berakhot 5b.

considering the essential uncertainty of the character and force of the Talmudic prescription on the matter (Principle 1), Rabbi Epstein sees no need to adopt or even be seriously concerned for the prohibition codified by Maimonides (Principles 5 and 6).
Methodological Principles: 1, 5, 6, 8.

Example #6 – *Arukh HaShulchan* §4:9

The *Shulchan Arukh* rules that water that is disqualified for use for washing before a meal—such as water that looks like another liquid, is dirty, smells bad, or was used for some kind of labor[6]—may nonetheless be used to fulfill the rabbinic obligation to wash one's hands before praying.[7] Rabbi Karo reasons that while washing before a meal is a ritual requirement and therefore requires ritually clean water, washing before morning prayers is merely a functional practice to ensure cleanliness while praying for which any liquid that results in clean hands will suffice.

The *Arukh HaShulchan*, exercising independent judgment, rejects the *Shulchan Arukh*'s view and rules that water used for washing one's hands before prayer must meet the same qualifications as water used for washing before meals (Principle 1). Rabbi Epstein argues that the *Shulchan Arukh* is mistaken in distinguishing between pre-prayer and pre-meal handwashing in light of the fact that Maimonides appears to have held that the same rules apply to both kinds of handwashing (Principle 3). Maimonides is fairly explicit on this point and writes that the Talmudic Rabbis legislated that one should wash one's hands and recite the blessing of *al netilat yadayim* "whether for eating, for reciting the *Shema*, or for prayer,"[8] thus indicating that washing before prayer and washing before a meal are manifestations of the same rabbinic enactment and subject to the same conditions.
Methodological Principles: 1, 3.

Example #7 – *Arukh HaShulchan* §4:10

Rabbi Karo rules in his *Shulchan Arukh* that, while dipping one's hands into water instead of pouring water over them is sufficient to fulfill the obligation to wash one's hands before prayers, it does not suffice to remove the *ruach ra'ah* that comes to rest on one's hands while sleeping during the night, and which must be removed before one may touch food or one's mouth, eyes, ears, or other bodily orifices. The *Shulchan Arukh* then suggests that dipping one's hands consecutively into three different containers of water might suffice to remove the *ruach ra'ah*, though he remains unsure about this.[9]

Here too, the *Arukh HaShulchan* disagrees with Rabbi Karo's codified view and holds that dipping one's hands in water definitely does not satisfy the requirements for pre-prayer washing (Principle 1). Rabbi Epstein again relies on the correlation between washing before meals and washing before prayer, as adopted by Maimonides and others, and he rules that just as dipping one's hands in water cannot fulfill the requirement for pre-meal washing, it also cannot fulfill the need for pre-prayer washing (Principle 3). Rabbi Epstein then expresses surprise at the *Shulchan Arukh*'s uncertainty regarding the effectiveness of dipping one's hands into three different

---

6   *See* Shulchan Arukh, Orach Chaim 160:1-4.
7   *See* ibid. 4:1.
8   *See* Mishneh Torah, Hilkhot Berakhot 6:2.
9   *See* Shulchan Arukh, Orach Chaim 4:12.

containers of water. The *Arukh HaShulchan* argues that since the *Zohar* affirms that dipping one's hands in water cannot affect the removal of the *ruach ra'ah*, the *Shulchan Arukh* should have codified that view as the correct rule of law (Principle 10).
Methodological Principles: 1, 3, 10.

Example #8 – *Arukh HaShulchan* §4:11

The *Shulchan Arukh* rules that when washing one's hands before prayer, one does not need to fulfill all the conditions associated with ritual washing before a meal, such as the need for washing using a cup or other vessel, the requirement that the water wash over the hands as a result of human effort, and the requirement that one use as least a *revi'it* of water to complete the washing.[10] Once again, the *Arukh HaShulchan* disagrees and rules that washing before prayer must satisfy all the requirements for valid washing before a meal (Principle 1).[11] He relies primarily on Maimonides's equating washing for meals with washing for prayer (Principle 3), and also on the similar views of the *Rosh* and the *Rashba*, both of whom rule that various requirements associated with washing for food must also be observed when washing for prayer. Finally, Rabbi Epstein notes that the *Zohar*, too, affirms this position (Principle 10).
Methodological Principles: 1, 3, 10.

Example #9 – *Arukh HaShulchan* §4:12

Both Rabbi Joseph Karo and Rabbi Moses Isserles rule that one should not recite the blessing of *al netilat yadayim* when washing one's hands in the morning after not having slept the night before.[12] The *Shulchan Arukh* explains that the reason for this ruling is that it is unclear whether the rabbinic requirement to wash one's hands in the morning applies to situations where one did not sleep the night before. Since there is a doubt about whether such handwashing is legally required, one should avoid reciting the possibly unnecessary blessing upon washing one's hands so as to avoid taking God's name in vain, just in case the washing was not actually mandated.

This uncertainty regarding the obligatory nature of washing one's hands in the morning after not sleeping the night before stems from a rabbinic dispute about the nature of the rabbinic prescription of morning handwashing. According to Rabbi Asher ben Yechiel, author of the important *halakhic* compendium known as the *Rosh*, the reason for the original rabbinic obligation of morning handwashing was that a person's hands become dirty during the night, since people move their hands about during their sleep and inevitably touch unclean or usually covered parts of their bodies. Based on this view, the rabbinic requirement should not apply to a person who did not sleep, and who therefore need not be assumed to have unknowingly touched unclean body parts. Rabbi Solomon ben Aderet, the *Rashba*, offers a different rationale for the rabbinic enactment and suggests that a person who awakes from a night's sleep is akin to having been "created anew," and one must therefore rededicate their hands to serving God. According to the *Rashba*, too, then, the handwashing rule should not apply to a person who did not sleep during the night and is therefore not a newly created being the following morning. An alternative view, however, argues that the rabbinic enactment of morning handwashing was legislated as

---

10 *See* ibid. 4:6-7.
11 *See* Arukh HaShulchan, Orach Chaim 4:9.
12 *See* Shulchan Arukh, Orach Chaim 4:13.

a categorical duty. Thus, since there is no record of the Talmudic Rabbis having included any exemptions from this requirement in cases where a person did not sleep during the night, the obligation remains in place, and a person who was awake all night must still wash and recite the appropriate blessing. In any case, according to Rabbis Karo and Isserles, this uncertainty about the applicability of the Rabbis' enactment to a person who did not sleep during the night raises doubts about whether such a person must wash their hands. Following the general *halakhic* rule of decision that one should not recite a blessing in cases where the obligation to do so is uncertain, the *Shulchan Arukh* and the *Rema* rule that one should wash without reciting the blessing.

The *Arukh HaShulchan*, however, rejects the codified views of Rabbis Karo and Isserles and rules that a person who did not sleep during the night must nevertheless wash their hands and recite the appropriate blessing before doing so (Principle 1). While this ruling seems to cut against the ordinary rule that doubts about whether a blessing should be recited should be resolved by not reciting the blessing—a rule that Rabbi Epstein himself relies on regularly (Principle 4)—Rabbi Epstein justifies this conclusion by affirming that there is no doubt in his mind that a person who was awake all night is still rabbinically obligated to wash his hands. He argues that the Talmud does not record any built-in exceptions to the general enactment that Jews must wash their hands in the morning, and the suggested rationales for the enactment offered by the *Rosh* and the *Rashba* are merely speculative and cannot control the application of the categorical rule. In Rabbi Epstein's view, his confidence in the correctness of his understanding of the Talmudic rule at issue here is sufficient to justify requiring people to recite a blessing over handwashing in cases where other authorities think such a blessing would be unnecessary and a violation of the biblical prohibition against taking God's name in vain (Principle 1). Methodological Principles: 1, 4.

Example #10 – *Arukh HaShulchan* §4:19

The *Arukh HaShulchan* rules that in cases where a person does not have water available to fulfill the rabbinic obligation to wash one's hands in the morning, one should wipe and clean one's hands using a rock, sand, a wooden board, or any other abrasive medium that can affect cleanliness. When doing so, however, Rabbi Epstein rules that one should not recite the ordinary blessing of *al netilat yadayim* ("on washing hands"), but should instead use the alternative formulation, *al nekiyut yadayim* ("on the cleanliness of hands").

Rabbi Epstein notes that in truth, he thinks that even when one cleans one's hands using something other than water, one could recite the ordinary blessing of *al netilat yadayim*, since, as he previously concluded, the rabbinic enactment of handwashing is uniform and categorical and does not include exemptions for special cases.[13] Nevertheless, Rabbi Epstein concludes that it is proper to recite the blessing of *al nekiyut yadayim* in such cases in deference to the views of the *Rosh* and the *Arbah Turim*, who explicitly prescribe the alternative form of the blessing for situations where one is forced to clean one's hands instead of washing them due to the unavailability of water. Here, it appears that the *Arukh HaShulchan* does not feel compelled to rule in accordance with his own understanding of the issue, and he instead defers to the views of the *Arbah Turim* and the *Rosh* because his own view that the rabbinic enactment is categorical does not truly preclude the validity of reciting the alternative *al nekiyut yadayim* blessing, and thus one can uphold the views of the *Arbah Turim* and *Rosh* without affirmatively violating the *Arukh HaShulchan*'s preferred understanding of the Talmudic issue (Principle 1).

---

13   *See* Arukh HaShulchan, Orach Chaim 4:12.

Methodological Principles: 1.

Example #11 - *Arukh HaShulchan* §6:6

The *Arukh HaShulchan* rejects the custom of some people who do not recite the blessing of *al netilat yadayim* on washing their hands in the morning, the blessing of *asher yatzar* recited after relieving oneself, and the blessing of *elokai neshamah* at home, and instead recite these blessings as part of the rest of the morning blessings after they arrive at the synagogue for morning prayers. While Rabbi Karo takes note of this custom in the *Shulchan Arukh* without rejecting it as a matter of law, Rabbi Epstein concludes that "this custom has no source or substance," (Principle 8) thereby rejecting the *Shulchan Arukh*'s implied tolerance for that practice (Principle 1). Rabbi Epstein observes that the predominant practice is to recite these blessings at home in the morning upon waking up, relieving oneself, and washing one's hands, and strongly prescribes that mode of practice as the correct one (Principle 8).
Methodological Principles: 1, 8.

Example #12 - *Arukh HaShulchan* §8:19

Rabbi Moses Isserles, or the *Rema*, rules that if a person has many four-cornered garments with *tzitzit* strings attached, then removes one such garment that he had previously donned after saying the appropriate blessing, and afterword seeks to put on another four-cornered garment, he must recite a second *al mitzvat tzitzit* blessing before putting on the second garment.[14]

The *Arukh HaShulchan* expresses his support for the *Rema*'s ruling here, advancing the independent line of reasoning that, when it comes to repeating the same blessing on numerous successive performances of the same *mitzvah*, the operative concern is whether or not the person in question has broken his intent to continue to fulfill that same *mitzvah*. If one has continuous intent to fulfill the *mitzvah*, the original blessing suffices for all subsequent performances of that *mitzvah*; but once one concludes the performance of a *mitzvah*, any subsequent performance of that *mitzvah*—even if temporally linked to the earlier performance—requires a new blessing. Thus, Rabbi Epstein writes, when one removes a four-cornered garment, one has demonstrated that he has concluded the performance of that *mitzvah* and must therefore make a new blessing when putting *tzitzit* back on thereafter (Principle 1).

Despite his agreement with the *Rema*'s ruling in principle, in practice Rabbi Epstein prescribes that one should not recite a new blessing when putting on a pair of *tzitzit* after having previously removed another pair of *tzitzit*. This is because Rabbi Epstein notes that the consensus of *halakhic* authorities disagrees with the *Rema*'s view, and "the law follows the majority" (Principle 2). Rabbi Epstein's respect for the consensus view stands even as he presents his own arguments for the weaknesses in the reasoning of those authorities that disagree with the *Rema*. Thus, while the *Arukh HaShulchan* is generally willing to rule in accordance with his own understanding against individual but important authorities like the *Shulchan Arukh*, he is far more deferential to the *halakhic* consensus, even when it runs counter to his own preferred understanding of the substantive issue—at least in this case where his own view would require the recital of a blessing that the consensus view deems to be made in vain.
Methodological Principles: 1, 2.

---

14 See Rema *to* Shulchan Arukh, Orach Chaim 8:12.

Example #13 – *Arukh HaShulchan* §9:25

Rabbi Joseph Karo rules that one may not put linen *tzitzit* strings on a silk garment because some kinds of wool look like silk, and one may inadvertently tie linen strings to a wool garment, thinking that the garment is made of silk, and thereby inadvertently violate the biblical prohibition of *shatnez*—wearing garments made of mixed wool and linen threads. The *Rema* takes this concern further and rules that one should not use linen for *tzitzit* strings at all, and instead the strings should be made out of wool, which may then be used on any garments, except ones made of linen (which in the absence of proper blue-colored *tekhelet* strings would constitute *shatnez*).

The *Arukh HaShulchan* rejects this limitation on the use of linen strings (Principle 1). While Rabbi Epstein agrees, of course, that one may not tie linen strings to a wool garment, he rules that one may put linen strings on a silk garment in order to fulfill the obligation of *tzitzit*. Rabbi Epstein reasons that in his own time and place there is no known variety of wool that appears to be and can be confused with silk, and so, the risk noted by both Rabbis Karo and Isserles is no longer a matter of concern. In light of this changed reality, the *Arukh HaShulchan* rules that the rule prohibiting the use of linen *tzitzit* strings on silk garments no longer applies (Principle 9). Importantly, however, Rabbi Epstein pays due deference to the codified opinions of the *Shulchan Arukh* and *Rema* by presenting his permission to tie linen *tzitzit* to a silk garment as only a measure of last resort. He writes: "If one only has linen strings, then one should make *tzitzit* out of the linen, even on a silk garment" (Principle 1).

Methodological Principles: 1, 9.

Example #14 – *Arukh HaShulchan* §11:6

The *Shulchan Arukh* observes that Maimonides and the *Rosh* disagree about the validity of *tzitzit* strings that are spun by a Gentile while an observant Jew supervises the spinning and instructs the non-Jewish spinner to perform the spinning *lishmah* – with the specific intent to produce strings for use as *tzitzit*.[15] According to Maimonides, such strings are invalid for use as *tzitzit*; according to the *Rosh*, however, the strings would be usable. Rabbi Moses Isserles suggests that one may avoid having to mediate between these two major authorities by having an observant Jew help the non-Jewish worker with some of the spinning. If a Jew participates in the spinning process even minimally, and does so *lishmah*, the strings may be used. This, Rabbi Isserles argues, follows from an analogy to the rules governing the preparation of parchment used for writing Torah scrolls or *tefillin*, which must be de-haired *lishmah* (with the intent that the resulting parchments will be used for Torah scrolls or *tefillin*). Just as parchment produced by a Gentile is acceptable so long as an observant Jew took part in the process with proper intentions, likewise, *tzitzit* strings spun by a Gentile may be used provided that an observant Jew contributed in some way to the spinning process *lishmah*.

The *Arukh HaShulchan* rejects Rabbi Isserles's leniency, however, and rules that strings produced by non-Jews may not be used for *tzitzit* (Principle 1). Rabbi Epstein rejects the *Rema*'s analogy between the spinning of *tzitzit* strings and the de-hairing of animal skins as part of the parchment making process. He argues that while it makes sense to say that the participation of a Jew in some aspect of the de-hairing of a particular animal skin is sufficient to render that skin as a whole as having been de-haired *lishmah*, the same cannot be said for a Jew's participation in

---

15 *See* Shulchan Arukh, Orach Chaim 11:2.

some small part of the spinning process, as this means that many, many strings will be produced from wool that the Jew took no part in spinning (Principle 1).
Methodological Principles: 1.

Example #15 – *Arukh HaShulchan* §11:24

Maimonides rules that one cannot make *tzitzit* strings from stolen wool. Several commentators note that this ruling seems to cut against an established *halakhic* principle that changes to a stolen item affect the acquisition of that item by the thief. In the case of producing *tzitzit* strings from stolen wool, the process of spinning stolen raw wool into strings should affect the thief's acquisition of the strings, rendering the *tzitzit* strings not stolen and permitted for use. Commentators therefore offer a variety of explanations for Maimonides's troubling view. Rabbi Joseph Karo suggests that Maimonides restricts the use of strings made from stolen wool only prior to the original owner's having given up hope of recovering his lost property, which would prevent the thief from acquiring the wool by virtue of transforming it into *tzitzit* strings. Others suggest that spinning wool into strings is a change that can be undone (by unraveling the strings), which prevents the change from affecting the thief's acquisition of the wool even if the owner has given up hope of recovering his property. Still, others suggest that the *halakhah* imposes more stringent requirements for a thief to acquire stolen property when that property will be used to perform a *mitzvah* that would typically be required, and so spinning the wool into strings, coupled with the original owners losing hope of recovering the wool, would still be insufficient to affect the thief's acquisition of wool used for *tzitzit* strings.

The *Arukh HaShulchan* rejects these attempted explanations of Maimonides's view, demonstrating how the premises of each are incorrect (Principle 1). Rabbi Epstein, however, is hesitant to abandon Maimonides's prohibition on the use of *tzitzit* strings woven from stolen wool (Principle 3), and instead offers his own novel explanation of Maimonides's ruling (Principle 2). Rabbi Epstein argues that the reason why one may not use strings woven from stolen wool, despite the change affected in the wool and even after the original owner gave up hope of recovering the wool, is that the thief would not have acquired the wool until after it had been transformed into *tzitzit* strings. Since the spinning of the wool into strings must be done *lishmah*, and since at the time of spinning the wool into strings the thief would not yet have acquired it, and the wool would still be considered stolen, it would be impossible for the spinning to have been done in a ritually proper manner. Ultimately, Rabbi Epstein seems unconvinced by his own creative justification for Maimonides's ruling; nevertheless, he is willing to rely on what he views as a possible, reasonable explanation of Maimonides's position, rather than to discard Maimonides's opinion out of hand—especially as rejecting Maimonides's ruling on this issue would amount to a serious leniency in a matter of biblical law, effectively permitting the use of *tzitzit* strings made from stolen wool—which may be invalid—to fulfill the biblical commandment of wearing *tzitzit* (Principles 2 and 4).
Methodological Principles: 1, 2, 3, 4.

Example #16 – *Arukh HaShulchan* §13:2

One is permitted to wear a garment tied with *tzitzit* strings in a public domain on the Sabbath.[16] While it is normally prohibited to carry things in a public domain on the Sabbath,

---

16 *See* ibid. 13:2.

this stricture does not apply to items of clothing that are presently being worn, or to items that are not technically worn, but which nevertheless serve to adorn clothing that a person is wearing in a public domain. Thus, while—in contrast to the garment to which they are attached—*tzitzit* strings are not clothing, one is still permitted to wear a garment tied with *tzitzit* strings in a public domain on the Sabbath, since the *tzitzit* are necessary accoutrements to the clothing.

The *Arukh HaShulchan* notes that this reasoning should only suffice to permit wearing *tzitzit* strings on a garment that is actually obligated to be tied with *tzitzit*, while wearing *tzitzit* tied to a garment that is not *halakhically* obligated in the *mitzvah* of *tzitzit* in a public domain should in principle be prohibited. Strings tied to a garment that does not legally require *tzitzit* cannot be regarded as necessary adornments of the garment itself—wearing a garment with such strings attached would be considered carrying and would not be permitted on the Sabbath in a public domain. Based on this, Rabbi Epstein concludes that it should be prohibited to wear small garments that are of insufficient size to be obligated in *tzitzit* in the public domain on *Shabbat* (Principle 1).

Despite his opposition to the practice based on his understanding of the issue, Rabbi Epstein notes that people customarily do wear such small *tzitzit*-adorned garments in the public domain on the Sabbath (Principle 8), and he offers a half-hearted justification for this technically prohibited practice. Rabbi Epstein suggests—quite inventively—that perhaps since such small garments are not *halakhically* obligated to have *tzitzit*, any *tzitzit* strings attached to such items of clothing are considered entirely insignificant and are regarded as legally null and void. Thus, from the perspective of the *halakhah*, when a person wears such a garment, that person is not regarded as carrying or wearing the irrelevant *tzitzit* strings at all, thus obviating any concerns that one would be considered to be carrying the strings in a public domain in violation of the biblical prohibition (Principle 1).

Methodological Principles: 1, 8.

Example #17 – *Arukh HaShulchan* §14:9

When prescribing the obligation to tie *tzitzit* on a four-cornered garment, the Torah instructs: "You shall make for yourself twisted strings on the four corners of the garment with which you cover yourself."[17] Based on the verse's emphasis on the obligation to place *tzitzit* on one's own garment, the Talmud rules that as a matter of biblical law, if a person borrows a four-cornered garment, he may wear that garment even without attached *tzitzit* strings. The Rabbis, however, maintained that once the borrowed garment has been in the borrower's possession for more than thirty consecutive days, the borrower is rabbinically obligated to tie *tzitzit* to the garment. The Rabbis reasoned that after the borrower has possessed the garment for thirty consecutive days, he appears to be the owner and not merely the borrower of the clothing item; at that point, not tying *tzitzit* to the garment would give off the impression that he is disregarding the obligation to wear *tzitzit*.[18] While *halakhic* authorities permit a borrower to tie *tzitzit* to a borrowed garment even before he has possessed the item for thirty days, many argue that one should not recite a blessing when donning such a garment, since prior to the thirty-day mark, the garment is neither biblically nor rabbinically obligated in the *mitzvah* of *tzitzit*.

The *Arukh HaShulchan*, however, rules that the Talmudic exemption of borrowed garments from *tzitzit* obligations no longer applies (Principle 1). Rabbi Epstein argues that the

---

17 Deuteronomy 22:12.
18 *See* Babylonian Talmud, Chullin 110b.

Talmudic exemption for borrowed garments was formulated in a time and place in which people customarily wore four-cornered garments as regular clothing items. In contemporary times, however, where the only four-cornered garments typically worn are the *tallit gadol* and *tallit katan*—which are made and worn for the specific purpose of fulfilling the *mitzvah* of *tzitzit*—this rule does not apply (Principle 9). Instead, whenever one borrows such a four-cornered garment, it is obvious that he is doing so for the purpose of fulfilling the *mitzvah* of *tzitzit*, and the lender thus impliedly gifts the garment to the borrower so that the borrower will in fact become the owner of the garment and thus be obligated and able to tie *tzitzit* to the garment and recite the appropriate blessing when wearing it.
Methodological Principles: 1, 9.

Example #18 – *Arukh HaShulchan* §14:12

The *Shulchan Arukh* rules that a person may borrow another's *tallit*, or prayer shawl, without permission and recite the appropriate blessing on performing the *mitzvah* of *tzitzit*, provided that the borrower refolds the *tallit* in the same manner that it was found.[19] This permission is based on the assumption that people are generally willing to allow others to fulfill *mitzvah* obligations with their possessions, provided this does not cause them any loss; therefore, *tallit* owners are not particular about people borrowing their prayer shawls, so long as the garments are treated properly and returned.

Despite the *Shulchan Arukh*'s permissive ruling on this issue, the *Arukh HaShulchan* rules that, in fact, one may not borrow another's *tallit* without permission (Principle 1). Rabbi Epstein argues that while it may have once been true that people do not generally mind others borrowing their *tzitzit*, "we see [today] that in fact many people are quite particular about this, especially when the *tallit* is new and clean; indeed, there are people who never tolerate others wearing their clothes." Based on this changed and observed reality, Rabbi Epstein says, it is prohibited to borrow another's *tallit* without his permission (Principle 9). Doing so very much borders on theft, and making a blessing upon wearing such a possibly stolen *tallit* is offensive to God.
Methodological Principles: 1, 9.

Example #19 – *Arukh HaShulchan* §16:5

The Talmud rules that garments must be of a certain minimum size in order to be subject to the *mitzvah* of *tzitzit*. Specifically, the Talmud states that only garments large enough to cover the head and most of the body of a child and large enough that an adult would occasionally wear them in public are obligated to have *tzitzit* strings tied to their corners.[20] Rabbi Epstein notes that based on this Talmudic passage, many authorities have protested against the practice of wearing small *tallit katan* garments to which *tzitzit* strings are tied in the public domain on the Sabbath. According to these authorities, such small garments are not obligated in the *mitzvah* of *tzitzit*; those who wear them are not fulfilling the *mitzvah* at all, and more problematically, wearing such a garment in the public domain on the Sabbath would violate the biblical prohibition against carrying.[21]

---

19 *See* Shulchan Arukh, Orach Chaim 14:11.
20 *See* Babylonian Talmud, Menachot 40b.
21 *See* Turei Zahav *to* Shulchan Arukh, Orach Chaim 16:1.

The *Arukh HaShulchan* rejects this concern. He notes that while some early authorities did in fact rule that only garments large enough to cover a child's head and body are obligated in the *mitzvah* of *tzitzit*, this would mean that all of the small *tzitzit* garments customarily worn today by Jews all over the world in order to fulfill the *mitzvah* of *tzitzit* would be invalid. This, he says, would be an untenable conclusion; rather, the prevailing and widespread practice of wearing a small garment with *tzitzit* to fulfill the *mitzvah* strongly suggests that such garments are not invalid (Principle 8). This conclusion is reinforced, Rabbi Epstein argues, by the views of some other early authorities, including the *Ritva*, the *Nimukei Yosef*, and the *Beit Yosef*, who all held that any four-cornered garment worn on one's body is obligated in the *mitzvah* of *tzitzit*. In light of the prevailing practice, Rabbi Epstein suggests that the Talmudic source prescribing the minimum size for a *tzitzit* garment must be referring to the minimum size of a regular *tallit*, upon which we recite the blessing of *"Lehit'atef B'tzitzit"* ("to wrap in *tzitzit*"). This garment, which is worn over one's clothing as a kind of cloak or cape, must be large enough to wrap. The *tallit katan*, however, which is not an actual clothing item, but which is merely worn under one's clothes as a means of constantly fulfilling the *mitzvah* of *tzitzit*, has no required size and can be used to fulfill the *mitzvah* so long as it has the required four corners (Principle 1). Methodological Principles: 1, 8.

Example #20 – *Arukh HaShulchan* §18:7

It is universally accepted that the *mitzvah* of *tzitzit* is limited to the daytime when one can fulfill the Torah's command that "you shall see" the *tzitzit* strings. There is, however, a dispute about in what sense the nighttime suspends the obligation to wear *tzitzit*. According to Maimonides, the nighttime exemption from *tzitzit* is tied to the time of day: once night begins, four-cornered garments may be worn without *tzitzit*; during the daytime, all four-cornered garments require *tzitzit* strings. The *Rosh*, however, rules that the nighttime exemption for *tzitzit* applies not to the time between sunset and sunrise, but to garments worn at night. Based on this view, quintessentially nighttime garments like pajamas may be worn without *tzitzit*, even if donned during the daytime hours.

According to Rabbi Epstein, these two different *halakhic* positions reflect a fundamental dispute between the Babylonian Talmud, which supports Maimonides's view, and the Jerusalem Talmud, which supports the *Rosh*'s view. The Babylonian Talmud's support for Maimonides's position does not lead Rabbi Epstein to reject the *Rosh*'s view, however. The Jerusalem Talmud's support for the *Rosh*'s rule tying the nighttime exemption from *tzitzit* to nightclothes leads Rabbi Epstein to prescribe that one should follow both positions (Principle 1). This conclusion is supported by the general principle that one should not recite blessings (which are generally only rabbinic obligations) when one is in doubt as to whether the *mitzvah* upon which the blessing will be said is in fact obligatory. Since the conflicting views of Maimonides and the *Rosh* make the obligatory nature of wearing *tzitzit* in cases that straddle the divide between the two uncertain, one should avoid reciting the blessing on *tzitzit* at night and during the day when wearing night clothes— a view supported by Rabbi Moses Isserles (Principle 4).[22]

Despite this nighttime *tzitzit* exemption, however, Rabbi Epstein prescribes that following the prevailing custom, those performing public religious functions—such as a *shliach tzibbur*, or prayer leader, leading congregational prayers; a scholar teaching Torah; or a *mohel* or *sandek* officiating at a circumcision—should wear a *tallit* even at night (Principle 8). This is based on the

---

22 *See* Rema *to* Shulchan Arukh, Orach Chaim 18:1.

Talmudic teaching that God wore a *tallit*, so to speak, when he related his Thirteen Attributes to Moses and forgave the Jews for the sin of the Golden Calf. Rabbi Epstein argues that this teaches that all those performing public religious functions on behalf of the community should wear a *tallit* out of respect for the congregation (Principle 1).

Rabbi Epstein further notes that the *Magen Avraham* recommends that a *shliach tzibbur* leading prayers at night should wear a *tallit* only while reciting *barechu*, the opening call to the congregation to begin the prayer, after which he should immediately remove the *tallit* in recognition of the nighttime exemption from *tzitzit*. Rabbi Epstein rules that this is not necessary, however, noting that doing so is impractical in practice and that "the Torah was not given to angels" with superhuman abilities (Principle 10). Nevertheless, Rabbi Epstein concludes by noting that it was in fact the mystically motivated practice of Rabbi Isaac Luria, the *Arizal*, to carefully avoid wearing his *tallit* after sundown, implying that one may – but definitely does not have to – adopt the *Magen Avraham*'s prescription in order to respect this mystical tradition (Principles 6 and 7). Methodological Principles: 1, 4, 6, 7, 8, 10.

Example #21 – *Arukh HaShulchan* §20:3

The Talmud rules that one may not purchase a *tallit* with *tzitzit* already attached from a Gentile, unless the seller is a professional merchant.[23] The concern here is that, since Gentiles are not scrupulous or independently trustworthy with regard to their observance of Jewish laws and practices, it is possible that the Gentile seller is selling a garment that appears to be a valid *tallit*, but which in fact is made with *tzitzit* that were not produced *lishmah* in accordance with *halakhic* requirements. This concern, however, only applies to private sellers who are suspect of misrepresenting their merchandise, since they have no real disincentive to do so. A merchant, however, stands to lose the trust of his customers if caught selling invalid prayer shawls that were in fact produced without the requisite intent. This provides a strong incentive for merchants to accurately describe the good they are selling and thus provides a basis for trusting a Gentile merchant when he presents the *tallit* he is selling as *halakhically* valid.[24] Many later *halakhic* authorities limit this permission to the purchase of an actual garment to which *tzitzit* strings have already been tied. These scholars reason that since non-Jews do not normally tie *tzitzit* strings to garments, it is reasonable to assume that these *tzitzit* were tied with the proper intent by a Jew who then sold the garment to the Gentile merchant. It is this reasonable assumption, combined with the assumed trustworthiness of merchants' representations about their wares, that permits a Jew to purchase a *tallit* from a Gentile merchant. Importantly, these authorities note that the same permission does not then apply to the purchase of actual *tzitzit* strings from a Gentile [Cuthean], even if the seller is a merchant. When purchasing *tzitzit* strings, one cannot rely on the assumption that the strings must have been spun by a Jew with proper intent, since unlike the tying of *tzitzit* strings to four-cornered garments, which is done almost exclusively by Jews, spun wool strings can be and are produced by Gentiles as well.[25]

The *Arukh HaShulchan* argues that a correct understanding of the relevant Talmudic passage indicates that in fact one may buy both a *tallit* garment and stand-alone *tzitzit* strings from a Gentile merchant, relying on the trustworthiness of merchants with respect to their

---

23 *See* Babylonian Talmud, Menachot 43a.
24 *See* Rashi *to* Menachot 43a (s.v. *min ha-oved kochavim*).
25 *See* Taz *to* Shulchan Arukh, Orach Chaim 20:1; Magen Avraham *to* Shulchan Arukh, Orach Chaim 20:1.

representations about their merchandise. Rabbi Epstein reasons that the Talmud explicitly permits purchasing a *tallit* garment from a Gentile not to impliedly prohibit the purchase of *tzitzit* strings, but to correct the possible misconception that since it is rabbinically prohibited to sell or give a *tallit* to a Gentile, it is also prohibited to purchase a *tallit* from a Gentile. In light of his understanding of the Talmudic passage at issue, Rabbi Epstein argues that one is in fact permitted to purchase both *tallit* garments and *tzitzit* strings from non-Jewish merchants (Principle 1). Nevertheless, Rabbi Epstein's read of the Talmud here is not dispositively clear. Consequently, Rabbi Epstein defers to the weight of the consensus of later *halakhic* authorities, who prohibited purchasing *tzitzit* strings from Gentile merchants (Principle 2).

Methodological Principles: 1, 2.

Example #22 – *Arukh HaShulchan* §21:7

The *Shulchan Arukh* instructs that a person must be careful to ensure that his *tzitzit* do not drag on the floor.[26] This rule is grounded in an opinion expressed by the *Sefer HaAgur*, which cites the *Mordechai* and holds that one who lets his *tzitzit* drag on the floor is subject to the verse, "I will sweep it with the broom of destruction."[27] The *Arukh HaShulchan* disagrees, however, and rules that "there is no concern if sometimes one's *tzitzit* drag on the ground" (Principle 1).

Rabbi Epstein notes that other authorities have noted that several Talmudic sources seem to contradict the *Sefer HaAgur*'s rule. In one source, Rabbi Chiya criticized Rabbi Yochanan for allowing his *tzitzit* to drag over graves while walking in a cemetery; Rabbi Chiya argued that this was disrespectful to the dead who could no longer perform the *mitzvah* of *tzitzit*.[28] Importantly, Rabbi Chiya's focus on respect for the dead indicates that, if Rabbi Yochanan's *tzitzit* had been dragging on ordinary ground rather than a cemetery, there would have been no problem. In another source, the Talmud approvingly notes that a man by the name of Ben Tzitzit HaKeset was so-called because he made sure that *tzitzit* strings only ever dragged on cushions (*keset*) out of respect for the *mitzvah*.[29] This suggests that Ben Tzitzit HaKeset was somehow especially pious for making sure his own *tzitzit* did not touch the ground; ordinary people's *tzitzit*, however, did apparently drag on the ground without any concern.

While some authorities defend the *Shulchan Arukh*'s prohibition and offer a variety of explanations to rectify this rule with the seemingly contradictory Talmudic sources, Rabbi Epstein rejects the prohibition against letting one's *tzitzit* drag on the ground. Rabbi Epstein offers several reasons for his permissive ruling. First, in light of his understanding of the relevant Talmudic sources, he suggests that the correct rule might only prohibit letting one's *tzitzit* drag on the ground in a manner that is particularly disrespectful, or the prohibition might only apply when one is actually donning the *tzitzit* and reciting the appropriate blessing rather than the entire time one is wearing the *tzitzit*. Ultimately, however, Rabbi Epstein rejects even a more limited prohibition against dragging one's *tzitzit* on the ground, pointing out that as a practical matter, if one is supposed to wear *tzitzit* while engrossed in prayer or Torah learning, it would be impossible to be adequately aware so as to ensure that the strings do not touch the ground (Principle 10). Indeed, Rabbi Epstein goes further and argues against the practice of tucking one's *tzitzit* strings into one's belt to ensure that they do not touch the ground. Since the

---

26   *See* Shulchan Arukh, Orach Chaim 21:4.
27   Jeremiah 14:23.
28   *See* Babylonian Talmud, Berakhot 18a.
29   *See* Babylonian Talmud, Gittin 56a.

halakhah does not prohibit one from allowing his *tzitzit* to touch the ground, and since it is therefore not disrespectful for *tzitzit* to drag on the ground, there is no reason to be concerned for this or to take steps to prevent it from occurring (Principle 6).
Methodological Principles: 1, 6, 10.

Example #23 - *Arukh HaShulchan* §25:13

The *Shulchan Arukh* and the *Rema* famously disagree about how many blessings one should recite when putting on *tefillin*, the black leather boxes, or phylacteries, worn on the arm and head during morning prayers. Rabbi Karo codifies the dominant view of the Sephardic that one recites a single blessing for both the head and arm *tefillin*. Rabbi Isserles, by contrast, affirms the accepted Ashkenazic practice that one recites two blessings when putting on *tefillin*, one on the arm *tefillah* and another on the head *tefillah*. The *Rema* adds, however, that "it is good to say *baruch shem kavod malkhuto le'olam va'ed* after reciting the second of these two blessings," which is the standard practice after one recites God's name unnecessarily, such as when one mistakenly recites a blessing that did not have to be made.[30]

The *Arukh HaShulchan* questions this explanation of the *Rema*'s directive to say *baruch shem kevod malchuto le'olam va'ed* after making a second blessing on the *tefillah shel rosh*, the phylactery that is placed on the head. Rabbi Epstein wonders: if we are certain that the Talmud does indeed require the recitation of two blessings on the *tefillin*, then we should not say *baruch shem kavod malchuto le'olam va'ed*, which is only said after having said God's name in vain. Conversely, if we are uncertain as to whether we should be reciting both blessings on the *tefillin* (and this uncertainty about the second blessing is the reason the *Rema* instructs the recitation of *baruch shem kavod malchuto le'olam va'ed*), then we ought not be reciting the second blessing at all, in accordance with the general decisional principle that one should not recite a blessing in a situation where the obligation to make that blessing is uncertain, since reciting the blessing unnecessarily would involve taking God's name in vain (Principle 4).[31]

While Rabbi Epstein thus questions the sensibility of the *Rema*'s position, he nevertheless acknowledges that in fact the custom of Ashkenazic communities is to recite two blessings when putting on *tefillin*, and to say *baruch shem kavod malchuto le'olam va'ed* after the second blessing (Principle 8).

Rabbi Epstein goes on to offer a novel understanding of the second *tefillin* blessing recited by Ashkenazic Jews that helps explain why it makes any *halakhic* sense to recite two blessings while also saying *baruch shem kavod malchuto le'olam va'ed* after the latter blessing (Principle 1). Rabbi Epstein suggests that the recitation of *baruch shem kavod malchuto le'olam va'ed* following the second *tefillin* blessing is actually unrelated to any doubts about whether *tefillin* require one or two blessings. Rabbi Epstein argues that while the first blessing of *lehaniach tefillin* is indeed a blessing marking the performance of the *mitzvah* of wearing *tefillin*, the second blessing of *al mitzvat tefillin* is a *birkhat hoda'ah* (a blessing of thanksgiving) expressing appreciation to God for enabling people to become connected to Him through wearing *tefillin*. Since the essence of the connection to God affected by wearing *tefillin* is symbolized by the verse of "*Shema Yisrael Hashem Eloheiu Hashem echad*," we follow up the blessing that thanks God for this connective opportunity by reciting *baruch shem kavod malchuto le'olam va'ed*, which is closely connected with the *Shema*.

---

30 Rema *to* Shulchan Arukh, Orach Chaim 25:5.
31 *See* Arukh HaShulchan, Orach Chaim 25:11.

Thus, according to Rabbi Epstein, the Ashkenazic practice of reciting two blessings on wearing *tefillin* works as follows: the first blessing marks the performance of the *mitzvah* of wearing *tefillin* and is no different than any other single blessing made prior to performing a specific *mitzvah*; the second blessing does not preface the performance of the *mitzvah*, but instead expresses gratitude to God for providing Jews with an opportunity to connect with the Divine through wearing *tefillin*; and finally, the recitation of *baruch shem kavod malchuto le'olam va'ed* affirms the nature of this connection and its association with the ideas expressed through the *Shema*.

Methodological Principles 1, 4, 8.

Example #24 – *Arukh HaShulchan* §25:15

As a rule, blessings recited when doing *mitzvot* are said immediately prior to engaging in the act that constitutes performance of the obligation. Consequently, the *Shulchan Arukh* rules that one should not say the blessing for *tefillin* until after the *tefillin* box is positioned properly on one's arm; then, one should recite the blessing and immediately affix the *tefillin* to one's arm by tightening the strap—which constitutes the fulfillment of the *mitzvah* of "putting on *tefillin*."[32] The *Rema* adds that Ashkenazic Jews, who recite a second blessing when putting the *tefillin shel rosh* on their heads, should likewise recite the blessing immediately before affixing the *tefillin* to their heads.[33] The *Magen Avraham* explains that in order to follow the *Rema*'s rule, one should first place the *tefillin* on one's head, then recite the blessing, and then fix the *tefillin* in place so that the blessing is recited immediately before fulfilling the *mitzvah* without the need to delay placing the *tefillin* on one's head after the blessing.[34]

The *Arukh HaShulchan* notes that the process prescribed by the *Rema* and the *Magen Avraham* poses practical difficulties. In order to recite the blessing, one must ensure that one's head is not uncovered; but, Rabbi Epstein notes, everyone who has ever tried putting the *tefillin shel rosh* on one's head knows that this is very difficult to do while keeping one's head covered with a hat or *kippah*. While this difficulty might be dealt with by placing one's *tallit* over one's head and *tefillin*, this solution does not help unmarried men who customarily do not wear prayer shawls (Principle 10). In light of this pragmatic difficulty, Rabbi Epstein rules that one may follow the custom of holding the *tefillin shel rosh* in one's hands very close to one's head, then recite the blessing while one's head remains covered, and then quickly remove one's head covering and fix the *tefillin* in place (Principles 1 and 8). In light of the practicalities of the situation, Rabbi Epstein rules, this procedure can be regarded as satisfying the requirement to recite *mitzvah* blessings immediately prior to performing the *mitzvah* act.

Methodological Principles: 1, 8, 10.

Example #25 – *Arukh HaShulchan* §25:22

The *Arbah Turim* rules that one is obligated to recite a new blessing on one's *tefillin* any time one replaces one's *tefillin* after they have moved from their correct positions on one's arm

---

32 Shulchan Arukh, Orach Chaim 25:8.
33 *See* Rema *to* Shulchan Arukh, Orach Chaim 25:8.
34 *See* Magen Avraham *to* Shulchan Arukh, Orach Chaim 25:13.

or head.³⁵ When one intentionally removes the *tefillin* with the intent to shortly replace them, however, one does not recite a new blessing when putting the *tefillin* back on.³⁶ According to the *Arbah Turim*, this is because it is only an unintentional interruption of fulfilling the *mitzvah* of *tefillin* that requires one to recite a new blessing; purposeful removal of the *tefillin* with intent to replace them, however, is not regarded as an interruption of one's mindful fulfillment of the *mitzvah*, and therefore does not require a new blessing when putting the *tefillin* back on later.³⁷ Rabbi Joseph Karo disagrees with this position, however, and rules that one who removes his *tefillin* to use the restroom must recite a new blessing when replacing the *tefillin*, even if at the time he initially removed them he had intended to put them back on shortly thereafter.³⁸ The *Rema* endorses the *Arbah Turim*'s position on this matter, noting that the accepted custom is to not repeat the blessing on one's *tefillin* when putting them back on shortly after removing them with the intent to replace them.

The *Arukh HaShulchan* goes further, however, and notes that the custom is to not repeat the blessing on *tefillin* even when the *tefillin* become unintentionally dislodged from their correct positions on the head and arm (and certainly when they are removed with the intent to replace them shortly thereafter). Rabbi Epstein candidly acknowledges that he does not know the reason for this custom, since all previous authorities agreed that one must repeat the *tefillin* blessing if one's *tefillin* accidentally moved from their proper positions. Nevertheless, Rabbi Epstein accepts the practice as normative and attempts to provide some rational justification for it (Principle 8). He suggests that since we only wear *tefillin* while praying, we are constantly mindful of our present fulfillment of the *mitzvah* of *tefillin*; therefore, even when the *tefillin* get unintentionally dislocated, our focus is still on fulfilling the *mitzvah*. Since there has been no break in the wearer's concentration on fulfilling the *mitzvah*, the *tefillin* can be replaced without having to recite a new blessing.³⁹ While Rabbi Epstein goes on to explain why this justification cannot possibly work in theory, he nevertheless maintains the normativity of the accepted custom to not repeat the blessing on *tefillin* if the *tefillin* need to be repositioned after accidentally becoming dislodged from their proper places on one's head and arm.

Rabbi Epstein goes on to argue, however, that perhaps this custom actually reflects a correct understanding of the relevant Talmudic sources. Rabbi Epstein notes that the principal source for the *Arbah Turim*'s rule requiring one to repeat the *tefillin* blessing anytime his *tefillin* accidentally move from their proper places on his arm or head is a comment in the Talmud that records that the "students of the School of Rav Ashi would repeat the *tefillin* blessing any time they touched their *tefillin*,"⁴⁰ which the *Rosh* understands as meaning that they would recite the blessing whenever their *tefillin* became dislodged from their proper places. Rabbi Epstein points out, however, that as a general rule of Talmudic interpretation, the correct *halakhah* does not follow the view of "the students of the School of Rav Ashi" (Principle 1), and that, moreover, Maimonides does not record any rule about having to repeat the *tefillin* blessing based on this Talmudic passage (Principle 3). Moreover, while he does not explicitly say so, Rabbi Epstein's acceptance of the popular practice of not repeating the *tefillin* blessing is likely also driven by the fact that the recitation of this blessing is a rabbinic requirement and is thus subject to the

---

35 *See* Arbah Turim, Orach Chaim 25.
36 *See* ibid. 8.
37 *See* Arukh HaShulchan, Orach Chaim 25:21.
38 *See* Beit Yosef *to* Arbah Turim Orach Chaim 25:12.
39 *See* Arukh HaShulchan, Orach Chaim 25:22 (quoting Magen Avraham *to* Shulchan Arukh, Orach Chaim 25:21).
40 Babylonian Talmud, Sukkah 46a.

general secondary rules of decision that discourage the recitation of blessings in cases of doubt and instruct that doubtful rabbinic obligations need not be performed (Principle 4).
Methodological Principles: 1, 3, 4, 8.

Example #26 – *Arukh HaShulchan* §25:29

The *Arukh HaShulchan* clearly delineates his approach to the use of the *Zohar* as a source of *halakhah* and proper religious practice. Rabbi Epstein notes that there are numerous practices connected to various *mitzvot* that are sourced in the mystical wisdom of the Kabbalah, and he proceeds to articulate a three-part rule for how one should approach the use of kabbalistic sources when making judgments about *halakhic* practice. As a general principle, Rabbi Epstein adopts the view that in principle the *Zohar* and the Talmud do not disagree, and that therefore, cases of apparent conflict between the kabbalistic prescriptions of the *Zohar* and Talmudic rulings should be resolved by—to the extent reasonably possible—creatively interpreting these sources so as to render them consistent with each other. When the Talmud and post-Talmudic *halakhic* authorities do disagree with the mystical practices prescribed by the *Zohar*, Rabbi Epstein holds that proper practice follows the rulings of the Talmud and conventional *halakhic* authorities, which take precedence over mystical sources in cases of conflict. This rule applies only when the *Zohar* permits that which the Talmud prohibits, however. When the *Zohar* prescribes stricter standards of conduct than those required by the Talmud, one may, if one so chooses, act strictly in accordance with the *Zohar*. Finally, Rabbi Epstein notes that when the *Zohar* prescribes kabbalistic practices with respect to matters not considered by the Talmud at all, "it is certainly appropriate to act in accordance with the words of the *Zohar*" (Principle 7). However, while Rabbi Epstein encourages the adoption of kabbalistic practices with respect to matters not regulated by the Talmud, he makes clear that such practices are entirely supererogatory, not obligatory, and that no one should be compelled to follow such mystical prescriptions (Principle 6).
Methodological Principles: 6, 7.

Example #27 – *Arukh HaShulchan* §27:9

The Talmud records a dispute between anonymous Tannaitic scholars, the *Tanna Kama* and the *Acherim*, regarding the *tefillin* obligation of a person whose arm is missing. According to the *Tanna Kama*, a person whose lower arm is missing is exempt from any obligation to wear the *tefillin shel yad*, the phylactery placed on one's arm. The *Acherim* disagree and rule that a person who is missing the lower half of his arm, but who still has a bicep upon which to place his *tefillin*, remains obligated to do so. The Talmud clarifies that the reason for the *Acherim*'s position is that when the Torah prescribes the obligation of *tefillin* on the hand—"*yadekha*"—it does so by spelling the word *yadekha* usually with a "*hey*" at the end. This suggests that the "hand" to which the Torah refers includes even an incompletely formed arm.[41]

The *Arukh HaShulchan* notes that the Talmud does not explain the reason for the *Tanna Kama*'s exempting an amputee from *tefillin*, but Rabbi Epstein suggests that the reason is that a person missing his hand cannot possibly place *tefillin* "on his hand" as the Torah commands and is thus exempt from the obligation to do so (Principle 1).[42]

---

41 *See* Babylonian Talmud, Menachot 37a.
42 *See* Arukh HaShulchan, Orach Chaim 27:7.

After noting with some surprise that the major early codifiers of Jewish law—including the *Rif*, Maimonides, the *Semag*, the *Rosh*, and the *Arbah Turim*—do not mention the issue at all, Rabbi Epstein suggests that this is because a careful reading of the relevant Talmudic sources indicates that the position of the *Acherim* is rejected, and it is therefore patently obvious that an amputee is exempt from wearing *tefillin*. Rabbi Epstein explains that the *Acherim*'s position is based on the very same Torah spelling of *"yadekha"* that in another place is used to establish that *tefillin* should be placed on the left hand. Since this latter exposition of the word *"yadekha"* is accepted as a matter of Talmudic law, the *Acherim*'s alternative explanation of this verse as obligating an amputee to wear *tefillin* is implicitly rejected. Without scriptural support for the view of the *Acherim*, then, the correct *halakhah* would default to the *Tanna Kama*'s position that, in the absence of a hand, a person cannot be required to fulfill the *mitzvah* that required him to place *tefillin* "on his hand."[43] *Tosafot* disagrees with this view, seemingly adopted by the majority of early authorities, that an amputee is exempt from the obligation to wear *tefillin*. Instead, *Tosafot* follows the view of the *Acherim* (with whom *Tosafot* thinks the *Tanna Kama* actually agrees), and rules that a person lacking a hand remains obligated to wear *tefillin*, so long as he still has an upper arm so that the *tefillin* can be placed properly. The *Rema* follows *Tosafot*'s view, obligating a hand-amputee to wear *tefillin*, but instructs that such a person don *tefillin* without reciting a blessing in deference to the view of the *Or Zarua*, who exempts an amputee from wearing *tefillin*. In light of legal doubt created by the dispute between *Tosafot* and the *Or Zarua*, the *Rema* rules that an amputee should wear *tefillin* (a biblical obligation) but should refrain from reciting the blessing (a rabbinic duty).

After discussing the possible Talmudic readings that underlie the positions of both the *Or Zarua* and *Tosafot*, the *Arukh HaShulchan* remains unconvinced that either understanding of the Talmudic dispute between the *Tanna Kama* and *Acherim* is unequivocally correct. While Rabbi Epstein is inclined to adopt his own explanation of the Talmudic sources—which would lead him to adopt the view of the *Tanna Kama* that a hand amputee is exempt from wearing *tefillin* (Principle 1)—he defers to the *Rema*'s ruling that such a person should wear *tefillin* without reciting a blessing because "once [this view] has gone forth from the mouth of our master teacher, the *Rema*, it is hard to violate his words." Thus, in the absence of a clear, confident, and independent judgment about the correct Talmudic rule, Rabbi Epstein adopts what he views as the broad consensus of early authorities—these sages defaulted to the *Tanna Kama*'s view requiring an amputee to wear *tefillin* (Principle 2) while also incorporating the *Rema*'s instruction to not recite a blessing when doing so. Here they follow the general rule regarding doubt: while doubts about biblical obligations should be resolved stringently, doubts about rabbinic duties should be resolved leniently (Principle 4).

Methodological Principles: 1, 2, 4.

Example #28 - *Arukh HaShulchan* §27:14

In his *Beit Yosef*, Rabbi Karo rules that if a person has an injury or other medical issue that prevents him from placing his *tefillin shel rosh* directly on his head, that person may place his *tefillin* on top of his hat, which is preferable to his not wearing *tefillin* at all.[44] While the accepted rule is that in order to fulfill the *mitzvah* of *tefillin* one must place the *tefillin* directly on and with nothing separating between his arm or head, here Rabbi Karo adopts the rejected view of the

---

43 *See* ibid. 27:6-7.
44 *See* Beit Yosef *to* Arbah Turim, Orach Chaim 27:5.

Rashba, who questioned whether the *tefillin shel rosh* must really rest directly on the head. While Rabbi Karo is willing to accept the *Rashba*'s permission in these extenuating circumstances, however, he further rules that a person who places his *tefillin* on top of his hat due to a head injury should do so without reciting a blessing, and he should also cover the *tefillin* box so that others will not see how he is wearing the *tefillin* and mistakenly conclude that one does not need to have the *tefillin shel rosh* resting directly on one's head.

The *Arukh HaShulchan* rejects Rabbi Karo's ruling. Rabbi Epstein thinks that it is obvious that the Talmud's prescription that the *tefillin shel yad* must rest directly on one's arm necessarily applies with equal force to the *tefillin shel rosh*, and that it is therefore impermissible for even an injured person to wear his *tefillin* on top of a hat (Principle 1). Rabbi Epstein acknowledges that there may be good reason to think that it is preferable to wear *tefillin* in this way in reliance on the rejected view of the *Rashba*—rather than to not wear *tefillin* at all—but nevertheless rejects the viability of relying on the thoroughly rejected position of the *Rashba* (Principle 5). Methodological Principles: 1, 5.

Example #29 – *Arukh HaShulchan* §31:4

The Talmud rules that one may not wear *tefillin* on the Sabbath or holidays because *tefillin* are worn as an "*ot*," a "sign."[45] One therefore is only obligated to wear *tefillin* on days when a sign of God's covenant is necessary; the Sabbath and holidays are themselves referred to as "signs," and it is therefore unnecessary and inappropriate to add another "sign" by wearing *tefillin*.[46]

Early authorities disagreed about whether the same rule should apply to wearing *tefillin* on *Chol HaMoed*, the intermediary days of holidays that reflect a festival character in some respects and are like ordinary weekdays in other respects. One school of thought, exemplified by the views of the *Rosh*, the *Mordechai*, the *Maharam MeRutenberg*, *Tosafot*, and the *Rema*, rules that one must wear *tefillin* on *Chol HaMoed* and even recite the appropriate blessing when doing so. According to these authorities, the symbolic "sign" of the Sabbath and holidays that precludes wearing *tefillin* on these days is tied to the biblical prohibition on performing *melakhah*, proscribed labors, on these days. Since the Torah does not prescribe a prohibition against doing *melakhah* on *Chol HaMoed*, those intermediate days do not carry any intrinsic "sign" that would preempt wearing *tefillin*, and one should therefore don the "sign" of *tefillin* after reciting the proper blessing like on any other day. A second group of authorities, including the *Ri* and *Semak*, maintain that on *Chol HaMoed*, one should wear *tefillin*, but should not recite the usual blessing. This view is based on these authorities' uncertainty regarding the correct Talmudic rule. Given doubts about the obligation to wear *tefillin* on *Chol HaMoed*, one should wear them (a biblical obligation), but should avoid reciting the appropriate blessing (a rabbinic obligation that risks taking God's name in vain in case *tefillin* ought not be worn). A third school of thought rules that one should not wear *tefillin* on *Chol HaMoed* at all. This position, which is held by the *Rashba*, *Raabad*, and *Beit Yosef*, is premised on the view that *melakhah* is in fact biblically prohibited on *Chol HaMoed*, just as it is on the Sabbath and regular holiday days. Since the prohibition on labor creates the necessary covenantal "sign" on *Chol HaMoed*, one should not wear *tefillin*, which superfluously add to that "sign" on those days.[47]

---

45 *See* Exodus 13:16.
46 *See* Babylonian Talmud, Menachot 36a.
47 *See generally* Arukh HaShulchan, Orach Chaim 31:4.

The *Arukh HaShulchan* considers the persuasiveness of each of these views, noting that the dispute seems to be dependent on how one understands what exactly the "sign" of the Sabbath and holidays inheres in, and whether or not that sign is similarly present on *Chol HaMoed* (Principle 1). Rabbi Epstein avoids reaching a definitive conclusion on this point, however, and refers to the various schools of thought here as all being "the words of the living God." The *Arukh HaShulchan* then notes that by his time, "All the Sephardim don't wear *tefillin* [on *Chol HaMoed*], while all the Ashkenazim do wear them – albeit without reciting a blessing." While Rabbi Epstein endorses the Ashkenazic practice of wearing *tefillin* on *Chol HaMoed* without reciting the blessing, he does so not as a matter of law but because this is the prevailing custom in the time and place in which he lived and wrote. This is clear from the fact that Rabbi Epstein goes on to say that given the lack of any clear Talmudic ruling on this question and the widespread disagreement and lack of consensus among earlier authorities, "Each person should hold fast to his custom" (Principle 8). Methodological Principles 1, 8.

Example #30 – *Arukh HaShulchan* §32:16

The *Arbah Turim* rules that *tefillin* scrolls must be written by the right hand of a right-handed scribe and by the left hand of a left-handed scribe.[48] This is based on an exegetical derivation from the juxtaposition of the verses that command, "You shall tie [the *tefillin*]" and "You shall write them [the biblical verses recorded on *tefillin* scrolls]."[49] Just as the *tefillin* are tied onto the left arm using the right hand, so too, the scrolls themselves must be written using the right hand so as to render the text a "full" or "complete" writing, a requirement which connotes that the text must be written richly, boldly, and with proper scribal skill.[50]

Commenting on this ruling, Rabbi Joseph Karo in his *Beit Yosef* rules that not only must one write *tefillin* using his right hand in the first instance, but also that *tefillin* written by the left hand are ritually invalid even *ex post* unless the writer was ambidextrous.[51] In his *Shulchan Arukh*, however, Rabbi Karo rules that even an ambidextrous person must write *tefillin* using his right hand – and if he uses his left hand, the *tefillin* are ritually invalid so long as another pair written properly by a right hand is available.[52] Many commentators explain that Rabbi Karo's permission to use *tefillin* written by the left hand of an ambidextrous scribe if no other *tefillin* are available extends even to *tefillin* written by the left hand of a right-handed scribe (or by the right hand of a left-handed scribe). While one should not recite the appropriate blessings when donning such *tefillin*, one may nevertheless wear them if no other properly written *tefillin* are available.

Rabbi Epstein strongly disagrees with this view. He thinks that it is fundamentally erroneous to read Rabbi Karo's ruling as permitting one to wear *tefillin* written by a scribe's non-dominant hand, even if those are the only *tefillin* available. Rabbi Epstein argues that the clear Talmudic rule is that any writing done by a person's non-dominant hand is not considered writing for ritual purposes; thus, while it is prohibited to write on the Sabbath, one is not liable for writing with one's left hand on the Sabbath. Likewise, Rabbi Epstein argues, *tefillin* written by a right-handed scribe's left hand are entirely invalid for ritual purposes—they may not be worn with or without

---

48 *See* Arbah Turim, Orach Chaim 32.
49 Deuteronomy 6:8-9.
50 *See* Babylonian Talmud, Menachot 37a.
51 *See* Beit Yosef *to* Arbah Turim, Orach Chaim 32:8.
52 *See* Shulchan Arukh, Orach Chaim 32:5.

reciting the blessing on *tefillin*, whether or not there are any properly written *tefillin* available as an alternative (Principle 1).
Methodological Principles: 1.

Example #31 – *Arukh HaShulchan* §40:6

The *Arbah Turim* and *Shulchan Arukh* rule that *tefillin* that are presumed to be properly written and ritually valid need not be opened up in order to examine the scrolls to confirm that the text is properly written and that the ink is still legible.[53] Rabbi Epstein notes, however, that while this is true from a strictly *halakhic* standpoint, in his own time a more stringent practice should be followed. He writes that it is well known that the kinds of ink used to write *tefillin* scrolls in his own time and place tend to become dry and chip off the surface of the parchment over the course of several years. In light of this present reality, he rules that it is not sufficient to rely on the earlier rulings of Rabbi Karo and the *Arbah Turim*, and that instead *tefillin* must be checked from time to time to ensure that the scrolls are still valid (Principles 1 and 9).
Methodological Principles: 1, 9.

Example #32 – *Arukh HaShulchan* §42:3

In observance of the rabbinic principle "We increase sanctity but do not decrease sanctity," it is prohibited to take the *tefillin shel rosh* and transform it so that it can be used as a *tefillin shel yad*. This is because the head-*tefillin*, which contains four separate scrolls and features two of the three letters of God's name (the *shin* and *dalet* of "Shakkai"), is of greater sanctity than the arm *tefillin*, which includes only a single parchment scroll and features only one letter of God's name (the *yud* of "Shakkai").[54] Authorities disagree, however, about whether the leather straps used to fix the arm *tefillin* to the arm may be reversed in a case where the strap broke close to the *tefillin* box, leaving too short a length of leather strap still attached to the box to allow the *tefillin* to be properly tied. According to some authorities, one may reverse the strap by reattaching the original loose end of the strap to the *tefillin* box and leaving the end of the strap that was previously attached to the *tefillin* box to become the loose end of the strap that will be wrapped around the arm. Other authorities argue, however, that this is prohibited, as it entails demoting the original sanctity of the end of the strap that had been attached to the box with a *yud*-shaped knot (which, together with the *shin* and *dalet* contained in the head *tefillin* form God's name, "Shakkai") by now having that end of the strap used to fix the *tefillin* to the arm.[55]

Rabbi Epstein rules in accordance with those who prohibit altering the straps of the arm *tefillin* in this manner. According to Rabbi Epstein, one may not alter the straps of *tefillin* that have been tied into the shape of a *yud* (on the arm *tefillin*) or a *dalet* (on the head *tefillin*). As Rabbi Epstein explains elsewhere, he thinks that on the basis of kabbalistic sources, the parts of the *tefillin* that are shaped to form the letters of God's name, "Shakkai," are biblically required, and therefore they carry a greater level of sanctity than the rest of the leather straps (Principle 7).[56]
Methodological Principles: 7.

---

53 *See* Arbah Turim, Orach Chaim 39; Shulchan Arukh, Orach Chaim 39:10.
54 *See* Arukh HaShulchan, Orach Chaim 42:1.
55 *See* ibid. 42:3.
56 *See* ibid. 27:10.

Example #33 – *Arukh HaShulchan* §45:1

The Talmud rules that one may not wear *tefillin* within four cubits of a dead body because openly displaying one's performance of a *halakhic* obligation mocks, so to speak, the deceased, who are no longer able to do so.[57] In his codification of this rule, Rabbi Joseph Karo writes: "It is forbidden to enter a cemetery, or to be within four cubits of a corpse, with *tefillin* on one's head because this amounts to mocking the dead."[58] As some authorities note, this formulation suggests that Rabbi Karo went beyond the Talmudic prohibition against wearing *tefillin* within four cubits of a corpse and ruled that if one is inside the precincts of a cemetery, one may not wear *tefillin*, even if one is more than four cubits distant from any of the graves. Rabbi Epstein rejects this rule, however. He notes that the Talmudic standard is clear: one may not wear *tefillin* within four cubits of a dead body (Principle 1), and that any added legal strictures above and beyond the Talmudic norm are not binding (Principle 6).
Methodological Principles: 1, 6.

Example #34 – *Arukh HaShulchan* §46:9

The Talmud prescribes that each of the rabbinically mandated *Birkhat HaShachar*, or "morning blessings," should be recited by each individual at the appropriate point in that person's morning routine. Thus, for instance, when a person awakes at dawn, they should recite, "Blessed is God, Lord of the Universe, Who endowed the rooster with the understanding to discern between day and night;" and when a person opens their eyes in the morning, they should say, "Blessed is God, Lord of the Universe, Who opens the eyes of the blind;" and when one gets dressed, one says "Blessed is God, Lord of the Universe, Who clothes the naked;" and so on.[59] Rabbi Epstein notes, however, that this was only true during Talmudic times, when people were generally holy and careful to avoid touching unclean parts of their bodies, even while sleeping. Thus, such people were able to pray immediately upon waking up and recite each blessing at its appropriate place in the morning routine. However, Rabbi Epstein writes that this is no longer true: people wake up with unclean, impure hands, and they therefore cannot recite these blessings immediately, but only after having washed (Principle 9). Modern sleeping practices and mindsets make it impracticable for anyone to recite the blessings in the manner prescribed by the Talmud, and therefore Rabbi Epstein says, the Talmudic ordering of the blessings no longer needs to be observed (Principle 10). Instead, Rabbi Epstein endorses the current custom whereby each individual recites all the morning blessings at home after having washed and cleansed his or her self from the previous night's sleep, and whereby the entire series of blessings is repeated publicly in the synagogue as part of the morning prayer service for the benefit of less educated or less scrupulous Jews who would not have recited the blessings on their own at home (Principle 8).
Methodological Principles: 8, 9, 10.

---

57 *See* Babylonian Talmud, Berakhot 18a.
58 Shulchan Arukh, Orach Chaim 45:1.
59 *See* Babylonian Talmud, Berakhot 60b.

Example #35 – *Arukh HaShulchan* §48:3

Rabbi Moses Isserles notes that some scrupulous people have the custom to shake and wave their bodies while listening to the public Torah reading, which mimics the giving of the Torah itself, which was revealed with "trembling." Likewise, many have the custom to shake and sway their bodies while praying as a fulfillment of the verse in Psalms, "all my bones say to you, oh God."[60] Rabbi Epstein notes that some people do indeed sway while praying, while others specifically avoid moving their bodies at all while they stand in prayer. Rather than prescribe either course of conduct as normative, Rabbi Epstein says that each person should adopt the practice that is most conducive to mindful and intentional prayer in accordance with his or her own constitution (Principle 6). Rabbi Epstein does note, however, that the *Zohar* provides "a venerable explanation" for the practice of swaying during prayer (Principle 7).
Methodological Principles: 6, 7.

Example #36 – *Arukh HaShulchan* §52:1

Rabbi Epstein questions the standard custom to recite the Torah passage of *Shirat HaYam* at the conclusion of the introductory *Pesukei D'Zimra* section of the morning prayer liturgy. This is problematic, Rabbi Epstein says, because *Pesukei D'Zimra* consists of readings from Psalms, and it is inappropriate to place readings from the Torah itself after readings from Psalms during the same sequence of prayers. It is for this reason, Rabbi Epstein suggests, that Maimonides instructs that the *Shirat HaYam* passage be recited not at the conclusion of *Pesukei D'Zimra*, but as the introduction to the recitation of the *Shema*, the liturgy sequence that follows the introductory prayers of *Pesukei D'Zimra*.[61] Nevertheless, Rabbi Epstein notes that accepted contemporary practice does not follow Maimonides's liturgy, and the placement of the *Shirat HaYam* is thus problematic.

Despite this concern, Rabbi Epstein accepts the settled custom to recite the *Shirat HaYam* at the close of *Pesukei D'Zimra* (Principle 8) and seeks to justify the practice by references to the *Zohar* (Principle 7). The *Zohar* raises the question posed by Rabbi Epstein about the proper placement of the *Shirat HaYam* in the liturgy and responds in a somewhat mystical vein that it is precisely because of the elevated holiness of the *Shirat HaYam* that this passage was placed at the very end of the *Pesukei D'Zimra* as a kind of crescendo in the liturgical lead-up to the recitation of the *Shema*.
Methodological Principles 7, 8.

Example #37 – *Arukh HaShulchan* §52:5

Rabbi Joseph Karo rules that if one arrived late to the synagogue without enough time to recite the *Pesukei D'Zimra* prayers on his own and still join the rest of the congregation in the recital of the *Amidah*, the central prayer of each of the three daily prayer services, one should skip *Pesukei D'Zimra*, recite the *Amidah* together with the congregation, and then go back and recite all of the *Pesukei D'Zimra* prayers following the *Amidah*, albeit without the usual

---

60 *See* Rema *to* Shulchan Arukh, Orach Chaim 48:1.
61 *See* Mishneh Torah, Hilkhot Tefillah 7:13.

introductory and concluding blessings typically included with *Pesukei D'Zimra* liturgy.[62] Rabbi Epstein explains that introductory and concluding blessings of *Pesukei D'Zimra* were placed in the liturgy only in order to properly bookend the praises of the *Pesukei D'Zimra* Psalms as a prelude to the primary prayers of the *Shema* and the *Amidah*. Once one has said the *Amidah*, however, it no longer makes sense to recite *Pesukei D'Zimra* in this manner, and accordingly Rabbi Karo rules that the blessings should be omitted (Principle 1).

Rabbi Epstein further notes that it is unlikely that Rabbi Karo meant to prescribe the post-*Amidah* recital of *Pesukei D'Zimra* as a genuine *halakhic* obligation. After all, Rabbi Epstein points out, Rav Natronai Gaon (d. 858) maintained that one should not recite *Pesukei D'Zimra* at all once the *Amidah* has already been said, and the *Arbah Turim* endorses this view.[63] Rabbi Karo himself explained that Rav Natronai Gaon must have only intended to proscribe the post-*Amidah* recital of *Pesukei D'Zimra* with its attendant blessings; after all, one is always permitted to recite Psalms during the day, and reciting the Psalms that comprise *Pesukei D'Zimra* should be no different, provided that one does not also recite the attendant blessings, which should only be said when *Pesukei D'Zimra* is recited as part of the standard prayer liturgy.[64] Based on Rabbi Karo's explanation of Rav Natronai Gaon's rulings, Rabbi Epstein concludes that Rabbi Karo himself only permitted the recital of *Pesukei D'Zimra* after the *Amidah* as a supererogatory practice – no different than an ordinary recital of Psalms—and then only so long as one does so without reciting the liturgical blessings, which may only be said when *Pesukei D'Zimra* is recited as part of the ordinary order of the morning prayer service.[65]

Rabbi Epstein questions Rabbi Karo's recommendation to recite *Pesukei D'Zimra* following the *Amidah*, however. First, Rabbi Epstein points out that Rabbi Karo's understanding of Rav Natronai Gaon's ruling on which this recommendation is based is mistaken. Rav Natronai Gaon himself ruled that one should not recite the *Pesukei D'Zimra* Psalms following the *Amidah* in a case where one had already recited the introductory and concluding *Pesukei D'Zimra* blessings prior to the *Amidah*. Thus, it cannot be that Rav Natronai intended merely to proscribe the post-*Amidah* recital of *Pesukei D'Zimra* without the attendant blessings; since he was dealing with a case where the blessings had already been said before the *Amidah*, there was no possibility that the blessings could have been repeated afterward in any case. Rather, Rav Natronai Gaon must have intended to prohibit any post-*Amidah* recital of *Pesukei D'Zimra*, with or without the attendant blessings. Moreover, Rabbi Epstein notes that some authorities explicitly prohibit any post-*Amidah* recital of the *Pesukei D'Zimra* Psalms, even without saying the attendant blessings, because the *Pesukei D'Zimra* Psalms as a liturgical group of prayers were organized specifically as an introduction to the *Shema* and the *Amidah*, and they should not be recited on their own afterward.

Rabbi Epstein therefore rejects Rabbi Karo's rule (Principle 1). Instead, he writes that it is better to not say *Pesukei D'Zimra* after the *Amidah* because in general it is best passively to not act rather than to act in a manner that may violate *halakhic* norms (Principle 4). This is especially so, he argues, in light of the fact that a strong consensus of earlier authorities concurs with Rav Natronai Gaon's ruling (Principle 2). Moreover, Rabbi Epstein notes that this conclusion is supported by kabbalistic sources, which attribute special importance to the role of *Pesukei D'Zimra* as a specifically introductory prayer prior to the recital of the *Shema* and the *Amidah* (Principle 7).

---

62 Shulchan Arukh, Orach Chaim 52:1.
63 *See* Arbah Turim, Orach Chaim 52.
64 *See* Beit Yosef *to* Arbah Turim, Orach Chaim 52:2.
65 Arukh HaShulchan, Orach Chaim 52:4.

Methodological Principles: 1, 2, 4, 7.

Example #38 – *Arukh HaShulchan* §53:21

Rabbis Joseph Karo and Moses Isserles both rule that any individual member of the community can object to and prevent the appointment of a particular *chazzan*, or public prayer leader.[66] Rabbi Epstein questions this remarkable rule, however, as it appears to constitute a stark departure from the ordinary rules governing communal appointments and *halakhic* decision-making in general, which endorses majority rule and does not permit the blockage of communal enactments or appointments on the basis of individual preferences.[67] Rabbi Epstein explains this rule on the basis of a responsum of the *Or Zarua*, who suggested that the role of the *chazzan* is to represent the entire community in public prayer and to fulfill the congregants' prayer obligations through his own recitals of the liturgy. It would be impossible for the *chazzan* to discharge the prayer obligations of a congregant who opposes his representing the congregation, and thus, even when only one member of the community opposes the appointment of the *chazzan*, the *chazzan* cannot assume his role as the community's prayer representative. Moreover, the *Or Zarua* writes that just as a priest could not offer a sacrifice on behalf of an unwilling donor, a *chazzan* cannot offer prayers—which the Talmudic Rabbis instituted to replace Temple sacrifices—without the consent of all the members of the congregation he is representing.

Based on this reasoning, Rabbi Epstein rules that Rabbi Karo and Rabbi Isserles's ruling no longer applies, and a *chazzan* may be appointed so long as he enjoys the support of a majority of the congregation (Principle 9). In past eras, most congregants were not sufficiently educated to pray on their own, and the function of the *chazzan*, the "congregational agent," really was to discharge congregants' prayer obligations by reciting the prayers loudly as the members of the congregation listened attentively and responded "amen" where appropriate. In this context, it made sense that any single person could prevent an appointee from taking on the role of *chazzan* because the nature of the *chazzan*'s role demanded that every member of the congregation consent to his prayer agency on their behalf. Rabbi Epstein notes, however, that in his own time and place virtually all Jews can and do pray on their own, and the role of the *chazzan* is thus more ceremonial and aesthetic than strictly ritually necessary. Under these circumstances, the absence of consent to the *chazzan*'s position by less than a majority of the community does not undermine the legitimacy of his office.

Rabbi Epstein further notes that even under the circumstances that prevailed in previous eras, the rule prescribed by Rabbis Karo and Isserles must necessarily be limited. A broad rule permitting any individual's dissent to invalidate the ritual authority of the *chazzan* would be completely unworkable in practice, and so, Rabbi Epstein prescribes a number of conditions to which this rule must be subject (Principle 10). For instance, Rabbi Epstein says that an individual cannot dissent to the appointment of a particular *chazzan* after previously assenting to the appointment.[68]

Methodological Principles: 9, 10.

---

66 Shulchan Arukh, Orach Chaim 53:19.
67 Arukh HaShulchan, Orach Chaim 53:19.
68 *See* ibid. 53:20.

Example #39 – *Arukh HaShulchan* §55:3

Rabbi Epstein explains that the early Second Temple period rabbinic synod known as the Men of the Great Assembly legislated the recitation of the *Kaddish*, a prayer designed to punctuate the standard prayer liturgy and other important occasions with acknowledgments of God's greatness.[69] Rabbi Epstein notes that many people are accustomed to punctuating the morning prayer service by reciting *Kaddish* many times—indeed, more times than the Talmudic Rabbis themselves prescribed. Taking the Talmudic prescription of the correct number of times that *Kaddish* should be said during the morning prayer service as normative, Rabbi Epstein rejects this common custom (Principle 1). While generally Rabbi Epstein treats customs with deference (Principle 8), he views the custom of reciting *Kaddish* more than legally necessary as a supererogatory practice that has negative repercussions (Principle 6). He notes that according to one major authority, reciting *Kaddish*, which contains God's name, is akin to reciting blessings; and, "just as it is good to be frugal with reciting blessings, it is likewise good to be frugal with the recitation of the *Kaddish* prayer." Thus, following the general principle that one does not recite unnecessary blessings, which involve the possible violation of the biblical injunction against taking God's name in vain, Rabbi Epstein prohibits the unnecessary recital of *Kaddish* and prescribes that *Kaddish* should be said only at those points in the prayer service at which it is legally required (Principle 4).

Methodological Principles: 1, 4, 6, 8.

Example #40 – *Arukh HaShulchan* §55:5

Maimonides states that after ten or more Jews engage in Torah study—even of non-legal or homiletical matters—one member of the group must recite *Kaddish DeRabbanan*, a special *kaddish* prayer used to mark the end of a public Torah study session. Rabbi Epstein asserts that implicit in Maimonides's statement is that, if fewer than ten Jews learn Torah, they are not permitted to recite the *Kaddish*. Indeed—though Rabbi Epstein does not say this explicitly—when Maimonides requires the recitation of *Kaddish* if "ten or more" study Torah, the qualification "or more" emphasizes that ten is the minimum and excludes the possibility of reciting *Kaddish* for less than ten. On the basis of his interpretation of Maimonides's rule (Principle 3), Rabbi Epstein rebukes those who customarily recite *Kaddish* alone after learning Torah to commemorate the anniversary of a loved one's death (Principle 8). Moreover, in limiting the recitations of *Kaddish*, Rabbi Epstein rules strictly to prevent future Jews from reciting the name of God in vain (Principle 4).

In addition, Rabbi Epstein cites the *Magen Avraham*,[70] who records that many have the custom to recite the *Kaddish* only after studying non-legalistic parts of the Torah, but not after studying only *halakhic* matters. Due to this practice, many have the custom to recite some brief non-legal Torah thought after studying *halakhic* matters to ensure the fulfillment of this stringency. Rabbi Epstein, however, explains that Maimonides implies the opposite; he ruled that a member of the study group must recite the *Kaddish* prayer even after studying non-legal matters, which certainly implies that the *Kaddish* should be recited after the study of legal matters as well. In light of Maimonides's position, Rabbi Epstein adopts this view (Principle 3) and rejects as mistaken the custom recorded by the *Magen Avraham* (Principle 8).

---

69 *See* Babylonian Talmud, Berakhot 3a.
70 *See* Magen Avraham *to* Shulchan Arukh, Orach Chaim 54:103.

Methodological Principles: 3, 4, 8.

Example #41 – *Arukh HaShulchan* §61:13

The Talmud states that one who is reciting the *Shema* prayer may not repeat the first word or first line of the prayer because it gives the impression that they believe that there are two authorities in the Heavens.[71] In fact, the Talmud instructs that one who is overheard repeating the *Shema* prayer should be silenced. *Rashi* and *Tosafot* disagree, however, about which offense is considered worse: repeating the first word, *Shema*, or repeating the entire first line of the prayer, "Hear Israel, Hashem is God, Hashem is One." *Rashi* maintains that repeating the first line of the prayer is the more serious infraction and requires silencing; repeating just the word, *Shema*, though still prohibited, does not demand that one be silenced. *Tosafot* takes the opposite position. According to this view, repeating the word *Shema* is the more serious transgression and the one which demands silencing.

Since the Talmud itself does not lend any particular support to either of these two approaches, the *Arukh HaShulchan* takes a stringent approach and rules that one should be silenced whether they repeat the first word or the first line. While it is unusual for Rabbi Epstein to prescribe a mode of practice designed to satisfy two competing rabbinic opinions (Principle 5), in this case Rabbi Epstein's ruling seems rooted in the ultimate indeterminacy of the Talmudic standard, and in the fact that the Talmud's underlying concern here relates to avoiding the appearance of polytheistic worship—a serious sin (Principle 4). Moreover, Rabbi Epstein advises that one should not even read the entire opening paragraph twice, an extralegal caution likely designed to further protect against the Talmud's concerns for the appearance of idolatrous worship (Principle 6). Rabbi Epstein notes, however, that this rule prohibiting the repetition of the *Shema* prayer does not apply to one who is reciting the *Shema* prayer before going to sleep because ideally one should fall asleep with the words of the *Shema* on their lips, and practically speaking this often necessitates saying the prayer several times before finally falling asleep (Principle 10). Nevertheless, Rabbi Epstein notes that there are authorities who object to this as well, and in deference to the concern for the appearance of polytheistic worship, even when repeating the *Shema* prayer while trying to fall asleep, one should skip the opening line (Principle 6).

Methodological Principles: 4, 5, 6, 10.

Example #42 – *Arukh HaShulchan* §62:4

The Mishnah rules that the *Shema* and the *Amidah* prayers may be recited in any language the praying individual understands.[72] This permission to pray in any language that a person understands is codified by Maimonides, the *Shulchan Arukh*, and others.[73] Rabbi Epstein, however, rules that while this rule was valid in the Talmudic era, one should not pray in a language other than the Hebrew and occasional Aramaic in which the traditional liturgy was originally written (Principle 9). Rabbi Epstein argues that the Mishnah only sanctioned reciting prayers in the vernacular if one translated them word-for-word, exactly and in their entirety (Principle 1). In the Talmudic era, the exact meaning of the words and phrases found in the prayers was known,

---

71 Babylonian Talmud, Berakhot 32b.
72 Mishnah, Sotah 7:1.
73 Shulchan Arukh, Orach Chaim 62:2; Mishneh Torah, Hilkhot Kri'at Shema 2:10.

and thus praying in another language using a precise translation of the original Hebrew was feasible. However, according to Rabbi Epstein, this is no longer the case as the meaning of many words and phrases are now a matter of debate among exegetes. For example, the verse, "Hear Israel," which opens the *Shema* prayer, can be understood in several different ways. Likewise, the literal meanings of the terms *tzitzit* (the fringes worn on four-corner garments) and *totafot* (a reference to *tefillin*) remain obscure. Even more critically, the meaning of the Tetragrammaton (the four-letter name of God) can no longer be rendered accurately. For this reason, not only can the *Shema* and *Amidah* prayers no longer be accurately rendered into another language, but in fact all blessings must be recited in the original Hebrew. Indeed, concludes Rabbi Epstein, this ruling was promulgated by the 'greatest authorities' around 80 years ago, which helped establish a settled and accepted practice to pray only in Hebrew (Principle 8). Additionally, based on comments Rabbi Epstein makes elsewhere in the *Arukh HaShulchan*,[74] it appears that he thought that even if the Talmud may permit praying in the vernacular, and even if in principle that permission should apply in later eras, people should still adopt the extralegal stricture of praying only in Hebrew in order to strengthen traditional ritual practice in the face of heterodox movements that made praying in the vernacular a cornerstone of their reformist program (Principle 6). Methodological Principles: 1, 6, 8, 9.

Example #43 – *Arukh HaShulchan* §63:5

The Talmud states that one may not say the *Shema* prayer while lying down.[75] *Rashi* understands this to mean that one may not recite the *Shema* while lying on one's back, but that one may recite the *Shema* while lying flat on one's front. Maimonides disagrees and rules that the Talmud prohibits reciting the *Shema* while lying down, whether in a supine or prone position.[76]

Rabbi Epstein explains that this prohibition is grounded in a concern for proper respect for the prayer, as it is disrespectful to pray while lying down. The *Rema* goes so far as to say that if possible, one should sit up fully before reciting the *Shema*.[77] Rabbi Epstein, however, rejects this requirement, noting that since the vast majority of rabbinic authorities have understood the Talmud to prohibit praying while fully lying down,[78] it is sufficient to pray while lying on one's side (Principle 2), and Rabbi Isserles's extralegal recommendation to sit up before praying is not obligatory (Principle 6).

While Rabbi Epstein thus rules that in principle the *halakhah* requires one to turn to their side before reciting the *Shema* while lying in bed, this rule does not apply to someone who is very ill or obese and is therefore unable to do so. Such people, Rabbi Epstein rules, may remain supine and merely lean over slightly as a sign of respect for the prayer before beginning their recital of the *Shema*; and if they are unable to do even that, they may nevertheless say the prayer lying down (Principle 10).

In connection to the prohibition against praying while lying down, Rabbi Epstein also addresses the issue of proper positioning of one's body when going to sleep. While not strictly required from a legal vantage, Rabbi Epstein nonetheless recommends that healthy males should

---

74 *See* Arukh HaShulchan, Orach Chaim 185:2.
75 Babylonian Talmud, Berakhot 13b.
76 Mishneh Torah, Hilkhot Kri'at Shema 2:2.
77 Rema *to* Shulchan Arukh, Orach Chaim 63:1.
78 *See* Arbah Turim, Orach Chaim 63, Shulchan Arukh, Orach Chaim 63:1; Magen Avhraham *to* Shulchan Arukh, Orach Chaim 63:1.

try to sleep on their side rather than lying prone or supine on the bed because doing so serves a valuable religious purpose (Principle 6). In his commentary on the Talmud, *Rashi* explains that a male should avoid sleeping on his back because he may become sexually aroused during the night, and "many others [in the room] may see this," leading to his becoming embarrassed. Rabbi Epstein, while referencing *Rashi*'s commentary, gives a different explanation of this practice. He explains that sleeping on one's front or back—as opposed to on one's side—is more likely to lead to a man becoming sexually aroused while sleeping and may also lead to nocturnal seminal emissions. To avoid this, one should sleep on one's side, though this is not legally required (Principle 6). Notably, it is possible that Rabbi Epstein's subtle departure from *Rashi*'s explanation of this rule is grounded in a recognition of the different sleeping arrangements common in his own time as opposed to during the Talmudic or medieval periods. It was rare in the times of the Talmud or *Rashi* for people to sleep alone and with privacy, and thus, becoming embarrassed by others seeing how one became sexually aroused while asleep may have been a real concern. By Rabbi Epstein's time, however, sleeping in private quarters was far more common—this obviated *Rashi*'s stated concern for the sleeping individual's personal embarrassment. Rabbi Epstein thus offers an expanded and more contemporaneously relevant rationalization of the Talmud's caution against sleeping on one's back, expressing a pious concern for avoiding unnecessary seminal emissions (Principles 1 and 9).

Methodological Principles: 1, 2, 6, 9, 10.

Example #44 - *Arukh HaShulchan* §65:4

Rabbinic authorities agree that one may continue performing a ritual obligation that one was earlier forced to interrupt, provided that the length of the interruption was shorter than the amount of time it would have taken to complete the performance of the *mitzvah* had no interruption occurred.[79] Halakhic authorities disagree, however, about how to proceed in cases where the length of the interruption is equal to or greater than the amount of time it would normally take to perform the entire ritual observance that one was engaged in at the time of the interruption. According to Maimonides, the *Rif*, and Rabbi Joseph Karo, the proper approach depends on the kind of ritual observance one was performing before being interrupted. If one was interrupted while in the middle of praying the *Amidah*, the central liturgy of each of the three daily prayer services, and the interruption lasted long enough to have said the entire prayer, one must begin reciting the *Amidah* from the beginning of the prayer after the conclusion of the interruption. When it comes to all other observances, however, one need not repeat the entire practice following a lengthy interruption. An alternative view is offered by *Tosafot*, the *Arbah Turim*, and many other authorities. These scholars rule that the *halakhic* standard depends on the nature of the interruption rather than the nature of the ritual observance that was interrupted. If the interruption was voluntary, then one need not restart the observance, no matter how long the interruption because it is as if the person intended to return and finish the observance the entire time. If, however, the lengthy interruption was involuntary, one must begin the ritual observance anew after the interruption ends.

The Talmudic sources that discuss this issue offer no determinative guidance, and Rabbi Epstein therefore adopts the second approach of *Tosafot* and the *Arbah Turim* because it is endorsed by a strong consensus of other *halakhic* authorities (Principle 2).[80]

---

79 Shulchan Arukh, Orach Chaim 65:1.
80 Arukh HaShulchan, Orach Chaim 65:4.

Rabbi Epstein's ruling that one need only restart a ritual observance following a lengthy interruption if the interruption was involuntary does not fully resolve the issue, however. This is because those authorities that endorse the second approach described above disagree amongst themselves about what kinds of interruptions qualify as "involuntary." According to the *Raabad* and the *Baal HaMaor*, only interruptions that are imposed by the *halakhah* are truly involuntary; other interruptions, however, are not. Thus, for instance, since Jewish law prohibits praying in an unclean place, if one interrupts one's prayers in order to use a restroom, the interruption is regarded as involuntary, and if the interruption was long enough one must begin reciting the interrupted prayer from the beginning. By contrast, if one's prayers were interrupted by other, non-legal causes, such as a fire, animal attack, or other phenomena, the interruption would be considered voluntary and one would not need to restart the prayer afterward, no matter how long the interruption lasted. Many other authorities disagree with the *Baal HaMaor* and *Raabad*. This second view maintains that "involuntary" interruptions include all interruptions that one does not willingly create, including natural events like attacks by bandits or animals for which the *halakhah* itself does not prescribe an interruption.[81] On this question, Rabbi Epstein rules in accordance with the first position of the *Baal HaMaor* and *Raabad* that only *halakhically* imposed interruptions are considered truly "involuntary," since in Rabbi Epstein's assessment, this view, too, is supported by rabbinic consensus (Principle 2).

Rabbi Epstein thus rejects the views of Maimonides on the issue of which kinds of interruptions require one to restart an observance, as well as the views of those authorities that rule that all unwilled interruptions are considered "involuntary." Nevertheless, Rabbi Epstein utilizes both of these rejected opinions in the specific case of one who takes a long pause in the recital of the *Amidah* prayer due to an interruption not imposed by the *halakhah*. In such a case, Rabbi Epstein rules that one must begin the *Amidah* prayer anew. This is because the case of an interrupted *Amidah* prayer involves the intersection of both the view that any interruption of the *Amidah* requires one to restart the prayer from the beginning, and the view that "involuntary" interruptions include even non-legally imposed pauses in a ritual performance. While each of these opinions is normatively rejected in isolation, in Rabbi Epstein's view the confluence of both opinions in the same case works to justify the ritually stringent conclusion that one must repeat the entire *Amidah* prayer after an extended involuntary interruption (Principle 5).[82]

Methodological Principles: 2, 5.

Example #45 – *Arukh HaShulchan* §70:5

The Mishnah rules that a groom who is marrying a virgin is exempt from reciting the *Shema* prayer on the wedding night.[83] The Talmud explains that this is because generally speaking the groom's mind will be preoccupied with fear that he will discover that his bride is in fact not a virgin; since the recitation of the *Shema* prayer requires mindful concentration on the prayer, such a preoccupied person is exempted from the duty to recite the prayer.

Rabbi Epstein notes that there is a disagreement among *halakhic* authorities as to whether a groom who nevertheless wishes to be stringent and say the *Shema* may do so. The *Rosh* rules that he may not recite the *Shema* because once the law has exempted him from the obligation, it would appear haughty to recite the prayer anyway as if he alone—in contrast to all other grooms

---

81 Ibid. 65:2.
82 Ibid. 65:4.
83 Mishnah, Berakhot, 2:5.

in the world—is able to maintain proper concentration on the prayer.[84] The *Rif* and Maimonides, however, rule that the groom may recite the *Shema* on the wedding night if he wishes to do so.[85]

Rabbi Epstein argues that this discussion is now purely academic. A groom's exemption from reciting the *Shema* only applied "in their days" when under ordinary circumstances people were capable of reciting the prayer with proper devotion and intention. In that context, a groom's special circumstances justified an exemption from the otherwise attainable obligation to recite the *Shema* with proper attention. Rabbi Epstein says that in modern times, by contrast, no one is really capable of mustering the proper mindful intent needed to properly recite the *Shema* under even ordinary conditions. We recite the prayer anyway, since it would be absurd to abandon the ritual duty to recite the *Shema* in response to this human failing (Principle 10), but in this context there is no special reason to exempt a groom from reciting the prayer (Principle 9). Even if the groom were to recite the prayer without proper attention due to his preoccupation with consummating the marriage, he would not thereby be any worse off than the general population who fail to recite the prayer properly themselves. Rabbi Epstein continues, however, and rules that not only are modern-day grooms no longer exempt from reciting the *Shema*, but they may not purport to act stringently in conformity to the Talmudic rule and avoid reciting the *Shema* on their wedding nights. Given the new reality, Rabbi Epstein argues, a groom's *not* reciting the *Shema* would appear haughty, as if to imply that ordinarily he recites the *Shema* with proper intent and will therefore avoid saying the prayer on his wedding night when such intent is unlikely to be maintained (Principle 6). To support his position, Rabbi Epstein notes that the widespread custom is for grooms to recite the *Shema* on their wedding nights and says that this custom should be followed (Principle 8).

Methodological Principles: 6, 8, 9, 10.

Example #46 – *Arukh HaShulchan* §75:7

The *Shulchan Arukh* rules that a man may not recite the *Shema* while standing in view of a woman's hair which she is accustomed to covering.[86] In this context, Rabbi Epstein laments that for many years married women have been ignoring the *halakhic* requirement to cover their hair. Indeed, he decries the fact that in his own day this shameful state of affairs has become endemic. As a result of this, however, Rabbi Epstein rules that men may now pray and recite the *Shema* in front of a married woman's uncovered hair. Rabbi Epstein offers several reasons for this. First, the common practice of married women not covering their hair undercuts the Talmud's characterization of hair as "nakedness," in the presence of which one could not recite the *Shema* (Principles 8 and 9). Second, Rabbi Epstein references the view of the *Mordechai*, who held that the hair of an unmarried woman is not considered "nakedness," and one may therefore recite prayers in the presence of the uncovered hair of an unmarried woman.[87] The *Mordechai* reasoned that, since men are accustomed to seeing the uncovered hair of unmarried women, such hair is not distracting and poses no impediment to prayer. Rabbi Epstein independently extends the *Mordechai*'s position to married women as well, arguing that since men are long accustomed to seeing the hair of even married women, unlike during Talmudic times, there is no fear of improper thoughts (Principles 1 and 9).

---

84 *Rosh to* Babylonian Talmud, Berakhot 16b.
85 Rabbi Isaac Alfasi, Rif, Berakhot 10a; Mishneh Torah, Hilkhot Kri'at Shema 4:7.
86 Shulchan Arukh, Orach Chaim 75:2.
87 Mordechai to *Berakhot* ch. 3.

Methodological Principles: 1, 8, 9.

Example #47 – *Arukh HaShulchan* §82:3

According to the Talmud, one may not recite the *Shema* prayer while standing next to a place where someone has urinated.[88] Later authorities note that this is so even if much of the urine has already been absorbed into the ground; if the ground is still wet enough to moisten one's hand were one to touch it, one may not pray in the presence of that spot.

Rabbi Epstein notes, however, that some authorities take a more lenient approach. According to these decisors, the Talmudic prohibition applies only to a spot where the ground is so wet that something placed upon it would itself become wet enough to dampen other items. Rabbi Epstein concludes that this opinion may be relied upon as the prohibition against praying near a piece of ground upon which someone had recently urinated is only rabbinic in nature. Since the correct parameters of this rule are subject to dispute, and since the Talmud itself does not determinately resolve the question, the doubt as to the correct rule must be resolved leniently (Principle 4). Thus, Rabbi Epstein rules that one may pray near a piece of ground upon which someone recently urinated so long as the urine is not still so wet as to be capable of moistening a cloth that would be capable of moistening a person's hand in turn. Moreover, since the stricter view is rejected as a result of the applications of the *halakhah*'s own doubt-resolving rules, there is no need to be stringent in such situations (Principle 5), especially as doing so offers no appreciable benefit (Principle 6).

Methodological Principles: 4, 5, 6.

Example #48 – *Arukh HaShulchan* §88:2

The Talmud records that the biblical prophet Ezra legislated that a man who experiences a seminal emission may not study Torah or recite the *Shema* prayer until after he immerses in a *mikvah*, a ritual bath used for purification from ritual impurities.[89] Maimonides, however, notes that following Ezra's enactment, observance of this rule fell out of practice because it proved too difficult to observe.[90] The Talmud itself, however, suggests that the Talmudic Rabbis themselves disestablished Ezra's rule.

Rather than rejecting Maimonides's position in favor of the Talmud's alternative account of how observance of Ezra's rule fell into disuse, Rabbi Epstein attempts to synthesize the two. He concludes that observing Ezra's stricture became too burdensome for the masses who were unable to observe such high standards of ritual purity—people thus became accustomed to ignoring this ritual purity requirement, and in response to this pragmatic reality, the Talmudic Rabbis repealed Ezra's ban on praying and studying without immersing in a *mikvah* following a seminal emission (Principles 1, 8, and 10). Rabbi Epstein notes, however, that since the Rabbis only repealed Ezra's rule in response to its already having fallen into popular disuse, those individuals who wish to continue observing this stricture may continue doing so (Principle 6). However, Rabbi Epstein warns that one must not supererogatively seek to observe Ezra's

---

88 *See* Babylonian Talmud, Berakhot 25a.
89 Babylonian Talmud, Berakhot 22a.
90 Mishneh Torah, Hilkhot Kri'at Shema, 4:8.

enactment if doing so would result in one's failing to recite the *Shema* at the appropriate time for want of a ritual bath (Principle 6).
Methodological Principles: 1, 6, 8, 10.

Example #49 – *Arukh HaShulchan* §90:7

The Talmud states that one must pray in a building that has windows.[91] According to *Rashi*, this is because windows allow one to look out at the Heavens and "submit their heart" to God, thus creating the proper mindset for prayer. Rabbi Epstein notes that this and other explanations offered by Talmudic exegetes make it clear that they understand the Talmud to prescribe that one not only pray in a building with windows, but also that one should pray while facing a window. However, Rabbi Epstein notes that in practice, the general custom is to not be particularly scrupulous about this rule (Principle 8). Indeed, Rabbi Epstein observes that in synagogues people generally choose to pray specifically in front sections of the wall that do not have any windows in order not to be distracted by others walking past outside (Principle 9). Moreover, the rabbi of the congregation is typically seated beside the ark, where there is no window. Rabbi Epstein accepts the common custom to not be careful about praying opposite a window and seeks to justify this departure from the apparent Talmudic rule by suggesting—in opposition to other commentators—that while the Talmud demands that synagogues have windows, it does not explicitly require one to pray facing those windows (Principle 1). Rabbi Epstein further supports the conclusion that one need not pray opposite a window by referencing a mystical teaching of the *Zohar*. The *Zohar* states that one may not pray in a building without windows as the 'earthly' synagogue must mirror the 'heavenly' synagogue by having twelve windows.[92] It is clear from this that the *Zohar* does not demand that one pray in front of a window, but only that a synagogue has twelve windows in its designated prayer space (Principle 7). Rabbi Epstein concludes by stating that, based on this mystical idea, it is a *mitzvah*—though not truly obligatory—to follow the *Zohar* and design synagogues to be constructed with twelve windows (Principle 6).
Methodological Principles: 1, 6, 7, 8, 9.

Example #50 – *Arukh HaShulchan* §94:17

The Talmud rules that one who is riding an animal while traveling on a journey does not need to dismount and stop their trip in order to recite the *Amidah* prayer. While the *Amidah* prayer must normally be said while standing reverently in place and facing towards Jerusalem, the Talmud explains that when one is traveling on the road these requirements are suspended because a traveler forced to dismount and face a particular direction while praying will not be able to properly concentrate on his prayers. It is thus preferable for the traveler to recite the *Amidah* prayer while still mounted and moving in the direction of their destination and directing their thoughts to God and Jerusalem.[93] Following the well-settled *halakhic* rule, Rabbi Epstein says that this dispensation similarly applies to a person traveling on foot: such a person does not need to halt their journey to pray the *Amidah*, since their preoccupation with the journey would impinge on their concentration in any case, and they can instead recite the prayer while

---

91 Babylonian Talmud, Berakhot 31a.
92 *See* Zohar, Pekudei, 251a. *See also* Beit Yosef *to* Arbah Turim, Orach Chaim 90:4.
93 Babylonian Talmud, Berakhot 30a.

continuing to walk (Principle 10). While this is indeed the normatively acceptable view, Rabbi Epstein suggests—but does not require—that those who are able to muster the proper mindfulness and concentration even while traveling should indeed halt their journey and recite the *Amidah* properly while standing in place and facing Jerusalem, since doing so offers the benefit of enhancing one's prayers (Principle 6).

Methodological Principles: 6, 10.

Example #51 – *Arukh HaShulchan* §97:3

Since one must pray the *Amidah* with great reverence in the manner that one would appear and stand before a king, the *halakhah* proscribes spitting while reciting the *Amidah* prayer. Maimonides rules, however, that in the case of a person who is simply unable to avoid having to spit during the prayer—such as one with a bad cold or cough—one should "throw [the spittle] behind him using his hand." As Rabbi Epstein points out, it seems that according to Maimonides, one who cannot avoid having to spit during the *Amidah* should spit into his hand and then toss the spittle behind him rather than turn his head from the proper prayer direction in order to surreptitiously spit to the side or behind him. In his *Beit Yosef* commentary on the *Arbah Turim*, Rabbi Karo argues that Maimonides could not have meant that a person should literally spit into their hand and then toss the spittle behind them, since a squeamish or sensitive individual would never design to do so, and thus Maimonides's apparent recommendation would fail to provide a workable way for those who cannot avoid spitting accumulated saliva out of their mouths to do so during the *Amidah* prayer.[94] Instead, Rabbi Karo suggests, Maimonides meant that a person should either spit into a cloth that is in his hand or turn his head and spit behind him. Following his reading of Maimonides's ruling, Rabbi Karo in his *Shulchan Arukh* takes a different approach to this issue and rules that rather than spit into one's hand and throw the spittle to the rear, one who cannot avoid spitting during the *Amidah* should either spit into a handkerchief or else turn his head and spit behind himself.[95]

The *Arukh HaShulchan*, however, disagrees with Rabbi Karo's approach. According to Rabbi Epstein, even an overly sensitive person can tolerate momentarily spitting into his hand and immediately depositing the saliva behind him, such that there is no reason to read Maimonides's ruling on this issue in any way other than in accordance with its plain and obvious meaning—permitting a person to spit into his hand and toss the spittle to the rear, all so long as he does not turn his head from the direction towards which the *Amidah* prayer is being directed. Thus, Rabbi Epstein adopts the plain understanding of Maimonides's position against the opinions of the *Shulchan Arukh* and other authorities, and rules that when an overly sensitive person feels the need to spit during the *Amidah*, he should spit into his hand and immediately deposit the saliva behind him (Principles 1 and 3).

Methodological Principles: 1, 3.

Example #52 – *Arukh HaShulchan* §100:3

Normative *halakhah* requires that on days of the year in which the mandated prayers are different from the rest of the year, such as the first day of a new month and on holidays, one must

---

94 Beit Yosef *to* Arbah Turim, Orach Chaim 97:2.
95 Shulchan Arukh, Orach Chaim 97:2.

either read the prayers from a prayer book or prepare the prayers prior to reciting them from memory. However, the *Arukh HaShulchan* notes that the common practice is to say even these less commonly recited prayers from memory, without having prepared them earlier (Principle 8). To justify this custom, Rabbi Epstein cites the normatively rejected opinion of the *Rif*, who maintained that a person can fulfill his or her daily prayer obligations by listening to the congregational prayer leader's own recitation of the liturgy rather than by necessarily having to recite all the prayers on one's own. While the *Rif*'s view is widely disputed and rejected as a matter of normative *halakhah*, Rabbi Epstein utilizes this outlying rabbinic opinion to justify the common practice of reciting special liturgies from memory. While those who try to say rarely recited prayers from memory are unlikely to do so properly, they can ultimately fulfill their own prayer obligation by listening to the liturgy recited by the *shliach tzibbur*, the congregation's prayer leader (Principle 5).

Methodological Principles: 5, 8.

Example #53 – *Arukh HaShulchan* §106:9

There is a dispute among some early rabbinic authorities over whether the obligation to pray is of biblical or rabbinic origin.[96] Maimonides famously held that daily prayer is a biblical duty, while others maintained that it is merely a rabbinic obligation. Rabbi Aryeh Gunzberg, author of the eighteenth-century work *Shaagat Aryeh*, sought to demonstrate that prayer is in fact only a rabbinically imposed duty from a Mishnaic ruling that prescribes that one must interrupt one's Torah studies in order to recite the *Shema*, but one should not do so in order to pray.[97] Rabbi Gunzberg reasons that the most plausible distinction between the *Shema* and other prayers that would help explain the Mishnah's distinguishing between the two is that, while reciting the *Shema* is a biblical obligation, prayer is merely a rabbinic duty. Thus, while one should interrupt one's Torah study to fulfill a time-limited biblical obligation like reciting the *Shema*, one should not do so in order to satisfy the rabbinic duty to pray.[98]

Rabbi Epstein rejects the *Shaagat Aryeh*'s attempt to prove that prayer is a rabbinic duty. Rabbi Epstein references a passage in the Jerusalem Talmud not cited by any previous *halakhic* scholars who addressed this issue, which provides several possible reasons for the Mishnah's distinguishing between interrupting Torah study to recite the *Shema* and doing so to pray (Principle 1). While some of these explanations are rooted in the assumption that prayer is only a rabbinic obligation, others rely on the premise that prayer is actually biblically mandated. Rabbi Epstein thus observes that both approaches to the question of the nature of the obligation to pray are deeply rooted in the rabbinic tradition, and that the Mishnah does not dispositively prove or disprove either view given the varied explanations offered by the Jerusalem Talmud.

Methodological Principles: 1.

Example #54 – *Arukh HaShulchan* §108:5

Jewish law prescribes three daily prayers that one is obligated to recite at particular times of the day. The correct way to address having failed to recite the appropriate prayer during

---

96 *See* Arukh HaShulchan, Orach Chaim 106:5-7.
97 *See* Mishnah, Shabbat 9b; Shaagat Aryeh, Orach Chaim, no. 14.
98 *See* Shaagat Aryeh, Orach Chaim, no. 14.

the allotted time of day, however, depends on the reason for which the prayer was missed. As Maimonides explains: "If one intentionally failed to pray, he has no way to correct his error and does not recite a make-up prayer. However, if [he missed the prayer] by accident, or was subject to some situational duress, or was otherwise busy, he makes up the missed prayer at the time he prays the next obligatory prayer of the day."[99] In other words, those with some excuse for why they missed a prayer are afforded the opportunity to rectify this by making up the prayer at a later time; those who intentionally skip a prayer, however, are considered more culpable and are therefore not given the benefit of correcting their failure by reciting a makeup prayer.

When defining the kinds of excuses that render one less than fully culpable for missing a prayer and thus entitle one to correct the error by making up the prayer later, Rabbi Epstein provides an expansive understanding that takes careful account of the pressures and human issues that may understandably lead people to forget to pray at the proper time (Principles 1 and 10). For instance, Rabbi Epstein writes that one's missing a prayer is understandably excusable and not treated as intentional if he missed the prayer time because he mistakenly thought he would finish a task in time to pray, but that task ended up taking much longer than anticipated, thus causing him to miss the prayer time. If one was busy with work or a business venture and did not halt his activities in order to pray out of concern that doing so would result in a financial loss, Rabbi Epstein writes that this is also understandably excusable. Remarkably, Rabbi Epstein goes so far as to rule that one's missing prayers is considered excusable if it resulted from simply forgetting to pray on time because people do in fact forget things, and such forgetfulness is therefore considered a form of situational duress (Principle 10).
Methodological Principles: 1, 10.

Example #55 - *Arukh HaShulchan* §108:6

While failing to recite an obligatory prayer at the prescribed time for some excusable reason justifies making up the prayer later, Rabbi Moses Isserles points out that this applies only *after* a prayer has already been missed and the relevant prayer time has passed. "However," Rabbi Isserles rules, "in the first place, while the prayer can still be recited at the proper time, one may not allow the time to pass [and thus miss reciting the prayer] on account of some financial loss" that one expects to suffer if one stops what one is doing to pray.[100] Rabbi Epstein, however, argues that such a categorical rule that fails to account for situations in which praying on time would cause a person to suffer serious financial losses cannot be correct. He notes that Jewish law clearly maintains that one need not spend inordinate amounts of one's money in order to fulfill even biblical obligations, and the same should certainly be true for a rabbinically imposed duty like praying the daily prayers at their prescribed times (Principle 1).[101] Rabbi Epstein therefore rules that while one is not excused from praying at the correct time on account of speculative concerns that one may possibly suffer a financial loss as a result, people are excused from having to pray on time if doing so is reasonably likely to cause a financial loss (Principle 10).[102]
Methodological Principles: 1, 10.

---

99 Mishneh Torah, Hilkhot Tefillah 3:8.
100 Rema *to* Shulchan Arukh, Orach Chaim 108:8.
101 *See* Arukh HaShulchan, Orach Chaim 108:6.
102 Ibid. 108:7.

Example #56 - *Arukh HaShulchan* §108:11

Jewish law prescribes that if one failed to recite one of the daily prayers at its proper time due to some valid excuse, one may make up the prayer later by reciting the *Amidah* twice during the next scheduled daily prayer. Rabbi Moses Isserles explains that when making up a previously missed prayer during a presently obligatory prayer, one first recites the current prayer and thereafter makes up the missed prayer. The *Rema* rules that if one mistakenly failed to recite *Minchah*, the afternoon prayer, and one therefore plans to recite the *Amidah* twice when praying *Maariv*, the evening prayer, one should first recite the *Maariv* prayer with its proper *Amidah*, then recite the *Ashrei* prayer, which introduces the *Minchah* liturgy, and then one should pray the *Amidah* once again to make up for the previously missed *Minchah* prayer.[103] The *Arukh HaShulchan* rejects Rabbi Isserles's ruling, however, and holds that one should not recite the *Ashrei* prayer after concluding the *Amidah* for *Maariv* and before beginning the makeup *Amidah* for the missed *Minchah* service (Principle 1). Rabbi Epstein bases this conclusion on a teaching of the *Zohar* that discourages the recitation of the *Ashrei* prayer after the proper time for reciting the *Minchah* service has passed (Principle 7).[104]
Methodological Principles: 1, 7.

Example #57 - *Arukh HaShulchan* §111:2

Rabbis Joseph Karo and Moses Isserles disagree about whether one should respond "*amen*" to the prayer leader's recitation of the blessing of *Gaal Yisrael*, a blessing which concludes the recitation of the *Shema* and introduces the silent recitation of the central *Amidah* prayer during the morning prayer service. Rabbi Karo rules that one may not interrupt one's prayers between the recitation of the blessing of *Gaal Yisrael* and the start of the *Amidah* because the Talmud itself places great importance on the juxtaposition of these two parts of the prayer service. Rabbi Isserles disagrees, however, and rules that one may say "*amen*" following this blessing because saying "*amen*" does not constitute a true interruption in the prayers, as it is part of the normal responsive liturgy.[105] The Talmud does not definitively resolve this issue (Principle 1), and Rabbi Epstein ultimately endorses Rabbi Karo's more stringent view because it is also supported by the *Zohar* (Principle 7).
Methodological Principles 1, 7.

Example #58 - *Arukh HaShulchan* §128:64

While the Talmud establishes that *Kohanim*, those belonging to the priestly family of Aaron, are obligated to perform and recite the congregational *Birkhat Kohanim*, the "Priestly Blessing" service, every day, Rabbi Moses Isserles notes that the custom among Jews in European lands is to only perform the Priestly Blessing on holidays. Rabbi Isserles explains that the Priestly Blessing can only be recited in a state of happiness and contentment—in the difficult economic and political circumstances faced by European Jews, such happiness only occurs on holidays. Moreover, even on holidays, such joy is present only during the *Musaf* service, which takes

---

103 Shulchan Arukh, Orach Chaim 108:8.
104 *See* Zohar, Pinchat 226b; Arukh HaShulchan, Orach Chaim 108:11.
105 Shulchan Arukh, Orach Chaim 111:1.

place right before the people leave the synagogue to head home and enjoy their holiday meals. Therefore, the *Rema* says, the Priestly Blessing is only recited as part of the *Musaf* prayer on holidays and not at other times.

Rabbi Epstein takes strong issue with the general custom observed by the *Rema*. After all, he says, how can one justify a custom that abrogates a clear biblical obligation to recite the Priestly Blessing daily? Rabbi Epstein therefore characterizes this practice as "a loathsome custom." Nevertheless, Rabbi Epstein writes that while several scholars have tried to reinstitute the daily recitation of the Priestly Blessing, their efforts were frustrated and came to naught, and "it is as if a voice has gone forth from the Heavens preventing us from saying the Priestly Blessing every day" (Principle 8). Furthermore, Rabbi Epstein attempts to provide a post hoc justification for this custom on the basis of the *Zohar*'s mystical teaching that from a strictly legal perspective, the Priestly Blessing can only be recited while the priests are in a state of joy, just like Aaron and his sons were during the original biblical recitation of the Priestly Blessing as part of the dedication of the Tabernacle in the wilderness (Principle 7). While such joy may have been present among some Jewish communities living in other times and places, this is no longer the case, and thus the original daily obligation to recite the Priestly Blessing daily no longer holds true (Principle 9).

Methodological Principles: 7, 8, 9.

Example #59 – *Arukh HaShulchan* §131:2

It is widely accepted that following the recitation of the *Amidah*, a penitential prayer known as *Tachanun* is recited. When discussing this issue, the *Arbah Turim* references a ruling by Rav Natronai Gaon, who ruled that reciting the *Tachanun* prayer is not truly obligatory. The *Arbah Turim* rules accordingly, noting that one may easily dispense with reciting the *Tachanun* prayer for relatively minor reasons.

Rabbi Epstein rules, however, that while it may be true that the *Tachanun* prayer was not strictly obligatory during the times of Rav Natronai Gaon and the *Arbah Turim*, the same is no longer the case (Principle 9). The simple reality is that Jews have widely accustomed themselves to recite the *Tachanun* prayer every day, and this has transformed this once optional prayer into something approximating an obligation (Principle 8). While reciting the *Tachanun* prayer is not formally obligatory from a strictly legal perspective, it remains a very weighty and important matter that should be taken seriously.

Methodological Principles: 8, 9.

Example #60 – *Arukh HaShulchan* §135:4

When the Torah is read in public as part of the morning prayer services on Mondays and Thursdays, three men are called to read from the Torah. First, a *Kohen* is called to read; then a Levite; and only afterward an ordinary Jew reads to complete the public Torah reading. The *Mordechai* writes, however, that if there are two ordinary Jewish bridegrooms present in the synagogue on a Monday or Thursday morning, both should be called to read from the Torah. A *Kohen* should be called to read first, then a Levite, and then the two bridegrooms in turn, though this will mean adding a fourth reader during the weekday Torah services. The *Rema* affirms this rule and explains that since the seven days following a wedding are considered a holiday for the bridegroom, it is appropriate to honor both bridegrooms, even if this requires a small addition and change to the ordinary weekday Torah reading service.

While Rabbi Epstein does not directly dispute Rabbi Isserles's ruling, he notes that he has never seen anyone actually implement this recommendation (Principle 8). Moreover, he notes that in principle it would seem that the underlying reasoning for the *Rema*'s rule renders it inapplicable in the current era when the general custom is to not add additional Torah readers on holidays. Since additional readers are not added to the congregational Torah reading service even on genuine holidays, there is no reason for additional readers to accommodate the bridegrooms' quasi-holiday (Principle 9). Still, while in principle Rabbi Epstein thus thinks that one should not add additional readers to the weekday Torah service in order to accommodate multiple bridegrooms in the synagogue, if honoring only one of the two bridegrooms with reading from the Torah will lead to conflict, the congregation may rely on the *Rema*'s ruling and allow both bridegrooms to read (Principle 10).
Methodological Principles: 8, 9, 10.

Example #61 – *Arukh HaShulchan* §136:2

When members of the congregation are called to read from the Torah during the public Torah reading service, a *Kohen* is called to read first, then a Levite, and after that a series of ordinary Jews complete the day's prescribed Torah reading. The Mishnah explains that the Rabbis instituted this set ordering of the public Torah reading service in order to promote and preserve harmony between people. Rather than having those chosen to read earlier feel themselves superior to those who read later, or having those chosen to read later bear some animosity to those chosen to inaugurate the day's Torah reading, the Rabbis prescribed a fixed order for the reading based on biblical distinctions between Jews belonging to priestly, Levite, and all other family groups.[106] The Talmud further explains that among the ordinary Jews selected to read the Torah after the *Kohen* and Levite, first Torah scholars accepting positions of communal leadership should read, then scholars fit to serve in such roles, then the sons of communal leaders, then the lay leaders of the congregation, and then any others.[107]

Rabbi Epstein notes that the Talmudic order of preference for participating in the public Torah reading indicates that after the first two readings—first by a *Kohen* and next by a Levite—there is no inherent sanctity or significance to any one of the subsequent readings over any others. All of the opportunities to read from the Torah scroll are equal, and people are selected to read in an order of precedence that relates to the reader's relative importance within the community, but not to the worth of that particular position in the sequence of readings itself. Rabbi Epstein observes, however, that the common practice in his own time was for people to treat the third and sixth portions of the weekly public Torah readings as especially important, and to call upon respected scholars or leaders to read at those points in the service (Principle 8). While this practice departs from the Talmud's own prescriptions for precedence in Torah readings, Rabbi Epstein notes that attributing special importance to the sixth reading is grounded in a mystical teaching of the *Zohar* (Principle 7). Moreover, Rabbi Epstein justifies the current custom by arguing that the Talmudic ordering no longer applies because from a Talmudic vantage, contemporary scholars and communal leaders are not truly qualified to serve in these roles. In the absence of the kinds of rabbinic and leadership figures that the Talmud envisioned, the Talmud's preferences for the ordering of non-*Kohen* and non-Levite Torah readers no longer apply (Principle 9). Rabbi Epstein goes on to argue that while the Talmudic order of preference

---

106 Babylonian Talmud, Gittin 59a.
107 Babylonian Talmud, Gittin 60a.

no longer applies and the contemporary custom carries normative weight, congregational leaders should still work to dispel the mistaken notion that any particular opportunity to read from the Torah is inherently more honorable or significant than any other. This recommendation is grounded in the observed reality that believing that some readings are better than others leads to animosity and fights between people over who should be given the choicest position in the Torah reading sequence (Principle 6).
Methodological Principles: 6, 7, 8, 9.

Example #62 – Arukh HaShulchan §137:3

The Talmud relates that the prophet Ezra legislated that on Mondays and Thursdays, the public Torah reading service should constitute a total of three people reading no less than a total of ten verses from the Torah. This means, of course, that while two of the Torah readers will each read three verses, the third reader will have to read four verses in order to ensure that ten verses are read. The Talmud rules, however, that it does not matter which of the three readers reads four verses. Rabbi Epstein points out that there are good reasons why each of the three could reasonably read the extra verse: the first reader should read the extra verse because he is first; the third reader because in general Jewish law seeks to "add sanctity rather than diminish it"; and the middle reader might read the extra verse because the middle flame on the Temple *menorah* lamp was the most ritually important (Principle 1). Based on this, *Rashi* writes that "if there are enough extra verses in that week's Torah reading section, each of the three should read four verses."

Rabbi Epstein, however, questions *Rashi*'s recommendation. First, he argues that *Rashi*'s prescription is nonsensical on its own terms, since in fact, there are always additional verses in the weekly Torah reading that would permit each of the three weekday Torah readers to read four verses. Next, he wonders why, if *Rashi* is correct, did the Talmudic Rabbis not simply prescribe the recitation of four verses by each reader? Perhaps, Rabbi Epstein says, the Rabbis did not require each reader to read four verses because this would take more time and burden the congregation's time and patience (Principle 10); but, he says, if that were so, then why would *Rashi* recommend doing otherwise? In light of these questions, Rabbi Epstein offers an alternative explanation of *Rashi*'s position. He suggests that *Rashi* merely sought to rule against an inequitable distribution of verses among readers for those Torah portions where for reasons related to permissible divisions of Torah sections into recited portions, every reader must read more than three verses. In any case, Rabbi Epstein notes that the common practice is not to observe *Rashi*'s stricture and to instead have various readers read different numbers of verses, depending on the topical arrangement of verses in any given Torah portion (Principle 8).

Rabbi Epstein notes that the common practice of reading only a total of nine verses from the Torah portion known as *Parshat VaYelech* seems to violate the Talmud's rule that weekday Torah readings must comprise at least ten verses. He nevertheless seeks to justify this practice by suggesting that this is permitted as to *Parshat VaYelech* because that Torah portion is already quite short. Reading more than nine verses would actually require the weekday reading to extend to include nearly half the total portion, which is not appropriate because the entire portion will be read publicly on the Sabbath in any case (Principle 8).
Methodological Principles: 1, 8, 10.

Example #63 - *Arukh HaShulchan* §139:2

The *Arbah Turim* and the *Shulchan Arukh* both rule that one should practice the Torah portion two or three times before one reads that portion publicly as part of the congregational Torah reading service. This ruling is based on a Midrashic account of the Talmudic sage Rabbi Akiva refusing to read from the Torah when asked because he had not previously practiced the portion. The Midrash goes on to explain that Rabbi Akiva derived this practice from God, who, the scripture implies, recited the Torah four times before finally communicating it to the Jewish people.

Rabbi Epstein questions the basis for the *Shulchan Arukh* and *Arbah Turim*'s conclusion, however. He notes that by its own terms the Midrash indicates that one should review the Torah portion he will later read for the congregation four times—not the two or three times prescribed by the *Shulchan Arukh*. To justify this ruling, Rabbi Epstein notes that another Midrashic passage indicates that the Rabbis and Rav Acha disagreed about how many times God reviewed the Torah before communicating it to Moses (Principle 1). According to Rav Acha, God reviewed the Torah four times, while the Rabbis argue that God reviewed the Torah twice. The law follows the view of the Rabbis, and thus the *Shulchan Arukh* rules that one should practice the Torah reading two or three times before reading it during the congregational service. In truth, the Midrash referenced by the *Shulchan Arukh* merely reflects the rejected position of Rav Acha, and it is cited by the *Shulchan Arukh* only for the normative support provided by the account of Rabbi Akiva's refusal to read publicly from the Torah without having previously practiced the portion.

Ultimately, however, Rabbi Epstein rejects the *Shulchan Arukh*'s requirement that each Torah reader must practice the reading before publicly reciting his portion. Rabbi Epstein argues that this rule made sense in past eras where the custom was to have different individuals read designated Torah portions of the week's Torah reading. Now, however, congregations use a professional Torah reader to read the entire weekly Torah portion, and each individual "reader" honored with being called to participate in the Torah reading service merely reads along with the official reader in an undertone (Principle 8). Under these conditions, there is no need for each "reader" to practice the portion before the public Torah reading (Principle 9).
Methodological Principles: 1, 8, 9.

Example #64 - *Arukh HaShulchan* §142:3

Maimonides rules that if the one reading the Torah publicly errs in his reading—"even in the precise pronunciation of just one letter"—the reader must be made to repeat the reading correctly. The *Arbah Turim* disagrees with Maimonides's position, however. A Midrashic source teaches that if one mistakenly reads the word "Aaron" as "Haran," he nevertheless has fulfilled his Torah reading obligation. Based on this, the *Arbah Turim* rules that errors in the reading do not preclude the ritual validity of the public Torah reading, and the reader should therefore not be corrected so as to avoid causing him embarrassment.

Rabbi Epstein questions the *Arbah Turim*'s ruling, however, in light of the fact that the Jerusalem Talmud rules explicitly that when the reader makes mistakes, even minor ones and even in the traditionally recited translation of the previously read Torah verses, the reader must be corrected and repeat the incorrectly read text properly (Principle 1). Rabbi Epstein further notes that the context of the Midrashic source used to support the *Arbah Turim*'s more permissive position is discussing the recitation of Torah verses by a child or other ignorant person. Such people would be unlikely to be reading the Torah as part of the congregational service, and thus, it is unlikely that this source can be reasonably read as having anything to say about the permissibility of errors in the public Torah reading service (Principle 1). Finally, Rabbi Epstein adds that the *Arbah Turim*'s own use of this Midrashic source appears inapplicable to the issue of public Torah readings because, while the ignorant or juvenile reader under discussion might become embarrassed when corrected, a properly trained Torah reader is able to easily correct himself and would not be embarrassed by his mistakes being pointed out.

In light of these questions, Rabbi Epstein accepts Maimonides's position as the proper rule (Principle 2), but also offers an alternative explanation of the *Arbah Turim*'s ruling that reconciles it with Maimonides's opinion. It is inconceivable, Rabbi Epstein writes, that the *Arbah Turim* is suggesting that genuine substantive errors in the reading need not be corrected. Rather, what the *Arbah Turim* means is that slight errors in pronunciation do not need to be corrected; such mistakes are not truly errors in the reading, and thus one should not risk causing embarrassment by pointing them out and correcting them. Substantive errors, however, must be corrected, as prescribed by Maimonides.

Methodological Principles: 1, 2.

Example #65 – *Arukh HaShulchan* §146:1

The Talmud states that the verse "Those who abandon God are consumed" refers to people who leave the synagogue while the Torah scroll is open and being read.[108] While the Talmud there clearly permits a person to walk out of the synagogue in between each individual section of the Torah reading service, it leaves unresolved the question of whether a person may leave in between the reading of one verse and the next.[109]

The *Arukh HaShulchan* notes that while the Talmud itself leaves the question unresolved, in contemporary times it is certainly prohibited to leave the synagogue in between two verses. Rabbi Epstein explains that the Talmud's uncertainty on this matter stems from the fact that during Talmudic times, the Torah reader would pause in between each verse to allow another person, known as the *meturgaman*, or "translator," to loudly call out the Aramaic translation of the previous verse for the benefit of less educated members of the congregation who might not understand the Torah's original Hebrew. This pause for the translator creates a lull in the reading and thus offers a possible reason to permit a congregant to leave the room without being considered to be "abandoning God." Today, however, the Torah reader does not pause for a verse-by-verse translation of the text, and so a person may not leave the synagogue during the momentary pause between each verse (Principles 1 and 9).

Rabbi Epstein further rules that despite the Talmud's permission to leave the synagogue in between each section of the Torah reading, one should not do so unless it is truly necessary and otherwise unavoidable. Normally, Rabbi Epstein does not instruct others to undertake such supererogatory behavior that goes beyond the strict letter of the law. In this case, however, he seems to view such pious conduct as serving an important religious value based on the rabbinic aphorism, "Honoring the Torah is greater than honoring the Divine Presence." It is so important to give honor to the Torah itself, that one should take advantage of the Talmud's broad permission to leave the synagogue in between the readings of Torah portions only in very pressing circumstances (Principle 6).

Methodological Principles: 1, 6, 9.

---

108 Babylonian Talmud, Berakhot 8a.
109 *See* ibid.

Example #66 - *Arukh HaShulchan* §146:2

The prophet Nehemiah records that when Ezra opened the Torah scroll to read it before the Children of Israel, "the entire nation stood [silently] at the entranceway."[110] Based on this verse, the Talmud rules that one may not speak while the Torah scroll is open and being read as part of the public congregational Torah reading. This prohibition applies even to speaking about Torah study, and the Talmud therefore prohibits one from verbally responding to questions about matters of Jewish law during the congregational Torah reading service.[111]

Rabbi Moses Isserles limits the Talmud's proscription by ruling that "rulings of the moment"—that is, responses to questions of *halakhah* that demand an immediate answer and cannot wait—may be provided even while the Torah is being publicly read. Rabbi Epstein explains that the *Rema*'s position means that every situation must be considered on its own merits; the answers to some kinds of questions can wait, while other kinds of questions demand immediate answers. Rabbi Epstein rules that when a question is imminently relevant and demands an immediate answer—such as a question regarding a possible error found in the Torah scroll that is being read, or a question concerning a sick person—the question can and should be answered, even during the Torah reading (Principles 1 and 10). The *Arukh HaShulchan* confirms that this is indeed the common custom (Principle 8), and that *halakhic* authorities can and should answer such questions, while waiting to respond to less urgent matters until the end of the Torah portion currently being read.
Methodological Principles: 1, 8, 10.

Example #67 - *Arukh HaShulchan* §146:5

While the Talmud records a prohibition to speak even words of Torah during the public Torah reading,[112] another Talmudic passage records that Rav Sheshet would turn his head and study Torah on his own. Rav Sheshet justified his conduct merely by saying, "They do theirs and we will do ours."[113] Commentators offer a variety of different explanations for Rav Sheshet's disregard for the general prohibition on speaking during Torah readings, and these Talmudic readings became codified exceptions to the Talmudic rule. Thus, Rabbi Joseph Karo rules that one may study Torah during public Torah readings as long as (1) he does so quietly; (2) there is a quorum of ten men that are focused on the Torah reading; (3) he is a full-time professional Torah scholar; or (4) he turns to face away from the congregation, thereby indicating that one wishes to study on one's own rather than participate in the congregational Torah reading.[114]

Rabbi Epstein disagrees with the *Shulchan Arukh*'s formulation of the exceptions to the Talmud's prohibition on speaking during Torah readings. According to Rabbi Epstein, the various syntheses of the two Talmudic passages offered by the commentators must be read in concert with each other rather than as separate, alternative exceptions. Thus, he says, the correct Talmudic rule is that one may not speak or study during the public Torah reading unless one is a professional scholar who turns away from the congregation and studies quietly while there is a *minyan*, or quorum, left listening to the reading (Principle 1).

---

110 Nehemiah 8:5.
111 Babylonian Talmud, Sotah 39a.
112 *See* ibid.
113 Babylonian Talmud, Berakhot 8a.
114 *See* Shulchan Arukh, Orach Chaim 146:2.

Nevertheless, Rabbi Epstein rules that today, in practice it is absolutely prohibited to study during the public Torah reading. He explains that while it may be technically permitted to study if one conforms to all the conditions listed above, doing so in modern times will lead uneducated Jews to treat the public Torah reading laxly and without sufficient reverence (Principle 9). In light of this contemporary reality, and in order to avoid the religiously negative result of people disrespecting the Torah reading, Rabbi Epstein requires people to conduct themselves beyond the technical requirements of the Talmudic rule and not study privately during public Torah readings (Principle 6).
Methodological Principles: 1, 6, 9.

Example #68 – *Arukh HaShulchan* §149:1

The Talmud rules that the congregation may not leave the prayer service taking place in a synagogue until after the Torah scroll used for the public congregational Torah reading has been rolled up, covered, and returned to the ark.[115] While the *Shulchan Arukh* codifies this rule, the *Rema* qualifies the prohibition as applying only to instances where the entire congregation leaves the synagogue at once. Individuals, however, may leave one by one, even before the Torah scroll is returned to the ark.[116]

The *Arukh HaShulchan* rejects the *Rema*'s permissive view. Rabbi Epstein asserts that a correct understanding of the relevant Talmudic passage shows that the prohibition on leaving the synagogue prior to the Torah being returned to the ark applies to every individual member of the congregation, not merely to the congregation as a whole. This, Rabbi Epstein says, is implicit from the context of the Talmudic ruling, which involves several discussions about individuals' obligations as good members of a prayer congregation, and it is likewise consistent with *Rashi*'s explanation of that Talmudic passage (Principle 1).
Methodological Principles: 1.

Example #69 – *Arukh HaShulchan* §150:9

Maimonides rules that the *bimah*, the large lectern from which the Torah scroll is publicly read and public lectures in the synagogue are given, should be placed in the middle of the synagogue, and Rabbi Moses Isserles rules accordingly. Rabbi Epstein notes, however, that in his own time some agitators were seeking to alter this customary placement of the synagogue lectern and instead position the *bimah* to one side of the sanctuary. Rabbi Epstein takes strong issue with this because, as he writes, "what is right in God's eyes is to not alter our ancestral customs in this matter [of the organization and set up of the synagogue]" (Principle 8).
Methodological Principles: 8.

Example #70 – *Arukh HaShulchan* §151:5

The Talmud teaches that contemporary synagogues are holy places that reflect on a somewhat reduced level of the sanctity of the Temple in Jerusalem.[117] Consequently, one must conduct

---

115 Babylonian Talmud, Sotah 39b.
116 Rema *to* Shulchan Arukh, Orach Chaim 149:1.
117 *See* Babylonian Talmud, Megillah 29a.

themselves respectfully within a synagogue and may not engage in "lightheadedness." Both the *Arbah Turim* and *Shulchan Arukh* rule that the prohibition against lightheaded behavior within a synagogue includes engaging in "frivolous talk"—conversation not related to praying, studying Torah, or other appropriate religious activities.

    Despite this well-codified proscription, Rabbi Epstein observes that people are commonly lax about this issue and often speak about mundane matters in the synagogue following prayer services. Rabbi Epstein attempts to justify this practice by suggesting that perhaps such people follow the opinion of Nachmanides, who rules that synagogues only retain inherent sanctity while they are presently being used for sacerdotal purposes like prayer or Torah study. Based on this view, as soon as the prayer service ends, the synagogue's sanctity dissipates, and it may then be used for mundane purposes, including, for instance, "frivolous talk" (Principle 8). Notably, Rabbi Epstein elsewhere rejects Nachmanides's position in favor of the alternative theory suggested by Maimonides. According to Maimonides, synagogue buildings possess an inherent sanctity rather than the temporary sanctity that devolves while they are being used for sacral functions as Nachmanides suggests. Rabbi Epstein endorses Maimonides's position (Principle 3), especially since it is supported by a passage of the Jerusalem Talmud (Principle 1).[118] While Rabbi Epstein thus rejects Nachmanides's conception of the temporary sanctity of synagogues as a matter of normative *halakhah*, he nevertheless utilizes this position in an attempt to justify the common practice of engaging in "frivolous talk" following the conclusion of prayers (Principle 5).

    While Rabbi Epstein thus attempts to legitimize the common practice of engaging in frivolous speech in synagogues, he also strongly criticizes those who smoke in the synagogue—in his view, this is a serious breach of proper religious decorum (Principle 6).
Methodological Principles: 1, 3, 5, 6, 8.

Example #71 – *Arukh HaShulchan* §153:2

    While synagogues possess sanctity and may not be used for mundane purposes, a synagogue may be sold and then used for non-sacred functions because the synagogue's holiness devolves upon the money or other consideration provided in exchange for the transfer of the synagogue building. Given that the sale of a synagogue is only permitted due to its sanctity's being transferred to the medium of exchange—which must then only be used for sacred purposes—the Talmud records a dispute between Ravina and Rav Acha, two Talmudic sages, regarding whether a synagogue building may be gifted to later be used for non-sacred purposes in light of the fact that in the case of a gift, there is no purchase money to which the synagogue's holiness may devolve. According to one scholar, a synagogue may not be gifted because, in the absence of any valuable consideration offered in exchange for the synagogue building, the synagogue retains its sanctity and may only be used for holy purposes. Another Talmudic scholar argues, however, that a synagogue may be gifted, and that the building's sanctity is perforce transferred to whatever benefit the gifter received from giving the gift, since no one really gifts anything unless the gift provides them with some benefit.[119]

    Following the canon of Talmudic construction that "in a dispute between Ravina and Rav Acha, the law follows the more lenient view," post-Talmudic authorities universally adopt the view that a synagogue may indeed be gifted for mundane uses. Rabbi Epstein, however,

---

118 *See* Arukh HaShulchan 153:3-4.
119 *See* Babylonian Talmud, Megillah 26b.

questions this conclusion. Ultimately, he wonders, how the gifted synagogue's sanctity is actually removed from the building—where does it go? While in the case of a synagogue sale the building's sanctity devolves upon the medium of exchange (which then becomes sacred and must be used only for holy purposes), in the case of a gift there is no tangible medium of exchange or consideration to which the synagogue's holiness might be transferred.

Rabbi Epstein records three different rabbinic responses to this concern. According to Nachmanides, a synagogue may be gifted because in truth synagogues do not possess any inherent holiness. Instead, synagogues have the same sanctity as other objects used to perform religious obligations, which possess sanctity while being used for sacred purposes but not while not in use. Consequently, the sanctity of a synagogue need not be transferred at all; once gifted and no longer in use for religious purposes, the synagogue's sanctity dissipates, and the building may be used for mundane functions. Rabbi Nissim Gerdoni offers a different explanation and argues that the sanctity of synagogues is a function of rabbinic legislation, and the Rabbis prescribed that synagogues may be gifted without impinging upon their holiness. Maimonides provides a third explanation for the legal permissibility of gifting a synagogue. According to Maimonides, the Talmudic principle that "the synagogues of Babylonia are built conditionally" means that all synagogues are built with an implicit condition permitting the alienation of the synagogue's inherent sanctity in accordance with the legal terms provided by the Rabbis. Since the Rabbis permitted the gifting of a synagogue, this is one of the implicit conditions included in the construction of any synagogue building, and thus the dissolution of the synagogue's sanctity as a result of the gift poses no legal concerns.

Rabbi Epstein rules in accordance with Maimonides's position for several reasons. First, Rabbi Epstein notes that this seems to be the most obvious understanding of the relevant Talmudic discussion about the nature of synagogue sanctity (Principle 1). Rabbi Epstein adduces further support from a passage in the Jerusalem Talmud, which refers to designating a courtyard as a synagogue as "sanctifying it," which suggests that synagogue sanctity is inherent and tied to the implicit and explicit nature of the designation (Principle 1). Rabbi Epstein further argues that the Talmud's original statement that "the synagogues of Babylonia are built conditionally" is grounded in the Talmud's understanding that synagogues in the diaspora are built with the understanding that communal leaders may make decisions about how to use and, if necessary, to alienate communal resources, including synagogues. While these Talmudic sources are not absolutely dispositive, and while it might be reasonable to support the alternative views of either Nachmanides or Rabbi Nissim Gerondi, Rabbi Epstein ultimately defaults to the normativity of Maimonides's view as the normative legal standard (Principle 3).
Methodological Principles: 1, 3.

Example #72 – *Arukh HaShulchan* §153:15

The Talmud rules that, while it is ordinarily prohibited to sell a Torah scroll, one may sell a Torah scroll if the proceeds from the sale are needed for the seller to be able to study Torah or to get married.[120] Many authorities extend this rule to also permit selling a Torah scroll in order to pay for weddings for orphans. In all these cases, the holiness of the Torah scroll itself is subordinated to the financial support needed to fund Torah study or to build new families, since "of what use is a Torah scroll if there is no one to study it?"

---

120 *See* Babylonian Talmud, Megillah 27a.

Rabbi Epstein notes, however, that some later authorities disagree about whether the permission to sell a Torah scroll in order to help orphans get married extends only to male orphans or to both male and female orphans. Some authorities rule that Torah scrolls may only be sold to help male orphans get married, since only males are biblically obligated to marry and procreate. Rabbi Epstein disagrees with this position, however, and rules that Torah scrolls may be sold to help marry off both male and female orphans. This conclusion is based on Rabbi Epstein's own understanding of what he views as the relevant Talmudic sources (Principle 1). In a passage discussing default dowry amounts that communal charity administrators must provide when arranging for the marriage of indigent female orphans, the Talmud observes that charity fund administrators must prioritize the marriage of female orphans over male orphans because "unmarried women suffer greater embarrassment than unmarried men."[121] This comment indicates that the relative obligations of men and women to marry and procreate are not the only relevant concerns when it comes to helping orphans get married. The fact that the Talmud seriously values the social embarrassment suffered by orphaned women unable to marry indicates to Rabbi Epstein that Torah scrolls may be sold in order to provide for the marriage needs of both male and female orphans.

Methodological Principles: 1.

Example #73 - *Arukh HaShulchan* §153:22

The Talmud rules that one may not demolish an existing synagogue—even an old and dilapidated synagogue—until after having built another synagogue as a replacement for the building that is to be torn down. Based on this principle, Rabbi Epstein rules that when the Talmud permits the sale of a synagogue building, it does so with the implicit understanding that the synagogue may not be sold until after an alternative location for the synagogue has already been secured. However, this requirement may be satisfied so long as the first synagogue building is sold with the intent to use the proceeds to purchase a new building, and provided that there are no reasons to think that there will be difficulty in buying the new location in a timely manner (Principle 1).

Some authorities maintain that this restriction on the sale of a synagogue applies even in places where there are already a number of functioning synagogues, such that there is no actual concern that the sale of one synagogue, and the failure to immediately acquire a new building may result in a suspension of communal prayers. Rabbi Epstein strongly disagrees with this view, however. He argues that the Talmudic discussions of this issue offer no support for this counterintuitive rule. The reason why one may not demolish or sell a synagogue without having a replacement building already in place is due to the concern that doing so may force the cessation of synagogue services in that community. This concern does not apply, however, where there are already multiple functioning synagogues in town, and the temporary closure of one will not lead to an inability to hold congregational prayer services.

Methodological Principles: 1.

---

121 Babylonian Talmud, Ketubot 67b.

Example #74 – *Arukh HaShulchan* §154:1

The *Arbah Turim* and *Shulchan Arukh* rule that houses and courtyards that are occasionally used as prayer spaces do not have the status or sanctity of a regular synagogue, and thus, people do not need to observe the ordinary strictures attendant to synagogue sanctity—such as prohibitions on eating and drinking, discussing business matters, and using the space as a shelter from the weather—in those spaces.[122] This ruling is based on a Talmudic rule that although it was customary for people to gather and pray in the town squares on fast days, such places do not have the kind of sanctified status that normally attaches to synagogues.[123] According to the Talmud, the reason for this rule is that synagogue sanctity attaches only to regular and permanent prayer spaces; since prayers were not regularly held in the public square and the space was only occasionally used to host special prayer gatherings, the public square did not have the status and sanctity of a synagogue. Like the Talmud's public squares, private homes and courtyards are used as prayer spaces only occasionally and are not thereby endowed with synagogue sanctity. Rabbi Joseph Karo further rules that the same rule applies to rented homes or courtyards; even when used as prayer spaces, they are not accorded the *halakhic* status of synagogues.[124]

Rabbi Epstein however notes that, while a rented space does not have the full status of a synagogue, it is qualitatively different from the mundane status the Talmud assigns to public squares occasionally used for prayer gatherings. In the case of public squares, the absence of synagogue sanctity is a consequence of those spaces not being synagogues at all but rather being convenient locations for ad hoc gatherings for large groups of people. Synagogues located in rented properties, by contrast, are considered impermanent not because they are infrequently used for prayer, but because they remain subject to the willingness of the property owner to continue to renew the renter's lease (Principle 1). This difference is important, Rabbi Epstein argues, because it means that while a rented space does not have the full *halakhic* status of a synagogue, such spaces must still be treated with respect while they are used to house a regular and permanent (for the duration of the current rental term, at least) prayer gathering (Principle 6). Rabbi Epstein further extends this notion that spaces regularly used for prayer should be treated with respect, even when they do not have the technical *halakhic* status of a synagogue, by ruling that it is properly pious conduct to ensure that residential apartments built above technically impermanent prayer spaces should be kept clean in a manner that respects the informal and temporary holiness of a space regularly used for prayer (Principle 6).
Methodological Principles: 1, 6.

Example #75 – *Arukh HaShulchan* §154:11

The Talmud rules that items designated for sanctified ritual uses may not be used for mundane purposes and must therefore be placed in a *genizah*, or hidden ritual storage, once their ritual usefulness has passed.[125] Exempted from this restriction are items that were only conditionally designated for ritual uses. Thus, for example, a cloth used to cover the table upon which the Torah scroll is placed when being read is considered designated for ritual use, and it may not also be used as an ordinary mealtime tablecloth. However, if the cloth was designated

---

122 Arbah Turim, Orach Chaim 154:1; Shulchan Arukh, Orach Chaim 154:1.
123 Babylonian Talmud, Megillah 26a.
124 Shulchan Arukh, Orach Chaim 154:2.
125 Babylonian Talmud, Megillah 26b.

for ritual use on condition that it could also be used for mundane purposes, the cloth could be used interchangeably as both a mealtime tablecloth and a ritual table covering for public Torah reading services.[126]

While the Talmud seemingly requires that conditions on the designation of items for ritual use must be explicit, Rabbi Moses Isserles rules that one may use certain synagogue items for mundane purposes even without having made any explicit conditions to that effect at the time that the items were initially designated for holy uses. Rabbi Isserles explains that, since it is practically very difficult to ensure that such items are not used for any mundane purposes, it is as if "the court initially stipulated conditions on their sanctified use."[127] The *Rema*'s ruling is based on an earlier ruling by the *Terumat HaDeshen* who sought to justify what was in his own time the common practice of people utilizing synagogue accoutrements for mundane purposes, such as by using the table ordinarily used for public Torah readings to hold prayer books or by placing invalid Torah scrolls in the ark.

The *Arukh HaShulchan* notes that it is difficult to justify the view that the designation of all synagogue items includes an implicit condition permitting their use for mundane purposes in light of the Talmud's apparent failure to recognize the possibility and legal efficacy of such presumptively implicit conditions. Indeed, as Rabbi Epstein points out, even the *Terumat HaDeshen* himself finds the idea suspect and only suggests the existence of such a condition as a post hoc justification for the existing practice of using synagogue items for mundane purposes (Principle 1).

Despite his reservations about the Talmudic basis for the *Rema*'s implicit conditioning of the use of ritual objects, Rabbi Epstein ultimately accepts this approach in order to justify the common practice of using synagogue accoutrements for mundane purposes—practices that included using the ark curtains as marriage canopies and placing the Torah scrolls on the *bimah* and a candle in the ark on Hoshana Rabbah. While some authorities strongly criticized such practices as violations of the rule prohibiting the use of sanctified items for mundane purposes, Rabbi Epstein justifies these practices by relying on the implicit condition idea proposed by the *Terumat HaDeshen* and the *Rema* (Principle 8). Bound up in Rabbi Epstein's support for this view is the *Rema*'s additional consideration that, since it is practically very difficult to ensure that such items are not used for any mundane purposes, it is as if "the court initially stipulated conditions on their sanctified use" (Principle 10).[128]

Rabbi Epstein further supports the existence of implicit conditions permitting the use of synagogue items for mundane purposes by referencing a passage in the Jerusalem Talmud. The Jerusalem Talmud records that Rav Yirmiyah observed people placing mundane items in the synagogue ark. When he asked Rav Ami about this practice, the latter permitted it, reasoning that "they initially stipulated this about these items."[129] Rabbi Epstein argues that Rav Ami could not have known whether the original builders of the synagogue ark had actually stipulated to permit use of the ark for mundane purposes, and he therefore infers that Rav Ami maintained that one could reasonably infer that such an implicit condition was included in the original construction of the synagogue. Rabbi Epstein thus argues that this passage supports the idea that a stipulation permitting mundane uses can be assumed even in the absence of an explicit condition (Principle 1).
Methodological Principles: 1, 8, 10.

---

126 *See* Shulchan Arukh, Orach Chaim 154:8.
127 Rema *to* Shulchan Arukh, Orach Chaim 154:8.
128 Ibid.
129 Jerusalem Talmud, Megillah 3:1.

Example #76 – *Arukh HaShulchan* §158:1-2

The Talmud records that the Rabbis legislated a ritual obligation to wash one's hands before eating bread.[130] Elsewhere, the Talmud explains that this rabbinic duty was imposed in response to concerns related to the proper handling of foods consecrated to the Temple in Jerusalem, which could only be eaten or handled by the priests after first washing their hands to remove any ritual impurities.[131] Rabbi Mordechai Yaffe further explains that the Rabbis were concerned that unless people were in the regular habit of washing their hands before eating bread on a regular basis, they would eventually make the error of handling sanctified bread without first washing their hands.[132] Rabbi Yaffeh writes that while the laws regarding sanctified food no longer apply following the destruction of the Temple in 70 CE, the requirement of ritual handwashing before eating bread remains in force. This is because Jews eagerly anticipate the rebuilding of the Temple, at which point the rules governing sanctified foods will once again become practical, and it is therefore important that Jews remain in the habit of washing their hands before eating bread.

Rabbi Epstein accepts Rabbi Yaffe's explanation, but goes on to give an additional, novel reason for the rabbinic obligation to wash before eating bread (Principle 1). He begins by noting that the Talmud understands the biblical command to "sanctify yourselves"[133] as referring to ritual handwashing before eating bread. [134] Further, the Talmud also states that anyone who eats bread without drying their hands (after ritual handwashing) is viewed as if they had eaten bread that is ritually impure.[135] The prominent medieval commentator *Rashi* writes that this is because undried hands remain dirty, and being dirty is synonymous with being ritually impure. Rabbi Epstein expands upon this idea and suggests that if being dirty is akin to being impure, then being clean is akin to being holy, "for cleanliness brings to purity which brings to asceticism and holiness." Consequently, one must wash before eating bread not merely to preserve the technical demands of Temple-era ritual purity laws, but also as a more contemporaneously relevant means of sanctifying mundane actions like eating (Principle 1).

It is important to note that unlike Rabbi Yaffe's explanation, which is ultimately tied to the centuries-dormant rituals of Temple practice, Rabbi Epstein provides a rationale grounded in the development of personal piety, which is of more contemporary relevance in his own time and place (Principle 9).

Methodological Principles: 1, 9.

Example #77 – *Arukh HaShulchan* §158:3

While the Rabbis instituted the practice of washing one's hands before eating bread, the *Shulchan Arukh* rules that this requirement does not apply to all kinds of bread. According to Rabbi Karo, one must only wash one's hands prior to eating bread upon which one will recite the usual blessing recited before eating bread, *hamotzi lechem min haaretz* ("who brings forth bread from the earth"). Bread-like products upon which one would recite the blessing of *boreh*

---

130 Babylonian Talmud, Chagigah 17b.
131 Babylonian Talmud, Chullin 106a.
132 Levush Malkhut, Orach Chaim 158:1.
133 Leviticus 20:7.
134 Babylonian Talmud, Berakhot 53b.
135 Babylonian Talmud, Sotah 4b.

minei mezonot ("who creates kinds of sustenance") rather than *hamotzi*, however, may be eaten even without one's having washed his or her hands, provided that it is not being eaten as a formal meal.[136]

The *Arukh HaShulchan* disagrees with Rabbi Karo's ruling, however (Principle 1). Instead of distinguishing between breads upon which one recites either the *hamotzi* or *mezonot* blessings, Rabbi Epstein argues, following Maimonides's view on the matter, that the correct distinction to be drawn between having and not having to wash one's hands before eating bread is between bread eaten as a set meal and bread eaten merely as a snack (Principle 3). Rabbi Epstein rules that, when one eats bread as a formal meal, one must wash one's hands beforehand even if one would not recite the *hamotzi* blessing on this bread-like food.

Methodological Principles: 1, 3.

Example #78 – *Arukh HaShulchan* §158:5

The Talmud rules that in addition to the requirement of ritual handwashing before eating bread, one must also wash before eating other kinds of foods that have been dipped in liquid.[137] Rabbi Epstein notes that *halakhic* authorities are split as to the reason for this rule. According to some scholars, this law was enacted for the same reason as the obligation to wash before eating bread—out of concern for the sanctified foods that were donated to the Temple priests and which could only be eaten with ritually pure hands. Rabbi Epstein points out, however, that if this were correct, the *halakhah* should prescribe the recitation of a blessing when washing one's hands before eating foods dipped in liquid, just as a blessing is prescribed for washing before eating bread. The Talmud, however, requires no such blessing. By contrast, *Tosafot* and others argue that the duty to wash before eating foods dipped in liquids was legislated in order to prevent the liquid—rather than the food—from contracting ritual impurity from one's unwashed hands. Rabbi Epstein notes that according to this second explanation, one would not need to recite a blessing upon washing one's hands because, unlike washing before eating bread, this washing is wholly unconnected to the biblical commandment to "sanctify yourselves" (Principle 1). Moreover, Rabbi Epstein argues, according to the view of *Tosafot*, one need not observe this law in the post-Temple era. While Jews in Talmudic times customarily ate only in a state of ritual purity—and therefore washed before eating foods dipped in liquid to avoid transferring the ritual purity of their hands to the food—Jews in later times are not accustomed to scrupulously observing these ritual purity laws; thus washing before eating foods dipped in liquids is no longer necessary (Principles 8 and 9).

Rabbi Epstein rules that in light of the fact that very many authorities have endorsed the latter of the two approaches to this issue, there is no strict obligation to wash before eating foods dipped in liquid (Principle 2), though people may—and in fact sometimes do—wash as a supererogatory religious observance (Principle 6). Still, he writes that even those who do choose to act strictly in this matter and wash before eating foods dipped in liquid as a supererogatory measure should do so without reciting any blessing. This is because doubts regarding whether a blessing should be recited in a given case are almost always resolved by not reciting the blessing (Principle 4), and because in his own time and place it was virtually unheard of for anyone to actually recite a blessing when washing their hands before eating foods dipped in liquid (Principle 8).

Methodological Principles: 1, 2, 4, 6, 8, 9.

---

136 Shulchan Arukh, Orach Chaim 158:1.
137 Babylonian Talmud, Pesachim 115a.

Example #79 – *Arukh HaShulchan* §159:25

The Talmud rules that ritual handwashing must be performed using a vessel, which must be used to pour the water contained therein onto one's hands.[138] Based on this Talmudic standard, Rabbi Epstein rules that one cannot fulfill this ritual washing obligation by having water cupped in the palms of someone else's hands poured over one's own hands. Moreover, Rabbi Epstein rules that even pouring water from a proper vessel into one's cupped palm and then pouring that water onto one's other hand does not satisfy the need to perform ritual handwashing using a vessel (Principle 1). Rabbi Epstein notes, however, that some authorities have reached a contrary conclusion and have ruled that, since the water came from a vessel before it was poured into one's cupped palm and subsequently poured over one's hand, such washing does satisfy ritual requirements. Rabbi Epstein thinks that his own ruling on this matter is analytically correct and rejects the contrary view that permits this manner of ritual handwashing. Still, he acknowledges that the common practice is to rely on the contrary view expressed by his interlocutors, and therefore he urges people to adopt his more stringent position while also accepting the post hoc acceptability of following the more lenient view (Principles 6, 7, and 8).
Methodological Principles: 1, 6, 7, 8.

Example #80 – *Arukh HaShulchan* §160:8

Codifying a number of disparate Mishnaic rules, Maimonides rules that four kinds of water may not be used for ritual handwashing, including water that has previously been used for some form of *melakhah*, or "work."[139] Rabbinic authorities explain, for instance, that water that was used to cool down another hot liquid cannot subsequently be used for ritual handwashing because it was previously used for some form of labor.[140] Commenting on this ruling, Rabbi Epstein wonders at the common practice of people in his own time who would routinely place containers of food or drink into barrels of water in order to keep the contents of those containers cool in warm weather and then subsequently use the water from those barrels for ritual handwashing. While this practice appears to cut against the normative rule that water previously used to perform some kind of work cannot later be used for ritual washing, Rabbi Epstein attempts to justify the custom by suggesting that those who use such water for ritual handwashing follow the opinion of Rabbi Elijah Shapiro (Principle 8). According to Rabbi Shapiro, water is not considered to have been used to perform work unless it was used to effect a change of some kind. Thus, while water used to cool down something hot—such as the water a blacksmith uses to cool hot metal—cannot be used for ritual washing, water previously used to prevent already cool food from becoming too hot has not been used for "work" and may be used for ritual handwashing.[141] While Rabbi Shapiro's view is not widely accepted and seems to cut against the more common rabbinic understanding of Maimonides's rules governing the use of water for ritual handwashing, Rabbi Epstein nevertheless relies on Rabbi Shapiro's view to help explain the common practice (Principle 5).
Methodological Principles: 5, 8.

---

138 *See* Mishnah, Yadayim 1:2.
139 *See* Mishnah, Yadayim 1:3; Mishneh Torah, Hilkhot Berakhot 6:7.
140 Tosafot Rosh, Chullin 107a.
141 Eliyahu Rabbah 160:6.

Example #81 – *Arukh HaShulchan* §160:10

The Mishnah rules that one may not perform the ritual mixing of the ashes of a *Parah Adumah*, a red heifer,[142] with water from which an animal previously drank in order to effect ritual purification.[143] Some authorities draw an analogy between the red heifer purification procedure and ritual handwashing; they therefore rule that one may not use water from which a chicken or dog previously drank for ritual handwashing because animals drink by dipping their open mouths into the water, leaving bits of saliva in the water as a result. This dirties the water, rendering it unfit for ritual use in the same manner as water previously used for some kind of labor.

The *Arukh HaShulchan*, however, disagrees with this ruling. First, Rabbi Epstein argues that the Mishnaic restriction against using water from which animals drank for the red heifer ritual is premised not on a concern for the fact that the water was used for some form of labor, but on the understanding that such water does not meet the biblical requirement that water used for the red heifer ritual must be "running water, placed in a vessel."[144] Since this technical requirement does not apply to ritual handwashing, it is improper to analogize the conditions that invalidate red heifer water to those that invalidate water used for ritual handwashing. Moreover, Rabbi Epstein points out, even if the saliva left by animals drinking from the water does raise concerns that the water is left unfit for handwashing, any drops of animal saliva should be considered nullified as they become mixed with the water in accordance with the standard rules governing the nullification of substances in mixtures. Based on this analysis of the issue, Rabbi Epstein rules that water from which animals previously drank may be used for ritual handwashing (Principle 1). Nevertheless, the *Arukh HaShulchan* does recommend—though he does not require—that one should avoid performing ritual handwashing using water from which a dog or pig previously drank; these animals, Rabbi Epstein argues, are typically especially dirty and leave the water dirty as well after drinking, rendering it less than ideally proper for ritual use (Principle 6). Methodological Principles: 1, 6.

Example #82 – *Arukh HaShulchan* §161:7-8

There is a disagreement among medieval rabbinic authorities about which parts of the hand must be washed in order to fulfill the ritual handwashing obligation. According to the *Raabad* and the *Rosh*, one must at a minimum wash one's fingers up to the "third joint," which commentators understand to mean up to one's knuckles.[145] Maimonides rules similarly, prescribing that ritual handwashing must cover the entirety of the fingers, but no more.[146] Rabbi Isaac Alfasi disagrees, however, and rules that one must wash one's whole hand up to the wrist.

Rabbi Epstein rules that the law follows the more lenient view offered by Maimonides (Principle 3), especially because this position is further supported by the *Zohar*, which teaches that when performing ritual handwashing, one must be careful to wash "fourteen joints" on each hand—the two joints on the thumb and the three joints on each of the other four fingers (Principle 7). While the *halakhah* does not require one to wash the entire hand, Rabbi Epstein

---

142 *See* Numbers 19:17-19.
143 Mishnah, Parah 9:3.
144 Numbers 19:17.
145 *See* Tosafot Rosh, Chullin 106b.
146 Mishneh Torah, Hilkhot Berakhot 6:4.

notes that the widespread custom is to wash the whole hand in accordance with Rabbi Alfasi's view, and he therefore advises people to follow this practice (Principle 8). Still, since in his opinion the strict letter of the law requires washing only one's fingers, Rabbi Epstein notes that one need not be careful to wash one's entire hand in accordance with the custom in situations where doing so would be difficult or impracticable (Principles 6 and 10).
Methodological Principles: 3, 6, 7, 8, 10.

Example #83 – *Arukh HaShulchan* §164:5

Rabbinic authorities list several instances in which one would need to repeat the obligatory pre-meal ritual handwashing during the course of a meal while also repeating the appropriate blessing of *al netilat yadayim* ("on the cleaning of hands"). Scholars agree, for instance, that if one relieved oneself during a meal, they must perform the prescribed ritual handwashing and recite the appropriate blessing before continuing the meal. Similarly, Rabbi Joseph Karo rules that if one touched a part of the body that is typically kept covered or which is otherwise unclean, one must wash and repeat the blessing before resuming their meal.[147] The *Magen Avraham*, an important authority and commentator on the *Shulchan Arukh*, rules that this last rule applies even where one touched a dirty part of the body while still chewing a piece of bread—one must not swallow the food in one's mouth until after having washed one's hands and recited the proper blessing.[148] Rabbi Epstein, however, rejects this rule, calling it an "unnecessary stringency" (Principles 1 and 6). Rabbi Epstein supports his view by referencing a Mishnah, which teaches that one who is in the middle of eating sanctified *terumah* food designated for consumption by only priests and their families but discovers that their personal status renders them prohibited from eating *terumah* may swallow the food that is already in their mouth (Principle 1).[149]
Methodological Principles: 1, 6.

Example #84 – *Arukh HaShulchan* §167:6

Based on a discussion in the Talmud, the *Arukh HaShulchan* rules that after reciting the blessing of *hamotzi lechem min haaretz* over bread, one should cut an average-sized piece from the loaf; one should not, however, cut a very small piece, lest one appear stingy, nor a very large piece, lest one appear gluttonous. This novel ruling, which is not recorded by earlier authorities, is based directly on Rabbi Epstein's understanding of the normativity of a Talmudic teaching (Principle 1).[150] Rabbi Epstein notes, however, that this ruling applies only to breaking bread on weekdays; on the Sabbath, it is best to cut a piece of bread that is large enough to serve for the entire Sabbath meal. Likewise, even on a weekday, one who is reciting the *hamotzi* blessing on behalf of others eating together at the same table should cut a large enough piece from the loaf so that they may then apportion that piece to all the other people at the table. Rabbi Epstein notes that the common practice departs from this ideal method and that instead of portioning pieces of bread to the other diners from the same piece that the one reciting the *hamotzi* blessing cuts for himself, people typically cut a smaller piece for their own consumption and then apportion the rest of the bread to the other diners at the table (Principle 8). Rabbi Epstein seeks to justify

---

147 Shulchan Arukh, Orach Chaim 164:2.
148 *See* Magen Avraham *to* Shulchan Arukh, Orach Chaim 164:2, 7.
149 Mishnah, Trumot 8:2.
150 Babylonian Talmud, Berakhot 39b.

this departure from what he sees as the correct legal norm by pointing out that typical loaves of bread in his own time were much larger than those used in Talmudic times (Principle 9) and that this makes it impracticable to initially cut a piece of bread from the loaf large enough to serve all the diners at the table (Principle 10). When using a smaller loaf, however, Rabbi Epstein says one should ideally follow the normative Talmudic practice, though doing so is not strictly required given the established custom (Principle 6).

Methodological Principles: 1, 6, 8, 9, 10.

Example #85 – *Arukh HaShulchan* §170:2

The Babylonian Talmud states that one may not speak while eating for fear that food could become lodged in the windpipe instead of going down the esophagus.[151] Rabbi Epstein notes that the common custom seems to be to speak freely during meals in apparent disregard for this clear Talmudic rule, and he therefore seeks to justify the common practice (Principle 8). First, Rabbi Epstein argues that the Talmudic rule applied only in Talmudic times when people typically ate their meals while reclining on couches, when speaking while eating did indeed pose a reasonable risk of choking. Modern meals, however, are eaten sitting upright in chairs. This obviates the Talmud's underlying concern and therefore renders speaking during a meal permitted (Principle 9). Rabbi Epstein further suggests that a careful read of the Talmudic discussion itself provides some justification for the common practice (Principle 1). The Talmudic ban on speaking during meals is offered in response to a request made by a diner to hear words of Torah. A discussion of Torah topics, Rabbi Epstein suggests, is likely to be lengthy and perhaps even contentious, and it is that kind of deep discussion that the Talmud seeks to prohibit out of concern for choking. Making brief comments about mundane matters, however, may well fall outside the Talmud's concern and therefore be perfectly permissible. Indeed, Rabbi Epstein notes, that is in fact the common practice—people leave longer, involved discussion for the time between courses while limiting their speech during those points in the meal that they are actually eating.

Ultimately, however, Rabbi Epstein rejects the possibility that the Talmud only seeks to prohibit long, involved discussions during a meal because the Jerusalem Talmud teaches that not even one word should be spoken while eating (Principle 1).[152] Rabbi Epstein therefore invokes the rabbinic aphorism, "God protects the simple,"[153] as if to say that there is no good justification for speaking during a meal, but since so many people do so, God shields them from the danger of choking.

Methodological Principles: 1, 8, 9.

Example #86 – *Arukh HaShulchan* §180:1

The Talmud records that it was customary to remove the tables from before all the diners prior to the recitation of the *Birkhat HaMazon*, or Grace after Meals blessing, with the exception of the person leading the recital of the blessing, whose table would be left in front of him.[154] Rabbi Epstein rules, however, that in his own time one should avoid removing the tablecloth

---

151 Babylonian Talmud, Taanit 5b.
152 Jerusalem Talmud, Berakhot 6:6.
153 Psalms 116:6. *See also* Babylonian Talmud, Shabbat 129a.
154 Babylonian Talmud, Berakhot 42a.

or clearing the table until after reciting the *Birkhat HaMazon*. He supports this ruling by arguing that modern dining habits differ from Talmudic ones, which justifies this change in the law (Principle 9). He explains that during the times of the Talmud, each diner ate at their own small table; the tables were removed and the area was cleaned prior to the recitation of the *Birkhat HaMazon* in order to ensure that leftover food did not become wet and disgusting when individual diners washed their hands following the meal (before reciting the *Birkhat HaMazon*). While this concern justified removing the tables and food from in front of the diners, for several different reasons the table and food were left sitting before the diner who would lead the recitation of the *Birkhat HaMazon* (Principle 1). The Talmud teaches, for instance, that blessings only attach to something extant, and so the presence of the leftover food would provide something tangible on which the blessings requested from God in the *Birkhat HaMazon* might attach. Moreover, the presence of the food would help remind the diners to focus on thanking God for providing the meal they just enjoyed. Finally, the *Zohar* teaches that for mystical reasons one may not recite the *Birkhat HaMazon* over an empty table (Principle 7). For these reasons, the Talmudic practice was to remove all the personal dining tables prior to reciting the *Birkhat HaMazon*—except for the table being used by the person who would lead the blessing.[155] Modern dining practices depart substantially from the Talmudic custom, however, as today all diners eat together at the same large table and also wash their hands following the meal using some kind of basin (Principle 8). This obviates the Talmud's concern for washing water ruining food left on the table, and so, Rabbi Epstein argues, the proper practice should default to the importance of keeping food on the table at the time that the *Birkhat HaMazon* is recited for the reasons discussed above (Principle 9).

While Rabbi Epstein thus considers the original Talmudic rule requiring the removal of food prior to reciting the *Birkhat HaMazon* no longer normative, he approvingly notes that some have the custom specifically to place some of the leftover bread from the meal in front of the person who will lead the recitation of the *Birkhat HaMazon* (Principle 8), since doing so imitates and maintains continuity with the older Talmudic practice (Principle 6).

Methodological Principles: 1, 6, 7, 8, 9.

Example #87 – *Arukh HaShulchan* §181:5

The Talmud teaches that one is obligated to wash their hands following a meal before reciting the *Birkhat HaMazon*. While the Talmud connects this obligation to the biblical command "And you will be sanctified,"[156] it also provides a rational explanation for the practice. The Talmud reasons that some salt used at meals may be "salt of Sodom," which can blind a person if they rub their eyes while the salt is on their hands. It is therefore dangerous to not wash one's hands after eating, when one may have touched salt of Sodom.[157]

Tosafot and the *Arbah Turim* focus on the Talmud's latter, rational explanation for the obligation to wash after a meal, and they therefore rule that in their own times one need not follow this Talmudic prescription because salt of Sodom is exceedingly uncommon. They argue that since the underlying risk of harm the law sought to prevent no longer exists, the rule itself is no longer binding. The *Rosh* disagrees with this view, however. According to the *Rosh*, the Talmud's obsolete safety reason for requiring post-meal handwashing is only a supplementary justification

---

155 *See* Arukh HaShulchan, Orach Chaim 180:3-4.
156 Leviticus 20:7.
157 *See* Babylonian Talmud, Chullin 105a.

for the rule; the primary reason for this obligation is as a fulfillment of the biblical command to "become sanctified," and the duty therefore still remains in effect.[158]

Rabbi Epstein rules that washing after meals is obligatory even today. Importantly, Rabbi Epstein's ruling that handwashing remains obligatory is not a result of his concluding that the *Rosh*'s view—that the Talmudic prescription is a consequence of the biblical command to "be sanctified"—is in fact correct. On the contrary, Rabbi Epstein concludes that the Talmudic discussion of the issue indicates that the *Rosh*'s understanding of the issue is mistaken. Rabbi Epstein points out that if the post-meal handwashing obligation was indeed rooted in the fulfillment of this biblical command, authorities would agree that one should recite a blessing upon washing one's hands after eating, just as a blessing is prescribed for washing one's hands before a meal in observance of a similar biblical command to "sanctify yourselves." The general consensus of rabbinic opinion, however, rejects the recitation of a blessing over post-meal handwashing (Principle 2), which indicates that the fulfillment of the biblical command, "you will be sanctified" is not the main reason for the Talmud's handwashing obligation (Principle 1). Rabbi Epstein thus rejects the *Rosh*'s view on the matter and instead endorses the opinion of *Tosafot*—that the primary reason for the Talmud's prescribed handwashing obligation is to avoid the dangers of residue from salt of Sodom that might remain on one's hands following a meal—especially because this understanding of the Talmudic sources is also adopted by Maimonides (Principle 3). Rabbi Epstein argues, however, that while in principle the *Tosafot* are correct that the Talmudic obligation would be obviated if there were no genuine concerns about possible contact with salt of Sodom (Principle 9), in fact, there is reason to be concerned about coming into contact with salt of Sodom even today in any place where sea salt is used in cooking. Since the reason for the Talmudic obligation is still relevant, the handwashing obligation remains in force. Indeed, Rabbi Epstein goes further and argues that even the *Tosafot* themselves really held that one must wash one's hands after eating, and that their arguments regarding the contemporary irrelevance of the reason for the Talmudic obligation were merely an attempt to provide a *post facto* justification for widespread popular disregard of the practice (Principle 8). Rabbi Epstein further supports his conclusion—that even following the views of the *Tosafot* and Maimonides, handwashing after meals remains contemporarily obligatory—by noting that the *Zohar* and kabbalists all strongly endorse this practice (Principle 7).

Methodological Principles: 1, 2, 3, 7, 8, 9.

Example #88 – *Arukh HaShulchan* §185:1

The Babylonian Talmud rules that the *Birkhat HaMazon* need not be recited only in Hebrew, and may instead be said "in any language in which you wish to recite the blessing".[159] The *Arbah Turim* and *Shulchan Arukh* both codify this Talmudic rule and thus give blanket permission for people to recite the *Birkhat HaMazon* in any language they wish.[160]

The *Arukh HaShulchan* rejects this broad permission to say the *Birkhat HaMazon* in any language, however. Instead, Rabbi Epstein rules that one may only recite this blessing in a language other than Hebrew if one does not understand Hebrew. Rabbi Epstein supports this conclusion with a passage in the Jerusalem Talmud that parallels the Babylonian Talmud's discussion of this issue. There, the Jerusalem Talmud states explicitly that the *Birkhat HaMazon* may be

---

158 *See* Arukh HaShulchan, Orach Chaim 181:3.
159 Babylonian Talmud, Sotah 33a.
160 Arbah Turim, Orach Chaim 185; Shulchan Arukh, Orach Chaim 185:1.

recited in any language "so that the one reciting the blessing will know whom they are blessing." Similarly, the same passage teaches that the *Amidah* prayer may be recited in any language "so that one will know how to ask God for their needs."[161] Rabbi Epstein argues that this passage suggests that the Talmudic permission to pray in a language other than Hebrew is merely to ensure that the individual praying will understand the content of the prayers. It follows from this, then, that if one understands the original Hebrew liturgy, and if the need to comprehend the prayers is thus satisfied, one may not utilize another language instead of the rabbinically composed Hebrew text. This understanding is supported, Rabbi Epstein says, by another ruling of the Jerusalem Talmud, which teaches that while one may fulfill the obligation to read the book of Esther on the holiday of Purim by reading the text in any language one understands, if one understands the original Hebrew, one cannot fulfill their obligation by reading the book in another language. Rabbi Epstein argues that the aforementioned discussion of this issue in the Babylonian Talmud must be read in light of the non-contradictory passage in the Jerusalem Talmud. Thus, when the Babylonian Talmud rules that one may recite the *Birkhat HaMazon* in any language that one understands, it should be understood to mean that one may do so only when one cannot comprehend the originally composed Hebrew text of the blessing. Thus, Rabbi Epstein rules that one may only recite the *Birkhat HaMazon* in another language if one does not understand the original Hebrew (Principle 1).

Methodological Principles: 1.

Example #89 – *Arukh HaShulchan* §185:3

Rabbi Epstein takes strong issue with the Reform practice of praying and reciting the *Birkhat HaMazon* blessing in the vernacular rather than in Hebrew. He acknowledges that the Reform position relies on a simple reading of a Mishnah, which teaches that the *Birkhat HaMazon*, the *Amidah*, the *Shema*, and several other ritual and liturgical formulations "may be recited in any language."[162] Rabbi Epstein rejects this Reform position, first because he notes that the great scholars of the previous generation reached a consensus rejecting this practice (Principle 2). Moreover, Rabbi Epstein notes that the Reformers badly misunderstood the Mishnah's ruling. In addition to the correct understanding of the Mishnah's rule hinging on the clarifying discussion in the Jerusalem Talmud discussed earlier,[163] Rabbi Epstein notes that the Talmudic discussion of this Mishnah suggests that the Mishnah's permission to recite the *Birkhat HaMazon* in a language other than Hebrew is actually much narrower than the Reform position admits. While the Mishnah itself lists a number of prayers and recitations that "may be said in any language," the following paragraph of the Mishnah includes a list of prayers and recitations that may only be said in Hebrew. Commenting on the Mishnah, the Talmud questions why the prayers listed in the first Mishnah may be said in other languages while those listed in the second Mishnah may not, and he goes on to present a series of biblical verses that prove both that the various recitals listed in the first Mishnah may be recited in any language and also that those listed in the second Mishnah may only be said in Hebrew.[164]

Rabbi Epstein notes that the Talmud's approach—establishing on the basis of biblical proofs that both some prayers must be said in Hebrew and that others may be recited in

---

161 Jerusalem Talmud, Sotah 7:1.
162 Mishnah, Sotah 7:1.
163 *See supra* Example #86.
164 *See* Babylonian Talmud, Sotah 32b-33a.

any language—is logically problematic. If the default rational assumption is that all prayers must be said only in Hebrew, then the Talmud need only prove that those others may be said in other languages; and if the rational default is that prayers may be said in any language, the Talmud only should have demonstrated that some of the prayers must be said only in Hebrew. Rabbi Epstein explains that in truth the default assumption is that all ritual recitals must be said only in Hebrew based on the mystical idea that the Hebrew language is especially sacred, since it was used to create the world and is in some sense the blueprint of the universe (Principle 7). Based on this, Rabbi Epstein says, even those that do not understand Hebrew should have to recite all prayers only in this sanctified language, and the Talmud thus deploys several biblical verses to show that those who do not understand Hebrew can pray at least some prayers in other languages. At the same time, since these scriptural sources demonstrate that those that do not understand Hebrew can recite some prayers in other languages, the Talmud needs to also prove that certain other prayers can only be said in Hebrew, even by those who do not understand that language.

Ultimately, Rabbi Epstein argues, this approach to explaining the aforementioned difficulties in the Talmudic discussion of praying in the vernacular indicates that the Talmudic rule only permits the recitation of certain prayers in the vernacular if one does not understand the original Hebrew (Principle 1). This counters the Reform claim that such prayers may be recited in other languages as a matter of course. Rabbi Epstein goes further, however, and generally proscribes the recital of prayers in any language other than Hebrew. While the Talmud itself permits doing so in cases where one does not understand the Hebrew, Rabbi Epstein disallows it, either because in his own time and place people were sufficiently educated to understand such commonly recited prayers when said in Hebrew (Principle 9), or as a supererogatory measure warranted as a means of countering the spread of Reform practices (Principle 6).
Methodological Principles: 1, 2, 6, 7, 9.

Example #90 – *Arukh HaShulchan* §186:1

Following the general rabbinic rule that women are obligated to fulfill all positive commandments that are not time-bound, the Talmud takes for granted that women are obligated to recite the *Birkhat HaMazon* blessing. The Talmud debates—and does not clearly resolve—whether women's obligation to recite this blessing is biblical, or if it is merely a rabbinically legislated obligation, while the Torah itself leaves women exempt from reciting the *Birkhat HaMazon*.[165] Importantly, the question is not just theoretical. If women are biblically obligated to recite the *Birkhat HaMazon*, then they may do so on behalf of men who are likewise biblically obligated to recite this blessing after meals. However, women are only rabbinically obligated to say the *Birkhat HaMazon*—their recitation of the blessing cannot also serve to fulfill the obligation on behalf of men, since the latter carry a biblical duty to recite the blessing. Post-Talmudic authorities disagreed about how to resolve this issue. Some authorities, including the *Raabad* and *Rashba*, understand the Talmudic discussion to indicate that women are biblically obligated to recite the *Birkhat HaMazon*; Rabbeinu Yonah maintains that the Talmud concludes that women are only rabbinically obligated; and the *Rosh*, *Tosafot*, and Maimonides all conclude that the Talmud leaves the question unresolved, and that therefore women must avoid fulfilling the obligation to say the *Birkhat HaMazon* on behalf of men lest they in fact be only rabbinically obligated to do so.

---

165 Babylonian Talmud, Berakhot 20b.

While the Talmud itself does not definitively resolve the issue, and while later authorities are split on the question, Rabbi Epstein adopts the view that women's obligation to recite the *Birkhat HaMazon* should be treated as rabbinic, and therefore they should not seek to fulfill the obligation to recite the blessing on behalf of men, who are certainly biblically obligated. Rabbi Epstein supports this conclusion first with the novel—though admittedly inconclusive—argument that since husbands are legally obligated to provide food for their wives, women do not relate to God in the manner depicted in the *Birkhat HaMazon* as "the one who feeds all" and are therefore likely not biblically obligated to recite the blessing. Likewise, Rabbi Epstein argues that, since one of the essential parts of the *Birkhat HaMazon* refers to God as "the one who builds Jerusalem," only men—who are builders—but not women are biblically obligated to recite the blessing (Principle 1). Rabbi Epstein's conclusion is further supported by the fact that Maimonides finds the Talmudic discussion inconclusive and thus rules that women should not be assumed to have a biblical obligation to recite the *Birkhat HaMazon* (Principle 3), and by the *Zohar*, which definitively concludes that women's obligation to recite the blessing is only rabbinic (Principle 7). Moreover, Rabbi Epstein's conclusion—that women should assume that their obligation is merely rabbinic and that therefore they should not seek to fulfill the obligation to say the blessing on behalf of biblically obligated men—is consistent with the general Jewish legal rules for resolving doubts, which prescribe that uncertainties regarding biblical law must be treated strictly. Here, there is Talmudic uncertainty about the nature of women's *Birkhat HaMazon* obligation, and they therefore should not try to recite the blessing for men who are definitely biblically obligated and whose own obligation can only be vicariously performed by other biblically obligated individuals (Principle 4).

Methodological Principles: 1, 3, 4, 7.

Example #91 – *Arukh HaShulchan* §191:4

According to the Talmud, day laborers who are being paid for their time are not required to say all four of the blessings that comprise the *Birkhat HaMazon*. Instead, the Talmud prescribes that they should recite a truncated version so as not to take any unnecessary time away from their employers.[166] Rabbi Epstein rules, however, that this leniency applied only in the Talmudic era—modern workers must recite the entire *Birkhat HaMazon* after eating. This is because, unlike employers in the Talmudic period, modern employers who hire workers at an agreed daily rate are not overly concerned about losing a few minutes of productive time while their employees recite the *Birkhat HaMazon*, and it can therefore be assumed that all such employment agreements include an implicit understanding that workers may break from their labor to do so (Principle 9). Rabbi Epstein takes his position a step further, however, and innovatively rules that even if the contract between the workers and their employer explicitly requires the employees to recite the abridged version of the *Birkhat HaMazon* prescribed by the Talmud, they should still recite the entire blessing (Principle 1). This is because virtually everyone knows that the custom is for day laborers to recite the full *Birkhat HaMazon* without interference from their employers, and employers therefore have no right to "remove themselves from society" or to treat their workers differently from the established commercial standard (Principle 8).

Methodological Principles: 1, 8, 9.

---

166 Babylonian Talmud, Berakhot 16a.

Example #92 – *Arukh HaShulchan* §202:19

Rabbi Joseph Karo rules that before eating sweet, edible fruit seeds, one must recite the blessing of "*boreh pri ha'etz*," recognizing God as the "Creator of the fruit of the tree." When eating bitter fruit seeds, however, Rabbi Karo rules that one should not recite any blessing. Moreover, when one eats fruit seeds that are naturally bitter, but which have become sweet through some kind of cooking process, one should not recite the blessing of *boreh pri ha'etz*, which is only said on fruit itself, and should instead recite the blessing of "*shehakol nih'yeh bidvaro*," a residual blessing recited upon all foods that do not grow from the ground, and which recognizes that "all comes into being through His [God's] word."[167] Rabbi Karo's ruling is based on an earlier rabbinic interpretation of a Talmudic passage that teaches that the shells of nuts and the seeds of fruit are subject to the biblical law of *orlah*, which prohibits the consumption of fruit during the first three years of a tree's productive fruit bearing. According to *Tosafot* and the *Rosh*, this Talmudic ruling, which is not directly related to the laws of blessings, demonstrates that the *halakhah* views fruit seeds as fruit, and that seeds should therefore be subject to the blessing of *boreh pri ha'etz*. Following this understanding of the Talmudic precedent, Rabbi Karo rules that one recites the blessing of *boreh pri ha'etz* on edible seeds just as one would on the fruit itself. The *Rashba*, however, offers an alternative understanding of this Talmudic passage. He maintains that seeds are generally not regarded as fruit, and that the Talmud treats them as such for purposes of *orlah* laws only due to special scriptural indication. Consequently, when eating fruit seeds, one should recite the blessing of *"boreh pri ha'adamah"* ("Who created the fruit of the Earth") rather than *boreh pri ha'etz*.

Rabbi Epstein rejects Rabbi Karo's ruling and instead adopts the *Rashba*'s view that one should recite the blessing of *boreh pri ha'adamah* on fruit seeds. Rabbi Epstein argues that this result is justified because a consensus of important authorities supported the *Rashba*'s position (Principle 2), in part because this view is more consistent with the principle that doubts regarding the obligation to recite blessings—which are rabbinic, not biblical, obligations—should be resolved in a manner that avoids reciting possibly unwarranted blessings. As a rule, one may in principle recite the blessing of *boreh pri ha'adamah* on fruit, since they do in fact grow from the earth; one may not however recite the blessing of *boreh pri ha'etz* on a food that is not actually considered "fruit." Since the precise status of edible fruit seeds remains doubtful in light of the Talmud's failure to determinately resolve the question, a consensus of rabbinic scholars, as well as Rabbi Epstein himself, concluded that one should err on the side of caution and recite a *boreh pri ha'adamah* rather than a *boreh pri ha'etz*, when eating fruit seeds (Principle 4).
Methodological Principles: 2, 4.

Example #93 – *Arukh HaShulchan* §206:5

Rabbi Joseph Karo codifies the well-settled rule that blessings said prior to eating food must actually be verbalized—the words must "go out from the lips," and ideally they should also be said loudly enough for the one reciting the blessing to hear his own words.[168] Thus, Rabbi Karo rules, if one merely thinks the words of the blessing instead of properly verbalizing them, they have not fulfilled their obligation to recite the blessing and must repeat the blessing properly. Maimonides disagrees with this view and rules that while blessings should be verbalized

---

167 Shulchan Arukh, Orach Chaim 202:3.
168 Ibid. 206:3.

ex ante, if in fact one merely thought the words of a blessing, one has still fulfilled their obligation *ex post*. Based on this view, since the obligation to recite a blessing is minimally—though not ideally—fulfilled by thinking the blessing in one's mind, one who did so should not thereafter repeat the blessing verbally, since this would amount to unnecessarily reciting a blessing and thus taking God's name in vain.

While Rabbi Epstein is usually deferential to Maimonides's rulings (Principle 3), in this case he rules that one must repeat a blessing that was initially thought but not verbalized. Rabbi Epstein notes that a near-universal consensus of *halakhic* authorities rejects Maimonides's view (Principle 2). Moreover, this opposition to Maimonides's ruling is based on the well-settled Talmudic principle that thinking something is not the same as verbalizing it, which strongly suggests that a blessing that was thought but not verbalized is considered to have not been recited at all (Principle 1). The weight of consensus to establish the correct Talmudic norm is so strong here that it even overrides Rabbi Epstein's usual concern about making unnecessary blessings (Principle 4). According to Maimonides, the thought blessing is sufficient to fulfill one's ritual obligation—repeating the blessing verbally would thus amount to taking God's name in vain. However, for Rabbi Epstein, the rabbinic consensus rejecting Maimonides's view establishes the correct legal standard and thus preempts the doubt-resolving rule that instructs one not to make blessings in cases of doubt.

Methodological Principles: 1, 2, 3, 4.

Example #94 – *Arukh HaShulchan* §210:6

While one is obligated to recite a blessing before eating any amount of food or drink, one only recites a blessing after eating if one consumed more than the prescribed minimum amount. In the case of food, the minimum amount that one must consume in order to be obligated to recite a concluding blessing is a *kezayit*, a volume of food equal to the size of an olive.

Both the Jerusalem and Babylonian Talmuds relate an incident in which Rabbi Yochanan ate an olive and recited the appropriate blessing after he ate. In both passages, the Talmud questions how Rabbi Yochanan recited a blessing after eating the olive—since olives contain pits, and since Rabbi Yochanan surely did not eat the pit that took up the middle of his olive, in fact, when he ate the flesh of the olive, he ate less than the volume of a whole olive. If so, how was he permitted to recite the blessing after eating without consuming the requisite minimum amount? The two Talmudic passages give two different answers to this question, which have important practical ramifications. According to the Jerusalem Talmud, Rabbi Yochanan did in fact consume less than the minimum amount of olive needed to recite a blessing after eating. However, the Talmud says, this minimum amount does not apply in cases where one consumed a "*beryah*," a whole "creature." When one eats an olive, or a grape, or another whole entity, that entity is significant in its own right and merits a blessing after eating, even if the actual amount consumed is less than a *kezayit*.[169] The Babylonian Talmud gives a different explanation for Rabbi Yochanan's behavior. According to this second account, the olive that Rabbi Yochanan ate was especially large. The correct measure of a *kezayit*, the Talmud says, is the volume of an ordinary-sized olive; Rabbi Yochanan's olive was of a very large variety such that, even excluding the pit, the flesh of the olive amounted to a *kezayit* and thus warranted the recital of a blessing after he ate.

---

169 *See* Jerusalem Talmud, Berakhot 6:1.

Rabbi Epstein notes that the fact that the Babylonian Talmud did not attempt to resolve the original question about Rabbi Yochanan's behavior by saying, as did the Jerusalem Talmud, that consuming a whole olive or other *beryah* warrants a blessing, even if the amount consumed measures less than a *kezayit*, indicates that the Babylonian Talmud does not think that the Jerusalem Talmud's *beryah* exemption from the minimum *kezayit* amount needed to recite a blessing after eating is correct. True to his high regard for the legal significance of the Jerusalem Talmud, Rabbi Epstein proposes one possible way to read the Babylonian and Jerusalem Talmud passages in concert so as to avoid direct contradiction and preserve the Jerusalem Talmud's *beryah* exemption to the *kezayit* minimum (Principle 1). Rabbi Epstein notes, however, that this interpretation of the Talmud is merely speculative, and he is far from confident that it is correct. He therefore rules in accordance with the plain meaning of the Babylonian Talmud—that one may not recite a blessing after eating unless after having consumed at least a *kezayit* of food, even if one ate a full *beryah*. He notes that this conclusion is supported by a consensus of authorities, including Rabbis Joseph Karo and Moses Isserles (Principle 2), and is not contradicted by Maimonides, who does not mention any special rules governing the recital of blessings after eating a *beryah*, which indicates that he too rejects the Jerusalem Talmud's rule (Principle 3). Rabbi Epstein's ruling on this matter is also consistent with the principle that one should not recite blessings in cases of doubt—the doubt here having been created by the conflicting rulings of the Jerusalem and Babylonian Talmuds, and by the possibility that the two sources could be read in concert with each other. Given this doubt, one should not recite a blessing after eating a *beryah* that is less than a *kezayit* in size, since blessings are only rabbinic obligations, while reciting an unnecessary blessing entails a biblical violation of taking God's name in vain (Principle 4).
Methodological Principles: 1, 2, 3, 4.

Example #95 – *Arukh HaShulchan* §232:6

In general, the *Amidah* recited as part of the afternoon *Minchah* prayer is said in the same way as the *Amidah* recited during the morning *Shacharit* prayer service—everyone recites the *Amidah* quietly to themselves; then the prayer leader repeats it out loud while the community answers "*amen*" to each of the prayer's blessings recited by the prayer leader and also recites the *Kedushah* prayer. Post-Talmudic authorities have debated the proper way to recite the *Minchah* prayer in cases where the prayer is for some reason delayed until late in the day, not leaving enough time to recite the full afternoon service before nightfall.

Rabbi Joseph Karo rules that, in such cases, each member of the congregation should recite the *Amidah* quietly, and that afterwards the *shliach tzibbur*, or prayer leader, should repeat the first three blessings of the *Amidah* together with the *Kedushah* prayer. The prayer leader should not, however, recite these blessings out loud while the rest of the congregation recites the *Amidah* quietly because the primary prayer obligation is to recite the *Amidah* as a personal silent prayer, which the prayer leader would then fail to have done.[170] The *Rema*, however, rules that it is in fact preferable for the prayer leader to pray out loud while the community is praying silently, even though in that scenario the prayer leader will not say a silent prayer at all. Rabbi Epstein notes that each of these practices has drawbacks. Adopting Rabbi Karo's practice means that the prayer leader does not repeat the entire *Amidah*, as is proper, while following the *Rema*'s approach precludes the possibility that the members of the congregation, who are supposed to

---

170   *See* Arukh HaShulchan, Orach Chaim 232:3.

be praying silently during the prayer leader's recitation aloud, will be able to respond *"amen"* to the prayer leader's blessings.[171]

Rabbi Epstein rejects both Rabbis Karo and Isserles's approaches to dealing with the correct order of the congregational *Minchah* service when prayed close to nightfall. Rabbi Epstein instead endorses the general custom in his own time and place, which was for the prayer leader to say the first three blessings of the *Amidah* and *Kedushah* prayer aloud while the community answers *"amen"*, and for each member of the congregation to then recite the full *Amidah* quietly while the prayer leader continues silently from where he left off as well (Principle 8). Unlike Rabbi Isserles's model, this approach allows the congregation to respond *"amen"* to the prayer leader's recital of the first three blessings while also satisfying Rabbi Karo's concern that the prayer leader recite the *Amidah* quietly himself to fulfill his basic prayer obligation. Despite this common custom, Rabbi Epstein also references an alternative practice, which is also customary—though not as widely adopted—and which maintains that even when the congregation prays the *Minchah* prayer close to nightfall, the congregation and prayer leader should first recite the *Amidah* silently, and thereafter the prayer leader should repeat the entire *Amidah* out loud as is the ordinary procedure for congregational prayers. Rabbi Epstein notes that this view is supported by the *Zohar* and therefore seems to indicate that this approach too is fully justified (Principle 7).

Methodological Principles: 7, 8.

Example #96 – *Arukh HaShulchan* §234:2

Because the recitation of the *Amidah* prayer for *Minchah* is not proceeded by any other set preparatory prayers, the Talmudic Rabbis established that Psalm 145, known as *Ashrei*, should be said prior to saying the *Amidah*. The reason for this is that the Rabbis maintained that it is inappropriate to begin the *Amidah* prayer without any prior preparation; they thus legislated that the congregation first recite *Ashrei* followed by the *Kaddish* prayer, and then, once their minds are properly oriented and focused, they begin the *Amidah*.

Rabbi Epstein notes that some have the custom to recite additional passages that relate to the daily afternoon sacrifices once brought to the Temple prior to their beginning the *Amidah* prayer of *Minchah* (Principle 8). While the Talmud itself does not prescribe the recitation of such additional passages, Rabbi Epstein approves and encourages this supererogatory practice because it serves the positive religious purpose of recalling the afternoon Temple service—for which the *Minchah* prayer was established to replace—following the destruction of the Temple and the cessation of the sacrificial service (Principle 6).

Methodological Principles: 6, 8.

Example #97 – *Arukh HaShulchan* §242:26

The Talmud adduces that one of the basic principles governing liability for performing prohibited labors on the Sabbath is that only *melekhet machshevet*, "significant work," is biblically proscribed. This means that, among other things, one is not liable for performing an otherwise prohibited act on the Sabbath if one did so unintentionally. The Talmud discusses a variation on such unintended performance of Sabbath labor by positing a case where one intended to grab and lift a plant that was already detached from the ground, but instead grabbed and lifted

---

171 *See* ibid. 232:4-5.

a plant that was still attached to the Earth, thereby violating the biblical prohibition against harvesting on the Sabbath. According to the Talmudic sage Rava, such a person is not liable for this act because "he did not intend to perform a prohibited act of cutting" a plant from the ground. According to another Talmudic sage, Abaye, one is liable for this kind of inadvertent Sabbath violation because the actor accomplished precisely the intended act of lifting the plant he intended. While the actor was mistaken as to the fact of whether the plant he intended to pick up was attached or detached from the ground, according to Abaye, such a mistake of fact does not absolve the actor of liability when the act itself was fully intended.[172]

The Talmud establishes a rule that, in virtually all cases of disputes between Rava and Abaya, the *halakhah* follows the view of Rava. Early authorities disagree, however, over how to understand the case around which the Talmudic discussion revolves. According to *Rashi*, the case involves an individual who intended to pick up one plant that was indeed detached from the ground, but who accidentally grabbed a different plant that was attached to the ground. *Tosafot*, however, argues that it is obvious and would be unnecessary for the Talmud to explicitly rule that the plant picker would be exempt from liability in such a case, since in fact he did not do his intended act of picking the detached plant. Instead, *Tosafot* argues that the case involves a person mistakenly thinking that the plant he intends to pick up is detached, actually succeeding in picking up that plant, but discovering that in fact the plant had been attached to the ground the entire time. In that case, *Tosafot* explains, the picker is not liable because the Sabbath violation occurred by happenstance while he was trying to do something he believed was perfectly permitted.

Rabbi Epstein adopts *Rashi*'s understanding of the Talmudic rule, concluding that, while one is not liable for mistakenly picking the wrong plant that turns out to be attached, if his intent was to pick a different plant that was in fact detached, one is liable for picking an attached plant while mistakenly thinking it was detached. Rabbi Epstein argues that *Rashi*'s understanding of the Talmudic case is supported by a related passage elsewhere in the Talmud.[173] There, the Talmud clarifies that Rava's ruling, exonerating a person who mistakenly picks the wrong plant, applies only where the subject of his actual action differed from the subject of his intended action in such a way as to render the actually accomplished task different from the intended result—as is the case where one intends to pick plant A and accidentally picks plant B instead, or where one intends to pick a date but instead accidentally picks a grape. However, when the actually accomplished act is the same as the intended act—such as where one actually picks the plant they meant to pick—the Talmud indicates that Rava's exonerating ruling does not apply (Principle 1). Rabbi Epstein acknowledges that this understanding of the interplay between two complex Talmudic discussions is not entirely straightforward or determinative; indeed, *Tosafot* explicitly base their disagreement with *Rashi*'s view on the parameters of Rava's absolving mistaken actions from Sabbath liability on an apparently alternative read of this second Talmudic discussion. Still, Rabbi Epstein notes that Maimonides—as well as general consensus of Talmudic commentators—understands the Talmudic case and Rava's ruling in the same manner as does *Rashi*, which leads him to ultimately rule accordingly in the *Arukh HaShulchan* (Principles 2 and 3). Methodological Principles: 1, 2, 3.

---

172 Babylonian Talmud, Shabbat 72b.
173 *See* Babylonian Talmud, Keritot 19a-20a.

Example #98 – *Arukh HaShulchan* §248:6

The Talmud rules that it is prohibited to set off on a boat trip less than three days before the Sabbath.[174] Early Talmudic commentaries offered a variety of different explanations for this rule. According to Maimonides and Rabbi Isaac Alfasi, the reason for this rabbinic prohibition is that generally people are seasick for their first several days at sea—the Rabbis therefore prohibited beginning a sea journey close to the onset of the Sabbath so as not to ruin the traveler's enjoyment of the Sabbath day aboard the ship.[175] According to the *Baal HaMaor*, however, the Rabbis prohibited setting out on a sea journey late in the week because sea travel is dangerous, and when dangerous situations arise, the sea traveler may be expected to have to perform labors typically prohibited on the Sabbath. While such measures are, of course, permitted in order to avert life-threatening dangers, one may not plan in advance to be in a dangerous situation on the Sabbath that will necessitate performing prohibited labors. The *Baal HaMaor* argues that one who sets sail within three days of the Sabbath is akin to one who intentionally plans to be in a situation where Sabbath violations will be necessary; in order to avoid this, the Talmudic Rabbis proscribed setting out on such a journey late in the week.[176] Nachmanides offers yet a third explanation for the rule. According to Nachmanides, the prohibition applies only where the only passengers on the ship are Jewish and is premised on a concern for the appearance of Jews hiring Gentiles to perform forbidden labors for them on the Sabbath. When one leaves port late in the week, it appears that one has hired the ship's captain and crew to perform prohibited labors—such as tying knots in the ship's rigging—on one's own behalf on the Sabbath, which is prohibited. By leaving earlier in the week, one ensures that by the time the Sabbath arrives, any labors performed by the crew on the Sabbath are clearly done for their own benefit and not specifically on behalf of the Jewish passengers—once at sea, the crew must handle the ship to reach their next port, and they do so for their own safety and profit.[177] Rabbeinu Chananel provides a fourth explanation of this rule. He argues that this prohibition applies only to boats traveling in very shallow water less than ten handbreadths deep and is concerned about violating the Sabbath prohibition against one's traveling outside of the *techum*, or boundary, of the settled area in which one finds oneself at the start of the Sabbath. Such boundaries do not apply to areas that sit higher than ten handbreadths from the ground; thus, a ship moving through deep water constitutes its own settled area, and one may travel as far as one wishes while remaining aboard the vessel. A boat moving through very shallow water, however, is not regarded as its own settled domain, and one traveling on such a boat is subject to the ordinary *techum* restrictions, which prohibit traveling two thousand cubits beyond the outer edge of the settled area in which one finds oneself at the onset of the Sabbath. While traveling by boat in shallow water thus presents a *halakhic* problem, Rabbeinu Chananel explains that the Talmudic Rabbis only prohibited doing so if one embarked less than three days before the Sabbath, because this makes it appear that one is intentionally planning to violate the *techum* prohibition. If one boarded the vessel more than three days before the Sabbath, however, the Jewish passenger is viewed as being unwillingly forced to travel beyond the *techum*, since he cannot very well leave the ship.[178]

Rabbi Epstein notes that despite the Talmudic prohibition, Jews in his own time and place—and indeed, Jews "throughout the entire world"—regularly board ships on Friday, and

---

174 Babylonian Talmud, Shabbat 19a.
175 *See* Arukh HaShulchan, Orach Chaim 248:3.
176 *See* ibid. 248:4.
177 *See* ibid. 248:5.
178 *See* ibid. 248:2.

even on the Sabbath itself. Rabbi Epstein notes that, while this practice can be squared with Nachmanides's and Rabbeinu Chananel's explanations of the Talmudic stricture, since such ships travel in deep water and carry both Jewish and Gentile passengers, it is nevertheless a violation of the Talmudic rule as understood by the vast majority of scholars, including such authorities as Maimonides and Rabbi Alfasi (Principle 2).

Rabbi Epstein provides two different justifications for the common practice of boarding ships within three days of the Sabbath in light of the apparently normative standard that doing so is prohibited by the Talmud under all conditions (Principle 8). First, he suggests that Nachmanides's rule actually reflects the correct Talmudic norm; therefore, there is no reason to be seriously concerned about the fact that the common practice is inconsistent with Maimonides's understanding of the prohibition (Principle 1). When explaining the parameters of the prohibition, the Talmud notes that while one is prohibited to set out on a boat trip within three days of the Sabbath, one may do so if the trip is for a religious purpose so long as the Jewish traveler requests before beginning the journey that the ship not travel on the Sabbath itself. Once this request is made, the Talmud says, the ship's captain can later decide to travel on the Sabbath as he wishes, and the labor he performs is not counted as having been done on behalf of the Jewish passenger, since the passenger specifically requested that the ship not proceed on its voyage during the Sabbath.[179] Rabbi Epstein explains that the fact that the Talmud frames its permission to set out on a boat trip shortly before the Sabbath in terms of a concern about ensuring that the ship's captain and crew do not perform prohibited labor on behalf of the Jewish traveler on the Sabbath lends support to Nachmanides's view that the prohibition exists out of concern for labor performed on behalf of Jewish travelers (Principle 1). But, Rabbi Epstein notes, in modern times Jews are never the only passengers on ships; thus, any labors performed—regardless of prior stipulations or when the ship departs—cannot therefore be directly attributed to the Jewish passengers, and thus, the rationale that originally animated the Talmud's rule no longer applies, leaving Jews free to board ships within three days of the Sabbath (Principle 9).

Rabbi Epstein also argues that the common practice of boarding ships within three days of the Sabbath may be permissible even according to Maimonides. Rabbi Epstein notes that according to Rabbi Moses Isserles, when the Talmud permits people to embark on a ship within three days of the Sabbath if the journey is for a religious purpose, the Talmud does not mean that the goal of the journey has to be specifically religious. Instead, the Talmud means to permit people to begin a sea journey close to the Sabbath so long as the trip is not merely for pleasure. Business trips, trips to see friends and family, and other such voyages are all regarded as "religious" and permit a traveler to begin a sea voyage within three days of the Sabbath.[180] Based on this understanding of the Talmudic rule, virtually all trips taken by Jews where the ship departs within three days of the Sabbath can be justified as serving a "religious" purpose, rendering them permissible even according to the more restrictive understandings of the Talmudic prohibition (Principles 5 and 8).

Methodological Principles: 1, 2, 5, 8, 9.

---

179 *See* Babylonian Talmud, Shabbat 19a.
180 *See* Rema *to* Shulchan Arukh, Orach Chaim 248:4.

Example #99 – Arukh HaShulchan §251:4

The Talmud strongly discourages people from performing prohibited Sabbath labors on Friday afternoon.[181] In light of this Talmudic prescription, Rabbi Epstein questions the common practice of his own time, when people would continue working until close to the onset of the Sabbath at sundown on Friday without any apparent concern of compunction for the Talmud's stance on the issue. Rabbi Epstein offers several justifications for this practice (Principle 8). First, he suggests that people work until late in the day on Fridays due to their pressing need to earn an adequate living, and this would justify their disregard of the Talmud's teaching (Principle 10). Second, Rabbi Epstein notes that based on a passage in the Jerusalem Talmud, which is codified in *halakhic* discussions of employment law, wage-earning workers may continue to work on Friday afternoons until shortly before the start of the Sabbath. Based on this, Rabbi Epstein concludes that the Talmud's discouraging people from performing labor on Friday afternoons must only be referring to business owners and not to their employees. Thus, the general practice of working nearly the entire day on Fridays is justified because the vast majority of workers are not business owners but employees subject to the demands of their employers (Principle 1). Rabbi Epstein offers a third justification and suggests that perhaps the Talmudic principle no longer applies, since it was originally offered as a measure to ensure that workers had adequate time off on Friday afternoon to prepare for the Sabbath. Now, however, Rabbi Epstein writes, "The women prepare everything" while the men are at work, and thus, there is no longer any need for the men to leave work early on Friday afternoon to make Sabbath preparations (Principle 9).

Despite these justifications, however, Rabbi Epstein urges—though does not formally require—pious people to uphold the Talmudic principle and avoid forbidden Sabbath labors on Friday afternoons (Principle 6).
Methodological Principles: 1, 6, 8, 9, 10.

Example #100 – Arukh HaShulchan §255:3

The Mishnah rules that it is prohibited to light a fire late on Friday afternoon unless there is enough time for the fire to catch on most of the wood in the pile before the Sabbath begins. This is because the Rabbis were concerned that, if the wood did not fully catch fire before the Sabbath, one may inadvertently stoke the wood after the Sabbath begins in order to ensure that the flames do not go out. In the same Mishnah, however, Rabbi Judah rules that one may light a fire using coals, even if the fire will not fully catch to all of the coals before the Sabbath begins, because there is no real concern that a partially caught fire set in a bed of coals might become extinguished if it is tended.[182]

Maimonides does not mention Rabbi Judah's more lenient ruling in the case of a fire lit in a bed of coals, seemingly adopting the view that all kinds of fires must be fully kindled prior to the start of the Sabbath. The *Arbah Turim*, however, codifies Rabbi Judah's position, thus distinguishing between fires lit in coals, which do not have to be fully kindled before the Sabbath begins, and fires kindled using wood fuel, which must catch before the onset of the Sabbath. Rabbi Epstein notes that several authorities question the *Arbah Turim*'s ruling, which adopts Rabbi Judah's view about fires kindled in coals because the opinion of the Rabbis recorded in the Mishnah does not draw a distinction between wood-fueled and coal-fueled fires, and a dispute

---

181 *See* Babylonian Talmud, Pesachim 20a.
182 *See* Babylonian Talmud, Shabbat 19b-20a.

between the Rabbis and Rabbi Judah should be resolved in favor of the majority view expressed by the Rabbis.

While Rabbi Epstein acknowledges that indeed Rabbi Judah's view disputes the more categorical position of the Rabbis, he nevertheless endorses the *Arbah Turim*'s adoption of Rabbi Judah's ruling—even though doing so entails rejecting Maimonides's ruling on this matter. Rabbi Epstein justifies his position by noting that the Jerusalem Talmud explicitly rules in accordance with Rabbi Judah's view, and the correct resolution of this Mishnaic dispute is thus determined accordingly (Principle 1).

Methodological Principles: 1.

Example #101 – *Arukh HaShulchan* §257:17

The Talmud records that the Rabbis legislated that on Friday afternoon, one may not cover food with materials that add heat to the covered dish. This rule was enacted out of concern that people might use ashes containing live coals to cover a pot in order to keep it warm on the Sabbath and may then either seek to extinguish or to kindle the lit coal in violation of Sabbath labor laws.[183] To avoid this possibility, the Rabbis legislated a blanket prohibition on covering food with items that add heat to the covered dish on Friday afternoon.

Some early authorities distinguish between the ways in which one may use different kinds of heat-increasing materials to keep food warm prior to the onset of the Sabbath. Rabbi Isaac Alfasi and the *Rosh*, for instance, rule that while one may not place a pot of food on top of a pile of used olive husks and then cover the food with a material that does not add heat, one may place a pot of food on top of a pile of sesame seed husks and then cover the dish with a material that does not add heat. These authorities argue that while sesame seed husks do not add a significant amount of heat to a dish, olive refuse gives off substantial heat and must therefore be treated more strictly. Rabbi Epstein notes, however, that other major authorities—including Maimonides, the *Arbah Turim*, and *Shulchan Arukh*—do not differentiate between olive and sesame husks, indicating that they disagree with the position adopted by the *Rosh* and Rabbi Alfasi.

Rabbi Epstein rejects the categorical positions implicitly adopted by Maimonides, the *Arbah Turim*, and *Shulchan Arukh*. Instead, he endorses Rabbi Alfasi and the *Rosh*'s view that one may place a covered pot on top of heat-inducing materials other than olive refuse. Rabbi Epstein argues that the laws regulating the placement of potentially harmful substances next to other people's property indicates that olive husks should be treated as able to add more heat than other substances like sesame seed husks and therefore must be treated more strictly in connection to Sabbath laws. Rabbi Epstein points out that the law is that one may not place one's pile of olive husks within four cubits of another person's wall because the heat generated by the decomposing olive refuse may be expected to damage the wall. Since this law speaks of the need to distance a pile of olive refuse but does not refer to sesame seed husks, Rabbi Epstein concludes that a correct understanding of the issue supports the views of Rabbi Alfasi and the *Rosh* that one may place a covered food pot on top of a pile of sesame seed refuse on Friday afternoon without violating the rabbinic enactment (Principle 1).

Methodological Principles: 1.

---

183 *See* Babylonian Talmud, Shabbat 34b.

Example #102 – *Arukh HaShulchan* §260:6

Several later authorities rule that one should not cut one's hair or nails on Thursday because hair and nails begin to grow again on the third day after they have been cut, and if one cuts them on Thursday, they will begin to grow again on the Sabbath. Rabbi Epstein rejects this ruling, however, since it contradicts a Mishnaic instruction for the members of the group of priests scheduled to work in the Temple each week to cut their hair on the Thursday preceding the start of their service (Principle 1). Moreover, Rabbi Epstein argues, there is no conceivable prohibition that one might be violating by one's hair or nails growing on their own on the Sabbath (Principle 1). While Rabbi Epstein thus rejects any prohibition on grooming oneself on Thursday, he does recommend against doing so and instead urges—but does not prescribe—that people cut their hair and nails on Friday as a sign of respect for the approaching onset of the Sabbath (Principle 6). Still, he notes, if one will not have time to groom oneself on Friday, one certainly may do so the day before (Principle 10).
Methodological Principles: 1, 6, 10.

Example #103 – *Arukh HaShulchan* §272:7

The *Arbah Turim* rules that one may recite the Sabbath *kiddush* over raisin wine. This is based on a Talmudic passage that teaches that raisin wine was even *ex post facto* ritually fit for use as part of the offering services in the Temple.[184] If raisin wine is fit for Temple service, it is surely fit for use to fulfill the rabbinic obligation to recite the Sabbath *kiddush* over a cup of wine.[185] Virtually all authorities include an important caveat to this *halakhic* permission to use raisin wine for *kiddush*: the *Arbah Turim*, Maimonides, Rabbi Isaac Alfasi, and Rabbi Moses Isserles all rule that raisin wine is only ritually fit for use for reciting *kiddush* if it was produced from raisins that themselves still contained some small amount of grape juice within them. If, however, the wine was produced merely by steeping completely dry raisins in water for an extended period of time, the "wine"—which is in fact just raisin-flavored water—may not be used for the Sabbath *kiddush*.[186]

In light of the strong consensus of authorities that invalidates raisin wine made by steeping dry raisins in water for ritual purposes, Rabbi Epstein raises concerns about how in his own time and place people routinely use raisin wine for *kiddush* (Principle 2). This is problematic, he says, because "everyone knows that the small raisins we use to make raisin wine are extremely dry and have no moisture in them at all," which renders the "wine" made from these raisins unsuitable for ritual purposes.

Rabbi Epstein seeks to justify the local custom and therefore offers several different justifications for the widespread practice of using this kind of raisin wine for *kiddush* (Principle 8). First, he suggests that the view that wine made from dry raisins is not legally treated as wine is a view tied to another *halakhic* position held by Maimonides and Rabbi Alfasi but rejected by most Ashkenazic *halakhic* authorities. There is a basic dispute among early authorities regarding whether the Torah recognizes that the flavor of a food is considered to be the substance of the food, or if this principle is merely rabbinic in nature. According to Maimonides and others, this is merely a rabbinic rule—Rabbi Epstein suggests that this may be why Maimonides declines

---

184 *See* Babylonian Talmud, Bava Batra 97a.
185 *See* Arukh HaShulchan, Orach Chaim 202:15.
186 *See* ibid. 272:6.

to treat as wine drinks made from completely dry raisins, which do not contain any actual juice secreted from the raisins themselves. Ashkenazic authorities, however, maintain that flavor is regarded as substance even at a biblical level, and based on that line of reasoning, one might be able to treat even water flavored by dry raisins as wine (Principle 1). Rabbi Epstein offers a second justification for the common practice of using raisin wine for *kiddush* by arguing that what is legally considered "wine" depends on what people customarily regard as wine. Since people consider raisin wine made from dry raisins to be "wine," it may be used for *kiddush* (Principle 5). Third, Rabbi Epstein argues that it would be impracticable to *not* treat this commonly used raisin wine as ritually suitable wine, because in his time and place, proper wine was simply not readily available to most people, and raisin wine had to serve as an acceptable substitute (Principle 10). Finally, elsewhere, Rabbi Epstein offers a further argument that provides a normative justification for the practice of treating this kind of raisin wine as "wine." He argues simply and without further elaboration that "this was the custom of our fathers and forefathers [to treat raisin wine as proper wine]," and this, he apparently thinks, justifies the practice on its own terms (Principle 8).
Methodological Principles 1, 2, 5, 8, 10.

Example #104 – *Arukh HaShulchan* §288:4

Jewish law prohibits fasting on the Sabbath.[187] In his *Shulchan Arukh*, Rabbi Joseph Karo notes two important exemptions to this rule. First, one for whom eating is harmful need not eat and may instead avoid food—effectively fasting—on the Sabbath. Second, Rabbi Karo writes that "a person who fasts every day such that eating on the Sabbath will cause him pain or distress due to this change of routine—there are those who say that they saw many pious people who fasted on the Sabbath for this reason."[188] Rabbi Epstein expressly endorses both of these rulings and explains that a person for whom eating is harmful or dangerous is of course exempt from the obligation to eat on the Sabbath. However, even a person that won't be harmed by eating and will indeed actually enjoy and be energized by the food, will be somewhat distressed or suffer some indigestion after eating good food because he is used to fasting—is exempted from the usual prohibition against fasting on the Sabbath (Principle 10).[189]
Methodological Principles: 10.

Example #105 – *Arukh HaShulchan* §301:9

Carrying objects in a public domain is biblically proscribed as one of the kinds of work prohibited on the Sabbath. Maimonides rules, however, that one is only liable for violating this biblical injunction if one carried a "significant and useful amount" of whatever object or item is being carried. Thus, one is only liable for carrying food if he carried more than the equivalent of a kernel of grain.[190] Similarly, Maimonides rules that one is liable for carrying wine in a public domain if he carries a minimum drinking portion, or *revi'it*, of wine. This ruling is based on a Mishnaic principle that states that a *revi'it* of wine is suited for use in reciting a blessing, and that

---

187 *See* Shulchan Arukh, Orach Chaim 288:1.
188 Ibid. 288:3.
189 Arukh HaShulchan, Orach Chaim 288:4.
190 Mishneh Torah, Hilkhot Shabbat 12:9, 18:2.

wine should be diluted with water in a 1:3 ratio.[191] Thus, a *revi'it* of raw wine is a useful amount of wine from which one can create a full *revi'it* of properly diluted wine, and one is therefore liable for carrying that amount of wine in a public space on the Sabbath.

Rabbi Epstein questions Maimonides's ruling based on his assumption that the Talmudic reference to the amount of wine considered significant and the proper water-dilution ratio for that wine must be evaluated in historical context (Principle 9). Rabbi Epstein argues that the Talmud's determination that a *revi'it* of wine is significant because it should be diluted in three-times as much water was only relevant during that era. Contemporary wines, however, are weaker and are appropriately diluted in only much smaller amounts of water, if at all. Based on this, one should not be contemporaneously liable for carrying only a *revi'it* of wine on the Sabbath, as Maimonides holds. Rather, liability should attach only if one carried a full *revi'it* of wine. Rabbi Epstein further supports his rejection of Maimonides's ruling by arguing that the correct Talmudic rule actually requires a contextual evaluation. The actual language of the Talmudic rule is that the amount of wine considered significant is the amount "suitable for filling up a cup." Rabbi Epstein maintains that this indicates that the Talmudic standard is that whatever amount of wine is actually needed to fill a cup is what is to be considered significant; in Talmudic times, when wine would be diluted, this meant a *revi'it*, while in modern times this means a full *revi'it* (Principle 1).

Methodological Principles 1, 9.

Example #106 – *Arukh HaShulchan* §301:10

Maimonides rules that one is only liable for carrying an amount of water that is at least sufficient to rinse a mortar.[192] Rabbi Epstein rejects Maimonides's position, however, because it seems to contradict an explicit Talmudic determination that one is liable for carrying an amount of water to mix into an eye salve—an amount much smaller than what is needed to rinse a mortar.[193] Rabbi Epstein, however, justifies Maimonides's view by offering an alternative explanation of the Talmud, based on a passage in the Jerusalem Talmud (Principles 1 and 3). The Jerusalem Talmud indicates that the rule that one is liable for carrying enough water from which to mix an eye salve refers not to ordinary water but to dew. One is liable for carrying ordinary water, however, only if one carries an amount sufficient to rinse a mortar. While the relevant passage in the Babylonian Talmud does not make any explicit distinction between dew and other water, Rabbi Epstein nevertheless understands that Talmudic standard in light of the parallel passage in the Jerusalem Talmud, so as to justify and ultimately rule in accordance with Maimonides's view.

Methodological Principles 1, 3.

Example #107 – *Arukh HaShulchan* §301:11

The Talmud records that according to Rabbi Yochanan, one is not liable for carrying peas for a cow to eat on the Sabbath.[194] This is because peas are not a cow's usual food; a cow would only eat peas during a time of great need. According to Rabbi Yohanan, eating food that one

---

191 *See* Babylonian Talmud, Shabbat 77a.
192 Mishneh Torah, Hilkhot Shabbat 18:2.
193 Babylonian Talmud, Shabbat 76b.
194 Babylonian Talmud, Shabbat 76a.

would not normally eat due to some great need is not legally significant, and thus, carrying peas for a cow to eat would be considered legally insignificant and not result in liability for violating the Sabbath prohibition against carrying. Reish Lakish, another Talmudic sage, disagrees with Rabbi Yochanan's position. According to Reish Lakish, the act of eating during a time of great need is legally significant; therefore, one would be liable for carrying a mouthful of peas for a cow to eat.

Maimonides adopts the view that carrying food not usually consumed by animals with the intent of using it as animal feed does indeed incur liability for carrying on the Sabbath.[195] While Maimonides's ruling contradicts the settled rule of Talmudic interpretation that in cases of dispute between Rabbi Yochanan and Reish Lakish, the law follows the view of Rabbi Yochanan, Rabbi Epstein seeks to justify and uphold Maimonides's decision (Principle 3). First, Rabbi Epstein suggests that perhaps Maimonides was working with a version of the Talmud in which the dispute over this question is recorded not as having been between Rabbi Yochanan and Reish Lakish, but as taking place between Rabbi Yochanan and Rabbi Oshaya. In that case, Maimonides would be fully justified in adopting Rabbi Oshaya's opinion as against that of Rabbi Yochanan, since standard rules of Talmudic interpretation maintain that the law follows the view of Rabbi Oshaya in cases where he disputes with Rabbi Yochanan.

Rabbi Epstein further argues that even if the correct version of the Talmudic dispute involves Rabbi Yochanan and Reish Lakish rather than Rabbi Oshaya, a proper understanding of the Talmudic source justifies Maimonides's ruling. While normally disputes between Rabbi Yochanan and Reish Lakish are resolved in favor of the former, in this case, Reish Lakish's position is normative because elsewhere the Talmud concludes—consistent with Reish Lakish's opinion—that unusual food consumption under pressing circumstances is legally cognizable as eating. Moreover, the Talmud indicates that Rabbi Yochanan himself ultimately conceded the correctness of Reish Lakish's position on the matter, thus justifying Maimonides's ruling adopting Reish Lakish's view (Principle 1).
Methodological Principles: 1, 3.

Example #108 – *Arukh HaShulchan* §301:13

Since one is only liable for carrying a useful and significant amount of an object through a public domain on the Sabbath, Maimonides rules that one may not carry a reed large enough to be fashioned into a writing implement.[196] Rabbi Epstein argues that Maimonides's ruling no longer applies because in his own time and place, reeds were not used to fashion writing implements. Instead, one is only liable for carrying an object that is legally significant and useful in the local geographic and temporal context; and thus, Rabbi Epstein rules that one is only liable for carrying a reed if the reed is large enough to be used to fuel a fire that could cook a small amount of food (Principle 5).
Methodological Principles: 5.

---

195 Mishneh Torah, Hilkhot Shabbat 18:3.
196 Ibid. 18:4.

Example #109 – *Arukh HaShulchan* §302:3

The Babylonian Talmud states that it is forbidden to shake out a black cloak on the Sabbath, as this type of action would constitute a forbidden Sabbath labor. However, the Talmud does not identify the specific kind of forbidden Sabbath labor involved in shaking out a black cloak. The Talmud adds that this prohibition applies only when an individual prefers his clothing to be shaken. One who does not care whether or not his clothes are shaken out, however, is not prohibited from shaking them.[197] *Rashi* explains that the Sabbath prohibition at issue in the Talmudic discussion is the labor of "whitening," which in this case is violated by shaking dust off the cloak, thereby making it more clean. According to *Tosafot*, however, the Talmud is prohibiting shaking dew, not dust, off a cloak as a violation of the prohibition against "whitening," which encompasses forms of laundering. Shaking dust off a cloak, however, is not sufficiently significant as to constitute a violation of the prohibition against laundering clothes on the Sabbath.[198]

Rabbi Epstein points out that many medieval authorities, including the *Rosh, Ran, Rashba,* and *Raabad,* followed the interpretation of *Tosafot*: it is forbidden for one to purposely clean his black clothing by shaking it of dew, but shaking off dust is permitted. The *Arbah Turim* and *Shulchan Arukh* both adopted this ruling as well.[199] Maimonides, however, offers an entirely different understanding of this Talmudic prohibition. According to Maimonides, the Talmud prohibits shaking out a cloak because doing so would violate the prohibition against *makeh bipatish*—doing the final act of production that makes an object usable. Maimonides focuses on the Talmud's concern for the black color of the cloak; shaking tufts of white wool from a black cloak is the final finishing step in producing a usable black cloak, and this is why doing so is prohibited on the Sabbath.[200]

Rabbi Epstein rules that the law follows the view of *Tosafot*—since a consensus of scholars support that position (Principle 2)—and because he argues that the views of both *Rashi* and Maimonides are unable to adequately account for the Talmud's prohibition on shaking out specifically a black cloak and its limiting of this prohibition to one who cares to have his cloak shaken out in this manner (Principle 1).[201] Nevertheless, since the issue involves a possible violation of biblical Sabbath laws, and because the Talmudic discussion on the matter is genuinely indeterminate and does not admit an analytically clear standard, Rabbi Epstein rules that in practice one must avoid engaging in any of the acts that the various rabbinic understandings of this Talmudic norm contemplate (Principle 4).
Methodological Principles: 1, 2, 4.

Example #110 – *Arukh HaShulchan* §303:22

The Talmud records a rabbinic enactment forbidding women from walking in a public domain on the Sabbath while wearing certain items of jewelry. While one who is wearing jewelry is not "carrying" the jewelry and is thus not violating the biblical prohibition against carrying objects in a public domain on the Sabbath, the Rabbis nevertheless prohibited the wearing of some kinds of jewelry because they were concerned that the wearer may remove the piece to

---

197 Babylonian Talmud, Shabbat 147a.
198 *See* Arukh HaShulchan, Orach Chaim 302:1.
199 *See* Arbah Turim, Orach Chaim 302; Shulchan Arukh, Orach Chaim 302:1.
200 Mishneh Torah, Hilkhot Shabbat 10:18.
201 *See* Arukh HaShulchan, Orach Chaim 203:2.

show others while walking in a public area, thus inadvertently violating the biblical proscription against carrying.[202] While the Rabbis held that this restriction applies to wearing jewelry in both genuine public spaces as well as semi-public enclosed residential courtyards, the Talmudic sage Rav ruled that this rabbinic prohibition does not include the wearing of hats or wigs in such courtyards, so as to ensure that women may appear well made-up in front of their own husbands.[203]

Rabbi Epstein notes, however, that the common practice of women in his own time was to wear all kinds of jewelry in public on the Sabbath without any apparent regard for any Talmudic regulations. Moreover, Rabbi Epstein points out that contemporary rabbinic authorities seem to take no issue with this widespread practice. While some authorities do in fact maintain that this prevalent practice is prohibited by Talmudic law, they write that it is best not to inform people of this fact because the women likely will continue wearing their jewelry in public anyway, "and it is better that they sin unknowingly than intentionally."[204] Rabbi Epstein, however, is unsatisfied with this explanation of the issue because he is unwilling to accept that the widespread practice of otherwise observant women is sinful. Instead, he records a number of bases for justifying the general custom to wear jewelry in public on the Sabbath (Principle 8).

Rabbi Epstein notes that some rabbis have tried to justify the contemporary practice of wearing jewelry in public on the Sabbath by adopting the non-normative view expressed by Rabbeinu Tam that there are genuine "public domains" within which biblical proscriptions for carrying on the Sabbath no longer exist. Based on this view, modern public streets are legally akin to Talmudic courtyards. Relying on this view and also analogizing contemporary accessories worn by women to Talmudic hats, some authorities have justified the modern practice of women wearing accessories in public on the Sabbath on the basis of Rav's Talmudic exception to the general prohibition on wearing jewelry in public. Wearing jewelry in public in contemporary times is legally analogous to wearing a hat or wig in a courtyard in Talmudic times and is thus permitted (Principle 5).[205] Rabbi Epstein finds this justification for the common custom of wearing jewelry in public on the Sabbath unsatisfactory, however, because it relies on a view that is not universally accepted: that a biblically defined "public domain" must be a space used by six hundred thousand people, and because there are in fact cities where that requirement is met. Ultimately, the justification for this widespread practice that seemingly disregards an explicit rabbinic prohibition must rest on more solid foundations.

Instead, Rabbi Epstein offers several reasons for which the original Talmudic prohibition may no longer remain in force due to changes in social practices and norms in contemporary times (Principle 9). First, Rabbi Epstein suggests that, since in modern times—unlike in the Talmudic era, when jewelry was far rarer and more valuable—women regularly wear jewelry in public; therefore, there is no real concern that they might remove their accessories to show them to others. Additionally, Rabbi Epstein suggests that the Talmudic Rabbis were concerned that women might remove and show off their jewelry in public because women did not often leave their homes—when they did leave, there was a reasonable basis for being concerned that they would use that time to show their jewelry to each other. In modern times, however, women do leave their homes during the week and on the Sabbath, and thus there is no concern that meeting each other in the street poses any kind of special occasion that may result in their removing and displaying their jewelry.

---

202 Babylonian Talmud, Shabbat 62a; Arukh HaShulchan, Orach Chaim 303:1.
203 Babylonian Talmud, Shabbat 64b.
204 *See* Arukh HaShulchan, Orach Chaim 203:21.
205 *See* ibid.

The Ten Methodological Principles of the *Arukh HaShulchan* | 331

Methodological Principles: 5, 8, 9.

Example #111 – *Arukh HaShulchan* §306:11

The *Arbah Turim* and *Shulchan Arukh* rule that it is forbidden for one to receive wages for work done on the Sabbath, even if one does work to fulfill a religious need.[206] This ruling is based on a Talmudic derivation from a verse in the Book of Isaiah, which descriptively speaks of the Jews' abstaining from "pursuing business" on the Sabbath.[207] Based on this rule, the *Arbah Turim* concludes that it is prohibited to hire cantors to lead prayers for the congregation during Rosh Hashanah because, just as one may not receive wages for work done on the Sabbath, one may not pay another for work done on the Sabbath or holidays.[208] While the *Shulchan Arukh* notes that some authorities permit hiring a cantor to lead prayers on the Sabbath, Rabbi Karo rules that the normative standard is that doing so is prohibited.[209]

Despite the strong positions of both the *Arbah Turim* and *Shulchan Arukh* forbidding the hiring of cantors to work on the Sabbath or holidays, Rabbi Epstein cautions against prohibiting the practice—since the widespread custom in his time was to hire a cantor (*chazzan*) to lead services on Sabbaths and holidays (Principle 8). Rabbi Epstein therefore attempts to provide several legal justifications for hiring cantors to lead prayer services on the Sabbath and holidays. First, Rabbi Epstein notes the Talmud does not prohibit paying the "translator," who during Talmudic times would loudly repeat a scholar's Torah lectures so that they could be heard by the usually large audience in attendance. Similarly, a translator would recite the Aramaic translation of the weekly public Torah reading portion alongside the one reading the standard Hebrew text.[210] Based on this precedent, Rabbi David HaLevi Segal, author of a major commentary on the *Shulchan Arukh* known as the *Turei Zahav*, argues that those needed to perform Sabbath-specific communal religious functions on the Sabbath, such as cantors or translators, may be paid for their Sabbath work.[211] Ultimately, however, Rabbi Epstein is unwilling to rely on the *Turei Zahav*'s ruling because in his view, the fact that these professionals doing Sabbath-specific work—rather than general work that happens to be done on the Sabbath—leads to paying them even more for prohibited labor (Principle 1). Rabbi Epstein next cites the *Mordechai*, who offers a second possible justification for the practice of hiring and paying cantors for leading prayers on the Sabbath by arguing that it is generally and broadly permitted to pay individuals to perform religious needs on the Sabbath. Rabbi Epstein rejects this approach as well—the Talmud explicitly prohibits paying certain other individuals for serving religious functions on the Sabbath, thus undermining the credibility of the *Mordechai*'s blanket permission (Principle 1).

Instead, Rabbi Epstein justifies the common practice of hiring cantors for Sabbath prayers by arguing that since there is no other way to ensure that people will fulfill this important religious function except by paying them for their work on the Sabbath, doing so is permitted (Principle 10). This is especially true, Rabbi Epstein argues, because one may view such payments not as being for work performed on the Sabbath itself, but for preparatory work done during the

---

206 See *Arbah Turim, Orach Chaim* 306.
207 Isaiah 58:13; *see also* Babylonian Talmud, Shabbat 150a; Arukh HaShulchan, Orach Chaim 306:1, 9.
208 See *Arbah Turim, Orach Chaim* 585; Babylonian Talmud, Bava Metzia 58b.
209 Shulchan Arukh, Orach Chaim 306:5; 585:1.
210 See Babylonian Talmud, Pesachim 50b.
211 See Turei Zahav *to* Shulchan Arukh, Orach Chaim 306:7.

week. Rabbi Epstein notes that, in truth in his own time, the need to hire paid cantors is not so pressing, since there are very many laypeople capable of leading the prayers. Nevertheless, communities strongly prefer to hire professional cantors with beautiful voices, and in practice having skilled cantors—for which the community must pay—has become an important religious need for the community (Principle 5). Moreover, Rabbi Epstein suggests that the cantors themselves do not view their activities as work, since they genuinely enjoy leading the prayers, and in any case, payments to cantors are not expressly made for their services in leading the prayers, but are given as a "gift" in gratitude for the cantors' efforts. Consequently, Rabbi Epstein rules that under these circumstances the Talmudic prohibition against paying cantors for their Sabbath work does not apply (Principle 9), especially since the point at issue here is the possible violation of a rabbinic prohibition rather than any actual biblically proscribed Sabbath labor (Principle 4). Methodological Principles: 1, 4, 5, 8, 9, 10.

Example #112 – *Arukh HaShulchan* §307:3

The Talmud forbids reading "ordinary documents" on the Sabbath.[212] Both *Rashi* and *Tosafot* rule that this prohibition applies specifically to reading business-related documents based on a verse in the Book of Isaiah, which characterizes the Sabbath as a day when one "does not pursue their commercial affairs or speak about [business] matters."[213] According to these authorities, the Talmudic prohibition is limited; while one may not read business documents, reading ordinary letters and other neutral materials on the Sabbath—even if not religious texts—remains permitted. Maimonides and the *Semag*, however, offer a completely different reason for the Talmudic prohibition against reading "ordinary documents." They argue that the Talmudic Rabbis were concerned that one who reads non-religious texts on the Sabbath may inadvertently come to erase some of the text, thereby performing a biblically proscribed Sabbath labor.[214] Maimonides's understanding of this issue has several important implications for the scope of the rabbinic prohibition against reading "ordinary documents." *Rashi* and *Tosafot* view the prohibition as a function of Isaiah's forbidding people from speaking of business matters on the Sabbath, and thus hold that the prohibition applies only to reading business documents aloud on the Sabbath. Reading non-religious texts not related to business matters aloud or reading even business documents silently, so as not to "speak about [business] matters," remains permitted in this view. According to Maimonides, however, reading any non-religious texts—even if one does so silently—remains prohibited because diverting one's mind from religious concerns while reading risks one's forgetting oneself and accidentally erasing some of the text in violation of Sabbath laws.

Rabbi Epstein adopts Maimonides's more expansive understanding of the Talmudic prohibition against reading "ordinary documents" (Principle 3) and further attempts to demonstrate that Maimonides's view is also endorsed by a consensus of major codifiers of Jewish law, including the *Arbah Turim* and *Shulchan Arukh* (Principle 2). He notes that both the *Arbah Turim* and *Shulchan Arukh* prohibit reading all secular documents on the Sabbath.[215] Since the aforementioned verse from Isaiah admits no such broad prohibition, Rabbi Epstein infers that the *Arbah Turim* and *Shulchan Arukh* follow Maimonides's view that the Talmudic prohibition

---

212 *See* Babylonian Talmud, Shabbat 116b, 149a.
213 Isaiah 58:13.
214 Mishneh Torah, Hilkhot Shabbat 23:19.
215 Arbah Turim, Orach Chaim 307:13.

is broadly based on a general concern that one may come to erase texts that one reads on the Sabbath. Therefore, one may only read religious works, which help keep one's mind focused on the Sabbath and obviate the concern that one may erase the text being read.
Methodological Principles: 2, 3.

Example #113 – *Arukh HaShulchan* §308:14

In order to better preserve the restful and tranquil quality and atmosphere of the Sabbath, the Talmudic Rabbis enacted a number of laws prohibiting conduct that, while not violating biblical labor proscriptions, would undermine the restful character of the day. One of the most expansive of these rabbinic prohibitions is the doctrine of *muktzah*, which restricts the kinds of objects and items that can be moved or handled on the Sabbath. Typically, whether a particular object can be used or handled on the Sabbath depends on the nature of the item, and an important distinction is drawn between objects whose principal use is itself permitted on the Sabbath and objects whose primary purpose is for use in activities that constitute biblically proscribed forms of Sabbath labor. Maimonides explains the basic doctrine as follows:

1. There are utensils that are used for permitted purposes, *i.e.* a utensil that may be used on the Sabbath for the same purpose for which it is used during the week. For example, a cup to drink from, a bowl to eat from, a knife to cut meat or bread, a hatchet to crack open nuts, and the like.
2. There are utensils that are used for forbidden purposes, *i.e.* a utensil that is forbidden to be used on the Sabbath for the same purpose that it is [ordinarily] used. For example, a grinder, a mill, and the like—for it is forbidden to crush or grind on the Sabbath.
3. All utensils used for purposes that are permitted may be carried on the Sabbath . . . for the sake of the utensil itself, for the use of the place they occupy, or to use it [for a permitted activity]. All utensils used for purposes that are forbidden . . . may be moved for the use of the place [they occupy], or to use them [for permitted activities]. However, it is prohibited to move such utensils for their own sake.
4. For example, one may move a wooden bowl to eat from it, to sit in the place [where it is located], or so that it will not be stolen. The latter is [what is meant by the expression] "for the sake of [the utensil] itself." Similarly, [a utensil] may be taken out of the sun so that it will not become dried out and break. It may also be removed from the rain so that it will not become wet and deteriorate. These are considered "for the sake of [the utensil] itself" and are permitted, since the tasks performed with this utensil are permitted.
5. Similarly, one may move a mill or a grinder in order to crack nuts open on it or to climb up to a couch on it. This is [what is meant by the expression] "to use it [for a purpose that is permitted]." Likewise, [one may move it] to sit in the place where it is located. However, one may not move it so that it will not break, so that it will not be stolen, or the like [because this would be "moving it for its own sake," which is prohibited with respect to utensils used for forbidden purposes].[216]

---

216 Mishneh Torah, Hilkhot Shabbat 25:1-5.

Despite this general prohibition against handling items made to be used to perform activities that are forbidden on the Sabbath "for their own sake," Rabbi Epstein utilizes a passage in the Jerusalem Talmud to prescribe a method that would permit moving such items to avoid their becoming lost or damaged. The Jerusalem Talmud addresses a situation in which one left nets sitting outside in the sun on the Sabbath and is concerned that the sun will damage the nets. Nets, which are used for trapping—a prohibited Sabbath labor—cannot be moved "for their own sake," and can only be handled to put the nets themselves to some Sabbath-permitted use. The Jerusalem Talmud rules that one might successfully remove the nets from the sun to the shade in the following, somewhat duplicitous manner: one should think to oneself that one wants to use the nets as a pillow (a Sabbath-permitted use that would allow the handling of the nets), and then, once the nets are being moved for this "reason," they can be moved to a shaded area.[217] Based on this discussion, Rabbi Epstein rules that one may indeed move items that one is otherwise prohibited to handle on the Sabbath in order to protect them from becoming lost or damaged, provided that one can come up with some permitted pretext for moving the item in the first place (Principle 1). Rabbi Epstein acknowledges that such a fictitious pretext amounts to a *har'amah*, a kind of formalistic legal trickery, but maintains that this is justified in order to avoid financial loss (Principle 10).

Methodological Principles: 1, 10.

Example #114 – *Arukh HaShulchan* §308:29

The Talmud rules that pieces of reeds that became separated from the kinds of reed mats upon which people customarily sat during the Talmudic era may be handled and moved; they are not considered to be *muktzah*. While typically it is prohibited to handle useless or ruined household objects because they serve no useful purpose on the Sabbath and are thus classified as *muktzah*, this is not the case with respect to pieces of worn out reed mats. While such items are no longer useful to sit upon, they are still useful for covering up dirt or filth; they are therefore not *mutktzah* and may be handled and moved for any purpose that does not constitute a biblically prohibited Sabbath labor.[218] This rule is codified by the *Shulchan Arukh*, which teaches that unless a worn out mat or rug was thrown away in the trash prior to the Sabbath—thereby indicating that the owner sees it as having no further useful purpose—one may use worn out rugs or mats for any purpose otherwise permitted on the Sabbath.[219]

Rabbi Epstein rejects the *Shulchan Arukh*'s ruling, however, and maintains that the Talmudic permission to use worn out rugs or mats on the Sabbath no longer applies. Rabbi Epstein points out that in his own time and place, people do not generally sit upon rugs in the manner that people did during the times of the Talmud. Instead, the vast majority of rugs are merely commodities designated for commercial sale, and are thus classified as inherently *muktzah*, based on the fact that they are items whose primary function (being bought and sold) is prohibited on the Sabbath. Consequently, due to this changed reality of how rugs are utilized, Rabbi Epstein rules that the broad Talmudic permission to use rugs for other purposes on the Sabbath no longer applies. Unless specifically designated for use on the Sabbath, rugs may only be moved or handled if one needs the rug itself for some permitted purpose or if one needs to use the space in which the rug currently sits (Principles 8 and 9).

---

217 Jerusalem Talmud, Shabbat 4:2.
218 Babylonian Talmud, Shabbat 125a.
219 Shulchan Arukh, Orach Chaim 308:12.

Methodological Principles: 8, 9.

Example #115 – *Arukh HaShulchan* §310:15

Both the *Arbah Turim* and *Shulchan Arukh* rule that one is allowed to handle or move a vessel that contains both *muktzah* and non-*muktzah* items.[220] Thus, for example, it is permitted to move a pan which holds both ashes and twigs. Although the twigs are *muktzah*, the ashes are not because ashes are useful for covering up human or animal waste on the Sabbath. While typically one is not allowed to handle or move a vessel that contains *muktzah* items on the Sabbath, one may move such a vessel if it contains both *muktzah* and non-*muktzah* items. These authorities qualify this permission, however, by noting that one may only handle and move the vessel containing both *muktzah* and non-*muktzah* items if the non-*muktzah* items are "more important" relative to the *muktzah* items.

Rabbi Epstein observes that the rulings of the *Arbah Turim* and *Shulchan Arukh* on this issue fail to determine explicitly whether one may move a vessel that contains both *muktzah* and non-*muktzah* items in cases where both items are of equal importance. While some authorities rule that it is prohibited to handle the vessel in such a case, Rabbi Epstein notes that this conclusion is seemingly contradicted by the fact that the language of the *Arbah Turim* and *Shulchan Arukh* suggests that handling the vessel is only prohibited if the *muktzah* item is more important than the non-*muktzah* item, but not when both are of equal significance. On the other hand, he observes, one may read these sources and reach the opposite conclusion—that one may handle the vessel only when the non-*muktzah* item is more important, but not when both items are of equal importance.

Rabbi Epstein ultimately concludes that one may handle a vessel that contains both *muktzah* and non-*muktzah* items, even when the non-*muktzah* objects are not more important than their *muktzah* counterparts. As long as the *muktzah* items are not more significant relative to the non-*muktzah* items, the vessel in which both are contained may be handled and moved. Rabbi Epstein justifies this conclusion directly on the basis of his own understanding of the Talmudic discussion over when one may handle vessels that contain both *muktzah* and non-*muktzah* items.[221] Rabbi Epstein understands that the conclusion of this complex Talmudic discussion is that one may handle a vessel that contains both *muktzah* and non-*muktzah* objects, unless the non-*muktzah* item is legally nullified relative to the *muktzah* item (Principle 1). Rabbi Epstein further argues that this conclusion is also more logically sound because, when the two items are of relatively equal importance, neither item is legally nullified; since ultimately the non-*muktzah* object remains significant in its own right, one should be permitted to handle the vessel in order to move the non-*muktzah* items contained therein (Principle 1). While he does not say so explicitly, it is also likely that Rabbi Epstein is more confident in his lenient ruling because moving *muktzah* objects is ultimately a rabbinic prohibition and not a biblical one—any uncertainties about both the correct meaning of the relevant Talmudic discussion and the rulings of the *Arbah Turim* and *Shulchan Arukh* should therefore be resolved in favor of leniency (Principle 4). Methodological Principles: 1, 4.

---

220 *See* Arbah Turim, Orach Chaim 310; Shulchan Arukh, Orach Chaim 310:8.
221 *See* Babylonian Talmud, Shabbat 47a.

Example #116 – *Arukh HaShulchan* §314:11

One of the kinds of labor prohibited on the Sabbath is creating a finished vessel or product. In light of this stricture against creating a new vessel, the Talmud discusses the circumstances under which one may open a sealed barrel, effectively making the once-closed barrel into a newly usable vessel. The Talmud rules that, while one may perforate the sealed hole of a barrel that sits above the level of the wine sediment that settles at the bottom of the barrel, one may not perforate a sealed hole previously made very low on the wall of the barrel below the point where the sediment has settled.[222] Commentators explain that it is permitted to open a sealed hole situated high on the barrel because, since such seals are relatively weak and impermanent, opening the seal is more like reopening an already fully formed vessel than creating a new one. The seals on holes below the sediment line, however, are especially strong due to the pressure of all the sediment and wine pressing down on the seal. Such seals are considered quite solid, and the Talmud therefore views opening them as a violation of the prohibition against completing the making of a new vessel—in this case the barrel, which was previously useless and sealed, but is now able to be filled and emptied through the newly made hole.

Rabbi Epstein rules that this Talmudic standard means that one may, in accordance with the generally accepted custom, open the sealed spout of a glass bottle on the Sabbath, even if doing so requires the use of a tool in order to remove the well-attached bottle cap. This is because such bottle caps are located at the top rather than at the bottom of the bottle, and thus fall within the Talmudic permission to reopen sealed openings located above the sediment line of a barrel or other container (Principles 8 and 1).

Methodological Principles 1, 8.

Example #117 – *Arukh HaShulchan* §316:6

Trapping animals is one of the thirty-nine categories of labor that are biblically prohibited on the Sabbath. As is true with respect to other kinds of forbidden Sabbath labors, this kind of activity is only biblically proscribed when done in a significantly impactful way that truly alters the state of the target animal from being "free" to being "trapped." Rabbinic authorities thus discuss whether one is liable for trapping animals that are in some manner incapacitated, such that they are not truly "free" even before having been trapped. Rabbi Epstein adopts Maimonides's view that whether one is liable for trapping an incapacitated animal depends on the kind of present incapacitation of the animal. For instance, Maimonides rules that one is liable for violating the Sabbath laws if one traps a deer that is sleeping because this is merely a naturally temporary incapacitation, and if the deer were to awaken, it would be able to run free but for its having been trapped. The act of trapping such a deer is thus viewed as effective and significant, and therefore is prohibited on the Sabbath.[223] However, in situations where the deer is lame, sick, or old, one is not liable for trapping it; since the animal's natural state prevents it from being able to escape and having complete freedom of movement, trapping the animal is not truly effective at altering its state of being and does not make the trapper liable for violating the Sabbath. Likewise, Maimonides rules that one is not liable for trapping a very young deer, since such animals are naturally docile and would not seek to run away but for their having been trapped. Rabbi Epstein adopts Maimonides's rulings (Principle 3) and innovates some additional parameters for the

---

222 Babylonian Talmud, Shabbat 146b.
223 Mishneh Torah, Hilkhot Shabbat 10:24.

scope of the Sabbath prohibition against trapping based on his own analytic intuition (Principle 1). First, Rabbi Epstein rules that Maimonides's trapping exemptions for young or old animals do not apply to capturing fish. Fish, Rabbi Epstein argues, are neither docile when young nor infirm when old, and capturing them at any time violates the prohibition against trapping on the Sabbath. Likewise, he says, fish—even if injured—are never legally regarded as being "lame" and not subject to the prohibition against trapping because in reality even injured fish are able to freely swim around in the water, such that confining them in any manner necessarily constitutes genuine "trapping" within the meaning of the biblical Sabbath restriction.
Methodological Principles: 1, 3.

Example #118 – *Arukh HaShulchan* §345:18

Carrying objects through a "public domain" is one of the thirty-nine categories of labor biblically proscribed on the Sabbath. The Talmud identifies a "public domain" as an open area at least sixteen cubits wide that is accessible to the public at large. Post-Talmudic authorities disagreed, however, about whether an area must actually be utilized by some minimum number of people to be classified as a "public domain" under biblical law. Most early scholars, including Maimonides, maintained that any space that meets the Talmudic qualifications of being sixteen cubits wide and freely accessible to the public at large meets the definition of a "public domain" within which carrying objects on the Sabbath is biblically forbidden. This view is grounded in the simple fact that, while the Talmud spends a good deal of time defining and justifying its definition of the legal parameters of a biblical "public domain," it makes no mention of any minimum population threshold that must actually use the space in question for it to be considered "public." Other scholars, most notably among them *Rashi*, maintained that an area can only be considered a biblical "public domain" if, in addition to its satisfying the Talmud's other explicit requirements, it is also regularly used by six hundred thousand people. This view is based on the Talmud's derivation of the size and character of a biblical "public domain" from the Torah's descriptions of the Jews' desert encampment during their forty-year sojourn in the wilderness. Since the Torah describes the Jewish population following the exodus as comprising some six hundred thousand military-age men, these authorities argue that a "public domain"—which is understood to track the Jews' biblical encampment—is a space that is utilized by at least six hundred thousand people.

This dispute has important and obvious practical ramifications. According to the minority view held by *Rashi* that only spaces utilized by at least six hundred thousand people may be classified as public domains, Jews may routinely carry items through virtually all public streets on the Sabbath, since there are almost no public spaces that are regularly traversed and utilized by six hundred thousand individuals. According to the majority approach exemplified by Maimonides, however, carrying objects on the Sabbath in almost all public streets would be prohibited, since these spaces are wide enough and accessible enough to qualify as "public domains," where carrying is biblically prohibited.

In evaluating this issue, Rabbi Epstein expresses serious doubts about the Talmudic soundness and analytic reasonableness of the minority view expressed by *Rashi* that considers only spaces used by six hundred thousand people to be "public domains." As noted earlier, the Talmud itself makes no explicit mention of any minimum population threshold as a condition for categorizing spaces as public. Moreover, as a general rule, legal opinions endorsed by a majority of scholars—like Maimonides's view on this issue—are given greater weight than those held by only a minority of scholars. Finally, Rabbi Epstein points out that *Rashi*'s views appear to contradict a biblical verse in which the prophet Nechemiah chastises the people for carrying in public on the Sabbath at a time when the local population numbered much fewer than six hundred thousand people.[224]

Despite his own analytic concerns about the legal viability of *Rashi*'s view, Rabbi Epstein ultimately accepts this definition of a "public domain" as normative. He writes:

> However, in any case all this analysis does not matter now that there is widespread acceptance [that carrying in the streets is permitted] in most of the cities of the Jewish people these past several hundred years in reliance on this [minority] viewpoint. And it is as if a voice has gone forth from the Heavens, saying that "the *halakhah* is in accordance with this view."[225]

The widespread customary acceptance and practical implementation of *Rashi*'s opinion over an extended period of time is thus sufficient to justify this ruling (Principle 8).
Methodological Principles: 8.

Example #119 – *Arukh HaShulchan* §417:8

Before the destruction of the Second Temple and the disbanding of the *Sanhedrin*, the Jewish religious calendar was determined by the monthly testimony of witnesses who appeared before the *Sanhedrin* to testify on having seen the new moon, thus establishing the start of a new month. With the disbanding of the *Sanhedrin*, a fixed calendar was instituted, thereby obviating the need for witnesses to testify and for a rabbinic court to formally declare the start of each new month. Nevertheless, in commemoration of this ancient practice, the Rabbis also instituted a special prayer known as the *Birkhat HaChodesh*, or "the sanctification of the month," which is recited on the Sabbath preceding the start of a new month according to the fixed Jewish calendar.[226]

The *Arukh HaShulchan* notes that in his own time and place, the common custom was to recite the *Birkhat HaChodesh* blessing while standing, since during Temple times, the witnesses who appeared before the *Sanhedrin* to testify about their having seen the new moon would have done so while standing. Moreover, he observes that the custom is to also announce the *molad*, the precise time that the new moon is expected to appear over Jerusalem, according to the astronomical calculations upon which the fixed Jewish calendar is based. This custom, too, is rooted in a memorialization of the *Sanhedrin*'s practice of declaring each new month. While the *Sanhedrin* declared the start of a new month based on eyewitness testimony of the sighting of the new moon, members of the *Sanhedrin* would compare the witnesses' testimony to their own astronomical calculations and predictions about when and where the new moon would appear. Since knowledge of the *molad* was an important feature of the *Sanhedrin*'s sanctification of the new month, the announcement of the *molad* is an appropriate accompaniment to the modern custom of reciting the *Birkhat HaChodesh* (Principles 1 and 8).

Rabbi Epstein goes on to explain that the popular practice of reciting the *Birkhat HaChodesh* blessing on the Sabbath preceding the start of the new month rather than at some other time is rooted in a desire to announce the new month to the community at a time and place where large numbers of Jews gather together at once (Principle 1). Moreover, Rabbi Epstein points out this custom is actually grounded in and legitimated by a passage in the Jerusalem

---

224 *See generally* Arukh HaShulchan, Orach Chaim 345:16-18.
225 Ibid. 345:18.
226 *See* ibid. 417:6-7.

Talmud. The Jerusalem Talmud records that Rabbi Yosah said that he did not recite the *Musaf* prayer because he did not know how to calculate the start of the new month. Rabbi Epstein reasons that Rabbi Yosah cannot be speaking about praying the *Musaf* prayer of *Rosh Chodesh*—the first day of the new month—itself, since one would certainly know whether any specific day was or was not *Rosh Chodesh*, and this would not depend on being able to calculate the start of the new month in advance. Instead, Rabbi Epstein says, Rabbi Yosah must be referring to the *Musaf* prayer of the Sabbath preceding the start of the new month, meaning to say that he would not recite the *Birkhat HaChodesh* as part of the Sabbath *Musaf* service because he did not know how to calculate the start of the new month in advance. Thus, Rabbi Epstein says, the common custom of reciting the *Birkhat HaChodesh* on the Sabbath preceding the beginning of the new month is legitimated by the Jerusalem Talmud (Principles 1 and 8).
Methodological Principles: 1, 8.

Example #120 – *Arukh HaShulchan* §417:10

While it is permissible to perform *melakhah*—the kinds of labor prohibited on the Sabbath—on *Rosh Chodesh*, there is a custom among some women to refrain from engaging in such work on *Rosh Chodesh*. This custom is rooted in a passage of the Jerusalem Talmud, which records that in recognition of the righteousness of Jewish women who refused their husbands' demands to donate their jewelry for the creation of the Golden Calf, women were afforded this added day of rest from labor (Principle 1). Rabbi Epstein praises this practice and accords it significant *halakhic* weight (Principle 8). Thus, he notes that, if the local custom is to perform some kinds of labor and not others, one may do so, but only if one is certain as to which kinds of work are permitted by local practice; the *halakhic* presumption, however, is that women may not perform any kind of *melakhah* on *Rosh Chodesh*. Despite this strong *halakhic* presumption that all labor is prohibited on *Rosh Chodesh*, the *Arukh HaShulchan* records that custom in his community was for women who were not engaged in business or expert labor refrain from doing creative labor at all on *Rosh Chodesh*, but those engaged in business or trades are not to refrain from doing their usual work. While Rabbi Epstein appears unhappy with this custom and justifies it only as an exigency measure necessary to ensure that people's livelihoods are protected (Principle 10), he legitimates the local custom as setting the standard for normative religious practice (Principle 8), and he refrains from urging people to adopt the supererogatory practice of refraining from *melakhah* in order to uphold the original laudable custom recorded in the Jerusalem Talmud (Principle 6).
Methodological Principles: 1, 6, 8, 10.

Example #121 – *Arukh HaShulchan* §419:2

Following a passage in the Jerusalem Talmud, the *Arbah Turim* rules that one should enjoy a festive meal on *Rosh Chodesh* in the same manner that one holds a festive meal on the holiday of Purim. Indeed, the *Arbah Turim* thinks that this obligation is sufficiently important that he rules that in months when *Rosh Chodesh* occurs on the Sabbath, one should eat a festive meal on the following Sunday (since Sabbath meals displace any special *Rosh Chodesh* meal). The *Arbah Turim* and other authorities argue that various biblical verses lend support for this idea.[227]

---

227 Ibid. 419:1.

In light of this strong tradition and basis for eating a festive meal on *Rosh Chodesh*, the *Arukh HaShulchan* questions the common practice of his own time, which disregarded the apparent *halakhic* imperative to eat a festive *Rosh Chodesh* meal (Principle 1). Rather than rejecting the local custom of not eating a festive meal on *Rosh Chodesh*, Rabbi Epstein seeks to justify the custom (Principle 8). He posits that perhaps the reason for this custom is that the Babylonian Talmud makes no clear directive to eat a festive meal on *Rosh Chodesh*, and Rabbi Karo in his *Beit Yosef* dismisses the biblical proofs offered by the *Arbah Turim* to support the obligation. Thus, the *Arukh HaShulchan* concludes that, consistent with the local custom, there is no actual legal obligation to eat a festive *Rosh Chodesh*. Still, Rabbi Epstein indicates that while it is not obligatory to eat a festive *Rosh Chodesh* meal, it is still appropriate to do so, since, as the Jerusalem Talmud indicates, making special efforts to mark *Rosh Chodesh* is religiously positive (Principle 6). Rabbi Epstein limits his encouragement to eat a special festive meal on *Rosh Chodesh* because, as he notes, in his time and place, doing so could be financially stressful, and he therefore recommends merely eating some kind of special dish or food—rather than a whole meal—in honor of the day (Principle 10).

Methodological Principles: 1, 6, 8, 10.

Example #122 - *Arukh HaShulchan* §430:5

The *Arukh HaShulchan* notes that there is a popular custom to not fast and to have a bit more than usual to eat and drink on *isru chag*, the day following the three major Jewish holidays of Sukkot, Passover, and Shavuot, because these days are considered quasi-holidays. Rabbi Epstein endorses this custom (Principle 8) and attempts to support it by suggesting that indeed the day after a holiday is a holiday because the happiness of the holidays is tied to the opportunity to consume the meat of the *Shelamim* offering, which was offered over the holiday during Temple times. Since the meat of a *Shelamim* offering can be consumed for two days and a night after it is first slaughtered, and since the holiday *Shelamim* can be offered on the last day of the holiday, it would be possible for people to continue eating the meat of their holiday offerings on the day following the holiday itself. Thus, Rabbi Epstein says, the happiness of the holiday extends through the day following the festival. In modern times, without a Temple or animal offerings, this continuing joyfulness is memorialized through the popular custom of not fasting and eating and drinking a bit more than usual in celebration of the day (Principle 1).

Methodological Principles: 1, 8.

Example #123 - *Arukh HaShulchan* §432:3

As is the case with all blessings recited upon the performance of a *mitzvah*, it is prohibited to speak or otherwise interrupt one's concentration after reciting the blessing but before beginning the search for *chametz*, or leavened products, on the night before Passover. Some authorities go so far as to rule that one is prohibited from interrupting the *chametz* search even after it has begun until after the search has been completed, and that if one did interrupt the search, one would have to recite the blessing once again before resuming one's search for *chametz*.[228]

The *Arukh HaShulchan* rejects this rule (Principle 1). Rabbi Epstein reasons that it is unreasonable to suppose that people could possibly complete the search for *chametz* without

---

228 See Turei Zahav *to* Shulchan Arukh, Orach Chaim 433:1.

any interruptions; after all, the search for *chametz* is not merely a short ritual performed on the night before Passover, but is a process that continues up until and through the holiday itself—as long as one must ensure that no *chametz* is found in his or her possession. It would be absurd, Rabbi Epstein says, to demand that people recite a new blessing before each and every small act of searching for *chametz* or ensuring that no further *chametz* is found in one's property (Principle 10). Rather, just as reciting the blessing of *hamotzi lechem min haaretz* on bread at the start of a meal covers all the food eaten at the meal, even when one interrupts one's eating by speaking or the like, so too the entire *chametz*-search process is covered by the initial blessing that is recited at the beginning of the formal obligatory search on the night before Passover. Methodological Principles: 1, 10.

Example #124 – Arukh HaShulchan §433:6

The *Shulchan Arukh* rules that, when searching for *chametz*, one does not have to search the middle of one's courtyard, unless one knows for certain that *chametz* is present; if *chametz* merely *may* be present, however, one need not search that part of the courtyard, since one can rely on the likelihood that any *chametz* there will be eaten by birds prior to Passover.[229] The *Rema* points out, however, that in another ruling the *Shulchan Arukh* seems to contradict this position. Elsewhere, Rabbi Karo permits a person to put *chametz* in a location frequented by birds, which the *Rema* supposes means that one certainly would not have to be careful to remove known *chametz* from the middle of an open courtyard where birds are likewise present.[230]

Rabbi Epstein notes that later commentators offer several possible resolutions to these apparently contradictory rulings by the *Shulchan Arukh*. According to the *Bayit Chadash* and *Turei Zahav*, the two rulings refer to two different kinds of courtyards. The first ruling refers to a private courtyard owned by the person searching for *chametz*—since he owns the courtyard, he must make sure to remove any *chametz* that he knows is present, though the likelihood that present *chametz* will be eaten by birds ameliorates any need to search the courtyard for *chametz* if he does not know for certain that *chametz* is in fact present. The second ruling, however, refers to throwing *chametz* into the public street or an ownerless courtyard. In that case, the *chametz* may be left out and need not be actively destroyed, since the combination of the person's lack of ownership of the space and the likelihood that his *chametz* will be consumed by birds in any case removes any concerns that he will end up still owning the *chametz* when Passover begins.

The *Magen Avraham* and others offer a different distinction. Based on this view, the *Shulchan Arukh*'s second ruling refers to leaving *chametz* in an open location prior to the night of the fourteenth of Nissan when the *halakhic* obligation to search for and remove *chametz* actually kicks in. The *Shulchan Arukh*'s earlier ruling, by contrast, refers to a case in which a person is searching for *chametz* after the obligation to do so takes effect. In the latter case, one cannot rely on the possibility that birds will eat the *chametz* if he knows that *chametz* is indeed present in the courtyard, since a fundamental decisional principle of *halakhah* maintains "*ein safek motzi m'yidei vadai*"—possibilities do not override certainties. Since in that case the obligation to remove *chametz* presently exists, the definite presence of *chametz* in the courtyard cannot be rectified by relying on the mere possibility that birds will consume the *chametz* prior to the start of Passover.

---

229 Shulchan Arukh, Orach Chaim 433:6.
230 *See* Rema *to* Shulchan Arukh, Orach Chaim 433:6. *See also* Shulchan Arukh, Orach Chaim 445:3.

The *Arukh HaShulchan* rules in accordance with the distinction between public and private courtyards suggested by the *Bayit Chadash* and *Turei Zahav*. Based on his understanding of the way in which the Talmud applies the principle of *ein safek motzi m'yidei vadai* to the obligation to search for *chametz*, Rabbi Epstein concludes that the distinction proposed by the *Magen Avraham*—between searching for *chametz* before or after the night of the fourteenth of Nissan—is incorrect (Principle 1). He explains that the Talmud indicates that the principle of *ein safek motzi m'yidei vadai* applies to the need to search for *chametz* in locations in one's own property that one is legally obligated to ensure are *chametz*-free for Passover. Since the principle is dependent on *location*, it should make no difference whether any particular location is being searched before or after the night of the fourteenth of Nissan, and the time-based distinction drawn by the *Magen Avraham* between searching for *chametz* in the same kind of location before or after the *halakhic* obligation to search takes effect is thus incorrect.
Methodological Principles: 1.

Example #125 – *Arukh HaShulchan* §434:7

The *Arbah Turim* rules that, immediately after one finishes searching for *chametz* on the evening of the fourteenth of Nissan, one should verbally nullify one's *chametz*, so that one will not violate the prohibition against owning or seeing *chametz* in case *chametz* was not found and was left over in one's possession following the required search.[231]

The *Arukh HaShulchan* questions the veracity of this rule on the basis of the *Arbah Turim*'s rationale (Principle 1): how can a person violate the prohibition on owning *chametz*, Rabbi Epstein wonders, merely because unbeknownst to them *chametz* happens to be present in their possession? On the contrary, since "the Torah and its laws were not given to the angels," a person who has searched his property and possessions for *chametz* in the manner prescribed by *halakhah* should be considered blameless for any *chametz* remaining in his possession afterwards (Principle 10). While Rabbi Epstein recognizes that it is of course possible for a person to sin inadvertently (*b'shogeg*), he argues that the characterization of sins as "inadvertent" applies only to reckless or negligent sins, such as a case where a person who is unaware of any *chametz* in his possession does not bother searching his property to confirm this fact and ends up discovering some *chametz* in his possession on Passover. In that case, the person has committed an inadvertent sin because he did not even bother to fulfill the Torah's requirement that he search for *chametz* in order to ensure that none is found in his possession during Passover. However, Rabbi Epstein rules, if a person does search in the manner prescribed by the Torah but nevertheless finds *chametz* in his possession on Passover, that person is considered in *oness*, under duress, and is therefore blameless. Rabbi Epstein thus argues that the rationale offered by the *Arbah Turim* for the obligation to verbally nullify one's *chametz* after properly searching for and removing *chametz* in one's possession (that the nullification serves to forestall possible violations of the prohibition against owning *chametz*) is inadequate.

Instead, Rabbi Epstein suggests that the reason *chametz* should be verbally nullified even after the search is properly completed is to prevent a later violation of the law against owning *chametz* in case one finds a piece of *chametz* in one's property on Passover and forgets to or delays in destroying it. Although such a person would not be liable for initially having owned that *chametz* (since he had previously searched his property), any delays in removing *chametz* that is found on Passover would amount to an active violation of the prohibition against keeping *chametz* in one's

---

231 Arbah Turim, Orach Chaim 434:2.

possession on Passover. By nullifying all such *chametz* before Passover, one ensures that any *chametz* found in one's possession on Passover is not actually his, and delays in removing that *chametz* would therefore not result in any violation of the laws against owning *chametz* on Passover.
Methodological Principles: 1, 10.

Example #126 - *Arukh HaShulchan* §434:10

Many authorities, including the *Arbah Turim* and *Shulchan Arukh*, rule that just as one may appoint an agent to clean and search his or her property in order to remove all *chametz* prior to Passover, one may also appoint another person as an agent to verbally nullify one's *chametz*. These authorities explain, however, that an agent may only successfully nullify the principal's *chametz* if the principal explicitly authorized him to do so, and that designating an agent to search for *chametz* in one's property is not sufficient to authorize the agent to also perform a legally effective *bittul*, or "nullification" of the principal's *chametz*.

The *Arukh HaShulchan* disagrees with this qualification (Principle 1). Instead, Rabbi Epstein rules that in contemporary times, when a principal authorizes an agent to perform a search for *chametz* in the principal's property, this also includes an implicit authorization empowering the agent to verbally nullify that *chametz*. Rabbi Epstein explains that the *Shulchan Arukh*'s ruling requiring an explicit authorization of the agent to nullify the *chametz* was grounded in the technical *halakhic* reality that *bedikat chametz* (the search for *chametz*) and *bittul chametz* (the nullification of *chametz*) are two separate and distinct biblical commandments; therefore, empowering an agent to perform the former does not automatically include authorization to do the latter. In his own time, however, Rabbi Epstein says, people colloquially use the term *"bedikat chametz"* to refer to both searching for and nullifying *chametz*, and thus authorizing an agent to perform *bedikat chametz* implicitly encompasses an authorization to also perform *bittul chametz* (Principles 8 and 9).
Methodological Principles: 1, 8, 9.

Example #127 - *Arukh HaShulchan* §435:3

The *Arukh HaShulchan* notes that authorities disagree about whether a person who checked for and destroyed their *chametz* prior to Passover but finds *chametz* in their home on Passover itself should—when eradicating that *chametz*—recite the blessing of *"al bi'ur chametz,"* which marks fulfillment of the biblical command "to destroy *chametz*." Rabbi Epstein himself rules that one should not recite the blessing in accordance with the general rule that one should not recite blessings—which are only rabbinic obligations—in cases where it is doubtful in the circumstances whether there is any obligation to do so (Principle 4). He reasons that the blessing that one recites before searching for and destroying one's *chametz* on the night before Passover covers all legally required searching and removing of *chametz*, even though this process may take place over a long period of time and involve many interruptions.[232] Thus, performing the *mitzvah* of removing *chametz* found on Passover has likely already been sanctified by the blessing one recited prior to *bedikat chametz* on the night of the fourteenth of Nissan, and no new blessing should be recited.
Methodological Principles: 4.

---

232 *See* Arukh HaShulchan, Orach Chaim 432:3.

Example #128 – *Arukh HaShulchan* §442:23

Rabbi Epstein quotes Rabbi Joseph Karo,[233] who rules that cheese that was curdled through the use of *chametz* (e.g. vinegar) must be destroyed before Passover. This is because the vinegar is a *"ma'amid,"* an active ingredient that causes major chemical transformations in the production of certain foods. Rabbi Epstein quotes Nachmanides, who rules that one is required to destroy even a food product created using a fourth-degree *ma'amid*. For example, if someone took the lees of beer (a leavened material) and used them to ferment mead, then took the lees of that mead and used it to ferment more mead, etc., even the fourth iteration of such a process would still be considered *chametz*. Rabbi Shneur Zalman of Liadi rules that one need not destroy such a product if doing so would cause a substantial financial loss. Rabbi Shneur Zalman contends that after the third iteration of the process, the original power of the *chametz* is weakened.[234] Rabbi Epstein relies on this ruling against the ruling of Nachmanides in the case that one encounters an extenuating circumstance of financial loss (Principles 4 and 10).

If one catalyzed a reaction using a combination of both a *ma'amid* of *chametz* and a *ma'amid* made of a non-*chametz* material, Rabbi Epstein maintains that the resultant product is permitted. Rabbi Jacob Lorberbaum, however, rules that such a product is prohibited, claiming that it is no better than a fourth iteration of a *ma'amid* (which is prohibited).[235] Rabbi Epstein counters that even in a case of a fourth iteration, the chemical power is still rooted in the *chametz* alone, whereas in a combined *ma'amid*, its power is derived from a dual source. Thus, Rabbi Epstein argues that one cannot analogize the rule of a fourth-degree *ma'amid* made of *chametz* to a *ma'amid* made of a combination of both *chametz* and non-*chametz* products. Furthermore, Rabbi Epstein brings a proof from the laws of *kilayim* (prohibited mixtures) that a product created by mixing both a permitted and prohibited source is permitted (Principle 1). Thus, Rabbi Epstein garners independent reasoning and proofs to argue against Rabbi Lorberbaum's claims.
Methodological Principles: 1, 4, 10.

Example #129 – *Arukh HaShulchan* §442:27

Some authorities rule that one is not obligated to remove or destroy small pieces of *chametz* that are smaller than the volume of an olive, unless several small pieces could be combined into a piece larger than this minimal amount. Others disagree, however, and maintain that even trace amounts of *chametz* must be removed from one's possession and destroyed prior to Passover. While Rabbi Epstein is convinced that the more lenient position—that trace amounts of *chametz* must be destroyed only if they collectively amount to more than an olive's volume—is analytically correct (Principle 1). However, he notes that the common custom in his time and place is for people to be careful to destroy even small amounts of *chametz* and therefore endorses that more stringent mode of practice (Principle 8).
Methodological Principles: 1, 8.

---

233 *See* Shulchan Arukh, Orach Chaim 442:5.
234 *See* Shulchan Arukh HaRav, Orach Chaim 442:10.
235 *See* Mekor Chaim, Orach Chaim 442:6.

Example #130 - *Arukh HaShulchan* §444:6

On the Sabbath, Jews are required to eat three meals consisting of bread: one at night, one in the morning, and one in the afternoon. If the day before Passover falls out on the Sabbath, however, the third meal becomes quite difficult to accomplish. One may not eat *matzah*, nor may one eat *chametz* past midday. Rabbi Moses Isserles[236] writes that in his areas—where people did not eat "enriched *matzah*" (*matzah* made with egg, such that it can be eaten even on the day before Passover)—one's third meal should consist of fruits or meat and fish. The *Magen Avraham*[237] suggests that, because some say that even if the third meal is eaten in the morning it still fulfills one's obligation, one should split his morning meal into two different meals.

Rabbi Epstein quotes a passage in the *Zohar* which records that if the day before Passover fell on the Sabbath, Rabbi Shimon bar Yochai would study Torah in place of the third meal. Based on this passage in the *Zohar*, Rabbi Epstein claims that there is in fact no obligation to eat a third meal on the afternoon before Passover. The meal is impossible because any type of bread is prohibited, dissolving the obligation (Principle 10). Rabbi Epstein notes that this is similar to times in which Yom Kippur falls on the Sabbath, when one is certainly not obligated to eat three meals due to the obligation to fast. Based on this understanding, Rabbi Epstein posits that Rabbi Shimon bar Yochai merely studied instead of eating meat and fish because there was no obligation to eat a third meal at all when the Sabbath coincides with Passover Eve (Principle 1). Therefore, one need not split his morning meal in two, nor partake of meat and fruit in the afternoon. Thus, Rabbi Epstein fashions quite a novel understanding of the *halakhah* based on a reading of the *Zohar* (Principles 1 and 7).
Methodological Principles: 1, 7, 10.

Example #131 - *Arukh HaShulchan* §446:11

The Jerusalem Talmud rules that if a Jew's roof is adjacent to a Gentile's roof and the Gentile's *chametz* rolled onto the Jew's roof during Passover, one should push away the *chametz* using a stick.[238] One should not handle such *chametz* directly, however, since doing so risks the possibility that one may absentmindedly forget the Passover prohibition on *chametz* and accidentally eat the *chametz* being moved. Rabbi Epstein explains that the Jerusalem Talmud maintains that, while one may handle one's own *chametz* in order to burn it on the holiday, there is a prohibition of touching a Gentile's *chametz* on Passover. What accounts for the distinction is that in the former case, there is an obligation to burn the *chametz*, whereas in the latter example, there is none. When one is involved in the process of destruction, he will not come to eat the *chametz*, and there is therefore no prohibition of touching it. When handling a Gentile's *chametz*, there is no obligation to destroy it. In such a case, therefore, the absent-minded handler's hand may stray to his mouth (Principle 1).

Rabbi Epstein claims that, since the function of roofs has changed from Talmudic times to modern times, the requirement to remove or cover *chametz* on a roof is now nonexistent (Principle 9). In Talmudic times, roofs were flat and utilized frequently by the members of the dwelling. In Rabbi Epstein's surroundings, roofs are slanted and useless. Therefore, even if a

---

236 Rema *to* Shulchan Arukh, Orach Chaim 444:1.
237 *See* Magen Avraham *to* Shulchan Arukh, Orach Chaim 444:1.
238 Mishnah, Pesachim 2:2.

Gentile's *chametz* found its way onto a roof, one is not obligated to remove it since it will not pose a serious temptation to anyone.
Methodological Principles: 1, 9.

Example #132 – *Arukh HaShulchan* §448:23

Chametz that was owned by Jews during Passover may not be eaten even after the conclusion of the holiday. However, Rabbi Joseph Karo rules that if one sold one's *chametz* to Gentiles prior to the start of Passover, that *chametz* may be consumed after the holiday, even if at the time of the sale the Jewish seller knew that the Gentile buyer intended to hold the *chametz* for safekeeping and sell it back after the holiday.[239] Indeed, he rules that if the *chametz* is very difficult to move, one can even leave the *chametz* in its place in the Jewish seller's property and sell the room in which the *chametz* is being stored to a Gentile. The *Turei Zahav* and the *Magen Avraham* both rule, however, that in cases where one sells one's *chametz* but leaves it in his house, he must give the Gentile buyer access to the house by handing over a key. Without handing over the keys, the whole sale is merely a tricky way of circumventing the law and is therefore legally invalid.

Rabbi Epstein notes, however, that in his days, the government carefully regulates the most prevalent type of *chametz* sold before Passover—alcoholic spirits. Because of this change in governmental policy, it is impossible to hand over keys to large stores of alcohol like Jews used to do in conformity to the requirements outlined by the *Turei Zahav* and the *Magen Avraham* (Principle 9). In order to justify this practice, Rabbi Epstein relies on the singular view of the *Chok Yaakov*, who limits the requirement to hand over the keys (Principle 5). According to the *Chok Yaakov*, withholding a key is only problematic for the validity of the sale if they are withheld in order to prevent the buyer from accessing his purchase. However, if one withheld the key through legal necessity, the sale is still valid. Furthermore, the requirement for the product to be accessible is only at the time of the sale. Withholding the product from the buyer once the purchase has occurred does not damage the validity of the sale. Therefore, instead of requiring the seller to hand over the key, Rabbi Epstein suggests that one should tell the Gentile where the key is placed, so that the buyer can make use of his *chametz* at his leisure.
Methodological Principles: 5, 9.

Example #133 – *Arukh HaShulchan* §453:5

The Talmud states that one can only fulfill the obligation to eat *matzah* that is made from one of the five varieties of grain mentioned in the Torah: wheat, barley, spelt, rye, and oats. Similarly, *chametz* is only prohibited if it is composed of these five grains. Thus, fermented rice, millet, beans, lentils (and other beans), legumes, and grains aside from the five biblical varieties—known as *kitniyot*—are not *chametz* and may therefore be consumed on Passover.[240]

Rabbi Epstein writes that, even though both biblical and Talmudic laws permit the consumption of *kitniyot*, the well-established custom among European Jews for hundreds of years is to refrain from eating such foods on Passover. This is due to the fact that prohibited grains can often become mixed in with *kitniyot* products, so that the consumption of *kitniyot* may result in inadvertently eating actual *chametz*. Furthermore, *kitniyot* and the prohibited grains look

---

239 Shulchan Arukh, Orach Chaim 448:3.
240 Babylonian Talmud, Pesachim 35a.

very similar once cooked; someone might come to confuse the two. In line with the consensus of authorities and his own acceptance of *minhag* as legally binding, Rabbi Epstein upholds this custom and strongly opposes those who doubt its significance and act leniently regarding it (Principle 8).

Rabbi Epstein supports the *minhag* of refraining from eating *kitniyot* on Passover by quoting a passage from the Jerusalem Talmud (Principle 1). There, Rabbi Yochanan ben Nuri claims that rice is considered a type of grain and therefore a fully prohibited source of *chametz*. The Rabbis, however, claim that rice does not undergo the prohibited process of fermentation called *chimutz*, instead undergoing a parallel, albeit permissible, process called *sirkhon*.[241] Rabbi Epstein argues that, if even the great Rabbis of the Talmud disagreed about the nature of rice fermentation, people of average intelligence would surely be easily confused about the distinction between the two products. Someone might reason that, if fermented rice is permitted on Passover, other fermented grain—whose fermentation appears similar to that of rice—are likewise allowed. To avoid this eventuality, Jews became accustomed to not eating even *kitniyot* on Passover.

Incorporated into the accepted custom, Rabbi Epstein continues, is that in a case of drought or famine—when there is not enough grain to bake *matzah* to satisfy the impoverished—the rabbis of the famished area have the ability to permit *kitniyot* for that Passover (Principle 10). Rabbi Epstein limits this permission to times past, when the only sources of sustenance were grains or *kitniyot*. However, after the onset of the potato—which became a major source of non-*kitniyot* food for the European population—there is no such permission to eat *kitniyot* in a time of famine (Principle 9).
Methodological Principles: 1, 8, 9, 10.

Example #134 – *Arukh HaShulchan* §458:3

Each Jew is commanded to eat *matzah* on the first night of Passover. Rabbi Jacob ben Asher writes that one should not begin baking the *matzah* until after midday on the Eve of Passover.[242] He quotes a responsum which rules that, just as the Passover offering was ritually invalid if slaughtered prior to midday on Passover Eve, *matzah* baked prior to midday would also be invalid. Rabbi Jacob ben Asher rules that *matzah* is still valid for the commandment if baked prior to midday; however, he says, one should ideally try to bake the *matzah* after midday.

Rabbi Epstein suggests that the source of this position is that in past eras, *matzah* was baked and eaten during the holiday itself. If each day, people were eating warm *matzah*, then it would be improper that the fulfillment of the actual commandment to eat *matzah* on the first night of Passover—the only time that eating *matzah* is biblically commanded—would be significantly less pleasing and delicious than on other days (Principle 1). Rabbi Epstein further suggests that in past times people ate thick *matzah*, which tended to become hard and difficult to eat once the *matzah* cooled. Rabbi Epstein claims that these considerations pushed Rabbi Jacob ben Asher to rule that one should only bake *matzah* past midday. The connection between *matzah* and the Passover offering, while interesting, does not reflect the real reason behind this practice (Principle 1).

Rabbi Epstein goes on to point out that in the modern era nobody bakes *matzah* during the holiday itself and eating warm *matzah* is not the norm. Because of that, eating old *matzah* on the first night would not be any less dignified than the other days. Therefore, Rabbi Epstein

---

241 Jerusalem Talmud, Pesachim 2:4.
242 Arbah Turim, Orach Chaim 458.

rules that the reasoning behind the practice of baking *matzah* after midday no longer applies, and the *Rosh*'s rule need not be followed (Principle 9). Rabbi Epstein concludes by noting that in modern times only the most stringently observant Jews are careful to bake their *matzah* after midday on Passover Eve; the general populace is not even aware of this practice (Principle 8). As such, Rabbi Epstein rules that such a stringency is unnecessary (Principle 6).
Methodological Principles: 1, 6, 8, 9.

Example #135 – *Arukh HaShulchan* §459:3

Environmental factors can cause dough to leaven more or less quickly. Therefore, the normative *halakhah* is that one should not prepare dough for *matzah* under the sunshine, since the heat from the sun may quicken the leavening of the dough, causing it to become *chametz* before the usual eighteen-minute deadline. Kneading the dough outdoors but in the shade should therefore be permitted. The Talmud rules, however, that even on cloudy days, the sun's rays may be expected to peek through the clouds; therefore, one should not knead *matzah* dough outside, even if the sky is currently cloudy.[243]

Based on this Talmudic rule, the *Bayit Chadash* rules that *matzah* dough prepared in the sun may not be used on Passover. However, Rabbi Epstein notes that in northern countries, cloudy days are in fact good protection from sun—especially in the early spring when the air is still cool. Consequently, in this environment there is no need to prohibit the use of *matzah* dough that was prepared outdoors on a cloudy day (Principle 9). Still, in deference of the Talmudic rule, Rabbi Epstein writes that one should not intentionally knead dough outdoors, even if under cloud cover (Principle 6). However, if one did so, Rabbi Epstein rules that such *matzah* is valid for use on Passover.

Also based on the aforementioned Talmudic rule, Rabbi Moses Isserles rules that one should not knead *matzah* dough next to an open window, as exposure to the sunlight streaming through the window may hasten the leavening process and render the dough *chametz*.[244] The *Chok Yaakov*, however, rules that kneading next to a closed window is permissible even if the window is made of glass, since the glass deflects the heat of the sun's rays sufficiently to obviate any concerns over the dough becoming *chametz* more quickly than usual.[245] Rabbi Epstein qualifies both of these rulings by noting that each one merely reflects the lived experiences of a particular scholar in his specific environment. Rabbi Epstein, however, observes that a closed glass window can often create a great deal of heat on the surfaces opposite it, and he rules that in such a case one would need to cover the windowpane before preparing *matzah* dough nearby. At the same time, he argues that a closed window can cause a room—especially one with an oven in it—to become quite hot and stuffy, thereby quickening the leavening process. In such a case, one should open a window to increase cooling airflow in the room (Principle 9). Rabbi Epstein further notes that the common practice is indeed to approach this issue pragmatically, with each baker doing what is contextually appropriate to reduce the risk of unusually fast leavening in their own baking area (Principles 8 and 10).
Methodological Principles: 6, 8, 9, 10.

---

[243] Babylonian Talmud, Yoma 28a.
[244] Rema *to* Shulchan Arukh, Orach Chaim 459:1.
[245] Chok Yaakov *to* Shulchan Arukh, Orach Chaim 459:4.

Example #136 – *Arukh HaShulchan* §466:2

Because saliva causes leavening when mixed with grain, the Talmud rules that one should not chew wheat and then place the mixture on a wound as a salve during Passover.[246] The *Magen Avraham* rules, however, that one may chew and swallow raw wheat without being concerned that he will thereby end up eating *chametz* because the leavening does not take place immediately.[247] Rabbi Epstein rejects the *Magen Avraham*'s lenient position. He argues that it is almost inevitable that, when chewing and swallowing raw wheat, some of the grain will remain lodged between one's teeth long enough to become *chametz* through contact with one's saliva, and it is therefore prohibited to chew and swallow raw wheat on Passover. Rabbi Epstein supports this contention by referencing a Talmudic rule premised on the assumption that meat remains between one's teeth after eating and by analogizing the Talmudic rule regarding meat to the case of chewing raw grains on Passover (Principle 1).
Methodological Principles: 1.

Example #137 – *Arukh HaShulchan* §470:5

Rabbi Jacob ben Asher and Rabbi Joseph Karo both rule that firstborns must fast on Passover Eve. Both firstborns from the father as well as firstborns from the mother must fast because both kinds of firstborn were killed in the plague of the firstborns in Egypt. Based on this logic, some contend that even female firstborns should fast because they too were killed during the plague preceding the Exodus. Rabbi Epstein notes that, despite this persuasive rationale, the common practice is that firstborn daughters do not fast on Passover Eve. Rabbi Epstein justifies this custom by suggesting that the obligation to fast on Passover Eve depends on whether or not firstborns were consecrated to God following the Exodus. Since women were not included in the consecration of firstborn Jews to God following the Exodus, they also are not included in the requirement to fast on the Eve of Passover (Principles 1 and 8).

While Rabbi Epstein thus justifies the common practice of firstborn daughters not fasting on Passover Eve, he is appalled that by his own time it had become common practice for even firstborn sons to avoid fasting on this day by attending the completion of a Talmudic tractate that had been studied by someone else. Since the completion of a tractate of the Talmud is a joyous occasion that warrants eating a festive meal, participants in the event may eat and, once they have eaten, need not fast thereafter. Rabbi Epstein records that this custom of attending such celebrations was widespread, but he simply cannot see a reason to act so leniently aside from weakness (Principle 10). While he takes issue with this creative method of avoiding the obligation to fast, Rabbi Epstein nevertheless suggests that perhaps people do this out of concern that fasting on Passover Eve may distract them from the many important tasks that must be done before the holiday begins, or because people are worried that eating the bitter herbs at the Passover Seder will cause them pain on an empty stomach (Principles 8 and 10). Moreover, Rabbi Epstein notes that, while there is a strong custom for firstborn males to fast on Passover Eve, the practice is not prescribed anywhere in the Babylonian Talmud, and the Jerusalem Talmud even explicitly rejects any such obligation (Principle 1). Thus, fasting on this day may not be strictly obligatory but rather a supererogatory practice, which, while laudable and normative as a matter of custom, could also be avoided for good reasons (Principle 6). For these reasons, Rabbi Epstein notes that

---

246 Babylonian Talmud, Pesachim 39b.
247 *See* Magen Avraham *to* Shulchan Arukh, Orach Chaim 466:1.

the rabbinic decisors of his generation have generally tolerated the public's light treatment of the fast, and Rabbi Epstein does not respond negatively either (Principle 2).
Methodological Principles: 1, 2, 6, 8, 10.

Example #138 – *Arukh HaShulchan* §471:5

The Talmud states that one should not eat a meal during the afternoon of Passover Eve, so that later that night he will eat the *matzah* with a strong appetite.[248] Rabbi Epstein notes that some have the custom of refraining from eating bitter herbs on Passover Eve for a similar reason: to ensure their consumption of the bitter herbs at night is with an appetite. Rabbi Epstein disagrees, claiming that the consumption of the bitter herbs was not intended to be a pleasurable or positive experience. Because of that, there is no legal preference for it to be done with an appetite. Because this *minhag* is based on a mistaken premise, Rabbi Epstein sees no need to uphold its validity (Principle 8).
Methodological Principles: 8.

Example #139 – *Arukh HaShulchan* §472:6

When drinking the wine and eating the meal at the Passover Seder, one needs to recline to one's left in the manner that free men once dined in the ancient world. The Talmud rules, however, that a married woman need not recline.[249] The medieval commentator Rabbi Solomon ben Meir, or the *Rashbam*, explains the rationale for this exemption as follows: since married women are generally subservient to their husbands, it would be inappropriate for them to recline at the Passover Seder in a kind of false symbolism of freedom and leisure. At the same time, however, the *Rashbam* rules that this exemption does not apply to "important women" or those who enjoy significant social standing; since these women are indeed free, they are obligated to recline in the same manner as their husbands. Based on the *Rashbam*'s understanding of this Talmudic rule, unmarried women as well as married women whose husbands are not at home—women who are thus free to run their households—are obligated to recline at the Seder. Rav Achai Gaon, however, rules differently based on an alternative text of this Talmudic rule. In Rav Achai's version of the Talmudic text, the Talmud instructs that women should not recline at the Seder because that is not the usual manner that women eat their meals. According to this version, since women do not usually recline while eating, doing so at the Seder meal would not be an expression of freedom and leisure and therefore should not be done.[250] But, Rav Achai writes women of great social stature do recline when they eat, and they should therefore recline at the Passover Seder as well.

Rabbi Epstein observes that the common practice in his own time was for women not to recline at the Seder meal, including unmarried and important women. Rabbi Epstein notes that Rabbi Moses Isserles rules that, since the status of women in their families and in society has substantially changed—and indeed is much greater—than it was in Talmudic times, all women have the status of "important" and are therefore obligated to recline.[251] Nevertheless, Rabbi

---

248 Babylonian Talmud, Pesachim 99b.
249 Babylonian Talmud, Pesachim 108a.
250 Sheiltot D'Rav Achai Gaon, Parshat Tzav.
251 Rema *to* Shulchan Arukh, Orach Chaim 472:4.

Epstein initially attempts to justify the common custom of women not reclining by referencing the less prominent view of Rabbi Eliezer ben Joel HaLevi, or the *Raavyah*, who rules that because nobody reclines during meals in the modern era, the law in the Talmud no longer applies (Principles 5, 8, and 9). This account of the modern custom of women not leaning at the Seder is unsatisfying for two reasons. First, Rabbi Epstein wonders, if the custom of women not to lean relies on the view of the *Raavyah*, then men should not lean at the Seder either. Second, Rabbi Epstein is not fully comfortable with basing the custom on the isolated and non-normative view of the *Raavyah*, especially when the broad consensus of other authorities, including the *Rema*, reject that view. Still taking the common custom as a normative baseline, however, Rabbi Epstein suggests that the modern practice can be justified by relying on Rav Achai Gaon's alternative version of the Talmudic norm and his resulting view that women—but not men—should not recline because ordinary men and women conduct themselves differently at meals (Principle 1).
Methodological Principles: 1, 5, 8, 9.

Example #140 – *Arukh HaShulchan* §472:15

Each Jew is obligated to drink four cups of wine at the Passover Seder. This obligation, like most others that relate to the Passover Seder, applies to both men and women. Rabbi Epstein writes that one is also obligated to place at least a small amount of wine in front of one's minor children—boys and girls—in order to educate and habituate them in performing the rituals of the Seder. The obligation to educate one's children to perform the commandments, even while they are minors and not yet formally obligated to fulfill these obligations, generally only applies to sons and not daughters. Rabbi Epstein reasons, however, that one is equally obligated to educate both one's sons and daughters in the laws and practices of the Passover Seder. Because the Seder commemorates the Exodus from slavery, one of the most basic concepts in the Jewish faith, both sons and daughters must be taught to engage in the Seder as much as possible from a young age (Principle 1).
Methodological Principles: 1.

Example #141 – *Arukh HaShulchan* §473:8

Rabbi Isaac Alfasi, Maimonides, and the *Rashba* all write that one should use two whole *matzot* at the Passover Seder in the same manner as one uses two loaves of bread for Sabbath and holiday meals. This is true, these authorities write, even though the Seder ritual involves breaking one of the *matzot* in half early in the meal and saving one half to be eaten as a dessert in commemoration of the Passover offering, which was consumed at the Seder during Temple times. While this actually leaves a person with only one and a half—not two—*matzot* upon which to recite the *hamotzi* blessing and eat the Seder meal, these scholars maintain that both the Babylonian and Jerusalem Talmuds indicate that using two *matzot* for the Seder is indeed the correct procedure.[252]

The *Rosh* and *Tosafot* disagree with this prescription, however. These scholars argue that one needs to have two whole *matzot* to fulfill the general requirement on Sabbath and holidays to have two whole loaves of bread for the meal. Since the one *matzah* is broken in half prior to eating the Seder meal, they rule that one needs to have three *matzot* initially so that two whole

---

252 Babylonian Talmud, Berakhot 39b.

ones can remain after one is broken. Rabbi Epstein rules in accordance with the view of the *Rosh* and *Tosafot* because the common practice is to use three *matzot* for the Passover Seder (Principle 8).
Methodological Principles: 8.

Example #142 – *Arukh HaShulchan* §473:11

Part of the Passover Seder ritual involves placing a platter on the table on which various symbolic items and foods eaten as part of the Seder ritual are placed. Such items include *matzah*, bitter herbs, spring vegetables, saltwater, an egg, and a small shank bone. Rabbi Epstein writes that when setting up the Seder plate with all of the night's ritual objects, one arranges them on the plate in the order that they will be used. This helps avoid having to reach over unused items in order to reach other items that are presently needed, which would violate the *halakhic* principle of *"ein ma'avirin al hamitzvot,"* or "we do not pass over *mitzvot*." While arranging the Seder plate in this manner is thus analytically correct, Rabbi Epstein notes that the common custom is to place the shankbone on the top-right, the egg to its left, the bitter herbs in a depression in the center, the *charoset* mixture on the bottom right, the spring herbs in a depression on the bottom left, and the bitter herbs for the sandwich on the bottom center (Principle 8). While this approach does not avoid the issue of "passing over" some items in order to reach other items, it does fulfill Rabbi Epstein's own preferred method of arranging the Seder plate and is supported by various mystical reasons, and Rabbi Epstein thus declines to object to it (Principle 7).
Methodological Principles: 7, 8.

Example #143 – *Arukh HaShulchan* §483:1

One of the ritual obligations of the Passover Seder is for each person to drink four cups of wine. Rabbi Epstein writes that if one lives in a place where mead is a common beverage, mead takes on the status of "local wine" and then may be used to fulfill the obligation of drinking four cups of wine at the Seder if no wine is available (Principle 10). While some authorities prohibit the use of beverages other than wine for the Sabbath *kiddush*, Rabbi Epstein argues that this stricture does not apply on Passover. These authorities prohibit the use of non-wine beverages for *kiddush* on the Sabbath because they recognize that one may, if necessary, recite the *kiddush* on bread, and so there is no good reason to permit the recitation of *kiddush* on other beverages. However, one cannot possibly use bread (or *matzah*) to fulfill the obligation to *drink* four cups of wine at the Passover Seder, and one may therefore use other local drinks to fulfill this obligation when no wine is available (Principles 5 and 10). This is especially true, Rabbi Epstein says, in light of the fact that it is the generally accepted custom to recite the Sabbath *kiddush* on drinks other than wine all year long, in which case, the Passover Seder should be no different (Principle 8).
Methodological Principles: 5, 8, 10.

Example #144 – *Arukh HaShulchan* §531:4

The Talmud rules that subject to certain specific exemptions, it is generally prohibited to perform *melakhah*—the kinds of creative work prohibited on the Sabbath—during *Chol*

HaMoed, the intermediary days of the major holidays of Passover and Sukkot.[253] One of the major exceptions to this general prohibition permits the performance of work necessary to address one's needs on the holiday itself. Despite this important exception, the Talmudic Rabbis legislated that it is prohibited to shave or cut one's hair on *Chol HaMoed*. While these are activities that may be necessary to look properly groomed in honor of the holiday itself, the Rabbis forbid shaving on *Chol HaMoed* in order to encourage people to get haircuts and shave prior to and in honor of the first day of the holiday. Given the rationale for this rabbinic prohibition, the Rabbis also permitted people to shave on *Chol HaMoed* if, due to circumstances beyond their control, they were unable to shave prior to the start of the holiday. Thus, for instance, a person released from prison on *Chol HaMoed* may shave and get a haircut, since circumstances precluded him from doing so prior to the holiday.

Early rabbinic authorities disagreed, however, about whether a person who had taken a vow to not shave, and who was released from the vow on *Chol HaMoed* may then shave during the intermediate days of the holiday. According to Maimonides, such a person is permitted to shave on *Chol HaMoed* even if he could have gotten released from the vow prior to the holiday, since ultimately he was effectively prevented from shaving before the holiday by the force of his earlier vow. The *Arbah Turim*, however, rules that such a person may shave on *Chol HaMoed* only if he was genuinely unable to gain release from his vow prior to the holiday; if he could have lifted the vow but did not do so, he remains prohibited from shaving even after the vow is lifted on *Chol HaMoed* itself.

The *Arukh HaShulchan* agrees with Maimonides's ruling (Principle 3) and goes further to argue that even the *Arbah Turim* would agree that a person released from a vow to not shave on *Chol HaMoed* may shave if he had intended to keep the vow throughout the whole holiday—and if he only sought release from the vow on *Chol HaMoed* because it became unexpectedly too difficult for him to continue keeping the vow. Such a person, Rabbi Epstein argues, is most akin to one who was genuinely unable to shave before the holiday (since absent the unexpected difficulty in upholding the proscription, he had no real grounds for gaining release from his vow) — thus, even the *Arbah Turim* would permit him to shave once his vow was lifted on *Chol HaMoed*. While there are some authorities who reject this understanding of the *Arbah Turim*'s position, Rabbi Epstein demonstrates that the Jerusalem Talmud supports his own view that one who was unable to secure a dispensation from his vow prior to the holiday—such as a person who did not yet find it too difficult to keep the vow—is regarded as someone who was unavoidably unable to shave before the holiday and who can therefore shave on *Chol HaMoed* (Principle 1). Methodological Principles: 1, 3.

Example #145 – *Arukh HaShulchan* §532:2

Maimonides rules that one may cut one's fingernails during *Chol HaMoed* and even permits doing so using scissors in the same manner that one would cut them on an ordinary weekday. Several other important early authorities adopt this position as well. The *Arbah Turim*, however, quotes several authorities who rule that one may only cut one's nails on *Chol HaMoed* if one uses a knife rather than scissors, so as to distinguish this *melakhah* activity from regular weekday nail trimming. The *Arbah Turim* also cites a more stringent view that prohibits using any kind of tool to trim one's fingernails on *Chol HaMoed*.

---

253 Babylonian Talmud, Chagigah 18a.

Rabbi Epstein observes that due to the *Arbah Turim*'s more stringent position, the general custom is to avoid using any kind of tool to cut one's nails on *Chol HaMoed* unless necessary for some religious purpose. While Rabbi Epstein endorses this customary stringency (Principle 8), he rules that one may cut one's nails in the usual manner on *Chol HaMoed* if, due to extenuating circumstances, he were unable to trim his nails prior to the holiday. Since Maimonides and other important authorities permitted nail trimming, it is in principle permitted to cut one's nails on *Chol HaMoed* (Principle 3), and one need not observe the customarily adopted stringency of the *Arbah Turim* in extenuating circumstances (Principles 6 and 10).

Methodological Principles: 3, 6, 8, 10.

Example #146 – *Arukh HaShulchan* §533:2

The Talmud lists several kinds of *melakhah* activities that may be performed on *Chol HaMoed* if done to accomplish things needed on *Chol HaMoed* itself; it is, however, prohibited to engage in these activities if doing so is not necessary for the enjoyment of the holiday.[254] These activities include grinding grain, cutting wood, and brewing beer. However, the Talmud rules that if one permissibly engaged in these activities during *Chol HaMoed* to serve holiday needs, and if some of the ground grain, cut wood, or brewed beer was left over after the holiday, one is permitted to use these products, provided that one does not intentionally produce extra during *Chol HaMoed* in order to circumvent the prohibition on doing *melakhah*.

The *Arukh HaShulchan* extrapolates from the Talmud's relatively narrow list of *melakhah* activities to which this rule applies, and formulates a broader principle regarding the parameters of performing labor on *Chol HaMoed*. Rabbi Epstein writes that one is only allowed to do constructive labor on *Chol HaMoed* if the work involved something that could not have been done before the holiday started. Even if one is engaging in the *melakhah* activity in order to serve holiday needs, one may not perform work that could have been done before the holiday began. The only exceptions to this broad rule are *melakhah* activities that relate to food preparation, which can be performed as needed on *Chol HaMoed*, even if they could have reasonably been performed prior to the holiday. This is why, Rabbi Epstein argues, the Talmud specifies wood cutting, grain grinding, and beer brewing; these activities are needed to prepare food and thus may be done on *Chol HaMoed*, subject only to the Talmud's condition that they are necessary for serving holiday needs. Other non-food related activities, however, are subject to the additional requirement that they could not have been done prior to the holiday (Principle 1).

Methodological Principles: 1.

Example #147 – *Arukh HaShulchan* §533:3-4

Following the Talmudic prohibition against doing *melakhah* on *Chol HaMoed* for non-holiday related purposes, the *Shulchan Arukh* rules that while a person does not have to limit specifically how much grain he grinds or how much beer he brews on *Chol HaMoed*, to ensure he only does just enough *melakhah* as is necessary for the holiday, one may not intentionally use an artifice in order to grind extra grain or brew extra beer on *Chol HaMoed* to use after the holiday.[255] Rabbi Karo further states that one may not use an artifice to produce more flour or beer

---

254 Babylonian Talmud, Moed Katan 12b.
255 Shulchan Arukh, Orach Chaim 533:1.

when he already has some in storage. One may, however, bake fresh bread, even if one has already baked bread in storage, since hot bread is preferable to cold bread. Once the fresh bread has been made, the older bread may be saved for after the holiday. While it is thus prohibited to use tricks to circumvent the Talmudic prohibition against doing *melakhah* on *Chol HaMoed* for after the holiday, if one violated this stricture, he is allowed to partake of the foods or beverages that he produced after the fact. Maimonides, however, disagrees with Rabbi Karo's limitations and instead rules that even one who has foodstuffs already made may nevertheless circumvent the Talmud's prohibition by producing additional large amounts of those substances "for holiday use," and then saving the inevitable leftovers for after the holiday. Maimonides reasons that this manner of circumventing the Talmudic prohibition against preparing for after the holiday would not be apparent to onlookers as an artifice (since observers do not know whether one has already prepared foodstuffs available or not), such that it remains permitted. The *Raabad* disagrees with Maimonides, however, and argues that all forms of artifice used under any conditions to circumvent the rabbinic proscription against performing *melakhah* on *Chol HaMoed* for post-holiday use are prohibited. The *Raabad* supports this view by pointing out that the issue is in fact the subject of dispute in the Talmud, where the majority view is that using artifices in this manner is prohibited.[256]

The *Arukh HaShulchan* defends Maimonides's position (Principle 3). Rabbi Epstein points out that the Talmud frames the rabbinic dispute about whether or not one may use artifices to circumvent the prohibition against working on *Chol HaMoed* for post-holiday needs as a conflict between two Tannaitic texts. It is true, Rabbi Epstein acknowledges, that one of these texts reflects the view of several Mishnaic rabbis, while the other reflects the view of only a single scholar. However, he argues that since the Talmud presents the dispute merely by quoting the two conflicting texts, the passage is best understood as placing the two Tannaitic texts on equal footing (Principle 1). Since the Talmudic discussion of this issue thus leaves the issue in doubt due to the unresolved conflict between these two Tannaitic sources, the issue should be resolved leniently in accordance with Maimonides's view, as the question when artifice is permitted to circumvent prohibitions is a rabbinic concern and not a biblical one (Principle 4).
Methodological Principles: 1, 3, 4.

Example #148 – *Arukh HaShulchan* §533:7

Rabbinic authorities agree broadly that one may trap and salt fish on *Chol HaMoed* in order to have fish to eat for the holiday, and this is permitted even if one traps and salts more fish than one needs for the holiday itself and even if not all the salted fish will be ready for consumption before the holiday is over. While normally one may not engage in *melakhah* activities on *Chol HaMoed* if the byproducts of that labor are not for holiday use, these authorities note that trapping fish is different from other types of activities that are forbidden on *Chol HaMoed* because, in order to catch good fish, one needs to trap as many as possible. Once the fish are trapped, moreover, they are salted on *Chol HaMoed* because salting food is not really a prohibited *melakhah*, and in any case the fish will spoil unless preserved. Plus, it is generally permitted to perform *melakhah* on *Chol HaMoed* in order to prevent financial loss. These authorities further note that one is even allowed to fish in public, since people are aware that one is fishing in order to have food for the holiday.

---

256 Babylonian Talmud, Moed Katan 12b.

Rabbi Epstein notes that rabbinic authorities disagree, however, about whether or not professional fishermen, who typically fish not for their immediate food needs but for commercial purposes, may also do so on *Chol HaMoed*. Normally rabbinic law bars professionals from engaging in their regular work on *Chol HaMoed* because others will assume that they are performing *melakhah* for commercial reasons—rather than for their own holiday needs—and some scholars maintain that the same is true for professional fishermen. Other authorities, however, rule that while most professionals may not engage in their usual work on *Chol HaMoed*, commercial fishermen may do so because, since everyone knows that people need fish to eat over the holiday, no one will think that the fishermen are working for reasons other than providing food for the holiday.

The *Arukh HaShulchan* rules in accordance with the more lenient position that permits professional fishermen to work on *Chol HaMoed*. In his view, this opinion is supported by a strong consensus of authorities (Principle 2), and there is therefore no reason to be seriously concerned for the outlying rulings that prohibit the practice (Principle 5).

Methodological Principles: 2, 5.

Example #149 – *Arukh HaShulchan* §534:6

It is prohibited to launder clothes on *Chol HaMoed* because this is a *melakhah* activity that could have been done prior to the holiday. If people were permitted to do laundry on *Chol HaMoed*, many people would wait and launder their clothes on *Chol HaMoed* when they are not working and have more time. As a result, they would enter into the holiday wearing unclean clothes.[257]

Rabbi Epstein notes that, while some scholars record a custom to allow Jews to hire Gentiles to launder their clothes on *Chol HaMoed*, this practice is incorrect. He notes that, since laundering clothes on *Chol HaMoed* is prohibited in order to ensure that people clean their clothes before the holiday, the prohibition necessarily encompasses hiring Gentiles to launder one's clothes on *Chol HaMoed* as well, since if one could get one's clothes cleaned on *Chol HaMoed*, one may decide to wear dirty garments at the start of the holiday and to then have them laundered during *Chol HaMoed*. To avoid this negative outcome, Rabbi Epstein rules that even having non-Jews launder one's clothes must be prohibited (Principle 6). Moreover, Rabbi Epstein notes that this is in fact the generally accepted custom (Principle 8).

Rabbi Epstein also notes that the Talmud appears to permit laundering linen clothes on *Chol HaMoed* because linen is easy to wash and therefore does not involve very substantial labor. The *Arukh HaShulchan* argues, however, that the accepted custom is that one may not wash even linen garments on *Chol HaMoed* and that this custom is binding (Principle 8). Moreover, Rabbi Epstein argues that the practice of not washing linen clothes on *Chol HaMoed* is not merely a matter of custom, but the practice is actually required by law. He notes that in fact the Talmud records two different rabbinic opinions about washing linen on *Chol HaMoed*: one authority permits the practice, while another prohibits it. While the Talmud itself does not clearly determine the issue, Rabbi Epstein argues that the fact that the accepted custom is not to wash even linen clothes on *Chol HaMoed* confirms that the stricter position has been accepted as the normative standard (Principles 1, 2, and 8).

Methodological Principles: 1, 2, 6, 8.

---

257 Arukh HaShulchan, Orach Chaim 535:1.

Example #150 – *Arukh HaShulchan* §535:2

The Mishnah rules that one may not move homes during *Chol HaMoed* if the two houses are located in separate courtyards because such major moves are stressful and will detract from one's ability to enjoy the holiday.[258] Commenting on this Mishnah, the Jerusalem Talmud adds several additional qualifications to the rule. According to the Jerusalem Talmud, one may not move between equally nice houses if one owns both or neither of the two homes. However, if one is moving from a rented house to a home that one owns, one may move on *Chol HaMoed*—even from a nicer rented home to a less nice house that one owns, since the move from a rented to an owned home is cause for celebration, and the stress of the move will therefore not detract from enjoying the holiday. While the Jerusalem Talmud does not say so explicitly, the *Arukh HaShulchan* infers from this passage that one also may move to a nicer home on *Chol HaMoed*—even if not from a rented to an owned house—because the happiness that comes with improved living conditions also dispels any concerns that the stress of moving will ruin one's enjoyment of the holiday (Principle 1).[259] While Maimonides disagrees with this inference and rules explicitly that one may not move residences on *Chol HaMoed*—even from a less nice house to a nicer home—Rabbi Epstein rejects this view. The *Arukh HaShulchan* points out that the fact that the Jerusalem Talmud gives special permission to move from a nicer home to a less nice home in cases where one is moving from a rented to an owned property indicates that one may move to a nicer home in any case (Principle 1).
Methodological Principles: 1.

Example #151 – *Arukh HaShulchan* §537:11

Harvesting produce is one of the categories of *melakhah* that may not be performed on the Sabbath, and it is therefore likewise prohibited to harvest fields, to pick fruits or vegetables, or even to gather inside produce that has already been detached from the ground during *Chol HaMoed*. Like other kinds of *melakhah*, however, one may engage in harvesting activities in cases where produce likely will be lost or destroyed if one waits until after the holiday to pick or gather it. The *Arukh HaShulchan* points out that in an Eastern European context, this exemption from the general prohibition against harvesting on *Chol HaMoed* has very broad implications. Rabbi Epstein rules it is permitted to harvest potatoes during *Chol HaMoed* period of Sukkot because rain is common in Eastern Europe at that time of year, and the potato crop will rot if not dug out of the ground before the rains begin. It is similarly permitted to harvest crops negatively impacted by cold weather during *Chol HaMoed*, since frosts often arrive as early as Yom Kippur, and the need to protect these crops and prevent them from being lost justifies quickly gathering inside the produce from the fields before it is ruined by the cold (Principles 9 and 10).
Methodological Principles: 9, 10.

---

258 Babylonian Talmud, Moed Katan 13a.
259 Arukh HaShulchan, Orach Chaim 535:1.

Example #152 – *Arukh HaShulchan* §539:3

The Babylonian Talmud rules that it is prohibited to engage in any business transactions during *Chol HaMoed* except in cases where refraining from business activities will result in one's suffering substantial financial losses.[260] This rule is likewise prescribed by the Jerusalem Talmud.

Rabbi Epstein notes that even on the Sabbath and holidays when it is biblically prohibited to perform *melakhah*, there is no biblical prohibition against engaging in business activities. Thus, Rabbi Epstein argues, even those authorities who maintain that performing labor during *Chol HaMoed* is biblically prohibited would agree that the Talmud's restriction on engaging in business on these days is only rabbinic. In light of this fact, Rabbi Epstein says the Talmud's proscription against all business activities during *Chol HaMoed* seems overly restrictive, since even biblically prohibited labors are only prohibited if one does more than a certain minimal threshold amount of work. For instance, the biblical prohibition on writing on the Sabbath applies only to writing two or more letters—but not to forming just one letter. Why, Rabbi Epstein wonders, were the Talmudic Rabbis so strict about proscribing *all* business activity when the Torah itself sets certain minimum thresholds for Sabbath and holiday labor restrictions?

Rabbi Epstein explains based on a passage in the Jerusalem Talmud that the purpose of *Chol HaMoed* is to provide a time for the Jewish people to eat, drink, be merry, and learn Torah. The Talmudic Rabbis prohibited business activities on these days in order to better preserve the purpose and character of the holiday; if people were allowed to do business, they would spend all of their time working on their businesses and would not be able to properly enjoy the holidays (Principle 1). Thus, Rabbi Epstein argues, it is necessary to take the prohibition against business even more seriously in some ways than the biblical prohibition against creative labor in order to ensure that people enjoy the holiday and learn Torah properly (Principle 6).
Methodological Principles: 1, 6.

Example #153 – *Arukh HaShulchan* §540:7

It is prohibited to build on *Chol HaMoed*. One may not even build things that are needed on the holiday because construction activities needed for the holiday could have and should have been undertaken prior to the holiday. One is, however, permitted to build ovens or stoves on *Chol HaMoed*, provided that they will be used during the holiday, since even building is permitted in order to provide for food-related needs during the holiday.

Both Maimonides and the *Shulchan Arukh* rule that one may also build a platform upon which an oven can rest, and that one may add extra clay to the outside of an already built oven to make it hold its heat more efficiently. The *Arukh HaShulchan* questions these rulings, since they seem to permit doing labor that is not strictly necessary in order to use the oven, and since *melakhah* that is not necessary on *Chol HaMoed* is prohibited. Despite this concern, Rabbi Epstein nevertheless seeks to substantiate Maimonides's and Rabbi Karo's ruling (Principle 3). He argues that even though it is possible to bake in an oven that is not resting on a platform or is not heavily insulated, since these enhancements make the oven better, one is permitted to construct them on *Chol HaMoed* (Principle 10).
Methodological Principles: 3, 10.

---

260 Babylonian Talmud, Moed Katan 10b.

Example #154 – *Arukh HaShulchan* §542:2

It is generally forbidden to make money from doing creative labor done on *Chol HaMoed*. Rabbi Joseph Karo, however, rules that one who does not have enough money to buy food for the holiday may perform *melakhah* for wages and is even permitted to earn more than he strictly needs for food during the holiday itself, so long as the work he is performing is his usual craft or profession. Some authorities limit this permission to work for wages on *Chol HaMoed* to only business activities or ritual work like writing *tefillin*; performing actual *melakhah*, however, like building or planting, remains prohibited even for individuals who do not have enough money with which to buy food for the holiday.

The *Arukh HaShulchan* rejects this view, noting that while those who seek to limit the kinds of labor an indigent worker may do on *Chol HaMoed* support their view by referencing a passage in the Jerusalem Talmud, no such Talmudic reference actually exists (Principle 1). Instead, Rabbi Epstein rules that any kind of creative labor is allowed to be done on *Chol HaMoed* by a worker who otherwise would not have the means to eat on the holiday. Rabbi Epstein limits this broad permission only by forbidding even indigent workers from performing very public kinds of labor, which would ruin the communal holiday spirit (Principle 6). Likewise, Rabbi Epstein says, a poor laborer may not earn wages by giving haircuts or shaves during *Chol HaMoed* because the prohibition against personal grooming on *Chol HaMoed* derives not from the general proscription against doing *melakhah*, but from a specific rabbinic enactment designed to ensure that people make sure to properly honor the holiday by getting their hair cut before it begins (Principle 6). For example, such a worker is not allowed to give haircuts or to shave others for income in order to eat, since it is forbidden for people to get haircuts or to shave. If such a worker were allowed to do these actions, then of course people would take advantage of the situation to shave and to get haircuts.

Methodological Principles: 1, 6.

Example #155 – *Arukh HaShulchan* §544:6

The Mishnah rules that *melakhah* may be performed during *Chol HaMoed* if it is done to serve a public communal purpose. Thus, one may repair roads or may dig or fill in public wells or water systems, even if this work is not strictly needed for the holiday itself.[261]

Rabbi Epstein notes that some authorities have held that the Talmud's broad permission to perform *melakhah* on *Chol HaMoed* when engaged in public works projects does not apply in cases where some specific official is tasked with overseeing such projects. Where oversight over public works projects resides in a particular individual, that official may not engage in *melakhah* activities during *Chol HaMoed* to execute such communal projects because, since the official's job depends on effectively overseeing public works, his work on such projects amounts to an individual rather than communal need. The *Arukh HaShulchan* rejects this limitation on the Talmudic rule permitting *melakhah* on *Chol HaMoed* for public purposes. Rabbi Epstein argues that it is obvious that at the time that the Mishnah and Talmud were written there were individual rulers and government officials whose job it was to make unilateral decisions about public works projects. Clearly, then, when the Rabbis generally permitted performing *melakhah* on *Chol HaMoed* when engaged in public works, they intended this permission to extend even to government officials tasked with overseeing such projects as well; otherwise, the Mishnah would have delineated

---

261 Mishnah, Moed Katan 1:2.

the limits of this rule (Principle 1). The *Arukh HaShulchan* notes that this is especially true in his own time when government officials are part of large bureaucratic systems and do not have wide discretion over the implementation of public works projects, nor are they personally responsible for the success or failure of such projects. Under these circumstances, it is even more clear that when officials direct or engage in *melakhah* to serve public needs during *Chol HaMoed*, they are doing communal rather than personal work (Principle 9). Therefore, there is no reason to be concerned about the opinion expressed by some authorities that public officials may not engage in *melakhah* for communal needs on *Chol HaMoed* (Principle 5).

Methodological Principles: 1, 5, 9.

Example #156 – *Arukh HaShulchan* §545:6

Like other kinds of *melakhah*, writing is presumptively prohibited on *Chol HaMoed*. Rabbi Moses Isserles notes that there are two groups of authorities who reached different conclusions about how to apply the typical exemptions from *Chol HaMoed* labor prohibitions to writing. According to some scholars, one may write for public purposes—such as writing Torah scrolls—only if such writing is also needed for the holiday itself. Thus, for instance, if the community's Torah scroll became invalid, one may fix the scroll by rewriting sections in which errors were found, so that the scroll could be used for public Torah reading services during the holiday. However, if the community had other scrolls available, fixing the damaged scroll on *Chol HaMoed* would be unnecessary and therefore prohibited. Another group of authorities rule, however, that writing done for public purposes may be performed during *Chol HaMoed*, even if the writing is not strictly needed for the holiday itself. Rabbi Isserles himself follows the second, more lenient view because, as he says, writing is no longer considered specialized artisanal work.[262]

The *Arukh HaShulchan* expands on the words of the *Rema* and innovatively rules that all non-expert creative labor for public use is allowed on *Chol HaMoed*, even if it is not needed for the festival itself, while expert creative labor, even for public use, may be done on *Chol HaMoed* only if it is needed for the upcoming festival (Principle 1). Rabbi Epstein justifies this rule by arguing that communal needs are like a pot of food being overseen by two cooks, where each person relies on the other to cook the dish properly. In such circumstances, it is important that someone take responsibility to oversee the matter when both cooks are present; otherwise, the food is likely to be ruined. The same is true, Rabbi Epstein says, when it comes to communal matters. *Chol HaMoed* is a good time to make sure important public needs are taken care of because people are not working and are generally available to see to such matters. Therefore, one is justified in adopting lenient rulings when it comes to dealing with public concerns (Principle 1). Moreover, Rabbi Epstein notes that when it comes to writing, the general custom is to differentiate between writing in the Talmudic era, which was a specialized skill, and writing in modern times, which is not (Principles 8 and 9). Therefore in modern times, one may write for public purposes, even if the writings are not needed on the holiday itself—such as writing letters on behalf of the community that will not be sent until after the holiday. The *Arukh HaShulchan* further justifies his lenient treatment of writing for communal needs on *Chol HaMoed* by pointing out that in modern times *Chol HaMoed* is a time that the community gets together and has time to discuss important matters related to public concerns, and resolving such matters often requires writing. Taking a narrow and strict view of the permissibility of writing on *Chol HaMoed*

---

262   Rema *to* Shulchan Arukh, Orach Chaim 545:1.

would make it very difficult for the community to conduct necessary business, and therefore a more lenient ruling is warranted (Principle 10).
Methodological Principles: 1, 8, 9, 10.

Example #157 – *Arukh HaShulchan* §550:4

Rabbi Joseph Karo rules that, on the Sabbath preceding communal fast days, such as the Seventeenth of Tammuz, the Fast of Gedaliah, and the Tenth of Tevet, communal leaders should publically announce the date of the upcoming fast day.[263] Rabbi Epstein explains the reason for this practice by noting that according to the Talmud, these fast days are not absolutely obligatory: "if the community wishes to observe these fast days, it fasts, and if it wishes to not fast, it need not fast."[264] Based on this, Rabbi Epstein suggests that the reason for Rabbi Karo's prescription that the upcoming fasts should be publically announced is to approximate communal acceptance of the fast, consistent with the Talmud's view that these fasts need be observed only if the community elects to do so (Principle 1). Based on this rationale, Rabbi Epstein rejects the practice of publically announcing upcoming fasts as prescribed by Rabbi Karo (Principle 1). Noting that the custom among Ashkenazic Jews is not to announce upcoming fast days on the preceding Sabbath (Principle 8), Rabbi Epstein explains that, while this was a proper practice in previous eras, it is no longer necessary in modern times. Such public announcements were once a means of creating a communal commitment to observe the fast, consistent with the Talmudic rule that such fasts are not obligatory absent communal consent. In modern times, however, the observance of these fast days is already a well-established custom that has been upheld consistently by many generations of Jews.[265] The ancestral custom to observe these fasts is therefore binding (Principle 8), and there is no longer any need to affect any actual communal acceptance of each individual fast day through public announcements on the preceding Sabbath (Principle 9).
Methodological Principles: 1, 8, 9.

Example #158 – *Arukh HaShulchan* §551:10

As a sign of mourning over the destruction of the Temple, the Talmud rules that one may not wear freshly laundered clothes during the week preceding the fast of Tisha B'Av.[266] Following the views of several important early authorities, Rabbi Moses Isserles rules that this stricture applies even to the Sabbath preceding Tisha B'Av. While mourning practices are typically suspended in honor of the Sabbath, Rabbi Isserles rules that, on the Sabbath proceeding Tisha B'Av, one should continue to wear the same soiled clothes worn the entire preceding week (with the exception of one's undergarments), so as to maintain this expression of mourning for the Temple as Tisha B'Av approaches.[267]

Rabbi Epstein notes, however, that in his time and place, and for at least several generations preceding his own, the people did not conduct themselves in accordance with Rabbi Isserles's prescription. Instead, on the Sabbath preceding Tisha B'Av, they would wear regular,

---

263 Beit Yosef *to* Arbah Turim, Orach Chaim 450:4.
264 Babylonian Talmud, Taanit 29a.
265 *See* Arukh HaShulchan, Orach Chaim 150:1; 151:23.
266 Babylonian Talmud, Taanit 29b.
267 Rema *to* Shulchan Arukh, Orach Chaim 151:1.

clean Sabbath clothes, even when Tisha B'Av itself fell on the Sabbath, and as a result the fast day was pushed off until the following Sunday. Rabbi Epstein wonders at this relatively recent development of religious practice, which he worries has resulted in people completely forgetting that, as a matter of law, one may not wear clean Sabbath clothes on the Sabbath preceding Tisha B'Av, and which he says implies that earlier generations of pious Jews were mistaken in wearing dirty weekday garments on the Sabbath before Tisha B'Av. While he acknowledges that the contemporary practice is indeed a violation of the law, Rabbi Epstein nevertheless seeks to justify it, for "how can we abrogate their [the people's] custom?" (Principle 8).[268] To justify the modern practice of wearing clean Sabbath clothes on the Sabbath preceding Tisha B'Av, Rabbi Epstein suggests that there is a significant difference between the mode of Sabbath dress of previous generations and that of his own time. In Rabbi Isserles's era, Sabbath clothes looked the same as weekday clothes; the only difference between them was that Sabbath clothes were of better quality and more expensive. Because there was no apparent difference between one's Sabbath and weekday dress, the accepted *halakhah* was that, on the Sabbath preceding Tisha B'Av, one should wear one's weekday clothes, since doing so would effectively maintain proper mourning practices in the leadup to Tisha B'Av itself without detracting from the Sabbath, since one's external appearance would appear unchanged from that of one wearing proper Sabbath dress. In his own time, Rabbi Epstein writes, things are different. Sabbath clothes and weekday clothes are fundamentally different, and any observer can tell which kinds of clothes are being worn. Under these circumstances, it would be an inappropriate detraction from the honor due to the Sabbath for people to wear ordinary weekday clothes on the Sabbath preceding Tisha B'Av, as this would amount to a publicly observable expression of mourning on the Sabbath, which is prohibited. Thus, Rabbi Epstein says, the old rule that one should wear weekday clothes on the Sabbath preceding Tisha B'Av no longer applies; instead, people should maintain the established custom of wearing Sabbath clothes (Principle 9).
Methodological Principles: 8, 9.

Example #159 – *Arukh HaShulchan* §551:14

While the Talmud prohibits laundering clothes during the week preceding Tisha B'Av, it limits this prohibition to only a specific kind of fine laundering, which the Talmud calls *gihutz*.[269] Rabbi Epstein rules that, in principle, the Talmud's prohibition on laundering during the week of Tisha B'Av does not apply in his own time and place, since routine modern laundering is not as intensive as the *gihutz* laundering prohibited by the Talmud (Principle 9). While ordinary clothes laundering is thus technically permitted, Rabbi Epstein notes that the prevailing custom is to prohibit all manner of laundering during the period leading up to Tisha B'Av. He writes: "And since our forefathers accepted this prohibition [on laundering], by default this becomes legally prohibited to us" (Principle 8). This is especially so, Rabbi Epstein says, because the reasons that the Talmud permitted ordinary laundering processes no longer apply in Eastern Europe. According to Rabbi Epstein, the Talmud may have permitted some kind of laundering only because the water in Babylonia, where the Talmud was produced, was generally stagnant and could not clean clothes particularly well (Principle 1). But, Rabbi Epstein writes, this is not true in his own time and place, where the water is fresh and can clean clothing quite well, even

---

268 Arukh HaShulchan, Orach Chaim 151:11.
269 *See* Babylonian Talmud, Taanit 29b.

using only ordinary laundering processes that are less intensive than the *gihutz* prohibited by the Talmud (Principle 9).
Methodological Principles: 1, 8, 9.

Example #160 - *Arukh HaShulchan* §555:2

The Talmud rules that "all the commandments that apply to a mourner are practiced on Tisha B'Av." Thus, in addition to the regular fast day restrictions on eating and drinking, on Tisha B'Av, it is also prohibited to wash one's body, to rub oneself with oils, to wear leather shoes, to engage in sexual relations, and to study Torah.[270] Since the Tisha B'Av restrictions prescribed by the Talmud are tied to mourning practices, the *Rosh* writes that in truth one should be obligated to wear *tefillin* on Tisha B'Av, since mourners are obligated to wear *tefillin* after the first day following the death of a relative, and since mourning practices of Tisha B'Av are no more restrictive than those of mourning following the day of death.[271] Despite the lack of any clear Talmudic prohibition, however, the general practice is to not wear *tefillin* on the morning of Tisha B'Av. Some rabbinic scholars, including Rabbi Isaac Luria, attempted to straddle these competing *halakhic* imperatives by donning their *tefillin* privately at home on Tisha B'Av morning and then removing them before attending services at the synagogue.

Rabbi Epstein rejects this approach and holds that it is not necessary to attempt to satisfy both the view that *tefillin* should be worn, as well as the popular practice to avoid wearing them on Tisha B'Av (Principle 5). Instead, Rabbi Epstein rules that, as a matter of law, *tefillin* should not be worn on Tisha B'Av morning. While the Talmud does not instruct that the regular obligation to wear *tefillin* is suspended on Tisha B'Av, Rabbi Epstein thinks that the widespread popular custom not to wear *tefillin* on Tisha B'Av morning is determinative (Principle 8). This is especially true, he writes, because the underlying reasons for the Talmud's Tisha B'Av prohibitions—that on Tisha B'Av one should conduct oneself as a mourner—apply forcefully to the issue of wearing *tefillin*. It is technically true that mourners do wear *tefillin* during the seven days of intense mourning following the day of death. However, mourners do not wear *tefillin* on the day of mourning because *tefillin* are called a "crown," and it is inappropriate to adorn oneself with a crown on a "bitter" day, like the day on which one's close relation dies. According to Rabbi Epstein, this reasoning applies with greater force to Tisha B'Av, for "it is an extremely bitter day for the entire Jewish people" (Principle 1). Since the practice of not wearing *tefillin* on Tisha B'Av morning is thus supported by the Talmud's underlying reasoning, as well as by established custom, Rabbi Epstein rules that this is the correct practice. There is no need to act strictly to don *tefillin* in private, and indeed it would be inappropriate to do so as a supererogatory measure, since doing so is inconsistent with the mournful character of the day (Principle 6).
Methodological Principles: 1, 5, 6, 8.

Example #161 - *Arukh HaShulchan* §557:2

The Jerusalem Talmud instructs that on Tisha B'Av, one adds a special prayer—*Nachem*, which seeks comfort from God over the destruction of Jerusalem and the Temple—in the middle of the ordinary *Amidah* blessing of *Avodah*, which recalls and seeks the restoration of

---

270 *See* Babylonian Talmud, Taanit 30a.
271 *See* Rosh *to* Babylonian Talmud, Taanit 4:37.

the Temple service.[272] Contemporary practice runs counter to the Jerusalem Talmud's prescription. While the supplementary *Nachem* prayer is indeed recited, it is inserted at the end of the *Amidah* blessing of *Boneh Yerushalayim*, which beseeches God to rebuild Jerusalem. Rabbi Isaac Alfasi attempts to explain this practice by noting that, according to the Babylonian Talmud, additional supplicatory prayers can be inserted at the end of any of the *Amidah*'s blessings, so long as the additional supplication relates to the theme of that blessing. Thus, Rabbi Alfasi says, it is appropriate to insert the special *Nachem* prayer recited on Tisha B'Av after the blessing of *Boneh Yerushalayim*, since both the blessing and the additional supplication relate to the destruction and rebuilding of Jerusalem.

Rabbi Epstein questions both the contemporary practice and Rabbi Alfasi's attempted explanation of that practice. Per Rabbi Alfasi's explanation, the Babylonian Talmud merely permits (but does not mandate) the recital of *Nachem* at some other point in the *Amidah*; and given the Babylonian Talmud's ambivalence on the issue, the Jerusalem Talmud's instruction that *Nachem* be recited as part of the *Avodah* blessing should control.

Consistent with his respect for both established customs and the *halakhic* weight of the Jerusalem Talmud, Rabbi Epstein avoids resolving this problem by rejecting either the Talmudic prescription to recite *Nachem* in the *Avodah* blessing or the contemporary custom of reciting *Nachem* in the *Boneh Yerushalayim* blessing (Principles 1 and 8). Instead, Rabbi Epstein offers a novel read of the underlying rationale for the Jerusalem Talmud's instruction regarding the recital of *Nachem* (Principle 1), and concludes by noting that, since this rationale no longer applies, the Jerusalem Talmud's rule no longer applies (Principle 9). Relying on a Tannaitic text, Rabbi Epstein points out that originally the *Boneh Yerushalayim* blessing was combined with another blessing—*Tzemach David*—which beseeches God to restore the Davidic monarchy. Rabbi Epstein suggests that these two blessings were combined at the time the Jerusalem Talmud formulated its *Nachem* rule, and that because the theme of *Nachem* does not relate to the theme of *Tzemach David* blessing, the Talmud could not have prescribed the recital of *Nachem* at the end of the combined *Boneh Yerushalayim* and *Tzemach David* blessing, and instead instructed that this supplemental prayer be said as part of the *Avodah* blessing. Later, however, the long *Boneh Yerushalayim* and *Tzemach David* blessing was divided into two separate blessings. This allowed *Nachem* to be recited as part of *Boneh Yerushalayim*, with which its themes more closely align. Thus, Rabbi Epstein concludes, contemporary practice does not actually reject the Jerusalem Talmud's rule, but instead practice reflects the proper placement of the *Nachem* supplication, given a very different liturgical context than the one in which the Talmud initially prescribed that *Nachem* be recited in the *Avodah* blessing.
Methodological Principles: 1, 8, 9.

Example #162 – *Arukh HaShulchan* §560:4

All the major *halakhic* codes—including the *Rif*, Maimonides's *Mishneh Torah*, the *Arbah Turim*, and the *Shulchan Arukh*—rule that, in order to commemorate the destruction of the Temple and Jerusalem, one must leave a portion of one's home unfinished. Rabbi Joseph Karo thus writes: "When the Temple was destroyed, the sages of that generation decreed that one should not paint or adorn one's house with moldings like the houses of kings, but rather one should simply plaster one's house with mortar, and whitewash it with lime. And [even then] one should leave over a square cubit opposite the entrance that unfinished with mortar or

---

272 Jerusalem Talmud, Berakhot 4:3.

whitewash."²⁷³ Rabbi Epstein notes that in his own time this rule is widely ignored, and he seeks to provide a post hoc justification for the common practice of fully finishing new homes with plaster and paint (Principle 8). His justification for this practice relies on his own assessment of the correct Talmudic rule regarding the permissibility of finishing one's home with plaster and paint, as well as differences in the kinds of construction materials used in his own time, as compared with those used in earlier eras (Principles 1 and 9).

Rabbi Epstein points out that codified versions of this rule requiring one to leave a square cubit of one's home unfinished rely on a single Tannaitic source, whereas in fact three separate Tannaitic texts bear on this issue. In addition to the *Baraita* (Tannaitic source) that requires one to leave a square-cubit of one's home unfinished to commemorate the destruction of Jerusalem, another *Baraita* completely prohibits plastering the walls of one's home or beautifying the walls with painted murals and moldings, and a third *Baraita* rules that "one should not plaster one's home with lime, unless the lime is mixed with straw or sand."²⁷⁴ In order to synthesize these three contradictory instructions, Rabbi Epstein argues that the correct Talmudic rule—and the rule the major codifiers all meant to record, though their words do not explicate it—is that one must leave a square cubit of one's home unfinished, but only if the finishing will be done with unadulterated plaster. When plaster is mixed with straw or sand, however, one may use it to finish the walls of one's home without having to leave over a square cubit to commemorate the destruction of Jerusalem (Principle 1). Based on this rule, Rabbi Epstein says it made good sense for the major codifiers entirely to prohibit plastering all of one's home, since in their times, it was most common to use pure plaster. But, Rabbi Epstein writes, in his own era, plaster is mixed with large amounts of sand, which the Talmud itself permits, and which is why observant Jews commonly do not leave any part of their homes unfinished to commemorate the destruction (Principle 9). Methodological Principles: 1, 8, 9.

Example #163 – *Arukh HaShulchan* §571:1

There is a Talmudic dispute over the religious propriety of fasting when not obligated by biblical or rabbinic law. According to one view, someone who undertakes supererogatory fasts is considered "holy," while another view holds that such a person is regarded as a "sinner" for depriving oneself of the permitted material enjoyment of God's world.²⁷⁵ The Talmud does not clearly endorse either of these two views, and Rabbi Epstein therefore concludes that both are correct—"these and those are the words of the living God." He argues that these two Talmudic opinions do not actually conflict with each other, and that whether someone who engages in supererogatory fasts is holy or sinful depends on the circumstances. Here, Rabbi Epstein lays out his basic approach to supererogatory religious conduct in general (Principle 6). It is never mandatory to undertake supererogatory fasts, but, where such fasting may prove religiously beneficial for a particular individual, it is commendable to do so. Thus, an individual who is in general sinful should undertake supererogatory fasts in order to cry, to pray, and to seek forgiveness from God—goals for which fasting is typically conducive. Likewise, any individual who can undertake fasting without this adversely impacting one's health or one's ability to conscientiously fulfill their basic religious duties is considered holy for fasting and thereby cleansing their sins. But, when fasting is likely to have negative religious or health effects, one should not undertake

---

273 Shulchan Arukh, Orach Chaim 560:1.
274 *See* Arukh HaShulchan, Orach Chaim 560:1-2.
275 *See* Babylonian Talmud, Taanit 11a-b.

supererogatory fasts, and one who does so is called a "sinner." Thus, if supererogatory fasting will weaken a person and prevent one from fulfilling genuine *halakhic* obligations, one should not fast. Likewise, Rabbi Epstein recommends that Torah scholars not undertake fasting, and instead they should devote their energies to increased Torah study. Teachers, communal functionaries, and hourly workers should also avoid fasting, since fasting is likely to negatively impact their ability to do their jobs.

Methodological Principles: 6.

Example #164 – *Arukh HaShulchan* §572:1

The Talmud rules that the Rabbis may not legislate public fast days on Thursdays, so as to avoid the possibility of marketplace price gouging. If marketplace vendors see people buying extra food on Thursday in anticipation of the end of the fast, they may raise the prices of food, which will cause customers to have to buy Sabbath food at a premium the next day.[276] Rabbi Joseph Karo rules that this prohibition applies even in times and places in which such price gouging is not a serious concern, such as in a city where most of the population is not Jewish, so that Jewish food-buying habits will not significantly impact market prices.[277] Rabbi Epstein, however, adopts the view of the *Magen Avraham*, who rules that the Talmud's proscription does not apply in modern times, when it is exceedingly rare for retailers to take advantage of temporary fluctuations in demand to raise prices dramatically (Principle 1). Since the underlying reason for the Talmudic rule no longer applies, the rule itself is no longer applicable (Principle 9), and, Rabbi Epstein notes, this is indeed the accepted custom (Principle 8).

Methodological Principles: 1, 8, 9.

Example #165 – *Arukh HaShulchan* §581:7

The *Zohar* instructs that the community should be very careful when choosing an individual to lead the congregation in High Holiday prayers and to blow the *shofar* on Rosh Hashanah. Specifically, the *Zohar* writes that the designated prayer leader (*shliach* tzibbur) should seclude himself for three days prior to the holiday, so as to avoid contracting any ritual impurity and in order to spend time in self-introspection and repentance. While Rabbi Epstein considers the *Zohar*'s suggestion seriously enough to quote it (Principle 7), he nevertheless finds this instruction impractical in his own time, concluding that, "due to our sins, we are unable to demand such" (Principle 10).

Methodological Principles: 7, 10.

Example #166 – *Arukh HaShulchan* §582:9

The Midrash records that the great and pious leaders of the generation would fast on the day before Rosh Hashanah. Rabbi Epstein notes that in his own times many common people also have the custom to fast on the day before Rosh Hashanah (Principle 8). He notes that, while there is good reason to avoid many kinds of supererogatory practices—especially those typically

---

276   *See* Babylonian Talmud, Taanit 15b.
277   *See* Shulchan Arukh, Orach Chaim 572:1. *See also* Be'er Heitev *to* Shulchan Arukh, Orach Chaim 572:1.

associated with particularly pious people, since the adoption of such practices by common Jews has the appearance of presumptuous hubris, fasting on Rosh Hashanah is a positive practice even for common Jews. This is because there is an obvious personal benefit to any individual who fasts in repentance for their sins, especially on the last day of the year prior to the day of judgment on Rosh Hashanah (Principle 6).
Methodological Principles: 6, 8.

Example #167 – *Arukh HaShulchan* §586:3

There is a basic dispute between Maimonides and Rabbi Joseph Karo regarding the proper characteristics of the kind of *shofar* that is suitable for ritual use on Rosh Hashanah. According to Maimonides, only the curved horn of a male ram may be used;[278] according to Rabbi Karo, however, any horn is ritually fit, except that of a cow—though it is preferable to use a curved ram's horn, if possible.[279] This dispute is rooted in a disagreement about the correct understanding of several Talmudic passages that provide a number of different formulations of the ritual requirements for the Rosh Hashanah *shofar*. In one passage, the Talmudic sage, Rabbi Avahu indicates the Rosh Hashanah *shofar* should be a ram's horn: "Why do we blow with a ram's horn [on Rosh Hashanah]? [It is as if] 'God said, blow a ram's horn before me so that I will recall the sacrifice of Isaac the son of Abraham [who at the last minute was exchanged for a ram], and consider it as if you have offered yourselves as sacrifices before me.'"[280] The Mishnah, however, rules that "all horns are fit for use as a *shofar*, except the horn of a cow."[281] Another Mishnah teaches that "the *shofar* of Rosh Hashanah is a straight horn from an Ibex ... and Rabbi Judah said, on Rosh Hashanah we blow a male ram's horn."[282] According to Maimonides, the law follows the view of Rabbi Judah and Rabbi Avahu who held that the *shofar* must be a curved horn from a ram, since in its discussion of the relevant Mishnah the Talmud expressly endorses that view.[283] The contrary view that all kinds of horns may be used as a shofar except cow horns is grounded in an alternative secondary principle of *halakhic* methodology and Talmudic interpretation, which holds that the law follows the view expressed by an anonymous Mishnah. Since the Mishnah anonymously states that "all horns are fit for use as a *shofar*, except the horn of a cow," Rabbi Karo maintains that this is the correct *halakhic* rule.

The correct Talmudic rule is thus uncertain; while the principle of Talmudic interpretation that instructs that the law follows anonymous Mishnaic opinions would yield that any horn not from a cow may be used as a *shofar*, the Talmudic text itself strongly indicates—though does not absolutely and determinately prescribe—that the law follows Rabbi Judah's view that a *shofar* must be a curved ram's horn. Rabbi Epstein notes that there is no rabbinic consensus supporting either view. *Rashi, Tosafot*, the *Semag*, and *Hagahot Maimoni* all agree with Maimonides's view that only a curved ram's horn is valid for use as a *shofar* on Rosh Hashanah; the *Rosh, Raabad, Ran*, and *Arbah Turim*, however, line up in support of Rabbi Joseph Karo's view that any

---

278 *See* Mishneh Torah, Hilkhot Shofar, Sukkah, V'Lulav 1:1.
279 Shulchan Arukh, Orach Chaim 586:1.
280 Babylonian Talmud, Rosh Hashanah 16a.
281 Mishnah, Rosh Hashanah 3:2.
282 Mishnah, Rosh Hashanah 3:4.
283 *See* Babylonian Talmud, Rosh Hashanah 26b. *See also* Arukh HaShulchan, Orach Chaim 586:3.

non-bovine horn may be used as a *shofar*, though there is a preference for using a curved ram's horn *ex ante* (Principle 3).

Rabbi Epstein rules in accordance with Maimonides's view, and provides several reasons for doing so. First, consistent with his general approach to resolving cases where the right Talmudic rule is uncertain, he adopts Maimonides's view, absent serious difficulties with this position (Principle 3). Second, he adopts Maimonides's view because blowing a ritually suitable *shofar* is a biblical obligation, and Maimonides's view, which is more restrictive of the kinds of horns that may be used as a *shofar*, is the stricter of the two positions. Thus, the doubt-resolving rule, "doubts about biblical rules are resolved strictly," demands the adoption of Maimonides's ruling (Principle 4). Finally, Rabbi Epstein notes that the "custom of the entire Jewish people" is to use a curved ram's horn, which lends further support to Maimonides's positon relative to Rabbi Karo's view (Principle 8).

Methodological Principles: 3, 4, 8.

Example #168 – *Arukh HaShulchan* §586:21

Rabbi Joseph Karo rules that, if a *shofar* is cracked around most of its width, it may not be used for ritual purposes on Rosh Hashanah; if the crack runs across less than half the width of the *shofar*, the *shofar* may be used. However, even a *shofar* that is cracked around most of its width may be used, if the crack is situated far enough away from the horn's mouthpiece that the *shofar*, measured from the mouthpiece to the crack, is large enough to be ritually valid, even if the cracked section were removed.[284] This view is supported by the *Rosh, Ran, Baal Ha'Ittur, Semak, Semag*, and possibly Maimonides.[285] Rabbi Karo records another position, however, which maintains that a *shofar* cracked along most of its width is usable even if there is not enough length from the mouthpiece to the crack to constitute a valid *shofar*, so long as the crack does not produce a distortion in the sound the *shofar* makes when blown. Rabbi Epstein endorses the first view because, he says, it is supported by a consensus of authorities (Principle 2). Moreover, unlike some other authorities who raise the possibility of relying on the more permissive second view in cases of need,[286] Rabbi Epstein does not consider the normatively rejected view viable at all (Principle 5).

Methodological Principles: 2, 5.

Example #169 – *Arukh HaShulchan* §589:6

The Mishnah rules that a *cheresh*, one who is deaf and mute, a *shoteh*, one who is legally mentally incompetent, and a *katan*, a minor, cannot blow the *shofar* for others in order to help them fulfill their obligation to hear the sound of the *shofar* on Rosh Hashanah. The Mishnah explains that this limitation is a consequence of the general rule that "one who is not obligated in a ritual matter cannot perform that ritual on behalf of others in order to fulfill their obligation."[287] Rabbi Joseph Karo rules that the Mishnah's exclusion of a *cheresh* from the obligation to hear and the ability to blow the *shofar* for others does not apply to a person who can hear and

---

284 Shulchan Arukh, Orach Chaim 58:9.
285 *See* Be'er HaGolah *to* Shulchan Arukh, Orach Chaim 586:21:2.
286 *See, e.g.*, Mishnah Berurah, Orach Chaim 586:56.
287 Mishnah, Rosh Hashanah 3:8.

merely does not speak, since the Talmudic classification of *cheresh* applies only to people who are both deaf and mute. Nevertheless, Rabbi Karo writes one who is deaf, even if he can speak, is still not obligated to hear the *shofar*, and cannot blow the *shofar* for others in order to enable them to fulfill their obligation to hear the *shofar* on Rosh Hashanah.[288] Rabbi Karo explains that one who cannot hear is himself exempt from the commandment to hear the sounds of the *shofar*, since it would be impossible for him to hear the sounds; and because such a person is not himself obligated to hear the *shofar*, he cannot help other hearing individuals fulfill their own obligation to hear the *shofar* by blowing it himself.

Rabbi Epstein strongly disagrees with Rabbi Karo's ruling. First, Rabbi Epstein notes as a general matter that the Talmud itself teaches that any time "the Rabbis refer to a *cheresh*, it refers to a person who can neither speak nor hear; but a person who can hear and not speak, or speak and not hear is still obligated [to fulfill ritual obligations]."[289] This principle should apply to the Mishnah's ruling about who is able to blow the *shofar* as well, and thus, someone who can speak but not hear, who is excluded from the legal category of a *cheresh*, should be able to blow the *shofar* for others. Moreover, Rabbi Epstein reasons that the fact that an individual cannot hear should not create a special exemption from the *shofar* obligation on account of this obligation's being dependent on one's ability to hear the *shofar* sounds. The actual commandment, Rabbi Epstein says, is to blow the *shofar*—hence, in the Talmud's terminology, "Everyone is obligated to blow the *shofar*..."[290]—though hearing the *shofar* satisfies this obligation as well. The essence of the obligation, however, is blowing the *shofar*. Based on this, Rabbi Epstein finds it difficult to believe that someone who can speak but cannot hear, who is not a *cheresh* and therefore not formally exempt from the *shofar* obligation, is exempted from the commandment by virtue of his lack of hearing. Such an exemption cuts against both the general rule that someone who speaks but cannot hear is bound by *halakhic* obligations like anyone else, and the principal duty associated with the *shofar*, which is to *blow*—and not necessarily to *hear*—the sounds of the *shofar*. If an exemption from the obligation for a person who is deaf but can speak exists, as Rabbi Karo maintains, then, Rabbi Epstein argues, the Talmud should have made this counterintuitive exemption explicit.[291]

Rabbi Epstein also questions Rabbi Karo's ruling on the basis of a Talmudic dispute regarding whether a person must hear what they are saying when they recite the *Shema* or *Birkhat HaMazon*, Grace After Meals. According to Rabbi Judah, a person that does not hear himself say these prayers nevertheless satisfies the obligation to recite them; Rabbi Yossi disagrees, however, and holds that, if one recites these prayers without hearing the recitation, that person has not fulfilled the obligation to recite the prayer and must do so again. In light of this passage, Rabbi Epstein makes the following argument: if Rabbi Karo was correct that a deaf individual is exempt from the *shofar* obligation because he cannot hear the *shofar* sounds, then Rabbi Karo should also rule, following Rabbi Yossi's view, that a deaf individual is also exempt from having to recite the *Shema* and *Birkhat HaMazon*, since, like the *shofar*, these obligations are fulfilled through hearing the recital of the prayer, which a deaf person cannot do. But, Rabbi Epstein points out, in fact neither Rabbi Karo himself, nor anyone else for that matter has ever entertained the notion that a deaf person is exempt from reciting the *Shema* or the Grace After Meals for this reason. Rather, Rabbi Epstein argues, it must be that it is only those who are physically able to hear that must hear their own recital of these prayers; those physically unable to hear, of course, cannot be

---

288 *See* Shulchan Arukh, Orach Chaim 589:1; Beit Yoseph, Orach Chaim 589:2.
289 Babylonian Talmud, Chagigah 2b.
290 Babylonian Talmud, Rosh Hashanah 29a.
291 *See* Arukh HaShulchan, Orach Chaim 189:4.

expected to do so, but must still recite the prayers, provided they can speak (Principle 10). The same is true, he argues, regarding the *shofar*: while a hearing person must hear the sounds being blown, a deaf person who is not a *halakhic cheresh* need not hear the *shofar*, though he remains obligated to blow the *shofar* nonetheless.

Based on his understanding of the Talmudic sources, Rabbi Epstein rejects Rabbi Karo's rulings. Instead, he prescribes the innovative rule that a person who is deaf but can speak must blow the *shofar* for himself, since he cannot fulfill his obligation by hearing the sounds of a *shofar* blown by another (Principle 1). Nevertheless, Rabbi Epstein writes that, since a great authority like Rabbi Karo ruled that such a person is not obligated to blow the *shofar* at all, such a person should not recite a blessing when doing so in deference to Rabbi Karo's stringent position (Principle 3), and because the obligation to recite the blessing is merely rabbinic, while doing so when not actually obligated violates the biblical injunction against taking God's name in vain (Principle 4).

Methodological Principles: 1, 3, 4, 10.

Example #170 – *Arukh HaShulchan* §590:14

The *Arbah Turim* rules that, if one blows a full three-sound series of blasts from a *shofar* in a single breath, without taking a new breath in between each of the three sounds, the sounds are not ritually valid and do not count towards the fulfillment of the obligation to blow the proper number of sounds with a *shofar* on Rosh Hashanah.[292] This is also the view of the *Rosh* and is supported by a Tannaitic *Tosefta*, which explicitly invalidates a series of *shofar* sounds if the individual sounds were not separated from each other by separate breaths. Rabbi Epstein notes, however, that the Jerusalem Talmud offers a contrary ruling, and holds that, if all the sounds were produced with a single breath, one still fulfills the obligation to hear the *shofar* through those blasts. Rabbi Epstein rules in accordance with the Jerusalem Talmud, and against the *Arbah Turim* and the *Tosefta*, since the Babylonian Talmud does not directly contradict the Jerusalem Talmud's ruling (Principle 1).

Methodological Principles: 1.

Example #171 – *Arukh HaShulchan* §600:4

While Rosh Hashanah is a two-day holiday, it is different from every other major holiday that is celebrated for two days outside the Land of Israel. Other major holidays are celebrated for one day in the Land of Israel and for two days in the diaspora in order to ensure that diaspora communities actually celebrate the holiday on the correct calendar date. During Talmudic times, the calendar was set by the *Sanhedrin*'s formal declaration of the start of each new month, based on a local sighting on the new moon. Since it took time to communicate this information to far-flung communities across the diaspora, the Rabbis declared that Jews outside the Land of Israel should celebrate each one-day holiday for two days, as this would ensure that one of the two celebrated days would be the correct biblically prescribed calendrical date of the holiday. Rosh Hashanah, however, is celebrated for two days, even in the Land of Israel. This is because, since Rosh Hashanah occurs on the first day of the month of Tishrei, it was often the case that the *Sanhedrin* would receive testimony about a new moon sighting on the previous night late in the

---

292   Arbah Turim, Orach Chaim 590.

day. This resulted in that entire day being in fact, the first of Tishrei, and thus Rosh Hashanah, but without the proper ritual observances having been practiced, since it was not known that the day was Rosh Hashanah until the appearance of witnesses later that afternoon. To avoid this, Tannaitic authorities legislated that all should observe Rosh Hashanah for two days following the twenty-eighth day of the previous month, Elul.

The extension of Rosh Hashanah into a two-day holiday and the two-day observance of other holidays in the diaspora are thus qualitatively different. While other holidays were observed for two days due to genuine doubts as to the correct calendar day, Rosh Hashanah was observed for two days in order to avoid the religious and ritual concerns that would otherwise result from sometimes beginning a day thinking it was the twenty-ninth day of the previous month only to discover later that afternoon, following the appearance of witnesses to the previous night's new moon, that the entire day had actually been the first of Tishrei, Rosh Hashanah. Consequently, while each of the two days of other holidays were considered distinct days for ritual purposes—with the second day essentially constituting a complete ritual repetition of the first day—the two days of Rosh Hashanah took on a different character, and were in some sense thought of as "one long day."[293]

The hybrid character of the two-day celebration of Rosh Hashanah led to an early rabbinic dispute regarding whether or not one should recite the *Shehechiyanu* blessing, which recognizes the uniqueness of the day on the second day of the holiday. On other holidays, all agree that the *Shehechiyanu* blessing is recited, since the second day is celebrated out of doubt, and thus may in fact be the true and correct date for the holiday celebration. This is not so, however, with respect to the second day of Rosh Hashanah. According to *Rashi*, one should recite the *Shehechiyanu* blessing upon the second day of Rosh Hashanah because the Torah establishes Rosh Hashanah as a one-day holiday, and therefore the blessing should be recited for each of the current two one-day holidays rather than only one time for an extended two-day holiday. Some earlier authorities disagreed with *Rashi*, however, and ruled that one should recite the *Shehechiyanu* blessing only on the first day of Rosh Hashanah.

Rabbi Epstein accepts *Rashi*'s view because it is supported by a consensus of *halakhic* authorities, virtually all of whom have endorsed the view that each day of Rosh Hashanah gets a separate *Shehechiyanu* blessing (Principle 2). While adopting *Rashi*'s view, Rabbi Epstein commends the practice of wearing a new item of clothing or including a new fruit as part of the evening meal on the second day of Rosh Hashanah. Since the occasion of eating a new fruit or wearing new clothes justify the recitation of the *Shehechiyanu* blessing in their own right, one can recite the blessing with the intent that it covers both the incidence of the second day of Rosh Hashanah and the new fruit or garment. In this way, one can recite the blessing as required by *Rashi* without having recited an unnecessary blessing, even according to those who think no blessing should be recited on the second day of Rosh Hashanah. While typically Rabbi Epstein does not feel the need to construct *halakhic* practices that help satisfy rejected opinions (Principle 5), here he does endorse a practice designed to fulfill the views of both those who support and those who oppose the recitation of the *Shehechiyanu* on the second day of Rosh Hashanah because, as he notes, "it is the established custom in all our lands" to do so (Principle 8). Moreover, doing so helps avoid the possibility of reciting a possibly unnecessary blessing (Principle 4).
Methodological Principles: 2, 4, 5, 8.

---

293 *See* Arukh HaShulchan, Orach Chaim 600:1-2.

Example #172 – *Arukh HaShulchan* §603:2

Based on a passage in the Jerusalem Talmud, the *Arbah Turim* instructs that one should be especially careful to "eat in purity" during the seven days between Rosh Hashanah and Yom Kippur as an expression of piety and special scrupulousness in *halakhic* observance in preparation for Yom Kippur.[294] For instance, the *Arbah Turim* writes that it is appropriate that those who during the year eat bread baked by Gentiles should, during the Ten Days of Repentance, be careful to eat only bread baked by fellow Jews.

While he recognizes the religious value of this practice, Rabbi Epstein makes clear that one should only undertake such added religious strictures with respect to matters that are not actually prohibited by *halakhah*. One should not, however, undertake supererogatory behaviors as expressions of piety during the Ten Days of Repentance by acting strictly in matters that are subject to *halakhic* dispute, as doing so could have negative consequences. Rabbi Epstein notes, for instance, that there are some practices that some authorities prohibit, but which we have customarily treated as permitted in rejection of the more stringent views. One should not conduct oneself strictly in such matters during the Ten Days of Repentance because such supererogatory conduct would amount to undertaking to follow the more stringent view on that issue, and thereby preclude a return to practicing the normatively accepted permissible view after Yom Kippur. In short, while supererogatory behavior during the Ten Days of Repentance can be religiously valuable, Rabbi Epstein discourages such conduct when it could lead to negative results (Principle 6).
Methodological Principles: 6.

Example #173 – *Arukh HaShulchan* §605:5

Rabbi Epstein notes the existence of the widespread and very old Yom Kippur Eve custom of *kapparot*, which involves symbolically transferring one's sins to a live chicken, which is then slaughtered and its meat distributed to the poor for their pre-fast meal. While many authorities have endorsed this custom, including many *Geonim*, *Rashi*, and Rabbi Moses Isserles, many others, including Nachmanides and Rabbi Joseph Karo, have voiced strong opposition to the practice, arguing that it smacks of witchcraft and modes of foreign worship.[295]

Consistent with his respect for customary practices, Rabbi Epstein attempts to blunt many of the traditional criticism leveled against *kapparot* (Principle 8). He argues that the claim that *kapparot* resembles sorcery and forms of foreign worship pertains only to the extreme practice of some Jews who specifically seek to perform this ritual with white chickens or birds that would be suitable for use as Temple offerings. The general practice, however, is not inherently problematic. Still, Rabbi Epstein takes issue with *kapparot*, and argues that, while in past eras the custom was acceptable, the manner in which it is performed in his own times makes him unsupportive. He notes that in his time and place, *kapparot* are performed on a very large scale right before Yom Kippur; this requires the ritual slaughterers to work very fast to dispatch the large number of birds being used, and this in turn results in ritual slaughterers becoming tired and careless. At the very least, Rabbi Epstein writes, even the most well-meaning slaughterers are bound to make mistakes under such difficult working conditions. This inevitably results in many of the birds being passed off as kosher, when according to *halakhah* they are unfit for

---

294 *See* Arbah Turim, Orach Chaim 603.
295 *See* Arukh HaShulchan, Orach Chaim 605:1-2.

consumption. This change in circumstances leads Rabbi Epstein to question the continued propriety of this once valid custom (Principle 9). Still, and despite his reservations, Rabbi Epstein notes that many before him have tried to end the practice of *kapparot* and failed, since for some reason the Jews have become incredibly attached and committed to this practice. Recognizing the impracticality of banning the practice outright, he therefore makes the pragmatic recommendation that at least *kapparot* ceremonies should begin several days before Yom Kippur, so as to allow more time for careful and proper slaughtering of the birds (Principle 10).
Methodological Principles: 8, 9, 10.

Example #174 – *Arukh HaShulchan* §609:2

The *Arbah Turim* refers to a Geonic ruling according to which it is prohibited to insulate hot food prior to the start of Yom Kippur in order to have warm food ready to eat immediately after the fast ends. Both the *Arbah Turim* and Rabbi Joseph Karo raise strong questions on this prohibition, since there is no conceivable prohibition against preparing food on a weekday to be eaten on another weekday (as opposed to preparing food on a Sabbath or holiday for consumption on another day, which is prohibited). Nor is it prohibited to leave food in a warming device of some kind prior to Yom Kippur, as there is no such prohibition with respect to the Sabbath.[296]

Despite these objections, Rabbi Epstein notes that the widespread custom among Ashkenazic Jews is to respect this Geonic prohibition, and he therefore attempts to provide several novel justifications for what he obviously regards as a legally unnecessary religious stricture that is nonetheless normative due to its widespread acceptance as a binding custom (Principles 1 and 8).
Methodological Principles 1, 8.

Example #175 – *Arukh HaShulchan* §612:9

While the Torah prohibits eating and drinking on Yom Kippur, as with all Torah-based dietary prohibitions, one who violates this stricture is punished for their sin only if they ate or drank more than a certain minimal amount. In the case of Yom Kippur, one is liable only for eating more than the size of a large date, and for drinking a *revi'it*, more than a cheek-full.[297] There is an early dispute, however, over the amount of time within which one must have consumed the requisite minimum amount of food or drink to be liable. According to *Rashi*, one is liable for eating or drinking on Yom Kippur only if one consumes the requisite amount within the amount of time it takes to eat a piece of bread—approximately a few minutes.[298] According to Maimonides, however, one is liable for eating or drinking on Yom Kippur only if the minimum amount is consumed during the amount of time it takes to drink a *revi'it*, about four fluid ounces.[299] Rabbi Epstein notes that many authorities question Maimonides's position here, and while Maimonides represents a stricter view, and while this issue is a question of biblical law, Rabbi Epstein rules in accordance with *Rashi*'s more permissive opinion because it is supported by a strong consensus of other authorities (Principle 2).

---

296 *See* Beit Yosef *to* Arbah Turim, Orach Chaim 509:1.
297 *See* Babylonian Talmud, Yoma 80b.
298 Babylonian Talmud, Keritot 13a.
299 Mishneh Torah, Hilkhot Yom Kippur 2:4.

Methodological Principles: 2.

Example #176 – Arukh HaShulchan §616:3

One of the five categories of special restrictions for Yom Kippur is the prohibition on washing oneself and rubbing oils into the skin for pleasure or comfort. Like the prohibitions on eating and drinking, these restrictions apply only to adult Jews; children do not fast, and they may wash themselves as well. However, Rabbi Epstein rules that an adult Jew should not wash or oil a child on Yom Kippur, since when doing so one also washes or oils oneself in violation of the laws of Yom Kippur. Therefore, if children need to be washed on Yom Kippur, it best to ask a Gentile to do so. This is true, Rabbi Epstein argues, even though the Talmud rules explicitly that a Jew is permitted to wash children on Yom Kippur, even using soothing hot water from which the Jewish washer will certainly derive enjoyment.[300] Rabbi Epstein maintains that the Talmudic rule no longer applies due to changed hygienic practices for children (Principle 10). In Talmudic times, children would regularly wash and have moisturizing oils rubbed into their skin, and therefore, they were permitted to have the same done to them on Yom Kippur, since withholding such from children would be distressing, and unlike adults, children have no *halakhic* obligation to "afflict" themselves on Yom Kippur. But, Rabbi Epstein writes, in his own time, children did not wash or have their skin moisturized with oils on any regular basis, and not doing so on Yom Kippur itself therefore would not create any particular distress or hardship for them. Consequently, Rabbi Epstein rejects the earlier ruling, and instead maintains that children should not be washed or anointed with oil on Yom Kippur.
Methodological Principles: 10.

Example #177 – Arukh HaShulchan §618:9

Rabbi Epstein notes that some people have the custom to stand on their feet for the full length of all the prayer services on Yom Kippur. Likewise, even many of those who do not stand for the entire service make sure to stand while the holy ark is open and the Torah scrolls are displayed to the congregation (Principle 8). Rabbi Epstein, however, notes that people who find standing for these extended lengths of time is difficult or impractical need not do so (Principle 10). Moreover, he recommends against adopting the supererogatory practice of staying awake for the entire night of Yom Kippur in prayer, which he says tends to make it difficult or even impossible to properly pray the required prayers during the following day (Principle 6).
Methodological Principles: 6, 8, 9.

Example #178 – Arukh HaShulchan §619:9

Rabbi Joseph Karo rules that on Yom Kippur an attendant should be placed on either side of the *chazzan* who leads the communal prayers.[301] Rabbi Epstein notes, however, that the contemporary custom in his own time and place is to not follow Rabbi Karo's prescription (Principle 8). Rabbi Epstein creatively explains that Rabbi Karo's ruling is based on the idea that, on communal fast days, attendants should flank the *chazzan* on either side while he prays, which

---

300 *See* Babylonian Talmud, Yoma 78a.
301 Beit Yosef *to* Arbah Turim, Orach Chaim 619:4.

symbolizes the way Aaron and Chur stood on either side of Moses, supporting him while he prayed to God for victory in the Jews' battle against the Amalekites shortly after they left Egypt (Principle 1). Rabbi Epstein notes, however, that normative Jewish law maintains that formal public fasts days are not observed by communities outside the Land of Israel. Thus, while it made sense for Rabbi Karo, who lived in Safed, to prescribe a Yom Kippur practice that would mimic the ritual observances of a public fast day, such a practice would be out of place in Eastern Europe or other locations outside the Land of Israel (Principle 9).
Methodological Principles: 1, 8, 9.

Example #179 - *Arukh HaShulchan* §624:6

At the conclusion of Yom Kippur, one recites the *havdalah* prayer, which symbolizes the transition from the sanctified time of Yom Kippur to the mundane time of the ordinary weekday. The Yom Kippur *havdalah* service, like the post-Sabbath *havdalah*, includes a blessing made over a flame. However, while the post-Sabbath *havdalah* blessing is recited over a flame that has been newly kindled after Sabbath has ended, the flame used in the post-Yom Kippur *Havdalah* service must be "a flame that rested"—a flame that was lit prior to and remained burning throughout Yom Kippur.

Rabbi Epstein raises the question of what to do in case one does not have a preexisting flame for use in the Yom Kippur *havdalah* service. In such a case, should one simply skip the blessing over a fire because at the close of Yom Kippur this blessing is only recited on a preexisting flame, or should one use a newly kindled flame because the *halakhic* prescription of a preexisting flame applies only if one is available? Rabbi Epstein responds initially by noting that the way in which most authorities express the preexisting flame rule suggests that, if no preexisting flame is available, one should simply omit that blessing from the *havdalah* service. For instance, Rabbi Karo writes: "And after Yom Kippur, one does not recite a blessing on a newly kindled flame."[302] While this is the normative rule and is widely accepted by virtually all authorities, the *Kol Bo*, an early medieval authority, rules that one may recite a blessing on a flame that was lit from another newly kindled flame. While the *Kol Bo* here represents a minority view and is not accepted in practice, Rabbi Epstein rules that in a case where no preexisting flame is available, one may rely on the opinion of the *Kol Bo* and recite the *havdalah* blessing on a flame that has been lit from another newly kindled flame (Principle 5). While Rabbi Epstein typically rules that one should avoid reciting blessings in doubtful cases (Principle 4), here the *Arukh HaShulchan* prescribes recitation of the blessing. Rabbi Epstein explains that the blessing over a flame in the Sabbath *havdalah* commemorates the creation of fire at the conclusion of the first Sabbath following creation and therefore requires the use of a newly created flame. The blessing over a flame during the Yom Kippur *havdalah*, by contrast, is an expression of thanks to God for making fire available for human use after the conclusion of Yom Kippur when restrictions on performing *melakhah* proscribed benefiting from fire (Principle 1). In line with this idea, Rabbi Epstein says, it makes sense to use a fire that had been lit before Yom Kippur began, and which was not used during the day. Based on this rationale, however, it seems that using a preexisting flame is an appropriate practice rather than a strict requirement, and thus can be dispensed with in situations where no preexisting flame is available for use (Principles 6 and 10).
Methodological Principles: 1, 4, 5, 6, 10.

---

302 Shulchan Arukh, Orach Chaim 624:4.

Example #180 – *Arukh HaShulchan* §626:9

The Talmud states that a *sukkah*, the temporary booth lived in during the holiday of Sukkot (Tabernacles)—is invalid for ritual use if it was built beneath a tree. This is because one of the central requirements of a ritually valid *sukkah* is that it be covered with *skhakh*—natural foliage that has been detached from the ground—and only with *skhakh*.[303] Rabbi Joseph Karo cites two different understandings of the parameters of this Talmudic rule.[304] *Rashi* and *Tosafot* qualify the Talmudic rule by maintaining that the Talmud actually intends to distinguish between two different kinds of *sukkah* coverings—one which is mostly closed, creating more shade than sunlight within the *sukkah*, and one which is mostly open, letting in more sunlight than shade. According to this view, the Talmudic rule applies categorically only if the canopy of the overhanging tree is mostly closed; in that case, the tree itself constitutes a "roof" over the *sukkah*, and the *sukkah* is therefore invalid. If, however, the tree's canopy is mostly open, the *sukkah* standing under the tree will be valid, provided that the *skhakh* covering the *sukkah* is itself mostly closed. In that case, the dense *skhakh* provides a ritually valid covering for the *sukkah*, while the sparse foliage of the overhanging tree does not constitute a genuine "roof" over the *sukkah* and leaves the *sukkah* ritually valid. Moreover, if both the tree canopy and the *skhakh* are sparse and are mostly open to the sky, the *sukkah* still will be valid if one lowers the branches of the overhanging tree, so that they intermingle with the foliage of the proper *skhakh*. In that case, the tree foliage is too sparse to qualify as an invalidating "roof," and as long as most of the *sukkah* covering is made of proper *skhakh*, the *sukkah* can be considered covered in accordance with *halakhah*. In addition to the foregoing understanding of the Talmudic invalidation of a *sukkah* built under a tree, Rabbi Karo refers to the more stringent opinion of the *Rosh*. According to the *Rosh*, the *sukkah* is invalid, even if the canopy of the overhanging tree is sparse, and if the *skhakh* is dense and mostly closed, provided that the *skhakh* foliage lines up under the tree canopy. In that case, the fact that the valid *skhakh* covering lines up directly under the tree foliage means that, in effect, the *sukkah* is ultimately covered by the tree rather than the *skhakh* and is therefore invalid.

Commenting on Rabbi Karo's treatment of this issue, Rabbi Epstein cites two additional opinions—those of Maimonides and the *Baal HaMaor*—which offer alternative understandings of the Talmud's stricture against building a *sukkah* under a tree. Based on the Talmud's permitting the use of a *sukkah* built under a tree only when one "cut off" the tree's branches, Maimonides argues that a *sukkah* built under a tree is only valid if one cut off the branches of the tree and placed them on top of the *sukkah* together with the original *skhakh*. The *Baal HaMaor*, by contrast, reads the same words in the Talmud as permitting the use of a *sukkah* built beneath a tree only if one "shook" the branches, which he takes to mean that a *sukkah* built under a tree can be rendered ritually fit only by shaking the leaves off the tree's branches, which demonstrates that one does not desire to use the overhanging tree to provide shelter or shade for the *sukkah*.

That Talmudic passage discussing this issue is genuinely ambiguous, and easily lends itself to at least four different understandings, as demonstrated by the competing explanations of *Rashi*, the *Rosh*, Maimonides, and the *Baal HaMaor*. While Rabbi Karo does not include Maimonides's opinion in his *Shulchan Arukh*, Rabbi Epstein himself regards Maimonides's view as significant and not so easily dismissed (Principle 3). Ultimately, Rabbi Epstein rules that one should build one's *sukkah* in a manner that conforms to all four of these views. While normally Rabbi Epstein prefers to reach a definitive ruling and eschews prescribing modes of religious practice designed to satisfy multiple opinions (Principle 6), in this case, no particularly

---

303 Babylonian Talmud, Sukkah 9b.
304 Shulchan Arukh, Orach Chaim 626:1, 4.

halakhic standard enjoys any more Talmudic support than any other. Accordingly, since the issue involves the ritual validity of a *sukkah*—a question of biblical law, Rabbi Epstein rules that one must act strictly to satisfy all of the viable *halakhic* opinions (Principle 4).
Methodological Principles: 3, 4, 6.

Example #181 – *Arukh HaShulchan* §626:25

Rabbi Epstein observes that in his own time many people build their *sukkah* beneath a removable roof by installing ritually valid *skhakh*—a temporary covering for the *sukkah* made of cut foliage—beneath a regular permanent roof, and then later removing the permanent roof in order to sit and eat in the *sukkah* under the *skhakh* as prescribed by Jewish law. Rabbi Epstein notes that this practice could be viewed as problematic because the *halakhah* requires that a *sukkah* be ritually valid at the time of its construction; if the *sukkah* was built in a ritually invalid manner, it remains invalid even after the impediment to its ritual validity is later removed. Here the *sukkah* is built beneath roof, which renders it invalid; thus, the later removal of the roof should not succeed in validating the originally invalid *sukkah*.

Based on his analysis of the Talmudic principle that a *sukkah* must be valid at the time of construction, however, Rabbi Epstein argues that this requirement applies only to invalidating features of the *sukkah* itself rather than the presence of external factors at the time of construction that are later removed. Thus, for instance, a *sukkah* that is covered with foliage that is still attached to the ground is invalid at the time of construction, and later cutting the *skhakh* from the ground will not make the *sukkah* ritually valid. By contrast, while the presence of a permanent roof hanging over an otherwise valid *sukkah* does indeed render the *sukkah* presently invalid, this invalidating factor is distinct from the *sukkah* itself, and so the later removal of the roof, which leaves the otherwise valid *sukkah* sitting properly beneath the open sky, will render the *sukkah* ritually fit for use (Principle 1).

Ultimately, however, Rabbi Epstein declines to apply this speculative understanding of the Talmudic principle that a *sukkah* must be valid at the time of construction, which enjoys no explicit support in the Talmudic text itself. Instead, he defers to the more stringent interpretation of this principle offered by Rabbi Moses Isserles, who rules that the post-construction validation of a *sukkah* is ineffective, even with respect to the removal of invalidating features external to the *sukkah* itself (Principle 2). Rabbi Epstein notes that Rabbi Isserles's understanding of the issue is widely accepted as the customary *halakhic* standard, and should therefore not be disregarded (Principle 8). Therefore, Rabbi Epstein rules that if one intends to build a *sukkah* under a retractable roof, one must ensure that the roof is left open at the time the *sukkah* is built, so as to render the *sukkah* ritually valid from the time of construction.
Methodological Principles: 1, 2, 8.

Example #182 – *Arukh HaShulchan* §629:2

Rabbi Epstein notes that in northern areas snow often falls during the Sukkot holiday, completely covering the *skhakh* of people's *sukkah* huts. The *Be'er Heitev* and *Shaarei Teshuva*, two important commentaries on Rabbi Karo's *Shulchan Arukh*, rule that, in a case where a *sukkah* is fully covered with snow, the *sukkah* will still be valid, despite the fact that it is covered with a material which is not acceptable for *skhakh*. They claim that, since snow is considered a permeable material in terms of ritual impurity, it is also not considered a ceiling, such that it will invalidate *skhakh*. Rabbi Epstein disagrees with their reasoning by bringing the counterexample of vegetables that are still attached to the ground. Vegetables when still attached to the ground definitely invalidate a *sukkah* if they cover the *skhakh*, despite the fact that they are considered a permeable barrier in terms of ritual impurity (Principle 1). Nonetheless, Rabbi Epstein suggests that a snow-covered *sukkah* will be valid because snow fulfills both requirements to be ritually valid *skhakh*. The Talmud states that in order for *skhakh* to be valid, it must grow from the ground and not be subject to ritual impurity.[305] Rabbi Epstein quotes another passage from the Talmud to prove that snow does not contract ritual impurity,[306] as well as a ruling of the *Mordechai* showing that the *halakhah* regards snow as something that "grows from the ground." Despite the fact that Rabbi Epstein himself considers snow to be acceptable *skhakh*, in this question of biblical law, he defers to the more stringent opinion of Rabbi Joseph Karo, who rules that snow is not something that "grows from the ground," and therefore snow invalidates a *sukkah* (Principles 3 and 4). Methodological Principles: 1, 3, 4.

Example #183 – *Arukh HaShulchan* §629:32

The Talmud records that the Rabbis legislated that one may not use wooden planks as *skhakh* to form the roof of a *sukkah* if the planks are wider than four handbreadths.[307] Rabbi Epstein explains that the reason for this rule is that one who uses such wide planks as *skhakh* may come to think that the roof of a *sukkah* is no different than the roof of a house (since regular roofs are also made of wide wooden boards), and may then mistakenly spend the Sukkot holiday in his regular house, which is certainly invalid for ritual use as a *sukkah*.[308] By its own Talmudic terms, however, this rule is limited to wood planks that are more than four handbreadths wide; only such wide planks may be confused for regular roofing, and narrower boards may therefore be used as *skhakh* for a *sukkah*.[309] While the Talmudic enactment only invalidates a *sukkah* covered with wide planks, Rabbi Joseph Karo notes that the customary practice is to avoid using even such narrower boards for *skhakh*.

In his own ruling on the matter, Rabbi Epstein goes even further. Keeping with his conviction that Talmudic norms must be applied contextually, Rabbi Epstein rules that in his own time, even a *sukkah* covered with wooden boards narrower than four handbreadths is ritually invalid because narrow planks are regularly used to build regular roofs, and therefore a *sukkah* covered by narrow boards may be easily confused for regular roofing (Principle 9). Rabbi Epstein's understanding of the correct application of the Talmudic rule in his own context thus results in the normative rejection of Rabbi Karo's nominal permission to use narrow planks to cover a *sukkah* (Principle 1). Still, Rabbi Epstein rules that, in a case where one is unable to find any other *skhakh*, one may rely on Rabbi Karo's understanding of the limits of the original Talmudic decree and build a *sukkah* using narrow planks. While he rejects Rabbi Karo's position that it is merely customary—and not strictly prohibited—to use narrow planks as *skhakh*, Rabbi Epstein is willing to use this otherwise rejected opinion in the extenuating circumstance where one cannot find any other more suitable *skhakh* material (Principles 5 and 10). Methodological Principles: 1, 5, 9, 10.

---

305 Babylonian Talmud, Sukkah 12a.
306 Babylonian Talmud, Niddah 17a.
307 *See* Babylonian Talmud, Sukkah 14a.
308 Arukh HaShulchan, Orach Chaim 629:30.
309 *See* Shulchan Arukh, Orach Chaim 629:18.

Example #184 – Arukh HaShulchan §632:4

The Talmud rules that a three-walled sukkah whose *skhakh* is split by a strip of invalid material like metal or woven mats running from its middle wall to its unwalled side is invalid, provided the strip of invalid covering is at least four handbreadths wide. In *halakhah*, four handbreadths are considered to be a "significant space." Consequently, a strip of invalid *skhakh* material four handbreadths wide effectively splits the three-walled *sukkah* into two separate structures, each composed of only two walls. Since a *sukkah* must have at least three walls to be ritually valid, a three-walled *sukkah* divided in two in this manner by a strip of invalid roofing four handbreadths wide is effectively two separate *sukkah* huts, each with two walls, and is unfit for use during the holiday.[310] The law is different, the Talmud says, when the strip of invalid roofing material runs adjacent to any of the *sukkah*'s walls rather than down the middle of the booth. In such cases, the *sukkah* remains valid unless the strip of invalid *skhakh* is wider than four *cubits*—roughly four times the width of the four handbreadths of invalid roofing required to invalidate a *sukkah* when the invalid *skhakh* runs through the middle of the structure. The reason for this discrepancy is the Talmudic doctrine of *Dofen Akumah*, or "Bent Wall," which views up to four cubits of invalid *skhakh* material that is adjacent to one of the *sukkah*'s walls as a continuation of the wall itself rather than as ritually unfit roofing. A strip of invalid *skhakh* adjacent to a wall will therefore not separate the wall from the rest of the *sukkah*, leaving the *sukkah* itself with only two walls, because the invalid *skhakh* itself is seen to be the horizontal continuation of that wall. When the invalid roofing material adjacent to the wall is more than four cubits wide, however, the *halakhah* no longer treats it as a continuation of the wall, but as roofing, which would result in the invalidation of the *sukkah*.

While Jewish law does not generally require the walls of a *sukkah* to touch the *skhakh*—instead demanding only that the walls be at least ten handbreadths tall and that they line up with the *skhakh*—the *Ran* rules that the principle of *Dofen Akumah* can only be used to validate a *sukkah* if the regular vertical *sukkah* wall is tall enough so that it actually meets the edge of the invalid roofing material that is to be treated as a horizontal extension of the wall. The *Rosh* disagrees with this limitation on the application of the *Dofen Akumah* principle, and instead rules that this doctrine may be used to validate a *sukkah* where the edge of the *skhakh* is made of invalid material as long as the top of the real wall lines up with—even if it does not actually touch—the roof above it.

Rabbi Epstein rules in accordance with the *Ran*'s more stringent standard for applying the principle of *Dofen Akumah* to validate a *sukkah* where part of the roofing is made of invalid *skhakh*. This is because dwelling in a valid *sukkah* during the holiday is a biblical obligation, and doubts must therefore be resolved stringently to ensure that the *sukkah* is indeed valid (Principle 4). Methodological Principles: 4.

Example #185 – Arukh HaShulchan §639:3

The Talmud states that one must live in a *sukkah* in the way that one generally lives in one's house.[311] Thus, one should, for example, bring mattresses and normal household items into the *sukkah*. The Talmud qualifies this rule, however, and instructs that one should not bring

---

310 Babylonian Talmud, Sukkah 17a.
311 Babylonian Talmud, Sukkah 26a.

his "eating vessels" into the *sukkah*.³¹² According to *Rashi*, the Talmud means that one should not leave vessels that have been used for dining in the *sukkah* once they have been dirtied, since leaving soiled dishes and cutlery in the *sukkah* would disrespect the *mitzvah* of *sukkah*. *Tosafot* offer a more lenient interpretation of the text. Based on this view, the Talmud only prohibits bringing vessels used for food preparation into the *sukkah* while it permits leaving soiled dishes and cutlery in the *sukkah* after a meal. *Tosafot* reason that cooking is not usually done in one's house, but in a kitchen space located away from one's living quarters; therefore, bringing cookware into the *sukkah* amounts to an inappropriate use of the *sukkah* itself, which is supposed to act as one's living quarters—not one's kitchen—during the Sukkot holiday.

The *Arbah Turim* and Rabbi Joseph Karo both codify *Rashi*'s more restrictive understanding of the Talmudic prohibition.³¹³ Rabbi Epstein notes that the common practice is to leave dirty dishes in the *sukkah* in accordance with the view of *Tosafot*. However, in this case, the *Arukh HaShulchan* rules against the general custom and instructs that people should not leave dirty dishes in the *sukkah*. Here, the custom conflicts with the settled view of the major *halakhic* codifiers, who rejected *Tosafot*'s opinion allowing one to leave dirty dishes in the *sukkah* (Principles 2 and 8), and who followed *Rashi*'s stricter view, reinforcing the respect due to the *sukkah* booth used to observe an important biblical commandment (Principle 6).
Methodological Principles: 2, 6, 8.

Example #186 – *Arukh HaShulchan* §639:13

The Talmud rules that because one is obligated to live in a *sukkah* during the holiday of Sukkot in the same manner that one lives in one's home, a person is obligated to sleep in a *sukkah* during the holiday. Indeed, the Talmud states that one is not even allowed to take a short nap outside of the *sukkah*.³¹⁴ Troubled by the fact that in his time many people were lax about observing this rule, Rabbi Moses Isserles offers two justifications for the fact that people in his time and place generally did not sleep in the *sukkah* during the holiday.³¹⁵ First, the *Rema* suggests that, perhaps in the cold, wet, Eastern European fall climate, people are generally exempt from the obligation to sleep in the *sukkah* due to the Talmudic rule that one who is distressed or uncomfortable in the *sukkah* need not remain there. The cold weather common in Eastern Europe makes sleeping in the *sukkah* quite uncomfortable for many, and therefore those who experience discomfort are exempt. Additionally, Rabbi Isserles points out that one is only obligated to sleep in the *sukkah* in the same manner in which one ordinarily would sleep in one's own home. Since men sleep beside their wives at home but cannot do so in a *sukkah* shared by many, married men are exempt from sleeping in a *sukkah*. Rabbi Isserles does suggest that people should attempt to arrange for their own private *sukkah*, so that they might then sleep in the *sukkah* with their wives and thereby fulfill the obligation.

Rabbi Epstein rejects the *Rema*'s second justification for the common custom to not sleep in the *sukkah*. He points out that the Talmudic view that the obligation to live in the *sukkah* in the same manner as one lives in one's home includes sleeping in the *sukkah* together with one's wife reflects the view of the Talmudic sage Abaye. Another scholar, Rava, disagrees with Abaye's ruling, however, and as a matter of Talmudic interpretation, in disputes between Abaye

---

312 Babylonian Talmud, Sukkah 29a.
313 Shulchan Arukh, Orach Chaim 639:1.
314 Babylonian Talmud, Sukkah 26a.
315 Rema *to* Shulchan Arukh, Orach Chaim 639:2.

and Rava, the law follows the view of the latter (Principle 1).[316] Still, Rabbi Epstein defends the general custom of not sleeping in the *sukkah* by pointing to the cold, harsh climate in many European countries. Because sleeping in the *sukkah* can often be quite uncomfortable and even dangerous, Rabbi Epstein explains that most are likely exempt from this requirement (Principle 8). While an obligation to sleep in the *sukkah* made sense in the Talmudic context of the Middle East, it does not generally apply in cold, wet climates like that of Eastern and Northern Europe (Principle 9).
Methodological Principles: 1, 8, 9.

Example #187 – *Arukh HaShulchan* §645:11

The Torah prescribes that, on the holiday of Sukkot, each Jew is required to gather together and take four different plant species—a *lulav*, or date palm branch; myrtle branches; willow branches; and an *etrog*, or citron.[317] When considering the necessary characteristics of a ritually valid *lulav*, the Talmud rules that a palm branch with a split *tiyomet* cannot be used to fulfill the biblical obligation.[318] Early rabbinic authorities disagreed over the precise definition of the *tiyomet*. Rabbi Isaac Alfasi and Maimonides note that every leaf on a palm frond is actually made up of two leaves that are joined along one long edge. These scholars maintain that, when the Talmud invalidated a *lulav* with a split *tiyomet*, the Talmud was referring to the long connected edge where every two *lulav* leaves are joined, and a *lulav* is until a majority of its leaves are split along this conjoined side. *Rashi*, however, rules that the *tiyomet* refers not to the conjoined edge of every two leaves on a palm branch but specifically to the spine of the *lulav*, which splits into two separate leaves. Based on this view, a split *tiyomet* refers to a split in the spine of the *lulav* itself between the two leaves that extend from the spine higher up on the branch. Some later authorities note that, in fact, the palm fronds that they are familiar with do not comport with *Rashi*'s description. Rather than having two leaves protruding from a central spine, every *lulav* has a single double leaf joined along one side that extends upward from the top of the *lulav*'s spine. In light of this observed reality, and based on a slightly different definition of the *tiyomet* that *Rashi* provides in a different Talmudic discussion, some authorities, including the *Terumat HaDeshen*, define the Talmud's "split *tiyomet*" as a split in the *lulav*'s single doubled-over middle leaf that extends upward from the spine. Rabbi Joseph Karo rules in accordance with the position of Maimonides and the *Rif*—which was also adopted by many other authorities—that a *lulav* is only invalidated by a split *tiyomet* if most of its leaves are split along their conjoined edges, and Rabbi Karo does not even refer to the alternative definition of the *tiyomet* offered by *Rashi*.[319] However the *Rema*, following the accepted custom of his time, rules that a *lulav* is invalid when its middle leaf is split from the top down to the spine and that people should try to find palm fronds on which the middle leaf extending upward from the spine is not split at all.

Rabbi Epstein expresses great surprise at Rabbi Isserles's decision to adopt *Rashi*'s minority view against the position of Maimonides, which was endorsed subsequently by the vast majority of rabbinic authorities. This is especially astounding, Rabbi Epstein says, because there is not even clarity about *Rashi*'s definition of the *tiyomet*, given his two inconsistent comments on the topic and the apparent incongruity between *Rashi*'s description of palm fronds and the actual

---

316 Babylonian Talmud, Sukkah 28b.
317 Leviticus 23:40.
318 Babylonian Talmud, Sukkah 32a.
319 Shulchan Arukh, Orach Chaim 645:3.

appearance of *lulav* branches. Thus, Rabbi Epstein rules that, as a matter of law, the majority view of Maimonides—that a *lulav* is invalid only if most of its leaves have been split in half—is correct (Principles 2 and 3). Despite this conclusion, however, Rabbi Epstein rules that, in practice, people should follow Rabbi Isserles's stricter view and find a *lulav* with an intact middle leaf—though he declines to rule that a *lulav* with a split middle leaf is actually invalid (Principle 6). He justifies this conclusion by noting that the mere fact that this position was prescribed by the *Rema*, the preeminent codifier of Ashkenazic practice, justifies encouraging people to adhere to this higher standard for the suitability of *lulav* fronds (Principle 6). Likewise, the *Rema* adopts this view at least in part because it reflects the established practice of Ashkenazic communities, and this lends further support for the standard (Principle 8). Moreover, the obligation to take ritually fit palm fronds on Sukkot is biblical, and thus warrants concern for the stricter, albeit non-normative standard expressed by Rabbi Isserles (Principles 4 and 5). Still, Rabbi Epstein notes that one should only be concerned with obtaining a *lulav* that meets the *Rema*'s quality standard if doing so is practicable; if one can only obtain palm branches with split middle leaves, these may be used, since the law actually follows Maimonides's more lenient position (Principle 10). Thus, Rabbi Epstein writes that in his time, where most of the palm fronds available in Eastern Europe do in fact have split middle leaves, one need not be overly concerned with following the *Rema*'s strict view (Principle 10).

Methodological Principles: 2, 3, 4, 5, 6, 8, 10.

Example #188 – *Arukh HaShulchan* §645:15

The Talmud rules that a dry *lulav* branch may not be used to fulfill the ritual obligation to take the four species on Sukkot. According to Rabbi Joseph Karo, a *lulav* is considered "dry" once it loses its green color and once its leaves whiten. The *Rema*, however, rejects Rabbi Karo's position and argues instead that, due to the difficulty of obtaining fresh palm branches in Eastern Europe, the *halakhah* follows the view of *Tosafot*, who ruled that a *lulav* is not classified as "dry" until it has become so desiccated that it can be flaked off with one's fingernail.[320]

Rabbi Epstein writes that, while the *Rema*'s position adopting the more lenient and less normative view of *Tosafot* was correct given the challenges of obtaining fresh palm branches in time and place (Principles 5 and 10), one should no longer rely on this view. Rabbi Epstein notes that by his own time, shipping had become faster and more reliable, and many more palm branches were shipped and available in Northern and Eastern Europe than were available during the *Rema*'s life—indeed, by Rabbi Epstein's time even local greenhouse-grown palms are available. Since the exigent circumstances that motivated Rabbi Isserles's reliance on the more lenient view of *Tosafot* no longer exist, Rabbi Epstein rules that one must instead follow Rabbi Karo's standard for determining whether a *lulav* is dry (Principle 10). This is especially so, since taking the four species on Sukkot is a biblical obligation, and it is therefore appropriate to adopt the stricter position in order to ensure that the *mitzvah* has been fulfilled (Principle 4).

Rabbi Epstein further rules that if soaking the *lulav* in water helps the branch recover some of its original green color, the *lulav* is no longer considered dry. He bases this novel ruling on a comparison to rules of ritual impurity. The Talmud rules that materials which will not cause impurity when dry will cause impurity if through soaking they return to their initial appearance. Rabbi Epstein claims that the same is true of a *lulav* (Principle 1).

Methodological Principles: 1, 4, 5, 10.

---

320   Rema *to* Shulchan Arukh, Orach Chaim 645:5.

Example #189 - *Arukh HaShulchan* §645:21

Rabbi Epstein notes that, since the plants of the four species are native to Mediterranean climates, people in Eastern and Northern Europe had recently begun cultivating some of these plants locally in indoor grow houses. The seventeenth century code *Chayei Adam* raised doubts about the validity of such greenhouse-grown plants for use in fulfilling the obligation to take the four species. Rabbi Epstein rules that such plants are perfectly valid for use. He notes that, when discussing the parameters of the biblical prohibition of *orlah*—the stricture against eating fruit from a tree during its first three years of growth—the Jerusalem Talmud concludes that a tree grown indoors is legally regarded as an *etz*, or "tree," and is therefore subject to the laws of *orlah*. Since the Torah repeatedly refers to both the *lulav* and myrtle branches taken for the four species as "trees," Rabbi Epstein argues that any of the species that the Talmud regards as a "tree"— including those grown indoors—qualifies for use as part of the four species (Principle 1). Rabbi Epstein further notes that the practice of growing some of the four species locally in greenhouses has become common and longstanding, and *"minhag yisrael torah hi"*—the custom of Jewish people is law—and the ritual validity of such plants to fulfill the obligation to take the four species is therefore validated by custom (Principle 8). Additionally, while unstated, Rabbi Epstein elsewhere notes the difficulty attendant to obtaining adequate specimens when the plants must be shipped to Russia from their natural growing climates, and thus alleviating some of the practical difficulty in obtaining the four species may also indicate that greenhouse-grown plants should be ruled acceptable (Principle 10).
Methodological Principles: 1, 8, 10.

Example #190 - *Arukh HaShulchan* §646:3

The Torah, when referring to the myrtle branch, one of the four species, calls it *"anaf etz avot,"* or "the branch of a leafy tree."[321] The Talmud explains that this refers to the myrtle tree, whose branches are very numerous and whose leaves cover the branches, as three leaves protrude from and surround the branch at each of the points from which they grow along the length of the branch. Thus, if one of the leaves in these three-leaf groups grows from the branch either above or below the other two leaves, the specimen is called a *"hadas shoteh,"* or "defective myrtle," and the branch is unfit for ritual use.[322] In his glosses on the *Shulchan Arukh*, Rabbi Moses Isserles notes that the common practice is to use such defective myrtles for the holiday, and therefore rules in accordance with a variant rabbinic opinion recorded in the Talmud that maintains that a myrtle branch remains ritually valid so long as two of the leaves in each three-leaf grouping grow from the same spot on the branch.[323]

Rabbi Epstein, too, acknowledges the common custom of using myrtle branches where some of the leaves grow from different points of the branch. Rejecting the *Rema's* reliance on the non-normative view recorded in the Talmud, however, Rabbi Epstein seeks to justify this customary practice by offering a novel reading of the relevant Talmudic discussion itself (Principles 1 and 8). In the discussion, the Talmudic scholar Rav Kahana claims that a myrtle branch is valid even when one of the leaves in its three-leaf groups is growing from a different point of the branch than the other two leaves. The Talmudic sage Rav Acha rebuffs Rav Kahana's

---

321 Leviticus 23:40.
322 Babylonian Talmud, Sukkah 32b.
323 Rema *to* Shulchan Arukh, Orach Chaim 646:3.

position by noting that the Rabbis referred to such a myrtle branch as a *hadas shoteh*, a "defective myrtle." While those who rule that such a myrtle is indeed ritually invalid understand Rav Acha's statement to indicate that a "defective myrtle" is ritually invalid, Rabbi Epstein claims the fact that such a branch is called "defective" does not necessarily mean that it is ritually unfit for use. Instead, Rabbi Epstein argues that, based on other Talmudic uses of the term, the word *"shoteh"* merely implies that this kind of myrtle branch is less than ideal for ritual use and that there are other specimens better suited for fulfilling the biblical obligation to take the four species. Rabbi Epstein further claims that based on other biblical uses of the word *"avot"* (as in *"anaf etz avot"*), the word is best understood as referring to two leaves and thus strongly implies that as long as two of the leaves in the three-leaf grouping are aligned, the myrtle remains valid. Based on these understandings of the Talmudic discussion, Rabbi Epstein supports the prevailing practice to use such myrtles as part of the four species.

Methodological Principles: 1, 8.

Example #191 – *Arukh HaShulchan* §647:6

The Torah describes one of the four species as *"arvei nachal,"* or "willows of the brook." The Talmud explains that while the plain meaning of this verse may indicate otherwise, any willow branches are acceptable for use when taking the four species, even if they grow in mountainous areas watered by the rain rather than on river banks.[324] *Rashi* argues, however, that, while any willows *may* be used, one should ideally use willows that grew in river banks or in brooks, thereby fulfilling the plain meaning of the Torah's command. *Tosafot* go even further, however, and argue that the Talmud's permission to use any kind of willow branch for the four species actually reflects the opinion of a scholar whose ruling on this matter is rejected as a matter of normative *halakhah*. Instead, *Tosafot* argue that only brook willows may be used to fulfill the *mitzvah* of taking the four species and that all other kinds of willows are ritually invalid.

Rabbi Epstein notes that the universal custom is not only to use any kind of willow for the four species, but also not even to maintain any kind of preference for brook willows as prescribed by *Rashi*. While Rabbi Epstein accepts the normativity of the general custom (Principle 8), he also attempts to justify this widespread disregard of the views of both *Rashi* and *Tosafot*. He argues that when the Torah referres to *"arvei nachal,"* the word *nachal* does not only mean a stream or brook as is commonly thought, but *nachal* also can refer to a valley or flatland devoid of water (Principle 1). Based on this reading, Rabbi Epstein suggests that, when *Rashi* and *Tosafot* indicate a preference or requirement for willows of the *nachal*, they could be referring not only to willows that grow in rivers, but also to willows that grow in flatlands and valleys. Based on this view, the general custom of using not only river willows but also willows gathered from other locations actually does accord with the views of *Rashi* and *Tosafot*.

Methodological Principles: 1, 8.

Example #192 – *Arukh HaShulchan* §648:10

One of the four species that the Torah obligates Jews to take on Sukkot is the *etrog*, or citron fruit. As in the case of the other species, the *etrog* must meet certain standards of wholeness and quality in order to be considered fit for ritual use on the holiday. Maimonides rules that

---

324 Babylonian Talmud, Sukkah 33b.

a *etrog* that has been punctured all the way through the fruit is invalid for ritual use. Additionally, an *etrog* that is punctured on its surface may not be used ritually if the defect is larger than the size of an *issar* coin, though if the puncture actually resulted in the removal of any of the fruit's flesh, the *etrog* is unfit for ritual use no matter how small the defect.[325] The *Raabad* disagrees with Maimonides, however, and argues for a more lenient approach to the quality standards of an *etrog*. According to the *Raabad*, an *etrog* is only invalidated by defects that cause some of the fruit's flesh to become detached from the rest of the *etrog*. Thus, even a fully punctured *etrog* is ritually valid so long as the puncture merely compressed the fruit of the *etrog* around the puncture and did not result in the removal of any of the *etrog*'s fruit. Moreover, the *Raabad* rules that in cases where only the surface of the *etrog* has been punctured, the fruit is valid for ritual use so long as the amount of the fruit that has been removed by the puncture is less than the volume of an *issar* coin. In his *Shulchan Arukh*, Rabbi Karo endorses Maimonides's more stringent view, though he also quotes the *Raabad*'s alternative position. The *Rema*, too, adopts Maimonides's approach, ruling that any actual deficiency in the flesh of an *etrog* invalidates the fruit for ritual use. Rabbi Isserles does, however, note that one may rely on the *Raabad*'s more lenient position in extenuating circumstances when no other *etrog* is available.

In light of its general acceptance by the most important and prominent *halakhic* codifiers, Rabbi Epstein rules in accordance with Maimonides's view (Principles 2 and 3) and also writes that one should not rely on the alternative view offered by the *Raabad*. While he thus rejects the *Raabad*'s position as non-normative, the *Arukh HaShulchan* nevertheless writes that, in extenuating circumstances, one may indeed rely on the *Raabad*'s rejected position, permitting the use of an *etrog* that is damaged, so long as it is not missing any of its flesh (Principles 5 and 10).

Rabbi Epstein further notes that in practice it is often quite difficult to determine whether or not an apparently damaged *etrog* has merely had its flesh compressed around a puncture or if some of its flesh is actually missing. In such cases, where the *etrog*'s ritual fitness is thus in doubt, Rabbi Epstein rules that the *etrog* may be used. He argues that the invalidation of citrons that are missing some of their flesh is only rabbinic, and since such an *etrog* is ritually valid under biblical law in any case, one may, in doubtful circumstances, follow the principle that doubts of rabbinic law are resolved leniently and treat the *etrog* as valid (Principle 4).
Methodological Principles: 2, 3, 4, 5, 10.

Example #193 – *Arukh HaShulchan* §650:3

The Talmud rules that a *lulav* must be at least four handbreadths long. Maimonides writes that this means that a *lulav* must be at least sixteen thumb-widths long.[326] However, the *Rosh* and the *Raabad* agree that the *lulav* is valid, even if it is only thirteen and a third thumb-widths long. These authorities argue that Maimonides mistakenly used the larger definition of a handbreadth—four thumb-widths long—which resulted in his longer minimum size for a ritually valid *lulav*. Because of the general agreement among *halakhic* decisors that, in the case of the size of a *lulav*, the law uses the definition for a smaller handbreadth, Rabbi Epstein rules against Maimonides that a thirteen and a half thumb-width long *lulav* is valid (Principle 2). Rabbi Epstein does write, however, that one who is able to practice stringently and obtain a *lulav* that fits even Maimonides's length requirement should try to do so, since such supererogatory

---

325 Mishneh Torah, Hilkhot Shofar, Sukkah, V'Lulav 8:7.
326 Mishneh Torah, Hilkhot Shofar, Sukkah, V'Lulav 7:8.

conduct respects Maimonides's prime place in the hierarchy of *halakhic* authorities (Principles 3 and 6), and also seeks to act strictly in order to be careful to fulfill the biblical obligation of taking the four species (Principles 4 and 6).
Methodological Principles: 2, 3, 4, 6.

Example #194 – *Arukh HaShulchan* §651:6

The Talmud rules that biblical law does not require that the *lulav*, willow branches, and myrtles, taken together as three of the four species, be bound together in order to be ritually valid.[327] However, both Maimonides and the *Rosh* write that, although binding the species together is not required, one should still do so in order to fulfill the biblical imperative to beautify the performance of *mitzvot*.[328] Indeed, *Rashi* goes so far as to rule that there is an obligation to bind the species together in a bundle in order to make them more beautiful. Since binding the species together in a kind of bouquet or arrangement makes them more aesthetically impressive, there is value in doing so, even if binding the species together is not strictly necessary from the perspective of their ritual fitness for fulfilling the obligation to take the four species on Sukkot. The *Rosh* rules that in order to fulfill the obligation to beautify the four species, one should bind them together using a proper double knot, which the *halakhah* regards as a legally effective binding. Rabbi Moses Isserles disagrees with this position. He argues that rather than tying the *lulav*, myrtle, and willow together using a double knot, one should instead wrap the three species together with a string, and thread the loose end of the string into one of the loops, encircling the branches.[329]

Rabbi Epstein supports Rabbi Isserles's view because in his view it makes more sense to fulfill a directive to beautify the species bundle by tying the items together with looped string than with a double knot, especially since according to the Talmud there is no *halakhic* need to bind the species together, and thus a full double knot is unnecessary (Principle 1). While the *Arukh HaShulchan* thus prefers the *Rema*'s approach to that of the *Rosh*, he notes that in his own time the custom was not to bind the species with a knot or a loop of string. Instead, people fashion a three-chamber holder made from braided palm leaves into which the *lulav*, myrtle, and willow branches are placed. While this custom departs from the *Rema*'s prescription, Rabbi Epstein notes that it fulfills the same beautifying objective in an even better way, and therefore endorses this practice (Principle 8).
Methodological Principles: 1, 8.

Example #195 – *Arukh HaShulchan* §657:2

Both the *Rosh* and Rabbi Joseph Karo rule that once a minor knows how to wave the four species, his father is obligated to buy him a set of the species, so that the child may fulfill the obligation to take them on Sukkot.[330] The *Turei Zahav*, however, quotes the position of Rabbi Solomon Luria, who disputes that view. A minor child is not obligated to take his own set of four species on Sukkot until he reaches the age of majority, and therefore, in cases where a minor is mature enough to perform the four species ritual, the father may simply let the child borrow

---

327 Babylonian Talmud, Sukkah 33a.
328 *See Mishneh Torah*, Hilkhot Shofar, Sukkah, V'Lulav 7:9.
329 *See* Rema *to* Shulchan Arukh, Orach Chaim 651:1.
330 *See* Shulchan Arukh, Orach Chaim 657:1.

his own four species rather than buy an additional set for the child's own use.[331] While a plain reading of the classic legal authorities suggests that the view of the *Rosh* and *Shulchan Arukh* is normative, and that a father who must indeed provide his mature minor son with his own set of the four species with which to fulfill the obligation to take the species on Sukkot, Rabbi Epstein ultimately adopts the less normative ruling of the *Turei Zahav*. He notes that it would be completely impracticable for most people who "struggle to afford even one set of the four species for the whole family," to acquire a separate set for each minor child sufficiently mature to perform the *mitzvah*. Rabbi Epstein thus rules that there is only an obligation on the father to buy a set of the four species for his son if he can afford it (Principles 5 and 10).
Methodological Principles: 5, 10.

Example #196 – *Arukh HaShulchan* §671:24

The Talmud teaches that since the purpose of Hanukkah candles is to publicize the miracle of Hanukkah, the candles should not be placed indoors, and they should instead be placed outside the home close to the doorway so that passersby will see the lit candles.[332] Rabbi Epstein notes, however, that the prevalent practice in his own time and place is not to place the candles outside one's house, even in cases where the Talmud's own dispensation for situations in which placing the candles outside poses some kind of danger does not apply. This custom is normative (Principle 8), and Rabbi Epstein explains that this departure from this Talmudic rule is justified because conditions in Eastern Europe are very different than those in the Land of Israel. In contrast with the generally dry and mild climate of the Middle East, in Eastern Europe, Hanukkah falls in the winter, when heavy snow, rain, and strong winds surely would extinguish any candle that one would try to light outside. This makes lighting the candles outdoors entirely impracticable and justifies the common custom of lighting indoors (Principle 10). While this problem could be remedied by enclosing one's Hanukkah candles in a glass case, Rabbi Epstein notes that such extraordinary measures are unnecessary (Principle 10), especially since enclosing the candles in glass detracts from the ability of passersby to see clearly the number of candles that have been lit, which is an essential feature of publicizing the miracle by lighting outside (Principle 6).
Methodological Principles: 6, 8, 10.

Example #197 – *Arukh HaShulchan* §670:8

Since Hanukkah is not a biblical holiday, it is generally permitted to do *melakhah*—creative labor on Hanukkah. The *Arbah Turim*, however, records that it is the custom that women not do creative labor during the time that the Hanukkah candles are burning, since they played an important part in some of the famous events during the war between the Hasmonean militias and the Seleucid armies. The *Arukh HaShulchan* endorsed this practice and writes that "we must not be lenient with them" by permitting women to perform *melakhah* while the candles are burning (Principle 8). Rabbi Epstein records other customs to not perform labor for the entire eight days of Hanukkah, or at least for the first and last days of the holiday, but rules that there is no need to observe such customs, since they were in fact neither known nor practiced in his own time and place (Principle 8).

---

331 *See* Turei Zahav *to* Shulchan Arukh, Orach Chaim 657:1.
332 *See* Babylonian Talmud, Shabbat 21a.

Methodological Principles: 8.

Example #198 – *Arukh HaShulchan* §676:1

Early rabbinic authorities disagreed about the correct wording of the first of the two blessings prescribed for the lighting of the Hanukkah candles. Maimonides and the *Arbah Turim* rule that the blessing reads, "*lehadlik ner **shel** Chanukah*" ("to light a candle *of* Hanukkah"), while the *Shulchan Arukh* instructs that one should recite, "*lehadlik ner Chanukah*" ("to kindle the Hanukkah candle"). Rabbi Karo reasons that, while the blessing recited when lighting Sabbath candles is "*lehadlik ner **shel** Shabbat*," the blessing over Hanukkah candles does not follow this formulation. A Sabbath candle may be used for any purpose, and indeed is meant to provide light, thus making it the special signifier in the blessing, indicating that the candle is being lit in honor of the Sabbath appropriate. Hanukkah candles, by contrast, are not allowed to be used for any purpose other than to fulfill the *mitzvah* obligation, and it is therefore unnecessary to specifically designate them as candles of Hanukkah.

The *Arukh HaShulchan* notes that, while Rabbi Karo's distinction between Sabbath and Hanukkah candles and their appropriate blessings is compelling, in truth the exact wording of the blessing does not matter very much, since both versions of the blessing mean essentially the same thing. While Rabbi Epstein thus has no strong analytic preference for one version of the blessing over the other, he notes that in his own time and place the general practice is to recite Rabbi Karo's version of the blessing, and one should therefore act in accordance with the custom (Principle 8).

Methodological Principles: 8.

Example #199 – *Arukh HaShulchan* §676:3

The Talmud prescribes two blessings to be recited over the lighting of the Hanukkah candles. One blessing—"*lehadlik ner shel Chanukah*" ("to light the Hanukkah candles")—marks the observance of the *halakhic* obligation to light the candles; the second blessing—"*she'asah nisim laavoteinu*" ("Who made miracles for our fathers")—gives thanks for the miraculous events commemorated by lighting candles during Hanukkah. The widely accepted text of this second blessing is "*she'asah nisim laavoteinu bayamim hahem bazman hazeh*," which means "Who made miracles for our fathers in those days at this time." Rabbi Epstein notes, however, that this version of the text is redundant, and instead endorses an alternative but uncommon version of the blessing that reads, "*she'asah nisim laavoteinu bayamim hahem **u'bazman** hazeh*," which means, "Who made miracles for our fathers in those days, **and** at this time" (Principle 5). While this addition changes the meaning of the blessing entirely, the *Arukh HaShulchan* prefers this version because it brings to light an important aspect of the miracles commemorated on Hanukkah. The more common version of the blessing makes it seem like God only performed the miracles for our fathers on this specific calendar date. However, the *Arukh HaShulchan* says, God actually performed miracles for our forefathers on many days leading up to the currently observed dates of Hanukkah, as the wars that culminated in the rededication of the Temple on these days lasted for years. Thus, in addition to the miracle of the oil in the Temple *menorah* lasting eight days, which occurred "at this time," Hanukkah also recalls the victory of the Hasmonean forces of the Seleucid armies "in those days." Therefore, while the common practice is to recite the first version of the blessing, Rabbi Epstein endorses the less common alternative, which he views as

giving better expression to the true nature of the holiday and the events it aims to commemorate (Principles 1, 6, and 8).
Methodological Principles: 1, 5, 6, 8.

Example #200 – Arukh HaShulchan §677:2

The Talmud rules that a person staying in an inn is obligated to light Hanukkah candles, even though he is not at home, but that he may fulfill this obligation by giving a bit of money to the owner of the inn and thereby become a partner in the owner's own Hanukkah candles. A traveler may also fulfill his Hanukkah candle-lighting duty by having his wife or other family members lighting candles in his regular permanent residence.[333]

Both Rabbi Isaac Alfasi and Maimonides rule that the Talmud's allowance for a traveler to fulfill his obligation to light Hanukkah candles through the inn owner or his family back home applies only to guests staying in places where they do not have their own separate entrance to the public street. However, if the guest has a separate entrance from the street into his own rooms—as would be the case in a motel, for instance—he remains obligated to light his own Hanukkah candles, even if his family will be lighting their own candles at his regular home. These authorities reason that if such a guest does not light his own candles at his own private entrance to his rooms at the inn, other people will suspect him of not fulfilling his obligation. To dispel this impression, he is obligated to light his own candles.

The *Arukh HaShulchan* writes that this ruling made sense in past eras when people lit outside in the entrances to their courtyards or homes. In modern times, however, when the general custom is for people to light Hanukkah candles inside their homes, there is no longer any reason to think that an absence of candles at a guest's private entrance to his rooms would lead others to assume that he did not light Hanukkah candles at all (Principles 8 and 9). In places where the general custom is for everyone to light their own Hanukkah candles, however, Rabbi Epstein recommends that even a guest should light his own candles rather than partnering with the inn's proprietor or relying on his wife or family lighting back at home (Principle 8).
Methodological Principles: 8, 9.

Example #201 – Arukh HaShulchan §687:3

While one is obligated to read the Book of Esther on both the night of Purim and during the day of Purim, *Tosafot*, the *Rosh*, and the *Ran* all rule that the central obligation of reading the Book of Esther and of publicizing the miracle of Purim is during the day and not at night. They base this conclusion on the fact that all of the other obligations of Purim—eating a festive meal, giving charity, and giving gifts of food—apply specifically during Purim day and not at night. Since the primary obligation to read the Book of Esther thus applies to Purim day, these authorities rule that, while one recites the *Shehechiyanu* blessing thanking God for bringing us to the special time and to the opportunity to observe the once-a-year ritual of reading the Book of Esther before reading the text on Purim night, one should nevertheless repeat the *Shehechiyanu* blessing before reading the Book of Esther a second time during the day of Purim. Maimonides, however, disagrees with this view, and rules that the *Shehechiyanu* blessing should only be recited

---

333 Babylonian Talmud, Shabbat 23a.

before reading the Book of Esther on Purim night, since that is the first time that the *mitzvah* of reading the text is being performed.

While typically Rabbi Epstein prescribes that, in cases of doubt, one should avoid reciting a possibly unnecessary blessing (Principle 4), in the case of reading the Book of Esther, he rules that the *Shehechiyanu* blessing should be recited at night and repeated before the Book of Esther is read again on Purim day.[334] This is because the *Shehechiyanu* blessing can be recited during the day without any real concern that it may be unnecessary, since the blessing can be recited with the intent for it to also mark the performance of the other main obligations of Purim—eating a festive meal, giving charity, and exchanging gifts of food—which apply only during the day. Moreover, Rabbi Epstein notes that it is the universal custom to recite the *Shehechiyanu* blessing before reading the Book of Esther on Purim day with the intention that the blessing apply also to these other observances (Principle 8).

Rabbi Epstein notes that there is an important practical consequence of the view that distinguishes between the centrality of reading the Book of Esther on Purim night and of reading the text on Purim day. Namely, if the daytime reading is in fact more central or important than the nighttime reading, then according to *Tosafot*, the *Rosh*, and the *Ran*, a person who for some reason can only read the Book of Esther once during Purim should preferably forego reading it at night and instead read it during the day. According to Maimonides, however, since there is no difference in the centrality of the two readings, one should read the Book of Esther at the first opportunity—on Purim night—rather than waiting until the following morning. Rabbi Epstein, however, rejects any conclusive analogies between these authorities' views on whether one should recite the *Shehechiyanu* blessing on the daytime reading of the Book of Esther and whether one should preferably read the book at night or during the day in cases where one can only read the text once. He notes that even Maimonides might agree that one should read the Book of Esther in the day because the daytime reading is more central, and Maimonides merely holds that once one has recited the *Shehechiyanu* blessing at night one cannot repeat it the next day for performing the same obligation. Likewise, while *Tosafot*, the *Rosh*, and the *Ran* view the daytime reading as more central, they may also hold that one should read the Book of Esther at the first opportunity—on Purim night—rather than waiting until the next day. Rabbi Epstein follows the later view—that one who can only read the Book of Esther once should do so immediately at night rather than passing up the opportunity and waiting to read until the next day, since in principle "we do not pass over the opportunity to perform a *mitzvah*" (Principle 4). Methodological Principles: 4, 8.

Example #202 – *Arukh HaShulchan* §689:5

The *Tosefta* teaches that, while all men are obligated to read the Book of Esther on Purim, and therefore also can read the book for others who fulfill their own obligation by hearing the text read, women are not obligated to read the Book of Esther, and therefore cannot read the text for others in order for the listeners to fulfill their own obligation thereby. Despite the *Tosefta*'s ruling, Rabbi Epstein notes that the accepted *halakhah* is that both men and women are obligated to read the Book of Esther on Purim. While this is a positive obligation that devolves only at a specific time-bound category of *halakhic* duties from which women are generally exempt, women are nevertheless obligated to fully participate in the observance of Purim practice because they were deeply involved in bringing about the events that the holiday commemorates.

---

334 Arukh HaShulchan, Orach Chaim 692:2.

Rabbi Epstein points out that in fact this accepted rule is not incompatible with the text of the *Tosefta* that seemingly excludes women from the obligation to read the Book of Esther. He notes that if indeed the *Tosefta* thinks that women are exempt from this duty, then there would be no reason for the *Tosefta* to note both that women are exempt from the obligation to read the Book of Esther and also that they cannot read it on behalf of others. If they are themselves exempt, perforce they cannot fulfill the obligation on behalf of others who are not exempt. Rather, Rabbi Epstein argues, the *Tosefta* itself strongly implies that women are indeed obligated to read the Book of Esther on Purim, and only distinguishes between male and female duties in this regard by noting that, while men may read the text on behalf of others, women may not (Principle 1). This rule is adopted by both the *Arbah Turim* and *Shulchan Arukh*, who rule that while women are obligated to read the Book of Esther themselves, they may not do so on behalf of others as having the text read by a woman, as part of a public service would detract from the "honor of the congregation."

Rabbi Epstein questions the logic of the rule that women are obligated to read the Book of Esther but may not enable others to fulfill their own obligation by reading the text on their behalf. After all, standard rules of *halakhic* practice teach that anyone who is obligated to perform a certain duty can also perform that duty on behalf of others who are likewise obligated. Even if one grants that it would dishonor the congregation for a woman to read the Book of Esther publically in the synagogue on behalf of all the other members of the community, this does not explain why a woman may not read the text privately on behalf of a few individuals.

Rabbi Epstein notes that Rabbi Moses Isserles accounts for this usual *halakhic* framework by arguing that women's and men's obligations with respect to the Book of Esther are different. While men are obligated to *read* the Book of Esther on Purim, women are obligated to *hear* the text read on Purim. Because their obligations are qualitatively different, the *Rema* argues, a woman reading the Book of Esther—which is merely a means for her hearing the text rather than a fulfillment of the obligation to read the book herself—cannot facilitate a man's fulfilling his obligation to read the text. Rabbi Epstein notes that this explanation accounts for the discrepancy between men's and women's ability to read the text for others, and also accounts for the text of the *Tosefta*, which can be understood as commenting specifically on the obligation to *read* the Book of Esther (from which, based on this view, women are indeed exempt). However, Rabbi Epstein questions the basis for the claim that male and female obligations with respect to the reading of the Book of Esther on Purim are indeed different; since women were involved in the unfolding of the Purim story, and since this historical book serves to include them in the duty to observe an obligation from which they would otherwise be exempted, on what basis might one conclude that there is any qualitative difference between their obligations?

To answer this question, Rabbi Epstein offers a novel insight into two different jurisprudential mechanisms whereby women are brought within the scope of obligation for certain time-bound positive commandments. Rabbi Epstein points out that the Talmud concludes that women are obligated to eat *matzah* on Passover—a positive, time-bound obligation—because, following the principle that there is correspondence between positive and negative obligations, since women are obligated to observe the prohibition against eating *chametz* on Passover, they are also obligated to eat *matzah*. From the fact that the Talmud does not simply argue that women must be obligated to eat *matzah* because "they too were involved in the occurrence of the miracle" of the Exodus, Rabbi Epstein concludes that bringing women within the ambit of a positive duty through the principle of "they too were involved in the occurrence of the miracle" does not create absolute correspondence between male and female obligations. Thus, while the obligations of men and women to eat *matzah* are exactly the same, the obligations of men and women with respect to Purim are qualitatively different: men are obligated to *read* the Book of Esther, while women are obligated to *hear* the book read. Thus, Rabbi Epstein concludes, while women may read the Book of Esther on behalf of other women (since both have the same kind of obligation), women may not read the text on behalf of men. Rabbi Epstein maintains this view, which he understands to be the best analytic understanding of the nature of men's and women's obligations with respect to reading the Book of Esther on Purim, despite what he acknowledges to be the consensus view of most major authorities—including Maimonides—that women may indeed read the Book of Esther on behalf of men (Principle 1).

Notably, based on this understanding of the kinds of women's obligations created through the principle of "they too were involved in the occurrence of the miracle," Rabbi Epstein also innovates a new rule regarding the lighting of candles on Hanukkah. Since the Talmud concludes that women must light Hanukkah candles—a positive, time-bound duty from which women are presumptively exempt—because they were important participants in the Hanukkah story, Rabbi Epstein concludes that men's and women's Hanukkah obligations are different. While men are obligated to *light* Hanukkah candles, women are only obligated to *observe* lit Hanukkah candles and thereby recall the miraculous salvation that took place during the Hanukkah story. Therefore, Rabbi Epstein says, women may not light Hanukkah candles on behalf of men (Principle 1). Methodological Principles: 1.

Example #203 – *Arukh HaShulchan* §695:5

The Talmud teaches that "one is obligated to become intoxicated on Purim until he can no longer tell the difference between the blessing of Mordechai and the curse of Haman."[335] The *Arukh HaShulchan* questions the simple understanding and application of this prescription, since fulfilling the Talmud's imperative would appear to require one to become as drunk as the biblical Lot—who in his drunkenness fathered children with his own daughters. The drunkenness of Lot is a paradigmatic rabbinic example of impermissible behavior, and thus Rabbi Epstein questions how to correctly fulfill this Talmudic teaching.

First, Rabbi Epstein notes that Maimonides rules merely that on Purim a person should simply drink until he is drunk enough to fall asleep; Maimonides makes no mention, however, of the need to become so intoxicated as to be incapable of distinguishing between Haman and Mordechai. Rabbi Moses Isserles takes a similar position, and rules that a person should drink a little more than he is accustomed to generally and should fall asleep, and while sleeping will be unable to distinguish between Haman and Mordechai. Rabbi Epstein not fully satisfied with these rulings, however, because, he argues, if the Talmud meant merely that a person should drink and then fall asleep, it surely could have said so (Principle 1). Rather than reject Maimonides's view out of hand as incompatible with the Talmudic sources, however, Rabbi Epstein suggests that Maimonides understood that this teaching, while recorded in the Talmud, is not to be taken as normative and obligatory at all. This is especially true because the Talmud following its prescription to become excessively drunk on Purim with a story involving one rabbi killing another while the two were drunk on Purim. This narrative functions to reject any extreme application of the Talmudic imperative to become drunk on Purim, and instead urges a softer reading of the obligation—namely, to drink and to fall asleep.

Rabbi Epstein goes on to consider a number of other alternative explanations of the Talmudic imperative to drink on Purim, all of which attempt to soften the impact of the obligation, either by emphasizing that the duty is to drink rather than to get drunk or by substantially

---

335 Babylonian Talmud, Megillah 7b.

lowering the threshold level of drunkenness one must reach. Rabbi Epstein notes, however, that all of these explanations fail to adequately account for the plain and obvious meaning of the Talmudic rule, which states simply that one must become so drunk as to no longer be able to distinguish between the hero and villain of the Purim story; and he observes that Rabbi Karo does in fact simply record the Talmud's directive, and unlike others, makes no attempts to soften its scope of impact.

As a matter of practice, however, Rabbi Epstein rules in accordance with Maimonides's view that one should merely drink more than usual and then sleep a bit (Principle 3). This is especially true in light of the many negative religious and moral consequences that come with excessive drunkenness, which strongly indicates that this should be avoided (Principle 6).
Methodological Principles: 1, 3, 6.

Example #204 – *Arukh HaShulchan* §695:17

On Purim, every Jew is obligated to send a gift of at least two food items to at least one other person. This practice, known as *mishloach manot*, is recorded in the Book of Esther itself as one of the ways in which the Jews of Persia celebrated their salvation from Haman's genocidal plans and is one of the *mitzvot* uniquely associated with the holiday of Purim.

The *Arukh HaShulchan* questions whether or not one may fulfill their *mishloach manot* obligation by sending a package of foodstuffs to a friend before Purim so that the package is received on Purim itself. On the one hand, the sender is not obligated to send *mishloach manot* until Purim day, and perhaps a gift sent too early does not, therefore, serve to fulfill the obligation. On the other hand, perhaps the fact that package is received on Purim is sufficient to fulfill the sender's *mishloach manot* obligation. Rabbi Epstein notes that some authorities have ruled that gifts of food sent before Purim and received on Purim do fulfill the obligation of *mishloach manot*. Rabbi Epstein himself, however, disagrees and rules that such gifts do not satisfy the *mishloach manot* obligation, which requires that gifts of food be sent and received on Purim itself. Rabbi Epstein reasons that a simple understanding of the source for this practice in the Book of Esther indicates that the gifts must be sent on Purim day. He further argues that the essential purpose of sending *mishloach manot* is to generate joy and goodwill between Jews, and that this goal is not fully achieved by people receiving gifts that had been previously dispatched. Instead, fulfilling this obligation requires a more direct link between givers and receivers, which can be best achieved when the food is both sent and received on Purim day (Principle 1).
Methodological Principles: 1.

Bibliography

Adler, Cyrus, and Emil G. Hirsch. "Shemoneh Esrei." In *The Jewish Encyclopedia*. Vol. 11. New York: Funk & Wagnalls, 1906.
Alfasi, Rabbi Isaac ben Jacob HaKohen (the Rif). *Rif*.
Alfasi, Rabbi Isaac ben Jacob HaKohen (the Rif). Responsa *Rif*.
Albrecht, Alt. "The Origins of Israelite Law." In *Essays on Old Testament History and Religion*. Translated by R. A. Wilson. Garden City, NY: Doubleday, 1966.
Ashkenazi, Rabbi Zvi Hirsch ben Yaakov (Chacham Tzvi). *Responsa Chacham Tzvi*.
Assaf, Simchah. *Gaonica: Gaonic Responsa and Fragments of Halachic Literature from the Geniza and Other Sources*. Jerusalem: Darom, 1933.
Avot D'Rabbi Natan.
Azulai, Rabbi Chaim Yosef David (Chida). *Birkei Yosef to Shulchan Arukh*.
Babylonian Talmud.
Bar-Ilan, Rabbi Meir. *MiVolozhin Ad Yerushalayim: Zikhronot*. Tel Aviv: Yalḳuṭ, 1939.
Bar-Ilan, Rabbi Meir, and Shelomoh Yosef Zevin, eds. *Encyclopedia Talmudit*. Jerusalem: Mossad HaRav Kook, 1947-.
Batnitzky, Leora Faye. *How Judaism Became a Religion: An Introduction to Modern Jewish Thought*. Princeton, N.J.: Princeton University Press, 2011.
Bechhofer, Rabbi Yosef Gavriel. *The Contemporary Eruv: Eruvin in Modern Metropolitan Areas*. Charleston: BookSurge, 2002.
Ben Asher, Rabbi Jacob (Tur). *Arbah Turim*.
Ben Asher, Rabbi Jacob (Tur). *Responsa Zichron Yosef to Shulchan Arukh*.
Ben Attar, Rabbi Chaim (Or HaChaim). *Pri Toar to Shulchan Arukh*.
Ben Baruch, Rabbi Meir (Maharam). *Responsa Maharam MeRutenberg*.
Ben Betzalel, Rabbi Chaim. *Vikuach Mayim Chaim to Rema*.
Ben Isaac, Rabbi Abraham. *Hilkhot Sefer Torah*. In *Sefer HaEshkol*, edited by Benjamin Hirsch Auerbach. Halberstadt: H. Meyer, 1868.
Ben Jacob, Rabbi Moses. *Sefer Mitzvot Gadol*.
Ben Maimon, Rabbi Moses (Maimonides). *The Guide to the Perplexed*.
Ben Maimon, Rabbi Moses (Maimonides). *Introduction to the Mishnah*.
Ben Maimon, Rabbi Moses (Maimonides), *Mishneh Torah*.

Ben Nachman, Rabbi Moses (Nachmanides). *Chiddushei HaRamban al HaTalmud.*
Ben Nachman, Rabbi Moses (Nachmanides). *Grama B'Nezikin.*
Ben Nachman, Rabbi Moses (Nachmanides). *Milchamot Hashem to Rif.*
Ben Nachman, Rabbi Moses (Nachmanides). *Perush HaRamban al HaTorah.*
Ben-Sasson, Haim Hillel, ed. *A History of the Jewish People.* Cambridge: Harvard University Press, 1985.
Ben Solomon Zalman, Rabbi Elijah (Vilna Gaon). *Biur HaGra to Shulchan Arukh.*
Ben Yechiel, Rabbi Asher (Rosh). *Responsa Rosh.*
Bension, Ariel. *The Zohar in Moslem and Christian Spain.* New York: Hermon Press, 1974.
Berlin, Rabbi Naftali Tzvi Yehudah (Netziv). *HaEmek Davar.*
Berlin, Rabbi Naftali Tzvi Yehudah (Netziv). *HaEmek Sheilah on Sheiltot D'Rav Achai Gaon.* Jerusalem: Mossad Harav Kook, ed., 1975.
Biale, David, David Assaf, Benjamin Brown, Uriel Gellman, Samuel Heilman, Moshe Rosman, Gadi Sagiv, and Marcin Wodziński. *Hasidism: A New History.* Princeton: Princeton University Press, 2018.
Birnbaum, Pierre., and Ira. Katznelson, eds. *Paths of Emancipation: Jews, States, and Citizenship.* Princeton: Princeton University Press, 1995.
Blackstone, William. *Commentaries on the Laws of England.* London: Printed by his Majesty's Law Printers, 1780.
Blidstein, Gerald J. "Capital Punishment - The Classic Jewish Discussion." *Judaism* 14, no. 2 (1965): 159-171.
Bokser, Ben Zion. *The Maharal: The Mystical Philosophy of Rabbi Judah Loew of Prague.* Lanham, MD: Jason Aronson Inc., 1977.
Brody, Robert. *The Geonim of Babylonia and the Shaping of Medieval Jewish Culture.* New Haven: Yale University Press, 1998.
Brown v. Allen, 344 U.S. 443 (1953).
Broyde, Michael J. "Custom as a Source of Jewish Law: Some Religious Reflections on David J. Bederman's Custom as a Source of Law." *Emory Law Journal* 61 (2012): 1037-1045.
Broyde, Michael J. "The Intercircuit Tribunal and Perceived Conflicts: An Analysis of Justice White's Dissents from Denial of Certiorari during the 1985 Term." *New York University Law Review* 62, no. 3 (1987): 610-650.
Broyde, Michael J. "May the Jewish Daughter of a Gentile Man Marry a Kohen?" *Journal of Halacha and Contemporary Society*, no. 52 (2009): 97-126.
Broyde, Michael J. "The Yerushalmi as a Source of Halacha." Hirhurim - Torah Musings. May 3, 2011. Accessed December 25, 2018. https://www.torahmusings.com/2011/05/the-yerushalmi-as-a-source-of-halacha/.
Broyde, Michael J., and Akiva R. Berger. "Jewish Ethics in Torah Reading: Balancing Hatred, the Ways of Peace, Holiness, Communal Dignity, and the Obligation to Read Torah on Shabbat when Five Israelite Men are not Present." *Hakirah* 23 (2017): 181-196.

Broyde, Michael J., and Ira Bedzow. "The Codification of Jewish Law and an Introduction to the Jurisprudence of the Mishna Berura." *Hamline Law Review* 35, no. 3 (2012): 623-654.

Buchman, Asher Ben-Zion. "King Solomon's Takanah: Rambam's Eruv." *Hakirah: The Flatbush Journal of Jewish Law and Thought* 3, (2006): 181-212.

Burnet v. Coronado Oil & Gas Co., 285 U.S. 393, 406 (1932) (Brandeis, J., dissenting).

Cardozo, Benjamin N. *The Nature of the Judicial Process*. New Haven: Yale University Press, 1921.

Cardozo, Nathan Lopes. "The In-Authenticity of Codifying Jewish Law." David Cardozo Academy. December 6, 2017. Accessed May 16, 2019. https://www.cardozoacademy.org/thoughts-to-ponder/codifying-jewish-law-not-authentic/.

Chaim, Rabbi Yosef. *Ben Ish Chai*.

Chajes, Rabbi Zvi Hirsch. *Darkhei Horaah,* in Kol Kitvei Maharitz Chajes.

Chazzan, Rabbi Refael Yosef. *Responsa Chikrei Lev*.

Da Fano, Rabbi Menahem Azariah (Rama MiPano). *Responsa Rama MiPano*.

Davis, Joseph M. *The Shulchan Arukh and Sixteenth Century Jewish Law*. New York: Oxford University Press, 2012.

De Vidas, Rabbi Elijah. *Reishit Chochmah*.

Derbaremdiker, Rabbi Avraham Yehoshua Heschel. *Seder HaDin* (2010).

Dworkin, Ronald. "Hard Cases." *Harvard Law Review* 88, no. 6 (1975): 1057-109.

Dworkin, Ronald. "No Right Answer?" In *Law, Morality, and Society: Essays in Honor of HLA Hart*, edited by P.M.S. Hachler and Joseph Raz, 58-84. Oxford: Clarendon Press, 1977.

Efrati, Rabbi Baruch. "Tokfam Shel HaMinhagim B'Yisrael." Daat. August 8, 2005. Accessed December 31, 2018. http://www.daat.ac.il/daat/toshba/maamarim/tokpam-2.htm.

Eisenstadt, Rabbi Abraham Tzvi Hirsch ben Yaakov. *Pitchei Teshuva to Shulchan Arukh*.

Ellenson, David. *After Emancipation: Jewish Religious Responses to Modernity*. Cincinnati: Hebrew Union College Press, 2004.

Ellenson, David. "Antinomianism and Its Responses in the Nineteenth Century." In *The Cambridge Companion to Judaism and Law*, edited by Christine Hayes, 260-286. New York: Cambridge University Press, 2017.

Elon, Menachem. *Jewish Law: History, Sources, Principles*. Translated by Bernard Auerbach & Melvin J. Sykes. Philadelphia: Jewish Publication Society, 1994.

Elyashiv, Rabbi Yosef Shalom. *He-arot al Mesekhet Pesachim*.

Epstein, Rabbi Baruch HaLevi. *Mekor Baruch*. New York: Ḥayil, 1954.

Epstein, Rabbi Yechiel Mikhel. *Arukh HaShulchan*.

Epstein, Rabbi Yechiel Mikhel. *Kitvei Arukh HaShulchan*.

Etkes, Immanuel. *The Gaon of Vilna: The Man and His Image*. Berkeley and Los Angeles: University of California Press, 2002.

Feinstein, Rabbi Moses. *Igrot Moshe*.

Fine, Lawrence. "New Approaches to the Study of kabbalistic Life in 16th-Century Safed." In *Jewish Mysticism and Kabbalah: New Insights and Scholarship*, edited by Frederick E. Greenspahn, 91-111. New York: NYU Press, 2011.

Fishbane, Simcha. *An Analysis of the Literary and Substantive Traits of Rabbi Israel Mayer Hacohen Kagan's Mishnah Berurah; Sections 243-247, 252*. Dissertation. Ottawa: National Library of Canada, 1988.

Fishbane, Simcha. *The Boldness of an Halakhist: An Analysis of the Writings of Rabbi Yechiel Mechel HaLevi Epstein the Arukh HaShulchan*. Boston: Academic Studies Press, 2008.

Fishbane, Simcha. *The Method and Meaning of the Mishnah Berurah*. Hoboken, NJ: Ktav Pub. House, 1991.

Francis, Rabbi Shlomo, and Rabbi Yonason Glenner. *The Laws of Eruv: A Comprehensive Review of the Laws of Eruvin and Their Practical Applications*. Lakewood, NJ: Israel Bookshop Publications, 2013.

Friendly, Henry J. "The Courts and Social Policy: Substance and Procedure." *University of Miami Law Review* 33, no. 1 (1978): 21-42.

Galeza, Dorota. "Hard Cases." *Manchester Student Law Review* 2, (2013): 240-266.

Ganzfried, Rabbi Solomon. *Kitzur Shulchan Arukh*.

Gaon, Rabbi Saadia. *Emunot V'Deot*.

Gerondi, Rabbi Jonah. *Commentary on Mishnah Avot*.

Gerondi, Rabbi Nissim. *Drashot HaRan*.

Glatt, Ephraim. "The Unanimous Verdict According to the Talmud: Ancient Law Providing Insight into Modern Legal Theory." *Pace International Law Review* 3, no. 10 (2013): 316-335.

Goldfarb, Michael. *Emancipation: How Liberating Europe's Jews from the Ghetto Led to Revolution and Renaissance*. New York: Simon & Schuster, 2009.

Goldish, Matt. "Halakhah, Kabbalah, and Heresy: A Controversy in Early Eighteenth-Century Amsterdam." *The Jewish Quarterly Review* 84, no. 2/3 (1993-1994): 153-176.

Goldstein, Daniel. "The Role of Humrot." *Hakirah: The Flatbush Journal of Jewish Law and Thought* 1, (2004): 11-24.

Gottheil, Richard. "Censorship of Hebrew Books." *The Jewish Encyclopedia*. Vol. 3. New York: Funk & Wagnalls, 1906. 650-52.

Grunfeld, Isidore, trans. *Horeb: A philosophy of Jewish Laws and Observances*, edited by Samson Raphael Hirsch. New York: Soncino Press, 2002.

Guthrie, Chris, Jeffrey J. Rachlinski, and Andrew J. Wistrich. "Blinking on the Bench: How Judges Decide Cases." *Cornell Law Review* 93, no. 1 (2007): 1-43.

HaKohen, Rabbi Shabbataiben Meir (Shakh). *Klalei Horaah B'Issur V'Hetter*. In Shulchan Arukh. Vol. 15. Jerusalem: Machon Yerushalayim, 2016.

HaKohen, Rabbi Shabbatai ben Meir (Shakh). *Nekudat HaKesef to Shulchan Arukh*.

HaKohen, Rabbi Shabbatai ben Meir (Shakh). *Sifsei Kohen to Shulchan Arukh*.

Halbertal, Moshe. *People of the Book: An Artistic Exploration of the Bible*. Cambridge: Harvard University Press, 1997.

HaLevi, Rabbi Chaim David. *Responsa Aseh Lecha Rav*.

Hallamish, Moshe. *HaKabbalah B'Tefillah, B'Halakhah, U'b'Minhag*. Ramat Gan, Israel: Bar-Ilan University Press, 2002.

HaNagid, Rabbi Shmuel. "Introduction to the Talmud." In *Aids to Talmud Study*, edited by Aryeh Carmel, 68-73. Jerusalem: Feldheim, 4th ed., 1980.

Hart, Herbert Lionel Adolphus. *The Concept of Law*. Oxford: Oxford University Press, 2nd ed., 1997.

Hart, Herbert Lionel Adolphus. "Positivism and the Separation of Law and Morals." *Harvard Law Review* 71, no. 4 (1958): 593-629.

Harvey, Warren Zev. "Law in Medieval Judaism." In *The Cambridge Companion to Judaism and Law*, edited by Christine Hayes, 157-86. Cambridge: Cambridge University Press, 2017.

Hayes, Christine. "The Torah Was Not Given to Ministering Angels: Rabbinic Aspirationalism." In *Talmudic Transgressions: Engaging the Work of Daniel Boyarin*, edited by Charlotte Elisheva Fonrobert et al., 123-160. Boston: Brill, 2017.

Hecht, Neil S., B. S. Jackson, S. M. Passamaneck, Daniela Piattelli, and Alfredo Rabello, eds. *An Introduction to the History and Sources of Jewish Law*. New York: Oxford University Press, 1996.

Helfgot, Nathaniel. "Minority Opinions and Their Role in Hora'ah." In *Milin Havivin - Beloved Words; an Annual Devoted to Torah, Society and the Rabbinate* 4 (2010): 36-60.

Heller, Rabbi Aryeh Leib. *Ketzot HaChoshen to Shulchan Arukh*.

Heller, Rabbi Yom Tov Lipmann. *Ma'adnei Yom Tov to Rosh*.

Heller, Rabbi Yom Tov Lipmann. *Tosafot Yom Tov*.

Henkin, Eitam. *Ta'arokh Lefanai Shulchan: Chayo Zemano U'Mepaalo Shel HaRav Yechiel Mikhel Epstein Baal Arukh HaShulchan*. Jerusalem: Magid, Hotsa'at Koren, 2019.

Henkin, Rabbi Yehuda. *Responsa Bnei Banim*.

Heschel, Abraham Joshua, and Gordon Tucker. *Heavenly Torah: As Refracted Through the Generations*. New York: Continuum, 2005.

Hess, Jonathan M. *Germans, Jews and the Claims of Modernity*. New Haven: Yale University Press, 2002.

Hidary, Richard. *Dispute for the Sake of Heaven: Legal Pluralism in the Talmud*. Providence: Brown Judaic Studies, 2010.

Holmes Jr., Oliver Wendell. "The Path of the Law." *Harvard Law Review* 10, no. 8. (1897): 457-478.

Iancu, Carol. "The Emancipation and Assimilation of the Jews in the Political Discourse Regarding the Granting of French Citizenship to the French Jews During the French Revolution." *Studia Judaica* 18 (2010): 89-115.

Ibn Migash, Rabbi Joseph (Ri Migash). *Responsa Ri Migash*.

Ibn Nachmias, Rabbi Joseph. *Commentary on Pirkei Avot*.

Ibn Zimra, Rabbi David ben Solomon (Radbaz). *Divrei David to Mishneh Torah*.

Ibn Zimra, Rabbi David ben Solomon (Radbaz). *Responsa Radbaz*.

Isserles, Rabbi Moses (Rema). *Darkhei Moshe to Arbah Turim*.

Isserles, Rabbi Moses (Rema). *Rema to Shulchan Arukh*.

Jachter, Howard, and Broyde, Michael J. "Electrically Produced Fire or Light in Positive Commandments." *Journal of Halacha and Contemporary Society*, no. 25 (1993): 89-126.

Jackson, Jeffrey D. "Blackstone's Ninth Amendment: A Historical Common Law Baseline for he Interpretation of Unenumerated Rights." *Oklahoma Law Review* 62, no. 2 (2010): 167-222.

Jackson, Jeffrey D. "Putting Rationality Back into the Rational Basis Test: Saving Substantive Due Process and Redeeming the Promise of the Ninth Amendment." *University of Richmond Law Review* 45, no. 2 (2011): 491-548.

Jacobs, Joseph, and Isaac Broyde. "Zohar." *The Jewish Encyclopedia*. Vol. 12. New York: Funk & Wagnalls, 1906. 689-691.

Jerusalem Talmud.

Kaplan, Aryeh. *Meditation and Kabbalah*. York Beach, ME: Red Wheel/Weiser, 1986.

Karo, Rabbi Joseph. *Beit Yosef to Arbah Turim.*

Karo, Rabbi Joseph. *Kessef Mishnah to Mishneh Torah.*

Karo, Rabbi Joseph. *Shulchan Arukh.*

Katz, Bentzion. "L'Toldot HaTzenzurah Shel HaSifrut HaYisraelit: Reshamim V'Zikhronot." *HaToren* 9 (1923): 41-48.

Katz, Bentzion. "L'Toldot HaTzenzurah Shel HaSifrut HaYisraelit: Reshamim V'Zikhronot." *HaToren* 10 (1923): 43-51.

Katz, Bentzion. "L'Toldot HaTzenzurah Shel HaSifrut HaYisraelit: Reshamim V'Zikhronot." *HaToren* 12 (1923): 48-60.

Katz, Benzion, ed. "B'H." Advertisement. *HaZman* (St. Petersburg-Vilna), Nissan 19, 5672, section 2:68.

Katz, Jacob. *Halakhah and Kabbalah: Studies in the History of Jewish Religion, Its Various Faces and Social Relevance.* Jerusalem: Magnes Press, 1984.

Katz, Jacob. *Out of the Ghetto: The Social Background of Jewish Emancipation, 1770-1870.* Syracuse, N.Y.: Syracuse University Press, 1998.

Katz, Jacob. "Post-Zoharic Relations Between Halakhah and Kabbalah." In *Divine Law in Human Hands: Case Studies in Halakhic Flexibility.* Jerusalem: Magnes Press, The Hebrew University, 1998.

Kellner, Menachem Marc. *Maimonides on the "Decline of the Generations" and the Nature of Rabbinic Authority.* Albany: State University of New York Press, 1996.

Kirschenbaum, Aaron. *Equity in Jewish Law: Halakhic Perspectives in Law: Formalism and Flexibility in Jewish Civil Law.* Library of Jewish Law and Ethics; v. 15. Hoboken, NJ: Ktav Publishing House, 1991.

Klier, John D. "1855–1894: Censorship of the Press in Russian and the Jewish Question." *Jewish Social Studies* 48, no. 3 (1986): 257-268.

Kook, Rabbi Abraham Isaac. *Igrot HaRayah.*

Kook, Rabbi Abraham Isaac. *Orach Mishpat.*

Lampel, Rabbi Zvi. *The Dynamics of Dispute: The Makings of Machlokess in Talmudic Times.* New York: Judaica Press, 1991.

Levine, Samuel J. *Jewish Law and American Law: A Comparative Study.* New York: Touro College Press, 2018.

Lewin, Benjamin Manasseh, ed. *Otzar HaGeonim*, 13 vols. Jerusalem: Hebrew University Press Association, 1928-1943.

Lipschitz, Rabbi Israel. *Tiferet Yisrael to Mishnah*.

Litowitz, Douglas. "Dworkin and Critical Legal Studies on Right Answers and Conceptual Holism." *Legal Studies Forum* 18, no. 2 (1994): 135-161.

Loew, Rabbi Judah. *Derekh Chaim on Pirkei Avot*.

Loew, Rabbi Judah. *Netivot Olam*.

Loew, Rabbi Judah. *Tiferet Yisrael*.

Lorberbaum, Menachem. "Rethinking Halakhah in Modern Eastern Europe: Mysticism. Antinomianism, Positivism." In *The Cambridge Companion to Judaism and Law*, edited by Christine Hayes, 232-259. New York: Cambridge University Press, 2017.

Lorberbaum, Yair. "Reflections on the Halakhic Status of Aggadah." *Diné Israel*, no. 24 (2007): 29-64.

Luria, Rabbi Solomon (Maharshal). *Yam Shel Shlomo*.

Luria, Rabbi Solomon (Maharshal). *Responsa Maharshal*.

Luzzatto, Rabbi Moses Chaim (Ramchal). *Mesilat Yesharim*.

Mann, Daniel. *Living the Halakhic Process: Questions and Answers for the Modern Jew*. Jerusalem: Devora Publishing, 2007.

Marbury v. Madison, 5 U.S. 137 (1803).

Medini, Rabbi Chaim Hezekiah. *Sdei Chemed*.

Meiri, Rabbi Menachem. *Beit HaBechirah*.

Meiri, Rabbi Menachem. *Responsa Meiri Magen Avot*.

Mekhilta D'Rabbi Shimon bar Yochai.

Meyer, Michael A. "Modernity as a Crisis for the Jews." *Modern Judaism* 9, no. 2 (1989): 151-164.

Meyer, Michael A. *Response to Modernity: A History of the Reform Movement in Judaism*. New York: Oxford University Press, 1988.

Mintz, Adam. "Halakhah in America: The History of City Eruvin, 1894-1962." Doctoral Dissertation, New York University, 2011.

Mintz, Adam. *It's a Thin Line: Eruv from Talmudic to Modern Culture*. Brooklyn, NY: Ktav Publishing House, 2014.

The Mishnah.

Margoliyot, Rabbi Chaim. *Shaarei Teshuva to Shulchan Arukh*.

Neiman, Moshe Chanina, and Dovid Oratz. *Tefillin: An Illustrated Guide to Their Makeup and Use*. Jerusalem: Feldheim, 1995.

Nekritz, Rabbi Yehudah Leib. "Yeshivot Beit Yosef Navaredok." In *Mosdot Torah B'Yiropah; Be-binyanam Uve-hurbanam*, edited by Samuel Kalman Mirsky. New York: Ogen, 1956.

Noonan, John T., Jr., and Edward McGlynn Gaffney. *Religious Freedom: History, Cases and Other Materials on the Interaction of Religion and Government*, Jr. New York: Foundation Press, 3rd ed., 2011.

Pereira, Shlomo M. "Codes of Jewish Law and their Commentaries: Historical Notes." Bar-Ilan University. The Lookstein Center. Iyar 25, 5763. Accessed May 19, 2019. http://lookstein.org/resource/jewish_law_codes.pdf.

Pill, Shlomo. "Jewish Law Antecedents to American Constitutional Thought." *Mississippi Law Journal* 85, no. 3 (2016): 643-696.

Pill, Shlomo. "Law as Engagement: A Judeo-Islamic Conception of the Rule of Law for Twenty-First Century America." Doctoral Dissertation, Emory University, 2016.

Pill, Shlomo. "Leveraging Legal Indeterminacy: The Rule of Law in Jewish Jurisprudence." *The Journal Jurisprudence* 33 (2017): 221-302.

Pill, Shlomo. "The Political Enforcement of Rabbinic Theocracy? Religious Norms in Halakhic Practice." *Studies in Judaism, Humanities, and the Social Sciences* 2, no. 1 (2018): 23-36.

Pill, Shlomo. "Recovering Judicial Integrity: Towards a Duty-Focused Disqualification Jurisprudence Based on Jewish Law." *Fordham Urban Law Journal* 39, no. 2 (2011): 511-576.

Posner, Richard A. *The Problems of Jurisprudence*. Cambridge: Harvard University Press, 1993.

Rabbeinu Tam. *Sefer HaYashar*.

Rabinowitz Teomim, Rabbi Elijah David, and Rabbi Tzvi Judah Rabinowitz Teomim. *Shevet Achim*. Jerusalem: Ahavat Shalom, 1994.

Rabinowitz, Rabbi Isaac HaLevi. *Dorot Rishonim*.

Reifman, Daniel. "Teaching Talmudic Hermeneutics Using a Semiotic Model of Law." In *Turn It and Turn It Again: Studies in the Teaching and Learning of Classical Jewish Texts*, edited by Jon A. Levinson and Susan P. Fendrick, 81-104. Brighton, MA: Academic Studies Press, 2013.

Reischer, Rabbi Jacob ben Joseph. *Responsa Shevut Yaakov*.

Rosenbloom, Noah H. *Tradition in an Age of Reform: The Religious Philosophy of Samson Raphael Hirsch*. Philadelphia: Jewish Publication Society of America, 1976.

Rosman, Moshe. *Founder of Hasidism: A Quest for the Historical Baal Shem Tov*. Berkeley: University of California Press, 1996.

Russ-Fishbane, Elisha. *Judaism, Sufism, and the Pietists of Medieval Egypt: A Study of Abraham Maimonides and His Times*. Oxford: Oxford University Press, 2015.

Sagi, Avi. *The Open Canon: On the Meaning of Halakhic Discourse*. London: Continuum, 2007.

Saiman, Chaim N. *Halakhah: The Rabbinic Idea of Law*. Princeton: Princeton University Press, 2018.

Salanter, Rabbi Israel. *Ohr Yisrael*.

Schäfer, Peter. "The Ideal of Piety of the Ashkenazi Hasidim and Its Roots in Jewish Tradition." *Jewish History* 4, no. 2 (1990): 9-23.

Schiffman, Lawrence H. *From Text to Tradition: A History of Second Temple and Rabbinic Judaism*. Hoboken, NJ: Ktav Publishing House, 1991.

Schochetman, Eliav. *Seder HaDin: Le'Or Mekorot HaMishpat Ha'Ivri, Takanot HaDiyun U'Fesikat Batei HaDin HaRabbanim B'Yisrael*. Jerusalem: Sifriyat Mishpat Ha'Ivri, 1988.

Schreiber, Aaron M. *Jewish Law and Decision-Making: A Study Through Time*. Philadelphia: Temple University Press, 1979.

Schreiber, Rabbi Moses (Chatam Sofer). *Responsa Chatam Sofer.*
Searle, John R. *The Construction of Social Reality.* New York: Free Press, 1995.
Segal, Rabbi David HaLevi (Taz). *Turei Zahav to Shulchan Arukh.*
Sifri.
Silber, Michael K. "The Emergence of Ultra-Orthodoxy: The Invention of a Tradition." In *The Uses of Tradition: Jewish Continuity in the Modern Era,* edited by Jack Wertheimer, 23-84. Cambridge: Harvard University Press, 1992.
Silber, Michael K. "The Historical Experience of German Jewry and Its Impact on Haskalah and Reform in Hungary." In *Towards Modernity: The European Jewish Model,* edited by Jacob Katz, 107-157. New Brunswick: Transaction Books, 1987.
Sinai, Yuval. "The Religious Perspective of the Judge's Role in Talmudic Law." *Journal of Law and Religion* 25, no. 2 (2009): 357-377.
Sirkis, Rabbi Joel (Bach). *Bayit Chadash to Arbah Turim.*
Slonik, Rabbi Benjamin Aaron Ben Abraham. *Responsa Masat Binyamin.*
Sofer, Rabbi Jacob. *Kaf HaChaim to Shulchan Arukh.*
Soloveitchik, Haym. "Rupture and Reconstruction: The Transformation of Contemporary Orthodoxy." *Tradition: A Journal of Orthodox Jewish Thought* 28, no. 4 (1994): 64-130.
Sperber, Daniel. *Minhagei Yisrael: Mekorot V'Toladot.* Jerusalem: Mossad HaRav Kook, 1998-2007.
Steinsaltz, Rabbi Adin. *The Essential Talmud.* Translated by Chaya Galai. New York: Basic Books, 2006.
Steinsaltz, Rabbi Adin. *The Talmud:* A Reference Guide. New York: Random House, 1989.
Stern, Eliyahu. "Enlightenment Conceptions of Judaism and Law." In *The Cambridge Companion to Judaism and Law,* edited by Christine Hayes, 215-231. West Nyack, NY: Cambridge University Press, 2017.
Stern, Eliyahu. *The Genius, Elijah of Vilna and the Making of Modern Judaism.* New Haven: Yale University Press, 2014.
Sussmann, Yaacov. "The Scholarly Oeuvre of Professor Ephraim Elimelech Urbach." In *Ephraim Elimelech Urbach: A Bio-Bibliography,* edited by David Assaf, 7-116, 64-65. Jerusalem: The World Union of Jewish Studies, 1993.
Tamanaha, Brian Z. "Good Casuistry and Bad Casuistry: Resolving the Dilemmas Faced by Catholic Judges." *University of St. Thomas Law Journal* 4, no. 2 (2006): 269-279.
Ta-Shma, Israel M. "The Law Is in Accord with the Later Authority - *Hilkhata Kebatrai*: Historical Observations on a Legal Rule." In *Authority, Process and Method: Studies in Jewish Law,* edited by Hanina Ben-Menahem and Neil S. Hecht, 101-128. Australia: Harwood Academic Publishers, 1998.
The Torah.
Tosafot to Babylonian Talmud.
Tosefta to Babylonian Talmud.
Twersky, Yitzchak. "Make a Fence Around the Torah." *Torah U-Madda Journal* 8 (1998): 25-42.
United States v. Carolene Products Co., 304 U.S. 144, 152-53 n.4 (1938).

Urbach, Ephraim Elimelech. *The Halakhah: Its Sources and Development*. Jerusalem: Massada, 1986.

Volozhin, Rabbi Chaim. *Ruach Chaim on Avot*.

Walter, Rabbi Moshe. *The Making of a Halachic Decision: A Comprehensive Analysis and Guide to Halachic Rulings*. Brooklyn: Menucha Publishers Inc., 2013.

Warburg, A. Yehudah. *Rabbinic Authority: The Vision and the Reality*. Vol. 1. Jerusalem, Israel: Urim Publications, 2013.

Washofsky, Mark. "Taking Precedent Seriously: On Halakhah as a Rhetorical Practice." In *Re-Examining Reform Halakhah*, edited by Walter Jacob and Moshe Zemer, 2-70. New York: Berghahn Books, 2002.

Weil, Rabbi Nathaniel. *Korban Netanel to Babylonian Talmud*.

Werblowsky, R. J. Zwi. *Joseph Karo, Lawyer and Mystic*. Philadelphia: Jewish Publication Society of America, 1980.

Werblowsky, R. J. Zwi. "The Safed Revival and Its Aftermath." In *Jewish Spirituality: From the Sixteenth-Century Revival to the Present*, edited by Arthur Green, 7-33. London: SCM Press, 1989.

Whitman, James Q. "No Right Answer?" In *Crime, Procedure and Evidence in a Comparative and International Context: Essays in Honour of Professor Mirjan Damaska*, edited by John D. Jackson, Maximo Langer, and Peter Tillers, 371-392. Portland: Hart Publishing, 2008.

Woolf, Jeffrey R. "The Parameters of Precedent in Pesak Halakhah." *Tradition: A Journal of Orthodox Jewish Thought* 27, no. 4 (1993): 41-48.

Yerushalmi, Eliezer. *Pinkas Navaredok: Memorial Book*. Tel Aviv: Alexander Harkavy Navaredker Relief Committee in U.S.A. and Navaredker Committee in Israel, 1963.

Yosef, Rabbi Yitzchak. *Ein Yitzchak*. Jerusalem: 2009.

Yosef, Rabbi Yitzchak. *Yalkut Yosef*.

Zacuto, Rabbi Abraham. *Sefer HaYuchsin HaShalem*

Index of Biblical and Rabbinical Works Cited

Biblical Texts:

Genesis, 163-164, 210, 226
Exodus, 22, 54, 92, 102, 131, 161, 194, 225-226, 274
Leviticus, 105, 118, 154, 158-159, 161-162, 210, 228, 305, 311, 381, 383
Numbers, 59, 104, 139, 147, 188, 308
Deuteronomy, 54, 59, 73, 75, 104, 124, 126, 139, 147, 162, 194, 196, 210-211, 224-225, 264, 275
Isaiah, 331-332
Ezekiel, 108-109
Malachi, 22n75
Psalms, 100-101, 182, 225, 278-279, 310
Ecclesiastes, 16n52
Song of Songs, 22
Proverbs, 99, 191
Esther, 96, 313, 389-393
Nehemiah, 200, 298

Talmudic and Classical Rabbinic Texts:

Midrash Rabbah, 164, 210, 225-226
Mekhilta D'Rabbi Shimon bar Yochai, 23
Sifri Numbers, 147
Sifri Deuteronomy, 12n43, 75, 124
Avot D'Rabbi Natan, 164
Mishnah
    Berakhot, 131, 143, 158
    Terumot, 309
    Shabbat, 215
    Rosh Hashanah, 116-117, 191-192, 367-368
    Moed Katan, 261
    Sotah, 282, 313
    Eduyot, 142
    Avot, 2, 99, 113, 158, 160
    Chullin, 159
    Parah, 308
    Yadayim, 307
Tosefta, 95-96, 370, 390-391
    Sanhedrin, 100
    Eduyot, 142
Jerusalem Talmud, 4, 13, 29, 51, 65-66, 78, 84, 93-97, 169, 219, 252, 255-256, 290, 296, 300-301, 312-313, 317-318, 323-324, 327, 334, 339-340, 345, 347, 349, 351, 353, 357-359, 363-364, 370, 372, 383
    Berakhot, 310, 317, 364
    Peah, 195
    Shabbat, 241, 334
    Eruvin, 150
    Pesachim, 139, 191, 347
    Rosh Hashanah, 150
    Megillah, 304
    Sotah, 313
    Bava Metzia, 163
    Horayot, 125
Babylonian Talmud
    Berakhot, 88, 92, 94, 97, 111, 120, 131, 133, 143, 151, 158, 166-167, 186, 195, 201, 219, 225, 227, 230, 239, 257, 268, 277, 281-283, 286-288, 297-298, 305, 309-310, 314-315, 351

406 | Index of Biblical and Rabbinical Works Cited

Shabbat, 89, 111, 128, 139, 160, 201, 211, 217, 221, 226-227, 231-232, 237, 257, 310, 320-324, 327, 329-332, 334-336, 387, 389
Eruvin, 137, 151
Pesachim, 161, 165, 191, 193-196, 198, 201, 232, 235, 306, 323, 331, 346, 349-350
Yoma, 105, 220, 228, 231, 348, 373-374
Sukkah, 94, 107, 118, 144, 152, 154, 191, 231, 271, 376, 378-381, 383-384, 386
Beitza, 117, 126, 187, 191-192, 211, 213-216
Rosh Hashanah, 105, 116-117, 145, 191, 206, 367, 369
Taanit, 165, 170, 186, 192, 202, 220, 310, 361-363, 365-366
Megillah, 145, 168, 203, 299-301, 303, 392
Moed Katan, 129-130, 158-159, 354-355, 357-358
Chagigah, 16, 71, 129, 305, 353, 369
Yevamot, 13, 100, 164, 194, 197
Nedarim, 187-188
Nazir, 212
Sotah, 93, 125, 298-299, 305, 312-313
Gittin, 215, 268, 294
Kiddushin, 108, 225, 228-229, 234
Bava Kamma, 8, 73, 127, 163, 166, 213
Bava Metzia, 4, 88, 117, 161-162, 331
Bava Batra, 145, 204, 325
Sanhedrin, 8, 87, 100-102, 113, 125
Makkot, 210
Shevuot, 111
Avodah Zarah, 8, 103, 112, 216-217
Menachot, 148, 152, 195, 233, 265, 267, 272, 274-275
Chullin, 102, 109, 161, 201, 211, 216, 264, 305, 311
Keritot, 106, 320, 373
Meilah, 229
Niddah, 195, 378

Post-Tamudic Rabbinic Texts

Rif
    Berakhot, 286
    Eruvin, 94
    Megillah, 96
Mishneh Torah
    Introduction, 2, 73, 85n4
    Hilkhot Avodah Zarah, 198, 212

Hilkhot Tefillah, 182, 193, 240, 278, 291
Hilkhot Tefillin, 152
Hilkhot Tzitzit, 59, 127, 148, 233
Hilkhot Berakhot, 116, 131, 201, 258, 307-308
Hilkhot Shabbat, 129, 160, 241, 326-329, 332-333, 336
Hilkhot Yom Kippur, 106, 373
Hilkhot Yom Tov, 54, 129-130
Hilkhot Chametz U'Matzah, 220
Hilkhot Shofar, Sukkah, V'Lulav, 117, 367, 385-386
Hilkhot Kiddush HaChodesh, 150
Hilkhot Kri'at Shema, 282-283, 286-287
Hilkhot Gerushin, 95
Hilkhot Beit HaBechirah, 257
Hilkhot Sanhedrin, 87, 100-102
Hilkhot Mamrim, 7, 74-75, 160, 188, 196, 213-214
Hilkhot Melakhim U'Milchamot, 7
Arbah Turim, 6, 8, 10, 20-25, 31, 34, 40-41, 47, 52, 64, 70-71, 85n4, 96, 106, 113, 118, 128-129, 138n8, 145-146, 199, 235, 256-257, 260, 270-271, 275, 284, 293, 296-297, 300, 311, 323-325, 339-340, 343, 353-354, 364, 367, 380, 387-388, 391
    Orach Chaim, 6, 40, 92, 95, 120, 129, 148, 167, 169, 204, 218, 220, 234, 271, 273, 275-276, 279, 283, 288-289, 303, 312, 329, 331-332, 335, 342, 347, 361, 370, 372-374
    Yoreh Deah, 6, 40, 188
    Even HaEzer, 6, 40
    Choshen Mishpat, 6, 9, 40, 74, 86
Shulchan Arukh and Rema
    Orach Chaim, 24, 54, 57, 59, 61, 92-93, 96, 104-106, 116-117, 119-120, 129-131, 139, 141, 145, 148, 151, 153-154, 160, 166-168, 181-183, 188, 198, 216-219, 221, 231-232, 235-236, 239-240, 242, 255, 258-259, 261-262, 265-271, 275-284, 286, 289, 291-292, 298-299, 303-304, 306, 309, 312, 316, 322, 326, 329, 331, 334-335, 340-341, 344-346, 348-350, 354, 360-361, 365-369, 375-376, 378, 380-383, 386-387
    Yoreh Deah, 14, 24, 73-74, 86, 95, 144, 161, 187-191, 212, 216, 232
    Even HaEzer, 24-25, 57, 108
    Choshen Mishpat, 5, 12, 14, 74, 86-88, 100, 103-104, 112, 143, 162
Arukh HaShulchan HaAtid, 47n3
Artzot HaChaim, 256

Index of Biblical and Rabbinical Works Cited | 407

Baal HaMaor, 119, 146-147, 285, 321, 376
Baal Ha'Ittur, 105, 368
Baal Hilkhot Gedolot (Bahag), 65
Bayit Chadash (Bach), 20, 22n75, 220, 341-342, 348
Be'er HaGolah, 105, 368
Be'er Heitev, 29, 166, 366, 377
Beit HaBechirah, 19, 213, 215, 231-232, 257
Beit Shmuel, 25
Beit Yosef, 8-10, 20, 22-25, 31, 46-47, 56, 60, 70-71, 79, 85-86, 92, 138, 144, 169, 203, 253, 255, 266, 271, 273-275, 279, 288-289, 340, 361, 369, 373-374
Ben Ish Chai, 58, 178
Biur HaGra, 5, 29, 104
Birkei Yosef, 178
Chavot Yair, 87-88, 193
Chayei Adam, 30, 383
Chelkat Mechokek, 26
Chidushei HaRamban, 19
Chidushei HaRashba, 19
Chok Yaakov, 346, 348
Darkhei Horaah, 74, 89, 176
Darkhei Moshe, 24-25
Drashot HaRan, 103
Divrei David, 214
Drisha U'Prisha, 20
Ein Yitzchak, 5, 13, 73-74, 77, 111
Eliyahu Rabbah, 307
Emunot V'Deot, 210
Eshel Avraham, 29
Grama B'Nezikin, 22n75
HaEmek Davar, 94
Hagahot Maimoni, 117, 367
Hagahot Rabbi Akiva Eiger, 30
Igrot HaRayah, 201
Igrot Moshe, 22, 85, 91, 104, 190
Kaf HaChaim, 179
Ketzot HaChoshen, 101, 238
Ketzot HaShulchan, 217
Kessef Mishnah, 27, 95
Kitvei Arukh HaShulchan, 42-43
Kitzur Shulchan Arukh, 28, 30, 32
Klalei Horaah B'Issur V'Hetter, 9, 74
Kol Bo, 375
Korban Netanel, 35
Levush Malkhut, 305
Machatzit HaShekel, 29, 59
Maharam MeRutenberg, 64, 199, 274
Maharshal, 64

Magen Avraham, 26, 29-30, 32, 148, 216-217, 231, 236, 256, 267, 270-271, 281, 309, 341-342, 345-346, 349, 366
Maggid Meisharim, 174
Magid Mishnah, 64
Malbim, 256
Mekor Baruch, 37
Mekor Chaim, 344
Midrash Shmuel, 137
Milchamot Hashem, 15, 111
Mishbetzot Zahav, 29
Mishnah Berurah, xii, 34-36, 44-51, 53-68, 138-140, 161, 239n65, 250, 368
Mordechai, 57, 256, 268, 274, 286, 293, 331, 378
Nekudat HaKesef, 22n75
Netivot Olam, 89
Nimukei Yosef, 266
Ohr Yisrael, 10
Or LaYesharim, 37
Or Zarua (Riaz), 143-144, 273, 280
Orach Mishpat, 201
Otzar HaGeonim, 176
Pri Chadash, 29, 188
Pitchei Teshuva, 31, 87-88, 144, 187, 190
Pri Toar, 190-191
Pri Megadim, 29
Pri Haaretz, 59-60
Raabad, 32, 87, 118, 128, 130, 146-147, 201, 274, 285, 308, 314, 329, 355, 367, 385
Raavan, 64
Ran, 64, 105, 118, 128, 215, 329, 367-368, 379, 389-390
Rashbam, 64, 350
Rashi, 18, 30, 64, 93, 105-106, 117-119, 128-129, 151-152, 154-155, 183, 227, 282-284, 288, 295, 299, 305, 320, 329, 332, 337-338, 367, 371-373, 376, 380-381, 384, 386
Reishit Chochmah, 109
Ri HaLevi, 64
Ritva, 19, 64, 191, 266
Riva, 64
Rivash, 64
Responsa Bach, 90
Responsa Bnei Banim, 9n32, 46
Responsa Masat Binyamin, 177
Responsa Meiri Magen Avot, 10
Responsa Ginat Vradim, 232
Responsa Ri Migash, 86, 114
Responsa Chikrei Lev, 86
Responsa Chacham Tzvi, 173, 178
Responsa Chatam Sofer, 177, 179, 187n8

Responsa Maharam MeRutenberg, 186
Responsa Maharik, 94, 197
Responsa Radbaz, 177
Responsa Rama MiPano, 179
Responsa Rashba, 92, 197
Responsa Rif, 188, 196
Responsa Rosh, 144, 197, 215
Responsa Shevut Yaakov, 86
Responsa Zichron Yosef, 190
Ruach Chaim, 101
Sdei Chemed, 14
Seder HaDin, 5
Sefer HaAgur, 268
Sefer HaChinukh, 125, 131, 161
Sefer HaTerumah, 64, 199
Sefer HaYashar, 37, 176
Sefer HaYuchsin HaShalem, 178
Sefer Meirat Einayim (Semah), 26
Sefer Mitzvot Gadol (Semag), 9, 64, 105, 117, 199, 256, 273, 332, 367-368
Sefer Mitzvot Katan (Semak), 64, 105, 199, 274, 368
Sefer Hishtanut HaTevaim, 217
Sifsei Kohen (Shakh), 22n75, 26, 32, 95, 74n22, 216
Shaagat Aryeh, 290

Shaarei Teshuva, 29, 31n97, 377
Sheiltot D'Rav Achai Gaon, 137, 350
Shitah Mekubetzet, 160
Shulchan Arukh HaRav, 29, 37, 46, 179, 344
Tiferet Yisrael, 210, 215
Torah Temimah, 102
Torat HaChatat, 24
Tosafot, 18-19, 24n82, 30, 64, 88, 94, 117-119, 128-129, 131-133, 145-146, 160, 214, 216-217, 229, 232, 234, 257, 273-274, 282, 284, 306, 311-312, 314, 316, 320, 329, 332, 351-352, 367, 376, 380, 382, 384, 389-390
Tosafot Yom Tov, 5n14
Terumat HaDeshen, 154, 158, 165, 203, 304, 381
Turei Zahav (Taz), 22n75, 25, 55n35, 127, 216n36, 265, 331, 340-342, 346, 386-387
Vikuach Mayim Chaim, 89n24
Yad Malachi, 13n48, 73-74
Yalkut Yosef, 27n92, 68n69
Yam Shel Shlomo, 18, 26-27, 32, 64, 72, 90, 137, 214
Zohar, 26, 52-53, 80, 141, 172-184, 201, 224, 236, 253-254, 259, 272, 278, 288, 292-294, 308, 311-312, 315, 319, 345, 366

Index of Names and Subjects

Abaye, 320, 380
Abba Shaul, 257
Acharonim, 6, 55n35, 88
Adam, 163-164
aggadah, 175-176
al bi'ur chametz, 343
al mitzvat tzitzit, 261
al nekiyut yadayim, 106, 260
al netilat yadayim, 106, 116, 258-261, 309
amen, 120, 182, 280, 292, 318-319
Amidah (prayer), 120-121, 145, 147, 167, 181-182, 184, 278-279, 282-285, 288-289, 292-293, 313, 318-319, 363-364
Amoraim, 3-4, 87n15
angels, 81, 89n22, 101, 174, 225-235, 237-239, 254, 267, 342
Aseret HaDibrot, 255
Asham, 255
asher yatzar, 261
Ashkenazi, Ashkenazic, 17, 19-20, 24, 32n103, 39, 54, 56, 62, 155, 157n1, 198-201, 204, 235, 269-270, 275, 325-326, 361, 373, 382
Ashrei, 292, 319
Avodah, 363-364
b'shogeg, 234, 342
baal nefesh, 63, 161
baal tosif, 54-55
Bar Kokhba Revolt, 3, 75
barechu, 267
Baruch She'Amar, 120
baruch shem kavod malkhuto le'olam va'ed, 269-270
bat kol, 64
Batyah Miriam Berlin, 37
bedikat chametz, 343
beryah, 317-318
bimah, 193, 203, 299, 304
Birkhat HaChodesh, 338-339

Birkhat HaMazon (Grace after Meals), 310-315, 369
Birkhat HaShachar, 277
birkhat hoda'ah, 269
Birkhat Kohanim ("Priestly Blessing"), 292
bittul chametz, 343
Bobriusk, 36
Boneh Yerushalayim, 364
boreh minei mezonot, 305-306
Baraita, 365
Braynah Velbrinski, 37
Canon law, 8-9, 27n92
censors, 42-43
Chabad, 29, 37, 179-180
chametz, 139, 141, 219-220, 231-232, 234-235, 340-349, 391
Chatat, 255
chazzan (cantor), 120, 280, 331-332, 374
cherish, 368-370
Chol HaMoed, ix, 54-56, 129-130, 274-275, 353-360
Christine Hayes, 237
Code, codification, x-xii, 3, 6, 9n32, 15-21, 23-27, 29-32, 34-35, 37, 39-40, 44-51, 60, 67-68, 70, 72, 77, 86-89, 91, 113-115, 135, 166, 174-175, 212, 244, 250, 277, 364, 383
Dina D'Talmuda, 78, 81, 136, 252
Dofen Akumah, 379
Eidel Kahanov, 37
ein ma'avirin al hamitzvot, 352
ein safek motzi m'yidei vadai, 341-342
Eliezer Ze'ira, 165-166
elokai neshamah, 261
elu v'elu divrei Elokim Chaim, 27, 137
Emancipation, 33-34
eruv, 28n94, 61-64, 66
Esther
Etrog, 143, 381, 384-385

Europe, European, 10, 20, 26, 31, 33, 37-38, 42, 44-45, 62, 87, 174, 199-201, 221, 237, 292, 346-347, 357, 362, 375, 380-383, 387
Eve, 163-164
ex ante, 118, 149, 316-317, 368
ex post, 143, 148, 204, 275, 317, 325
Ezekiel, 108-109
Ezra, 287-288, 295, 298
Ezra's enactment, 287-288
fasting, 28n94, 141, 167-168, 170-171, 188-189, 242-243, 303, 326, 340, 349, 361-363, 365-367, 374-375
four species, 154, 382-384, 386-387
Gaal Yisrael, 182, 292
Garden of Eden, 163
gemara, 4, 16, 18, 35, 76, 86n9
Purim, 28n94, 96, 313, 339, 389-393
Rabban Gamliel, 113
Rabbi Abraham ben David of Posquieres (the Raabad), 32, 87, 118, 128, 130, 146-147, 201, 274, 285, 308, 314, 329, 355, 367, 385
Rabbi Abraham ben Yechiel Mikhel of Danzig, 30
Rabbi Abraham Chaim HaLevi, 232n38
Rabbi Abraham Chaim Naeh, 217n40
Rabbi Abraham HaLevi (Magen Avraham), 26
Rabbi Abraham Isaac Kook, 201n70
Rabbi Abraham Joshua Heschel, 175-176
Rabbi Abraham Zacuto, 178
Rabbi Akiva, 22, 296
Rabbi Akiva Eiger, 29-30
Rabbi Aryeh Gunzberg, 290
Rabbi Aryeh Leib Heller, 101, 238
Rabbi Asher ben Yechiel (the Rosh), 19, 24-26, 32n101, 64, 95, 105-106, 115, 118-119, 128, 132, 138n8, 181, 201-202, 256, 259-260, 262, 266, 271, 273-274, 285, 308, 311-312, 314, 316, 324, 329, 331, 348, 351-352, 363, 368, 370, 376, 379, 385-387, 389-390
Rabbi Avahu, 117, 367
Rabbi Baruch Halevi Epstein, 37n22
Rabbi Benjamin Slonick, 177
Rabbi Chaim ben Attar, 190-191
Rabbi Chaim ben Betzalel, 89n24
Rabbi Chaim Berlin, 43
Rabbi Chaim Hezekiah Medini, 14n50
Rabbi Chaim David HaLevi, 91
Rabbi Chaim Margoliyot, 29
Rabbi Chaim Volozhin, 101, 174

Rabbi Hezekiah da Silva, 29, 188n9
Rabbi Chiya, 162-163, 268
Rabbi David ben Solomon ibn Zimra (the Radbaz), 177, 214n25
Rabbi David HaLevi Segal (the Taz), 25-26, 29-30, 32, 331
Rabbi Dov Ber Epstein, 36-37
Rabbi Eitam Henkin, ix, 45n1
Rabbi Elazar HaKapar, 165
Rabbi Eliezer ben Joel HaLevi (the Raavyah), 57, 351
Rabbi Elijah de Vidas, 109n56
Rabbi Elijah Goldberg, 36
Rabbi Elijah ben Solomon Zalman Kramer of Vilna (the Vilna Gaon), 29-30, 46, 50
Rabbi Elijah Shapiro, 307
Rabbi Ezekiel Landau, 31
Rabbi Isaac Alfasi (the Rif), 16-17, 25-26, 62, 64, 94, 138n8, 145, 154, 196, 201-202, 204, 256, 273, 284, 286, 290, 308-309, 321-322, 324-325, 351, 364, 381, 389
Rabbi Isaac ben Moses of Vienna (Rabbi Isaac Or Zarua, the Riaz), 64, 143-144, 273, 280
Rabbi Isaac Elchanan Spektor, 38
Rabbi Isaac Luria (the Arizal), 174, 267, 363
Rabbi Israel Baal Shem Tov, 174
Rabbi Israel Meir Kagan, xii, 34-35, 45-50, 54-55, 58-59, 61-63, 67, 138-140, 239n65, 250
Rabbi Israel Salanter, 10n37, 38
Rabbi Jacob ben Asher, 6, 20, 22n75, 32n101, 113, 347, 349
Rabbi Jacob Berlin, 36
Rabbi Jacob Lorberbaum, 344
Rabbi Jacob Sofer, 179n28
Rabbi Joel Sirkis (the Bach), 20, 22n75, 90
Rabbi Jonah Gerondi, 99n2, 114n13, 159
Rabbi Joseph ben Meir Teomim, 29
Rabbi Joseph ibn Migash (the Ri Migash), 86n7, 114-115
Rabbi Joseph ibn Nachmias, 113n11
Rabbi Joseph Karo, 6, 9n32, 20-32, 34-35, 38-40, 42, 46-47, 61-62, 67, 77, 79, 86-87, 91, 95-96, 99, 103, 105, 110, 112, 115-121, 126-127, 130-132, 134, 138-139, 141, 145, 153-154, 166, 168, 174, 181-183, 188-189, 212, 217-218, 242, 250, 253, 255-263, 269, 271, 273-280, 284, 289, 292, 298, 303, 305-306, 309, 316, 318-319, 326, 331, 340-341, 344, 346, 349, 354-355, 358-359, 361, 364, 366-370, 372-378, 380-382, 385-386, 388, 393

Rabbi Joseph Steinhardt, 190
Rabbi Joseph Yozel Horwitz, 38
Rabbi Joshua Falk Kohen (the Sema), 20, 26
Rabbi Judah Ashkenazi, 29
Rabbi Yehudah Leib Nekritz, 38n26
Rabbi Judah Loew, 89-90, 99-100, 174, 210n6
Rabbi Judah the Prince, 3, 76
Rabbi Malachi HaKohen, 13n48, 73-74
Rabbi Meir Bar-Ilan, 41
Rabbi Meir ibn Gabbai, 137
Rabbi Menachem Meiri, 19
Rabbi Menachem Mendel Schneersohn of Lubavitch, 37, 180
Rabbi Menachem MiPano, 178-179
Rabbi Mordechai ben Abraham Yaffe of Prague (the Levush), 25
Rabbi Mordechai ben Hillel HaKohen (the Mordechai), 57, 256, 268, 274, 286, 293, 331, 378
Rabbi Moses ben Isaac Judah Lima, 26
Rabbi Moses ben Jacob of Coucy, 9n35
Rabbi Moses ben Maimon (Maimonides), *passim*
Rabbi Moses ben Nachman Girondi (Nachmanides), 15, 19, 64, 161-162, 196, 300-301, 321-322, 344, 372
Rabbi Moses Feinstein, 22n75, 85n4, 90-91
Rabbi Moses Isserles (the Rema), x, 22n75, 24-28, 38-40, 54-56, 92-93, 103-105, 107, 120, 126, 139-140, 143, 154-155, 182, 193, 203-204, 212, 218, 235-236, 240, 259-262, 266, 269-271, 273-274, 278, 280, 283, 291-294, 298-299, 304, 318-319, 322, 325, 341, 345, 348, 350-351, 360-362, 372, 377, 380-383, 385-386, 391-392
Rabbi Moses Sofer, 31, 177
Rabbi Naftali Tzvi Yehudah Berlin, 36-37, 137, 174
Rabbi Nathaniel Weil, 216n35
Rabbi Neria Gutel, 217n40
Rabbi Nissim Gerondi, 103, 301
Rabbi Oshaya, 328
Rabbi Samuel ben Nathan HaLevi Loew, 29
Rabbi Samuel Feibush, 25
Rabbi Samuel Uceda, 136
Rabbi Shabbatai HaKohen (the Shakh), 25-26, 32
Rabbi Shimon bar Yochai, 26n90, 143, 173, 177, 179, 345
Rabbi Shimon ben Lakish (Reish Lakish), 328
Rabbi Shimon ben Shetach, 163

Rabbi Shneur Zalman of Liadi, 29-30, 37, 46, 179, 344
Rabbi Solomon ben Aderet (the Rashba), 19, 64, 128, 132, 181, 197, 259-260, 274, 314, 316, 329, 351
Rabbi Samuel ben Meir (the Rashbam), 64, 350
Rabbi Solomon Ganzfried, 30, 32
Rabbi Solomon Luria (Maharshal), 26n91, 64, 137, 177, 386
Rabbi Solomon Yitzchaki (Rashi), 18, 30, 64, 93, 105-106, 117-119, 128-129, 151-152, 154-155, 183, 227, 282-284, 288, 295, 299, 305, 320, 329, 332, 337-338, 367, 371-373, 376, 380-381, 384, 386
Rabbi Tzvi Hirsch Ashkenazi, 178
Rabbi Zvi Hirsch Chajes, 176
Rabbi Yechiel Mikhel Epstein, *passim*
Rabbi Yehudah Henkin
Rabbi Yitzchak Yosef, 27n92, 68n69
Rabbi Yochanan, 161, 191, 193-194, 268, 317-318, 327-328
Rabbi Yochanan ben Nuri, 347
Rabbi Yom Tov ben Avraham Asevilli (the Ritva), 19, 64, 191n25, 266
Rabbi Yom Tov Lipmann Heller, 5n14, 18n63
Rabbi Yosef Eliyahu Henkin, 46n2
Rabbi Yossi, 369
Rabbi Yossi HaGlili, 194
Rabbeinu Chananel, 321-322
Rabbeinu Tam, 37, 64, 176, 183, 330
Rav, 257, 330
Rav Acha, 296, 300, 383-384
Rav Achai Gaon, 350-351
Rav Ami, 304
Rav Ashi, 93, 257, 271
Rav Assi, 108
Rav Hai Gaon, 94-95, 176
Rav Kahana, 257, 383-384
Rav Natronai Gaon, 279, 293
Rav Papa, 228
Rav Saadia Gaon, 17n57, 176, 210n6
Rav Sheshet, 298
Rav Yirmiyah, 304
Rav Yitzchak, 257
Rava, 320, 380-381
Ravana, 257
Ravina, 93, 300
red heifer, 308
restatement, x, xii, 3n6, 6, 16, 20, 24, 31, 35, 38, 42, 44-46, 70-72, 77, 86-87, 89, 113-115, 251

revi'it, 106, 259, 326-327, 373
Rishonim, 6, 10, 40, 50n19, 61, 64, 87-88, 95
ritual impurity, 92, 183, 236, 287, 305-306, 366, 377-378, 382
Robert Jackson, 12, 123
Rosh Hashanah, 95, 105, 116-118, 149-152, 169, 181, 183, 236, 331, 366-372
Roshka Berlin, 36
ruach ra'ah, 258-259
Russia, Russian, 36, 38, 42-44, 179, 201, 383
Sabbath, *passim*
Seder, 139, 349-352
Sephardi, Sephardic, 16, 24, 27n92, 39, 46, 56, 68n69, 196, 200, 269, 275
seudah, 139-140
Shacharit, 318
shatnez, 217-218, 233, 262
Shavuot, 28n94, 340
shehakol nih'yeh bidvaro, 131, 316
Shehechiyanu, 149, 151-152, 371, 389-390
Shelamim, 255, 340
Shema, 57, 116, 143, 182, 219, 227-229, 258, 269-270, 278-279, 282-283, 285-288, 290, 292, 313, 369
Shirat HaYam, 182, 278
shliach tzibbur, 266-267, 290, 318, 366
Shmuel, 108, 165, 224-225
shofar, 95-96, 105, 116-118, 183, 236, 366-370
shoteh, 368, 383-384
sirkhon, 347
Sodomite Salt, 311-312
the Sanhedrin, 7-9, 12, 14, 75-76, 102, 150, 191-192, 196, 213-215, 338, 370
sukkah, 107, 118-119, 152-153, 376-381
Sukkot, 28n94, 118, 143, 152, 154-155, 340, 353, 357, 376-378, 380-382, 384, 386-387
synagogue, 38, 57, 59, 93, 167-168, 181, 193, 203, 261, 277-278, 288, 293-294, 297, 299-304, 363, 391
ta'ut b'davar mishnah, 86-87
ta'ut b'shikul hada'at, 87-88, 103
Tachanun, 293
tallit, 60, 236, 265-268, 270
Tannaim, 87n15, 93, 95, 130-131, 142, 150, 272, 355, 364-365, 370-371
tashmishei kedushah, 203
techum, 321

tefillin, 54-56, 152, 166, 183, 202, 218, 230-232, 235-236, 257, 262, 269-277, 283, 359, 363
tekhelet, 218, 262
Temple, 2-3, 6, 14, 17n58, 20, 47n3, 75, 102, 124, 132, 161, 165, 191-192, 202, 204, 206, 212-213, 215-216, 220, 228-229, 233, 238, 255-257, 280-281, 295, 299, 305-306, 319, 325, 338, 340, 351, 361, 363-364, 372, 388
Ten Commandments, 92n41, 255
Ten Days of Repentance, 169, 372
terumah, 309
testimony, 150, 338, 370-371. *See also* witness
the Exodus, 337, 349, 351, 391
Tisha B'Av, 165, 192, 202, 220-221, 361-364
tiyomet, 154-155, 381
totafot, 283
Tree of Life, 163-164
Tzemach David, 364
tzitzit, 28, 59-61, 104, 126-128, 139-140, 147-149, 217-218, 233-234, 261-269, 283
vehilkheta, 9n33
Volozhin Yeshivah, 36, 179
vow, 73n18, 165, 188-189, 191, 353
wine, 160-162, 165, 188, 193, 203-205, 216, 325-327, 336, 350-352
witnesses, 150, 338, 370-371. *See also* testimony
yeridat hadorot, 89
yirat horaah, 100
yirat shamayim, 100
Yom Kippur, 28n94, 105-106, 141, 169-170, 181, 237, 345, 357, 372-375

Index of Examples by Methodological Principle

Principle One: 1, 2, 3, 5, 6, 7, 8, 9, 10, 11, 12, 13, 14, 15, 16, 17, 18, 19, 20, 21, 22, 23, 24, 25, 27, 28, 29, 30, 31, 33, 37, 39, 42, 43, 46, 48, 49, 51, 53, 54, 55, 56, 57,62, 63, 64, 65, 66, 67, 68, 70, 71, 72, 73, 74, 75, 76, 77, 78, 79, 81, 83, 84, 85, 86, 87, 88, 89, 90, 91, 93, 94, 97, 98, 99, 100, 101, 102, 103, 105, 106, 107, 109, 111, 113, 115, 116, 117, 119, 120, 121, 122, 123, 124, 125, 126, 128, 130, 131, 133, 134, 136, 137, 139, 140, 144, 146, 147, 149, 150, 154, 155, 156, 157, 159, 160, 161, 162, 164, 169, 170, 174, 178, 179, 181, 182, 183, 186, 188, 189, 190, 191, 194, 199, 202, 203, 204

Principle Two: 4, 12, 15, 21, 27, 37, 43, 44, 64, 78, 87, 92, 93, 94, 97, 103, 109, 112, 137, 148, 149, 168, 171, 175, 181, 185, 187, 192, 193

Principle Three: 6, 7, 8, 15, 25, 40, 51, 71, 77, 82, 87, 90, 93, 94, 97, 106, 107, 112, 117, 144, 145, 147, 153, 167, 169, 180, 182, 187, 192, 193, 203

Principle Four: 9, 15, 20, 23, 25, 27, 37, 39, 40, 41, 47, 78, 90, 92, 93, 94, 109, 111, 155, 127, 128, 147, 167, 169, 171, 179, 180, 182, 187, 188, 192, 193, 201

Principle Five: 5, 28, 41, 44, 47, 52, 70, 98, 103, 108, 110, 111, 132, 139, 143, 148, 155, 160, 168, 171, 179, 183, 187, 188, 192, 195, 199

Principle Six: 5, 20, 22, 26, 33, 35, 39, 41, 42, 43, 45, 47, 48, 49, 61, 65, 67, 70, 74, 78, 79, 80, 81, 82, 83, 84, 86, 89, 96, 99, 102, 120, 121, 134, 135, 137, 145, 149, 154, 160, 163, 172, 179, 180, 186, 187, 193, 196, 199, 203

Principle Seven: 20, 26, 32, 35, 36, 37, 49, 50, 56, 58, 61, 79, 82, 86, 87, 89, 90, 95, 130, 142, 166, 177

Principle Eight: 1, 4, 5, 11, 16, 19, 20, 23, 24, 25, 29, 34, 36, 39, 40, 42, 45, 46, 48, 49, 52, 58, 59, 60, 61, 62, 63, 66, 69, 70, 75, 78, 79, 80, 84, 85, 86, 87, 91, 95, 96, 98, 99, 103, 110, 111, 114, 116, 118, 119, 120, 121, 122, 128, 129, 133, 134, 135, 137, 138, 139, 141, 142, 143, 145, 149, 156, 157, 158, 159, 160, 161, 162, 164, 166, 167, 171, 173, 174, 177, 178, 181, 185, 186, 187, 189, 190, 191, 194, 196, 197, 198, 199, 200, 201

Principle Nine: 13, 17, 18, 31, 34, 38, 42, 43, 45, 46, 49, 58, 59, 60, 61, 63, 65, 67, 76, 78, 84, 85, 87, 89, 91, 98, 99, 105, 110, 111, 113, 114, 126, 131, 132, 133, 134, 135, 139, 151, 155, 156, 157, 158, 159, 161, 162, 164, 165, 173, 177, 178, 183, 186, 200

Principle Ten: 7, 8, 20, 22, 24, 34, 38, 41, 43, 45, 48, 50, 54, 55, 57, 60, 62, 66, 75, 82, 84, 99, 102, 103, 104, 111, 120, 121, 123, 125, 128, 130, 133, 135, 137, 143, 145, 151, 153, 156, 165, 169, 173, 176, 179, 183, 187, 188, 189, 192, 195, 196

www.ingramcontent.com/pod-product-compliance
Lightning Source LLC
Chambersburg PA
CBHW052054300426
44117CB00013B/2119